THE ROUTLEDGE HANI
OF PANPSYCHISM

> "This book provides a rich and novel discussion of one of the most exciting (and hardest) issues in philosophy, namely the nature of consciousness, by taking seriously panpsychism. It contains a large variety and number of quality contributions, both from a historical and a contemporary perspective, which makes it a book of reference indispensable for anyone interested in the field. A great read and an inspiring contribution to the philosophical debate about the nature of consciousness."
>
> *Jiri Benovsky, University of Fribourg, Switzerland*

> "The rise to prominence of panpsychism is a response to a growing disillusionment with orthodox physicalism. If you want to know the history, strengths and weaknesses of this surprising revival of an ancient metaphysics, this wide-ranging collection is an excellent place to start."
>
> *Howard Robinson, Central European University, Hungary*

Panpsychism is the view that consciousness – the most puzzling and strangest phenomenon in the entire universe – is a fundamental and ubiquitous feature of the world, though in a form very remote from human consciousness. At a very basic level, the world is awake. Panpsychism seems implausible to most, and yet it has experienced a remarkable renaissance of interest over the last quarter century. The reason is the stubbornly intractable problem of consciousness. Despite immense progress in understanding the brain and its relation to states of consciousness, we still really have no idea how consciousness emerges from physical processes which are *presumed* to be entirely non-conscious.

The Routledge Handbook of Panpsychism provides a high-level comprehensive examination and assessment of the subject – its history and contemporary development. It offers 28 chapters, appearing in print here for the first time, from the world's leading researchers on panpsychism. The chapters are divided into four sections that integrate panpsychism's relevance with important issues in philosophy of mind, philosophy of science, metaphysics, and even ethics.

1. Historical Reflections
2. Forms of Panpsychism
3. Comparative Alternatives
4. How Does Panpsychism Work?

The volume will be useful to students and scholars as both an introduction and as cutting-edge philosophical engagement with the subject. For anyone interested in a philosophical approach to panpsychism, the *Handbook* will supply fascinating and enlightening reading. The topics covered are highly diverse, representing a spectrum of views on the nature of mind and world from various standpoints which take panpsychism seriously.

William Seager is Professor of Philosophy at the University of Toronto Scarborough. He works primarily in the philosophy of mind and consciousness studies; his most recent book is *Theories of Consciousness* (2nd edition; Routledge, 2016).

ROUTLEDGE HANDBOOKS IN PHILOSOPHY

Routledge Handbooks in Philosophy are state-of-the-art surveys of emerging, newly refreshed, and important fields in philosophy, providing accessible yet thorough assessments of key problems, themes, thinkers, and recent developments in research.

All chapters for each volume are specially commissioned, and written by leading scholars in the field. Carefully edited and organized, *Routledge Handbooks in Philosophy* provide indispensable reference tools for students and researchers seeking a comprehensive overview of new and exciting topics in philosophy. They are also valuable teaching resources as accompaniments to textbooks, anthologies, and research-orientated publications.

ALSO AVAILABLE:

THE ROUTLEDGE HANDBOOK OF
EMERGENCE
Edited by Sophie Gibb, Robin Hendry, and Tom Lancaster

THE ROUTLEDGE HANDBOOK OF
THE PHILOSOPHY OF EVIL
Edited by Thomas Nys and Stephen de Wijze

THE ROUTLEDGE HANDBOOK OF
SOCIAL EPISTEMOLOGY
Edited by Peter Graham, Nikolaj Jang Lee, David Henderson, and Miranda Fricker

THE ROUTLEDGE HANDBOOK OF
PHILOSOPHY OF THE CITY
Edited by Sharon M. Meagher, Samantha Noll, and Joseph S. Biehl

THE ROUTLEDGE HANDBOOK OF
PANPSYCHISM
Edited by William Seager

THE ROUTLEDGE HANDBOOK OF
EMOTION THEORY
Edited by Andrea Scarantino

THE ROUTLEDGE HANDBOOK OF
PHILOSOPHY OF RELATIVISM
Edited by Martin Kusch

For more information about this series, please visit: www.routledge.com/Routledge-Handbooks-in-Philosophy/book-series/RHP

THE ROUTLEDGE HANDBOOK OF PANPSYCHISM

Edited by William Seager

Routledge
Taylor & Francis Group

NEW YORK AND LONDON

First published 2020
by Routledge
605 Third Avenue, New York, NY 10017

and by Routledge
2 Park Square, Milton Park, Abingdon, Oxon, OX14 4RN

First issued in paperback 2021

Routledge is an imprint of the Taylor & Francis Group, an informa business

Publisher's Note
The publisher has gone to great lengths to ensure the quality of this
reprint but points out that some imperfections in the original copies may
be apparent.

Library of Congress Cataloging-in-Publication Data
A catalog record for this book has been requested

ISBN 13: 978−1−03−223937−8 (pbk)
ISBN 13: 978−1−138−81713−5 (hbk)

DOI: 10.4324/9781315717708

Typeset in Bembo
by Apex CoVantage, LLC

CONTENTS

CONTRIBUTORS

Miri Albahari teaches philosophy at the University of Western Australia. She works in comparative philosophy, on the epistemology and metaphysics of mystical states.

Torin Alter is Professor of Philosophy at The University of Alabama. He writes mostly on consciousness and the mind-body problem

Andrew Bailey is Associate Professor in Philosophy, and Associate Dean (Research & Graduate Studies) for the College of Arts at the University of Guelph, Ontario, Canada. He works on the philosophy of consciousness, embodied cognition and the ethics of AI, as well as the thought of William James.

Pierfrancesco Basile is Lecturer in Philosophy at the University of Bern and at the KSA Luzern, Switzerland. His last book is *Whitehead's Metaphysics of Power: Reconstructing Modern Philosophy* (Edinburgh UP, 2017).

Michael Blamauer worked for several years in the field of philosophy of mind with special focus on panpsychism, notably editing *The Mental as Fundamental: New Perspectives on Panpsychism* (Ontos, 2011).

David Bourget is Associate Professor of Philosophy and Director of the Centre for Digital Philosophy at the University of Western Ontario. He has published a number of articles on consciousness, its role in the mind, and its place in nature.

Monima Chadha teaches philosophy at Monash University in Australia. She works in cross-cultural philosophy with special interest in Abhidharma Buddhism.

David Chalmers is University Professor of Philosophy and Neural Science and Co-Director of the Center for Mind, Brain, and Consciousness at New York University.

Sam Coleman is Reader of Philosophy at the University of Hertfordshire. His main interest is in reconciling scientific accounts of matter and the brain with what we glean from the personal perspective.

Daniel Dombrowski is in the Philosophy Department of Seattle University. Among his many publications is the book *Rethinking the Ontological Argument: A Neoclassical Theistic Response* (Cambridge UP, 2006).

Philip Goff is a philosopher and consciousness researcher at Durham University and author of *Galileo's Error: Foundations for a New Science of Consciousness* (Pantheon, 2019). His research focuses on how to integrate consciousness into our overall theory of reality.

Terry Horgan is Professor of Philosophy at the University of Arizona. He has published (often collaboratively) in philosophy of mind, philosophy of cognitive science, metaphysics, epistemology, and metaethics.

Steven Horst is Professor of Philosophy at Wesleyan University. He is the author of four books, including *Beyond Reduction* (Oxford UP, 2007), *Laws, Mind, and Free Will* (MIT, 2011), and *Cognitive Pluralism* (MIT, 2016).

Robert J. Howell is Dedman Family Distinguished Professor and Chair of the Philosophy Department at Southern Methodist University. His work mostly concerns the nature of subjectivity, the self, and the mind.

Graeme Hunter is Emeritus Professor of Philosophy at University of Ottawa and Research Professor of Philosophy at Dominican University College. He works for the most part on philosophers of the Early Modern Period.

Martin Lin is Professor of Philosophy at Rutgers University in New Brunswick, New Jersey. His research concerns metaphysics and philosophy of mind in the early modern period.

Freya Mathews is Adjunct Professor of Environmental Philosophy at Latrobe University, Australia. She has taught and published very widely in the field of environmental philosophy, particularly in ecological metaphysics.

Angela Mendelovici is Associate Professor of Philosophy at the University of Western Ontario. She has written numerous works on consciousness, intentionality, and the relationship between the two, including her recent monograph, *The Phenomenal Basis of Intentionality* (Oxford UP, 2018).

Hedda Hassel Mørch is associate professor of philosophy at Inland Norway University of Applied Sciences. She was previously a postdoc at Center for Mind, Brain and Consciousness at New York University and University of Oslo.

Yujin Nagasawa is H.G. Wood Professor of the Philosophy of Religion at the University of Birmingham, UK. He is the author and editor of many books including *God and Phenomenal Consciousness* (Cambridge UP, 2008) and *Consciousness in the Physical World* (with Torin Alter; Oxford UP, 2015).

Paavo Pylkkänen is Vice Dean of Research of the Faculty of Arts and Head of Department of Philosophy, History and Art Studies at the University of Helsinki, where he has worked as Senior Lecturer in Theoretical Philosophy. He is also Associate Professor in Theoretical Philosophy at the University of Skövde, Sweden. His research areas are philosophy of mind, philosophy of science, and the foundations of quantum theory. He is the author of *Mind, Matter and the Implicate Order* (Springer, 2007).

Luke Roelofs is a postdoctoral researcher at New York University, working on social cognition and the metaphysics of consciousness. His new book, ***Combining Minds*** (Oxford UP, 2019), address the combination problem for panpsychism.

William Seager is Professor of Philosophy at the University of Toronto Scarborough. His most recent book is *Theories of Consciousness* (2nd ed; Routledge, 2016).

Michael Silberstein is Professor of Philosophy at Elizabethtown College and Affiliated Faculty in the philosophy department at the University of Maryland, College Park, where he is also a faculty member in the Foundations of Physics Program and a Fellow on the Committee for Philosophy and the Sciences. His most recent book is *Beyond the Dynamical Universe: Unifying Block Universe Physics and Time as Experienced* (Oxford UP 2018).

David Skrbina is a senior lecturer in philosophy at the University of Michigan at Dearborn. His research interests include panpsychism, philosophy of technology, and environmental philosophy. His books include *Panpsychism in the West* (revised edition, MIT Press, 2017), *The Metaphysics of Technology* (Routledge, 2015), and most recently, *The Jesus Hoax* (Creative Fire Press, 2018).

Daniel Stoljar is Professor of Philosophy at the Australian National University in Canberra and a Fellow of the Australian Academy of the Humanities. He is the author of *Ignorance and Imagination: The Epistemic Origin of the Problem of Consciousness* (Oxford UP, 2006), *Physicalism* (Routledge, 2010), and *Philosophical Progress: In Defense of a Reasonable Optimism* (Oxford UP, 2017).

Galen Strawson holds the President's Chair of Philosophy at the University of Texas at Austin. His books include *Freedom and Belief* (Oxford UP. 1986), *The Secret Connexion* (Oxford UP, 1989), *Mental Reality* (MIT Press, 1994), *Selves* (Oxford UP, 2009), *Locke on Personal Identity* (Princeton UP, 2011), and *The Subject of Experience* (Oxford UP, 2017).

Donovan Wishon is Associate Professor of Philosophy at the University of Mississippi. He is the author of a number of papers on Bertrand Russell's theories of mind, matter, language, and knowledge, and his coedited volume *Acquaintance, Knowledge, and Logic* (with Bernard Linsky) received the 2016 Bertrand Russell Society book prize.

PREFACE TO THE HANDBOOK

Roughly speaking, panpsychism is the view that mentality is a fundamental feature of the world which exists ubiquitously throughout the world. The relevant kind of mentality is the most puzzling and strangest phenomenon in the entire universe: consciousness. The fundamental form of consciousness posited by panpsychism is presumably very remote from that of human consciousness and possessed of a primitive and unutterably simple nature. At a very basic level, the world is awake.

Mostly people intuitively find panpsychism implausible, but sometimes for bad reasons. For example, panpsychism does not imply that everything is conscious because not everything is a fundamental entity. Most things in the world are composite beings. Whether a particular composite being is conscious or not depends on the 'mental chemistry' which binds or transforms the fundamental consciousness of its constituents into more complex forms of consciousness. Some things, like us or our brains, have the right chemistry. Rocks do not. One of the major philosophical problems facing panpsychism – the so-called 'combination problem' – is to understand how mental chemistry works, or even to understand how it is so much as possible in the first place.

Still, panpsychism remains implausible to most. Yet it has experienced a remarkable renaissance of interest over the last quarter century. The reason for the rebirth of serious engagement is the intractable problem of consciousness. Despite immense progress in understanding the brain and its correlational relation to states of consciousness, we still really have no idea how consciousness could emerge from physical states and processes which are *presumed* to be entirely nonconscious in their fundamental nature. As Thomas Huxley famously quipped in 1876 'how it is that anything so remarkable as a state of consciousness comes about as a result of irritating nervous tissue, is just as unaccountable as the appearance of the Djinn, when Aladdin rubbed his lamp'. But somehow the physical world performs this feat on a regular basis. This suggests that consciousness is somehow a 'way of being physical'. My current experience is telling me something – something quite extraordinary – about the nature of the physical being I am. In the absence of belief in magical eruptions of metaphysically discontinuous properties, an almost inevitable line of thought drives us toward panpsychism.

Thinking about panpsychism brings together a host of core issues in the philosophy of mind, the philosophy of science, metaphysics, and even ethics. This book aims to introduce and explore such issues from a wide diversity of viewpoints.

I give a broad philosophical introduction to panpsychism and its place in current debates about consciousness and its place in nature in the initial chapter of this book, 'A Panpsychist Manifesto'.

Here I will very briefly introduce the handbook itself. The goal of the handbook is to provide a high-level comprehensive examination and assessment of panpsychism – its history and contemporary development. It will be useful both to students and scholars as both an introduction and cutting-edge philosophical engagement. For anyone with a lively intellect interested in a philosophical approach to things, the handbook should supply fascinating and enlightening reading. As noted, the topics covered are highly diverse, representing a spectrum of views on the nature of mind from various standpoints which take panpsychism seriously.

The handbook is divided into 28 chapters roughly sorted into a number of themes. The first is a set of historical reflections ranging from Ancient Greek philosophy, Buddhist thought, Early Modern philosophy to the rich period for panpsychism of the 19th and early 20th centuries.

The second section deals broadly with various forms of panpsychism. These encompass distinct kinds of consciousness which might form the basic building block of a panpsychic view of the universe as well as different ways that panpsychism might describe the world, notably in the distinction between micropsychism (which assigns primitive mental aspects to elementary physical entities) to cosmopsychism (which takes the entire universe to be the fundamental conscious entity).

Next, in the third section, panpsychism faces up to a number of critical alternatives which are distinctive for taking panpsychism seriously and confronting their preferred doctrine directly with it. These include less well-known approaches such as subjective physicalism and cognitive pluralism, as well as the better known alternatives of neutral monism and the modern rebirth of Russellian monism.

In the final section, the chapters provide a variety of viewpoints on how panpsychism would or could actually work or be articulated in a more precise form. These chapters consider, for example, the question of how or whether individual subjects of experience could be 'summed' or 'combined' into more complex subjects, whether quantum mechanics can help fund a panpsychic outlook, whether causation itself can underpin some form of panpsychism and the core question of the real nature of the infamous combination problem.

The handbook also contains two 'keynote' articles. One is by Galen Strawson, who has long been one of the most forceful advocates for the intelligibility and possible intellectual benefits of panpsychism. He provides a close examination of the relation between panpsychism and our understanding of the physical, *the* issue which is at the heart of panpyschism. The second is by David Chalmers, who played a large role in the rebirth of interest in panpsychism at the end of the 20th century with his famous invocation of the 'hard problem' of consciousness and has since done much to deepen our understanding of panpsychism. His paper examines a comprehensive set of forms of idealism, the connection with panpsychism, and considers the question whether idealism is the natural endpoint beyond panpsychism for those moved by the seeming intractability of the problem of consciousness.

I would like to thank all the contributors to the handbook who took my editorial interventions in good spirit and waited patiently for the publication to come together. I also thank the team at Routledge who have shown understanding and patience across a long gestation period, and who were always fully supportive, not least – to my mind – in tracking down the beautiful Emily Carr painting which graces the handbook's cover.

1

INTRODUCTION
A Panpsychist Manifesto

William Seager

The world is awake. That can stand as a slogan for *panpsychism*: the view that I will understand here as holding that consciousness is fundamental and ubiquitous in nature. This does not mean that everything is conscious. Whether a particular non-fundamental entity is conscious will depend upon the arrangement of its fundamental constituents given some presumed laws of 'mental chemistry'[1] which govern the emergence of complex forms of consciousness. So in bare outline panpsychism presents a familiar picture of fundamental features interacting in ways to generate more complex forms, it's just that the catalog of the fundamental includes consciousness. Nor does panpsychism entail that sophisticated, high-level, human-like consciousness is ubiquitous. The term 'consciousness' is notoriously hard to define and the victim of multitudes of more or less well motivated (re)definitions. I aim for a minimal conception. For contrast, compare this expansive notion of consciousness, plucked merely for illustrative purposes from Aaronson (2016): 'displaying intelligent behavior (by passing the Turing Test or some other means) might be thought a necessary condition for consciousness'. On the minimal conception, consciousness does not at all require that ability to pass the Turing test. Feeling pain (or any other sensation) alone is sufficient for consciousness; consciousness implies only sentience. It's worth noting this because there is a somewhat pernicious ambiguity lurking here, that between a property and the evidence we have for ascribing it. Although still inaccurate, Aaronson's dictum is closer to the truth if we change the final phrase to 'a necessary condition for the ascription of consciousness'. But note that we can have *theoretical* reasons for ascribing a property without there being any direct observational evidence for the ascription. So, the kind of minimal consciousness in question is not 'self-consciousness' or 'transcendental subjectivity', or awareness of the self as a subject, or awareness of one's own mental states, or the ability to conceptualize one's own mental states as such. Consciousness is simply sentience, or the way things are present (to the mind).

It is undeniable that panpsychism is intuitively implausible. It is frequently subject to derision by philosophers, being labeled 'absurd' (Searle 2013) and 'ludicrous' (McGinn 1999: 97). Even sympathizers have qualms. Thomas Nagel worries that panpsychism carries the taint of 'the faintly sickening odor of something put together in the metaphysical laboratory' (1986: 49). Such denigrations stem from a certain confidence – misplaced I think – in our pre-existing conception of the nature of the physical world and a rather strange lack of confidence in our conception of subjective consciousness. We think we know what matter is, and we think we thereby know that it just is *not* the kind of thing which is or could be intrinsically conscious. In fact, though commonplace the former belief is demonstratively mistaken, which leaves open the status of the latter claim.

This is not a new thought. In one form or another it dates back at least to 19th-century writers such as Ernst Mach and William James, and in the early 20th century to Bertrand Russell and Arthur Eddington. The basic idea that the nature of matter is not obvious just from our daily interactions with material objects forms the core of Noam Chomsky's intriguing but somewhat obscure views on the mind-body problem, seemingly leading to Chomsky requiring/expecting a physical-science revolution before consciousness can be understood as a natural phenomenon (see 2000: ch. 4). The staunch anti-panpsychist John Searle sometimes also suggests the need for a revolution in science in order to understand how consciousness is a 'biological phenomenon', likening the situation to that of physics prior to the introduction of the electromagnetic field (1992: 101 ff.). Searle's claim that there is no special problem of consciousness because of the 'biological powers' of the brain has always struck me as, therefore, rather strange and one wishes he would explain, not in the details that can be left to science, but just the general mechanism of emergence by which the biological generates consciousness which would then reveal to us where to look for the neurological details. There is considerable recent work devoted to understanding the nature of the physical (see e.g. Montero 2009; Wilson 2006) and much current interest in the associated doctrine of Russellian Monism (see e.g. Alter and Nagasawa 2015). This idea is forcefully expressed in defense of panpsychism in the work of Galen Strawson (see e.g. 2006, 2003 and Strawon's chapter in this volume).

In the face of this natural antipathy, consideration of the philosophical advantages of panpsychism is the best way for it to gain sympathy. The primary motivator for panpsychism is the problem of consciousness. Over the last fifty years we have witnessed staggering advances in our knowledge of the brain and our ability to observe it in action. As we enter into the search for the elusive neural correlates of consciousness there are truly remarkable developments in mapping the relations between states of consciousness and neural activity.

Perhaps the most astonishing example of our growing knowledge, which is now underpinning practical clinical interventions, is the work of Adrian Owen, who investigates people diagnosed as being in a profound vegetative state. Such patients are incapable of making any overt behavioral response which could signal residual consciousness and have been regarded as completely unconscious. Owen has found that a disturbing number of such patients are in fact 'locked in' – fully conscious but cut off completely from their bodies. Using real-time functional MRI, Owen is able to interact with supposedly vegetative subjects by asking them to imagine various activities, such as playing tennis, or walking around their home. It is possible to identify the (no doubt partial) neural correlates of what the subject is imagining and thus open up a channel of communication. Owen is currently working on non-MRI solutions which patients will be able to use outside his laboratory, perhaps even at home.[2] This is what we can do now. There is little doubt that our ability to discover and track neural correlates of conscious states will expand enormously over the next decades.

Nonetheless, the infamous 'explanatory gap' (see Levine 1983) between the physical states of the brain and consciousness remains. Finding neural correlates does not show us how the brain manages to generate or realize consciousness and thereby solve David Chalmers's 'hard problem' (see his 1995, 1996). It seems likely that we will in the near future discover deeper and much more specific neural signatures of conscious states, perhaps involving neural synchronization or distinctive neural or subneuron dynamical activity associated with consciousness. That too won't reveal how consciousness is produced by the brain: these mechanisms are only more fine-grained correlations. There is a problem of principle here.

Why is that? As hinted previously, the core of the problem is the apparent mismatch between the nature of the physical world as we understand our fundamental theories to have revealed and the subjective, 'what it is like' aspect of minimal conscious experience. It feels like something to be awake and this just seems utterly foreign to how we regard and, for many, how we *ought* to regard the material world.

I take it that physics provides our scientific understanding of that world at the most fundamental level. However, its theories are perpetually provisional and the more or less background metaphysical pictures which they both suggest and spring from have a distressing history of being radically over-turned by those of newer theories. And yet it is undeniable that we have accumulated knowledge. This is possible because the metaphysical picture which lurks within or behind our physical theories is not essential to their use and need not be preserved across scientific revolutions, even as explanatory and predictive power is retained and expanded. What is preserved is the relational or structural systems which physical theory maps out and by which it is confirmed and becomes predictively successful.[3] These structures are all, ultimately, relations between observable quantities for which we have labels such as 'mass', 'electric charge', 'momentum', etc., all definable in terms of observable *motion*. Over centuries of development, physical theory has become successively more complex (for example, many kinds of charge beyond that of electric are now recognized) but all new hypotheses link to the relations between observable quantities, albeit sometimes indirectly.

It is unsurprising that nowhere in this system do we find subjectivity, nor in the development of physics is there any need to posit a subjective aspect to nature. The explanatory gap is exactly the problem of how a world which is supposed to be completely described at the fundamental level by a science which has no place or need for subjectivity nonetheless somehow includes the subjective aspect of the world we call 'consciousness'.

The problem has been recognized for a very long time. In 1714 Leibniz expressed it with his 'mill argument' in the *Monadology*:

> Imagine there were a machine which *by its structure* produced thought, feeling, and percep-
> tion. We can imagine it as being enlarged while maintaining the same relative proportions,
> to the point where we could go inside it, as we would go into a mill. But if that were so,
> when we went in we would find nothing but pieces which push one against another, and
> never anything to account for a perception ... perception, and everything that depends on
> it, is inexplicable by mechanical principles.
>
> (1714/1989: 215, my emphasis)

Note that Leibniz makes the anti-structuralist point that the causal organization of the mill, or the brain, cannot provide an explanation of the appearance of consciousness even if it is correlated with it.[4]

Leibniz was targeting the so-called 'mechanical philosophy' which, roughly speaking, asserted that the material world was, as Newton put it, such that 'God in the Beginning form'd Matter in solid, massy, hard, impenetrable Particles, of such Sizes and Figures, and with such other Properties, and in such Proportion to Space, as most conduced to the End for which he form'd them' (1730/1979, Query 31). Of course, Newton did not stop with this characterization but left the strict mechanical view behind by adding that 'these Particles have not only a Vis inertiæ, accompanied with such passive Laws of Motion as naturally result from that Force, but also that they are moved by certain active Principles'. Gravity is but one example of such 'principles', which he also called 'Powers, Virtues, or Forces'.[5] Newton expected a scientific chemistry to emerge in time based upon them.

A philosophically purified version of mechanism was much later articulated by C. D. Broad which can stand as the mechanistic ideal, whose essence is:

(a) a single kind of stuff, all of whose parts are exactly alike except for differences of position and motion;
(b) a single fundamental kind of change, viz, change of position ...
(c) a single elementary causal law, according to which particles influence each other by pairs ...

(d) a single and simple principle of composition, according to which the behavior of any aggregate of particles, or the influence of any one aggregate on any other, follows in a uniform way from the mutual influences of the constituent particles taken by pairs.

(1925: 44–5)

This vision is so ethereal that nothing like it has ever been seriously entertained. But the actual mechanical worldview and its successors for a couple of centuries of furious and spectacularly successful development can be seen as implicitly inspired by this pure vision. It expresses well a picture of the world – let's call it 'LEGO® world' – formed of a very large number of very small parts which are metaphysically independent of each other, have individual identities (albeit ones of very little interest) but which can interact by local causation. The familiarity we have with things like this, think marbles or, indeed, LEGO bricks, is what funds confidence in our conception of matter or the physical and makes it seem intuitive and almost obvious . . . and very distant from subjectivity.

The mechanical world view leveraged this picture into an intuitive positive conception of the nature of matter: it came in chunks akin to the small particles we are familiar with in ordinary experience: impenetrable, capable of motion and – thanks ultimately to God's decree – observant of the fundamental rules or laws of nature which governed how these pieces interacted (e.g. conservation of energy). Exactly how and why these material units are 'forced' to obey the laws of nature remained (and remains) somewhat obscure. Perhaps the laws' power is just a primitive metaphysical fact which links properties with the appropriate level of modal force. Perhaps the laws somehow follow from the causal powers of the fundamental entities of the world. Maybe the laws are a mere catalog of universal regularities, or meta-regularities across a set of possible worlds (the 'nomologically possible worlds'). Perhaps the laws are an imposition of the conscious mind which 'imposes' them upon an intrinsically chaotic universe (we find laws of nature because we could not exist in those regions of possibility that were 'too' chaotic; a kind of anthropic Kantianism).

In any case, this conception of matter excluded consciousness as one of its properties (except perhaps if God directly and miraculously 'superadded' it to a material system[6]) and, in any case, there was no need to posit consciousness to generate all the forms and activities in which matter could participate. As to these forms, we now know that LEGO world is capable of implementing a Turing machine so such a world could at least simulate anything which can be computed (ignoring speculative hyper-computational devices), including quantum mechanics. Such a simulation might be very slow but one should not confuse the simulation runtime with the time internal to the simulation. Perhaps, so to speak, it might take seconds of simulation time to compute one yoctosecond of internal simulation time, but we can suppose that the simulation lives in an eternal and spatially infinite world so there is no principled limitation here (we can suppose the physics of the simulation world is unconstrained by anything except its being a LEGO world). Presumably, our entire universe, or at least the observable universe, can thus be simulated given that the number of possible initial conditions (the degrees of freedom of the big bang) is finite (which seems to be implied by current theory, e.g. the holographic principle and possible theories of quantum gravity).

So the LEGO world conception is in fact a spectacularly powerful one and it is based upon an intuitively attractive conception of the nature of matter. One reason panpsychism seems weird to people is that they have implicitly absorbed something like the mechanistic view of the material world and its conception of the nature of the physical. But notwithstanding the power of the LEGO world picture, its positive conception of the physical was exploded in the first half of the 20th century. Matter does not form the 'LEGO world' imagined by the early mechanists. It turns out that matter is nothing at all like 'matter' was supposed to be.

Of course, it is quantum mechanics that has revealed this to us. This lesson is perhaps the number one thing that quantum mechanics is 'trying to tell us'. Quantum entanglement seems to hint that nature is holistic and that a world of independent material parts is merely a kind of emergent approximation. This has been noted many times by physicists beginning almost from the birth of quantum mechanics:

- Erwin Schrödinger: a particle certainly is . . . not a durable little thing with individuality (1952: 241).
- Hans Primas: the idea . . . that the material world is . . . structured by some kind of interacting 'elementary systems' is in sharp contradiction [with] quantum mechanics (1998: 88).
- Basil Hiley: quantum phenomena require us to think in a radical new way, a way in which we will have to ultimately give up both the notion of particles and fields (1999: 116).
- David Bohm: the entire universe must, on a very accurate level, be regarded as a single indivisible unit in which separate parts appear as idealizations permissible only on a classical level of accuracy of description (1951: 167).

Our best quantum theory asserts that fundamental reality is composed not of material particles at all but rather strange universal fields, the temporary excitations of which can appear to our experiments as particle-like apparitions. These fields appear to exist in an extremely (infinite?) high-dimensional space which cannot be directly identified with the space and time of experience.

But despite the radical revision required by the quantum mechanical picture of the world, our new physics has no need to add *consciousness* to the quantum fields to generate the physical phenomena and structure that we can observe.[7] The structures and systems of relations amongst the physical attributes of the world are generated from the purely physical fundamental features posited by physics with no hint of intrinsic subjectivity. So the great revolution in physics occasioned by the discovery of quantum mechanics has not by itself closed the explanatory gap and solved the hard problem of consciousness. In fact, as noted, some aspects of quantum physics, most famously the nature of observation or measurement, may suggest a fundamental role for consciousness[8] but, even if it is real, it is a role which figures *outside* of the system described by physical theory, breaking the law which governs the evolution of the quantum state.

The end of LEGO world and the mechanistic, or neo-mechanistic, picture of the world means we have lost any viable positive conception of the fundamental nature of matter. What we are left with is nothing more than the relational structure linked to observables, which physics maps out for us with such stunning success. It is thus also the case that there is no direct impediment to the panpsychist hypothesis stemming from an acceptable positive conception of the nature of the physical.

Lacking an explanation of consciousness in physical terms and lacking any conception of material reality beyond the structural, the panpsychist steps into the opening and suggests that perhaps the fundamental reality of the physical world itself partakes of some aspect of subjective consciousness. Again, this does not mean that quantum field particle states are reflecting about their own existence, enjoying a rich inner life akin to our own (though some vast multi-particle states are, namely ourselves). But minimal, unsophisticated and unreflective consciousness is much more common than its opposite, as witnessed by the host of pretty clearly conscious animals, some of which must have extremely limited forms of awareness. All the panpsychist needs to posit is that some form of subjectivity, some kind of primitive feeling, is at the foundation of the physical world.

No positive conception of the physical precludes this posit, since we have no such conception. The hypotheses of physics, of course, make no mention of consciousness but this is no surprise given the structuralist constraints of physical science. But, roughly speaking, something beyond structure is needed to make reality concrete. This point was perhaps made most precisely and forcefully by Max Newman (1928) in his critique of Russell's attempt at a purely structural account of science. Given any system of entities, a merely abstract specification of structure as, say, sets of ordered n-tuples, is revealed to be already present (sets exist if their members do). Something has to 'select' a certain structure as 'real' or concrete and, obviously, this 'something' has to go beyond simply additional relational structure. This point should not be over interpreted. It does not imply the return of objects in the sense of independent units with persistent and genuine individuality. It is simply the requirement that some form of concrete reality is needed to, so to speak, realize what are otherwise pure abstractions.[9] Why not, asks the panpsychist, let the one nonstructural reality we are already acquainted with and for which we do have a positive conception, namely our own subjectivity, stand as this foundation?

I will concede that this sort of consideration does not make panpsychism exactly plausible. It strikes many as beyond strange to think of the world as awake and kind of 'humming' with a primitive consciousness suffused throughout it as if there was an extra dimension of basic subjectivity. Many or most would still prefer a physicalist metaphysics. But it seems to me that, at bottom, there are only two alternatives which abide with standard physicalism.[10]

The first is emergentism. Like the word 'consciousness', the term 'emergence' is fraught with ambiguity. The minimal sense of the notion is simply that of a system having properties which are not possessed by its parts. Familiar and uncontroversial examples abound: the liquidity of water, the vortex structure of a tornado or hurricane. Commonplace but more exotic and controversial forms are things like the collective intentionality of groups or nations. In any case, the world is awash in emergence: almost everything you could think of has properties which are not shared by the fundamental physical entities postulated by physics. But this sort of standard or conservative emergence based upon complexity does not engender an explanatory gap. When vast numbers of hydrogen and oxygen atoms, for example, get together just right (and noting that these atoms, and their constituent nucleons are themselves emergent entities of the same sort) we get liquid water, which is a remarkable substance whose complexities are still not fully understood, although we do more every day with 'ab initio molecular dynamics simulations' of critical temperatures, density changes and the like (see e.g. Morawietz et al. 2016). Such efforts reveal that there is no doubt about the general route from oxygen and hydrogen to the properties of water. From one point of view, this should not be at all surprising. The properties of water at issue are themselves purely structural and a natural target for the structure-based systems explored by more fundamental physics.

On a much grander level, we have learned a tremendous amount about the emergence of the classical world from its quantum underpinnings via decoherence (see the canonical text Joos et al. 2003) and the rise of effective field theory, understood via the renormalization group procedure, which reveals why the world is amenable to our theoretical descriptions even if we can be quite sure that these descriptions are in themselves incomplete and ultimately inaccurate. Thus quantum field theory itself is regarded as a merely empirically adequate emergent within a delimited sector of nature: 'we have learned in recent years to think of our successful quantum field theories . . . as "effective field theories", low-energy approximations to a deeper theory that might not even be a field theory' (Weinberg 1995: xxi). Note that from the structuralist viewpoint the prospect of potentially radical theoretical transformation is not a big problem. The predictive and explanatory successes of field theories remain since the structure they revealed remains after theory change.

Let's group this widespread and internally quite diverse form of emergence under the term of 'conservative emergence'. Its twin hallmarks are first, that there is an intelligible route from the constituents of a system, broadly conceived to include everything from atoms to field states to theoretical structures, to its emergent properties, even if complexity will often preclude precise predictions of exact values of the emergent features; and second, that the emergent features will be largely describable and explicable in terms of their own proprietary laws, albeit always subject to potential interference from the more fundamental submergent underpinnings. It is an amazing fact about our world that it is structured by a hierarchy of relatively autonomous emergent domains (of course, if it were not, we would not be here).

The emergence of subjectivity presents a problem of an entirely different order and seems to call for more than conservative emergence. Ever more complex calculations of the behavior of ever more complicated physical systems will not get us to consciousness, even if it should prove possible to model the behavior of human beings, say via sophisticated computational neural simulations. There is no intelligible route from the relational structures found in our physical science to the intrinsic property of subjectivity. We are thus left with a *radical* emergence in which subjectivity simply appears at some, seemingly arbitrary, point in the physical development of the universe rather like Locke's fantasy of God directly 'superadding' consciousness to matter. Although logically possible, such a radical emergence is entirely at odds with the whole point of the physicalist enterprise. Furthermore, there is no reason to think that a radically emergent feature is itself physical in nature; quite the opposite in fact, given that all the physical features we know are either fundamental or conservative emergents that arise from assemblages and interactions of, ultimately, the fundamental features of the physical world.

Absent emergence, the second alternative is denial. Perhaps there is nothing more to the world than the relational structures posited by physics, along with all the conservatively emergent outgrowths of basic physical processes. There are two immediate problems with such a heroic response. The first is that we are left in ignorance about the underlying nature of matter. I suppose the best physicalist reply is that this is simply an unavoidable and fundamental limitation to our knowledge, regrettable perhaps but not such as to recommend endorsing panpsychism over epistemic humility (see Langton 1998; Lewis 2009).

The second problem seems much more serious: denying the reality of subjective experience is a desperate measure and one of dubious coherence. The immediately most obvious argument for the incoherence of the position is very simple:

1. If consciousness is an illusion then it merely seems that it exists.
2. But if anything *seems* to exist, that seeming is a state of consciousness.
3. Therefore consciousness (states of consciousness) exists.

The most developed ultra-eliminativism about experience itself is that of Daniel Dennett which attempts, cleverly but ultimately unsuccessfully, to work around this argument. Dennett proposes that we suffer an illusion that subjective experience exists but that this illusion is a purely cognitive 'thought-illusion' which can be explained in terms of a science of entirely nonconscious intentional states (see e.g. Dennett 1991; for criticism see Seager 2017). Dennett exploits the fact that the term 'seems' has both an experiential and epistemic sense (contrast 'the sun seems to be rising' versus 'it seems that Trump will irreparably harm America'). The latter sense does not immediately demand any experiential component, which is why Dennett can say without falling into immediate contradiction that '[t]here seems to be phenomenology. . . . But it does not follow from this undeniable, universally attested fact that there really is phenomenology' (1991: 366).

Of course, this line of attack requires some explication of a purely cognitive, non-experiential theory of thought content which Dennett has attempted to supply with his theory of intentional stances. A particularly sophisticated deployment of this account leads to what he calls the method of heterophenomenology. Applying it to those misguided enough to believe in consciousness, heterophenomenology

> involves extracting and purifying texts from (apparently) speaking subjects, and using those texts to generate a theorist's fiction, the subject's heterophenomenological world. This fictional world is populated with all the images, events, sounds, smells, hunches, presentiments, and feelings that the subject (apparently) sincerely believes to exist in his or her (or its) stream of consciousness.
>
> (Dennett 1991: 98)

The basic problem with this approach, as I see it, is that it fairly obviously has a tacit dependence on the experience and consciousness of the notional 'researcher' who is performing the heterophenomenological exercise.

One way to see this is to take an epistemological route. Following the old path of Descartes, let us each ask ourselves whether we know that something exists, or that something is happening right now. It is evident that we have access to a realm of data which by itself guarantees that yes, indeed, something exists. But the relational structures of physics cannot provide that guarantee since their existence is not a certainty: what is certain is the realm of subjective experience. If we posit that this realm does not exist, then we are left with the disturbing possibility that, given how things are now, nothing at all exists. If anything is clear it is that that thought is self refuting as soon as it is consciously thought. We do have access to a realm of immediately available and unassailable self-knowledge, albeit of a quite limited form (which limitations Descartes also emphasized). Denying this is to undermine the claim that we can know we are thinking at all, or indeed, that we know that anything exists. It is much more plausible that consciousness exists than that we cannot unassailably assert certain propositions which we understand.

Granting that conscious experience exists (as if this were a concession!) does not entail panpsychism. We can retain an epistemic humility about the underlying nature of the material world along with the – in this context now somewhat puzzlingly assertive – denial that it involves subjectivity. And we can always retain the hope that a conservatively emergent path from neuroscience (or elsewhere in the sciences) will illuminate the generation of consciousness by a world bereft of fundamental subjectivity. But the former view is not mandatory and there is not the slightest hint of how the latter might be accomplished.

Panpsychism promises to integrate our scientific and 'personal' view of the world and do so in a way that respects both the completeness of the physical picture of the causal structure of the world it investigates and the role of consciousness itself. The price to pay is admission of subjectivity into the foundation of the world as one of its fundamental features.

Needless to say, panpsychism faces many problems beyond its initial air of implausibility. But these are problems which can be philosophically explored, analyzed and perhaps solved. For example, one might wonder why, if panpsychism is true, we see no sign of subjectivity at the fundamental physical level (electrons do not seem to be experiential subjects). But in fact the only direct revelation of subjectivity is in our own experience and the panpsychist interprets this as evidence, that 'consciousness . . . provides a kind of "window" on to our brains' thereby revealing 'some at least of the intrinsic qualities of the states and processes which go to make up the material world' (Lockwood 1989: 159). The fact that very simple physical systems do not exhibit complex behavior should not be surprising but it's hardly clear that this *shows* they lack a subjective aspect.

The most vexing difficulty facing panpsychism is the so-called 'combination problem' (see James 1890/1950: ch. 6; Seager 1995), which is the issue of how the primitive foundational aspect of subjectivity postulated by the panpsychist builds itself into the sophisticated and rich forms of consciousness which creatures like us enjoy. This is not the place to discuss this in detail. Suffice to say that recent work has offered a variety of possible approaches to the combination problem (see many of the papers in Brüntrup and Jaskolla 2016, especially Chalmers 2016 and Goff 2016, and many of the chapters in this volume). Some of these approaches use the reasonably familiar relation of co-consciousness, some use a relation of phenomenal blending, some devise a notion of phenomenal bonding and some develop the idea that primitive experiential aspects 'fuse' into new forms, superceding the originals. It is also possible to re-orient the problem by adopting a radical holism, in which the single fundamental entity is the universe as a whole. Panpsychism then becomes what is called 'cosmopsychism', and the combination problem becomes the 'de-combination' problem. This somewhat Spinozistic view is as yet little explored but see Goff (2017) as well as the chapters of Albahari and Goff in this volume. All of these ideas face serious objections, but they all stand as potential answers to the combination problem. The point here is that the combination problem is one that can be addressed fruitfully. It is not a showstopper.

Philosophical exploration and development of the panpsychism is possible and has already proved fruitful. Panpsychism is a viable solution to the traditional mind-body problem and addresses the more modern specific problem of consciousness. We can throw off the shackles of an outmoded and falsely restrictive conception of the physical and declare that the world is awake.

Notes

1. This term goes back to John Stuart Mill (see 1843/1963: 108–9); see also Nagel (1979).
2. Owen has written a beautiful and fascinating popular exposition of his work entitled *Into the Gray Zone* (2017); a scholarly presentation of methods and results can be found in Owen (2008).
3. For philosophical discussion of scientific structuralism, the doctrine that science provides only knowledge of structural or relational features of reality see French (2014).
4. Leibniz's celebrated solution to the mind-body problem, the pre-established harmony (1695/1997) between the material and mental realms, *predicts* the existence of neural correlates of consciousness. Leibniz (1696/1997) provides an interesting discussion of the three possible relations between matter and consciousness: causal, miraculous and harmony.
5. Newton's acceptance of such perhaps 'occult' powers was anathema to strict mechanists who denied both action at a distance and hoped for a physics based solely upon interparticle collision. Leibniz himself, along with several other luminaries, attempted to develop vortex-based accounts of planetary motion which avoided Newtonian gravitation with some incomplete success (see Aiton 1972).
6. Something Locke famously asserted was within the power of God and to which Leibniz agreed, though according to him it could be accomplished only via an objectionable 'perpetual miracle' (see 1704/1996: 67).
7. It may need to add consciousness to the picture in order to get determinate observations, but that is an extra feature that has always seemed unscientific. Very few, but not zero, physicists believe that the solution to the measurement problem essentially involves consciousness (see McQueen (2019) for a popular level philosophical discussion).
8. The specific idea that measurement requires the intervention of a conscious observer appears in somewhat veiled ways in Bohr and von Neumann. It is explicitly advanced in London and Bauer (1939/1983) and Wigner (1962). A modern proponent is Henry Stapp (e.g. 1993).
9. For discussion of the subtleties of Newman's objection to Russell see Demopoulos and Friedman (1985); see also van Fraassen (2007) and the radical pro-stucturalist discussion in Ladyman et al. (2007).
10. There are non-physicalist alternatives to panpsychism. Idealism, for example, retains defenders and has sparked some renewed interest in recent philosophy (see e.g. Foster 2008; Pelczar 2015; Chalmers's paper in this volume). Various forms of dualism are further alternatives that still have a few defenders (see e.g. Robinson 2004; Lavazza and Robinson 2014). Arguing for panpsychism over such non-physicalist views cannot be undertaken here, but roughly speaking it is panpsychism's ability to integrate with the scientific view of the world and provide a solution to the problem of mental causation that are its main advantages.

References

Aaronson, Scott (2016). 'The Ghost in the Quantum Turing Machine'. In S. Barry Cooper and Andrew Hodges (eds.), *The Once and Future Turing*. Cambridge: Cambridge University Press, pp. 193–296.

Aiton, Eric (1972). *The Vortex Theory of Planetary Motions*. London: Macdonald.

Alter, T., and Nagasawa, Y. (eds.) (2015). *Consciousness in the Physical World: Perspectives on Russellian Monism*. Oxford: Oxford University Press.

Bohm, David (1951). *Quantum Theory*. Englewood Cliffs, NJ: Prentice-Hall.

Broad, C. D. (1925). *Mind and Its Place in Nature*. London: Routledge and Kegan Paul.

Brüntrup, G., and L. Jaskolla (eds.) (2016). *Panpsychism*. Oxford: Oxford University Press.

Chalmers, David (1995). 'Facing Up to the Problem of Consciousness'. *Journal of Consciousness Studies*, 2 (3): 200–19. (Reprinted in J. Shear (ed.), *Explaining Consciousness*. Cambridge, MA: MIT Press, pp. 9–32, 1997).

Chalmers, David (1996). *The Conscious Mind: In Search of a Fundamental Theory*. Oxford: Oxford University Press.

Chalmers, David (2016). 'The Combination Problem for Panpsychism'. In G. Brüntrup and L. Jaskolla (eds.), *Panpsychism*. Oxford: Oxford University Press, pp. 229–48.

Chomsky, Noam (2000). *New Horizons in the Study of Language and Mind*. Cambridge: Cambridge University Press.

Demopoulos, William, and Friedman, Michael (1985). 'Bertrand Russell's the Analysis of Matter: Its Historical Context and Contemporary Interest'. *Philosophy of Science*, 52 (4): 621–39.

Dennett, Daniel (1991). *Consciousness Explained*. Boston: Little, Brown & Co.

Foster, John (2008). *A World for Us: The Case for Phenomenalistic Idealism*. Oxford: Oxford University Press.

French, Steven (2014). *The Structure of the World: Metaphysics and Representation*. Oxford: Oxford University Press.

Goff, Philip (2016). 'The Phenomenal Bonding Solution to the Combination Problem'. In G. Brüntrup and L. Jaskolla (eds.), *Panpsychism*. Oxford: Oxford University Press, pp. 283–304.

Goff, Philip (2017). *Consciousness and Fundamental Reality*. Oxford: Oxford University Press.

Hiley, Basil (1999). 'Active Information and Teleportation'. In D. Greenberger, W. Reiter, and A. Zeilinger (eds.), *Epistemological and Experimental Perspectives on Quantum Physics*. Dordrecht: Kluwer.

James, William (1890/1950). *The Principles of Psychology*, vol. 1. New York: Henry Holt and Co. (Reprinted in 1950, New York: Dover, ed.X. (Page references to the Dover edition.)).

Joos, Erich, Dieter Zeh, H. et al. (2003). *Decoherence and the Appearance of a Classical World in Quantum Theory*. Berlin: Springer-Verla.

Ladyman, James, Ross, Don et al. (2007). *Everything Must Go: Metaphysics Naturalized*. Oxford: Oxford University Press.

Langton, Rae (1998). *Kantian Humility: Our Ignorance of Things in Themselves*. Oxford: Oxford University Press.

Lavazza, A., and Robinson, H. (eds.) (2014). *Contemporary Dualism: A Defense*. London: Routledge.

Leibniz, Gottfried Wilhelm (1695/1997). 'New System of the Nature of Substances and Their Communication, and of the Union Which Exists Between the Soul and the Body'. In R. Woolhouse and R. Francks (eds.), *Leibniz's 'New System' and Associated Contemporary Texts*. Oxford: Oxford University Press, pp. 7–36.

Leibniz, Gottfried Wilhelm (1696/1997). 'Letter to Basnage'. In R. Woolhouse and R. Francks (eds.), *Leibniz's 'New System': And Associated Contemporary Texts*. Oxford: Oxford University Press, Clarendon Press, pp. 62–4. (See C. I. Gerhardt (ed.) *Die philosophischen schriften von Gottfried Wilhelm Leibniz*, vol. 4. Berlin: Weidmann, 1880, p. 496ff).

Leibniz, Gottfried Wilhelm (1704/1996). *New Essays on Human Understanding*. Cambridge: Cambridge University Press. (J. Bennett and P. Remnant (trans. and ed.). Although this work was not published by Leibniz it was an essentially complete work, composed around 1704–5).

Leibniz, Gottfried Wilhelm (1714/1989). 'Monadology'. In Roger Ariew and Daniel Garber (eds.), *G. W. Leibniz: Philosophical Essays*. Indianapolis: Hackett, pp. 214–24.

Levine, Joseph (1983). 'Materialism and Qualia: The Explanatory Gap'. *Pacific Philosophical Quarterly*, 64: 354–61.

Lewis, David (2009). 'Ramseyan Humility'. In David Braddon-Michell and Robert Nola (eds.), *Conceptual Analysis and Philosophical Naturalism*. Cambridge, MA: MIT Press, Bradford Books, pp. 203–22.

Lockwood, Michael (1989). *Mind, Brain and the Quantum*. Oxford: Blackwell.

London, Fritz, and Bauer, Edmond (1939/1983). 'The Theory of Observation in Quantum Mechanics'. In J. Wheeler and W. Zurek (eds.), *Quantum Theory and Measurement*. Princeton: Princeton University Press, pp. 217–59. (Originally published as 'La théorie de lobservation en mécanique quantique'. In *Actualités scientifiques et industrielles*, no. 775, Paris: Heinemann, 1939.).

McGinn, Colin (1999). *The Mysterious Flame: Conscious Minds in a Material World*. New York: Basic Books.

McQueen, Kelvin (2019). 'Does Consciousness Cause Quantum Collapse?'. *Philosophy Now* URL=https://philosophynow.org/issues/121/Does_Consciousness_Cause_Quantum_Collapse.

Mill, John Stuart (1843/1963). *A System of Logic*, vol. 7–8 of *The Collected Works of John Stuart Mill*. Toronto: University of Toronto Press.

Montero, Barbara (2009). 'What Is the Physical?' In B. McLaughlin, A. Beckermann, and S. Walter (eds.), *The Oxford Handbook of Philosophy of Mind*. Oxford: Oxford University Press, pp. 173–88.

Morawietz, Tobias, Singraber, Andreas et al. (2016). 'How van der Waals Interactions Determine the Unique Properties of Water'. *Proceedings of the National Academy of Sciences*, 113 (30): pp. 8368–73. www.pnas.org/content/113/30/8368.abstract.

Nagel, Thomas (1979). 'Panpsychism'. In *Mortal Questions*. Cambridge: Cambridge University Press, pp. 181–95. (Reprinted in D. Clarke, *Panpsychism: Past and Recent Selected Readings*. Albany: SUNY Press, 2004.).

Nagel, Thomas (1986). *The View from Nowhere*. Oxford: Oxford University Press.

Newman, M. (1928). 'Mr. Russell's Causal Theory of Perception'. *Mind*, 37: 137–48.

Newton, Isaac (1730/1979). *Opticks, or, a Treatise of the Reflections, Refractions, Inflections and Colours of Light*. New York: Dover, ed.X.

Owen, Adrian M. (2008). 'Functional Neuroimaging of the Vegetative State'. *Nature Reviews Neuroscience*, 9 (3): 235–43.

Owen, Adrian M. (2017). *Into the Gray Zone: A Neuroscientist Explores the Border Between Life and Death*. New York: Scribner.

Pelczar, Michael (2015). *Sensorama: A Phenomenalist Analysis of Spacetime and Its Contents*. Oxford: Oxford University Press.

Primas, Hans (1998). 'Emergence in Exact Natural Science'. *Acta Polytechnica Scandinavica*, 91: 83–98.

Robinson, William (2004). *Understanding Phenomenal Consciousness*. Cambridge: Cambridge University Press.

Schrödinger, E. (1952). 'Are There Quantum Jumps? Part II'. *The British Journal for the Philosophy of Science*, 3 (11): 233–42.

Seager, William (1995). 'Consciousness, Information and Panpsychism'. *Journal of Consciousness Studies*, 2 (3): 272–88. (Reprinted in J. Shear (ed.), *Explaining Consciousness*. Cambridge, MA: MIT Press, 1997.).

Seager, William (2017). 'Could Consciousness Be an Illusion?' *Mind and Matter*, 15 (1): 7–28.

Searle, John (1992). *The Rediscovery of the Mind*. Cambridge, MA: MIT Press.

Searle, John (2013). 'Can Information Theory Explain Consciousness'. *New York Review of Books*, January 10: 54–58.

Stapp, Henry (1993). 'A Quantum Theory of the Mind-Brain Interface'. In *Mind, Matter and Quantum Mechanics*. Berlin: Springer, pp. 145–72.

Strawson, Galen (2003). 'Real Materialism'. In L. Anthony and N. Hornstein (eds.), *Chomsky and His Critics*. Oxford: Blackwell, pp. 49–88. (Reprinted with new postscript, in T. Alter and Y. Nagasawa (eds.), *Consciousness in the Physical World: Perspectives on Russellian Monism*. Oxford: Oxford University Press, 2015, pp. 161–208.

Strawson, Galen (2006). 'Realistic Monism: Why Physicalism Entails Panpsychism'. *Journal of Consciousness Studies*, 13 (10–11): 3–31. (Reprinted in A. Freeman (ed.), *Consciousness and Its Place in Nature*. Exeter: Imprint Academic, 2006.).

van Fraassen, BasC. (2007). 'Structuralism(s) About Science: Some Common Problems'. *Proceedings of the Aristotelian Society Supplementary Volume*, 81 (1): 45–61.

Weinberg, S. (1995). *The Quantum Theory of Fields, vol. 1: Foundations*. Cambridge: Cambridge University Press.

Wigner, Eugene (1962). 'Remarks on the Mind-Body Problem'. In I. Good (ed.), *The Scientist Speculates*. London: Heinemann, pp. 284–302. (Reprinted in J. Wheeler and W. Zurek (eds.), *Quantum Theory and Measurement*. Princeton: Princeton University Press, 1983, pp. 168–81.).

Wilson, Jessica M. (2006). 'On Characterizing the Physical'. *Philosophical Studies*, 131 (1): 61–99.

PART I

Historical Reflections

2

PLATO AND PANPSYCHISM

Daniel Dombrowski

1. Introduction

David Ray Griffin's 1998 book *Unsnarling the World Knot: Consciousness, Freedom, and the Mind-Body Problem* alludes to a rope metaphor from Schopenhauer to the effect that the key philosophical problem since the 17th century (the mind-body problem) is, on prevailing assumptions, unsolvable. One can highlight several prominent philosophers of mind to illustrate why we have been tied in a 'world knot': William Seager has claimed that we have no idea whatsoever *how* consciousness 'emerges' from matter (1991: 195). Jaegwon Kim has held that we have reached a 'dead end' regarding the mind-body problem (1993: 367). Colin McGinn has alleged that we will *never* be able to understand the emergence of consciousness from the brain (1991: 1–2, 7). John Searle has suggested that most of mainstream philosophy of mind is 'obviously false' (1992: 3). And Galen Strawson has maintained that only a 'revolutionary' new way of thinking will enable us to respond adequately to the mind-body problem (1994: 92, 99). Although Daniel Dennett is a bit more optimistic regarding a solution to the mind-body problem on prevailing assumptions, even he has portrayed consciousness as a 'mystery' (1991: 21).

Some philosophers of mind think that panpsychism is the type of revolutionary thinking mentioned by Strawson that will enable us to unsnarl the world knot. In the context of the present chapter, however, Thomas Nagel's phrasing may be a bit more helpful when he says that 'radical' speculation is needed in order for such an unsnarling to be successful (1986: 10). I am taking the etymology of the word 'radical' seriously in that it comes from the Latin *radix* for 'root.' That is, contemporary panpsychists are offering an oxymoronic *radically new* approach to the mind-body problem as well as revitalizing an ancient solution to it. It is not often noticed in contemporary debates in philosophy of mind that panpsychism may very well be part of a *philosophia perennis* that goes back to Plato.

The spirit of the present chapter is captured well in a quotation from Josiah Royce, who once suggested that:

> Whenever I have most carefully revised my . . . standards, I am always able to see . . . that at best I have been finding out, in some new light, the true meaning that was latent in old traditions. . . . Revision does not mean mere destruction.
>
> (1908: 11)

When the questions are asked, how can experience arise out of, and act back upon, nonexperience?, or, how can consciousness arise out of, and act back upon, nonconsciousness?, the two major responses since the time of Descartes have been in terms of some form of dualism or some form of materialism. Indeed, the debate between dualists and materialists since the time of Descartes can be seen as entrenched.

But the situation is not as hopeless as it seems. This is due in part to the fact that some major philosophers of mind (e.g., Seager 1999; Strawson 2006) have moved toward panpsychism since the time when Griffin's book was published. The apparently entrenched character of the dualism–materialism debate should not prevent us from appreciating Plato's influence on Aristotle, Aristotle's influence on Leibniz, and the Leibnizian character of contemporary debates regarding panpsychism. For example, the whole point to Aristotelian and Thomistic hylomorphism was to suggest that matter without form and form without matter are the results of abstraction in that concrete reality is populated by 'formbodies' or 'mindbodies' or 'soulbodies,' to coin terms that try to capture the nondualistic character of hylomorphs. The Aristotelian idea that mind is, in a manner, all things is a protest against the view that mind is what is left over when one abstracts away from either behavior or matter. Rather, matter in motion just *is* mind in some fashion, hence, on one plausible reading of Aristotle, panpsychism is implicitly affirmed.

Leibniz is explicitly a panpsychist in his *Monadology*, but Leibniz's similarity to Aristotle is not often noticed. Newton insisted that an active principle had to be operative *in* nature, and not *ex machina* as in Descartes. But Leibniz thought that Newton did, in fact, unwittingly fall victim to use of the *ex machina* device. Leibniz's own defense of something fundamentally active in nature was seen by him as a return to Plato and Aristotle, specifically to the ideas that physical existents were characterized by *kinesis* (motion) and *dynamis* (dynamic power). It even makes sense to claim that an account of the universe as dynamic and vibratory would have surprised Plato less than it would Newton (see Whitehead 1978: 94). And Kant appears to rebuke those who ridicule Leibniz's panpsychism because, *if* we had to state what physical reality is in itself, we would have to follow Leibniz (1900: Part 1, Ch. 1).

I am obviously not doing justice to the rich history of panpsychism in this brief introduction. But I am trying to militate against the famous (or infamous) quip allegedly made by Quine that there are two quite different reasons why people enter philosophy: to do philosophy or merely to do history of philosophy. I am arguing that these two are not mutually exclusive. That is, thinking about the mind-body problem *is* historical thinking via major figures like Plato and Descartes, whether philosophers of mind realize it or not. Regarding the mind-body problem in general, and regarding panpsychism in particular, the following well-known quotation from Alfred North Whitehead seems most appropriate: 'The safest general characterization of the European philosophical tradition is that it consists of a series of footnotes to Plato' (Whitehead 1978: 39). In the present chapter I will be relying especially on the thought of Whitehead, Charles Hartshorne, and other process philosophers who have been quick to notice the panpsychist dimension of Plato's thought.

2. Some Panpsychist Passages

What does it mean to explain the world, in general, and human nature, in particular? On a Platonic basis such an explanation would seem to be in terms of either: (a) soul or (b) matter; or (c) both soul and matter. The second option would have been anathema to Plato. Further, there is considerable well-known evidence in Plato's dialogues in favor of the third option, leading many scholars to think of Plato as some sort of dualist. But the issue is complicated and not merely because of the understandable difficulty involved in determining Plato's own views in his dialogues. That is, there is also evidence in favor of the claim that the first, panpsychist option may be the best clue we have to understanding Plato's overall view. The main purpose of this chapter is to explore this option. In the course of this exploration I will also touch on the relationship between soul and Platonic forms as well as the importance of the World Soul in several of Plato's later dialogues. The forms and the World Soul make Plato's view somewhat unique in the history of panpsychism.

An initial passage to consider can be found at *Epinomis* 983d, where Plato's presumed spokesperson (the Athenian) suggests that soul is the universal cause of body. A key question is: how close do such passages take us to the claim that Plato was a panpsychist? His view seems to have been, at first glance at the *Phaedrus* (245e, also 246b, 275b) and *Laws* (896a, also 895c, 896d, 898d, 899a–b), that souls *initiate* change and transmit it to others, whereas bodies merely *receive* and transmit change. That is, soul is defined in terms of self-motion in the *Phaedrus* and *Laws* and, as a result, has a certain sort of ontological priority to body, a priority that is found in the *Epinomis* as well. (On the authenticity of the *Epinomis* as an epilogue to Plato's *Laws*, see Crombie 1962: 12, 329.)

For metaphysical or cosmological purposes, *psyche* is used by Plato to refer to experiencing, thinking, remembering, feeling, etc., and only for ethical or religious purposes does he use the term to refer to an enduring entity behind these processes. The dynamism of soul is evidenced in the new concrete reality that exists at each moment. Plato is well aware of the fact that the transition from motion to rest and from rest to motion does not occupy much of a stretch of time but occurs in an instant (*exaiphnes* – *Parmenides* 156). It is not illegitimate to infer that it is this self-moving, processual character of soul in Plato that is crucial in the effort to understand the relationship between soul and body.

An understandable mistake that could be made at this point would be to conclude that in Plato's dialogues soul is active whereas body is passive. But in the *Republic* it is clear that the degree of affective and cognitive adequacy in soul is due to the reliability of the influence it receives from the object that is experienced or known. This point enables us to see that it would indeed be a mistake to claim that in Plato souls are strictly active. In fact, one of the most obvious of the soul's powers is its ability to receive influence from others, as in perception. As one moves up the famous divided line in the *Republic* (509d–511e), what one finds is increasing adequacy of apprehension of the world due to an increasing ability of soul to receive influence from the reality apprehended: from imagination (*eikasia*), to belief (*doxa*), to hypothetical knowledge (*dianoia*), to the highest level of awareness (*noesis*).

The point of the present chapter is not to claim that Plato has to be viewed as a panpsychist, but rather that one does not have to view him as a dualist, as is commonly assumed. A key passage to consider in the effort to make intelligible the panpsychist tendency in his thought is *Sophist* 247d–e (also see 249a, 249d), where Plato's presumed spokesperson (the Eleatic Stranger) says the following:

> I suggest that anything has real being that is so constituted as to possess any sort of power either to affect anything else or to be affected, in however small a degree, by the most insignificant agent, though it be only once. I am proposing as a mark to distinguish real things that they are nothing but power.

Whitehead goes so far as to say that in this passage can be found the height of Plato's genius as a metaphysician (Whitehead 1967: 120). Being is here defined as power or *dynamis*, which is not accidentally the root of our word 'dynamic,' specifically the power to affect, or the power to be affected by, others. I take it that the 'or' (*eite*) in the preceding quotation does not refer to mutual exclusivity between influence and being influenced, hence 'and' (*kai*) might have better expressed the point. Further, the words 'nothing but power' in the preceding quotation might be better phrased in terms of the capacity for *dynamis*.

Plato's dialogue style betrays this idea. One does something with (not to) one's dialectical partner. This makes the dialogue style a good model for the general nature of reality. As opposed to authoritarian dictation, in dialectic it will not suffice to suggest that to speak and be heard are admirable, whereas to listen and to hear are not. Plato makes this point explicit in at least one dialogue, the *Gorgias* (508a). We will also see that to speak of the supreme soul (i.e., the World Soul) as persuading other souls is to presuppose that each lesser soul has the power to be moved.

Plato hints at the panpsychist position (in which only concrete singulars feel, and in which the abstract is real only in the concrete, thus soul is the inclusive type of reality) when he indicates that soul is coincident with every action and passion. But no ancient Greek thinker was in a position to fully understand the difference between singulars and aggregates in the smaller parts of nature. That is, there is a vast difference between soul as such or soul as a generic principle, on the one hand, and animal soul (including human soul), on the other. It is the lack of self-motion in everyday inanimate things that has caused materialists or dualists to suppose that the microscopic parts of these things also lack self-motion (see Hartshorne 1983: ch. 2–3).

In Plato's dialogues we learn that soul is the universal cause (*aitias tou holou* – *Epinomis* 988d), that it is (metaphysically rather than chronologically) prior to body (*presbyteras e somatos* – *Laws* 892a), that bodies are derived from soul (*soma de deuteron te kai hysteron* – *Laws* 896c), that we receive our being from soul (*Laws* 959a), and that soul is the primary source of all things (*psychen genesin hapanton einai proten* – *Laws* 899c). So although Plato could not fully understand the full significance of panpsychism in that he lived over two thousand years before the discovery of cells and other microscopic centers of power, it would be a mistake to think that he was totally ignorant of such significance by defending dualism *simpliciter*. (Also see *Philebus* 28d, 29a-31b; and *Timaeus* 30b–c, 31a, 40b–e, 69c–70e, 77b.)

William Lane Craig offers in formal outline something like the following argument (in abbreviated form), which indicates why the definition of soul in terms of self-motion is crucial in the effort to understand the panpsychist tendencies in Plato's thought. That is, a version of Craig's reconstruction of Plato's thought can be used not only to understand Plato's theology, but also to understand his flirtations with panpsychism:

a. Some things are in motion.
b. There are two kinds of motion: communicated motion and self-motion.
c. Communicated motion implies self-motion: (i) because things in motion imply a self-mover as their source of motion, otherwise there would be no starting point for the motion; and (ii) because things moved by another imply a prior mover.
d. If all things were at rest, only self-motion could arise directly from such a state: (i) because a thing moved by another implies the presence of another moving thing; (ii) but this contradicts the hypothesis that all things are at rest.
e. Therefore, the source of all motion is self-motion or soul

(Craig 1980: 4).

To say that there are strong grounds for thinking that Plato was a panpsychist is to say that self-motion is pervasive in Plato's cosmology, including the self-motion *of*, or self-motion *in*, plants, stars, the sun, and earth. That is, we would be wrong to assume that it is only human or animal souls that are capable of self-motion.

Although he finds the animism or panpsychism in Plato's dialogues (especially, the *Phaedrus*, the *Timaeus*, and the *Laws/Epinomis*) odd, Crombie emphasizes the importance of this aspect of Plato's thought. The self-motion of soul has not only intellectual, but also spiritual, significance in Plato's thought, as Crombie sees things, in that it is part of the effort to counteract the physicalist reductionism of the newly found atheists. The fact that Crombie himself does not find mechanism problematic is evidence in favor of the claim that he can be seen as an independent observer of Plato's animism or panpsychism (see Crombie 1962: 325–40).

3. The Forms and Soul

Two additional topics need to be considered in order to understand Plato's engagement with panpsychism. First, something has to be said about the relationship between soul and the forms in Plato. If the forms are seen as having causal power (and there is textual evidence that Plato viewed forms in this manner), then this might mean that whereas bodies can be moved by other moved things or by self-moved souls, souls can also be moved by the motionless forms. Yet if the forms are items in divine *psyche*, then soul in some sense is fundamental for metaphysical speculation and hence Plato came quite close to panpsychism. That is, panpsychism is compromised if too much emphasis is placed on forms or abstract objects as having causal power of their own or as having agency.

It is common to hear that the forms are 'independent,' even of the divine soul. It must be admitted that there are several passages in Plato's dialogues that support this interpretation. But if 'X is independent of Y' has any sharp meaning it must be that X could exist even if Y did not, which implies that Y is contingent. If X stands for the forms and Y for divine soul, then the nonexistence of God is being taken as possible. But this result conflicts with the treatments of divine soul in both the *Timaeus* and Book Ten of the *Laws*. It also conflicts with Plato's anticipation of the ontological argument (see Dombrowski 2006). That is, if God's existence is not contingent in Plato, then not only are the forms envisaged by divine soul, they could not lack this status. Both the forms and God are everlasting on Plato's view and as a result there can be no real independence of one from the other. God always exists as the ideal knower in Plato and the forms are the objects such an ideal knower would know. In different terms, on the extradeical view (where the forms have some sort of curious existence apart from both matter and soul) panpsychism is threatened, but on the more defensible intradeical view (where forms are items in divine psychical process) panpsychism is preserved.

It can be said that the greatest problem in Plato's metaphysics does not concern the theory of forms, but rather concerns the problem of how to sufficiently grasp the functions of soul as both receptive and creative. There are also the related problems of understanding internal and external relations in soul and how to come to terms with the way that soul interacts with body. Plato's analysis of becoming remains incomplete, because if knowing something is to change that something, as Plato sometimes indicates, then past events go on changing when we think about them. Plato probably flirted with this idea (that knowing something changes it) as a reaction to the opposite view that the past completely determines the present, in souls as well as in bodies. The self-motion of soul must mean that soul originates change, which is at least compatible with the view that necessary, although not sufficient, causal conditions are inherited from the past. Soul does not merely transmit tendencies from the past, nor just receive them, as in bodies.

4. The World Soul

Second, it is difficult to understand the topic of panpsychism in Plato without a consideration of his cosmology, dominated as it is by the concept of a World Soul. The concept of soul as self-moving or self-creative sheds light on Platonic theodicy in the sense that the lack of complete order in the world is explained by there being many souls that can get in each other's way. These many self-active agents imply indefinitely great if not complete disorder unless there is a supreme Soul to persuade the many lesser souls to conform to a cosmic plan. But they cannot *completely* fit such a plan for then they would not be self-determined.

The meaning of God as the World Soul having power over us is intelligible only if we see the World Soul as a self-moved mover of others who is also partially moved by these other self-movers. Such a God can rule the world only in the sense that such a soul sets optimal limits for free action. The divine can control the changes in us by inspiring us with novel ideas, hence by molding the divine life itself God presents us at each moment with a partly new ideal. But such a God is not omnipotent because omnipotent power would be a monopoly of power over the powerless, which is at odds with the aforementioned Platonic view that being *is* power.

The doctrine of the World Soul appears in at least five of Plato's later dialogues (*Statesman*, *Philebus*, *Timaeus*, *Laws*, *Epinomis*), indicating its importance to Plato. To help explicate both the characteristics of the World Soul and the implications of the World Soul for panpsychism in Plato, three levels of *psyche* can be distinguished.

P1 is *psyche* at the microscopic level of cells and atomic particles, where contemporary biology and physics can be seen to have vindicated Plato's forays into panpsychism. Reductionistic materialism in its various manifestations and determinism have faded, on the contemporary panpsychist view (see Griffin 1998), as reality in its fundamental constituents itself seems to have at least a partially indeterminate character of (Platonic) self-motion. That is, the sum total of efficient causes from the past does not supply the sufficient cause to explain the behavior of the smallest units of becoming in the world. Plato was wiser than he knew. Little did he realize that in 20th–21st-century science universal mechanism might give way to ubiquitous self-motion.

P2 is *psyche* per se, which involves feeling of feeling, found in animals and human beings, where central nervous systems enable 'higher' organisms as wholes to feel just as the constituent parts show at least prefigurements of feeling at a local level. And feeling *is* localized. Think of a knife stuck in the gut of any vertebrate or of sexual pleasure. P2 consists in taking these local feelings and collecting them so that an individual as a whole can feel what happens to its parts, even if the individual partially transcends the parts. If the reader thinks that all of this is foreign to Plato, it should be noted that in the *Republic* (462c–d) Plato makes it clear that if there is pain in one's finger (note, not the whole hand), the entire community (*pasa he koinonia*) of bodily connections is hurt. The organized whole of the individual is such that when one part is hurt there is a feeling of pain in the human being as a whole (*hole*) who has the pain in the finger. Of course, Plato's treatment of localized pain was not based on cell theory, but on obvious phenomenological evidence symbolized in the *Republic* by precisely localized intense pain in a finger rather than in an arm or a hand. Panpsychism helps us to better understand how, when one has pain in one's finger, the pain is in one sense mine and in another sense not mine. Further, there was some sort of dim awareness among the ancient Greeks of nerves (*neura*), which were significant parts of the ancient scientific view of the world (see Solmsen 1961).

P3 is divine *psyche*. If I am not mistaken, the following four-term analogy takes us to the heart of Plato's view of both panpsychism and the World Soul:

P1 : P2 :: P2 : P3

The universe is a societal organism (a World Soul), of which one member (the Demiurge) is preeminent, just as human beings are societies of cells (*neura* or 'nerves'), of which the mental part is preeminent.

Because an individual must, to maintain integrity, adapt to the environment, mortality is implied. But if we imagine the World Soul we must not consider an environment external to divinity, but an internal one: the world body of the World Soul (including the demiurgic divine mind). This cosmic, divine animal (*zoon* – *Timaeus* 30c) has such an intimate relation to the divine body that there must also be ideal ways of perceiving and remembering the bodily parts such that the World Soul can identify the microindividuals (P2) that are included. We can only tell when cells in our finger have been burned by the fire. We cannot identify the microindividuals as such.

Although the evidence in Plato's dialogues is somewhat unclear as to how matter could consist of multitudinous souls of extremely subhuman kinds, he had at least a glimmering that it was the multiplicity of souls that made general order possible (due to the persuasive influence of the World Soul on lesser souls) and absolute order impossible (due to the self-moving power of each soul). Each new divine state in the life of the World Soul harmonizes itself with both its predecessor and with the previous state of the *cosmos*. This is analogous to a human being harmonizing itself with its previous experience and bodily state, but with a decisive difference. The human soul must hope that its internal and the external environment will continue to make it possible for it to survive, whereas the World Soul has no such problem in that there is no external environment for the World Soul. But the differences between the World Soul and the human soul (the World Soul knows the microindividuals included within the divine life and the World Soul has no external environment) should not cloud the important similarities (the fact that self-change is integral to soul at all levels and the fact that the soul-body analogy used to understand the World Soul-world body helps us to better grasp the relationship between a human soul and the besouled parts of a human being). The autokinesis of soul at all levels (P1, P2, and P3) is precisely what enables Platonic panpsychism to avoid the bifurcation of the world (and the reductionistic reaction to such bifurcation) that has dominated philosophy since the time of Descartes.

The most important similarity lies in the fact that one's bodily cells (or *neura*) are associated, at a given moment, with one as a conscious supercellular singular, just as all lesser beings are associated with the society of singulars which in the *Timaeus* is called the divine animal or the World Soul. In a way, all talk of the World Soul short of strict univocity contains *some* negativity, in that God does not exist, know, love, etc. exactly as we do. With regard to the divine body, however, almost all theists in the Abrahamic religions have allowed this negativity to run wild by completely denying the divine body. This is perhaps why the World Soul strikes many or most contemporary readers as odd.

It did not strike Plato as odd, however. In fact, according to Plutarch, all of the ancient philosophers, except for Aristotle and the atomists, believed that the world was infused with a divine, animal soul (Plutarch III 1870: 133). In two passages in Plato's later dialogues (*Theaetetus* 176b–c; *Timaeus* 90a–d; also see *Republic* 500c–d) it is suggested that the goal of human soul is to become as much like divine soul as possible (*homoiosis theoi kata to dynaton*). This is possible because the World Soul and our souls are remotely akin, just as our souls are remotely akin to souls vastly inferior to our own, although these latter are at least proto-sentient centers of self-moving power. This *homoiosis* doctrine is at once metaphysical/cosmological, intellectual, moral, and aesthetic (from the Greek *aisthesis*, feeling). Plato's view strikes some people as odd (see Annas 1999; Mohr 1985) on the assumption that divinity necessarily involves otherworldliness or escape from this world. But belief in panpsychism and the related idea of a World Soul does not involve a flight beyond the natural world of becoming if the World Soul just *is* that world when considered as an integral, besouled whole.

5. Conclusion

It should now be clear why it is not necessary to view Plato as some sort of dualist. Scholars have always noticed the importance of *psyche* in the mesocosmos (P2). But they have paid insufficient attention to the macrocosmic significance of soul in Plato (P3). We are parts (P2) of the World Soul or of what is seen in the *Timaeus* as the divine animal (P3). This should give us a clue regarding the analogous part-whole relationship between the microcosmic parts (P1) that constitute us as mesocosmic wholes (P2). This clue has also largely been ignored by scholars, which perhaps explains why it is often assumed without argument that Plato was a dualist. The aforementioned four-term analogy actually runs both ways. Just as P3 helps to explain why there is a *universe* or a *cosmos*, in that the World Soul brings together what would otherwise be the scattered multiplicity of the bodily, so also there is a sort of *cosmos* or wholeness of an individual life (P2). That is, bodily life is *permeated by* besouled, dynamic power, hence it is a mistake to think of soul in Plato as having a sort of epiphenomenal existence hovering above body.

As was mentioned earlier, there is evidence in Plato's dialogues that is supportive of the claim that he can be viewed as a panpsychist. This evidence includes the ideas that: only soul is capable of self-motion; soul is the universal cause of body; soul is the only initiator of change in the universe; soul is both active and passive in the dynamic power it exhibits; and bodies are derived from soul, hence soul is metaphysically prior to body. The problem of how life (or consciousness) arises out of lifeless (or unconscious) matter is not one that even comes up on the basis of this evidence in that the dynamic power of being goes all the way down, on the view of Plato I am explicating in the present chapter.

On the panpsychist view, each event is a dynamic subject for itself and an object for others, hence no event is simply a subject or simply an object, contra dualism or materialism. That is, reality is characterized by the dynamic power in subjects that become objects. Interpreting Plato as a panpsychist thus enables us to better come to grips with a key feature of several of his later dialogues, which suggests that being has both an 'in itself' dimension and an 'in relation' character. *Psyche*, defined by Plato as self-motion, is required in order to understand the very dynamism of the world. This is because inactivity is inimical to soul, even when its amphibious qualities are taken into consideration: soul has one foot in the eidetic realm of changeless forms and one foot in the instantial camp of dynamic nature. Only soul has the right sort of contact to link up both the forms and ubiquitous flux. Indeed, the Greek *physis*, which is usually translated into English as 'nature,' might more accurately be translated as 'process,' as Whitehead argues (1967: 150).

Granted, Plato is his own worst enemy in the sense that he did a very good job in providing evidence for the widespread thesis that he was a dualist. But three disparate positions are clearly defended in ancient philosophy by Plato and others which, when put together by later thinkers, can lead to a credible version of panpsychism: (1) Plato's discovery in the *Sophist* of the metaphysical concept that being *is* dynamic power to both exert influence on, and to be influenced by, others; (2) his definition of *psyche* in the *Phaedrus* and *Laws* in terms of self-motion, a definition that is amplified by Aristotelian *kinesis*; and (3) the Epicurean belief that ultimate reality is atomic in character, a belief that is amplified by the ancient Greek discovery of *neura*, as detailed by Solmsen (1961).

6. Postscript: Skrbina's Interpretation

It will be helpful to see the extent to which the view of Plato presented in this chapter agrees with the magisterial study of the history of panpsychism authored by David Skrbina (2005), who agrees that there is something problematic in the familiar conclusion that Plato was a dualist. There is also something problematic in seeing the forms as the ultimate realities in Plato, as we have seen previously in defense of the intradeical interpretation of the relationship between the forms and divine soul. It must be admitted, however, as Skrbina notes, that Plato can also be read as something of a reverse epiphenomenalist. Epiphenomenalism consists in the belief that body is the fundamental reality, whereas mind has some sort of shadowy reality that derives from the body. The reverse epiphenomenalism in Plato noticed by Skrbina, however, has mind as the fundamental reality, whereas the body has a shadowy sort of reverse doppelganger existence derived from mind, as found, say, in the famous myth of the cave in the *Republic* (see Skrbina 2005: 6, 10, 14).

Skrbina thinks that the best interpretation of Plato is that he was a panpsychist, especially when his later dialogues are considered. (Things get confusing, however, when Skrbina claims that the Stoics were the first panpsychists. I assume that this is a typographical error and that what Skrbina wanted to say was that the Stoics were the first *pantheists* – 2005: 21.) Perhaps the biggest contribution that Skrbina makes to the view of Plato as a panpsychist is his argument that a belief in a panentheistic (not pantheistic) World Soul is different from a belief in panpsychism and that one could commit to a belief in a World Soul without committing to panpsychism in that to speak of soul/mind as a single universal being leaves open the question as to whether soul/mind is attributable to each thing in itself. Skrbina and I are in agreement that Plato can profitably be seen as *both* a defender of a panentheistic (literally, all is *in* God) World Soul *and* a panpsychist, given the proliferating pluralism of *psyche* in Plato (Skrbina 35, 39). However, Skrbina is for some unstated reason reluctant to view the World Soul in theistic terms.

Four arguments for panpsychism in Plato (and other ancient Greek philosophers) are detected by Skrbina. First, there is an argument from indwelling power in things (based on the evidence provided by things being capable of self-motion and being possessive of other sorts of dynamic power). Second, there is an argument from continuity (apparently based on the idea that we can notice various levels of dynamic power in the universe and have a sense that such powers are not to be found solely in human beings). Third, there is an argument from first principles wherein soul/mind is not derivative or incidental, but central and primary. And fourth, there is the well-known argument from design that has exerted a huge influence on the history of philosophy, an argument wherein the self-motion of divine soul is transmitted to other besouled beings throughout the *cosmos*. These arguments, far from striking ancient philosophers as odd, would have had a family resemblance to the hylozoism or animism or panpsychism of the presocratic philosophers. In fact, the first philosophers who defended the idea of matter without feeling were the atomists, on Skrbina's interpretation. That is, what would have struck most ancient thinkers as odd would be the unfeeling atoms (*atomoi apatheis*) of Leucippus and Democritus (Skrbina 2005: 25–8, 33, 40).

From the preceding it would be legitimate to conclude that I see a great deal of compatibility between my own view of Plato's panpsychism and Skrbina's view, contra the interpretation of Plato as a dualist, as found, say, in Guthrie (1962–81: 4, 420). Or again, whereas Plato *did* tend toward dualism in his middle period, in his later dialogues he tended toward panpsychism, although I would add that there are prefigurements of panpsychism in the middle dialogues (as in *Ion* 533–536, where the magnetic power of lodestones is discussed) and faint traces of dualism in the later dialogues. But Skrbina is surely correct about the tendency toward panpsychism in the later dialogues, as in *Philebus*, where soul is the cause of all things and where there are living presences in nature (896d, 899b). This tendency in Plato is both noticed and affirmed by Plotinus (*Ennead* VI. 7, 11). Indeed, Skrbina insightfully goes so far as to say that 'There appear to be no passages in the late dialogues that explicitly deny the panpsychist conclusion' (2005: 44, also 34–5, 42–3).

Works Cited

Annas, Julia (1999). *Platonic Ethics, Old and New*. Ithaca: Cornell University Press.

Craig, William Lane (1980). *The Cosmological Argument from Plato to Leibniz*. New York: Barnes and Noble.

Crombie, I. M. (1962). *An Examination of Plato's Doctrines*, vol. 1. London: Routledge and Kegan Paul.

Dennett, Daniel (1991). *Consciousness Explained*. Boston: Little, Brown.

Dombrowski, Daniel (1991). 'Hartshorne and Plato'. In Lewis Hahn (ed.), *The Philosophy of Charles Hartshorne*. LaSalle, IL: Open Court.

Dombrowski, Daniel (2005). *A Platonic Philosophy of Religion: A Process Approach*. Albany: State University of New York Press.

Dombrowski, Daniel (2006). *Rethinking the Ontological Argument: A Neoclassical Theistic Response*. New York: Cambridge University Press.

Griffin, David Ray (1998). *Unsnarling the World Knot: Consciousness, Freedom, and the Mind-Body Problem*. Berkeley: University of California Press.

Guthrie, W. (1962–81). *History of Greek Philosophy*, 6 vols. Cambridge: Cambridge University Press.

Hartshorne, Charles (1983). *Insights and Oversights of Great Thinkers: An Evaluation of Western Philosophy*. Albany: State University of New York Press.

Kant, Immanuel (1900). *Dreams of a Spirit-Seer*. Trans. Emmanuel Goerwitz and Frank Sewell. New York: Macmillan.

Kim, Jaegwon (1993). *Supervenience and Mind*. New York: Cambridge University Press.

Leibniz, Gottfried (1991). *Discourse on Metaphysics and Other Essays*. Trans. Daniel Garber and Roger Ariew. Indianapolis: Hackett.

McGinn, Colin (1991). *The Problem of Consciousness*. Oxford: Blackwell.

Mohr, Richard (1985). *The Platonic Cosmology*. Leiden: Brill.

Nagel, Thomas (1986). *The View from Nowhere*. New York: Oxford University Press.

Plato (1977). *Platonis Opera*. Ed. John Burnet, 5 vols. Oxford: Clarendon Press.

Plato (1999). *The Collected Dialogues of Plato*. Ed. Edith Hamilton and Huntington Cairns. Princeton: Princeton University Press.

Plutarch (1870). *Plutarch's Morals*. Ed. William Goodwin. Boston: Little, Brown.

Royce, Josiah (1908). *The Philosophy of Loyalty*. New York: Macmillan.

Seager, William (1991). *Metaphysics of Consciousness*. London: Routledge.

Seager, William (1999). *Theories of Consciousness*. London: Routledge.

Searle, John (1992). *The Rediscovery of the Mind*. Cambridge: MIT Press.

Skrbina, David (2005). *Panpsychism in the West*. Cambridge: MIT Press.

Solmsen, Friedrich (1961). 'Greek Philosophy and the Discovery of Nerves'. *Museum Helveticum*, 18: 150–67, 169–97.

Strawson, Galen (1994). *Mental Reality*. Cambridge: MIT Press.

Strawson, Galen (2006). *Consciousness and Its Place in Nature: Does Physicalism Entail Panpsychism?* Exeter: Imprint Academic.

Whitehead, Alfred North (1967). *Adventures of Ideas*. New York: Free Press.

Whitehead, Alfred North (1978). *Process and Reality*. Ed. David Ray Griffin and Donald Sherburne, corrected edition. New York: Free Press.

3

ABHIDHARMA PANPROTOPSYCHIST METAPHYSICS OF CONSCIOUSNESS

Monima Chadha

Panpsychism refers to a variety of doctrine that asserts that mental features are ontologically fundamental and ubiquitous. This definition in terms of mental features is not standard, but I think it will prove to be useful. The term 'mental features' is suitably ambiguous: it is neutral on whether mental features are restricted to phenomenal features or comprise non-phenomenal features as well and also on whether mental features are substances, or objects, or properties or some entirely new kind of thing hypothesised by physicists or contemplated by metaphysicians. To claim that mental features are ontologically fundamental separates out panpsychism not only from physicalism but also from eliminativism. Again, to claim that they are ubiquitous separates out the doctrine from Cartesian dualism and neutral monism. However, this fails to rule out idealism as a variety of panpsychist views. I think rightly so, as idealism is a version of panpsychism, indeed its most popular version in the nineteenth century (Seager and Allen-Hermanson 2015). The revival of panpsychism in recent times is not a version of idealist metaphysics; far from it. Most contemporary panpscyhists accept that the material and mental features are ontologically fundamental. Some, like Galen Strawson (2006), go so far as to claim that panpsychism is entailed by 'real physicalism' or 'realistic materialism'. Much more needs to be said to give a precise specification of panpsychism but this brief characterisation will suffice for my purposes here. I do not intend to give a precise answer to the question as to what is panpsychism; rather my interest here is to explore what Buddhist views of the mind have to offer to contemporary debates on panpsychism.

Contemporary interest in panpsychism is driven by the intractablilty of the "hard problem" (Chalmers 1996). Reductive physicalism is no longer the only game in town, even scientifically minded philosophers are willing to pursue other paradigms as live options. As a methodological approach, reductive physicalism, or the so-called orthodox naturalism of "eliminating or locating" (Jackson 1998: 5) non-physical features of the world in the physical, has given way to liberal naturalism (Strawson 1985). Liberal naturalists in philosophy of mind seek to explain consciousness without the metaphysical constraints of physicalism and of any ontological limitations on sorts of things that constitute the basic furniture of the world. Panpsychism as a prominent example of the liberal naturalist approach has the license to introduce a different kind of metaphysics to replace the current physicalist ontology and its settled categories. Panpsychists should not be restricted by ontological categories like those of substances, properties, atoms, subjects of experience and so on. Contemporary panpsychists, for example Nagel (1998) and Strawson (1999), contend that our current conceptions of mind and body, mental and physical are radically inadequate and in need of revision. In light of this, it could be useful to look at philosophical traditions other than our own Western tradition, particularly at traditions that have grappled, and continue to grapple, with cognate problems. I believe that the ancient Indian Buddhist tradition, and its contemporary philosophical forms, is quite germane here for several reasons.

First, Buddhist philosophy contains a wealth of material that is relevant to the concept of consciousness and that of mind. Panpsychists, and analytic philosophers more generally, can find valuable insights in it. However, Buddhist philosophy, and classical Indian philosophy more generally, is not easily integrated into mainstream Western philosophy because their interests (specifically, soteriological aims) and languages are foreign to contemporary philosophers and have been ignored for a very long time. It is only in the last decade or so that scholars, with the requisite philosophical training and knowledge of the relevant languages, have successfully extracted discussions of consciousness and mind from classical Buddhist sources and situated them in the corresponding contemporary philosophical debates (Dreyfus 2011; Thompson 2014; Ganeri 2012; Chadha 2015; Garfield 2015). Secondly, what makes the Buddhist tradition especially attractive to panpsychism as well as liberal naturalism is because its metaphysics is radical and revisionary in that it lacks a self and any other persisting entities. Thirdly, and most importantly, the reason in its favour is that panpsychism seems to have a natural affinity with Buddhism more generally as both views emphasise that the mental is *almost* a universal feature of living beings. This statement is possibly true but only because it is vague and imprecise. Buddhist philosophers will complain that Buddhist metaphysics contains a variety of views about the nature of mind, some of which clearly are not panpsychist. Garfield (2015), for example, argues that Buddhist texts can be of great use to contemporary physicalism since they contain insights that can be used to respond to the famous conceivability argument, in favour of dualism, for the possibility of zombies. Panpsychists will complain that 'almost' is not a part of the literal meaning of panpsychism. My response is that my interest is in elucidating *a* panpsychist Buddhist view of consciousness to explore ways of strengthening and enriching contemporary panpsychist positions in important ways by drawing on Buddhist thought. My response to the Buddhist is that there is no *one* view that qualifies as *the* Buddhist view of consciousness. Therefore, what I shall be exploring here is *a* Buddhist view of consciousness and this should answer any concerns of Buddhist philosophers. My focus will be on the Abhidharma Buddhist tradition, which flourished in the first millennium AD in India, and whose stated aim is to give an account of conscious experience. In particular, I want to draw attention to the view of consciousness defended by Sautrāntika-*Yogācāra* School, or what is commonly called the Buddhist Logic School (Siderits 2007: 208). This view is originally proposed by Vasubandhu in his formulation of the Sautrāntika doctrine in the *Abhidharmakośa-bhāṣya*, and later modified by rich insights from *Yogācāra* philosophers like Asanga, Dignāga and Dharmakīrti. The challenge for them is to give an account of conscious experience in the absence of self and indeed all other persisting and substantial entities. I will show that the Sautrāntika-Yogācāra view of consciousness presents a plausible version of panpsychism. And, that it can address some longstanding concerns about panpsychist theories, especially the combination problem. Furthermore, recent neuroscientific studies of Buddhist meditation practices give us some independent, some would say empirical, reasons to think that these views of the mind are plausible.

The plan of this chapter is as follows. In section 1, I present the Sautrāntika-Yogācāra view of consciousness. In section 2, I argue that this view, as a version of panprotopsychism, has the potential to offer an adequate solution to a major challenge that continues to plague various panpsychist views: the combination problem. To be clear, my aim is not to offer an Abhidharma Buddhist solution to the combination problem, but only to show how a panprotopsychist view might explore solutions to the combination problem. In his papers (Chalmers 2015, 2016) Chalmers lists various versions of panpsychism and the combination problem. These two papers together chalk out a conceptual map carving out the logical space into a set of locations, positions, or places occupied by various panpsychist views and the solutions to the combination problems explored by their advocates. One of the tasks of this chapter is to place the Abhidharma Buddhist view on this conceptual map as a first step in exploring an Abhidharma Buddhist-inspired solution to the combination problem. This is interesting because it offers an insight into what protophenomenal properties look like and how we may try to overcome the non-phenomenal/phenomenal gap which would be the most serious combination problem threatening panprotopsychist views.

1. Sautrāntika-Yogācāra Model of Consciousness

The Sautrāntika-Yogācāra is part of the Indian Abhidharma tradition in Buddhist philosophy. Like all other Buddhist schools, the Abhidharma schools endorse the no-self doctrine. In fact, the most important Sautrāntika-Yogācāra philosopher Vasubandhu endorses a really strong version of the no-self view: the no-subject view (Chadha 2015). The challenge for the Abhidharma philosophers to explain the phenomenology of experience in a selfless, or more precisely for Sautrāntika-Yogācāra in a subjectless world.

The Abhidharma analysis of experience reveals that what we experience as a temporally extended, uninterrupted, flow of phenomena is, in fact, a rapidly occurring sequence of causally connected events each with its particular discrete object; much the same way a rapidly projected sequence of juxtaposed discrete images is perceived as a movie. Sentient experience is explained in terms of mental and physical processes (*skandhas*) that arise and cease in a causal sequence.[1] The distinctive contribution of the Ābhidharmikas is that they reduce the time scale of sequential mental and physical processes and regard them as discrete momentary events or *dharmas* (Ronkin 2005: 66–78). These discrete momentary events (*dharmas*) exist only for an instant or moment (*kṣaṇa*), where a moment is the limit of time. There are various opinions regarding the duration of a moment. Vasubandhu says that there are sixty-four moments in the time that it takes for a healthy man to snap his fingers (*Abhidharmakośabhāyam* 3.85b–c); others even say that billions of mind moments elapse in the time it takes for lightning to flash or eye to blink. These discrete momentary events or '*dharmas*' are the only existents, and they alone are objects of knowledge. Abhidharma produces a complete account of reality in terms of this single category of ultimately real entities. In this Section, I first explain the Sautrāntika doctrine of nature of *dharmas* and then explain how they combine to constitute conscious experiences.

The Sautrāntika view of the nature of *dharmas* and the constitution of conscious experiences from the basic *dharmas* arises as a result of a series of critiques of the early Abhidharma Sarvāstivāda doctrine. Vasubandhu rejects the distinction between substance and attributes (Pruden 1988: 1348). It is wrong to think of *dharmas* as substances, since substances are independent existents. However, according to the Buddhist doctrine of dependent origination (*Pratītyasamutpāda*) there are no independent existents; everything that exists is conditioned by its causes. Furthermore, *dharmas* are not universals, for Vasubandhu argues against the existence of universals (2.41a). Also, *dharmas* are not composite entities: they are simple, without spatial or temporal parts. Vasubandhu argues that medium-sized physical objects that we normally regard as real like jars, heaps, streams, persons, etc., are composites or aggregates of *dharmas*. These composites, he argues, do not exist in the ultimate sense, they are real only with reference to conception (*prajñapti-sat*); only *dharmas* exist in the ultimate sense (*paramartha*-sat) (6.4). But, then, one may ask: what are these *dharmas*, these ultimate constituents of reality? The Sautrāntikas have very little to say on this. They claim that *dharmas* are of two kinds: conditioned and unconditioned.[2] Among the conditioned *dharmas*, there are material (*rūpa*) and mental (*citta, caitta, etc.*) *dharmas*. Material *dharmas* (*rūpa*) are in space, but consciousness 'not having a mass, is not situated in a place' (1.43a–b).

Contemporary Buddhist philosophers have proposed that the best way to understand a *dharma* is to think of it as 'an elementary quality or event or condition' (Goodman 2004: 393) or 'a thin property' (Ganeri 2001: 99); a 'trope' as in contemporary analytic philosophy: e.g., the particular white of this wall rather than whiteness as such. Tropes, like physical objects, are particulars, as they are located in a particular time and space, though not necessarily so. They can be individuated as primitive particulars without spatio-temporal dimensions (Maurin 2014). They are unlike universals, in that they are not wholly present in each instance although they point to groups of identical things. However, in some sense, they share features with universals, in that they are 'ways objects are'.[3] Trope theorists believe that both particulars and universals can be understood as aggregates or sets of tropes. So, for example, we can think of Vasubandhu as an aggregate of Vasubandhu's colour, Vasubandhu's shape, Vasubandhu's logical acumen, etc. and similarly we can think of intelligence as bundle of Vasubandhu's intelligence, Asanga's intelligence, Udayana's intelligence, etc. Likewise, the Abhidharma would analyse the middle-sized mental and physical objects as aggregates of *dharmas*. Thus, we can think of mental *dharmas* as tropes that have temporal dimensions only.[4]

Such a trope-theoretic interpretation of *dharmas* has been used to reconstruct an Abhidharma account of the physical world (Goodman 2004) as well as of the conscious experience (Ganeri 2012) by an appeal to the notion of Humean supervenience (Lewis 1986: ix). Humean supervenience is the view that everything supervenes on spatio-temporal distribution of intrinsic properties. Weatherson (2015) offers a useful picture to understand this thesis. Imagine that the world is like a giant video monitor. The facts about a monitor's appearance supervene, plausibly, on intrinsic qualities of the pixels, together with facts about the spatial arrangement of the pixels. However, I want to steer away from Humean supervenience in offering a reconstruction of conscious experiences for two reasons: (a) *dharmas* are not necessarily physical, and for this reason (b) they are also not necessarily spatial entities (see Pruden 1.43 a–b previous). Thus, Humean supervenience, which necessarily involves intrinsic properties instantiated at spatio-temporal points, is not suited to an Abhidharma analysis. My own reconstruction will use the notion of *dharma*-clusters, vertical causation and supervenience.

There is intense debate about whether the Ābhidharmika philosophers arrived at this view through logical analysis or through introspection. Ganeri favours the former in suggesting that it is best to think of *dharmas* as proto-intentional (proto-cognitive and proto-affective) psychologically primitive processes that combine to constitute conscious experiences (2012: 130). Dreyfus seems to favour the latter though with an important qualification. He notes that "the Abhidharma analysis of the mental is a description of the complexity of the components of mental processes as they are phenomenologically available, not an analysis of the ontological basis of mental processes, a basis that is not readily available to the kind of analysis central to its project" (Dreyfus 2011: 119). *Dharmas* can be thus thought of as the basic components of mental and physical processes, basic in the sense that they cannot be further analysed into more basic phenomenologically available components. Dreyfus adds the qualification that this should not be taken to mean that *dharmas* are directly given in introspection, for they may only be available to those who have had appropriate mental training, for example in mindfulness meditation. Note, however, that these two views are not mutually exclusive: we can think of *dharmas* as basic components that can be arrived at either through logical analysis or through mindfulness meditation training or through both; in fact Vasubandhu, in his magnum opus *Abhidharmakośa*, endorses precisely this dual route.

For Buddhist epistemology generally, sensory perception is the paradigm of conscious experience. According to most Abhidharma schools, sensory perception is always intentional, and is brought about by an interaction among the sense faculties (e.g., eye), the corresponding type of consciousness (e.g., visual consciousness) and their appropriate sense objects (e.g., form, colour, etc.). There are six kinds of consciousness: five corresponding to the sensory organs and the sixth the mental awareness (awareness of thoughts, feelings, etc.). Conscious experience, according to the Ābhidharmikas, is always directed at objects, i.e., it is *of* something. In this the Abhidharma philosophers agree with phenomenologists that intentionality is an essential feature of consciousness. What distinguishes the Abhidharma view is its analysis of object-directedness involving five universal mental features that accompany every conscious mental state. The role of these mental features in conscious experience becomes obvious if we take into account the fact that the mere coming together of an object and sense faculty is not sufficient for a conscious experience to arise. A cognitive event is initiated by contact, which the Ābhidharmikas describe as a relation between a sense faculty and sense object giving rise to a sensory consciousness. Such sensory consciousness, according to these philosophers, is always associated with affect or feeling. The object may be felt as pleasant or unpleasant or neutral, but it is never sensed without arousing feeling. Perception is the mental factor which plays the role of discerning or discriminating the object by distinguishing it from other things. Furthermore, each conscious state is also goal-directed in that it is always associated with volition or an intention to act. This together with feeling is responsible for determining the ethical quality of consciousness, that is to say, whether it decreases or increases suffering. Attention is the mental factor that is responsible for orienting consciousness towards its object, in that it guides other mental features towards the object of consciousness (Thompson 2014: 38). The senses always process a steady stream of sensory impressions; some clusters of these impressions generate a representational form of the object when attention directs the universal mental features towards it. Attention thus is necessary but not sufficient for conscious experience. Representational forms of experience are created by the interplay of these five mental features and occasionally involve some other associated mental factors. The Abhidharma has a long list of these occasional mental factors; indeed, there are significant disputes on exactly how many there are. A few of these occasional features are: anger, greed, mindfulness, compassion, wisdom, etc. Each of these features when accompanying a conscious state has the ability to affect the way we see objects and thus contribute to its representational form. Ganeri explains this succinctly:

> The great elegance and attraction of the [Abhidharma] theory lies in the fact that simultaneously it recognises the irreducibility of the phenomenal character of experience, it admits the joint contribution of sensation and conceptualisation in the constitution of experience, it acknowledges that experience is, as it were, saturated with affect, that appraisal is built into the fabric of experience, it maintains that every experience has, as a basic ingredient, a capacity or tendency to combine in various ways with various others, and it makes the attention intrinsic to experience.
>
> (2012: 127)

The Yogācāra account of mind adds two further consciousnesses to the six kinds of conscious states accepted by the Abhidharma schools mentioned earlier. These are the basic or storehouse consciousness (*ālaya-vijñāna*) and the afflictive mentation or ego-consciousness (*kliṣṭa-manas*). The first is a constant and neutral baseline consciousness that serves as repository of all basic habits, tendencies, and karmic latencies accumulated by the individual. The doctrine of basic consciousness is in large part an attempt to show that there is mental continuity within a lifetime and across lifetimes despite the *dharma* ontology in which there is no enduring substance.[5] The ego-consciousness, on the other hand, is an innate sense of self arising from the apprehension of basic consciousness as being a self (Dreyfus and Thompson 2007: 97). This self, however, is not an ontological reality: it is merely a conceptual fabrication resulting from the (mis)apprehension of basic consciousness.

In addition to these two new kinds of consciousnesses the Abhidharma-Yogācāra *philosopher* Dignāga *introduces the notion of 'self-awareness' in Pramāṇasamuccaya, his seminal work*. He defines self-awareness as a mode of awareness that provides immediate, non-conceptual access to how things subjectively appear to the mind. Dignāga was the first to articulate the idea that consciousness requires reflexive awareness. In Buddhist philosophy of mind the term "consciousness" does not stand for a faculty or a mysterious property of physical matter or non-physical substance. Consciousness is simply a conscious state, which for the Buddhist-Abhidharma philosopher is composed of a complex network of conscious momentary atoms (*dharmas*). Reflexive awareness can be understood as a kind of mental perception. It is "mental" in the sense that it is independent of the five external senses and it is "perception" in that it is an immediate and therefore non-conceptual awareness. And, insofar as it is a perception, self-awareness is a means of valid cognition (*pramāṇa*). Dharmakīrti explains this idea by appeal to a representational theory of perception: perception of an object is mediated by the direct apprehension of the mental representation that reveals an aspect (*ākāra*) of the object (Dreyfus 1997). Although the form of an object is produced by a causal link between the object and a sense organ, the form itself is a feature of the experience, not a feature of the object of experience. This is the unique Buddhist view that the representational form of the object is also the phenomenal form of the experience. That is to say, the mediating representation is Janus-faced. Dignāga's dual-aspect theory can be brought in to explicate this further. On this view perception is a cognitive episode that grasps an object, e.g., a glass of wine. This perception in its arising is associated with a pleasant feeling which is immediately grasped as what-it-is-like for me to perceive the glass of wine. Thus, this single cognitive episode must involve two aspects: the objective form and the subjective form. The first that is the objective form (*grāhyākāra*) is the representation of the external object and the second that is the subjective form (*grāhakākāra*) is the grasping or holding of this representational or objective form. The phenomenal form that reveals itself in self-awareness. Dharmakīrti expresses this by saying that when we are aware of something we are simultaneously aware of the awareness (*PV*, III: 266).[6] Basic consciousness and reflexive self-awareness are essential to explain full-bodied conscious experience, whereas ego-consciousness plays the role of explaining away the imaginary self. Let me use an example to lay out the details of the Yogācāra-inspired account of conscious experiences.

Consider a present conscious experience of having a coffee. The *dharmas* that constitute aroma, colour, warmth, etc., are simultaneously provided by various sense consciousnesses. But there are countless many other coffee-relevant *dharmas* available in the basic consciousness that have resulted from previous encounters with coffee, for example, *dharmas* of taste, the caffeine rush associated with drinking coffee, the smell of freshly roasted coffee beans, the sweetness of added sugar, the desire for coffee, etc. The conscious experience of coffee does not arise in the first moment of sensory contact with the coffee; rather, this sensory contact sets off a chain of horizontal and vertical processes that might, depending on the availability of universal and occasional mental factors, result in the production of the representational form of the coffee. The presentation of coffee gives rise to sensible qualities that constitute aroma, color, warmth, *and* so on. These sensible qualities horizontally cause contiguous corresponding (aroma, color, warmth, etc.) *dharmas* in the next moment. At the same time they vertically cause processes in the basic consciousness, which activate coffee-relevant *dharmas* (for example, desire to drink coffee, taste, the accompanying rush of caffeine, sweetness of sugar, etc.). These vertical activations produce new horizontal series. At a unique and propitious moment when all the relevant *dharmas* are co-present together with the requisite universal mental features (and other occasional mental factors) the representational form of the coffee is produced. Intention, although itself a universal mental feature and thus a *dharma* has a double role: it binds together the relevant *dharmas* to produce the representational form the object.[7] Attention too in the same way has a double role: it transforms this representational form into a phenomenal form. For these Abhidharma philosophers, conscious attention is top-down and conscious phenomenon, though intentional, may be partly unconscious. Conscious attention is what explains the for-me-ness of an experience. In other words, the production of the phenomenal form, which encompasses the subjective and the objective aspects, coincides with the awareness of the coffee and the awareness of the perception of the coffee. To summarize: a conscious experience of coffee and the awareness of that experience are simultaneously produced as a result of the production of the phenomenal form of the object, which supervenes on co-temporal *dharmas* that are vertically present at that moment.

There is evidence to suggest that such a picture of conscious experience is empirically plausible. Our sensory system constantly receives multiple inputs, which are usually perceived as a stream. Thus, perception is regarded as a continuous process. However, there is scientific evidence to believe that perception consists of discrete mind moments. Recently Baumgarten et al. (2015) have shown that neuronal oscillation cycles define discrete perceptual moments which constitute the basis for a discontinuous and periodic nature of somatosensory perception exactly as the Abhidharma believed. Furthermore, it makes sense if a brain/mind embeds within it what Varela et al. (2001) called a brainweb, a massive parallel distributed system of highly specialized processors. The "global neuronal workspace model" for conscious access imposes a temporal granularity on neural states in a stream of consciousness. This framework postulates that, at any given time, many modular cerebral networks are active in parallel and process information in an unconscious manner. Information is consciously represented when the neural population that represents it is mobilized by top-down attentional amplification into a brain-scale state of coherent activity (in Buddhist terms, the transformation of representational form into the phenomenal form) that involves neurons distributed throughout the brain. Global Workspace Theory (Baars 1988; Dehaene and Naccache 2001) suggests that consciousness does not make more information available; it just makes the representation available to multiple networks to cooperate and compete in solving problems. There is no central processor or subject that is conscious of the information. The representation itself is conscious merely because of its salience in the cerebral networks. This completes my account of Sautrāntika-*Yogācāra* view of conscious experiences.

2. What Kind of Panpsychist View Is Offered by Sautrāntika-Yogācara?

The foregoing section was meant to give the reader a sense of the panpsychist flavour of the Sautrāntika-*Yogācāra* analysis of conscious experience. The fact that mental *dharmas* are part of the basic furniture of the world, along with physical *dharmas*, naturally leads to the conclusion that the Sautrāntika-*Yogācāra view is a version of panpsychism or panprotopsychism* (Chalmers 2015). If we think that conscious states supervene on collections of present mental *dharmas* which are best thought of as proto-conscious or proto-intentional features as the result of logical analysis, then we favor the panprotopsychist option. Alternatively, if we hold that mental *dharmas* are potentially phenomenologically available as they can be discerned as such by experts who have mastered the art of mindfulness meditation, then we favour the panpsychist option. For my purposes here, I shall concentrate on the panprotopsychist option as it is more amenable to analytic philosophy. The panpsychist interpretations requires the inculcation and perfection of meditation skills which is too much to expect from ordinary folk and philosophers.

The Abhidharma phenomenology is unique in that it presents an analytic method to discern, list, and classify the momentary mental *dharmas*. It advances a model of mind, of mental states – conscious experiences, thoughts, etc. – in delineating the components of mentality and how they interact to produce conscious experiences. However, it is not a fixed list. Different Abhidharma thinkers and traditions offer different lists and leave open the option that the list may be expanded and reclassified by later thinkers. Chalmers (2015) notes that we must wait for a full panprotopsychist theory to get clear about the nature of protophenomenal properties. As a version of the panprotopsychist view, the Sautrāntika-Yogācāra gives us some idea of what protophenomenal properties could be like. More generally, Abhidharma philosophies offer detailed lists of the sort of mental features that constitute conscious experiences.

Mental *dharmas* are best understood as entities that play a constitutive role in the production of conscious states. *They are classified into types according to the role they play in the constitution of conscious experiences and thoughts.* The Abhidharma does not provide a fixed and final list of types of *dharmas* as a result of the reductive analysis. Rather each of the traditions offers a list of irreducible elements but these lists are open ended and not immune to revision. The Theravāda school of Abhidharma introduced a system of eighty-two *dharma* types, the Sarvāstivāda school, on the other hand, adopted a system of seventy-five basic types of *dharmas*. The teaching of Abhidharma is a kind of therapy for those who are confused about the nature of reality. To begin with the Abhidharma teaching focuses on ridding oneself of the false sense of self that is imposed on what really exists. Once we discharge the enduring sense of selfhood in favor of a dynamic system of constantly changing and interrelated dharmas, we undermine the fruitless activity of trying to grasp and fix the world of experience. The reexamination of basic features that constitute the world of experience through proliferating lists is itself a method for challenging our yearning for a fixed and stable sense of the world (Heim 2014). On this reading the Abhidharma view tells us that the variety of experience is explained by a relatively small number of *dharma* types. This is in agreement with what physics tells us about the basic ingredients of the world. Not only this, the fact that the Abhidharma attitude is that these lists are open-ended and revisable and that there is no "fixed" number of basic ingredients that describe the experiential world once and for all is very much in agreement with what we may call the scientific attitude.

Furthermore some of these mental features are universal in that they accompany every mental state; others are occasional mental features that accompany some thoughts. The occasional features are further classified into those that accompany "good" mental states, those that accompany "bad" mental states, and yet others that are indeterminate in that they accompany "neutral" states. The qualifications "good", "bad", etc., may seem odd to contemporary Western philosophers, but it must be remembered that in the Buddhist way of thinking most conscious experiences and thoughts are said to contribute to, and thus be responsible for, moral agency and actions. The moral quality of the mental state is determined by the quality of the constituting *dharmas*: "Good" mental *dharmas*, e.g. the feeling of compassion, the intention of sharing, etc., result in good mental states. "Bad" mental *dharmas*, greed, anger, etc., on the other hand, result in bad mental states. The Buddhists have a very simple way of measuring good, bad and neutral. That which reduces suffering is good, that which increases suffering is bad, and that which does not alter the suffering is neutral. Apart from these morally loaded *dharmas*, the Abhidharma lists also include: sensuous properties like redness, roughness and mellowness, etc.; feelings like joy, pride, etc.; intentions like good, bad, etc.; kinds of attention, meta-attention, calmness, lightness of body; and, so on. This very brief description is by no means a complete census of the many mental features that can be involved in conscious awareness. The task here is to give the reader a sense in which protophenomenal properties contribute to, and play a role in, the constitution of phenomenal properties. Protophenomenal properties determine the nature and character of phenomenal properties; they are not merely structural properties.

At this point, I want to turn my attention to the nature of combination among the *dharmas*. It is plausible to say that *dharmas* can combine with one another, but a lot turns on whether the rules for this combination are laws of nature (*a posteriori*, metaphysically contingent) or inherent in the nature of the combining things (*a priori*, metaphysically necessary). Panprotopsychism has an advantage over emergentism provided that the rules of combination are of the latter type (*a priori* and necessary), otherwise the view cannot be differentiated from emergentism. We have already mentioned that the Abhidharma ontology includes the following universal mental factors which must accompany all conscious experience: contact (*sparśa*), feeling (*vedanā*), perception (*saṃjñā*), intention (*cetanā*) and attention (*manasikāra*). The last two – intention and attention – are special factors. Intention, although itself a *dharma*, is characterised in the Theravāda as something that through its activity brings together the other mental features to produce the objects of experience as representational forms (Heim 2014: 105). Representational forms as objects of experience do not mirror the world out there; rather they are actively constructed by the cooperation of mental factors and external objects. Attention is what leads the mind to its object. An analogy used by Buddhaghosa suggests that attention is like a coachman, it drives other mental factors to an object (*ibid.*). Attention is what gives rise to the phenomenal form of the object or the subjective aspect of the experience. Reflexive awareness then provides the principle that ties together the subjective aspects of experience to give rise to the self-conscious states (Ganeri 2012). The important point to note here is that intention, attention and self-awareness are essential and intrinsic features of experience itself. Thus according to the Buddhist panprotopsychist, Abhidharma theories of the rules for combination are inherent in the nature of the combining things, thus they are metaphysically necessary and *a priori*. This ensures that Buddhist panprotopsychism is not vulnerable to the sort of objections that may be raised against the emergentists.

Panprotopsychism has some advantages over its rivals. Chalmers, for example, notes that in contrast to other panpsychist views, panprotopsychism does not need to posit subjects or proto-subjects at the bottom level. But it does suffer from the especially difficult combination problem that he labels the "non-phenomenal/phenomenal gap." This version of the combination problem, like the corresponding problems for other versions of panpsychism, is spelt out by means of a conceivability argument. The weight of the argument rests on the existence of protophenomenal zombies: beings that share our protophenomenal properties (and also all the physical properties) but can still be without phenomenal consciousness. Chalmers admits that the conceivability of protopanpsychist zombies is less obvious than the possibility of panpsychist zombies (2015). The foregoing Buddhist account gives us some idea about the protophenomenal elements that constitute phenomenal states of conscious awareness. This random list might lead one to question whether panprotopsychist zombies are really conceivable, a suspicion strengthened by the Abhidharma explanation of subjectivity without a self. As noted earlier, the Buddhist account does not accept that the usually unargued assumption that having a conscious experience necessarily entails a subject of experience, a subject for whom it is, somehow or other, like to have this experience. On this Buddhist account subjectivity is accounted for by the fact that conscious states are reflexively self-aware, they are not states of awareness in virtue of being owned or had by a subject of experience. Reflexivity is the very nature of consciousness; it defines what it is to be conscious. The no-self thesis is a corollary not only of the denial of persisting entities, but also of the denial of a substantialist metaphysics of independently existing entities. This very minimal metaphysics of momentary *dharmas*, property-particulars, eliminates the subject of experience completely. There are no subjects and no streams of experiences; only synchronically unified experiences. Such a denial of subjects of experience at the level of microexperiences and macroexperiences is much more radical than contemplated by Western philosophers, with the possible exception of Hume. This view of continually evolving causal series of momentary tropes has no room for the so-called non-subject/subject gap that is offered as a basis to argue for the plausibility of existence of panprotopsychist zombies.

Someone may object[8] that the Abhidharma are not really defending a no-subject view, rather they are only denying an eternal, metaphysically fundamental, incorruptible soul substance. Those who are concerned about the combination problem do not have such a subject in mind. The objection is as follows: let the subject be whatever it is that accounts for the subjectivity of conscious states. If reflexive awareness is what accounts for the subjectivity of conscious states and reflexive awareness is itself a *dharma*, then we do need to combine subjects after all. I think the Abhidharma must at this juncture claim that not all mental *dharmas* are reflexively aware and thus should be treated as subjects. The point is that reflexive awareness is triggered by the presence of attention. When you have attention, a phenomenal form is generated, which in turns triggers the *dharma* of reflexive awareness giving rise to a conscious momentary event. But there is only one of these for any conscious experience. There are further questions about the unity of consciousness at a time and over time. The Abhidharma, like all the other Buddhists, deny diachronic unity. Synchronic unity, they claim, can be explained by appeal to storehouse consciousness (for details about how such an account works see Chadha 2015).

Chalmers, however, suggests another justification which may help us to conceive protopanpsychist zombies: the nonquality/quality gap. But even this route is blocked by our Buddhist panprotopsychists: protophenomenal properties are not obviously nonqualitative properties. Protophenomenal properties range from what we straightforwardly conceive of as sensuous properties (e.g., redness) and feelings (e.g., pleasure, pain) or emotions (e.g., shame, fear) to mental faculties (e.g., attention), powers or dispositions (e.g., wisdom, concentration) and bodily properties (e.g., balance). On this Buddhist picture, I suggest, it is better to think in terms of degrees of consciousness, which in turn translates into degrees of qualitative or phenomenal awareness. The difference between phenomenal and protophenomenal properties is that of degree, not of kind. In other words, there is no unbridgeable nonquality/quality gap. Rather, what we have are the manifest and unmanifest states of conscious awareness. The unmanifest are not such that they cannot be consciously discerned but only that they are in the background of our manifest awareness. For example, in watching a beautiful sunset while walking on a rocky beach, I am manifestly aware of the beautiful red colour but there is a subtle unmanifest awareness of bodily balance in the background. The latter comes to the fore if I trip while walking. As already said, conscious awareness is an interplay of many different features and the intensity and character of the protophenomenal features determines the character of the phenomenal states.

This should give the reader an idea of the Abhidharma Buddhist view of consciousness and what it offers to the contemporary discussion of panpsychism. As I said before, my aim here has not been to present the Abhidharma Buddhist solution to various versions of the combination problem. I am only suggesting that these Buddhists ideas are worth exploring further if we are serious about investigating the solution space available to the panpsychists in addressing the combination problem.

Notes

1. *Skandhas* are aggregates of *dharmas* (1.7a–b).
2. The unconditioned *dharmas* are constituents of meditative states and liberation and are thus beyond the scope of this paper.
3. The idea that *dharmas* are tropes has been suggested in Mark Siderits (1997) and has also been developed by Ganeri (2001). Ganeri's focus is on an interpretation of Dignāga.
4. The talk about tropes is useful from a panpsychist point of view; it keeps the metaphysics of substance and universals at an arm's length. Mental *dharmas* as protophenomenal parts are just elements of reality. The Abhidharma philosophers, and Buddhists more generally, do not want to ascribe to a substance metaphysics or a realism about universals.
5. *Ālaya-vijñāna* is posited in what Schmithausen (1987: 12, 18) calls the "initial passage" in the Basic Section of the *Yogācārabhūmi*. It is described as an unmanifest consciousness that persists within the material sense faculties during the highest meditative state (*nirodha samāpatti*, literally translated as the "attainment of extinction," signifying the extinction of perception and feeling). The later sections of the *Yogācārabhūmi* also offer other proofs for the existence of *ālaya-vijñāna*, some of which aim to provide a fix for the problem of *karmic* continuity. However, it is important to note that *ālaya-vijñāna* is one of a number of fixes proposed to deal with this problem.
6. Dharmakīrti's *Pramāṇavārttika* is referred to as PV *in accordance with the standard practice*.
7. Intention here is not to be understood as in contemporary Western philosophy as a state formed on the basis of belief-desire reasoning but rather as a *dharma*, a proto-conscious event that accumulates, organises, and rallies together other *dharmas* for the production of an object of a resulting conscious event.
8. As does Luke Roelofs in personal communication.

References

Baars, Bernard J. (1988). *A Cognitive Theory of Consciousness*. Cambridge, MA: Cambridge University Press.

Baumgarten, T. J., Schnitzler, A., and Lange, J. (2015). 'Beta Oscillations Define Discrete Perceptual Cycles in the Somatosensory Domain'. *Proceedings of the National Academy of Sciences of the United States of America*, 112 (39): 12187–92.

Chadha, M. (2015). 'The Problem of the Unity of Consciousness: A Buddhist Solution'. *Philosophy East and West*, 65 (3): 746–64.

Chalmers, David (1996). *The Conscious Mind: In Search of a Fundamental Theory*. New York: Oxford University Press.

Chalmers, David (2015). 'Panpsychism and Panprotopsychism'. In T. Alter and Y. Nagasawa (eds.), *Consciousness in the Physical World: Essays on Russellian Monism*. Oxford: Oxford University Press.

Chalmers, David (2016). 'The Combination Problem for Panpsychism'. In G. Brüntrup and L. Jaskolla (eds.), *Panpsychism*. Oxford: Oxford University Press, pp. 229–48.

Dehaene, S., and Naccache, L. (2001). 'Towards a Cognitive Neuroscience of Consciousness: Basic Evidence and a Workspace Framework'. *Cognition*, 79: 1–37.

Dreyfus, G. (1997). *Recognizing Reality: Dharmakirti's Philosophy and Its Tibetan Interpretations*. Albany: State University of New York Press.

Dreyfus, G. (2011). 'Self and Subjectivity: A Middle Way Approach'. In M. Siderits, E. Thompson, and D. Zahavi (eds.), *Self, No-Self? Perspectives from Analytical, Phenomenological, and Indian Traditions*. Oxford: Oxford University Press, pp. 114–44.

Dreyfus, G., and Thompson, E. (2007). 'Asian Perspectives: Indian Theories of Mind'. In M. Moscovitch, E. Thompson, and P. Zezalo (eds.), *The Cambridge Handbook of Consciousness*. Cambridge: Cambridge University Press.

Ganeri, J. (2001). *Philosophy in Classical India*. New York: Routledge.

Ganeri, J. (2012). *The Self: Naturalism, Consciousness and the First-Person Stance*. Oxford: Oxford University Press.

Garfield, Jay L. (2015). *Engaging Buddhism: Why It Matters to Philosophy*. New York: Oxford University Press.

Goodman, C. (2004). 'The *Treasury of Metaphysics* and the Physical World'. *Philosophical Quarterly*, 54 (216): 389–401.

Heim, M. (2014). *The Forerunner of All Things: Buddhaghosa on Mind, Intention, and Agency*. New York: Oxford University Press.

Jackson, Frank (1998). *From Metaphysics to Ethics: A Defence of Conceptual Analysis*. Oxford and New York: Oxford University Press.

Lewis, David K. (1986). *On the Plurality of Worlds*. Oxford: Blackwell.

Maurin, A-S. (2014). 'Tropes'. In E. N. Zalta (ed.), *The Stanford Encyclopedia of Philosophy*, Fall edition. http://plato.stanford.edu/archives/fall2014/entries/tropes/.

Nagel, Thomas (1998). 'Conceiving the Impossible and the Mind-Body Problem'. *Philosophy*, 73 (285): 337–52.

Pruden, L. (1988). *Abhidharmakośabhāyam English Translation of Poussin, Louis de la Vallée., 1923–1931/1980. L'Abhidharmakośa de Vasubandhu*, 6 vols. Bruxelles: Institut Belge des Hautes Études Chinoises and Berkeley: Asian Humanities Press.

Ronkin, N. (2005). *Early Buddhist Metaphysics: The Making of a Philosophical Tradition* (Oxford Centre for Buddhist Studies Monograph Series). London and New York: Routledge-Curzon.

Seager, William, and Allen-Hermanson, Sean (2015). 'Panpsychism'. In E. N. Zalta (ed.), *The Stanford Encyclopedia of Philosophy*, Fall edition. http://plato.stanford.edu/archives/fall2015/entries/panpsychism/.

Schmithausen, L. (1987). *Ālaya-vijñāna: On the Origin and Early Development of a Central Concept in Yogacara Philosophy*. Tokyo: The International Institute for Buddhist Studies.

Siderits, Mark (1997). 'Buddhist reductionism'. *Philosophy East and West*, 47 (4), 455–478.

Siderits, Mark (2007). *Buddhism As Philosophy*. Indianapolis: Hackett.

Strawson, Galen (1999). 'The Self'. *Journal of Consciousness Studies*, 4 (5–6): 405–28. (Reprinted in S. Gallagher and J. Shear (eds.), *Models of the Self*. Thorverton: Imprint Academic, 1999.

Strawson, Galen (2006). *Consciousness and Its Place in Nature: Does Physicalism Entail Panpsychism?* Ed. A. Freeman. Exeter: Imprint Academic.

Strawson, P. F. (1985). *Skepticism and Naturalism: Some Varieties*. London: Methuen and New York: Columbia University Press.

Thompson, Evan (2014). *Waking, Dreaming, Being: Self and Consciousness in Neuroscience, Meditation, and Philosophy*. New York: Columbia University Press.

Varela, F., Lachaux, J-P., Rodriguez, E., and Martinerie, J. (2001). 'The Brainweb: Phase Synchronization and Large-Scale Integration'. *Nature Reviews – Neuroscience*, 2: 237.

Weatherson, B. (2015). 'Humean Supervenience'. In B. Loewer and J. Schaffer (eds.), *Blackwell Companion to David Lewis*. Oxford: Wiley-Blackwell.

4

SPINOZA'S PANPSYCHISM

Martin Lin

Spinoza is a panpsychist. For him, mentality is a pervasive and fundamental feature of the natural world. But he also believes the much stronger claim that every single physical thing – plants, rocks, stars, donkeys, the organs of a human body, etc. – has a mind. This is because he identifies each of God's ideas with a mind. Because God is omniscient and has an idea of each physical thing whatsoever, each physical thing has a mind. Why does he believe this and what does it mean?

Before we try to answer this question, it will be useful to review some basic features of Spinoza's metaphysics. To begin with, Spinoza thinks that there is only one fundamental being or substance, which he identifies with God or Nature (1p14[1]). That is, Spinoza naturalizes God or, alternatively, deifies nature. (Henceforth I will use 'Nature' with a capital 'N' to indicate this substance.) Nature is something that is "in itself" (1d3). By this, Spinoza means that there is nothing more fundamental than Nature in terms of which the existence of Nature can be understood. Nothing explains the existence of Nature, either causally or metaphysically, but the nature of Nature itself. For this reason, Spinoza says that Nature is self-caused (1p11 and 1p11d). Nature is also conceived through itself (1d3). That is, thinking about Nature does not require thinking about any other thing. Nature is conceptually self-contained. Spinoza thinks that these features entail that there can be only one Nature and it is infinite, eternal and necessary.

Nature, the one infinite substance, can be thought of in infinitely many ways. These ways of thinking about Nature are called 'attributes' and they express its essence (1d4). For reasons that are obscure, Spinoza thinks that we know only two of these attributes, thought and extension. 'Extension' is Spinoza's word for the physical. Leaving aside the unknown attributes, we can think about Nature as both mental (thinking) and physical (extended). Nature can be conceived under either attribute. The important point for our purposes is that Nature thinks. It has ideas, which constitute its thoughts. Nature is also physical. Bodies of all sorts (particles, human bodies, stars, etc.) are modes of Nature conceived physically. What does Nature think about? It thinks about itself conceived of physically. That is, its ideas represent its modes of extension including bodies.

It is important to emphasize that Nature conceived of as thinking is the very same thing as Nature conceived of as extended. Thought and extension are not two essential properties of this nature. Rather, they are different ways of thinking about the very same essence of the substance (2p7s). Thus, Spinoza is a conceptual dualist but not a metaphysical one. How can Nature be thought of in two different ways without those ways implying a metaphysical difference? The answer is that these different ways of conceiving do not say different things about Nature. Their contents are identical. They merely express those contents in a different format or present them differently. Because both thought and extension are equally fundamental, Spinoza is neither a materialist nor an idealist. Nature can be completely and accurately represented as either mental or physical.

Spinoza thinks that there is only one fundamental thing but that there are many derivative things. His terms for these non-fundamental beings are modes (1d5). Cabbages, kings, shoes and ships are all modes of nature. So too are the human body and mind (2d1 and 2d3).

The correct metaphysical analysis of these modes is a controversial matter. Many readers of Spinoza think that they are properties of Nature. In this chapter, I will proceed on the basis of an interpretation according to which modes are Nature insofar as it satisfies certain conditions. This should be understood on the model of a wave, which is a medium insofar as it oscillates, or a fist, which is a hand insofar as it is clenched. Bodies are thus like waves on the oceans of extension and minds are like waves on the oceans of thought. Modes so conceived are not properties. We can see this by considering the following example. The ocean insofar as it oscillates (a subject insofar as it satisfies some condition) is noisy. But the expression of the ocean insofar as it oscillates does not refer to a property. We can see this by considering the falsity of the statement the property of oscillation is noisy. Not only is this statement false but any statement that attributes the property of being noisy to a property is also false. And thus, generalizing from this case, we can conclude that any expression of the form x insofar as φ doesn't refer to a property but rather an object. Minds and bodies are modes and so, on this construal of modes, they are objects. Such objects as waves, fists, and dents are obviously derivative objects. We can say that they are constituted by the subjects that, in virtue of satisfying some condition, determine them to exist. Although I will proceed on the basis of this interpretation, none of my conclusions depend upon it. Those who prefer alternative interpretations are free to substitute them in what follows.

1. Mind in the Seventeenth Century

Spinoza's philosophy of mind is in many respects a response to a revolution introduced by Descartes. According to Descartes, the mind and body are two distinct substances that have nothing in common. Among the characteristic features of the mind are consciousness, simplicity, and being the cause of intelligent action. Mind is also the substance in which perceptions and volitions inhere.

The nature of body is three-dimensional Euclidean extension. Individual bodies are regions of three-dimensional extension that are capable of motion and rest. Because we can clearly and distinctly conceive of minds existing independently of bodies, Descartes concludes that the mind and body are distinct substances.

On this picture, the physical world is cleanly separated from the mental world insofar as they play no role in metaphysically constituting one another. Causal connections do, however, run between the mental and the physical. Inputs from the physical world causally explain sense perceptions in the mind. Outputs from the mental world causally explain the bodily motions that constitute intelligent action. Thus Descartes endorses mind-body substance dualism with causal interaction.

Many seventeenth-century philosophers who are otherwise sympathetic to Descartes's innovations in the philosophy of mind reject mind-body interaction. How can two substances with nothing in common causally interact? For many post-Cartesian philosophers, the answer is that they can't. Fire heats because it is hot. Donkeys beget donkeys because they are donkeys. Similarity is required for causation.

Spinoza is among those philosophers who are sympathetic to the Cartesian notion that mind and body are dissimilar but is hostile to interaction. Spinoza is hostile to the idea of interaction because there are no connections between the concepts of two things that have nothing in common. There must be, however, connections between the concept of an effect and the concept of its cause. Therefore, two things with nothing in common cannot causally interact.

It is not an easy thing to deny mind-body interaction because there are many correlations between the mental and the physical that strongly suggest interaction. When I want a beer and believe that there is beer in the fridge, I get up and walk over to the fridge. When you kick my shin, I experience pain. What explains the tight correlations that exist between mind and body such as these? Spinoza's answer to this question, his parallelism doctrine, is also the basis of his panpsychism.

2. The Parallelism Doctrine

In proposition 7 of part 2 of the *Ethics*, Spinoza says:

> The order and connection of ideas is the same as the order and connection of things.

This means that the mental realm and the physical realm are causally isomorphic. For every body there is an idea that represents it and for every idea there is a body represented by it. Moreover, there is a one-to-one mapping from causal relations between bodies to relations between ideas and vice versa.

The reason Spinoza believes the parallelism doctrine is most clearly expressed in the following passage (2p7s):

> Before we proceed further, we must recall here what we showed viz. that whatever can be perceived by an infinite intellect as constituting an essence of substance pertains to one substance only, and consequently that the thinking substance and the extended substance are one and the same substance, which is now comprehended under this attribute, now under that. So also a mode of extension and the idea of that mode are one and the same thing, but expressed in two ways. Some of the Hebrews seem to have seen this, as if through a cloud, when they maintained that God, God's intellect, and the things understood by him are one and the same. Therefore, whether we conceive nature under the attribute of Extension, or under the attribute of Thought, or under any other attribute, we shall find one and the same order, or one and the same connection of causes, i.e., that the same things follow one another.

That is, the parallelism follows from the fact that modes of thought and modes of extension are identical but conceived of differently. If they are identical, then they cannot differ with respect to their causal structure. This raises difficult questions about Spinoza's denial of mind-body interaction but they fall outside of the scope of this chapter.

3. Spinoza's Panpsychism

Recall that for every body, there is an idea that represents it. Human minds are ideas of human bodies. These ideas are in Nature conceived of as a thinking thing. The human mind is thus Nature's idea of our body. Spinoza thinks that there is nothing special about the human mind. Just as the human mind is Nature's idea of the human body, the idea of any body whatsoever is the mind of that body. Spinoza writes:

> For the things we have shown so far are completely general and do not pertain more to man than to other Individuals, all of which, though in different degrees, are nevertheless animate. For of each thing there is necessarily an idea in [Nature], of which [Nature] is the cause in the same way as [it] is of the idea of the human Body. And so, whatever we have said of the idea of the human Body must also be said of the idea of any thing.
>
> (2p13s)

This means that not only do human beings have minds, but also every part of the human body has a mind and every non-human body has a mind. In the case of non-human organisms that are reasonably complex, this result is more or less intuitive. Many people think that chimpanzees, dolphins, and even cats have minds. Perhaps more controversially, many people think that even less complex vertebrates have minds of some sort. But Spinoza extends the realm of the minded further to include invertebrates, plants, and even what we would classify as inanimate objects such as stars, planets, and tiny particles of matter. As the preceding text attests, Spinoza himself does not think that there are any truly inanimate objects. Everything has a mind, that is, is associated with an idea that represents it, and is to some degree alive.

4. Degrees of Mentality

Spinoza's thesis that each body has a mind, no matter how simple it is, raises several difficult questions. The first pertains to the relationship between the mind and intelligent behavior. In his *Discourse on the Method*, Descartes (1985: 140; AT VI: 56–7) claims that our evidence for mentality comes from intelligent behavior. According to Descartes, if some system can respond appropriately to an unlimited set of circumstances, then the causes of the behavior of that system are mental. For example, in competently using language, human beings can understand infinitely many novel sentences and in turn, can respond with infinitely many novel sentences. Thus we have evidence that human beings other than ourselves have minds. But if a system fails to exhibit such intelligent behavior, we have no evidence of mentality and attributing a mind to it would be unjustified. This is a plausible idea. Spinoza, on the other hand, attributes minds to systems that do not exhibit any intelligent behavior such as stones, tiny particles of matter, and stars. What could justify him in doing so?

Another difficulty stems from Spinoza's commitment to attributing minds to bodies that lack the degree of internal structure that we associate with mentality. For example, we observe a tight correlation between mental activity and the human central nervous system, which is very complex. We don't observe a tight correlation between mental activity and any much simpler system. This strongly suggests that only physical systems with a high degree of internal complexity can have minds. Spinoza, however, is committed to attributing minds to any bodies whatsoever, no matter how simple they may be. How could he argue for the plausibility of such attributions despite the observed correlation between complexity and mentality?

Two final difficulties come from Spinoza's claim that not only the human body, but also every part of the human body has a mind that is a part of my mind. Every atom, every cell, every organ composing my body has a mind. What is more, each of these minds is a part of my mind. The first difficulty is that I seem to be unaware of a great deal that happens in my body. For example, my pancreas is currently producing insulin. If my pancreas has a mind and that mind is part of my mind, why am I unaware of this? The second difficulty concerns how these various minds can compose a greater mind, viz., my own mind. This is a difficult question because, it is plausible to think, under no circumstances do human minds ever compose greater minds of which they are parts. This strongly suggests that minds in general do not compose.

Spinoza is aware of these problems. His response to the problems relating to intelligent action and complexity is to claim that all bodies are "to some degree" "animata" (1p13s). The word animata is generally translated as animate and although Spinoza does believe that all bodies are animate to some degree, I think the word is also meant to resonate with *animus*, which Spinoza uses as a synonym for mind (mens) (see for example 2a3). Thus, Spinoza is saying that all bodies to some degree are alive and have a mind.

The notion that the mental comes in degrees is crucial to Spinoza's claim that mind is pervasive throughout nature. It is more plausible to claim that stones and plants have minds if they have minds only to a very low degree than if minds are attributed to them without qualification. But what does it mean for mind to come in degrees?

Part of Spinoza's account of what it means for bodies to be animate to different degrees is given in the following text:

> I say this in general, that in proportion as a Body is more capable than others of doing many things at once, or being acted on in many ways at once, so its Mind is more capable than others of perceiving many things at once, And in proportion as the actions of a body depend more on itself alone, and as other bodies concur with it less in acting, so its mind is more capable of understanding distinctly. And from these [truths] we can know the excellence of one mind over the others.
>
> (2p13s)

Spinoza thinks that some minds are more capable of perceiving many things at once than others are and also that some minds understand things more distinctly than other minds do. He claims that the ability of the mind to perceive many things at once is proportional to its body's ability to do many things at once and the ability of the mind to understand things distinctly is proportional to the extent to which the actions of the body depend upon the body alone.

Why does Spinoza think that the mind's ability to perceive many things at once is proportional to the body's ability to do many things at once? The answer is found in Spinoza's account of sense perception and complex individuality. According to him, the primary content of the idea of the body, i.e., the mind, is the body itself. But when the body interacts with the external world, the state of the body depends not just on the nature of the body but also on the nature of the external causes that affect it. In this way, by representing the body, it represents a state of the body that carries information about the external world. The body's ability to acquire states that encode information about the external world depends upon its ability to do many things. To see why, we need to look at Spinoza's account of complex physical things like human bodies.

A complex body such as the human body is defined by a pattern of motion that obtains between its parts. Such a body survives the changes it undergoes just in case the pattern of motion and rest that characterizes it is preserved. So if environmental inputs alter the motions of the parts of a complex body, that body survives the resulting changes so long as these new motions are incorporated into the body in such a way that its overall pattern of motion and rest is preserved.

There are various ways in which encounters with external causes may be survived. A stone, for example, pursues a very simple strategy. It does one thing in response to all external causes: its parts remain bonded together and communicate the motions introduced in a more or less uniform way. Most significantly, it does not respond differentially to the way in which causal inputs from the environment are structured. For this reason, its states don't carry very much information about its external causes. But a human body pursues a much more complex strategy. In the response to external stimuli, it responds very differently depending on the structure of the stimuli. For example, while the stone is indifferent to anything but the total energy of the wave produced by the handclap, the human body responds differently depending on how that energy is structured. Wavelength, frequency, and amplitude all matter to the human body but not to the stone.

In this way, Spinoza explains the seeming lack of mentality on the part of bodies that do not possess complex internal structure. Very simple bodies encode very little information about their external causes and thus the minds associated with them perceive very little about the external causes of their states. Very complex bodies encode much more information about their external causes and so the minds of those bodies perceive much more about their external environment.

Let us now turn our attention to the claim that the more actions depend upon the body alone, the more the mind understands distinctly. Spinoza thinks that causal responsibility is a degreed notion. This is intuitively plausible. Suppose that by myself I cannot lift an object that weighs one hundred pounds because I can only generate enough force to lift ninety pounds. I fully exert myself and you help by contributing the force needed to go from ninety to one hundred. There is a clear intuitive sense in which I am doing more of the work than you. If through resistance training I go from an ability to lift ninety pounds to an ability to lift ninety-nine pounds, then the next time we lift the weight together, and I fully exert myself, then I have contributed even more of the work (I have adapted this example from Della Rocca 2008: 115).

Spinoza thinks that most human behavior is partially explained by environmental inputs. This is clearly the case where sense experience guides action because sense experience requires environmental inputs. Spinoza also thinks that our cognitive behavior is purely rational only when environmental inputs do not explain it in any way. Spinoza is a rationalist who thinks that sense experience is the source of error and confusion, so we are at our cognitive best when our thinking is free from the influence of sense experience. We engage in rational thinking fully divorced from sense perception when we are doing pure mathematics and when we engage in pure philosophical reasoning. But although we are not perfectly rational when environmental inputs help determine our thoughts and behavior, we can still be more or less rational, depending upon how much our own nature contributes to the explanation of what we do and think. The more it contributes, the more rational we are.

Spinoza relates structural complexity to power: the power of acting of a body and the correlative power of thinking of a mind are a function of complexity. Human beings are more capable of rational thought than, for example, fish or worms because our bodies and minds are so much more complex than theirs. Stones too have minds, but their bodies are even less complex than worms, and so they are, for all intents and purposes, incapable of rational thought. These conclusions help minimize the implausibility of attributing minds to creatures that lack the structural complexity that is correlated with mindedness.

This also helps to solve the problem of how Spinoza can attribute minds to bodies that don't exhibit intelligent behavior. Because Spinoza associates power with complexity, very simple bodies do not have much power of acting just as their minds do not have much power of thinking. The minds of such creatures are nothing more than mute representations that generate few effects. However, when such representations join together to form complex wholes, new powers of thought are generated. And as a consequence of the parallelism doctrine, new powers of action in the body are also generated. Intelligent behavior is characteristic only of such complex bodies.

It is sometimes alleged that Spinoza needs a distinction between (1) minds that are subjects of conscious experience and those that are not, and (2) ideas that are conscious and those that are not (see for example Wilson 1999: 133). The first distinction is needed because it is implausible to ascribe consciousness to, for example, stones because they lack the structural complexity that we associate with consciousness. The second distinction is needed because Spinoza is committed to the claim that the human mind contains an idea of every part of its body. But I am unaware of the action of my pancreas and many other events occurring in my body. Thus, if I have ideas that represent these things, they must be unconscious. It is further alleged that Spinoza has no way of consistently making out any such distinctions.

It is true that Spinoza cannot distinguish between conscious and unconscious minds, and conscious and unconscious ideas, but he has a related distinction that may serve just as well: he distinguishes degrees of consciousness.

Spinoza links power and complexity to consciousness. Consider the following passage:

> [H]e who, like an infant or child, has a Body capable of very few things, and very heavily dependent on external causes, has a Mind which considered solely in itself is conscious of almost nothing of itself, or of God, or of things. On the other hand, he who has a Body capable of a great many things, has a Mind which considered only in itself is very much conscious of itself, and of God, and of things.
>
> (5p39s)

We have already encountered the claim that a mind is more capable of perceiving more things at once and is more excellent the more powerful its body is. Here the claim is extended to consciousness as well. The more powerful a body is the more conscious its mind is (see Garrett 2008).

Spinoza's remarks on consciousness are sketchy at best, but perhaps he could be read as describing a kind of functional account of consciousness. A powerful bodily state entails, by virtue of the parallelism, a powerful idea. An idea that is powerful contributes more to the determination of the mind's future states. That is, the idea contributes more to reasoning. This could be likened to a kind of access consciousness: an idea is conscious to the degree that it contributes to determining the direction of thought and contributes content to it. It seems, however, less compelling as an account of phenomenal consciousness.

Because Spinoza links structural complexity with power and power to consciousness, stones are, due to their structural simplicity, conscious to only a very minimal degree. Likewise, thoughts about my pancreas do not determine my other thoughts to any appreciable degree. This suggests that they have only a very small amount of power. Consequently, they will be the subjects of only the dimmest conscious awareness. Thus, while Spinoza does not have the resources to draw a line between conscious and unconscious states and entities, he can place entities and states on a spectrum of consciousness.

The last problem we have to consider is how minds can compose minds. Recall that the human mind is just Nature's idea of the human body. Spinoza tells us that the human mind is not special in this regard and that we can consider Nature's idea of any body as the mind of that body. But the human body is composed of simpler bodies, each of which is represented by an idea in Nature's mind. Thus we must conclude that each idea of each part of the human body is a mind. The human mind is a complex mind each part of which is itself a mind.

This might be regarded as implausible. To see why, consider the putative fact that human minds never join together to form more complex superhuman minds. Indeed it's very difficult to see how that could ever happen in principle. This could be taken as evidence for the principle that minds don't compose minds.

But if we look at the details of how Spinoza thinks that simpler minds compose more complex minds, the account is not as implausible as it might first appear. To begin with, it must be emphasized that the human mind is not a substance, as it is for Descartes. Instead, Spinoza holds that it is a collection of ideas. In this way, it is not entirely dissimilar to the bundle theory of the mind familiar from Hume. The difference between the bundle theory and Spinoza's theory is that Spinoza adds the further claim that the ideas in the bundle compose a single complex idea. Thus, although it is strictly speaking correct to say that every part of the body has a mind, it's a bit misleading because Spinoza is deflating the mind not inflating ideas. The notion of a complex idea that is composed of simpler ideas is much more familiar (think of psychologically real complex concepts composed of simpler concepts), than the idea of complex minds composed of simpler minds. Spinoza just assimilates the latter to the former.

Moreover, Spinoza denies the claim that human minds don't compose with other minds to form more complex minds. Indeed, he repeatedly asserts that the human mind is part of the infinite intellect which is the mind of the totality of finite corporeal creatures. Thus Spinoza clearly believes that his claim that the human mind has parts that are themselves minds is not in conflict with any general principles prohibiting minds from composing.

5. Conclusion

Spinoza believes that each body – every animal, plant, particle, and star – has a mind. Moreover, every complex body composed of simpler bodies has a complex mind composed of simpler minds. And just as bodies are modes of extended nature, minds are modes of thinking nature. Minds are thus

Nature's ideas of the body. This view might seem to conflict with four plausible claims: (1) minds are possessed only by creatures capable of intelligent behavior; (2) minds are associated only with creatures with complex bodies; (3) we are unconscious of many things that happen in our bodies; and (4) minds do not compose. Spinoza responds to (1)–(3) with an account of degrees of power of thinking, which he associates with structural complexity. He is thus able to claim that although creatures incapable of any appreciable intelligent action and lacking structural complexity have minds with very little power of thinking. And because he arguably has a functionalist account of consciousness, many ideas/minds will have very low levels of consciousness. With respect to (4), he assimilates minds to ideas and thus the claim that minds compose is no more implausible than the claim that ideas compose. Because many thoughts are complex, this is not implausible at all.

Note

1. All citations from Spinoza are from Spinoza (1925). Most English translations are from Spinoza (1985), with occasional modifications. The citation method to the *Ethics* is to Book + Element + additional material (if any). For example, '1p13s' refers to Book 1, Proposition 13's scholium; '1d3' refers to Book 1, Definition 3.

References

Della Rocca, Michael (2008). *Spinoza*. London: Routledge.
Descartes, René (1985). *Philosophical Writings*, vol. 1. Ed. and Trans. J. Cottingham, R. Stoothoff, D. Murdoch. Cambridge: Cambridge University Press. (The 'AT' page reference is to *Oeuvres de Descartes*, C. Adam and P. Tannery (eds.), Paris: 1897–1910 and 1964–1978; Paris: Librairie Philosophique, J. Vrin (1996).).
Garrett, Don (2008). 'Representation and Consciousness in Spinoza's Naturalistic Theory of the Imagination'. In C. Huenemann (ed.), *Interpreting Spinoza*. Cambridge: Cambridge University Press, pp. 4–25.
Spinoza, Baruch (1925). *Spinoza Opera*. Ed. C. Gebhardt, 4 vols. Heidelberg: Carl Winter.
Spinoza, Baruch (1985). *The Complete Works of Spinoza*. Ed. and Trans. Edwin Curley, vol. 1. Princeton: Princeton University Press.
Wilson, Margret (1999). 'Objects, Ideas, and Minds: A Comment on Spinoza's Theory of Mind'. In her *Ideas and Mechanism*. Princeton: Princeton University Press.

5

MANY-MINDED LEIBNIZ'S MANY MINDS

Graeme Hunter

William Seager and Sean Allen-Hermanson (2015) begin the "Panpsychism" article in the *Stanford Encyclopedia of Philosophy* with a rough, but useful, taxonomy of a wide "range of possible positions" they classify as versions of panpsychism. The upshot for the key term, "mind" is that panpsychist accounts of it are distributed along three different continua. Mind can be anything from:

1. (a) Fully conscious *to* (b) unconscious,
2. (a) the only thing going (Idealism) *to* (b) something that resists explanation in non-mentalistic terms,
3. Ubiquitous: [Everything (a) *is* one (= Idealism), or, at least, (b) *has* one] *to* (c) rare.

Leibniz easily fits into this taxonomy. His alphanumeric panpsychic identifier is: 1a–b/2b/3b.
 Thus, for Leibniz:

1a–b. What I will call "minds" (subject to later clarification) can take every form from fully conscious (God) to devoid of consciousness (what Leibniz calls "simple substances" or "bare monads").
 2b. Minds are the *forms* of bodies and in human beings they are the substantial substrate of all those famously recalcitrant properties like consciousness, intentionality, freedom, moral obligation, and purpose, which *refuse* to be explained within the physical paradigm of matter in motion. (Leibniz believes that physics can't even explain its own laws of motion without bringing in *something like* mind.)
 3b. Finally, minds are ubiquitous, not to the extent that every real thing is a mind (Idealism), but to the extent that every real thing has a mind, or at least something like a mind (Leibniz's distinctive hylomorphism).

That is a rough outline of what I take to be Leibniz's view of *mind*. It needs a bit of refining though, and even when refined much about it will remain controversial. In this chapter I would like to address and remove three interesting points of controversy.

1. Does Leibniz Have a Concept of "Mind?"

It is not obvious that Leibniz had any concept falling within the range of what contemporary anglophone philosophers mean by "mind." Though he wrote philosophy fluently in three languages, none of those languages was English. He wrote in French to those who could understand it, because French was fashionable, particularly for diplomats like himself; in Latin to those who did not read French, or in writings that were primarily academic; and in German to German speakers who were not primarily academics. These three languages furnish Leibniz with nine different terms, each of which, in some circumstances, we translate as "mind." None, however, is semantically equivalent to "mind" as we use the word colloquially, let alone to its technical use in contemporary philosophy of mind. Finally, none of the nine terms at Leibniz's disposal is semantically equivalent to any of the others, though they all, together with "mind," occupy overlapping semantic fields.

In French there are "âme" and "esprit," which roughly correspond to "soul" and "spirit" in English. No French word gets closer to what contemporary anglophone philosophers mean by "mind," which obviously leaves a big gap between it and them. The French terms are etymologically and historically laden with religious, spiritualistic, or parapsychological connotations, from which philosophers purposely keep the English term free.

Contemporary French practitioners of *philosophie de l'esprit* become aware of the gap when they try to engage with the work of their anglophone counterparts. They may either stipulate definitions for the available French terms, turning them by fiat into semantic equivalents of "mind," or they may put to work the French adjective "mental," more about which to follow (see, e.g. Engel 1994: 1–3; Fisette et Poirier 2000: 1, 13).

Leibniz, on the other hand showed no hesitation in using "âme" and "esprit" to designate the non-corporeal components of his ontology. He welcomes, and for theological purposes exploits, the historical, spiritual and religious connotations with which contemporary philosophers of "mind" seldom wish to be involved.

Leibniz almost never resorts to the French adjective "mental." In the seven volumes of his philosophical writings edited by C.I. Gerhardt, comprising roughly 3500 pages, there are only five occurrences of 'mental', four of which are attributed to the character representing Locke in Leibniz's *Nouveaux essais*.[1] The fifth occurs in an article Leibniz sent to the *Journal des savants* in 1696 (GP IV: 502). All five occurrences seem to mean the same, as do his occasional uses of the Latin adjective "mentalis." Both are predicated of things whose existence is only "apparent" or "phenomenal."[2]

There is nothing, then, in Leibniz's French writings to suggest he possessed anything like our contemporary concept of "mind," or would have found it useful.

Not many of Leibniz's German writings are of interest in connection with his philosophical psychology, but the German language itself *is*. In addition to "Seele" and "Geist" (which are fairly close counterparts of "âme" and "esprit" respectively) German has "Gemüt," and Leibniz makes use of it in some of his more popular writings. Like "mind," "Gemüt" refers to our mental faculties and is free of spiritual connotations. In casual German its meaning can be indistinguishable from mind, as when Leibniz tells a philosophical layman that human souls (*menschliche Seelen*) are a species of the genus of rational *Gemüter* (GP 1: 53).[3]

However, unlike "mind" in its post-Cartesian philosophical sense, "Gemüt" is not characterized first and foremost by discursive thinking, but instead by *feeling*, in the sense of receptivity to stimuli. "Fühlende Seele" ("feeling soul") is the first substitute for "Gemüt" proposed by the *Wahrig Deutsches Wörterbuch* (1971). And that is the way Leibniz uses it throughout an early essay on peace of mind called *Gemütsruhe* (GP 7: 95–7). The subject of that essay, Leibniz writes, is "the enlivening and inward excitement of the *Gemüt*, bringing us the highest and most enduring delight of our lives."[4] You might get away with "mind" as a translation for "Gemüt" in that passage, though, given the popular nature of the text, "heart" would be preferable, because Leibniz is clearly discussing our affective capacity.

Feeling is very important for Leibniz, whether or not he is writing in German. Monads (as he comes to call all souls, spirits and *Gemüter*) are "windowless," meaning incapable of interaction either with bodies or with other immaterial beings (except for God) and hence each one, if it is to be in contact with its world, must feel (*empfinden*) everything in every part of the world, though each must generate its feelings from its own resources in the form of perceptions. In a verse epitome of his philosophy Leibniz defines *Geist* wholly in terms of "Empfindlichkeiten" (feelings or sensibilities).[5]

German practitioners of *Philosophie des Geistes* therefore face problems analogous to those their French counterparts meet when it comes to translating anglophone philosophy of mind. Peter Bieri, in a collection of anglophone philosophers of mind in translation, solves the problem summarily by adopting the German adjective "mental" as a "technical term" (Bieri 1981: 4). Its virtual absence from colloquial and conversational German facilitates its being pressed into technical service as a referent for the "non-physical." Two further advantages also recommend it: first, it is the same as the English adjective "mental" that anglophone philosophy associates with "mind." Secondly, it connects with the Cartesian *res cogitans*, which Descartes of course equates with the Latin *mens*.[6] Thus, the adjective "mental" serendipitously furnishes French, German and English philosophy of mind with a common term. Unfortunately, though, as pointed out previously, Leibniz's infrequent uses of this term do nothing to link *his* notion of the mental with ours.

A more promising avenue would be to explore the impact of the Cartesian "mens" on Leibniz's Latin writings. In Latin, "anima," and occasionally "animus," occupy similar semantic territory to "âme" and "Seele," while "spiritus" does the job of "esprit" and "Geist." But "mens" is a different story. Part of Descartes' contribution to philosophical psychology was to liberate the word "mens" from its association with semantically related Latin terminology, particularly with "anima" and "animus." As he tells Mersenne, "in good Latin 'anima' means air, or breath from the mouth, which, I think has been carried over into the meaning of 'mens,' which is why I said it is often taken for a corporeal thing."[7] Descartes' determination to avoid that confusion provides an excellent motive for keeping "mens" separate from "anima," even if it is Hobbesian materialism, rather than spiritualism, which Descartes is here concerned to sideline.

Strangely, though, Descartes allows the related word, "animus," to stand as a synonym for "mens" in his canonical introduction of "res cogitans" in *Meditation* II.[8] Later he finds it necessary to explain what he meant. He tells Hobbes that he only put "mens" and "animus" together because they are both colloquially (*vulgo*) taken to refer to something endowed with thought (AT 7: 174). And to Bourdin, who insists on thinking of "animus" as something corporeal, Descartes recommends that he try to get it through his thick head that for Descartes there are only two kinds of things: *corpus* and *mens*, i.e., body and mind (AT 7: 487).

Though Leibniz is a careful reader of Descartes, the Cartesian use of "mens" is not a significant influence. Leibniz is much more concerned with expanding the meaning of "mens" than with limiting it. A pure Cartesian conception of "mens" may pop up from time to time in his early writings,[9] but soon the word becomes enriched with the meanings and connotations of "entelechy," "soul," "spirit," "monad" and the rest. Nor is Leibniz consistent in the terms he picks to designate different patches of this wide semantic field. He varies his vocabulary not only according to context, but also according to the language he is using and especially, in his many correspondences, according to the preferred philosophical vocabulary of his correspondent.[10] Notwithstanding the surface variation in terminology, however, a consistent doctrine underlies it.

Leibniz provides a valuable snapshot of his mature philosophical psychology in 1710 after his secretary, Rudolph Christian Wagner, asks him to explain what he thinks about the "nature of the soul" (*animae natura*). The term "anima," Leibniz tells Wagner, has both a broad and a narrow sense.[11]

Broadly construed, "anima" denotes a vital principle (*principium vitale*) or a principle of internal action … existing in a monad (*principium actionis internae in … monade existens*). This internal action, which Leibniz considers to be the most basic characteristic of any real being, is what he calls "perception" (*perceptio*), defined as internal representation of what is external (*repraesentatio externi in interno*).

In this broad sense, Leibniz tells Wagner, soul (*anima*) may be attributed not only to animals but to all percipient things. Readers familiar with Leibniz will know that the other percipient things are not just men and angels, who are higher than animals in the great chain of being, but also a vast range of beings stretching down from animals, through plants, to entities which, though unaware of their perceptions, are yet percipient, and always something more than bare matter (*nuda materia*). These lowest beings, which he elsewhere calls by such names as "simple substances" and "bare monads," contain some principle of organization and perceptive activity which he often calls, as he does in the letter to Wagner, a primitive entelechy (*Entelechia primitiva*).

In a *strict* sense, however, "anima" applies only to the nobler form of life (*species vitae nobilior*) enjoyed by animals, whose perceptions involve sensation, attention and memory. But "mens," Leibniz continues, is something nobler still: it is a rational soul (*anima rationalis*). This picture is constant in Leibniz's mature (post 1686) thought, though the terminology in which he expresses it varies. In the closing sections of the Monadology (1714), as in other late French writings, reasonable souls (*mentes*) become known as "esprits."

Having thus carefully set out his terms, Leibniz is able to offer Wagner a lapidary summary of his philosophical psychology: mind is rational soul; soul is sensate life; life is a perceptive principle.[12] In so saying Leibniz implies that minds, in addition to their rationality, have the powers characteristic of lower-order souls as well. Here he reflects the Aristotelian and Scholastic traditions, according to which the rational soul also has powers of sensation, self-motion and self-nourishment.[13] But Leibniz's conception goes beyond theirs.

As mentioned, Leibniz is always trying to import content into his notion of mind. His ambition is to reconcile as many as possible of the divergent views of his predecessors. To his late correspondent, Nicolas Rémond, he describes his project this way:

> I have tried to unearth and re-combine the truth buried and scattered among the opinions of the different philosophical sects, and I believe I threw in something of my own just to advance things a little. The subjects I have been studying since childhood have all contributed to this project.
>
> (GP 3: 606)[14]

His early childhood studies, he tells Rémond, were Aristotle and the Scholastics, to which, he says, Plato and Plotinus also contributed something, as did other ancient schools he encountered later. Then, in his teenage years, he encountered the moderns, particularly Descartes. Leibniz's drive to understand and incorporate led him to the characteristically broad notion of soul we have already seen him to have. "This [path of education] is what brought me back to the entelechies," he continues,

> from the material to the formal, and led me at last to understand, after some corrections and improvements, that monads, or simple substances, are the only true substances. . . . This is what Plato and the later Academicians and even the sceptics glimpsed, though these epigones of Plato used the insight less effectively than Plato did.

Leibniz's attempt to deepen, reconcile and unify Western philosophy ultimately gives us the monadological metaphysics we associate with his name. In one of his fine phrases he describes it as "a kind of perennial philosophy (GP 3: 624 ff.).[15]

The upshot of this brief survey of his thought is that Leibniz had nothing corresponding to our modern concept of mind. Unlike current German or French philosophers of mind, however, he did not regret its absence. Had he wanted it, "mens" and "esprit," would have provided him with all or most of what "mind" contains, though in his usage both have also religious, spiritual, and teleological dimensions that contemporary philosophers of mind regard as unscientific, and zealously disregard.

Leibniz's instinct went in the opposite direction. He loads his own notion of mens/esprit with as many traditional connotations as it can bear, because it takes such a laden notion, he thinks, to be the bearer of science itself. "Incorporeal natures" *animae* in the broad sense, supply the necessary foundations even for physics and mathematics.[16] Philosophers today who have begun to suspect that minds could never have arisen in the physical world, if the mental had not been there from the beginning, are thinking Leibniz's thoughts after him.

2. Leibnizian Hylomorphism

My calling Leibniz a hylomorphist will raise a red flag for some readers. Many Leibniz scholars, perhaps still a majority, think him an idealist. It is true that Leibniz could continue to be a panpsychist on the Seager and Allen-Hermanson taxonomy, even if he turned out to be an idealist, but still it is preferable to know which kind of panpsychist he really is, especially because hylomorphism organizes Leibniz's thought in a more plausible way than idealism does. What draws people to Leibniz's philosophy are its three striking dimensions of breadth, depth and systematicity. What frequently disenchants these same readers is what they see as his three lapses into fantasy: his idealism, his denial of the possibility of interaction, and his optimism.

"Optimistic, orthodox, fantastic and shallow," were the words Bertrand Russell used to describe these aspects of his thought, which Russell tried to airbrush away as merely a "popular" philosophy, meant to win the approval of "princes and princesses" and to distract their attention from a far more interesting private philosophy which was logical and Spinozistic (Russell 1946: 604).[17]

Russell's "two philosophies" account has not stood up well to scrutiny, but if we are to regard Leibniz's idealism, denial of interaction, and optimism as bona fide parts of his philosophy, then it becomes all the harder to swallow. Leibniz's admirers therefore ought to hope he is a hylomorphist. If he is, one their three stumbling blocks goes away. And maybe two! Although I only have space for a quick sketch of Leibniz's hylomorphism, I will try to indicate how it also helps demystify the second "fairy tale" aspect of Leibniz's philosophy, the denial of interaction.

Donald Rutherford speaks for what may still be a majority view when he says that in "Leibniz's late writings" "material things do not form part of his fundamental ontology," and only "monads and their individual modifications" exist (Rutherford 1995: 143).[18] A seemingly definitive proof-text for this idealist picture can be found in Leibniz's late correspondence with the Dutch polymath Burcher de Volder. There he says:

> When the subject is considered accurately, we have to say that in nature (*rebus*) nothing but simple substances are found, and in them perceptions and appetites.
>
> (GP 2: 270)[19]

However Glenn Hartz has shown, I think definitively, that a huge amount of what Leibniz says in his later writings leans toward realism, in the sense of including among the most fundamental things in nature some that are neither minds nor mind-dependent (Hartz 2007: 6). Hartz does not conclude that Leibniz is a realist or a hylomorphist, however, but that he is a "theory dualist," meaning that Leibniz considers both realism and idealism to be *explanations* of the world, without affirming either as *true* of it. "[B]oth can be held rationally," Hartz says on Leibniz's behalf, "so long as they are regarded as mere hypotheses" (Hartz 2007: 155).

Though it is true that Leibniz appears to endorse idealism at least as often as realism, I cannot see theory-dualism as the best interpretive response. Hartz's irenic intention does not outweigh a reader's disappointment at having to conclude that, when Leibniz offered systematic accounts of the world, he was never aiming at the truth.

Hartz says defenders of realism inevitably "make a hash of" of Leibniz's idealist side (Hartz 2007: 155). This chapter will be an exception, though, if only because it will not have time to consider the idealist side.[20]

Leibniz is a hylomorphist because he follows Aristotle in thinking that mind is the form of the body. "Our body is the matter," he tells Arnauld in 1687, "and our soul the form of our substance." Then he adds, "the same holds of other corporeal substances" (GP 2: 119).[21] Living bodies of all kinds act as they do, Leibniz says, because of "a soul, or form analogous to soul, or a first entelechy, or a primitive force for acting, which is a law inscribed in it, impressed upon it by divine decree" (GP 4: 512).[22]

The many terms with which Leibniz clothes his notion of soul in such passages suggest that he is not just taking over Aristotle's definition of soul. The dynamic character he adds to it ripples through all his thought. In physics the form of the body reveals itself as *vis viva* or "living force"; in psychology it is appetite, the restless generator of perceptions; in public life it is the *I* of our *character*, by which we inscribe our unique signature upon the world. Finally, beyond our material existence in the world, our soul is the immortal spirit that fits or unfits us for the City of God.

"Entelechy" is an Aristotelian term meaning literally "having a plan within." It is our first-order substantial form, but it does not account for the plans we make and execute for our own reasons. We plan; we choose; we act. But we owe our ability to do these things to a first-order primordial entelechy within us. "All actions of bodies are mechanical and independent of souls" (GP 4: 540), Leibniz reminds us. But our *ability* to act in the ways we do must itself be explained by our soul or form.

Leibniz's hylomorphism does not reify the soul, but neither does it completely naturalize it. Soul is the *form* a body takes. Or even better: soul is the form which, at God's command, takes a body, enabling it to act in certain ways. Its most elementary appearance is as *force* in physics itself. In his "New System of the Nature of Substances" Leibniz calls *force*:

> a mid-point between power and action, which includes an effort, an activity (*acte*), and entelechy. . . . That is why I consider it to be constitutive of substance, being the origin of action, which is [a substance's] character.
>
> (GP 4: 472)

I think it reasonable to regard this picture as a form of hylomorphism, though I realize that I have not said nearly enough to *prove* that it is so. If I am right, though, hylomorphism frees Leibnizian metaphysics of one of its fantastical features, idealism.

Leibniz's views on interaction also become a little more tractable on this account. The appearance of interaction is not merely in the mind. Body A really does push body B. But A does *not* communicate its force to B, an idea of which, as Hume famously said, "we cannot form the most distant conception."[23] Instead, "no body suffers the impact of another except in virtue of a motion already within it, arising out of its own resources (*de son propre ressort*)" (GP 4: 476). When A pushes B, each body draws on its own force to accommodate itself to the changes in the other. The appearance of interaction is preserved and can be treated as real for the purposes of calculating its physical effects, yet without introducing paradox into metaphysics. The same thought adapted to the communications of mind and body avoids the impasse of Cartesian dualism. Leibniz calls that application of his doctrine "pre-established harmony."[24]

3. Does a Panpsychist Interpretation of Leibniz Have Direct Textual Support?

The Leibnizian hylomorphism I have just sketched fits naturally in the continuum of theories recognized as panpsychic in Seager and Allen-Hermanson's taxonomy. There is no obvious call for direct textual evidence of his panpsychism as such. However it would be wrong to ignore a paper by the Leibniz scholar, Andreas Blank (2000), which claims that support of that kind is lacking.

In the English summary that precedes his paper, Blank states his main contention as follows: "The interpretation of Leibniz's theory of simple substances as a philosophy of panpsychism has no direct support from Leibniz's texts." It is unclear here (and in Blank's paper) whether he is only defending the weak thesis that panpsychism can't be attributed to Leibniz on the strength of what he says about simple substances alone, or the stronger thesis, that what Leibniz says about simple substances makes it difficult or impossible to attribute panpsychism to him.

Blank's weaker thesis may be true without affecting what I have argued here. I made no claim that the ubiquity of what Leibniz loosely calls souls, namely simple substances, guarantees that souls in a stricter sense (e.g., minds or spirits) are also present everywhere.

However, my account would be in trouble if the stronger thesis were true. Does what Leibniz says about simple substances preclude any interesting reading of Leibniz as a panpsychist?

First, a terminological clarification: Blank uses the term "Seele" in his paper, and "soul" in his English summary, for what Leibniz means by the Latin "anima" and the French "âme." I shall use the word "soul" when reporting Blank's words, and I'll use other terms, as appropriate, when stating Leibniz's views or my own.

Blank's argument depends on two factual claims I will not dispute. The first is that an *ontological gap* exists between the powers of *simple substances* and those of *souls*. Simple substances produce complete representations of the world from their own resources, but lack what Blank calls the "second-order perceptions" (Blank 2000: 121)[25] of sensation, awareness and memory. Souls are equipped with both.

The ontological gap he is referring to can be presented as follows: if all Leibnizian substances were ordered according to the principle of least change, beginning with those with the least perceptive ability and ending with those who have most, the passage from least to greatest would not be gradual at all points. Between the most complex simple substance, S, and the simplest of minds endowed with "second-order perceptions," M, there would be a jump, an ontological gap. There would be no intermediate beings between S and M. Leibniz scholars find that problematic, because Leibniz is always assuring us that there are no jumps in nature (see, e.g., GP 2: 186; GP 3: 529; GP 4: 399).

It is tempting to try to explain this gap away by appeal to Leibniz's doctrine of "petites" (or subconscious) perceptions,[26] or by appeal to his more general views about continuity in nature. But Blank is successful, I think, in showing that neither doctrine can close this gap.

Blank's second factual claim, then, is that Leibniz's principle of continuity, as applied to the great chain of being, holds only for *possible* kinds of substances, not for those that exist in the actual world. In other words, logically speaking, there *could have been* creatures in the gap between S and M, but in fact there are none.

That there is an ontological gap, and that we can't explain it away, are factual claims I will not contest. But what significance does Blank's conclusion have for *my* claim that Leibniz, as I have previously described him, is a panpsychist? None that I can detect. Whether the gap between S and M can be filled by actual substances with intermediate substantial forms is an interesting question internal to Leibniz's metaphysics, but not determinative of whether or not he can be called a panpsychist.

Blank's point might still pose a challenge, however, if we were to apply his finding about the ontological gap to the corresponding "explanatory gap," which some philosophers of mind say arises when we look for a naturalistic evolutionary account of the origin of mental powers such as consciousness, beginning from a physicalistic starting point.

At first it might appear that naturalistic evolutionary explanations get a leg up in Leibniz's metaphysics. They are allowed to start from mind-like simple substances instead of from material bodies. But there is still that troublesome gap between S and M. The jump is still too great to figure in a wholly naturalistic explanation of how simple substances evolved into souls.

It is of course pleasant to speculate about how Leibniz would answer that question. But we can only conjecture. It's not his question. He holds that everything was created by God at the beginning of time, all living things *preformed* in their first ancestors' seed. Each individual of each generation develops (literally *unfolds*) according to what is prescribed by the entelechy given it by God at the beginning of time (CD §81).[27] All the beings that will ever be ensouled have been so from the beginning. No evolutionary explanation is required.

For that preformationist picture, entailing the ubiquity of the mental, there is, *pace* Blank, textual warrant. Though Leibniz never offered an evolutionary account of the human mind, he is still the ancestor of those thinkers today who suspect there can be no physicalistic and naturalistic account of it.

There is nothing, for Leibniz, that does not owe its type of existence either to mind itself, or to something resembling mind. Not even physics, he thinks, can be understood without considerations of regularity and purpose that presuppose and anticipate the mental (see e.g., DM §12; GP 4: 508). "Thus, entelechies must be everywhere," he tells Bayle, "and it is to have a small idea of nature's Author (who multiplies as much as possible these little worlds), if we associate them only with human bodies. In fact it is impossible that they not be everywhere" (GP 4: 557; compare also "De ipsa natura" §12, GP 4: 504 ff.).

Notes

1. In order of occurrence, they are: NE 2.12.7 (2x); NE 2.29.8; NE 4.5.1.
2. See NE 2.12.7, "en quelque façon mentale ou de phénomène;" GP 2: 486 ". . . de Relationibus censeo, . . . relationem communem utrique esse rem mere mentalem."
3. Letter to Johann-Friedrich, Duke of Brunswick-Lüneburg, May 21, 1671.
4. "Die Gemüths Ruhe ist eine belustigung des gemüths und innerliche vergnügung verursachende in uns die höchste und beständigste wollust unsers lebens" (GP 7: 95). In my translation I read "verursachend" for "verursachende."
5. Cited in Mahnke (1966: 17).
6. E.g.: "sum ergo praecise tantum res cogitans, id es, mens" AT 7: 27. We must remember, however, that "mens" becomes "esprit" in the French translation: AT 9: 21.
7. To Mersenne, April 24, 1641, AT 3: 362.
8. AT 7, 27: "sum igitur praecise tantum res cogitans, id est mens, sive animus, sive intellectus, sive ratio."
9. E.g. GP 1: 11: "res cogitans seu men[s]"; GP 4: 171: "Mentem voco ens cogitans."
10. As he tells his correspondent Burcher de Volder, GP 2: 232: "[M]ihi animus est notionem quaerere quae conveniat caeteris quoque et hominum usui consentiat."
11. All citations from this letter are taken from GP 7: 528f.
12. "mens est anima rationalis, ita anima est vita sensitiva, et vita est principium perceptivum" GP 7: 529.
13. Comp. Aristotle, *De anima*, 415a; Aquinas, *Summa Theologica* 1a q76 a4.
14. To Rémond, January 10, 1714.
15. To Rémond, August 26, 1714.
16. For a brief statement to this effect, see DM §23; for a full presentation see "De ipsa natura sive de vi insita actionibusque Creaturarum, pro Dynmaicis suis confirmandis illustradisque," GP IV: 504–16.
17. Russell had developed this view already in his influential book *A Critical Exposition of the Philosophy of Leibniz* (Russell 1900). For a discussion of some of the limitations of this approach see Hunter (1993).
18. R. M. Adams makes the most thorough case for an idealist reading in Adams (1994).
19. To de Volder, June 30, 1704.
20. In Hunter (2010: 581–4), I discuss an alternative to "theory pluralism" in a little more detail.
21. To Arnauld, Sept 1687.
22. "De ipsa natura . . . [materiam] . . . primam esse mere passivam, sed non esse completam substantiam; accedereque adeo debere animam, vel formam animae analogam, sive *entelecheian ten proten*, id est . . . vim agendi primitivam, quae ipsa est lex insita, decreto divino impressa."
23. Hume, *Enquiry Concerning Human Understanding*, 4.2.
24. See e.g., NE 2.2.28: "je soutiens que les âmes ne changent rien dans la force ni dans la direction des corps; que l'un serait aussi inconcevable et aussi déraisonnable que l'autre, et qu'il se faut servir de l'harmonine préétablie pour expliquer l'union de l'âme et du corps" (trans: "I maintain that souls change nothing either in the force of the direction of bodies, the one being as inconceivable and unreasonable as the other, and that we have to resort to pre-established harmony to explain the union of soul and body.").
25. "Perzeptionen zweiter Stufe."

26. By means of which some apparent gaps can be bridged, such as that between consciousness and unconsciousness in animals and in human beings. See Blank (2000: 121).
27. For more on this doctrine of Leibniz's see Catherine Wilson (1997).

Bibliography

Adams, R. M. (1994). *Leibniz: Determinist, Theist, Idealist*. Oxford and New York: Oxford University Press.

Bieri, Peter (ed.) (1981). *Analytische Philosophie des Geistes*. Königstein/Ts: Hain.

Blank, Andreas (2000). 'Leibniz und die panpsychistische Deutung der Theorie der einfachen Substanzen'. *Studia Leibnitiana*, 32 (1): 117–25.

Descartes, René (1996). *Oeuvres*. Ed. Charles Adam and Paul Tannery, 11 vols. Paris: Vrin. (Abbrev. "AT").

Engel, Pascal (1994). *Introduction à la philosophie de l'esprit*. Paris: La Découverte.

Fisette, Denis et Poirier, Pierre (eds.) (2000). *Philosophie de l'esprit*. Paris: Vrin.

Hartz, Glenn (2007). *Leibniz's Final System: Monads, Matter and Animals*. London and New York: Routledge.

Hunter, Graeme (1993). 'Russell Making History: The Leibniz Book'. In A. Irvine and G. A. Wedeking (eds.), *Russell and Analytic Philosophy*. Toronto: University of Toronto Press, pp. 397–414.

Hunter, Graeme (2010). 'Leibnizian Materialism'. *Dialogue*, 49: 573–88.

Leibniz, G. W. (1978). *Die Philosophischen Schriften*. Ed. C. I. Gerhardt. Hildesheim: Olms (Abbrev: "GP"). (Note: Works available in many editions and translation with common section-markers are identified according to the following key: CD = "Causa dei," an appendix to the *Theodicy;* DM = *Discours de métaphysique* = *Discourse on Metaphysics*; NE = *Nouveaux essais* = *New Essays on Human Understanding*).

Mahnke, Dietrich (1966). *Unendliche Sphäre und Allmittelpunkt*. Stuttgart: Frommann.

Russell, Bertrand (1900). *A Critical Exposition of the Philosophy of Leibniz*. London: George Allen and Unwin.

Russell, Bertrand (1946). *History of Western Philosophy*. London: George Allen and Unwin.

Rutherford, Donald (1995). 'Metaphysics: The Later Period'. In Nicholas Jolley (ed.), *Cambridge Companion to Leibniz*. Cambridge: Cambridge University Press, pp. 124–75.

Seager, William, and Allen-Hermanson, Sean (2015). 'Panpsychism'. In E. N. Zalta (ed.), *The Stanford Encyclopedia of Philosophy*. https://plato.stanford.edu/archives/fall2015/entries/panpsychism/. (Note this is not the latest version of the article, which has since been substantially updated.).

Wilson, Catherine (1997). 'Leibniz and the Animalcula'. In M. A. Stewart (ed.), *Studies in Seventeenth Century Philosophy*. Oxford and New York: Oxford University Press.

6

PANPSYCHISM IN THE 19TH CENTURY

David Skrbina

Upon its reemergence in the Italian naturalism of the Renaissance, panpsychism rapidly assumed a position of prominence in Western philosophy and by the early 1800s was a significant aspect of the metaphysical thinking of many prominent philosophers (for a detailed history, see Skrbina 2017). It was during the 19th century, however, that panpsychism witnessed a true resurgence. Primarily in Germany and Great Britain, the view became something of a mainstream idea in philosophy. Drawing from both the history of philosophy and the newly emerging sciences, philosophers found increasing reason to promote new variations on the panpsychist theme. In the present chapter, I cite some of the major figures of that time and give an outline of their views.

1. Schopenhauer

Of its many prominent advocates, panpsychism was perhaps the most central to the work of Arthur Schopenhauer. His *Die Welt als Wille und Vorstellung* (1819/1969) – completed when he was only 30 years old – is a landmark in the history of philosophy.[1] At nearly 1200 pages in length in its final edition, it's a monumental, highly detailed work, and yet the basic thesis is simply stated. Reality is comprehensible in two distinct but related ways. First there is the sense in which everything is known only as a mental image or impression, in the mind of the perceiver. When perceiving a given thing, what is presented in the mind is not the thing in itself but a representation of it as constituted by the sense impressions. When holding a red rose, for example, what one perceives is not the rose itself but a collection of colors, scents, and tactile sensations. What is known is only an idea or representation of a thing, not the thing-in-itself. The world, to the perceiver, is idea. This aspect is well-known; it was implicit in Descartes and Kant, and fully articulated in the idealism of Berkeley. The second way of conceiving of the world is deduced from human introspection. Our own body is obviously a material object, and we know it, in the first sense, as an object like any other. But we also know it in another way – from 'the inside,' as it were. Our mental lives offer many aspects to us: emotions, pains, pleasures, memories, beliefs, and so on. These things are primarily sensory, and thus related to our bodily perceptions. But most fundamentally, says Schopenhauer, is the fact that we know *desire*. Wanting, urging, striving, seeking . . . these are at the core of our bodily existence. We want food, drink, and sex. We desire and strive for material goods. We have myriad bodily urges, many of which we struggle to control. Desire is the foundation of our material being. For Schopenhauer, all these appetitive qualities are compressed into the word 'will.' Will, therefore, constitutes the essence of the human body, the thing-in-itself of our biological organism.

The argument is brought to a completion by acknowledging that the human body is simply an object like every other in the world. It's comprised of matter; it has an atomic structure; it produces ideas or representations in the mind of a perceiver; it is subject to the same natural laws as everything else. The human body, in its ontological construction, is not fundamentally different from any other object. Therefore, if the human body is essentially will, then so too is everything. Thus Schopenhauer reasons that all things, in themselves, are just will. Material objects are both, and at once, idea from the outside and will from the inside. As he says, "this world is, on the one side, entirely *representation*, just as, on the other, it is entirely *will*" (1819/1969: 4).

He takes pains to emphasize the ontological nature of his theory. It's not that things have a will or exert will – they *are* will. Material things are literally "objectifications of will," that is, physical manifestations, solidifications, or embodiments of it. This is clearly evident with the human body: "the whole body is nothing but objectified will" (100). Individual body parts are specific manifestations of different aspects of will, and bodily movements – whether voluntary or involuntary – are in reality motions of the will. But this holds for all material objects, since all are constructed on the same plan.

If everything in nature is objectified will, then this must hold true down to the smallest particles and to the most elemental forces. Natural forces must, indeed, be the simplest and purest manifestation of will. And in fact, says Schopenhauer, this is precisely what we see. "The most universal forces of nature exhibit themselves as the lowest grade of the will's objectification" (130). He elaborates:

> [C]ontinued reflection will lead [one] to recognize the force that shoots and vegetates in the plant, indeed the force by which the crystal is formed, the force that turns the magnet to the North Pole, the force whose shock [results] from the contact of metals of different kinds, . . . and finally even gravitation, which acts so powerfully in all matter, pulling the stone to the earth and the earth to the sun; all these he will recognize as . . . the same according to their inner nature. He will recognize them all as that which . . . is called *will*.
>
> (110)

The idea that all things are will, and express a kind of striving or desiring, is clearly reminiscent of Spinoza's conatus theory, and of his generally panpsychist outlook in which "all things are animate in varying degrees" (*Ethics* 2p13S). Unsurprisingly, Spinoza was a major influence in Schopenhauer's thinking.[2] We find the same themes elaborated in his later works. In *On the Will in Nature* (1836) he writes, "generally every original force manifesting itself in physical and chemical appearances, in fact gravity itself – all these in themselves . . . are absolutely identical with what we find in ourselves as *will*" (1836/1992: 20). Even though he finds in inorganic nature "absolutely no trace of a consciousness of an external world," yet in such things as "stones, boulders or ice floes" we see that "they are affected by an influence from without . . . which one can accordingly regard as the first step toward consciousness" (82). And plants, though likewise lacking true consciousness, experience "an obscure self-enjoyment" and "a feeble analogue of perception."

Panpsychism, and the notion of the world as will, is also central to Schopenhauer's final major work, *Parerga and Paralipomena*. In a notable passage, he decries the "fundamentally false contrast between *mind*[3] and *matter*" (1851/1974: 104). To the extent that one can speak of mind or matter in the real world, mind must be equally attributable to both organic and inorganic objects. Any two material objects, such as – to use his example – the human body and a stone, have internal qualities that are of necessity alike. Both are ruled by laws of nature, both are material, and both are thus describable in the same metaphysical terms. Where in one case we find mentality, so must we find it in the other:

> Now if you assume in the human head a *mind*, . . . you must also concede to every stone a *mind*. . . . In short, we can attribute matter to every so-called mind, but also mind to all matter, whence it follows that the contrast is false.
>
> (106)

Throughout his writings, Schopenhauer provides the first articulation of the so-called intrinsic nature argument for panpsychism.[4] Science, as a mechanistic philosophy, can only perceive external manifestations of force, mass, motion, and so on. What things are, in themselves, is completely unknown to mechanics:

> At bottom . . . [mechanistic] etiology does nothing more than show the orderly arrangement according to which the states or conditions appear in space and time. . . . But in this way we do not obtain the slightest information about the inner nature of any one of these phenomena. . . . The force itself that is manifested, the inner nature of the phenomena that appear in accordance with those laws, remain for it an eternal secret, something entirely strange and unknown.
>
> (1819/1969: 97)

And again later in *Parerga*, he writes that the mechanistic, scientific account of nature

> is restricted to determinations of space and time. . . . But as soon as we go, even in mechanics, beyond the pure mathematical . . . we are already face to face with manifestations that to us are just as mysterious as are thinking and willing in man; and thus we are confronted with that which is directly unfathomable.
>
> (106)

Unfathomable, that is, by science. With a true metaphysics, we can see that this "inner nature" is precisely the will; and that perceived matter is nothing other than the will objectified.

2. Fechner

Gustav Fechner was, in a sense, the antithesis of the pessimist Schopenhauer. Fechner adopted a vibrant, exuberant, life-enhancing perspective on the world. His worldview was intimately and openly linked to his panpsychist philosophy, perhaps more so than with any other major philosopher. He was also a first-rank scientist and mathematician. He virtually invented the science of psychophysics, and discovered 'Fechner's Law': the principle that the perceived strength of a sensation is proportional to the logarithm of the intensity of the stimulus.

Fechner's panpsychism was marked by his conception of the world as composed of a hierarchy of minds or souls (*Seele*). There are souls 'below' us, such as in plants, and there are souls 'above' us, in the Earth, the stars, and the universe as a whole. Humans are surrounded, at all levels of being, by varying degrees of soul. This is Fechner's "daylight view" – the human soul at home in an ensouled cosmos. This he contrasted to the then-standard materialist "night view" – humans alone, isolated points of light in a universe of utter blackness.

Consider separately his discussions of the 'lesser' (subhuman) and 'greater' (superhuman, or collective) minds. The former consists almost entirely of a discussion of plants, of which Fechner had no doubt that they possessed minds. The primary basis for this view was a continuity argument, or analogy with human beings, though he employed at least four other arguments for panpsychism. The Continuity argument appears repeatedly in his book *Nanna* (1848). For example:

> If we take a cursory glance at some of the outstanding points, is not the plant quite as well organized as the animal, though on a different plan, a plan entirely of its own, perfectly consonant with its idea? If one will not venture to deny that the plant has a life, why deny it a soul? For it is much simpler to think that a different plan of bodily organization built upon the common basis of life indicates only a different plan of psychic organization. . . .

[W]hether it be a plant or an animal, the complexity of structure and process is so completely analogous, except that the cells are differently arranged.

(1848/1946: 168–9)

Why are plant-souls important? Because they are the most direct indicators of the overall panpsychic nature of the world. As Fechner explained in *On the Soul-Question*:

[B]elief in the plant soul is just a little instance of the general situation . . ., for in this whole question the least and the greatest things are closely connected. . . . I considered that in the little soul of the plant I had found a little handle by which faith in the greatest things could be more easily hoisted to the big pedestal.

(1861/1946: 138–9)

Perhaps more important than Fechner's elaborations on the plant-soul was his discussion of, in the words of William James, the "superhuman consciousness" – the mind of society, of the Earth, of the stars, and of the cosmos. Fechner was the first scientist-philosopher to seriously examine these possibilities and to regard them as actual features of reality. James gives an excellent summary of the view:

In ourselves, visual consciousness goes with our eyes, tactile consciousness with our skin. . . . [T]hey come together in some sort of relation and combination in the more inclusive consciousness which each of us names his *self*. Quite similarly, says Fechner, we must suppose that my consciousness [and yours, though] they keep separate and know nothing of each other, are yet known and used together in a higher consciousness, that of the human race. . . . Similarly, the whole human and animal kingdoms come together as conditions of a consciousness of still wider scope. This combines in the soul of the earth with the consciousness of the vegetable kingdom, which in turn contributes . . . to that of the whole solar system, and so on from synthesis to synthesis and height to height, till an absolutely universal consciousness is reached.

(1909: 155–6)

Here we have a view of mind as a nested hierarchy, reaching from the lowest forms to the greatest. It is, as James said, "A vast analogical series, in which the basis of the analogy consists of facts directly observable in ourselves" (156).

Fechner's view was a pure pluralist panpsychism, and very close to that of James – sufficiently so that James was compelled to strongly emphasize the point that all these levels of hierarchy in the world possess, individually, their own minds. Elaborating on Fechner, he explains:

The vaster orders of mind go with the vaster orders of body. The entire earth . . . must have . . . its own collective consciousness. So must each sun, moon, and planet; so must the whole solar system. . . . So has the entire starry system as such its consciousness.

(152–3)

Fechner used a variety of arguments to defend his panpsychist claims. Earlier I cited a number of arguments by continuity, but he made use of at least four other techniques: (1) *In-Dwelling Powers*: plants have the power to take 'dead matter' and make it living, and in this sense they have more "vital force" than do animals. "Out of raw earth, water, air, and decaying substances the plant makes glorious forms and colors" (1848/1946: 184). (2) *Non-Emergence*: the Earth must be sentient, because "animate beings cannot arise from inanimate" (1861/1946: 156). (3) *Design*: the cosmos creates ensouled beings in order to attain full and complete enjoyment of existence. (4) *Theological*: Fechner admits that there is an element of faith involved here: "however we begin it or however we end, we shall not be able to discover and impart any exact proofs" (135). He notes that even in traditional theology, the Spirit of God is everywhere: "If one concedes a God who is at once omnipresent, omniscient, and omnipotent, then in a certain sense the universal animation of the world by God is already admitted" (1848/1946: 163–4).

In the end, Fechner made clear that his entire philosophical system was no mere poetic or romantic vision. It was not wishful thinking. It was intended as a metaphysical truth about reality. As he said in *On the Soul-Question*: "All this is not metaphorical, is not an hypothesis: it is a simple and literal statement of how things are" (1861/1946: 153).

3. Lotze, Clifford, and Other Scientist-Philosophers

Among German scientist-philosophers, Fechner was the outstanding proponent of a panpsychic worldview, but others held the same outlook, including Hermann Lotze. Lotze's chief work, *Microcosmos* (1856–64), is a comprehensive study on mind and matter. He prefaces the discussion by describing the antipathy between the philosophies of "mechanical science" on the one hand and what he calls the "Philosophy of the Feelings" on the other. The mechanist philosophers sought to describe everything in terms of forces and laws, but they overlooked the fact that such things "are not the ultimate components of the threads that weave the texture of reality" (xii). Later in the work he introduces a dual-aspect theory in which all matter has "a double life, appearing outwardly as matter, and as such manifesting . . . mechanical [properties, while] internally, on the other hand, moved mentally" (150). He speaks of this inner soul- or mental-life as being an "absolute indivisibility" (157), and proceeds to draw analogies between the soul and the indivisible atoms of matter.

Lotze's panpsychism is founded on the principle of the indivisibility of the atom. Matter as "infinitely divisible extension" is "an illusion" (354); rather, it consists of point-like atoms structured in a cohesive pattern by their respective forces. It is precisely this point-like nature of the atom that allows us to see it as a single unifying center of experience, with its own psychic life:

> The indivisible unity of each of these simple beings [atoms] permits us to suppose that in it the impressions reaching it from without are condensed into modes of sensation and enjoyment. [As a result,] no part of being is any longer devoid of life and animation.
>
> (360)

Like the ancient Greeks, Lotze accepted that motion is ultimately attributable to such a psyche: "We must . . . in general allow and maintain that all motion of matter in space may be explained as the natural expression of the inner states of beings that seek or avoid one another with a feeling of their need" (363).

In the end, panpsychism is not simply some abstract theory of metaphysics. For Lotze, it is the "beauty of the living form [that] is made to us more intelligible by this hypothesis" (366). And this, he says, is precisely why we must accept the view. Science itself neither wants nor needs panpsychism – rather, it's needed to satisfy the human spirit, to make the nature of the human soul comprehensible.

Not long after Lotze's primary work appeared, panpsychism began to gain attention in England. The physicist and philosopher William Kingdon Clifford argued that science had bridged the gap between organic and inorganic by describing the same atomic particles and same laws at work in each (1874/1903). This development naturally suggested a similar possible bridge between physics and consciousness. He concluded that mind was an active principle in nature, but because it was essentially non-physical, it had to function in a separate plane of existence. The physical and the mental thus operated as parallel systems: "the physical facts go along by themselves, and the mental facts go along by themselves" (53).[5] Clifford then applies a non-emergence argument in making his case for panpsychism. As we move down the chain of living organisms,

> it is impossible for anybody to point out the particular place . . . where [absence of con-
> sciousness] can be supposed to have taken place. . . . [E]ven in the very lowest organisms,
> even in the Amoeba . . . there is something or other, inconceivably simple to us, which is of
> the same nature with our own consciousness. . . . [Furthermore] we cannot stop at organic
> matter, [but] we are obliged to assume . . . that along with every motion of matter, whether
> organic or inorganic, there is some fact which corresponds to the mental fact in ourselves.
>
> (60–1)

Echoing Fechner, he notes that his doctrine "is no mere speculation, but is a result to which all the greatest minds that have studied this question in the right way have gradually been approximating for a long time" (61).

Clifford later expanded on his views, advocating a monist philosophy in which the basic constituent of reality is "mind-stuff." Neither mind nor consciousness, mind-stuff is rather the elements that combine together to form "the faint beginnings of Sentience." Mind is thus viewed as composed of 'mental atoms' that combine in an analogous manner as physical atoms do: "A moving molecule of inorganic matter does not possess mind, or consciousness; but it possesses a small piece of mind-stuff" (1878: 65). Intelligence and volition emerge only in higher-level complexes of mind-stuff, but elementary feelings are present in all things, at all levels.

At about the same time, Clifford's compatriot, Samuel Butler, was developing panpsychist ideas of his own. He discussed them in his 1880 book *Unconscious Memory*. Like many other thinkers of the time, Butler noted that scientists had determined that the nature of the organic is the same as the inorganic; vitalism was largely disproved, organic matter was shown to be identical with inorganic, and the same forces were everywhere present – the standard view to this day. The logical conclusion, then, was that certain core characteristics of the living must inhere, in some form, in the non-living. As he says, "if we once break down the wall of partition between the organic and inorganic, the inorganic must be living and conscious also, up to a point" (22). He continues:

> [I]t is more coherent with our other ideas, and therefore more acceptable, to start with
> every molecule as a living thing . . . than to start with inanimate molecules and smuggle
> life into them; . . . what we call the inorganic world must be regarded as up to a certain
> point living, and instinct, within certain limits, with consciousness, volition, and power of
> concerted action.
>
> (23)

At the conclusion of the book he offers this view as a useful and even morally enlightened perspective: "I would recommend the reader to see every atom in the universe as living and able to feel and to remember, but in a humble way" (273). That a moral perspective is engendered by panpsychism is perhaps not obvious: "True, it would be hard to place one's self on the same moral platform as a stone, but this is not necessary; it is enough that we should feel the stone to have a moral platform of its own" (275). Butler is thus one of the few modern commentators to cite the moral relevance of panpsychism. His statements show early signs of an ecological value system, one in which objects of nature have intrinsic moral worth.[6] Back in Germany, Ernst Mach's philosophical writings began to emerge in the early 1880s. An Austrian physicist known more for his scientific advances than his philosophy, he nonetheless made substantial contributions to the philosophy of science, and he was an early contributor to the field of logical positivism. For Mach, the aim of science was to predict and describe, and only secondarily to 'explain.' In his epistemology, he was strongly empiricist. He eventually developed a neutral monistic philosophy in which the primary substance of existence was neither mental nor physical but rather something that he called "sensations." This realization led him to a panpsychist conception of reality.

In his *Science of Mechanics* (1883) Mach articulated this view: "Properly speaking the world is not composed of 'things' . . . but of colors, tones, pressures, spaces, times, in short what we ordinarily call individual sensations" (1883/1974: 579). The view that 'all is sensation' is an interesting and novel development; it superficially resembles Berkeley's idealism, except that there is no observing mind involved. A more accurate description of his view may be that of an ontological pansensism – not of the usual form in which all things have the power to sense, but rather that they constitutionally are themselves sensations.

If Mach was less than clear on the details of his pansensism, he was unambiguous about his monist ontology and its panpsychist implications. He notes that both mechanistic monism and "animistic" monism are inadequate worldviews:

> Both [the mechanical and animistic mythologies] contain undue and fantastical exaggera-tions of an incomplete perception. Careful physical research will lead . . . to an analysis of our sensations. We shall then discover that our hunger is not so essentially different from the tendency of sulphuric acid for zinc, and our will not so greatly different from the pres-sure of a stone, as now appears. We shall again feel ourselves nearer nature, without its being necessary that we should resolve ourselves into a nebulous and mystical mass of molecules, or make nature a haunt of hobgoblins.
>
> (560)

Clearly Mach is sensitive to the close association between his view and animism, and he wants to make nature sensate without introducing personal spirits. He seems to draw inspiration from Scho-penhauer – note the comparison between 'will' and 'pressure of a stone' – and we know from his other writings that he was highly influenced by Fechner. His unique form of pansensism led the way for the soon-to-follow developments of James (radical empiricism) and Whitehead (process philosophy).

Another important thinker of the time was Ernst Haeckel. As among the first to see the philo-sophical implications of the newly emerging theory of evolution, he established himself as the lead-ing German Darwinist. He developed a panpsychic and even pantheistic monism in which both evolution and the unity of all natural phenomena played a major role.

Haeckel was explicitly panpsychist by 1892: "One highly important principle of my monism seems to me to be, that I regard *all* matter as *ensouled*, that is to say as endowed with *feeling* (pleas-ure and pain) and *motion*" (1892: 486). He offers here one argument for panpsychism, namely that "all natural bodies possess determinate chemical properties," the most important being that of "chemical affinity." This affinity, Haeckel argues, can only be explained "on the supposition that the molecules . . . mutually *feel* each other" (483). Elsewhere he employs evolution on behalf of a continuity argument, claiming that evolution shows "the essential unity of inorganic and organic nature" (1895: 3). Evolutionary monism strikes at the heart of both the religious worldview and the mechanical philosophy. "Our conception of Monism . . . is clear and unambiguous; . . . an immaterial living spirit is just as unthinkable as a dead, spiritless material; the two are inseparably combined in every atom" (58).

Haeckel's most famous work was *The Riddle of the Universe* (1899). Here he arrived at a neutral monist position in which his ultimate reality was "substance" which possessed two attributes or manifestations, matter and energy. Matter corresponded to 'body' and energy to 'spirit,' and the two aspects were then united in a parallel manner. All living creatures, for Haeckel, possess "conscious psychic action"; the inorganic world also possesses an inherent psychic quality, though he takes care to emphasize that this is unconscious rather than conscious mentality. This applies even to the atoms: "I conceive the elementary psychic qualities of sensation and will, which may be attributed to atoms, to be *unconscious*" (179).

Finally, Haeckel's *The Wonders of Life* (1904) is primarily an elaboration of his earlier ideas. In this work, though, he refers to himself for the first time as a hylozoist. He notes: "Monism is best expressed as hylozoism, in so far as this removes the antithesis of materialism and spiritualism (or mechanism and dynamism)" (88). And he here proposes a third fundamental attribute to his "substance"; in addition to matter and force, he adds "*psychoma*" or "general sensation." This is his response to charges that mere matter and force/energy are not in themselves 'psychic' enough to account for mind. He summarizes his view thusly: "(1) No matter without force and without sensation. (2) No force without matter and without sensation. (3) No sensation without matter and without force" (465).

4. Leading American Panpsychists

Physician and psychologist Morton Prince explored the philosophy of mind in his 1885 book *The Nature of Mind and Human Automatism*. Following Clifford, he proposes "mind stuff" as the 'thing-in-itself' of material objects. This view – a form of idealist monism – is offered as a contrast to mechanistic materialism: "matter is no longer the dead and senseless thing it is popularly supposed to be" (1885/1975: 163). Evolution suggests the unity of all phenomena. As a consequence, "the whole universe . . . instead of being inert is made up of living forces; not conscious [but] pseudo-conscious. It is made up of the elements of consciousness" (164).

Shortly thereafter, Josiah Royce developed his system of objective or absolute idealism. In his *Spirit of Modern Philosophy* (1892) he proposed a theory of the Universal Self – Logos, or World-Spirit, or God – as the cosmic mind which is the reality behind all physical phenomena. He combines this notion with a dual-aspect view of matter, roughly along Schopenhauerian lines.

As with many other thinkers of the time, Royce saw in evolution grounds for viewing all physical objects as subject to the same metaphysical principles. Humans unquestionably possess an inner mental life; hence so too does everything. This is the "relation of the inorganic world to our human consciousness" (1892/1955: 419). He explains:

> The theory of the 'double aspect,' applied to the facts of the inorganic world, suggests at once that they, too, in so far as they are real, must possess their own inner and appreciable aspect. . . . In general it is an obvious corollary of all that we have been saying.
>
> (419–20)

> [W]e know that there is no real process of nature that must not have, known or unknown to us, its inner, its appreciable aspect. Otherwise it could not be real.
>
> (426–7)

Royce counsels the reader not to view this as mere animism or anthropomorphism. It's simplistic and misleading to presuppose that "stones or planets" have anything like a human inner life: "it is not ours to speculate *what* appreciative inner life is hidden behind the . . . lifeless things of the world" (427).

Royce's final articulation of panpsychism came in *The World and the Individual* (1899–1901) where he asks the reader to "suppose that even material nature were internally full of the live and fleeting processes that we know as those of conscious mental life" (213). He concludes that the mental aspect of nature exists, but that it operates at a vastly different, and slower, time scale than our human consciousness, and therefore we cannot perceive it. He writes, we have no right whatever to speak of really unconscious Nature, but only of uncommunicative Nature, or of Nature whose mental processes go on at such different time-rates from ours that we cannot adjust ourselves to a live appreciation of their inward fluency.

(225–6)

The "very vast [mental] slowness in inorganic Nature," such as in a rock or the solar system, is no less extant that our own mentality. Time scale is entirely arbitrary; slower is not lesser. The mind in nature is fully conscious. Hence a mental life is to be found everywhere in nature:

Where we see inorganic Nature seemingly dead, there is, in fact, conscious life, just as surely as there is any Being present in Nature at all. And I insist, meanwhile, that no empirical warrant can be found for affirming the existence of dead material substance anywhere.

(240)

C. S. Peirce, known primarily for his pragmatism, logical philosophy, and semiotics, ventured into metaphysics in an important series of articles published in *Monist* between 1891 and 1893. The first of these, "The Architecture of Theories," addresses "the brick and mortar" of any viable metaphysical system: the relation of mind to matter. Dualism is no longer tenable for Peirce, and thus he concludes that some form of monism must be true. The version he favors involves the notion of "hylopathy" – the view that all matter 'feels.' Standard monisms, such as neutralism or materialism, fail to fully account for mind in a naturalistic way. We are thus left with an objective form of idealism:

The one intelligible theory of the universe is that of objective idealism, that matter is effete mind, inveterate habits becoming physical laws.

(1891/1992: 293)

Pierce is here referring to his "cosmogonic" thesis in which the universe originates in a condition of pure, chaotic feeling. It then becomes progressively "crystallized" into matter as this mind undergoes a kind of solidification, via the process of patterns of recurrence that Peirce calls "habits." Mind is thus at the core of reality. It exists in varying stages of solidification seen in one sense as matter, in another as mind.

He briefly returns to panpsychism in "The Law of Mind," where he observes that "*tychism* must give birth to an evolutionary cosmology … and to a Schelling-fashioned idealism which holds matter to be mere specialized and partially deadened mind" (1892a/1992: 312). At the end of the essay he reiterates that "what we call matter is not completely dead, but is merely mind hide-bound with habits" (331).

Peirce's most important article was the last in the series, "Man's glassy essence." Here he begins with a look at physics and chemistry, moving on to a discussion of primitive life forms and the protoplasm inside all living cells. Of all its properties, the most important one is that "protoplasm feels" (1892b/1992: 343) and it furthermore exhibits all essential mental qualities. This sensitivity and sentience are inferred, Peirce tells us, by analogy: "[T]here is fair analogical inference that all protoplasm feels. It not only feels but exercises all the functions of mind" (343). The analogy is based on such properties as the sensitive reaction to the environment, ability to move, to grow, to reproduce, and so on. And yet protoplasm is simply complex chemistry, a particular arrangement of molecules. Feeling cannot be accounted for by mechanistic laws; therefore, we are "[forced to] admit that physical events are but degraded or undeveloped forms of psychical events" (348). Peirce then presents his own dual-aspect theory of mind:

[A]ll mind is directly or indirectly connected with all matter, and acts in a more or less regular way; so that all mind more or less partakes of the nature of matter. … Viewing a thing from the outside, . . . it appears as matter. Viewing it from the inside, . . . it appears as consciousness.

(349)

The dynamic sensitivity of protoplasm necessarily results in an enhanced capability for feeling: "nerve-protoplasm is . . . in the most unstable condition of any kind of matter; and consequently, there the resulting feeling is the most manifest." Again, this sort of sensitivity is a general property of matter: "Wherever chance-spontaneity [i.e. unstable sensitivity] is found, there, in the same proportion, feeling exists." Peirce thus effectively introduces a new argument for panpsychism, based on the correlation between a specific physical characteristic – dynamic sensitivity – and a mental quality, feeling. All matter is dynamic to a greater or lesser degree, and thus all must be associated with an 'interior' that feels. Like the evolutionary argument, this approach incorporates elements of continuity and non-emergence. To these it adds a reference to the indwelling power of dynamical systems. Clearly Peirce was only sketching out his views here, and certainly the lack of a developed theory of dynamical systems restricted his ability to articulate himself. With the advent of chaos theory and nonlinear dynamics in the late 20th century, we now have new ways of expanding on Peirce's insight.[7] Finally, Peirce recognized that his generalized theory of mind applied not only to lower-order systems but also to those significantly larger and more comprehensive than the human being. People who interact strongly with each other produce a true group mind that is of like nature to all mind. Personhood or personality results when the lower-order minds are "in close enough connection to influence one another" (350). He continues: "there should be something like personal consciousness in [collective] bodies of men who are in intimate and intensely sympathetic communion." In other words, the degree of interaction and participation determines the degree of mind. Peirce adds that these ideas "are no mere metaphors. . . . [T]he law of mind clearly points to the existence of such personalities."

5. Nietzsche

Panpsychism in the writings of major philosophers is always controversial. In most cases, it's either denied or ignored by the experts. But we find something different in the work of Friedrich Nietzsche. In his case, scholars dispute whether he even articulated a panpsychist worldview; and if he did, whether he actually believed it. The evidence, however, is clear and decisive; Nietzsche did articulate and endorse a form of panpsychism, from his late 20s through the end of his life. Already in 1872 he observed "that the impact, the influence of one atom upon another is likewise something which presupposes sensation" (1979: 35) – indicative of an early orientation toward panpsychism.

Among Nietzsche's central metaphysical claims is the theory of 'will to power' (*der Wille zur Macht*). Appearing in his unpublished notebooks as early as 1876, the phrase shows up repeatedly in his various writings right until the very end. But its precise meaning is a matter of dispute. At a minimum, it seems to express Nietzsche's belief that all human motivation and actions are, at root, strivings for power of some sort. And he is clear that all living things likewise act on behalf of, or seek, power. The final extension of will to power to the inorganic world, however, generates much debate; it's here that panpsychism becomes explicit. I refer to this as the 'ontological will to power' thesis.

In much the same manner as Schopenhauer, Nietzsche suggests in several passages that things are, in themselves, will to power. The large majority of these appear in the notebooks, and many have been reproduced in the posthumous book *The Will to Power* (1906). Only in two instances did he publish explicitly ontological references to will to power. And only in one – in *Beyond Good and Evil* – does he give anything like an extended argument.

Consider the following passages. These are among his first clear ontological references, and all date from 1885. For example:

The victorious concept "force" . . . still needs to be completed: an inner will must be ascribed to it, which I designate as "will to power," i.e. as an insatiable desire to manifest power. . . . [O]ne is obliged to understand all motion, all "appearances," all "laws," only as symptoms of an inner event, and to employ man as an analogy to this end.

(1906/1967: § 619)

Elsewhere he casts it in terms of causation and forces. "There is absolutely no other kind of causality than that of will upon will. Not explained mechanistically" (§ 658). And yet more explicitly:

"Attraction" and "repulsion" in a purely mechanistic sense are complete fictions: a word. We cannot think of an attraction divorced from an intention. The will to take possession of a thing or to defend oneself against it and repel it – that we "understand."

(§ 627)

Section 655 remarks on "the will to power in every combination of forces," and observes that "the entire distinction" between the organic and the inorganic "is a prejudice." If all this appears vague, we have the strikingly explicit statement in section 1067: "*This world is the will to power – and nothing besides!* And you yourselves are also this will to power – and nothing besides!"

The following year he published *Beyond Good and Evil*. Among the more interesting passages is this:

Granted finally that one succeeded in explaining our entire instinctual life as the development and ramification of *one* basic form of will – as will to power, as is *my* theory . . . [then] one would have acquired the right to define *all* efficient force unequivocally as: *will to power*. The world seen from within, the world described and defined according to its "intelligible character" – it would be "will to power" and nothing else.

(1886/1973: § 36)

The passage is clear and explicit, but unfortunately Nietzsche elected to cast it in provisional and conditional terms, leading some to argue that he never really endorsed the view. But seen in light of his many other passages, over many years, it's clear that he was making a positive metaphysical claim here.

In 1887, a passing comment appears in *On the Genealogy of Morals*. In the Second Essay he makes reference to "the theory that in all events a *will to power* is operating" (§ 12).[8] But unfortunately there is no elaboration. Two notebook entries of the time, however, express a related sentiment: if all extant things are will to power, and they continually express this will, then they are, in a sense, alive: "Being – we have no idea of it apart from the idea of 'living' – How can anything dead 'be'?" (1906/1967: § 582). And again: "'Being' as universalization of the concept 'life' (breathing), 'having a soul,' 'willing, effecting,' 'becoming'" (§ 581).

In Nietzsche's final working year, 1888, we find several relevant passages in *Will to Power*:

- A quantum of power is designated by the effect it produces and that which it resists. . . . [E]very atom affects the whole of being. . . . That is why I call it a quantum of 'will to power' (§ 634).
- My idea is that every specific body strives to become master over all space and to extend its force (– its will to power) and to thrust back all that resists its extension (§ 636).
- [My theory would be] that all driving force is will to power, that there is no other physical, dynamic or psychic force except this (§ 688).
- The will to accumulate force is special to the phenomena of life, to nourishment, procreation, inheritance – to society, state, custom, authority. Should we not be permitted to assume this will as a motive cause in chemistry, too? – and in the cosmic order? (§ 689).

- [L]ife is merely a special case of the will to power (§ 692).
- [T]he innermost essence of being is will to power (§ 693).

The evidence thus shows that Nietzsche did seriously entertain the ontological, panpsychic thesis of will to power for most of his productive life. Published statements are rare, but the repeated notebook entries show that he continued to find value in the idea. He surely would not have continued to remark on the ontological thesis if at any point he found it to be irrelevant or untrue.

Nietzsche's untimely demise in 1900 not only brought the century to a close, it marked the end of perhaps the golden age of panpsychism in the West. It is true, there would be major panpsychist philosophers working into the 20th century, most notably James, Bergson, Whitehead, and in a less explicit manner, Russell. But overall the movement was on the decline. Scientific materialism and logical positivism would drive out classical metaphysics, and panpsychism along with it.

Fortunately this would be a temporary condition. The positivist stranglehold on philosophy has lessened in recent decades, and at least since the mid-1990s, the way has become clear for a renewed examination of panpsychism. Once again, as before, it is considered a viable and respectable approach to understanding the nature of mind.

Notes

1. Garvey (2006), for example, rates it among the top 20 books of all time.
2. Along with Aristotle, Plato, Goethe, and Kant, Spinoza is among the most-cited individuals in the book.
3. Reading 'mind' for *Geist*.
4. Recently this argument has become known as "Russellian," but in fact Schopenhauer articulated it more than 100 years earlier.
5. This is closely aligned with Spinoza's parallelism. But Spinoza goes further and views the two parallel sequences as identical; see *Ethics* (2p7).
6. For a recent discussion of this subject, in light of panpsychism, see Skrbina (2013).
7. For one such analysis, see Skrbina (2009b).
8. "*als mit der Theorie eines in allem Geschehn sich abspielenden Macht-Willens.*" *Geschehn* may be read as 'happenings' or 'occurrences.'

Bibliography

Butler, S. (1880/1910). *Unconscious Memory*. London: Longmans, Green.
Clifford, W. K. (1874/1903). 'Body and Mind'. In *Lectures and Essays*, vol. 2. London: Macmillan.
Clifford, W. K. (1878). 'On the Nature of Things in Themselves'. *Mind*, 3 (9): 57–67.
Fechner, G. (1848/1946). 'Nanna, or on the Soul-Life of Plants'. In R. Lowrie (trans.), *Religion of a Scientist*. New York: Pantheon.
Fechner, G. (1861/1946). 'On the Soul-Question'. In R. Lowrie (trans.), *Religion of a Scientist*. New York: Pantheon.
Garvey, J. (2006). *The Twenty Greatest Philosophy Books*. London: Bloomsbury.
Haeckel, E. (1892). 'Our Monism'. *Monist*, 2 (4).
Haeckel, E. (1895). *Monism as Connecting Religion and Science*. Trans. J. Gilchrist. London: A. and C. Black.
Haeckel, E. (1899/1929). *The Riddle of the Universe*. Trans. J. McCabe. London: Watts.
Haeckel, E. (1904). *The Wonders of Life*. Trans. J. McCabe. London: Watts.
James, W. (1909/1996). *A Pluralistic Universe*. Lincoln, NE: University of Nebraska Press.
Lotze, R. H. (1856–64/1971). *Microcosmos*. Trans. E. Hamilton and E. Jones. Edinburgh: T&T Clark.
Mach, E. (1883/1942). *The Science of Mechanics*. Trans. T. McCormack. London: Open Court Publishing.
Nietzsche, F. (1886/1973). *Beyond Good and Evil*. Trans. R. Hollingdale. London: Penguin.
Nietzsche, F. (1887/1967). *On the Genealogy of Morals*. Trans. W. Kaufmann. New York: Random House.
Nietzsche, F. (1906/1967). *The Will to Power*. Trans. W. Kaufmann and R. Hollingdale. New York: Random House.
Nietzsche, F. (1979). *Philosophy and Truth*. Ed. D. Breazeale. New York: Humanities Press.
Peirce, C. (1891). 'The Architecture of Theories'. *Monist*, 1 (1). (Reprinted in N. Houser and J. W. Kloesel (eds.), *The Essential Peirce*, vol. 1. Bloomington, IN: Indiana University Press, 1992.).

Peirce, C. (1892a). 'The Law of Mind'. *Monist*, 2 (2). (Reprinted in N. Houser and J. W. Kloesel (eds.), *The Essential Peirce*, vol. 1. Bloomington, IN: Indiana University Press, 1992.).

Peirce, C. (1892b). 'Man's Glassy Essence'. *Monist*, 3 (1). (Reprinted in N. Houser and J. W. Kloesel (eds.), *The Essential Peirce*, vol. 1. Bloomington, IN: Indiana University Press, 1992.).

Prince, M. (1885/1975). 'The Nature of Mind and the Human Automatism'. In *The Origins of Psychology*, vol. 1. Alan Liss.

Prince, M. (1904). 'The Identification of Mind and Matter'. *Philosophical Review*, 13 (4): 444–51.

Royce, J. (1892/1955). *Spirit of Modern Philosophy*. Boston: Houghton Mifflin.

Royce, J. (1898/1915). *Studies of Good and Evil*. New York: Appleton.

Royce, J. (1899–1901). *The World and the Individual*. New York: Macmillan.

Schopenhauer, A. (1819/1969). *The World as Will and Representation*. Trans. E. F. Payne, vol. 1. New York: Dover.

Schopenhauer, A. (1836/1993). *On the Will in Nature*. Trans. E. F. Payne. Oxford: Berg.

Schopenhauer, A. (1851/1974). *Parerga and Paralipomena*. Trans. E. F. Payne, vol. 2. Oxford: Clarendon Press.

Skrbina, D. (2009a). 'Panpsychism in History'. In D. Skrbina (ed.), *Mind That Abides*. Amsterdam: Benjamins.

Skrbina, D. (2009b). 'Minds, Objects, and Relations'. In D. Skrbina (ed.), *Mind That Abides*. Amsterdam: Benjamins.

Skrbina, D. (2013). 'Ethics, Eco-Philosophy, and Universal Sympathy'. *Dialogue and Universalism*, 23 (4): 59–74.

Skrbina, D. (2017). *Panpsychism in the West* (revised edition). Cambridge, MA: MIT Press.

Strong, C. (1904). 'Dr. Morton Prince and Panpsychism'. *Psychological Review*, 11 (1): 67–9.

7

WILLIAM JAMES, PURE EXPERIENCE, AND PANPSYCHISM

Andrew Bailey

William James (1842–1910) did not write very extensively about panpsychism. In all his voluminous published writings the topic is discussed in only half a dozen places (and the position is mentioned approvingly, but with no discussion, in a few others).[1] In his lecture notes and unpublished manuscripts there is somewhat more exploration of the idea of panpsychism, but still James' investigation of the theme there is relatively limited.

This relative reticence is quite surprising. The prospect of panpsychism – as James construed it – is intimately connected to issues that were of deep and often lifelong interest to James, and what's more he appears to have been increasingly aware of this as his thoughts developed from the 1890s onwards. These issues include the status of metaphysical monism versus dualism, and of a broadly 'empiricist' temper to human thought as opposed to a 'rationalist' one; the possibility of free will; the nature of the self, and its relation to God or the absolute; and the evidence for 'psychical' or supernatural phenomena such as telepathy, extrasensory perception, or communication with the dead.

James' lack of extensive overt attention to the issue is also surprising because panpsychism was very much a 'live option' at the time he was writing. James read, was influenced by or sympathetic to, and responded to, such panpsychist (in one way or another) authors as Charles A. Strong (1903), Henri Bergson (1907), Morton Prince (1904), Gustav Fechner (1861), William Kingdon Clifford (1874, 1878), Ernst Haeckel (1893), Josiah Royce (1892), and Gerardus Heymans (1905).

Why, then, was James – not an author to shy away from speculation, or one unwilling to follow a suggestive train of thought to see where it led – relatively silent on the topic of panpsychism? The answer, I suggest, is that panpsychism, while attractive or even necessary to him, gave James difficulties: the dualist or idealist forms of panpsychism that seemed to be available to him were not a good fit with – indeed, appeared to directly contradict – some of the central tenets of the pluralist radical empiricism that he was developing. As a result, James must have found himself reluctant to clearly state an allegiance to panpsychism in any of the various forms in which it was then understood. Yet, something panpsych-ish was evidently appealing to James' intellectual sensibilities, and was even something that might solve some of the remaining difficulties he felt with his radical empiricism. The result, I will argue here, is that we can trace in James' writings a unique form of panpsychism – or perhaps better a panprotopsychism – that does not resemble the leading (dualist or idealist) panpsychisms of his day nor is it a form of the perhaps somewhat more modern neutral monist forms of panpsychism, but is something else again.

I will begin by summarizing James' account of consciousness and its place in his metaphysics of pure experience. Although there is interpretive disagreement over whether James' account of experience is consistent or complete, either over the span of his writings or in its final form, I shall ignore that controversy here. My own view is that, at least in its broad strokes, a unified picture of the mind and its place 'in' the world can be seen emerging from James' writings, and that his later positions are consistent with and amplify his earlier views rather than rejecting them (Bailey 1998).

At the core of James' stance on consciousness is his close attention to the scope and limits of what is delivered through experience – his 'radical empiricism' has its roots in even the earliest of James' work on psychology. In addition, a common thread in his work on consciousness is the rejection of various dualities both within conscious experience and between consciousness and everything else; this compulsive blurring of ontological lines leads ultimately to James' metaphysics of 'pure experience' – which is not a monism but a cheerful pluralism.

According to James, "[t]he first and foremost concrete fact which everyone will affirm to belong to his inner experience is the fact that *consciousness of some sort goes on*" (1892: 140).[2] That is, states of consciousness exist, and – James asserts – form the basic data of the science of psychology. This positive thesis, however, is coupled with a well-known deflationary stance towards consciousness: while James is keen to assert that "thought goes on" (1890: 225), his view is that this is pretty much *all* that is delivered through introspection. He presents the following well-known list of what we know about consciousness from the first-person (1890, Chapter IX):[3]

1.   Every thought is part of a personal consciousness;
2.   Within each personal consciousness thought is always changing;
3.   Within each personal consciousness thought is sensibly continuous;
4.   Thought always appears to deal with objects independent of itself; and
5.   Thought is selectively attentive.

Consciousness, as we actually experience it, amounts to nothing more than a sequence of thoughts characterized by these five aspects: indeed, "I believe that 'consciousness,' when once it has evaporated to this estate of pure diaphaneity, . . . is on the point of disappearing altogether. It is the name of a nonentity" (1904a: 477).

Here, according to James, is what consciousness isn't: It isn't a container through which thoughts pass – it is the flux-like stream of thought itself and is natively selective. It isn't a soul or ego behind or within our experience; that is, we have no empirical, introspective evidence for such a thing. It isn't even identifiable as "a kind of impalpable inner flowing" (1904a: 479), the residuum postulated by the neo-Kantians of James' day even after they had abolished the dualism between knower and known.

> It seems as if consciousness as an inner activity were rather a *postulate* than a sensibly given fact, the postulate, namely, of a *knower* as correlative to all this known; and as if '*sciousness*' might be a better word by which to describe it. But 'sciousness postulated as an hypothesis' is practically a very different thing from 'states of consciousness apprehended with infallible certainty by an inner sense.'
>
> (1892: 400)

Furthermore, according to James, careful attention to the deliverances of introspection reveals that (a) we have no direct evidence that the stream of thought is a different kind of substance than the rest of the world; and (b) we have no direct evidence for any kind of duality between content and consciousness. Although we may suppose that we perceive our mental life

> as a sort of interior current, active, light, fluid, delicate, diaphanous, so to speak, and absolutely opposed to whatever is material . . . I believe . . . that this sort of consciousness is a

pure chimera, and that the sum of concrete realities which the word consciousness should cover deserves quite a different description.

(1905b: 56–60)

And although we may suppose that conscious thought is made up of content plus a mode of presentation of that content,

> [e]xperience, I believe, has no such inner duplicity; and the separation of it into consciousness and content comes, not by way of subtraction, but by way of addition – the addition, to a given concrete piece of it, of other sets of experiences. . . . [A] given undivided portion of experience, taken in one context of associates, play[s] the part of a knower, of a state of mind, of 'consciousness'; while in a different context the same undivided bit of experience plays the part of a thing known, of an objective 'content.'
>
> (1904a: 480)

The remaining dualism – "since [experience] can figure in both groups simultaneously we have every right to speak of it as subjective and objective both at once" (1904a: 480) – is not a mysterious or a metaphysical dualism. "[I]t becomes verifiable and concrete. It is an affair of relations, it falls outside, not inside, the single experience considered, and can always be particularized and defined" (1904a: 480).

Yet, for all of his emphasis on experience as a stand-alone phenomenon whose nature can be fully grasped without resort to relations to things outside of itself – either a knower/attender/valuer or a set of extra-mental referents – James was no idealist. On the other hand, he was not a materialist either. Although consciousness is clearly not for James a separate substance from the physical, nor is it to be identified with the physical; and this is true of James' thought even during the period he was writing his *Principles of Psychology*.

> Although we affirm that the *coming to pass* of thought is a consequence of mechanical laws . . . we do not in the least explain the *nature* of thought by affirming this dependence, and in that latter sense our proposition is not materialism.
>
> (1892: 13)

James lists many attributes of consciousness which he considers not to be predicable of the physical. For example, he dwells at some length on the fact that consciousness is unique in that it can have 'ends' or 'interests' (1878). Considered merely physically, the reactions of our brain

> cannot be properly talked of as 'useful' or 'hurtful' at all. . . . All that can be said of them is that *if* they occur in a certain way survival will as a matter of fact be their incidental consequence. The organs themselves, and the rest of the physical world, will, however, all the time be quite indifferent to this consequence, and would quite as cheerfully, the circumstances changed, compass the animal's destruction.
>
> (1890: 98)

This has the additional consequence that the fundamental character of consciousness, for James, is as a 'fighter for ends.' It is not purely cognitive – rather, cognition is subservient to ends (1890: 141).

Other central examples of non-physical predicates, for James, are the property of 'knowing' or 'reporting' and of being 'personal.' In addition, all sorts of things are true of 'mental objects' (that fire may play over them and not affect them, that they only came into existence moments ago) that are false of their corresponding 'physical' counterparts, and *vice versa* (1904a: 482).

So, according to James, the raw data of science is experience and what experience pre-theoretically reveals is that we have mental lives – a "personal consciousness" – but that this mental life is no more and no less than the constant flux of a "stream of consciousness." This flux is both thinner than we assume, containing within itself no evidence of things beyond itself (such as an ego) but also richer than we might have noticed because it has 'built in' many relations that we tend wrongly to treat as external to, or superposed on, experience.

> Every examiner of the sensible life *in concreto* must see that relations of every sort, of time, space, difference, likeness, change, rate, cause, or what not, are just as integral members of the sensational flux as terms are, and that conjunctive relations are just as true members of the flux as disjunctive relations are.
>
> (1909a: 279–80)

There is nothing about experience to show that it is 'made of' something other than whatever makes up the material world, yet there remains a clear distinction – revealed within experience – between the physical and the mental. What, then, is the relationship between mind and world?

> My thesis is that if we start with the supposition that there is only one primal stuff or material in the world, a stuff of which everything is composed, and if we call that stuff 'pure experience,' then knowing can easily be explained as a particular sort of relation towards one another into which portions of pure experience may enter. The relation itself is a part of pure experience; one of its 'terms' becomes the subject or bearer of the knowledge, the knower, the other becomes the object known.
>
> (1904a: 478)

Thus James introduces his notion of 'radical empiricism' – that the most fundamental stuff is not matter, nor mind, but pure experience. In a sense, *both* consciousness and the material (non-experiential) world are equally unreal.

> Let the case be what it may in others, I am as confident as I am of anything that, in myself, the stream of thinking (which I recognize emphatically as a phenomenon) is only a careless name for what, when scrutinized, reveals itself to consist chiefly in the stream of my breathing.... *The entity is fictitious, while thoughts in the concrete are fully real. But thoughts in the concrete are made of the same stuff as things are.*
>
> (1904a: 491)

James explores and motivates this idea with an example. We see a room, which commonsensically is a physical object in space, and which commonsensically we have 'in our mind.' How can the room be in two places at once: the world and the mind? It might be that what is in the mind is only a *representation* of the room; but "the reader's sense of life" knows no intervening image but seems to see the room immediately (1904a: 481). James' solution to this puzzle is the following: "Reality is apperception itself.... Our sensations are not small inner duplications of things, they are the things themselves in so far as the things are presented to us.... [T]his present actuality by which [public things] confront us, from which all our theoretical constructions are derived and to which they must all return ... is homogeneous – and not only homogeneous, but numerically one with a certain part of our inner life" (1905b: 57).

The commonsensical solution to the problem, James thus urges, is to hold that the room exists in two places at once just as a single point can be on two lines at once: if it is at their intersection. (1904a: 481). The two 'lines' or processes or sets of relations are:

a. the reader's personal biography, a set of mental, 'inner,' operations.
b. the history of the house of which the room is part, a train of physical operations.

That these two groups of operations are "curiously incompatible" (as James emphasizes) is a matter of their differing contexts only, "just as the same material thing may be both low and high, or small and great, or bad and good, because of its relations to opposite parts of an environing world" (1904a: 485). The difference between things perceived and things imagined is not a difference in kind: "It is simply that a present object has a vivacity and a clearness superior to those of the representation. . . . But this present object, what is it in itself? Of what stuff is it made? Of the same stuff as the representation. It is made of *sensations*; it is a thing perceived" (1905b: 58).

So what kind of 'stuff' is pure experience? According to James, there are as many stuffs as there are 'natures' in the things experienced. If you ask what any one bit of pure experience is made of, the answer is always the same: "It is made of *that*, of just what appears, of space, of intensity, of flatness, brownness, heaviness, or what not" (1904a: 487). What then accounts for the contrast James recognizes between the mental and the physical? As we might expect given the preceding, according to James the 'mental' and 'physical' do *not* differ in their natures, but only in their *relations*. "The general group of experiences that *act* . . . comes inevitably to be contrasted with the group whose members, having *identically the same natures*, fail to manifest them in the 'energetic' way" (1904a: 489, my italics). Thus, the thought of a fire *is* hot; the mental image of a metre-stick *does* have extension; it is just that the fire fails to warm my body, and the imagined metre-stick need not be in a stable 'spatial' relationship with other mental objects. "The two worlds differ, not by the presence of absence of extension, but by the relations of the extensions which in both worlds exist" (1904a: 489).

But how can one bit of pure experience *know* another? Indeed, how can a bit of pure experience 'know' anything? James has this to say:

> That which exists and constitutes the portion of truth that the word 'Consciousness' covers over is the susceptibility that the parts of experience possess to be reported or known. . . . This susceptibility is explained by the fact that certain experiences can lead some to others by means of distinctly characterized intermediary experiences, in such a fashion that some are found to play the role of things known, the others that of knowing subjects. . . . One can perfectly define these two roles without departing from the framework of experience itself and without invoking anything transcendent. . . . The attributes subject and object, represented and representative, thing and thought mean, then, a practical distinction that is of the utmost importance, but that is of a *functional* order only, and not at all ontological as classical dualism imagines it.
>
> (1905b: 63–4)

James' point is not that only 'mental' experiences are connected together such that one experience leads to another – *every* experience, whether functionally mental or physical, whether 'knower' or 'known', blends seamlessly into a continuum. "Sensational experiences *are* their 'own others,' then, both internally and externally. Inwardly they are one with their parts, and outwardly they pass continuously into their neighbors, so that events separated by years of time in a man's life hang together unbrokenly by the intermediary events" (1909a: 285). Rather, his idea is that there is a suite of relations that characterize experiences that 'play the role' of knowing subjects and another that is individuative of experiences 'playing the role' of things known.

Finally, a point that James found rather pressing, how can my *point of view* – my self – be accounted for? If 'mind' and 'matter' are fundamentally (intrinsically) the same, and all the universe is pure experience, then what is it that traces 'my' passage through 'the external world'? What makes an experience part of *my* personal consciousness? James' response, in part, is to say that

> the world experienced (otherwise called the 'field of consciousness') comes at all times with our body as its centre, centre of vision, centre of action, centre of interest. Where the body is is 'here'; when the body acts is 'now'; what the body touches is 'this'; all other things are 'there' and 'then' and 'that.'

> (1905a: 9)

That is, there is a constant relation (or type of relation) that all my experiences have in common – they are all related on one way or another to the set of experiences (changing over time) that constitute my body.

These then, in bare outline, are some of the main points of William James' thinking about consciousness and its place in the world. How does all of this relate to panpsychism?

James himself seems to have considered his "philosophy of pure experience" to be a stepping stone in the direction of panpsychism proper, but not yet to be panpsychic. In the concluding section to "A World of Pure Experience" (1904b), James writes:

> With this we have the outlines of a philosophy of pure experience before us. At the outset of my chapter, I called it a mosaic philosophy. In actual mosaics the pieces are held together by their bedding, for which bedding the Substances, transcendental Egos, or Absolutes of other philosophies may be taken to stand. In radical empiricism there is no bedding; it is as if the pieces clung together by their edges, the transitions experienced between them forming their cement. . . . Experience itself, taken at large, can grow by its edges. That one moment of it proliferates into the next by transitions which, whether conjunctive or disjunctive, continue the experiential tissue, can not, I contend, be denied. . . . These relations of continuous transition experienced are what make our experiences cognitive. In the simplest and completest cases the experiences are cognitive of one another. When one of them terminates a previous series of them with a sense of fulfilment, it, we say, is what those other experiences 'had in view.' The knowledge, in such a case, is verified; the truth is 'salted down.' Mainly, however, we live on speculative investments, or on our prospects only. . . . In this sense we at every moment can continue to believe in an existing *beyond*. . . . The beyond must, of course, always in our philosophy be itself of an experiential nature. If not a future experience of our own or a present one of our neighbor, it must be a thing in itself in Dr. Prince's and Professor Strong's sense of the term – that is, it must be an experience *for* itself whose relation to other things we translate into the action of molecules, ether–waves, or whatever else the physical symbols may be. . . . This opens the chapter of the relations of radical empiricism to panpsychism, into which I cannot enter now.

> (1904b: 568–9)

The contrast that James envisions here seems to be between a doctrine where everything that exists is both "of an experiential nature" and part of a human personal consciousness (which is a commitment of his philosophy of pure experience), and a view which supposes that there are experiences which are *not* part of a human personal consciousness – that there are experiences 'for themselves' which are not part of a mind; or alternatively, experiences that are part of a personal consciousness but not a human consciousness – perhaps the minds of plants or animals (as Fechner supposed, for example) or of some superhuman consciousness. It is this latter collection of views that James thought of as a form of panpsychism.

Although James appears to hold open these possibilities – and we will return to his positive stance on panpsychism shortly – there are other variants on panpsychism that he is concerned to rule out, in large part because they seemed to him incompatible with some of the commitments of radical empiricism.

Perhaps most importantly, he was unwilling to adopt the view that the world is any sense fundamentally mental: that the mental has any sort of priority over the physical. James was quite clear that pure experience – even though it is, after all, experiential; indeed, whenever we encounter it (though not necessarily always), part of a personal consciousness – is not inherently mental. In fact, it is no more closely allied to the mental than it is to the physical. Experiences "having identically the same natures" might be either mental or physical depending on how they stand in relations to other experiences. Furthermore, at least in James' view, this is not merely some ersatz physical: it is the very physical world we meet with in experience, the empirical bedrock of science. Plants, animals, rocks, fire, gravity, the predictions of the laws of physics and chemistry – all are perfectly real, non-mental, correspond to our best science, and are constituted by pure experience.

Secondly, famously, James would have found unconvincing any form of panpsychism that views personal conscious states as being compounded from simpler psychic or protopsychic atoms. James argued in *Principles of Psychology* (1890) that what he called 'atomistic hylozoism' or the doctrine of 'primordial mind-dust' cannot work.

> *All the 'combinations' which we actually know are* EFFECTS, *wrought by the units said to be 'combined,'* UPON SOME ENTITY OTHER THAN THEMSELVES. Without this feature of a medium or vehicle, the notion of combination has no sense. . . . In other words, no possible number of entities (call them as you like, whether forces, material particles, or mental elements) can sum *themselves* together. Each remains, in the sum, what it always was; and the sum itself exists only *for a bystander* who happens to overlook the units and to apprehend the sum as such; or else it exists in the shape of some other *effect* on an entity external to the sum itself. Let it not be objected that H_2 and O combine of themselves into 'water,' and thenceforward exhibit new properties. They do not. The 'water' is just the old atoms in the new position, H-O-H; the 'new properties' are just their combined *effects*, when in this position, upon external media, such as our sense-organs and the various reagents on which water may exert its properties and be known. . . . Where the elemental units are supposed to be feelings, the case is in no wise altered. Take a hundred of them, shuffle them and pack them as close together as you can (whatever that may mean); still each remains the same feeling it always was, shut in its own skin, windowless, ignorant of what the other feelings are and mean. There would be a hundred-and-first feeling there, if, when a group or series of such feelings were set up, a consciousness *belonging to the group as such* should emerge. And this 101st feeling would be a totally new fact; the 100 original feelings might, by a curious physical law, be a signal for its *creation*, when they came together; but they would have no substantial identity with it, nor it with them, and one could never deduce the one from the others, or (in any intelligible sense) say that they *evolved* it. Take a sentence of a dozen words, and take twelve men and tell to each one word. Then stand the men in a row or jam them in a bunch, and let each think of his word as intently as he will; nowhere will there be a consciousness of the whole sentence.
>
> (1890: 158–60)

In *Principles of Psychology* James briefly considers the prospects for an uncompounding 'mind dust' theory, which he calls polyzoism, or multiple monadism (1890: 179–80). On this view each neuron – or even each atom – has its own consciousness, unconnected to all the others; the fact of our own individual, unitary consciousness then requires a "central cell" or "arch-cell", to which all other neurons in the brain are subservient. But James admits this is both physiologically and metaphysically implausible. In short, according to James, any sort of mind-dust theory – what Chalmers calls "constitutive panpsychism" (2016) – must be abandoned.

Other variants or components of panpsychism are also ruled out explicitly by James in his unpublished writings. In his manuscript notes for his 1906–7 course at Stanford, Philosophy D, "General Problems of Philosophy" (see James 1988), he discusses what he terms 'weak' panpsychism – which he equates with epiphenomenalism – and 'strong' panpsychism, which he calls idealistic panpsychism. He finds fault with both of them.

Thus, he was opposed to the kind of double-aspect or neutral monist theory that treats the mental as something like the 'subjective aspect' or intrinsic nature of the building blocks of reality while the physical is their 'objective aspect' or extrinsic nature. (E.g. Schopenhauer 1859: Bk II, § 17; Peirce 1892; Strawson 2006). James' objection to this was that it rendered the mental epiphenomenal: it reserves all the causal or 'active' power for the physical and renders the mental a mere subjective accompaniment. As is well known, James argued vehemently against such a position (1879, 1890) – he was opposed to any view that "banishes [consciousness] to a limbo of causal inertness" (1890: 135), where it exists more like a "melody," or a "shadow" than like a "real thing." "It is to my mind quite inconceivable that consciousness should have *nothing to do* with a business which it so faithfully attends" (1890: 136).

He also had qualms throughout his life about absolute idealism, and it was this that led him to withhold his allegiance to strong or idealistic panpsychism. Part of the problem, as we have seen, is idealism's tendency to privilege the mental over the physical, which James rejected. His robustly commonsense view was that consciousness is causal (and moreover causal in a way that the physical is not – it is a chooser of ends), but that not *only* consciousness is causal; the physical world also exerts causal powers, in the ways described by science. Furthermore, James was throughout his life a metaphysical pluralist and he found himself unable to whip up real enthusiasm in himself for absolutism or indeed any form of austere monism. (His 'pure experience,' recall, far from being monistic, has as many different and diverse concrete natures as are required to account for the "blooming, buzzing confusion" of our experienced reality: while the nature of fire as a physical phenomenon may be the same as that of fire as a conscious experience, the nature of fire – though still 'pure experience' – may be quite different from the nature of an apple or a desk.)

James' pluralism is rooted in his empiricism, and also in his commitment to leaving a space for free will – for individual choices to make a difference – in the universe. "Instead of defining the parts in light of the (unexperienced) whole, empiricism begins with the parts experienced, and proceeds towards whatever wholes seem factually indicated" (Lamberth 1999: 194). This leaves space for genuine novelty, and also, since our own actions influence the flux, it leaves room for genuine morality. What happens depends not on some universal telos or final cause but on the actual, piecemeal, contingent playing out of history.

Let us now turn away from James' negative pronouncements on panpsychism and towards the sources of its undeniable attraction for him. Put a bit crudely, these attractions were mainly religious and supernatural for James, though they do also address the rather thorny metaphysical question of how pure experience as we encounter it in our own personal consciousness is to be understood – if it can be understood – as potentially existing apart from any human personal consciousness.

On the question of God, James writes in *A Pluralistic Universe* (1909a):

> Only one thing is certain, and that is the result of our criticism of the absolute: the only way to escape from the paradoxes and perplexities that a consistently thought-out monistic universe suffers from as from a species of auto-intoxication – the mystery of the 'fall' namely,

of reality lapsing into appearance, truth into error, perfection into imperfection; of evil, in short; the mystery of universal determinism, of the block-universe eternal and without a history, *etc.*; – the only way of escape, I say, from all this is to be frankly pluralistic and assume that the superhuman consciousness, however vast it may be, has itself an external environment, and consequently is finite.

(1909a: 140)

James was interested not only in holding open a space for God (or at least something god-like) in his metaphysics, but also in the role of 'superhuman consciousness' in giving us a reason to feel at home in the universe. In the first few pages of *A Pluralistic Universe*, James distinguishes between cynical and sympathetic philosophical outlooks. On the former view (which, though dualistic, is a view James associates with 'narrow' empiricism and with a materialist approach to the universe), the human 'soul' is foreign to the universe. On the latter, there is no sharp distinction to be made between soul and matter – humanity is much more at home with, and integrated into, the non-human universe. This tends towards a 'spiritualistic' philosophy, where there is some spiritual – and hence soul-like – principle central to the universe.

> Materialistic and spiritualistic philosophies are the rival types that result: the former defining the world so as to leave man's soul upon it as a soil of outside passenger or alien, while the latter insists that the intimate and human must surround and underlie the brutal. This latter is the spiritual way of thinking.
>
> (1909a: 23)

In this context, James proposes an alliance between "the thicker and the more radical empiricism" and the religious life.

> We are indeed internal parts of God and not external creations, on any possible reading of the panpsychic system. Yet because God is not the absolute, but is himself a part when the system is conceived pluralistically, his functions can be taken as not wholly dissimilar to those of the other smaller parts, – as similar to our functions consequently. Having an environment, being in time, and working out a history just like ourselves, he escapes from the foreignness from all that is human, of the static timeless perfect absolute.
>
> (1909a: 138)

In addition, James' interest in psychical phenomena – which he had from his early years of training as an MD right until his death (for a period he was the president of the Society for Psychical Research) – led him to postulate that the most reasonable explanation for certain supernatural phenomena, such as telepathy, extrasensory perception, or communication with the dead, was the impingement of some broader cosmic consciousness upon our individual personal consciousness.

> Every bit of us at every moment is part and parcel of a wider self, it quivers along various radii like the wind-rose on a compass, and the actual in it is continuously one with possibles not yet in our present sight. And just as we are co-conscious with our own momentary margin, may not we ourselves form the margin of some more really central self in things which is co-conscious with the whole of us? May not you and I be confluent in a higher consciousness, and confluently active there, tho we now know it not?
>
> (1909a: 131)

That is, though perhaps without lending it his full-throated support, James was clearly attracted to what we might now call a form of 'cosmopsychism' (Jaskolla and Buck 2012; Shani 2015; Goff 2017).

> Out of my experience, such as it is (and it is limited enough) one fixed conclusion dog-matically emerges, and that is this, that we with our lives are like islands in the sea, or like trees in the forest. The maple and the pine may whisper to each other with their leaves, and Conanicut and Newport hear each other's fog-horns. But the trees also commingle their roots in the darkness underground, and the islands also hang together through the ocean's bottom. Just so there is a continuum of cosmic consciousness, against which our individuality builds but accidental fences, and into which our several minds plunge as into a mother-sea or reservoir. Our "normal" consciousness is circumscribed for adaptation to our external earthly environment, but the fence is weak in spots, and fitful influences from beyond leak in, showing the otherwise unverifiable common connection. Not only psychic research, but metaphysical philosophy, and speculative biology are led in their own ways to look with favor on some such "panpsychic" view of the universe as this. Assuming this common reservoir of consciousness to exist, this bank upon which we all draw, and in which so many of earth's memories must in some way be stored, or mediums would not get at them as they do, the question is, What is its own structure? What is its inner topog-raphy? . . . What are the conditions of individuation or insulation in this mother-sea? To what tracts, to what active systems functioning separately in it, do personalities correspond? Are individual "spirits" constituted there? How numerous, and of how many hierarchic orders may these then be? How permanent? How transient? And how confluent with one another may they become?
>
> (1909b: 589)

Where does all this leave us? I shall conclude by trying to summarize a sort of Jamesian panpsy-chism (or, since he insists that it is not the mental that is fundamental, but 'pure experience' which is neither yet potentially both mental and physical) panprotopsychism. It is, at least, a position quite distinct from most of those that ply the main currents of the contemporary panpsychist debate. I leave it to the reader to judge how attractive or plausible the position it is.

For James, it is not true that the fundamental building blocks of the universe are conscious. Those building blocks – or, in Jamesian terms, substantive parts of the flux, which is itself smoothly and endlessly continuous – are pure experiences. But to be a pure experience, for James, is not thereby to be conscious or in any sense self-aware or a knower. A pure experience has, intrinsically, a robust and distinct nature – and the diversity of natures is at least as great as the diversity of our experience – but it is in itself neither physical nor mental. It 'becomes' physical or mental only in virtue of being embedded in a set of *relations* with other pure experiences . . . and (I take it) every pure experience is so embedded, such that all pure experiences are either mental or physical.

James notes that

> [C]onsciousness, however small, is an illegitimate birth in any philosophy that starts with-out it, and yet professes to explain all facts by continuous evolution. If evolution is to work smoothly, consciousness in some shape must have been present at the very origins of things.
>
> (1890: 149)

And James' ultimate philosophy satisfies this condition, not by making consciousness a sort of 'mind-dust' that is sprinkled on the original components of the universe, but by marking the differ-ence between the conscious and the non-conscious by a set of relations that can be participated in naturalistically by original, non-conscious elements. No additional magic 'glow' is needed. Similarly, the emergence of a personal consciousness, a self, is to be explained wholly in terms of relations (primarily, relations between experiences and another set of privileged experiences that characterise a body). This is not, though, functionalism (or at least it doesn't seem so to me) because the what-it-is-likeness of consciousness – the heat of fire or the taste of blackberries – is contributed by the intrinsic nature of the pure experience. Finally, significantly, this intrinsic nature is the *same* as the intrinsic nature of (objective) fire and blackberries – this is why our being related in certain ways to these pure experiences counts as knowing, not just about how blackberries seem to us, but how they *are*.

Finally, although each pure experience we encounter is, perforce, part of our personal consciousness (otherwise we would not be encountering it) – even if a physical thing, it is on a trajectory that crosses the trajectory of our conscious point-of-view – there is (for James) something attractive about a view that answers the question: what is a pure experience when we do not encounter it? with the suggestion: it is a part of a (pluralistic, non-absolute) cosmic consciousness. On this basis, the universe is made a friendly, familiar place rather than an impersonal one. Is there evidence for its truth? James hoped there was, through religious experience and through otherwise unexplained psychic phenomena. Perhaps in this sense everything is, after all, part of a mind.

Notes

1. The key passages are as follows. Panpsychism is mentioned for the first time by James, offhand but apparently approvingly though in the same breath as idealism, in 1881's "Reflex Action and Theism". Chapter 6, "The Mind-Stuff Theory," in Principles of Psychology (1890), although not directed at panpsychism per se – but rather at an atomistic, compositional theory of mind – is often taken to be a classic early expression of the combination problem for panpsychism. In *Varieties of Religious Experience* (1902) James expresses his own sympathy for panpsychism, and in the lecture notes for his course on philosophy at Harvard (1902–03) he expresses his allegiance for the first time to "pluralistic panpsychism." The 1904–5 lectures that became his Essays in Radical Empiricism (1912) reconfirm this panpsychist commitment, as did his 1907–8 Hibbert Lectures, published as A Pluralistic Universe (1909a). In both 1904's "A World of Pure Experience" and 1905's "The Experience of Activity" James notes that radical empiricism is related to panpsychism, but declines to enlarge on those connections. In "The Confidences of a 'Psychical Researcher'" (1909b) he postulates a 'cosmic consciousness' – a possibility he also mentions in Varieties of Religious Experience – as a way of explaining certain parapsychological phenomena.
2. Italicized phrases in this and all the following quotations are in the original, unless otherwise noted.
3. See also James (1884) and (1892: Chap. XI).

References

Bailey, Andrew (1998). 'The Strange Attraction of Sciousness: William James on Consciousness'. *Transactions of the C. S. Peirce Society*, 34 (2): 414–34.

Bergson, Henri (1907). *L'Évolution créatrice*. Paris: Félix Alcan. (*Creative Evolution*, trans. Arthur Mitchell. New York: Henry Holt, 1911.).

Chalmers, David (2016). 'Panpsychism and Panprotopsychism'. In Godehard Brüntrup and Ludwig Jaskolla (eds.), *Panpsychism*. Oxford: Oxford University Press, pp. 19–47.

Clifford, W. K. (1874). 'Body and Mind'. *Fortnightly Review*, December. (Reprinted in *Lectures and Essays*, vol. II. London: Macmillan, 1879.).

Clifford, W. K. (1878). 'On the Nature of Things in Themselves'. *Mind*, January. (Reprinted in *Lectures and Essays*, vol. II. London: Macmillan, 1879.).

Fechner, Gustav (1861). *Ueber die Seelenfrage*. Leipzig: C.F. Amelang. (*On the Soul-Question*, trans. W. Lowrie, in *Religion of a Scientist: Selections from Gustav Th. Fechner*. New York: Pantheon, 1946.).

Goff, Philip (2017). *Consciousness and Fundamental Reality*. Oxford: Oxford University Press.

Haeckel, Ernst (1893). *Der Monismus als Band zwischen Religion und Wissenschaft*. Bonn: Emil Strauss. (*Monism as Connecting Religion and Science*, trans. J. Gilchrist, London: A. & C. Black, 1895.).

Heymans, Gerardus (1905). *Einführung in die Metaphysik, auf Grundlage der Erfahrung*. Leipzig: Barth.

James, William (1878/1978). 'Remarks on Spencer's Definition of Mind as Correspondence'. In *Essays in Philosophy*. Cambridge, MA: Harvard University Press, pp. 27–8.

James, William (1879). 'Are We Automata?' *Mind*, 4 (13): 1–22.

James, William (1881/1897). 'Reflex Action and Theism'. In *The Will to Believe: And Other Essays in Popular Philosophy*. New York: Longmans, Green & Co., pp. 111–44.

James, William (1884). 'On Some Omissions of Introspective Psychology'. *Mind*, 9 (33): 1–26.

James, William (1890/1950). *The Principles of Psychology*, vol. I. New York: Henry Holt. (References are to the Dover edition).

James, William (1892/1984). *Psychology: Briefer Course*. New York: Henry Holt. (References are to the Harvard University Press edition).

James, William (1902). *Varieties of Religious Experience*. New York: Longmans, Green & Co.

James, William (1904a). 'Does "Consciousness" Exist?' *Journal of Philosophy, Psychology and Scientific Methods*, 1 (18): 477–91.

James, William (1904b). 'A World of Pure Experience'. *The Journal of Philosophy, Psychology and Scientific Methods*, 1 (20): 533–43; 1 (21): 561–70.

James, William (1905a). 'The Experience of Activity'. *The Psychological Review*, 12 (1): 1–17.

James, William (1905b). 'La Notion de Conscience'. *Archives de Psychologie*, 5: 17. (References are to the translation by Jonathan Bricklin, *Journal of Consciousness Studies*, 12 (7): 55–64, 2005.)

James, William (1909a). *A Pluralistic Universe*. New York: Longmans, Green & Co.

James, William (1909b). 'The Confidences of a "Psychical Researcher"'. *The American Magazine*, 68: 580–9.

James, William (1912). *Essays in Radical Empiricism*. New York: Longmans, Green & Co.

James, William (1988). *Manuscript Lectures*. Ed. I. K. Skrupskelis. Cambridge, MA: Harvard University Press.

Jaskolla, L., and Buck, A. J. (2012). 'Does Panexperiential Holism Solve the Combination Problem?' *Journal of Consciousness Studies*, 19 (9–10): 190–9.

Lamberth, David C. (1999). *William James and the Metaphysics of Experience*. Cambridge: Cambridge University Press.

Peirce, C. S. (1892). 'Man's Glassy Essence'. *The Monist*, 3 (1): 1–22.

Prince, Morton (1904). 'The Identification of Mind and Matter'. *Philosophical Review*, 13 (4): 444–51.

Royce, Josiah (1892). *The Spirit of Modern Philosophy*. Boston: Houghton Mifflin.

Schopenhauer, Arthur (1859). *Der Welt als Wille und Vorstellung*, 3rd edition. Leipzig.

Shani, Itay (2015). 'Cosmopsychism: A Holistic Approach to the Metaphysics of Experience'. *Philosophical Papers*, 44 (3): 389–437.

Strawson, Galen (2006). *Consciousness and Its Place in Nature: Does Physicalism Entail Panpsychism?* Ed. A. Freeman. Exeter: Imprint Academic.

Strong, C. A. (1903). *Why the Mind Has a Body*. New York: Macmillan.

8

OVERCOMING THE CARTESIAN LEGACY

Whitehead's Revisionary Metaphysics

Pierfrancesco Basile

We are now so used to the materialistic way of looking at things, which has been rooted
in our literature by the genius of the 17th century, that it is with some difficulty that we
understand the possibility of another mode of approach to the problems of nature.
—*Alfred North Whitehead (SMW: 42[1])*

1. Introduction: The Language Problem

In terms of current philosophical classifications, Whitehead is an exponent of "process philosophy."[2]
Philosophical denominations are difficult to pin down to a precise definition. But in this case there
is a clear-cut criterion for distinguishing between process and non-process thinkers. Common sense
takes it for granted that all activities and happenings are to be traced back to some preexisting entity.
It is Anne, we say, who let our aunt's precious cup fall on the ground; and the falling is not a ghostly
floating occurrence: it is the falling *of* the aunt's cup. In our ordinary conceptual scheme, permanent
things have priority over events. They are, to use Peter Strawson's apt terminology, the "basic particulars" (see Strawson 1959: 38–58).

Whitehead does not question that the commonsense view is pragmatically useful. But he takes a
revisionary approach when questions of basic ontology are at stake. At a metaphysically fundamental
level, he posits *processes* rather than *things* as the building blocks of reality. The idea that the category
of process is ontologically fundamental is not easy to understand. What kinds of processes are basic?
How is their nature to be discovered? How are permanence and stability to be accounted for in a
world whose basic elements are in constant flux? Before considering Whitehead's answers to these
questions a word is in order concerning one major difficulty that any process philosophy has to
face. Process metaphysics effects a radical alteration of our ordinary conceptions. Such modes of
thought are very old, however, and have impressed themselves upon our language. A truly revisionary metaphysics must therefore not solely provide a new conceptual scheme, but also a new language
in which to articulate it (PR: 11). As Whitehead rightly notices, the ontology of enduring things is
mirrored in the subject-predicate structure of our ordinary sentences. In order to correctly express a
radically different conceptual scheme one would thus have to revise not solely the available vocabulary, but grammar as well (AI: 228). This sounds like an impossible task. It is as if the revisionary
metaphysician had to attempt either an extraordinary transmutation of ordinary language or to communicate his worldview from within a medium that incorporates opposite theoretical commitments.

How is one to deal with this difficulty? Whitehead takes the only course open to him and tries to steer a middle path, *twisting* ordinary language in the hope to elicit new meanings. The (almost legendary) obscurity of his books and the queerness of his terminology are not a result of incapacity, but the proper response to a real problem. To appeal to this feature of his writings as an argument against his philosophy would demonstrate failure in understanding the enterprise he is engaged in, not superior philosophical *acumen*.

2. The Inner Nature of Being: The Phenomenological Perspective

The other fundamental doctrine in Whitehead's metaphysics is his panpsychism or, as it is also sometimes called, his panexperientialism.[3] Whitehead's new metaphysics is offered as an alternative to

> the fixed scientific cosmology which presupposes the ultimate fact of an irreducible brute matter, or material, spread throughout space in a flux of configurations. In itself such material is senseless, valueless, purposeless. It just does what it does, following a fixed routine imposed by external relations which do not spring from the nature of its being.
>
> (SMW: 17)

As against this view, Whitehead raises what is nowadays called the hard problem of consciousness. The absolute *heterogeneity* of mind and matter prevents us from understanding how the former could be derived from the latter. Since human minds undoubtedly exist and have originated in the course of evolution, he argues, they must be derived from constituents that are (at least in part) themselves mental. This is a brief yet very powerful argument, provided that one admits that philosophy cannot rest satisfied with a mere recording of facts, but must aim at an intellectual grasp of the nature of things. For surely, there is nothing in the concept of a purely extended bit of matter that explains why that bit must also be endowed with *experiences*.[4]

What does this argument tell us about the intrinsic nature of reality? The rejection of materialism is consistent with two different views of its basic principles: (1) on one conception, such principles are psycho-physical units, that is, they possess a mental as well as a physical side; (2) on another (idealistic, or as it should perhaps better be called, mentalistic) conception, such units are purely mental, fully resolved in their experiential doings. Whitehead explicitly favors the psycho-physical conception. Nowhere does he attempt to reduce the physical world to a phenomenal appearance in the way sometimes suggested by Leibniz, a philosopher Whitehead greatly admired. The best way to overcome the mind/matter dualism (the "bifurcation of nature") that has plagued modern thought since Descartes is not by privileging mind over matter as the idealists do, but to elaborate a novel conception in which matter and mind are viewed as different yet mutually correlated sides of a single event. As he puts it, the world "is not merely physical, nor is it merely mental" (AI: 190).

Isn't panpsychism a ludicrous view, one that should be rejected without further ado by any thinking person?[5] Charges of intrinsic implausibility are always difficult to adjudicate. The danger is that we condemn as absurd all views inconsistent with our longstanding prejudices. Whitehead tries to mitigate any initial resistance we may have by reminding us that the notion of senseless matter is a conceptual construction, a *cultural product* that, as such, can be subjected to criticism, revised or even totally abandoned. Shortly before the rise of Cartesianism, he observes, even a methodologically cautious author like Francis Bacon found it appropriate to write in his *Natural History* a sentence such as the following: "It is certain that all bodies whatsoever, though they have no sense, yet they have perception" (SMW: 41). A panpsychist view of nature, Whitehead also explains, would not be unscientific. Appealing to a condensed version of what is nowadays called "the intrinsic nature argument,"[6] he contends that there is a division of labour between physical science and metaphysics: "Science ignores what anything is in itself. Its entities are merely considered in respect to their extrinsic reality, that is to say, in respect to their aspects to other things" (SMW: 153). Since science and philosophy ask different questions, there can be no incompatibility between them. A panpsychist view of the ultimate constituents of reality is not solely coherent with science; it may even be what is needed in order to give some content to its rather empty abstractions. The happenings in nature, Whitehead reminds us, are always more than the theories we have ingeniously devised to handle them: "a complete existence is not a composition of mathematical formulae, mere formulae. It is a concrete composition of things illustrating formulae" (AI: 158).

In spite of his explicit rejection of metaphysical idealism, Whitehead does not hesitate to draw his metaphysical categories from an examination of his own subjectivity. Imagine you are reading a book in your chamber when you hear someone walking along the street. The steps suddenly enter your conscious awareness, while many of the pleasant phantasies and sensations associated with the reading vanish. Some contents have been retained, others have been excluded. At the same time, you experience the steps as an evolving series. They seem to be arising from the past, but there is also a suggestion in your present consciousness that they will continue in the immediate future. Each moment of experience is a Janus-faced entity. It has a selective relationship with the past, while also foreshadowing events to come. In Whitehead's hands, this phenomenological analysis develops into the metaphysical hypothesis that reality is made up of temporally extended quanta of feeling (*actual occasions*), each of which absorbs (*prehends*) aspects of previous ones. Furthermore, each such occasion is conceived as a subject that begins its life by incorporating aspects of its precursor occasion, before suffering deposition by becoming itself a datum for a new occasion. In retrospect, an individual's psychical life is a "chain" of moments of experience that have become publicly available – it is a series of *subjects-becoming-objects*.

The new ontology Whitehead settles for is one of serially interconnected experiential events: "The soul is nothing else than the succession of my occasions of experience, extending from birth to the present moment" (MT: 163). As experiences such as the hearing of sounds or our understanding of a sentence wonderfully illustrate, an experience requires a timespan in which to unfold. Thus, Whitehead concludes, each occasion must be conceived as possessing *duration*. Whitehead appeals to James's analyses in *Some Problems of Philosophy* to substantiate this claim:

> Either your experience is of no content, of no change, or it is of a perceptible amount of content or change. Your acquaintance with reality grows literally by buds or drops of perception. Intellectually and on reflection you can divide these into components, but as immediately given, they come totally or not at all.
>
> (James 1911: 155; PR: 68)

Obviously enough, not all aspects of our past are incorporated within a novel moment of experience. This leads Whitehead to conceive of a mental occasion – "a drop of experience" – as the outcome of a genetic process that involves selection as well as integration into a novel experiential whole. Since the occasion of mentality that constitutes a person's mind at any one moment is the outcome of a synthetic process, however, the question immediately arises as to the nature of the unifying agent. *Who is doing the synthesis?* Surprisingly enough, Whitehead argues that there is literally nothing to the genetic process than the process itself – the process already *is* the self. As he puts it in a truly remarkable passage:

> the philosophies of substance presuppose a subject which then encounters a datum, and then reacts to the datum. The philosophy of organism [Whitehead's own philosophy] presupposes a datum which is met with feelings, and progressively attains the unity of a subject.
>
> (PR: 155)

Whitehead uses the term "concrescence" (literally meaning *growing together*) to designate the process in the course of which many feelings acquire the unity of a moment of experience. Insofar as it is considered as the outcome of the concrescing process, he furthermore explains, what is usually termed "subject" should be called "superject." The actual occasion – whose full nature consists of both process and outcome – is therefore best characterized as *subject-superject*. The view is stated thus:

> It is fundamental to the metaphysical doctrine of the philosophy of organism, that the notion of an actual entity as the unchanging subject of change is completely abandoned. An actual entity is at once the subject experiencing and the superject of its experiences. It is subject-superject, and neither half of the description can for a moment be lost sight of.
>
> (PR: 29)

This is a perplexing doctrine. But if Whitehead is right in claiming that Aristotelian ontology shapes our thoughts as well as our modes of expression, this is precisely the sort of notion that – at the present stage of metaphysical inquiry – we should find it difficult to grasp as well as to articulate clearly.

3. Towards a Process Philosophy of Nature: Basic Principles

What about the relation between the fleeting occasions and the more "robust" objects of everyday life? Even a mountain can be conceptualized as an event if one considers its existence within the horizon of millennia instead of years. But surely the mountain does not exist in a flash in the way the momentary actual occasions do. In order to account for permanence, Whitehead introduces into his philosophy the concept of *eternal object*. Among the basic categories of his system, he explains, "actual entities and eternal objects stand out with a certain extreme finality" (PR: 22). "Eternal objects" is, roughly, Whitehead's designation for what are traditionally called Universals which he conceives after the guise of Aristotle as the forms of things, as existing only *in rebus* rather than as independent entities. Another crucial category introduced by Whitehead to ground the possibility of permanence in a world of flux is that of *nexus*, by which Whitehead means "any particular fact of togetherness" (PR: 20) between actual occasions. The togetherness in question is "the fact of relatedness" that is realized when an actual occasion "prehends" another one.

A special class of nexuses is constituted when the actual occasions form a particularly cohesive group in virtue not merely of their prehensive relationships, but because they are able to sustain and to transmit to their successor occasions a common form (eternal object). Such nexuses are termed "societies" and can be of two types, according as to whether they are composed by a single historic route of actual occasions or by many such routes. The former type is called a *temporal society*, the latter *spatiotemporal*. What we are used to regarding as enduring things are really societies of occasions of one of these two types. A fundamental physical entity like an electron or a proton, Whitehead speculates, is a temporal society: it can be conceived as a "worm" of experiential occurrences, each of which inherits from its predecessor a common form (PR: 91). Another example of such a society is the human soul, which consists of a single line of inheritance. Such societies are termed "personal" not because they have conscious mentality, but in the sense expressed by the Latin *persona*: each such nexus "sustains a character" (PR: 35). Macroscopic objects such as chairs and tables are on the contrary spatiotemporal societies. They are composed of many interacting streams that collectively sustain a given structure over a longer period of time.

Nature also includes living organisms – plants, the so-called "lower" and "higher" animals, and human beings. How are we to explain the differences between them? The metaphysical moral involved in the social analogy is simple enough: different types of enduring objects must be differently structured. On this account, what distinguishes an inert enduring object such as a rock from a living organism such as a dog is that the latter possesses a hegemonic centre. A temporal society with personal order (what we would familiarly term the dog's "soul" or "mind") exerts control over the other parts of the larger spatiotemporal society within which it exists (the dog conceived as the union of his mind and the whole body). In the case of an inanimate object such as a rock, no such dominant unit has emerged. Lower animals and plants present still a different structure; in this case, no single dominant centre exists: many centres exert control over the organism within which they are embedded; such organisms resemble "democracies" rather than "monarchies."

The division of societies into three classes – those with one dominant centre (a dog), those with more than one (a tree), and those with none (a rock) – provides the framework within which Whitehead addresses the mind-body problem. Within this spectrum, a human being can be viewed as a society in which the stream of experiences that constitute the enduring self has taken some significant amount of control over the remaining parts of the organism, especially of the brain. This theory is basically a version of Leibniz's theory of the mind as the body's "dominant" or "hegemonic" monad. It entails a non-Cartesian form of dualism in which the mind is *numerically* yet not *qualitatively* different from the brain. Mind and body are both societies of actual occasions – the former being a temporal society, the latter a spatiotemporal one.

Whitehead explains his view as follows:

> in an animal body the presiding occasion . . . is the final node, or intersection, of a complex structure of many enduring objects. . . . The human mind is thus conscious of its bodily inheritance. . . . This route of presiding occasions probably wanders from part to part of the brain, dissociated from the physical material atoms.
>
> (PR: 109)

One may wonder why Whitehead does not identify the mind with the brain instead of representing it, picturesquely, as "wandering" within our heads. But consider what the suggested alternative would amount to. Whitehead conceives of each of the ultimate physical particles constituting the body as a personal society, hence *de facto* as a kind of low-level mind. If the human mind were identical with the brain, then he would have to explain how myriad lower minds could fuse into the higher mind of a human being. He would then have to solve what in the recent literature about panpsychism has been called the combination problem. By drawing a numerical distinction between the mind and the brain, he is now able to sidestep this momentous difficulty.

But there is a loose end to this solution. The view that the mind is numerically distinct from the brain but "interacts" with its several constituents needs to be supplemented by a detailed explanation of such an intercourse. What is needed is precisely what Leibniz declared to be impossible when he called his monads "windowless": to provide a theory of monadic causation, however, may turn out to be as difficult as solving the combination problem.[7]

Furthermore, Whitehead's account remains problematic in another fundamental respect. At one point, he provides the following description of the thinking subject:

> The simplest example of a society in which the successive nexus of its progressive realization have a common extensive pattern is when each such nexus is purely temporal and continuous. The society, in each stage of realization, then consists of a set of contiguous occasions in serial order. A man, defined as an enduring percipient, is such a society.
>
> (AI: 205)

How adequate is Whitehead's explanation of the nature of the self as a single line of successive occasions? Since each occasion is a novel creation, what grounds our identity over time? The riddle of personal identity is too complex to be discussed here at any reasonable length. Nevertheless, it is unclear whether Whitehead's process ontology provides sufficient resources for dealing with it appropriately. According to him, "the only strictly personal society of which we have direct discriminative intuition is the society of our own personal experience" (AI: 206). But I am hardly aware of there being a common pattern or form that remains identical throughout all – or even only a signifi-cant portion of – my experiential occasions. An explanation of endurance in terms of momentary events and a recurring pattern sounds plausible with respect to objects such as electrons and protons, but it lacks all evidence when the nature of the self is at stake.

4. Experience as a Physical Phenomenon: The Naturalist Perspective

As we have seen, Whitehead's account of the actual occasion as an emergent moment of human mentality is puzzling enough. Can it be reconciled with his further claim that actual occasions are genuine constituents of the physical world? Whitehead forcefully argues that the Newtonian view of time and space as great "containers" of all things has been made obsolete by both relativ-ity theory and quantum theory (SMW: 118). Specifically, quantum theory forces us to renounce the notion of atoms moving continuously along linear trajectories; the basic constituents of reality make "jumps" (SMW: 129) from one spatiotemporal location to another. This suggests that the ultimate particles are to be conceived as event-like, as *occurrences* rather than as *continuants*. Further-more, the permanent features we observe do not have to be interpreted in terms of continuously existing entities, but in terms of a *reiteration* of fundamental patterns within successive, existentially *discontinuous* events:

> The discontinuities introduced by the quantum theory require revision of physical con-cepts in order to meet them. In particular . . . some theory of discontinuous existence is required. What is asked from such a theory, is that an orbit of an electron can be regarded as a series of detached positions, and not as a continuous line.
>
> (SMW: 135)

Relativity theory compels us to rethink another main feature of the worldview of scientific materialism. Space and time are more closely tied than previously thought, eventually collapsing into a unified concept, *space-time*. Moreover, Whitehead goes on to argue, the theory of relativity points to an essential connection between space and time on the one hand, and the particular occurrences of nature on the other. Although this involves a significant – and therefore very difficult – departure from ordinary modes of thought, we must conceive space and time as *abstractions* from the intricate texture of concrete natural events.

> The new relativity associates space and time with an intimacy not hitherto contemplated; and presupposes that their separation in concrete fact can be achieved by alternative modes of abstraction . . . But each mode of abstraction is yielding attention to something which is in nature; and thereby is isolating it for the purpose of contemplation.
>
> (SMW: 118)

As an alternative to the Newtonian view, Whitehead introduces the notion that actual occasions are inherently spatiotemporal. While coming into being, they cumulate to form an intricate spati-otemporal block, an ever-growing manifold of interrelated occasions. Actual occasions are not *in* time or *in* space; rather, they *constitute* space-time. Whitehead means it literally when he says: "The actualities of the Universe are processes of experience, each process an individual fact. The whole Universe is the advancing assemblage of these processes" (AI: 197).

This is not the place to enter further into a discussion of Whitehead's philosophy of space and time.[8] For the purposes of the present chapter, the question to be raised is this: how can actual occa-sions have spatio-temporal properties, if they are subjects of experience? Apparently, we are left with two incompatible characterizations of the actual occasion. On the one hand, (1) the actual occasion is said to be a quantum of experience: "each actual occasion is a throb of experience including the actual world within its scope" (PR: 190). On the other hand, (2) it is described as a spatio-temporal quantum: "There is a spatial element in the quantum as well as a temporal element" (PR: 283).

Can the appearance of inconsistency be dispelled? For the sake of expository simplicity, the temporal and the spatial aspects of the actual occasion may be considered separately. It could be thought that there is no special problem in conceiving of an actual occasion as temporal, since each possesses internal duration. But Whitehead also identifies "physical time" with the successive series of durational wholes. This relegates the process of concrescence, quite mysteriously, to a pre-temporal or non-temporal realm of existence. "The actual entity," Whitehead says, "is the enjoyment of a certain quantum of physical time. But the genetic process [the concrescence] is not the temporal succession" (PR: 283). Several problems arise at once. How can a process, such as the concrescence is said to be, fail to have a temporal dimension? How can what is not temporal, the concrescence, bring about a temporal product, the subjectively enjoyed duration? Or is Whitehead only talking metaphorically when he describes the concrescence as a process that issues in a definite result? These questions find no easy answer in Whitehead's metaphysics.[9]

Analogously, it could be argued that there is an obvious sense in which our mind can be said to be "spatial," since we do have perceptions of voluminous things located in space. In describing actual occasions as spatial quanta, however, Whitehead is conceiving of them as constituents of real space, *not simply as having internal spatial representations*. This means that actual occasions have to be thought of as being themselves voluminous. This must be so, it should be noted, if the natural world, of which the actual occasions are the basic building blocks, has to be more than a phenomenal appearance. But conceived as a quantum of experience (that is, as a subject-superject), it is truly difficult to see how an actual occasion could be subsumed under spatial categories.

Alternatively, one may try to make the two descriptions (1) and (2) consistent by taking them to refer to successive phases of an actual occasion's career. The occasion would then begin its life as a causally open process (the concrescence); evolve creatively into a unified moment of experience (the superject); and eventually become an object in the double sense that (a) it is "objectifed" (prehended) by other actualities and (b) turns into a constituent of the physical world. Such a suggestion makes the contrast between (1) and (2) less strident, but it fails as a philosophical theory. Unless our ordinary understanding of space and experience are flawed in some fundamental way, that an *experiential* process should issue in a *spatial* quantum appears to be as magical a leap as the alleged origination of mind from merely extended matter. The heterogeneity problem arises again, only in a reversed order.

5. Conclusion: Insight or Delusion?

What are we to make of all this? The metaphysician who aims at overcoming Cartesian dualism must necessarily carve his ultimate notions from different starting points. Conceptions derived from physical science and from one's own experience will have to be carefully balanced against one another, changed so as to be made mutually consistent, till they will eventually converge into a few basic notions of the highest generality. As Whitehead puts it,

> any doctrine which refuses to place human experience outside nature, must find in descriptions of human experience factors which also enter into the description of less specialized natural occurrences. . . . We should either admit dualism, at least as a provisional doctrine, or we should point out the identical elements connecting human experience with physical science.
>
> (AI: 185)

Given the complexity of the enterprise Whitehead is engaged in, we cannot hope for his notion of an actual occasion to be an easy one to grasp. This concept is one of those ultimate metaphysical generalities that can be fully articulated only when metaphysical knowledge has achieved full completion. To the best of my knowledge, nowhere does Whitehead suggest that he has taken anything more than a first step in this direction.

Still, a doubt remains: If Whitehead really wanted to overcome the Cartesian legacy, why did he retain such terms as "experience," "mind," "subject," and the like? Aren't the objections that have just been raised against the notion of the occasion as an experiential/physical unit simply due to the fact that we are still thinking within the inhibiting framework set by Cartesian metaphysics and forms of expressions? Why, then, not cut the Gordian knot and abandon all this philosophically loaded language? In the end, Whitehead suggests, this is what we should have to do. Consider what he says about his use of the word "feeling":

> This word 'feeling' is a mere technical term; but it has been chosen to suggest that functioning through which the concrescent actuality appropriates its datum so as to make it its own.

(PR: 164)

This is a striking passage. To say that a word has a technical sense is to say that it diverges in some important respect from its ordinary usage. But how significant is this divergence? What we face here is a particularly important instance of the general problem that language poses to the revisionary metaphysician that has been discussed at the very beginning of this chapter. We sense that language is stretched up to its breaking point when encountering a passage such as the following: "The final facts are, all alike, actual entities; and these actual entities are drops of experience, complex and interdependent" (PR: 18).

Eventually, each reader is called upon to decide whether she or he understands what Whitehead, here and in many other analogous places, means to convey. Does he disclose a radically new conceptual horizon, or is he simply talking nonsense? It lies in the nature of the case that there will be no noncontroversial answer to this, all decisive, question.

Notes

1. See References for a guide to the abbreviations used for Whitehead's works.
2. A brief yet comprehensive survey of this philosophical orientation is provided in Rescher (1996).
3. Whitehead did not refer to his philosophy as a form of "panpsychism;" his own preferred denomination was the more general "philosophy of organism." Whiteheadians like David Ray Griffin prefer the term "panexperientialism" (see Griffin 1998: 78).
4. A particularly strong version of the argument for panpsychism based upon the heterogeneity problem has been provided in Strawson (2006).
5. As John Searle contends in his (2004: 149–50). Even authors otherwise very appreciative of Whitehead's philosophy reject this aspect of his thought. A notable example is Simons (2006).
6. This argument is discussed at some length in Seager (2006).
7. For a more elaborate discussion of this point see Basile (2010).
8. For a recent analysis see McHenry (2015).
9. These difficult issues are ably discussed in Lango (2001).

References and Suggested Readings

Primary Sources

Whitehead, A. N. (1920/2000). *Concept of Nature*. Cambridge: Cambridge University Press.
Whitehead, A. N. (1925/1967). *Science and the Modern World*. New York: Free Press. **[SMW]**
Whitehead, A. N. (1927). *Symbolism: Its Meaning and Effect*. New York: Macmillan.
Whitehead, A. N. (1929/1958). *The Function of Reason*. Boston: Beacon.

Whitehead, A. N. (1929/1978). *Process and Reality: An Essay in Cosmology*. Ed. D. R. Griffin and D. W. Sherburne, corrected edition. New York: Free Press. **[PR]**

Whitehead, A. N. (1933/1967). *Adventures of Ideas*. New York: Free Press. **[AI]**

Whitehead, A. N. (1938/1969). *Modes of Thought*. New York: Free Press.

Secondary Sources

Basile, P. (2009). *Leibniz, Whitehead and the Metaphysics of Causation*. Basingstoke and New York: Macmillan.

Basile, P. (2010). 'Materialist vs. Panexperientialist Physicalism: Where Do We Stand?' *Process Studies*, 39 (2): 264–84.

Cobb, J. and Griffin, D. R. (eds.) (1977). *Mind and Nature: Essays on the Interface of Science and Philosophy*. Washington, DC: University Press of America.

Christian, W. (1959). *An Interpretation of Whitehead's Metaphysics*. New Haven: Yale University Press.

Emmett, D. (1966). *Whitehead's Philosophy of Organism*. Westport: Greenwood Press.

Ford, L. (1984). *The Emergence of Whitehead's Metaphysics: 1925–1929*. Albany: State University of New York Press.

Griffin, D. R. (1998). *Unsnarling the World-Knot: Consciousness, Freedom and the Mind-Body Problem*. Berkeley, Los Angeles and London: University of California Press.

Haack, S. (1979). 'Descriptive and Revisionary Metaphysics'. *Philosophical Studies*, XXXV: 361–71.

Hartshorne, C. (1970). *Creative Synthesis and Philosophic Method*. London: SCM Press.

Hartshorne, C. (1977). 'Physics and Psychics: The Place of Mind in Nature'. In J. Cobb and D. Griffin (eds.), *Mind and Nature*. Washington, DC: University Press of America, pp. 89–96.

Hosinsky, T. E. (1993). *Stubborn Fact and Creative Advance: An Introduction to the Metaphysics of Alfred North Whitehead*. New York: Rowman & Littlefield.

James, W. (1911). *Some Problems of Philosophy: A Beginning of an Introduction to Philosophy*. New York: Longmans, Green.

Kraus, E. M. (1988). *The Metaphysics of Experience: A Companion to Whitehead's "Process and Reality"*. New York: Fordham University Press.

Lango, J. (1972). *Whitehead's Ontology*. Albany: State University of New York Press.

Lango, J. (2001). 'The Time of Whitehead's Concrescence'. *Process Studies*, 30 (1): 3–21.

Leclerc, I. (1958). *Whitehead's Metaphysics*. London: George Allen & Unwin.

Lowe, V. (1985/1990). *Alfred North Whitehead: The Man and His Work*, 2 vols. Baltimore and London: Johns Hopkins University Press.

McHenry, L. (2015). *The Event Universe: The Revisionary Metaphysics of Alfred North Whitehead*. Edinburgh: Edinburgh University Press.

Nobo, J. L. (1986). *Whitehead's Metaphysics of Extension and Solidarity*. Albany: State University of New York Press.

Rescher, N. (1996). *Process Metaphysics*. Albany: State University of New York Press.

Seager, W. (2006). 'The Intrinsic Nature Argument for Panpsychism'. In A. Freeman (ed.), *Consciousness and Its Place in Nature*. Exeter: Imprint Academic, pp. 129–45.

Searle, J. (2004). *Mind: A Brief Introduction*. Oxford: Oxford University Press.

Sherburne, D. W. (1996). *A Key to Whitehead's Process and Reality*. Chicago: University of Chicago Press.

Simons, P. (1998). 'Metaphysical Systematics: A Lesson from Whitehead'. *Erkenntnis*, (XLVIII): 377–93.

Simons, P. (2006). 'The Seeds of Experience'. In A. Freeman (ed.), *Consciousness and Its Place in Nature*. Exeter: Imprint Academic, pp. 146–50.

Strawson, G. (2006). 'Realistic Monism: Why Physicalism Entails Panpsychism'. In A. Freeman (ed.), *Consciousness and Its Place in Nature*. Exeter: Imprint Academic, pp. 3–31.

Strawson, P. (1959). *Individuals: An Essay in Descriptive Metaphysics*. London and New York: Routledge.

9

RUSSELL'S NEUTRAL MONISM AND PANPSYCHISM

Donovan Wishon

The difference between physics and psychology is analogous to that between a post man's knowledge of letters and the knowledge of a recipient of letters. The post man knows the movements of many letters, the recipient knows the contents of a few.

—Bertrand Russell, An Outline of Philosophy *(1927)*

1. Introduction

Bertrand Russell's writings on neutral monism continue to exercise a profound influence on much work on panpsychism – the view that mind (*psyche*) is in some way a fundamental and pervasive (*pan*) feature of the physical universe. Neutral monism is the view that both mental and material phenomena arise from a single kind of more basic reality (*monism*) which is neither mental nor material (*neutral*).[1] On the surface, these are two radically different accounts of the place of mind and matter in reality. Yet many believe that Russell's version of neutral monism has a more intimate relation to panpsychism than its name suggests.

So what exactly is Russell's view? As a first pass, one can say that revolutionary advances in twentieth-century physics and psychology convinced him that the traditional distinction between 'mind' and 'matter' is unfounded and that the subject matter of both physics and psychology concerns collections of causally ordered space-time events. Some of them – ones occurring in the brains of humans and other biological organisms – compose mental episodes such as those we experience. At the same time, some (including those composing our minds) compose the physical systems investigated by physics, chemistry, physiology, and the rest of the natural sciences. Aside from certain of our conscious mental episodes, our knowledge of these space-time events is indirect and limited to the abstract structural descriptions provided by the physical sciences. We are otherwise left completely in the dark about their underlying qualitative natures.

Many interpret Russell's neutral monism as ultimately constituting, entailing, or strongly *suggesting* some form of panpsychism. After all, if the only occurrences we know otherwise than through the abstract spatio-temporal and causal descriptions of the sciences are mental ones, and if the basic elements[2] of concrete reality share a common nature, then it is natural to conclude that they too are mental in character. From such reasoning, Sir Arthur Eddington concludes that 'the stuff of the world is mind-stuff [that is] more general than our individual conscious minds; but we may think of its nature as not altogether foreign to the feelings in our consciousness' (1928a: 276). Yet while Russell admits that this view could be correct, he insists that there are better grounds for thinking otherwise.

2. Russell's Mind-Matter Dualism

Russell is an avowed neutral monist for roughly the last half-century of his long career (Eames 1967). However, prior to adopting the doctrine in 1918, Russell is one of its sharpest critics. In order to understand better why he comes to embrace it, as well as the particular form his version takes, it is worthwhile to trace the development of his early views on mind and matter.

Influenced by his Cambridge teachers G. F. Stout, James Ward, and especially John McTaggart, Russell is initially a devotee of absolute idealism, which had for several decades dominated the British philosophical world. Inspired by Kant, Hegel and Leibniz, absolute idealism is the view that all human knowledge is mediated through conceptual structures which modify and distort the raw materials of experience, thereby obscuring the true fundamentally mind-like nature of reality. Some versions hold that reality consists entirely of a community of immaterial conscious beings, while others hold that all of reality is ultimately a single, indivisible conscious whole.[3] In either case, absolute idealists typically hold that the universe as we ordinarily experience and conceive of it is mere appearance and that no truth about reality, as it is in itself, can be known without apprehending it as a whole.

Despite this initiation into absolute idealism, Russell (alongside Moore and others) soon launches a wide-ranging, self-proclaimed 'revolt' against it (1959: 54–64). A number of the ensuing philosophical skirmishes concern broad issues in metaphysics, epistemology, and logic beyond the scope of this chapter. But others focus specifically on the nature of the mind, its place in nature, and its role in human knowledge. Here, Russell's preliminary target is the idealist claim that all human knowledge and experience is mediated through the distorting lenses of conceptual structures (Hylton 2003).

Russell contends that our most basic form of experience is constituted by our direct, unmediated awareness of elements of reality as they are independent of human thought.[4] Following William James (1890), Russell calls such direct empirical awareness 'knowledge by acquaintance'. But unlike many contemporary philosophers, he conceives of it as a special epistemic relation holding between our minds and objects which are generally outside of our minds. Echoing Franz Brentano (1874), Russell proclaims that 'the faculty of being acquainted with things other than itself is the main characteristic of a mind . . . it is this that constitutes the mind's power of knowing things' (1912: 66–7).

Contrary to popular belief, Russell does not think acquaintance provides us with infallible, indubitable, or comprehensive knowledge about the existence, identities, features, or nature of its objects (Wishon 2017).[5] Even our most careful acquaintance-based beliefs about objects admit of the possibility of substantial error and ignorance. Indeed, he stresses on a number of occasions that 'all or any of our beliefs may be mistaken, and therefore all ought to be held with at least some degree of doubt' (1912: 39–40, 210).[6]

Russell sees acquaintance as playing several indispensable epistemic roles for our thought and talk. Acquaintance directly *presents* objects to us in experience without the need for a mediating inference or conception of them. It both supplies empirical evidence about the elements of reality we encounter and puts us in a position to attend to them, identify them, analyze them, and form some conception of their character and features. This enables us to acquire factual knowledge about the world in a piecemeal fashion, without any need for us to grasp it as a whole. We can also combine our conceptions of particular objects of our experience with our general conceptions of how the world works and thereby acquire inferential knowledge 'by description' of elements of reality beyond our experience. Acquaintance is thus the fundamental enabling condition for all of our thought and knowledge about the universe, its constituents, and its most general features.

Russell initially believes we have sensory acquaintance with the familiar objects of common sense and science. But a number of empirical considerations soon convince him that the qualities and relations we directly encounter in sensation (such as experienced color, shape, orientation, tone, texture, and so on) cannot be properties of material objects. For one thing, the sensory qualities and relations we ordinarily attribute to material objects can change based on perspective and circumstance when those objects and their relations do not (1912: 11–18). For another, we can experience these same sensory features while dreaming, hallucinating, or having our sense organs (or brains) directly stimulated when no corresponding material objects are present (34–7, 55–6).[7] In fact, given the time it takes stimuli to travel from their sources to our sense organs, ordinary sensory experiences concern physical objects and events only as they were in the past (52–3).

Russell thus concludes that the immediate objects of our sensory awareness – or 'sense-data' as he calls them – are concrete particulars that are external to the mind, causally dependent upon our physiology, but not inherent in our physical environments.[8] Rather, they are indirect 'signs' of the material objects, features, and relations around us due to the systematic physiological effects they have on us in various circumstances (1912: 16, 45).

For Russell, the indirect nature of our knowledge of material objects has profound implications. Whereas we are in a position to know without inference that objects presented in our experience exist, we must infer the existence of material objects based upon experienced patterns of sense-data (1912: 93–4, 207–9). Moreover, our lack of acquaintance with material objects, features, and relations (including causal and spatio-temporal ones) leaves us in the dark about their underlying intrinsic natures (54). In fact, he denies that we have any grounds for supposing sense-data and physical reality resemble each other intrinsically (45, 55–6).

Russell thus concludes that our conception of physical reality is entirely abstract and structural in character. From experienced patterns of sense-data in egocentric space and time, we can only legitimately infer the ordering or arrangement of physical objects in the 'public' space and time of physics but not their intrinsic natures (1912: 45–53). In fact, even our grasp of physical spatio-temporal and causal relations is abstract and logical in character. At best, we can only know of physical reality that it includes such-and-such elements (the natures of which are unknown to us) standing in such-and-such mathematically describable relations (the natures of which are unknown to us) based on their presumed correspondence with what is presented to us in sensory experience (49–50).

One consequence of the abstract character of physics, Russell notes, is that it allows idealists to claim that the underlying nature of physical reality 'must be in some sense mental' (1912: 56). Such a conclusion, he stresses, 'is not to be dismissed as obviously absurd' since both sensory experience and science leave us 'completely in the dark as to the true intrinsic nature of physical objects' (58–9). He insists 'the truth about physical objects *must* be strange' (59). Even so, Russell thinks the arguments offered in support of idealism are fallacious, and so they give us no grounds to abandon our instinctive belief that physical reality is 'something radically different from minds and the contents of minds' (1912: 57–9). What is more, he thinks idealism conflicts with our introspective evidence that our mental acts differ greatly in intrinsic character from the mind-independent objects of sensation, memory, and conception (79). Such evidence suggests that we have no reason to think matter – whatever its true nature might be – is anything but insentient and unthinking.

3. Constructing Minds and Matter

Russell soon becomes dissatisfied with this account of our physical knowledge. For one thing, the entire subject matter of physics would then consist of entities and relations that lay beyond all possible human experience and thus preclude direct empirical verification of scientific theories. For another, it holds the truth of physics hostage to kinds of entities whose existence is speculative and natures are mysterious. Lastly, it renders knowledge of physical reality dependent upon precarious inferences from sense-data using philosophically controversial principles of reasoning.

Seeking a firmer foundation, Russell sets out to 'logically construct' physics from our more secure knowledge of sense-data together with some tentative theoretical assumptions. Presuming the continuity and simplicity of nature, he proposes the possibility of constructing physics entirely from (1) the sense-data we experience firsthand, (2) those that others presumably experience, and (3) transitory sensible qualities and relations of the same nature that are posited as making up the rest of material reality despite not being sensed by anybody.[9] In other words, he offers as a theoretically fruitful possibility a roughly 'panqualityist' picture according to which physical reality is composed of the same kinds of mind-independent qualities and relations we encounter in sensory experience.[10] Though emphatically speculative, he thinks it 'has a better chance of being true than any of its present competitors' (1915: 107). It also has the merit of implying that we have sensory acquaintance with at least some of the mind-independent qualities, spatio-temporal relations, and causal relations that make up physical reality.

Soon afterwards, Russell considers the possibility of similarly constructing our self-knowledge entirely on the basis of introspected (and remembered) thoughts, experiences, and other psychological episodes (1918: 149–50). But he seemingly does not think this project can be wholly successful because such logical constructions leave unexplained our introspective evidence for the relational character of our psychological acts. Moreover, they cannot adequately account for the difference in immediacy between what is and is not experienced, the selectiveness of attention, or egocentric and demonstrative thought – all of which, Russell maintains, seem to require a subject who bears psychological relations to distinct objects. He thus concludes that we cannot fully divorce self-knowledge from a commitment to the existence of a substantial self, even if it is knowable only by inference (*Papers* 7: 15–32).[11]

4. Russell's Neutral Monism

Despite his resistance to neutral monism, Russell becomes persuaded of its truth in 1918 (Russell 1959: 134). In particular, he becomes convinced that 'William James had been right in denying the relational character of sensations' (134). He concludes that we lack introspective evidence for either the existence of a substantial self or the relational character of mental episodes (1919: 25). He also gains confidence that intrinsically relational mental acts are not required for explaining our various cognitive and conative episodes. Hence, we have neither empirical nor theoretical grounds for supposing that mental episodes consist of relations between subjects and objects which are typically not mental.

Russell thus becomes free to treat minds as constructions out of the same sensible qualities and relations that construct matter. Following James (1904), he proposes that the transitory qualities we experience are intrinsically neither mental nor material, but rather 'neutral' in character.[12] They become mental or material (or both) by being part of causal processes that are either psychological or physical (or both). Thus, Russell argues, 'the mental and the physical are not distinguished by the stuff of which they are made, but only by their causal laws' (1919: 299). He suggests that

> a sensation may be grouped with a number of other occurrences by a memory-chain, in which case it becomes part of a mind; or it may be grouped with its causal antecedents, in which case it appears as part of the physical world.
>
> (1959: 139)

Russell takes neutral monism to have a number of attractive features beyond fitting our introspective evidence. On the philosophical side, he argues that considerations of ontological continuity and parsimony prescribe neutral monism 'as preferable to dualism if it can possibly be made to account for the facts' (*Papers* 7: 21). But unlike idealism or materialism, neutral monism achieves such ontological unity and simplicity without subordinating matter to mind or mind to matter (1927a: 10). It also promises to avoid the issue of how minds and matter can causally interact with each other. 'It used to be thought 'mysterious',' he says, 'that purely physical phenomena should end in something mental [such as a sensation]. That was because people thought they knew a lot about physical phenomena, and were sure they differ in quality from mental phenomena' (1927b: 117). On a neutral monist view, minds and matter are composed of the same underlying 'stuff' which can occur equally as part of physical causal processes and/or psychological causal processes. Thus, what we ordinarily regard as the effects of mind on matter or of matter on mind are simply cases in which episodes composing a mind occur as a beginning or ending part of chains of physical causation (119).

On the scientific side, Russell sees neutral monism as better coinciding with revolutionary advances in twentieth-century physics and experimental psychology. New theories about the relativity of space and time, the structure of the atom, and the strange realm of quantum phenomena forced radical revisions to traditional conceptions of matter. Russell sees physics as having dispensed with the idea that the universe is composed of small 'bits' of matter located at specific points in space, crowding out other such bits, and enduring through various changes in their features. In its place, physics characterizes 'matter' as a complex, causally connected series of transitory and sometimes overlapping occurrences unfolding within relativistic four-dimensional space-time. Thus, Russell declares, 'matter, in modern science, has lost its solidity and substantiality; it is becoming a mere ghost haunting the scenes of its former splendors' (1927b: 235).

In the case of psychology, an increasing emphasis on empirical methodologies put similar pressure on the traditional notion of minds as persisting immaterial substances. Behaviorists, such as Watson (1914) and Thorndike (1911) and introspectionists, such as Wundt (1874), James (1890), and Titchener (1909) alike agreed that a substantial self is not observable to careful introspection and thus lies outside of the subject matter of a properly empirical psychology. At the same time, scientists rapidly amassed increasing evidence of robust correlations between psychological phenomena and physiological processes. Russell thus concludes that psychology, like physics, better accords with a causally connected system of transitory occurrences than the notion of a substantial self.

Thus buttressed by both philosophy and science, Russell advances the thesis that 'everything in the world is composed of "events"', where an event is 'something having a small finite duration and a small finite extension in space; or rather, in view of the theory of relativity, it is something occupying a small finite amount of space-time' (1927b: 222). These events constitute the shared subject matter (and evidential basis) of both physics and psychology – which diverge from each other only in terms of the different causal laws and groupings of events they investigate.

Russell thus takes neutral monism to reveal a hidden unity among the physical and psychological sciences. He even speculates about the possibility of our developing a more fundamental unifying science which he dubs 'chrono-geography' (1927b: 227). As he imagines it, such a science would directly investigate different series of the neutral events composing the universe without, even for practical purposes, treating some systems of them as 'matter' and others as 'minds' (227–8). Russell is quick to emphasize, however, that the question of whether physical or psychological *causal relations* can be reduced to one another, or both to something neutral between them, is largely an empirical one (227–32).[13]

5. The Analysis of Matter

Russell's adoption of neutral monism obliges him to refashion his account of matter and our knowledge of it (Russell 1927a). No longer seeing sensation as a direct awareness relation between subjects and sensible qualities and relations outside the mind, he proposes that it is simply the occurrence of events exhibiting sensory features within a larger system of events organized by psychological causal relations. At the same time, he insists, 'the sensation that we have when we see a patch of colour [for example] simply is that patch of colour, an actual constituent of the physical world, and part of what physics is concerned with' (1921: 142). In other words, the same sensory events that are parts of our minds are parts of a vast system of qualitied events ordered in relativistic space-time in terms of physical causal relations.[14] And without the same need to distinguish the acts and objects of sensing, he replaces the term 'sense-data' with 'percepts', which strikes him as a more neutral label and does not wrongly suggest that sensory features are located in the surrounding environment.

In fact, Russell believes that there is compelling physical and physiological evidence that our percepts are, in some sense, located in our brain. He argues that the natural sciences show that perception involves elaborate causal processes that are typically initiated by a complex series of events in the environment, produce relevant physiological changes in our sensory organs, and ultimately terminate in neurological events in our brain (1927a: 320). Moreover, the sensible qualities and relations we ordinarily ascribe to our environment become present within our experience only at the very end of such causal processes. And these very same sensory elements can also be present in hallucinatory or illusory experience when relevant neurological events occur in the absence of their normal intermediate and remote causes. From all of this, Russell draws the notorious conclusion that 'what a physiologist sees when he examines a brain is in the physiologist, not in the brain he is examining' (320).

Russell thus comes to regard the core epistemological problem of matter as that of explaining how we get from the presence of percepts in our brain to our knowledge of physics. He proposes that such knowledge rests on non-demonstrative inferences from our percepts using a number of reasonable, but unprovable, assumptions about how they relate to events outside of our brain. Russell thinks that such inferences (and background assumptions) are ordinarily automatic, unreflective, and 'physiological' in nature; they become explicit only after careful analysis by a theorist or scientist (1927a: 190). Among other things, he argues, we assume that percepts have spatio-temporal and causal continuity with other events in space-time, that differences in percepts result from differences in their causes, and that different causal chains unfold along distinguishable spatio-temporal paths (1927a: 398–402, 1948: 506–15). Against this background, we rely on the changing patterns of our percepts to infer the existence of various systems of events outside our experience, their relative positions in space-time, and the causal relations they bear to other events, including our percepts. In this way, the physical sciences strive to describe the spatio-temporal and 'causal skeleton of the world' (1927a: 391).

But despite the incredible achievements of the natural sciences, Russell insists that they leave us completely in the dark about the intrinsic natures of the events they describe. In fact, the only exceptions to our otherwise complete ignorance in this respect are the qualities and relations of certain percepts and other psychological events in our brain. Hence, he says, 'as regards the world in general, both physical and mental, everything that we know of its intrinsic character is derived from the mental side, and almost everything that we know of its causal laws is derived from the physical side' (1927a: 402). Russell thus urges caution when speculating about the intrinsic nature of events outside the brain. They might greatly resemble the qualities of our percepts, but they might also be 'totally different in strictly unimaginable ways' (1959: 13). Turning received wisdom on its head, he declares that 'physics is not mathematical because we know so much about matter, but because we know so little' (1927b: 125).

6. The Analysis of Mind

Russell's analysis of matter constitutes only part of his overall neutral monist project. Russell sees it as equally important for providing an empirically and theoretically adequate analysis of minds and our knowledge of them. The core of his view is that 'minds' are complex systems of qualitied space-time events organized by psychological causal relations. A proper analysis of mental phenomena, then, requires accurate descriptions of these causal relations. But since naïve introspection is limited, unreliable, and easily biased, they must be investigated using careful experimental methods and controls (1921: 223–6). Russell's analysis thus incorporates various branches of experimental psychology, including behaviorist psychology, psychoanalysis, gestalt psychology, abnormal psychology, perceptual psychology, and self-observational psychology, among others.[15]

Russell argues that the widespread belief in 'an impassable gulf' between mind and matter is deeply rooted in erroneous doctrines about the essential characteristics of mental phenomena (1921: 9–10). The most notable of these mistakes is the popular belief that 'consciousness' is the most central feature of mentality (11). This is problematic because there is no reason to think that there are classes of mental episodes that never occur unconsciously (288). Furthermore, he asserts, many who think 'consciousness' is essential to mind carelessly run together very different senses of the term.[16] Specifically, 'conscious experiences' are variously described as psychological episodes that possess special intrinsic qualities, episodes that supply direct awareness of objects, and/or episodes that are themselves objects of direct awareness (112–13). Russell contends that each notion requires its own analysis and that none constitutes the ultimate essence of the mind.

Of the three notions, Russell initially devotes the least attention to whether consciousness is a special kind of intrinsic quality. In part, this simply reflects his long-standing opposition to ascribing a mental nature to the sensory qualities and relations we encounter. But he also objects that (1) minds are composite systems of elements rather than a simple kind of stuff possessing a quality unique only to it, and (2) our ignorance of other events precludes us from knowing whether their intrinsic qualities radically differ from, or closely resemble, those of our conscious episodes (1921: 113, 134–6).

Russell sees more promise in defining 'conscious experiences' as episodes which make us aware of something else. But as he no longer thinks such awareness is direct, he contends that it involves external causal relations between our mental episodes and the objects and features in our environment. The relation of episodes of awareness to their objects is roughly akin to that of uncles to their nephews: 'a man becomes an uncle through no effort of his own, merely through an occurrence elsewhere' (1921: 113). Specifically, qualited events constitute episodes of objectual awareness in virtue of their bearing the right causal relations to remote space-time events and occurring as part of a system of events exhibiting a marked degree of (1) sensitivity and (2) 'mnemic' responsiveness (1927b: 171).

A system 'is 'sensitive' to a certain feature of the environment if it behaves differently according to the presence or absence of that feature' (1921: 260).[17] By this measure, 'iron is sensitive to anything magnetic' (260). Scientific instruments are designed so that changes in their sensitive components serve as signs of causally related features which are remote, otherwise unobservable, and/or useful to measure.[18] Similarly certain events in the nervous systems of humans and other biological organisms reliably signal the presence or absence of various distal features to which they are sensitive (131–6). And while scientific instruments can be more reliable and accurate, humans and higher animals are sensitive to a greater variety of stimuli, can respond using information pooled from different sources, can increase some sensitivities through practice, and are often sensitive to stimuli that, in normal circumstances, are useful for promoting their biological and/or individual purposes.[19]

Episodes constitute objectual awareness only if they also occur in the right way within a system displaying a pronounced degree of 'mnemic' responsiveness. Systems possess this characteristic just in case their responses to stimuli tend to be shaped considerably by earlier episodes in their biographies. Accordingly, mnemic responses are ones whose 'proximate cause consists not merely of a present event [the stimulus], but this together with a past event' (Russell 1921: 85). Russell notes that this characteristic can be present in 'dead matter' (such as when steel is magnetized), but argues that it occurs more frequently in humans, animals, and plants, and plays a more central (and often biologically advantageous) role in their behavior (78). Notable examples of mnemic phenomena include acquired habits, images 'copied' from sensations, psychological associations, non-sensational elements in perception, and memories, among other things (79–82, 198–203, 285–6).

Mnemic causal relations are also crucial components of various other paradigmatic 'mental' characteristics. First, they distinguish sensations (qualited episodes caused by external stimuli and resulting in certain mnemic responses) from images (qualited episodes caused by other internal episodes that only sometimes result in further ones) (1921: 150–1). Second, they unify events in small regions of space-time into 'perspectives' and different perspectives along continuous space-time paths into mental biographies or 'minds' (129). Third, systems organized in these ways also exhibit subjectivity – 'the characteristic of giving the view of the world from a certain place' – based on how they are situated with respect to other events in space-time (296). And fourth, it is precisely when qualitied episodes bear the right mnemic relations to others within the same subjective mental biography that they are transformed from mere happenings into 'experiences' (129).

On Russell's neutral monist analysis, there are three different ways we can achieve 'self-consciousness' regarding our occurrent mental episodes. Most primitively, we in some sense 'feel' our sensory episodes and their qualities simply by experiencing them – that is, merely by having them occur in the right way within our subjective mental biography (Russell 1921: 139–42). Second, we can also 'notice' such episodes when they produce memory images in us that are sensitive to them, resemble them in some way, and are accompanied by feelings we might express as '*this* is occurring' or '*this* occurred' (1921: 288–9). And third, we can 'notice' our mental images by associating them with other episodes in our mental biography with the same (or roughly similar) contents (290–1).

Russell takes all of this to show that 'consciousness is far too complex and accidental to be taken as the fundamental characteristic of mind' (1921: 292). And the same goes for other mental phenomena, such as belief, desire, memory, intelligence, volition, and so on, which are likewise wholly composed of qualitied events and various mnemic causal relations (300). But while he takes these naturalistic analyses to support neutral monism, some see a distinctly panpsychist strain in them.

7. A Case for Panpsychism?

Russell's neutral monism has a long history of being closely associated with panpsychism. Most interpreters merely note that it has certain elements that make it consistent with panpsychist readings, which Russell acknowledges. But some take him to endorse positions that either constitute or imply some form of panpsychism.[20] This sentiment is often fueled by his own early descriptions of his project as an attempt to construct matter from sensations and 'constituents analogous to sensations' and later remarks that these elements more closely resemble 'mental' events than traditional 'matter' (1921: 306, 1927a: 388). So, it is easy to see why some interpret Russell's view as an idiosyncratic form of phenomenalism or idealism (1921: 306).[21] Nevertheless, such readings conflict with both his explicit disavowals of phenomenalist and idealist theories and his repeated insistence that mind as well as matter is composed of intrinsically neutral qualitied elements.[22]

Even so, many argue that Russell's neutral monism collapses, in one way or another, into a form of panpsychism. The most common argument holds that panpsychism is the most reasonable result of epistemic, explanatory, and metaphysical theses Russell accepts. First, it accepts his repeated claims that the only intrinsic qualities we know other than merely descriptively are those of our own mental episodes. Second, it adopts his view that we ought to use a number of non-demonstrative principles (or postulates) when reasoning from our best empirical evidence to theories about the nature of reality, especially his preference for theories exhibiting greater simplicity, uniformity, and comprehensiveness.[23] And third, it agrees with him that these considerations favor whichever form of stuff monism (but pluralism about particulars) best fits our evidence and scientific theories.

However, critics contend that panpsychism, rather than neutral monism, best satisfies these desiderata. For if our empirical evidence for intrinsic qualities is restricted solely to mental phenomena, and we are to prefer the most parsimonious and comprehensive theory that fits this evidence, then we should conclude that the intrinsic nature of the stuff science describes abstractly and structurally is also mental or experiential in character.[24] Many panpsychists further insist that the intrinsic qualities of mental episodes *cannot* be continuous with those of elements devoid of any mental, experiential, or experience-involving character.[25] In fact, some argue, if our empirical evidence for intrinsic qualities is exhausted by those of an experiential nature, we might wonder why we should ever suppose there to be ones of any other kind.

Many of these elements are present in Sir Arthur Eddington's review of *The Analysis of Matter*. Indeed, he begins:

> Russell's neutral stuff is intended to be the common basis of mental and physical manifestations, but approaching it through the physical manifestations we reach only the symbolic scheme of its structure, whereas approaching through the mental manifestations we reach a 'concrete' statement of its nature.
>
> (1928b: 95)

Thus, in Eddington's estimation describing the basic stuff of the world as 'mind-stuff' is preferable to neutral stuff. In his 1928 Gifford Lectures, he again makes roughly the same point:

> It is sometimes urged that the basal stuff of the world should be called 'neutral stuff' rather than 'mind-stuff', since it is to be such that both mind and matter originate from it. . . . [But this] implies that we have two avenues of approach to an understanding of its nature [when in actuality] we have only one approach, namely, through our direct knowledge of mind.
>
> (1928a: 280)

And given that our mental episodes are our only source of knowledge of intrinsic character, he urges, 'It seems rather silly to prefer to attach it to something of a so-called 'concrete' nature inconsistent with thought, and then to wonder where the thought comes from' (259).

Charles Hartshorne similarly presses Russell on the basis of his (alleged) admission that 'no neutral qualities are known to us, . . . and no qualities of dead matter, but only the qualities of mental events which are located in the brain' (1937: 222). If this is so, Hartshorne surmises, Russell's allegiance to neutral monism is seemingly based on materialistic prejudice, obstinate agnosticism about the qualities of inorganic events, and a cavalier positing of 'an absolutely unimaginable meaning for the word 'quality'' (221–2).

And there are other ways one might derive panpsychism from Russell's neutral monism. For instance, Skrbina points out that Russell regularly describes a broad range of both organic and inorganic phenomena in strikingly mentalistic terms (2007: 178–9). As noted previously, a key component of his analysis of objectual awareness is something's being 'sensitive' to features of the environment. And this, he acknowledges, is a characteristic present to some degree not just among biological organisms but also in stones, pieces of iron, scientific instruments, and perhaps everything in nature.[26] Similarly, even mundane inorganic phenomena such as magnetized iron and steel, unwound rolls of paper, and watercourses exhibit mnemic reactions – responses in which something's behavior is the joint result of past and present stimuli.[27] At various points, Russell also ascribes 'subjectivity' to photographic plates, 'intelligence' to calculating machines, 'habit-memory' to gramophones, and rudimentary forms of 'thought' to river beds.[28] He even entertains the remote possibility that the sun is 'intelligent' or that atoms have 'a kind of limited free will'.[29] It is altogether unsurprising that many suspect him of being a panpsychist.

8. Russell's Case for Neutral Monism

Though Russell would agree with panpsychists that mental phenomena are likely present to some degree wherever there is biological life, he takes the overall evidence to suggest that mind is neither a ubiquitous nor fundamental feature of the universe. In some cases, he admits that his grounds for preferring neutral monism to panpsychism or idealism are somewhat weak. But in other cases, he takes the considerations favoring neutral monism to carry a good deal of weight.

For starters, Russell holds that neutral monism better accords with our instinctive, commonsense, and scientifically informed belief that minds are relatively rare occurrences in the universe. While he readily admits that our preconceptions about reality are often misguided and rooted in prejudice, he thinks our most basic beliefs still deserve provisional assent in the absence of stronger arguments to the contrary. Conversely, he sees little attraction in attempts to 'humanise the cosmos' or to ascribe to mind 'a cosmic importance which it by no means deserves' (1959: 12, 97). For his own part, Russell reports,

> I accept without qualification the view that results from astronomy and geology, from which it would appear that there is no evidence of anything mental except in a tiny fragment of space-time, and that the great processes of nebular and stellar evolution proceed according to laws in which mind plays no role.
>
> (1959: 12)

Russell also holds that neutral monism better accounts for the continuity mental phenomena appear to have with the rest of the universe. By his lights, panpsychists and idealists too hastily account for such continuity by ascribing primordial mental aspects to the basic elements of nature. Russell contends that 'observations of the differences between living and dead matter coupled with inferences based on analogy or its absence' suggest that this is a remote possibility (1948: 246–7). In fact, given the great differences in structure and behavior between the biological organisms to which we ordinarily ascribe minds and most physical phenomena, he thinks it more likely that most physical occurrences – especially those too simple to exhibit mnemic responses – are wholly devoid of mentality (246–7).

Russell believes that the continuity of mind with the rest of nature is more likely due to their being wholly composed of simpler qualitied elements and causal relations that are not intrinsically mental. Russell intends from the very start for his analysis of mind to be fully naturalistic in this sense. These motivations are plain in his first manuscript notes on the topic: 'I was anxious [as a dualist] to rescue the physical world from the clutches of idealism. . . . But if I could rescue the so-called 'mental' world from him too! Then the reason for making a gulf between the mental and the physical would disappear' (*Papers* 8: 255). To these ends, his neutral monism sets out to 'reduce everything cognitive to 'pure natural events'', and in this respect 'its bias or flavour is materialistic' (254). In later writings, Russell even describes his theory as a form of 'non-materialist naturalism' (*Papers* 10: 371–5).[30]

Russell thinks that an analysis of mind must account for two different sorts of continuity in nature. Firstly, it should emphasize the evidence of mental continuity among humans and the rest of the biological domain, including animals, plants, and even the simplest unicellular organisms.[31] Russell argues that 'from the protozoa to man there is nowhere a very wide gap either in structure or in behavior . . . [and so] it is a highly probable inference that there is also nowhere a very wide mental gap' (1921: 41). Indeed, he is inclined to ascribe varying degrees of cognition, conation, and feeling to all animals, 'learning' and 'habit–memory' to plants and animals, and goal-directed environmental sensitivity and responsiveness in even the simplest organisms.[32] He even entertains the possibility that 'each cell in the body has its own mental life, and that that only selections from these mental lives go to make up the life we regard as ours' (1927b: 231).

Secondly, such analyses must accord with mounting scientific evidence for the continuity of biological life and mind with the plethora of inanimate phenomena in the universe. As Russell sees it, 'the evidence, though not conclusive, tends to show that everything distinctive of living matter can be reduced to chemistry, and therefore ultimately to physics' (1948: 46). And this goes equally for the mental characteristics of biological organisms, thus suggesting that 'mind is merely a cross-section in a stream of physical causation' (1927b: 156). But while the basic ingredients of mental phenomena (including qualitativity, subjectivity, sensitivity, and mnemic responsiveness) are plentiful in the inorganic domain, it is only when they combine in sufficiently complex causal systems that life and mentality result (1948: 50).

Russell arguably comes to see this as the most pressing challenge for panpsychism and idealism: that all mental phenomena (including consciousness, sensation, memory, thought, volition, personality, and so on) are composed of more basic elements whose natures are not intrinsically mental. Indeed, he says, 'I think 'mental' is a character, like 'harmonious' or 'discordant', that cannot belong to a single entity in its own right, but only systems of entities' (1927b: 161). Russell reiterates this point on several occasions, including as a rejoinder to Eddington:

> Professor Eddington disagrees with neutral monism, and holds instead to the doctrine of 'mind-stuff', although he is careful to explain that this need not be either mind or stuff. I disagree with this doctrine, because I hold that mentality is a form of organization, not a property of individual events, just as, say, democracy is a property of a community and not of an individual citizen.
>
> (Papers 10: 53–4; Papers 10: 62)

But if mentality can only be exhibited by the right kinds of complex systems, then it presumably cannot be an ultimate or pervasive feature of the universe. Moreover, Russell stresses, 'it must not be assumed that part of a mental state must be a mental state' (1927a: 320).

Russell simply does not share the conviction of panpsychists and idealists that mental phenomena cannot be wholly composed of elements that themselves are not intrinsically experiential in nature. This strikes him as pure metaphysical dogma, as introspection shows us nothing about our mental episodes which precludes them from being systems of neutral qualities and relations. Indeed, while Eddington and Hartshorne are correct that we can experience the intrinsic qualities *of* our mental episodes, it does not follow that these qualities are *themselves* intrinsically mental. For our introspective evidence is equally compatible with the view that such episodes and their qualities become 'mental' or 'experiential' only due to extrinsic causal relations they bear to other such elements. For the same reason, the charge that neutral monism appeals to an illegitimate and incomprehensible notion of 'quality' is baseless.

Russell holds that panpsychism and idealism often rest on misconceptions about the intimacy and comprehensiveness of our introspective knowledge. As he sees it, many panpsychists ascribe to our introspective 'knowledge' of percepts a directness which applies instead only to our 'experience' of them (*Papers* 10: 53 and 61–2). In actuality, while we directly 'feel' such episodes simply by their occurring in the right way within our mental biography, any thoughts or judgments about them require our 'noticing' them via causally mediated images. As a result, our cognitive grasp of our experiences and their features lacks the transparency, security, and comprehensiveness many presume it to have. And this goes for Eddington, who 'is very well aware how little physics tells us about the physical world, but being no psychologist he somewhat exaggerates what psychology [and introspection] can tell us about the mental world' (53).

As for himself, Russell reports, 'I am prepared to admit that we are nearer to knowing about our own minds than about anything else, because the causal chain from an event to my knowledge of it is shorter when it is in my own brain than when it is anywhere else' (*Papers* 10: 53). But even though our introspective beliefs track certain features of our mental episodes with a high degree of reliability and accuracy, it does not follow that they fully capture the nature of such episodes or their features, even in ideal circumstances. So although 'we know the intrinsic character of the mental to some extent', we can still have many misconceptions and a good deal of ignorance about our experiences and their qualities (1927b: 238). Panpsychists such as Eddington thus cannot simply assume that the intrinsic characters of the 'phenomena he regards as mental' are essentially and fundamentally experiential (*Papers* 10: 62). In fact, Russell thinks our introspective evidence strongly suggests that our experiences have imperceptible parts and structure that outrun our capacities for introspective discrimination (1927a: 281–3 and 386).[33] And while they could turn out to be more rudimentary mental elements, he thinks such speculations go beyond our introspective evidence and what is most reasonable to infer from it.

Russell's overall attitude concerning panpsychism is particularly clear in his 'Mind and Matter' (1956). In this late paper, he considers the question: 'What is the difference between things that happen to sentient beings and things that happen to lifeless matter?' (142). His reply is that lifeless objects 'move and undergo various transformations, *but they do not 'experience' these occurrences* whereas we do 'experience' things that happen to us' (142, emphasis added). These remarks are important both because he expressly denies that inorganic systems are sentient and because the italicized parts are Russell's late additions to the chapter's page proofs, presumably included precisely to forestall panpsychist readings of his neutral monism.[34]

8. Conclusion

Much more can be said about Russell's neutral monism, its history, and the arguments he offers for it and against panpsychist and idealist alternatives. What is plain is that the relationship between Russell's theory and contemporary versions of panpsychism is a complicated one. On one hand, his analysis of matter has a number of features attractive to panpsychists. Among them are its claims that the physical sciences only provide abstract descriptions of the causal and spatio-temporal structure of the natural world, that all of its basic elements share the same kind of intrinsic character, and that the only such characters with which we are acquainted are certain qualities and relations of our mental episodes.

On the other hand, Russell's analysis of mind is largely at odds with panpsychism. For even though it ascribes features such as qualitativity, subjectivity, sensitivity, and mnemic responsiveness to many different organic and inorganic systems, only the first of these features can be exhibited by individual events as opposed to systems of them. Moreover, none of these features are to be interpreted in a mentalistic way in their most basic forms. On Russell's view, experience and mentality only result when the right combinations of these features are exhibited by sufficiently complex causal systems, such as in the case of humans, animals, plants, and other biological organisms.

Russell's neutral monism thus should not be of interest to contemporary philosophers of mind only for its landmark treatment of matter. It also offers a remarkably sophisticated naturalistic account of the mind that both gives a central place to the experimental results of physics, biology, and psychology and anticipates a number of widely accepted contemporary philosophical theories by roughly a half-century. It also directly challenges some of the core epistemological, metaphysical, and methodological assumptions behind panpsychism in ways that go well beyond the so-called 'incredulous stare'. In particular, philosophers today would do well to give more attention to Russell's arguments concerning the scope and limits of introspective knowledge, the imperceptible complexity of our conscious episodes, and the grounds for thinking that the intrinsic qualities of our experiences are themselves intrinsically experiential.[35]

Notes

1. Stubenberg (2018) notes that neutral monism is sometimes understood in other, conflicting, ways.
2. I am here using 'basic elements' in a way that is intended to be neutral about whether they occur at the microlevel of particles, macrolevel of humans and animals, and/or at the cosmic level of the entire universe as a whole.

3. McTaggart 1921 and 1927 is of the former kind while Bradley 1893 is (arguably) a case of the latter. For more on absolute idealism and/or its influence on Russell, see Hylton 1990; Griffin 1991; McDaniel 2016; Candlish and Basile 2017; Guyer and Horstmann 2018; Levine 2018.
4. The following is based on Russell's 1911, 1912, and his posthumously published 1913 manuscript (*Papers* 7).
5. See Gandon 2017 for a similar discussion about Moore.
6. See Proops 2014, 2015; Linsky 2015; Wishon 2017, 2018.
7. For more on Russell's views about sensation, hallucination, imagination, and dreams, see Carey 2015.
8. While Russell grants that sense-data might be mental, he sees no good reason to give up our 'instinctive' belief that they are not. Arguably, Russell views them as concrete particulars that are neither mental nor material (Quinton 1972; Wishon 2017). But Pears (1967: 33–4) thinks they are events in the nervous system and Landini (2011: 238–9) argues that they are transitory physical particulars that are signs of the four-dimensional continuants of physics.
9. See Russell 1914a, 1914b, 1915, and posthumously published 1912 'On Matter' (*Papers* 6: 80–95).
10. It is not a pure panqualityism, however, as there are mental subjects and acts above and beyond the sense-data and 'unsensed sensibilia' composing physical reality. Also, we should not presume that the posited sensible qualities and relations must be ones that humans can experience.
11. Russell thinks these considerations also pose a grave challenge to neutral monism (1918: 86–7 and 153). See Pincock 2018 and Wishon 2018.
12. Russell credits the term 'neutral stuff' to Henry Sheffer rather than James, who preferred to describe the basic stuff as 'pure experience'. His other influences include Mach (1886) and the American New Realists.
13. For more on Russell's changing views on causation and our knowledge of it, see Eames 1989 and Bostock 2012. See Maclean 2014 for more on whether Russell views such causal relations as mental, physical, or neutral.
14. Landini offers a conflicting reading of Russell's neutral elements according to which they 'are without intrinsic phenomenal character' (2011: 297), though see Stubenberg (2018) for a plausible response.
15. The behaviorist elements of Russell's analysis of mind are well-known. See Blackwell 1989; Hatfield 2003; Kitchener 2004; Landini 2011; Pincock 2018. But his use of other branches of psychology is rarely mentioned.
16. Russell unfairly includes Stout (1896 and 1899) among those making this mistake.
17. Russell's analysis of objectual awareness is rarely recognized for anticipating more recent naturalistic theories of content. Notable exceptions are Baldwin 2001; Stevens 2006a, 2006b; Kitchener 2007; Levine 2009; Landini 2011.
18. See Russell 1921: 255–61, 1927b: 47, 70, 225, 1940: 13, 1959: 19, 103.
19. See Russell 1921: 46, 259–61, 1927b: 47–8, 75–6.
20. See Eddington 1928a; Hartshorne 1937; Popper and Eccles 1977; Skrbina 2007; Coleman 2009; Strawson 2017, this volume. Note that Coleman 2017 defends a panqualityism that closely resembles Russell's neutral monism.
21. See Savage and Anderson 1989; Maxwell 1972; Strawson 1994; Brüntrup 2017.
22. See Russell 1921: 10, 1927a: 388, 1959: 107, and *Papers* 9: 32.
23. See Russell 1927a: 10, 1959: 103–4, and *Papers* 8: 147.
24. See Strawson 2017, this volume and Goff 2016, 2017.
25. See Russell 1921: 40, 90, 1935: 203, 1948: 215, 1959: 15, and *Papers* 9: 284, Hartshorne 1937; Strawson 2017, this volume; Goff 2016, 2017.
26. See Russell 1935: 131 and footnote 26 above.
27. See Russell 1921: 78, 1927b: 237–8, 1935: 132, 1956: 153–5.
28. See Russell 1921: 130–1, 166, 1956: 155, 1959: 183.
29. See Russell 1927b: 241, 1948: 247. He does, however, take the former possibility to be 'of the order of 'pigs might fly'' and the latter to be one expressed 'more or less fancifully'.
30. There are longstanding debates about whether Russell's 'neutral monism' develops into a form of physicalism. See Banks 2014; Bostock 2012; Landini 2011; Pincock 2018; Stubenberg 2015, 2018; Wishon 2015.
31. See Russell 1921: 40, 1927b: 161, 1935: 202–4, 1948: 160, 1959: 95.
32. See, for instance, Russell 1921: 40–4, 51–7, 64–5, 77–90, 167, 259–61. He cautions against assuming that other organisms have mental lives closely resembling our own:

> If you pick up a mossy stone which is lightly embedded in the earth, you will see a number of small animals scuttling away from the unwonted daylight. . . . Such animals are sensitive to light, in the sense that their movements are affected by it; but it would be rash to infer that they have sensations in any way analogous to our sensations of light.
>
> *(1921: 44)*

33. Russell mentions at least two ways we might infer our experiences have imperceptible parts and structure (1927a: 281–3, 386). First, we do so from so-called 'phenomenal continua cases' in which we cannot discern differences between qualities a and b, nor b and c, but we can do so regarding a and c, thereby suggesting that b is distinct from both a and c even though we cannot discern it to be so. Second, if indiscernible experiences lead to different results in the same circumstances, we might infer they have imperceptible parts just as we do with analogous cases in natural science. See Wishon 2017 for more on Russell's treatment of phenomenal continua cases.

34. My thanks to the Bertrand Russell Archives at McMaster University for providing me access to these page proofs.

35. I thank Galen Strawson, Leopold Stubenberg, Bernard Linsky, Nick Griffin, Sandra Lapointe, Ken Blackwell, Gülberk Koç Maclean, Matt Duncan, Kevin Morris, David Beisecker, Barbara Montero, Aaron Graham, David Harmon, and Celine Geday for helpful discussions at various stages of writing this chapter. I also thank the University of Mississippi for support during my Spring 2019 sabbatical leave. Finally, I give special thanks to William Seager for his immense patience and helpful editorial guidance, without which this chapter would not have been completed.

References

Baldwin, T. (2001). 'Russell on Memory'. *Principia: An International Journal of Epistemology*, 5 (1–2): 187–208.

Banks, E. (2014). *The Realistic Empiricism of Mach, James, and Russell: Neutral Monism Reconceived*. Cambridge: Cambridge University Press.

Blackwell, K. (1989). 'Portrait of a Philosopher of Science'. In C. W. Savage and C. A. Anderson (eds.), *Minnesota Studies in the Philosophy of Science*, 12: 281–93.

Bostock, D. (2012). *Russell's Logical Atomism*. New York: Oxford University Press.

Bradley, H. (1893). *Appearance and Reality*. London: George Allen and Unwin.

Brentano, F. (1874). *Psychologie vom empirischen Standpunkt*. Leipzig: Verlag von Dunckner und Humblot.

Brüntrup, G. (2017). 'Emergent Panpsychism'. In G. Brüntrup and L. Jaskolla (eds.), *Panpsychism: Contemporary Perspectives*. New York: Oxford University Press, pp. 48–71.

Candlish, S., and Basile, P. (2017). 'Francis Herbert Bradley'. In E. Zalta (ed.), *The Stanford Encyclopedia of Philosophy*, Spring edition. https://plato.stanford.edu/archives/spr2017/entries/bradley/.

Carey, R. (2015). 'Seeing, Imagining, Believing: From *Problems* to *Theory of Knowledge*'. In D. Wishon and B. Linsky (eds.), *Acquaintance, Knowledge, and Logic: New Essays on Bertrand Russell's the Problems of Philosophy*. Stanford, CA: CSLI Publications, pp. 107–27.

Coleman, S. (2009). 'Mind Under Matter'. In D. Skrbina (ed.), *Mind That Abides: Panpsychism in the New Millennium*. Philadelphia, PA: John Benjamins Publishing, pp. 83–107.

Coleman, S. (2017). 'Panpsychism or Neutral Monism: How to Make Up One's Mind'. In G. Brüntrup and L. Jaskolla (eds.), *Panpsychism: Contemporary Perspectives*. New York: Oxford University Press, pp. 249–82.

Eames, E. R. (1967). 'The Consistency of Russell's Realism'. *Philosophy and Phenomenological Research*, 27: 502–11.

Eames, E. R. (1989). 'Cause in the Later Russell'. In C. W. Savage and C. A. Anderson (eds.), *Minnesota Studies in the Philosophy of Science*, 12: 264–80.

Eddington, A. (1928a). *The Nature of the Physical World*. Cambridge: Cambridge University Press. (Citations from 2012 Cambridge University Press edition.).

Eddington, A. (1928b). 'The Analysis of Matter: By Bertrand Russell'. *Journal of Philosophical Studies*, 3 (9): 93–5.

Gandon, S. (2017). 'Sidgwick's Legacy? Russell and Moore on Meaning and Philosophical Inquiry'. *Journal for the History of Analytical Philosophy*, 6 (1).

Goff, P. (2016). 'Bertrand Russell and the Problem of Consciousness'. In S. Leach and J. Tartaglia (eds.), *Consciousness and the Great Philosophers*. London: Routledge, pp. 185–91.

Goff, P. (2017). *Consciousness and Fundamental Reality*. Oxford: Oxford University Press.

Griffin, N. (1991). *Russell's Idealist Apprenticeship*. Oxford: Clarendon Press.

Guyer, P., and Horstmann, R. P. (2018). 'Idealism'. In E. N. Zalta (ed.), *The Stanford Encyclopedia of Philosophy*. https://plato.stanford.edu/archives/win2018/entries/idealism/.

Hartshorne, Charles (1937). *Beyond Humanism: Essays in the New Philosophy of Nature*. New York: Willett, Clark & Co.

Hatfield, G. (2003). 'Behaviourism and Psychology'. In T. Baldwin (ed.), *Cambridge History of Philosophy, 1870–1945*. Cambridge: Cambridge University Press, pp. 640–8.

Hylton, P. (1990). *Russell, Idealism, and the Emergence of Analytic Philosophy*. Oxford: Clarendon Press.

Hylton, P. (2003). 'The Theory of Descriptions'. In N. Griffin (ed.), *The Cambridge Companion to Bertrand Russell*. Cambridge: Cambridge University Press, pp. 202–40.

James, W. (1890). *The Principles of Psychology*, vol. 1. New York: Henry Holt.

James, W. (1904). 'Does Consciousness Exist?' *Journal of Philosophy, Psychology and Scientific Methods*, 1 (18): 477–91.

Kitchener, Richard F. (2004). 'Bertrand Russell's Flirtation with Behaviorism'. *Behavior and Philosophy*, 32 (2): 273–91.

Kitchener, Richard F. (2007). 'Bertrand Russell's Naturalistic Epistemology'. *Philosophy* 82 (1): 115–46.

Landini, G. (2011). *Russell*. New York: Routledge.

Levine, J. (2009). 'From Moore to Peano to Watson: The Mathematical Roots of Russell's Naturalism and Behaviorism'. *The Baltic International Yearbook of Cognition, Logic, and Communication, Volume 4: 200 Years of Analytical Philosophy*: 1–126.

Levine, J. (2018). 'Russell and Idealism'. In R. Wahl (ed.), *The Bloomsbury Companion to Bertrand Russell*. New York: Bloomsbury Academic, pp. 17–58.

Linsky, B. (2015). 'Acquaintance and Certainty in *The Problems of Philosophy*'. In D. Wishon and B. Linsky (eds.), *Acquaintance, Knowledge, and Logic: New Essays on Bertrand Russell's the Problems of Philosophy*. Stanford, CA: CSLI Publications, pp. 65–85.

Mach, E. (1886). *Beiträge zur Analyse der Empfindungen*. Jena: Verlag von Gustav Fischer.

Maclean, G. K. (2014). *Bertrand Russell's Bundle Theory of Particulars*. New York: Bloomsbury.

Maxwell, G. (1972). 'Russell on Perception: A Study in Philosophical Method'. In D. F. Pears (ed.), *Bertrand Russell: A Collection of Critical Essays*. Garden City, NY: Doubleday, pp. 110–46.

McDaniel, K. (2016). 'John M. E. McTaggart'. In E. N. Zalta (ed.), *The Stanford Encyclopedia of Philosophy*. https://plato.stanford.edu/archives/win2016/entries/mctaggart/.

McTaggart, J. (1921). *The Nature of Existence*, vol. I. Cambridge: Cambridge University Press.

McTaggart, J. (1927). *The Nature of Existence*, vol. II. Cambridge: Cambridge University Press.

Pears, D. (1967). *Bertrand Russell and the British Tradition in Philosophy*. London: Fontana.

Pincock, C. (2018). 'Neutral Monism'. In R. Wahl (ed.), *The Bloomsbury Companion to Bertrand Russell*. New York: Bloomsbury Academic, pp. 312–33.

Popper, K., and Eccles, J. C. (1977). *The Self and Its Brain: An Argument for Interactionism*. London: Springer-Verlag.

Proops, I. (2014). 'Russellian Acquaintance Revisited'. *Journal of the History of Philosophy*, 52 (4): 779–811.

Proops, I. (2015). 'Certainty, Error, and Acquaintance in *The Problems of Philosophy*'. In D. Wishon and B. Linsky (eds.), *Acquaintance, Knowledge, and Logic: New Essays on Bertrand Russell's the Problems of Philosophy*. Stanford, CA: CSLI Publications, pp. 45–63.

Quinton, A. (1972). 'Russell's Philosophy of Mind'. In D. F. Pears (ed.), *Bertrand Russell: A Collection of Critical Essays*. Garden City, NY: Doubleday, pp. 80–109.

Russell, B. (1911). 'Knowledge by Acquaintance and Knowledge by Description'. *Proceedings of the Aristotelian Society*, 11: 108–28. Also in *Papers 6*.

Russell, B. (1912). *The Problems of Philosophy*. London: Williams and Norgate.

Russell, B. (1914a). *Our Knowledge of the External World*. London: Open Court.

Russell, B. (1914b). 'The Relation of Sense-Data to Physics'. *Scientia*, 16: 1–27. Also in *Papers 8*.

Russell, B. (1915). 'The Ultimate Constituents of Matter'. *The Monist*, 25: 399–417. Also in *Papers 8*.

Russell, B. (1918). 'The Philosophy of Logical Atomism'. Reprinted in D. Pears (ed.), *The Philosophy of Logical Atomism*. Peru, IL: Open Court, 1985. Also in *Papers 8*.

Russell, B. (1919). 'On Propositions: What They Are and How They Mean'. *Proceedings of the Aristotelian Society*, Supplementary Volume, 2: 1–43. Also in *Papers 8*.

Russell, B. (1921). *The Analysis of Mind*. London: George Allen and Unwin.

Russell, B. (1927a). *The Analysis of Matter*. London: Kegan Paul, Trench, and Trubner. (Citations from 1954 Dover edition.).

Russell, B. (1927b). *An Outline of Philosophy*. London: George Allen and Unwin. (Citations from 1993 Routledge edition.).

Russell, B. (1935). *Religion and Science*. London: Thornton Butterworth. (Citations from 1997 Oxford University Press edition.).

Russell, B. (1940). *An Inquiry into Meaning and Truth*. London: George Allen and Unwin.

Russell, B. (1948). *Human Knowledge: Its Scope and Limits*. London: George Allen and Unwin. (Citation from 1992 Routledge edition.).

Russell, B. (1956). 'Mind and Matter'. In *Portraits from Memory*. London: George Allen and Unwin. Also in *Papers 11*.

Russell, B. (1959). *My Philosophical Development*. London: George Allen and Unwin. (Citations from 1993 Routledge edition.).

Russell, B. (1984). *The Collected Papers of Bertrand Russell, Volume 7: Theory of Knowledge, the 1913 Manuscript*. Ed. E. R. Eames and K. Blackwell. London: George Allen and Unwin. [*Papers 7*].

Russell, B. (1986). *The Collected Papers of Bertrand Russell, Volume 8: The Philosophy of Logical Atomism and Other Essays 1914–19*. Ed. J. G. Slater. London: George Allen and Unwin. [*Papers* 8].

Russell, B. (1988). *The Collected Papers of Bertrand Russell, Volume 9: Essays on Language, Mind and Matter 1919–26*, Ed. J. G. Slater with the assistance of B. Frohmann. London: Unwin Hyman. [*Papers* 9].

Russell, B. (1992). *The Collected Papers of Bertrand Russell, Volume 6: Logical and Philosophical Papers 1909–13*. Ed. J. G. Slater with the assistance of B. Frohmann. London: Routledge. [*Papers* 6].

Russell, B. (1996). *The Collected Papers of Bertrand Russell, Volume 10: A Fresh Look at Empiricism 1927–42*. Ed. J. G. Slater with the assistance of P. Köllner. London: Routledge. [*Papers* 10].

Russell, B. (1997). *The Collected Papers of Bertrand Russell, Volume 11: Last Philosophical Testament 1943–68*. Ed. J. G. Slater with the assistance of P. Köllner. London: Routledge. [*Papers* 11].

Savage, C. W., and Anderson, C. A. (1989). 'Introduction'. In C. W. Savage and C. A. Anderson (eds.), *Minnesota Studies in the Philosophy of Science*, 12: 3–23.

Skrbina, D. (2007). *Panpsychism in the West*. Cambridge, MA: The MIT Press.

Stevens, G. (2006a). 'Russell's Re-Psychologising of the Proposition'. *Synthese*, 151 (1): 99–124.

Stevens, G. (2006b). 'On Russell's Naturalism'. *The Bertrand Russell Society Quarterly*, 130.

Stout, G. F. (1896). *Analytic Psychology*, 2 vols. New York: Macmillan.

Stout, G. F. (1899). *A Manuel of Psychology*. New York: Hinds and Noble.

Strawson, G. (1994). *Mental Reality*. Cambridge, MA: The MIT Press.

Strawson, G. (2017). 'Mind and Being: The Primacy of Panpsychism'. In G. Brüntrup and L. Jaskolla (eds.), *Panpsychism: Contemporary Perspectives*. New York: Oxford University Press, pp. 75–112.

Strawson, G. (2019). 'What Does "Physical" Mean? A Prolegomenon to Physicalist Panpsychism'. In this volume.

Stubenberg, L. (2015). 'Russell, Russellian Monism, and Panpsychism'. In T. Alter and Y. Nagasawa (eds.), *Consciousness in the Physical World: Perspectives on Russellian Monism*. Oxford: Oxford University Press, pp. 58–90.

Stubenberg, L. (2018). 'Neutral Monism'. In E. Zalta (ed.), *The Stanford Encyclopedia of Philosophy*. https://plato.stanford.edu/archives/fall2018/entries/neutral-monism/.

Thorndike, E. L. (1911). *Animal Intelligence*. New York: Macmillan.

Titchener, E. B. (1909). 'The Psychology of Feeling and Attention'. *Journal of Philosophy, Psychology and Scientific Methods*, 6 (3): 64–77.

Watson, J. (1914). *Behavior: An Introduction to Comparative Psychology*. New York: Henry Holt.

Wishon, D. (2015). 'Russell on Russellian Monism'. In T. Alter and Y. Nagasawa (eds.), *Consciousness in the Physical World: Perspectives on Russellian Monism*. Oxford: Oxford University Press, pp. 91–118.

Wishon, D. (2017). 'Russellian Acquaintance and Frege's Puzzle'. *Mind*, 126 (502): 321–70.

Wishon, D. (2018). 'Russell on Introspection and Self-Knowledge'. In R. Wahl (ed.), *The Bloomsbury Companion to Bertrand Russell*. New York: Bloomsbury Academic, pp. 256–85.

Wundt, W. (1874). *Grundzüge der physiologischen Psychologie*. Leipzig: Engelmann.

10

PANPSYCHISM RECONSIDERED

A Historical and Philosophical Overview

David Skrbina

Perhaps no position in the history of philosophy is at once as neglected, as misunderstood, and yet as potentially important as panpsychism. Denigrated or ignored for most of the 20th century, panpsychism is now of resurgent interest. It is being reexamined and reconsidered as a potentially fruitful approach to mind generally, and specifically as a potential resolution to the long-standing question of emergence. Panpsychism has far-reaching philosophical implications, affecting such diverse areas as metaphysics, epistemology, and ethics. The time is right to revisit this venerable, seminal, surprising, and challenging approach to philosophy of mind.

Though the concept is ancient, the term 'panpsychism' comes to us from the work of Italian philosopher Francesco Patrizi, and his *Nova de universis philosophia* of 1591. The word derives from *pan* ('all') + *psyche* ('mind' or 'soul'). Broadly conceived, it is the notion that all things possess some degree of mind, consciousness, or subjectivity. In principle this reaches down to the smallest physical ultimates, and upward to the cosmos as a whole. It admits of a surprisingly wide variety of interpretations.

One way to begin clarifying the concept is to say what panpsychism is *not*. First, it is not animism – which is the view that spirits or souls inhabit all natural entities. Animism is most widely cited with respect to indigenous or archaic cultural traditions, and has a quasi-religious connotation. Suffice to say that philosophical panpsychism has little connection with such traditional animism. Modern panpsychists take a much more abstract and analytical view of mind and tend to avoid discussion of any quasi-spiritual entities.

Secondly, panpsychism is not hylozoism – the view that all things are alive (*hyle* ['matter'] + *zoe* ['life']). The term 'hylozoism' appeared in the 17th century and was used to refer to certain ancient Greek views in which life adhered in all things. But in ancient times, of course, the notion of life was poorly understood. We can see, for example, how early thinkers might have viewed a lodestone as alive since it had the power to move small bits of metal. Or how rubbed amber might be seen as living, given that it attracted scraps of paper or cloth. Over the centuries, as people gained a better understanding of the mechanisms of life, hylozoism generally ceased to be an active theory.

Interestingly, though, it never completely died out. A handful of 19th-century philosophers claimed to be hylozoists, including Ernst Haeckel and Friedrich Paulsen. Josiah Royce wrote about an "appreciative inner life [that] is hidden behind the describable but seemingly lifeless things of the world (1892/1955: 427). Later he remarked that "where we see inorganic Nature seemingly dead, there is, in fact, conscious life" (1899: 240). Francis Bradley concurred: "we cannot call the least portion of Nature inorganic" (1893/1930: 240). Into the 20th century, John Haldane (1932, 1934) argued that all matter was alive, as did Wilfred Agar (1943). Even as late as 1982, the physicist-philosopher David Bohm claimed that "in a way, nature is alive . . . all the way to the depths" (1982: 39). Apart from these few cases, however, hylozoism is rarely cited in recent literature.

Thirdly, panpsychism is not pantheism – the view that the universe is God. Like panpsychism, pantheism has a long and noble legacy. Found in rough form in Plato,[1] the originating conception of pantheism is generally attributed to the Stoic philosophers, and it was notably resurrected by Spinoza in the mid-1600s. But it has no necessary connection to panpsychism; the fact that all things are enminded, even the universe as a whole, does not entail divinity. Confusion here is understandable, though, given that virtually all major pantheists in history – Plato, the Stoics, Spinoza – were also panpsychists.

Apart from these three terms, we find in the literature a handful of other related concepts: pan-biotism, pansensism, panentheism, panexperientialism. I myself have coined and employed the term 'hylonoism' (Skrbina 2009a). And other variants exist.

Panpsychism, then, is not spiritism, life, or god. It's not mythological, and it's not supernatural. The 'psyche' of panpsychism is mind, subjectivity, experience – not soul. Panpsychism is a serious, rational, naturalistic, and far-reaching conception of mind.

1. Panpsychism as Meta-Theory

Panpsychism occupies a unique status in philosophy of mind, if only because of its conceptual stand-ing. It's a theory, not *of* mind, but of what things *have* mind. It does not necessarily attempt to explain what one means by 'mind' – though many panpsychists do this. It does not necessarily attempt, or promise, to resolve any of the long-standing mind-body problems. It does not necessarily assume a representationalist or intentional stance. It does not necessarily address any of the many issues sur-rounding qualia, or supervenience. Panpsychism is neither monist, dualist, nor pluralist. It's not a theory of mind at all; it is, rather, a meta-theory. It simply holds that, however one conceives of mind, all things – suitably defined – possess it.

This is important because certain modern-day critics argue that panpsychism cannot deliver on its "promises." Or they claim that it offers "no solution." Or that it is "empty." Or worse. In fact, panpsychism holds only as much value as the underlying theory of mind. Virtually every conven-tional theory is formally open as to the extent of mind. Most contemporary thinkers grant mind or mentality to the so-called higher animals, at least. Many go further. Some extend mind outside the physical body, to (unspecified) external devices and objects. Panpsychism simply says: Extend mind to all things. It's a potential adjunct to nearly any current conception.

As such, proponents of panpsychism must adopt a different approach than ordinary philosophers of mind, if they are to mount a viable defense. Empirical data is problematic here, if not impossible. Scientific analyses are arguably inapplicable. Defenders must therefore argue indirectly: from plausi-bility, or parsimony, or first principles, or evolutionary continuity. In the following I will outline some general categories of panpsychist arguments, from an historical standpoint.

2. The Question of Emergence

One of the strongest arguments for panpsychism today springs from the intrinsic weakness of its main competitor: emergentism. Nearly every modern-day philosopher of mind is an emergentist. They believe that, in the distant past, mind did not exist. Today, it does. Ergo, it must have emerged, in an absolute sense, from an organic milieu that was devoid of mind. Yes, they say, this must have happened; admittedly, they are not sure when or how, but self-evidently, it must have occurred. In any case, no further need for philosophers to ponder the matter. This is a question for paleontology or physiology, not philosophy. No important philosophical issues attach to it – or so they believe.

Panpsychists reply: Not so fast. When spelled out, the emergentist position is found to be rife with problems, questions, and profound implications.

Let's recount the emergentist position a bit more carefully. They believe, explicitly or implicitly, that there was a point in the past history of the Earth – say, a few hundred million years ago – when there were no mind-bearing organisms in existence. Before Homo sapiens, before mammalian life, before any 'higher animals' at all, there were no experiencing beings on the planet. Biology ran strictly on unthinking, unperceiving, unfeeling instinct. There was no sadness, no happiness, no pain, no joy – anywhere at all on Earth. Hunger merely triggered a biological reflex to seek out food. A quenched thirst felt like nothing – rather, it was like the fuel gauge on a car: one drank, the needle 'rose,' the body was sated. When fleeing a predator, there was nothing at all like a sensation of fear; organisms simply ran, hid, or fought back. Sexual intercourse was in no sense enjoyable, but strictly a physical act that perpetuated the species.

Then, at some crucial point in organic evolution, the first enminded creature appeared. That is, *suddenly* appeared. Some first select species – and indeed, some *first individual organism* – suddenly 'felt' the world. Suddenly, the light bulb went on. Suddenly, for the first time in the known universe, an entity actually experienced reality. Pleasures and pains actually felt a certain way. Fear, happiness, anger, jealously . . . these actually now meant something. For the first time ever, it was *something to be like* a living organism (Nagel 1974).

How, panpsychists ask, did this miracle happen? How could it be that, two parental organisms – that were not 'slightly' enminded, or 'proto' enminded, but completely and utterly devoid of mind – could give birth to an offspring that, for the first time ever, experienced the world? Was it a genetic fluke? An abnormality? A naturalistic miracle? And the same miraculous event must then have occurred over and over again, countless times, to many different sets of unminded parents. And then, later, to many other species – if we accept that enmindedness extends beyond our own. The end result is that, today, we and – a few? a hundred? a thousand? – other species actually experience pain and pleasure, actually feel things, and thus are true ontological subjects.

The miraculous nature of such an event is hard to overestimate. Mind came from that which was utterly devoid of mind. Enminded children came from utterly unminded parents. Mentality, subjectivity, qualia, suddenly appeared, like a bolt from the blue, having never existed in the known universe. This is called brute emergence. Panpsychists say that's a miracle, and that miracles don't exist. Mind could never have emerged from no-mind. Therefore, it was there all along. And if it was there all along, panpsychism obtains.

Now, it's clear that this is not to say that *nothing* emerges. Emergence happens all the time, and it always has. In fact, nearly everything that we see around us emerged. Every structured being in the universe – animals, plants, rocks, planets, stars – all, at some point, did not exist; now they do; therefore they did indeed emerge.

But not everything can plausibly do so. Time, for instance, seems inconceivable to have ever emerged from a timeless cosmos. So too with space; we simply cannot conceive how spatiality could have come into being in a universe that was non-spatial. Time and space must have always existed, everywhere. They are 'pan' qualities of reality. Other entities likely fall into this non-emergent category. Mass/energy may be one. And certain subatomic qualities, like spin, charge, and quantum state, may be the same. Panpsychists add one more item to the list: mind. Experientiality, subjectivity, qualia . . . the emergence of such things is inconceivable, from a universe utterly without them. If they did, it's a true miracle. Panpsychists prefer a rational, naturalistic, and non-miraculous universe. And in such a universe, mind must have always been present.

In addition to this historical emergence problem, there are two other forms. One is what we may call the phylogenic question: Among the organisms living today, which ones possess mind? Nearly everyone grants awareness and experience to the so-called higher animals, at least. And yet no one feels competent to define these fortunate creatures. Primates, dolphins, and whales? Surely. Dogs and cats? Probably. But mice? Goldfish? Earthworms? Fruit flies? Jellyfish? Amoeba? Sponges? We can see the problem. Again, conventional philosophers can declare this a non-issue, or simply relegate it to those exploring the fringe topic of 'animal minds.' But from a perspective of understanding the ontology of mind, we need to know: Where can we draw the line? And how can we justify drawing it there? And if we can't justify it, perhaps the line does not exist. Perhaps all life, at least, is experiential.[2]

The third form of the emergence problem is ontogenic. Consider a developing human fetus. When, in the span of those nine months, does the fetus suddenly acquire a mind? For the emergentist, a fertilized egg is utterly mindless, whereas a newborn infant (presumably) is fully experiential. So the emergentist must ask, At what point in the process does the light suddenly switch on? But any answer he gives will be deficient. Is it on at 12 weeks? If so, why not at 11 weeks and 6 days? What magic happens when the fetus grows from, say 500 million cells to 500 million plus one? This is clearly ridiculous. The emergentist has no plausible and defensible answer. The panpsychist thus has the stronger case: No sudden switch happens. There is no one magic cell that turns on the light. The fetus is enminded and experiencing from Day 1 – even if at an extremely low level. For that matter, so are the unfertilized egg and every individual sperm cell.

The bottom line seems quite clear: One is either an emergentist, or one is a panpsychist. I generally try to avoid black-and-white distinctions, but this one is fairly clear cut. There is no middle ground. Either the early Earth – and the early universe – was mindless, or it wasn't. If we claim that it was originally mindless, we have an obligation to explain the miraculous, brute emergence of the experiencing subject. If we cannot explain it, the panpsychist case becomes all the stronger.

Now, all this is not to say that panpsychists don't have their own version of an emergence problem: the so-called combination problem. If, say, our individual cells are experiential, how do their lesser minds relate to our one, unified, higher-order mind? Do they compose it? If so, how does this work? Do they exist in parallel? Do we then in fact have many minds in our bodies? If so, why don't we sense this? And in any case, where does our higher-level mind come from? These are important problems that the panpsychist must address. But I emphasize: *These are lesser-order problems than that posed by brute emergence*. It is intrinsically more difficult to explain the absolute appearance of some quality, than to explain how it complexifies. If one must have problems, one generally prefers that they are at least tractable. The complexifying, combinatorial nature of mind is a riddle, but we have analytic methods to address it. Brute emergence of mind is a miracle, and little more can be said.

3. Standard Arguments: Pro and Con

Panpsychism has been an active theory in philosophy from the very beginning. The first philosopher, Thales (ca. 600 BC), was a panpsychist, and it was sustained through the pre-Socratics, Plato, Aristotle, the Stoics, and perhaps the Epicureans. It subsided during the early Christian era, but even then, the neo-Platonists held to a loose form of panpsychism, as did St. Francis. It was revived in the Renaissance by the Italian naturalists, who were in turn followed by Spinoza and Leibniz. Some two dozen major philosophers defended forms of panpsychism in the 18th and 19th centuries, and into the 20th we find it articulated by the likes of Bergson, James, Whitehead, and Russell, among many others.

Looking across the millennia, we find a recurring set of core arguments for panpsychism. Here I will briefly summarize ten of these, and list a few of their more prominent defenders. Needless to say, these are generally not analytic arguments. Nonetheless, important thinkers have found merit in them, and we owe it to ourselves to at least understand their reasons for holding such a view. Naturally, this categorization involves a fair amount of interpretation. Many individuals put forth more than one of these arguments. And some of them clearly overlap. I cannot elaborate here, but some of these individuals are examined in detail in the present volume, and in my own works (2003, 2009b, 2017).

(1) *Indwelling Powers.* All material objects exhibit certain powers or abilities that can plausibly be ascribed to some mind-like quality. Typically these relate to motion, energy, or self-preservation. Originated by Thales, attributable to such diverse thinkers as Heraclitus, Spinoza, and Fechner.

(2) *Continuity.* There is a metaphysical and ontological continuity among all objects; in humans, this accounts for our mind or soul; therefore all things possess something analogous to it. Originated by Anaximenes, attributable to the Stoics, Schopenhauer, Peirce, Whitehead.

(3) *Design.* The ordered, complex, and persistent nature of physical objects suggests the presence of an intrinsic mentality. Originated by Plato, attributable to Patrizi, Maupertuis, Fechner.

(4) *Non-Emergence.* As explained previously; sometimes called the 'genetic' argument. Originated by Epicurus, attributable to Campanella, William Clifford, and Teilhard de Chardin. Modern, analytic version of this argument presented by Galen Strawson.

(5) *Theological Argument.* God is mind and spirit; God is omnipresent; therefore mind also is omnipresent. Originated by Campanella, attributable to Henry More and Fechner.

(6) *Authority.* The sheer number of prominent panpsychists in history suggests that the view has credibility. The intuitions of great minds cannot be discounted. Originated by Bruno, attributable to Clifford, Paulsen, Hartshorne.

(7) *Naturalized Mind.* If the human mind is not to be considered an eternal mystery or a divine miracle, it must be fully integrated into the natural world, and nothing does this better than panpsychism. Attributed to Hartshorne, David Ray Griffin, and recent process philosophers.

(8) *Greater Virtue.* Panpsychism has a number of beneficial consequences for ethics, the environment, and society generally. It is a positive, generous, and expansive approach to mind. Pragmatically, it works to the benefit of all. Attributable in diverse ways to such thinkers as Plato, Campanella, Fechner, Paulsen, and others.

(9) *Last Man Standing.* The nature of mind and its relation to the body is generally a very difficult question. Every mind-body theory has major, unresolved problems. But when carefully thought through, panpsychism is the least problematic, and hence the most plausible view. Formulated by Hartshorne and Griffin, and lately appealed to by Strawson.

(10) *Intrinsic Nature.* Our knowledge of the physical world is extrinsic – that is, based on observation and physical relations. Science provides wonderfully detailed theories about these relations but tells us nothing about any possible intrinsic or 'inner' nature of material things. However, our own first-hand experience suggests that something experiential or mind-like resides at the inner core of existence. This suggests that all things, intrinsically, are mind-like or experiential. Anticipated by Leibniz and Kant, developed by Schopenhauer and Nietzsche, and made explicit by Russell. Today this approach is known as 'Russellian.'

By contrast, panpsychism has come in for criticism throughout the years, though not always of a high caliber. Due to its unconventional nature, it is more susceptible to jest and ridicule than most philosophical positions. But of course, such things do not qualify as valid counterarguments. To simply mock a panpsychist position, or to launch ad hominem attacks against a proponent, is to do nothing to refute the thesis. And we furthermore know that many times in history the apparently 'absurd' or 'outrageous' thesis has proven to be true. The following are a few examples of philosophical critiques launched at panpsychism over the years. I begin with a sampling of the polemical, superficial, and dismissive remarks, followed by the more serious arguments that have been presented.

For most of history, few felt compelled to challenge panpsychism. For reasons that are not entirely clear, we have virtually no recorded critiques prior to the 17th century; and even then, we find only indirect attacks for the next three centuries. In fact it was not until the early 1900s that philosophers began to specifically target panpsychist views for criticism. In the 1920s, for example, Yale philosopher Charles Bennett worried about the ethical implications: "Put me in a world where all is in some sense (however obscure) spirit . . . and you embarrass me strangely. Now I no longer feel free to treat any part of the material world merely as means" (1922: 89). In the 1950s, Wittgenstein gave short shrift to the view: "Can anyone imagine a stone's having consciousness?" he asked; from an analytical perspective, "such image-mongery is of no interest to us" (1953: 119). Two decades later Madden and Hare (1971: 23) wrote that panpsychism is "an unmitigated disaster in the eyes of a great majority of contemporary philosophers."

Amidst a critical analysis of dualism, Geoffrey Madell (1988: 3) remarked that

> the sense that the mental and the physical are just inexplicably and gratuitously slapped together is hardly allayed by adopting either a panpsychist or a double aspect view of the mind, for neither view has any explanation to offer as to why or how mental properties cohere with physical.

It's true that most panpsychists take mind as a brute fact of existence. But all metaphysical theories accept certain things as brute; why this counts against panpsychism is unclear. Gerald Edelman (1992: 212) briefly cited panpsychism as the "most extreme form" of attempts to "make mind and consciousness direct properties of matter." This whole approach to mind, for Edelman, is "spooky and mystical." It has no value to a rigorous scientific mind: "Most good physicists are hardly committed to notions of panpsychism."

Psychologist Nicholas Humphrey occasionally dabbles in philosophy of mind, and he too is quick to dismiss panpsychism. It is "one of those superficially attractive ideas that crumble to nothing as soon as they are asked to do any sort of explanatory work" (1992: 203). He is aware of the demand that, within a strictly materialist worldview, consciousness must, at some point, have suddenly and dramatically arisen from an utterly unminded material substrate. Panpsychists, as we saw, view this putative event as an inexplicable miracle. But Humphrey is unfazed: "consciousness quite suddenly emerged" at some unknown point in evolutionary history, he says confidently. Indeed, he is willing to designate the time before this monumental event as "BC": "before consciousness."[3]

Colin McGinn has repeatedly trash-talked panpsychism. He calls it "metaphysically and scientifically outrageous," and then asks, "Are we to suppose that rocks actually have thoughts and feelings . . .?" (1997: 34). Elsewhere he mocks the idea that consciousness is omnipresent by comparing it to the claim that "Elvis is everywhere" (1999: 95). As he sees it, panpsychism entails that "electrons and stars . . . literally feel pain, see yellow, think about dinner." It is "very hard to take . . . the theory seriously," precisely because "it is empty." More recently McGinn has declared the view to be "a complete myth, a comforting piece of utter balderdash" (2006: 93), adding: "Isn't there something vaguely hippyish, i.e. stoned, about the doctrine?" To his credit, he has also articulated some precise counterarguments; I examine those later.

John Searle is another prominent foe, who famously remarked that panpsychism is "absurd" and "breathtakingly implausible" (1997: 48). "There is not the slightest reason to adopt panpsychism," he adds (50). He repeated the same thought some years later. "Consciousness cannot be spread across the universe like a thin veneer of jam" (2013) – as if this were the view of current panpsychists. One cannot call the view false, he says; in fact, "it does not even get up to the level of being false. It is strictly speaking meaningless."

4. Substantive Critiques

Once we set aside the jokes, superficial remarks, and ad hominem attacks, we find a handful of serious counterarguments to panpsychism. I offer a relatively detailed discussion of the first – the combination problem – and then cite some representative views for the others.

(1) **The combination problem**. For centuries it has been recognized that there is a potentially serious problem if one considers the possibility that mind exists simultaneously at both

higher and lower scales of being. If, for example, the cells that make up an animal are presumed to be sentient or conscious in any fashion, a question immediately arises: How do the minds of the cells relate to, or perhaps constitute, the mind of the whole organism? If the lesser minds are distinct, why are we not aware of competing subjects within ourselves? If the lesser minds constitute or compose 'our' mind, how, exactly, does this work? It seems impossible to imagine how, for example, a billion individually sentient neurons could give rise to a singular and unified sense of consciousness at all.

And there are other issues. Our neural cells, for example, are themselves composed of smaller structures like molecules, atoms, and subatomic particles. Does each level of organization possess its own mind? If so, then any complex being is a nested hierarchy of vast mental complexity.[4] Nietzsche believed this to be the case; he held that "our body is but a social structure composed of many souls" (1886/1973: § 19). And furthermore, does the nesting process continue 'upward,' that is, to higher orders of being? To a social mind? A global mind? Or a cosmic mind? Is the universe a vast cosmopolis of enminded beings?

Needless to say, this situation poses, if not a 'problem,' then at least a very large question for any panpsychist. Perhaps the first to recognize, and criticize, panpsychism on this basis was Ralph Cudworth. He criticized the materialist "hylozoick atheists," of whom Spinoza was the leading culprit, writing as follows:

> Moreover, this hylozoick atheism was long since, and in the first emersion thereof, solidly confuted by the atomic atheists, after this manner: if matter as such had life, perception, and understanding belonging to it, then of necessity must every atom or smallish particle thereof, be a distinct percipient by itself. From whence it will follow that there could not possibly be any such men and animals as now are, compounded out of them, but every man and animal would be a heap of innumerable percipients, and have innumerable perceptions and intellections. Whereas it is plain that there is but one life and understanding, one soul or mind, one perceiver or thinker in everyone.
>
> And to say that these innumerable particles of matter do all confederate together – that is to make every man and animal, to be a multitude or commonwealth of percipients and persons, as it were, clubbing together – is a thing so absurd and ridiculous, that one would wonder, the Hylozoists should not choose to recant that their fundamental error of the life of matter, than seek shelter and sanctuary for the same, under such a Proteus.
>
> For though voluntary agents and persons, may many of them, resign up their wills to one, and by that means have all but as it were one artificial will, yet can they not possibly resign up their sense and understanding too, so as to have all but one artificial life, sense, and understanding. Much less could this be done by senseless atoms, or particles of matter supposed to be devoid of all consciousness or animality.
>
> (1678/2011: 290)

Less than a century later, Diderot acknowledged the problem but found it to be no real obstacle to establishing the existence of a collective mind. Referring to a swarm of bees, he wrote that "the cluster is a being, an individual, an animal of sorts." Tight interaction – "continual action and reaction" – is sufficient to establish the unity of the collective mass. "It seems to me that contact, in itself, is enough" (1769/1937: 67, 76).

In one of his early writings, Kant made a passing reference to the combination problem. Reflecting on Leibniz's panpsychism, he wrote,

> Everybody recognizes [that] even if a power of obscure conception [i.e. perception or intelligence] is conceded to . . . matter, it does not follow thence that matter itself possesses

power of conception, because many substances of that kind, united into a whole, can yet never form a thinking unit.

(1766/1900: 54)

The same thought recurred in his *Critique of Pure Reason* (1781), in which he argued that material composites are possible and occur via simple aggregation but that this is not possible with mental substances:

Every *composite* substance is an aggregate of several substances, and the action of a composite, or whatever inheres in it as thus composite, is an aggregate of several actions or accidents, distributed among the plurality of the substances. . . . But with thoughts, as internal accidents belonging to a thinking being, it is different. For suppose it be the composite that thinks: then every part of it would be a part of the thought, and only all of them taken together would contain the whole thought. But this cannot consistently be maintained. For representations (for instance, the single words of a verse), distributed among different beings, never make up a whole thought (a verse), and it is therefore impossible that a thought should inhere in what is essentially composite. It is therefore possible only in a *single* substance, which, not being an aggregate of many, is absolutely simple.

(1781: A352)

Mental combination, it seems, is impossible, on Kant's view.

William James is well known for addressing the combination problem, and for his evolving opinion of it. Early in his career, he viewed it as an insurmountable problem, at least for any 'mind stuff' theory of consciousness. The very notion of lower-order mental subjects, or mind-atoms, compounding into more complex minds is "logically unintelligible" because such entities would have to combine upon some non-mental basis (1890/1950: 149–55). His mature thinking, however, reversed this view. In *A Pluralistic Universe* (1909) James dedicates an entire chapter to "the compounding of consciousness." Here he recalls his earlier thinking with disdain:

Twelve thoughts, each of a single word, are not the self-same mental thing as one thought of the whole sentence. The higher thoughts, I insisted [earlier], are psychic units, not compounds. . . . The theory of combination, I was forced to conclude is thus untenable.

(189)

"For many years I held rigorously to this view," he writes. Now, though, he realizes that it "is almost intolerable. . . . It makes the universe discontinuous" (206). If analytic logic drives one to believe in isolated minds, "so much the worse for logic." Hence his final view: "the self-compounding of mind in its smaller and more accessible portions seems a certain fact. . . . Mental facts do function both singly and together, at once" (292). Composition of minds is an evident truth; any so-called combination problem does not exist.

But the issue retains force even to the present. McGinn (2006) calls it the 'derivation problem.' Physical or spatial combination yields many possibilities, but "there is no analogous notion of combination for qualia . . . you can't put qualia end-to-end" (96). Thus, he says, "we cannot envisage a small number of experiential primitives yielding a rich variety of phenomenologies; we have to postulate richness all the way down, more or less." And this, he implies, is unacceptable. Lycan makes a similar point: high-level mental properties "must be a function of the mental properties inhering in their subjects' ultimate components. How could that be?" We cannot even imagine "in what way a mental aggregate [could] consist of a host of smaller mentations" (2011: 362).

Perhaps. But then again, *all* theories of mind and body yield outcomes that are presently "hard to imagine." It's true that the panpsychist needs to explain the emergence of complex mind from simpler mind, but as I stated earlier, this emergence problem is much more tractable than the miraculous, brute emergence of mind from no-mind. Our current concepts in physics, in fact, give us some models by which to conceive panpsychist emergence – field theory, for example, in which distinct fields combine, overlap, and sum up to larger, more complex fields. Quantum physics may provide yet other options, including superposition. Any of these is preferable to imagining the unimaginable: mind, consciousness, and experience emerging from that which is utterly without.

(2) **Brute emergence**. Perhaps, says the critic, brute emergence is not so inconceivable after all. To this most difficult question, Paul Edwards (1972) has a "simple answer" – essentially, reductive materialism combined with epiphenomenalism. The strong or brute emergentist need simply claim that matter, at some sufficient level of complexity, causes the appearance of mind, but that this same mind has in turn no causal effect back on the material substrate. "Granting that awareness is not a physical phenomenon, it does not follow that it cannot be produced by conditions that are purely physical" (27). But what these special and unique conditions are, he does not say. And his theory naturally implies that human minds are epiphenomenal as well – something that few philosophers accept.

Karl Popper (1977) also defends brute emergence. Solidity, he says, radically emerges when a liquid is cooled. Hence radical emergence is no miracle at all. And when a child grows into an adult, its mind correspondingly grows in complexity, but this does not imply that the food the child eats, and uses to build its brain, is itself enminded or proto-mental. The unminded food particles, when properly integrated into a nervous system, do in fact yield consciousness. Hence, once again, brute emergence is clearly possible. But of course, all this is just an assertion: it *must* happen, and therefore it does. This is question-begging.

As I noted earlier, Humphrey too accepts the thesis of radical emergence. Feedback loops, he says, have an all-or-nothing quality. And the nervous system is a kind of complex feedback loop. "Hence, we may guess that, as the sensory loops grew shorter in the course of evolution and their fidelity increased, there must have been a threshold where consciousness quite suddenly emerged" (1992: 205–6). A "guess," however, is not a rational argument. It would take much more theorizing, backed by some considerable indirect empirical evidence, before such a thesis could be accepted.

(3) **Inconclusive analogy**. Also known as the 'not mental' objection. This is functionally a response to both the continuity and intrinsic nature arguments mentioned previously, and was first raised by Edwards. Continuity panpsychists attempt to make a comparison between organic and inorganic things, but "the analogies are altogether inconclusive" (1972: 28). Edwards grants that such things as atomic structure, hierarchical organization, persistence, and laws of physics may be common to all material objects, but he argues that we have no reason to associate these with mental properties. A similar argument is discussed by Seager (1995) and Lycan (2011), who cast it in terms of intrinsic natures. Lycan briefly cites two objections: First, "what grounds the assumption that the ultimate constituents of the physical world must have intrinsic properties at all?" (360). Perhaps, he suggests, extrinsic relationships and properties are all there are to such particles. Second, even if we decide that they must have some intrinsic nature, why assume it is mental, or conscious?

But panpsychists have a ready reply: Mind and experience is the most basic fact of human existence, and physicalism still must account for it. At present, it cannot. It's plausible that physicalism is inherently unable to this, since it has access only to the 'outsides' of things – their properties and relationships. And yet we know, on the 'inside,' that mind exists. Our inner nature certainly seems to be mental, and it's very likely that the same holds for the higher animals, at least. But then we cannot justify stopping anywhere along the phylogenetic chain, and hence panpsychism obtains.

(4) **Not testable**. Also known as the 'no signs' objection. Edwards (1972: 28) states that there can be no empirical evidence for panpsychism, hence it is unverifiable, hence non-scientific. "It would probably be pointless to try to 'prove' that panpsychism is a meaningless doctrine." McGinn (1999: 96–7)

says, "regular matter gives no sign of having such mental states: things simply do not behave as if they are in pain or want a drink of water." Furthermore,

> physicists have discovered no reason to attribute sensations and thoughts to atoms and stars. They get on perfectly well without supposing matter in general to have mind ticking away inside it. If electrons have mental properties, these properties make no difference to the laws that govern electrons.
>
> (1999: 97)

Paul Churchland (1997: 213) remarks that "modern atomism's experimental and explanatory successes" are vast and well-documented, whereas that of panpsychism "is approximately zero." Modern science can explain chemical elements, formation of stars, evolution, functioning of the nervous system – on and on. "At present panpsychism can do none of these things. Not even one. . . . No pressing explanatory job exists for it to do." And likewise for Lycan: "panpsychism's most obvious liability is the absence of scientific evidence" (2011: 361).

In principle, however, this is little different than arguing that neuro-chemical transactions in the brain are sufficient to explain human behavior, and that we therefore have no need to posit the existence of a mind. At a physical level, brain action can – theoretically – account for everything we do. As with humans, it's unreasonable to demand "tests" or "signs" of subjectivity.

5) **Supervenience**. McGinn asks, "Are the [experiential] properties of particles supervenient on their non-[experiential] properties or not?" This is the standard view of reductive materialists; mind supervenes on the brain. Either way that the panpsychist answers this question, says McGinn, he runs into trouble. If not, then two particles could be physically identical and yet have radically different experiential states. But this leads back to the 'no signs' problem, and it suggests epiphenomenalism (see next). If particle minds do supervene on their physical properties, "it will be hard to avoid accepting that there is *emergence* there – that combining the [non-experiential] properties in that way gives rise to the [experiential] properties" (2006: 94–5).

6) **Epiphenomenalism**. "A more worrying difficulty for the panpsychist is the threat of epiphenomenalism," says Lycan (2011: 362). Physics is causally closed, and thus any putative atomic minds have no causal role to play. "They are brought into existence only to do nothing at all." This is an *a priori* 'no signs' problem – not only are there no signs of mentality, there can *never* be any signs. The panpsychist, of course, can simply respond that epiphenomenalism holds for all minds, human and atom alike. This may be distasteful to some, but there is no logical problem in holding such a view.

7) **Irrelevance**. As a final counterargument, some ask: What's the point of positing atomic minds if we do not, and cannot, have any conception whatsoever of what they are like? "What kinds of [experiential] properties do particles have?" asks McGinn (2006: 95). Presuming that atomic minds somehow contribute to or compose our high-level mental states, "they are going to have to be rich and wide-ranging: not just sensory states but also emotional states, conative states, and cognitive states." But such things are inconceivable. We cannot simply postulate their existence. "This is a game without rules and without consequences," he says. Lycan (2011: 363) makes a similar point. "What sorts of mental properties in particular do the smallest things have?" To presume the existence of sensory or intentional states is "ludicrous." "How could [an atom] see, hear, or smell anything? What would be the contents of its beliefs or desires?"

In sum, these counterarguments generally raise valid and important points. But none of them are insurmountable. In large part, they are calls for details. In order to be more widely accepted, panpsychists need to articulate a clear theory of mind and justify its universal extent. They need to delineate precisely which objects are enminded, and in what way. And they need to clearly demonstrate the philosophic payoff – conceptually, metaphysically, ethically – in accepting the truth of panpsychism.

On the other hand, some critics seem to be terminally dissatisfied. Either they have ruled out panpsychism *a priori*, and thus no case, no matter how compelling, can win them over; or they make outrageous and impossible demands of the thesis. A good example of the latter is Churchland. He closes his short critique with the following:

> Unless panpsychism constructs . . . theoretical proposals and testable hypotheses, and unless it achieves some systematic successes in experimental predictions and technological control, it will continue to appear to be . . . a theoretical hangover from a less knowledgeable time.
>
> (1997: 212)

Is it reasonable to demand of any theory (or meta-theory) of mind that it yield "testable hypotheses," "experimental prediction," and "technological control"? Surely not. Such things apply only to mechanistic conceptions; if these are prerequisites for acceptable solutions, the space of possibilities becomes absurdly small.

The following point must be emphasized: When it comes to the mind, we are faced with an array of difficult propositions. Every theory has significant, unresolved problems, open issues, or distasteful implications. This is striking, given that the mind is the one thing in this universe with which we are most intimately acquainted – precisely because we *are* that thing. Matter is much more poorly understood; we know its extrinsic, functional, and structural nature, but really nothing more. We presume that there is nothing mental about matter, but this is sheer presumption, and a baseless one at that. As Strawson (2015: 203) emphasizes, "There is no evidence – there is precisely zero evidence – for the existence of non-experiential reality." The famed causal closure of physics says nothing against experiential matter. Matter can follow all its usual deterministic or quantum laws, without infringing one iota on experiential or even intentional qualities. Epiphenomenalism may hold after all. Or, as I have argued elsewhere, the causal closure of the physical may be mirrored by the causal closure of the mental (Skrbina 2014: 240).

In the end, a strong case can be made that panpsychism is in fact the most plausible, the most reasonable, and hence the most likely true conception of mind. Strawson puts the point well:

> One should, I believe, endorse the thesis of the *theoretical primacy of panpsychism*. According to this thesis, unprejudiced consideration of what we know about concrete reality obliges us to favour some version of panpsychism . . . over all other positive substantive theories of the intrinsic non-structural nature of reality. . . . In its strongest form, the thesis is not just that it would take extraordinarily hard work to justify preferring any substantive metaphysical position that isn't panpsychist. . . . It's rather that it can't be done.
>
> (2015: 203)

This is a remarkably forceful assessment. Panpsychism, he says, should be considered the default conception of mind – only to be displaced on the (highly unlikely) possibility that it can be rationally demonstrated to be false. We have good reason to accept it, and none to dispute it.

Yet this will hardly impress panpsychism's critics. Mainstream philosophers of mind are explicitly or implicitly committed to mechanistic materialism and brute emergence of mind, and they are loath to give them up. This suggests an interesting situation: that we have the makings of a classic paradigm shift. Often it happens, in science and in philosophy, that the majority viewpoint on some controversial topic becomes entrenched and cannot be dislodged by rational argumentation. Despite the growing strength of a new opposing view, the majority clings tenaciously to its traditional position. Nothing will dissuade them. And yet the opposing view grows in strength and numbers, typically among the younger members of the discipline. In the end, the majority never changes their minds; they simply die off. And then the new view ascends to prominence.

Perhaps something of the sort will happen here. In this case, of course, it is not something that is 'new,' but rather something *renewed* – rediscovered, refurbished, reexamined. From the 16th through 19th centuries, panpsychism was a commonplace, even dominant position in philosophy. It was articulated in different ways by many of the leading thinkers of the day. With the coming of analytic philosophy and logical positivism in the early 20th century, panpsychism was driven down, and then largely forgotten for nearly a century. Only in the 1990s did the panpsychist movement reawaken. With skepticism growing about the viability of mechanistic materialism, and with the ongoing failure to resolve mind-body problems within this dominant paradigm, the time may be approaching where panpsychism is once again accorded a large degree of respect. It may once again be accepted as a true and naturalistic account of the mind.

Notes

1. "This world . . . is a blessed god" (*Timaeus* 34b). See also *Timaeus* (55d, 92c).
2. There are obvious implications here for environmental ethics and animal rights. As I stated earlier, panpsychism has important ethical consequences. For one approach, see my (2013).
3. In a particularly striking example of an ad hominem attack, Humphrey issued a public diatribe in 2011 against Galen Strawson, calling him "not only an intellectual ass but unscholarly and lazy too." "His ideas about panpsychism have made him a laughing stock," wrote Humphrey; hence we must "consign him to the nursery." See Skrbina (2017: 295).
4. Leibniz's monadology proposed something very close to this view.

Bibliography

Agar, W. (1943). *A Contribution to the Theory of the Living Organism*. Melbourne, Australia: Melbourne University Press.
Bennett, C. (1922). 'Review of *Volonte et Conscience*'. *Philosophical Review*, 37: 86–90.
Bohm, D. (1982). 'Nature as Creativity'. *ReVision*, 5 (2): 35–40.
Bradley, F. (1893/1930). *Appearance and Reality*. Gloucestershire: Clarendon Press.
Churchland, P. (1997). 'Panpsychism: A Brief Critique'. In C. Butler (ed.), *History as the Story of Freedom*. Amsterdam: Rodopi, pp. 211–16.
Cudworth, R. (1678/2011). 'The True Intellectual System of the Universe'. In W. Uzgalis (ed.), *The Correspondence of Samuel Clarke and Anthony Collins*. Peterborough, ON: Broadview, pp. 285–92.
Diderot, D. (1769/1937). 'D'Alembert's Dream'. In J. Steward and J. Kemp (trans.), *Diderot: Interpreter of Nature*. London: Lawrence and Wishart.
Edelman, G. (1992). *Bright Air, Brilliant Fire*. New York: Basic.
Edwards, P. (1972). 'Panpsychism'. In *Encyclopedia of Philosophy*. New York: Macmillan.
Haldane, J. B. S. (1932). *The Inequality of Man*. London: Chatto & Windus.
Haldane, J. B. S. (1934). 'Quantum Mechanics as a Basis for Philosophy'. *Philosophy of Science*, 1: 78–98.
Humphrey, N. (1992). *A History of the Mind*. London: Chatto & Windus.
Hutto, D. (2000). *Beyond Physicalism*. Amsterdam: Benjamins.
James, W. (1890/1950). *Principles of Psychology*. New York: Dover.
James, W. (1909/1996). *A Pluralistic Universe*. Lincoln, NE: University of Nebraska Press.
Kant, I. (1766/1900). *Dreams of a Spirit-Seer*. New York: Macmillan.
Kant, I. (1781/1965). *Critique of Pure Reason*. New York: St. Martin's.
Lycan, W. (2011). 'Recent Naturalistic Dualisms'. In A. Lange et al. (eds.), *Light Against Darkness*. Göttingen: Vandenhoeck & Ruprecht, pp. 348–63.
Madden, E., and Hare, P. (1971). 'The Powers That Be'. *Dialogue*, 10 (1): 12–31.
Madell, G. (1988). *Mind and Materialism*. Edinburgh: Edinburgh University Press.
McGinn, C. (1997). *The Character of Mind*. Oxford: Oxford University Press.
McGinn, C. (1999). *The Mysterious Flame*. New York: Basic.
McGinn, C. (2006). 'Hard Questions'. In A. Freeman (ed.), *Consciousness and Its Place in Nature*. Exeter: Imprint Academic, pp. 90–9.
Nagel, T. (1974). 'What is It Like to Be a Bat?' *Philosophical Review*, 83 (4): 435–50.
Nietzsche, F. (1886/1973). *Beyond Good and Evil*. Trans. W. Kaufmann. New York: Penguin.

Partridge, E. (1984). 'Nature as a Moral Resource'. *Environmental Ethics*, 6 (2): 101–30.

Popper, K., and Eccles, J. (1977). *The Self and Its Brain*. Berlin: Springer.

Royce, J. (1892/1955). *Spirit of Modern Philosophy*. Boston: Houghton Mifflin.

Royce, J. (1899). *The World and the Individual*. New York: Macmillan.

Seager, W. (1995). 'Consciousness, Information, and Panpsychism'. *Journal of Consciousness Studies*, 2 (3): 272–88.

Searle, J. (1997). 'Consciousness and the Philosophers'. *New York Review of Books*, 44 (4).

Searle, J. (2013). 'Can Information Theory Explain Consciousness?' *New York Review of Books*, 60 (1).

Skrbina, D. (2003). 'Panpsychism as an Underlying Theme in Western Philosophy'. *Journal of Consciousness Studies*, 10 (3): 4–46.

Skrbina, D. (2009a). 'Minds, Objects, and Relations'. In D. Skrbina (ed.), *Mind That Abides*. Amsterdam: Benjamins, pp. 361–82.

Skrbina, D. (2009b). 'Panpsychism in History'. In D. Skrbina (ed.), *Mind That Abides*. Amsterdam: Benjamins, pp. 1–32.

Skrbina, D. (2013). 'Ethics, Eco-Philosophy, and Universal Sympathy'. *Dialogue and Universalism*, 23 (4): 59–74.

Skrbina, D. (2014). 'Dualism, Dual-Aspectism, and the Mind'. In A. Lavazza and H. Robinson (eds.), *Contemporary Dualism*. London: Routledge, pp. 220–44.

Skrbina, D. (2017). *Panpsychism in the West*, revised edition. Cambridge, MA: MIT Press.

Strawson, G. (2006). 'Realistic Monism: Why Physicalism Entails Panpsychism'. In A. Freeman (ed.), *Consciousness and Its Place in Nature*. Exeter: Imprint Academic, pp. 3–31.

Strawson, G. (2015). 'Postscript to "Real Materialism"'. In T. Alter and Y. Nagasawa (eds.), *Consciousness in the Physical World*. Oxford: Oxford University Press, pp. 201–8.

Wittgenstein, L. (1953). *Philosophical Investigations*. New York: Macmillan.

PART II

Forms of Panpsychism

11

BEYOND COSMOPSYCHISM AND THE GREAT I AM

How the World Might be Grounded in Universal 'Advaitic' Consciousness

Miri Albahari

Manifestation needs time and space, but the source of [personalised] consciousness was there before manifestation took place.

(Maharaj 1985: 86)

It is because consciousness is unborn and undying that the millions of forms get created and destroyed; it is a continuous process. . . . Please understand that . . . you are the form-less, timeless unborn. It is because of your identification with the body as an entity that your consciousness, which is universal consciousness, thinks that it is dying. Nobody is dying, because nobody was born. . . . Only that in which consciousness manifests itself is limited and created and destroyed. The total potential of consciousness remains. It is unlimited.

(Maharaj 1994: 32–3)

1. Introduction

In 1946, Aldous Huxley proceeded to collate what he took to be evidence for an 'inexhaustible' and 'perennial' theme first expressed in writing 25 centuries ago and subsequently recurring from within the ambit of many religious traditions, including those of Christian mysticism, Taoism, Hinduism and Buddhism. This theme, says Huxley, expresses a metaphysics that:

recognises a divine Reality substantial to the world of things and lives and minds; the psy-chology that finds in the soul something similar to, or even identical with, divine Reality; the ethic that places man's final end in the knowledge of the immanent and transcendent Ground of all being – the thing is immemorial and universal.

(1946: 9)

The core ideas have arguably found their most explicit articulation within the Advaita Vedanta tradi-tion, whose Upanisadic origins owe their particular formulation to 8th-century figure Adi Sankara, and whose philosophy has found expression in the words of recent figures acclaimed to have awoken to its ultimate reality (the opening quotes by Nisargadatta Maharaj are from such a figure). From the body of Advaitic writings can be extrapolated four main tenets which, following Huxley, I allude to as the 'Perennial Philosophy':

1. All that appears as concrete reality – the spatio-temporal universe with its furniture of tables, pebbles, stars, atoms, cats, human beings – is fundamentally grounded in 'universal consciousness', which is beyond the subject/object division, beyond the bounds of space and time, completely self-subsistent.
2. Universal consciousness forms the common backdrop to all individual conscious experience.
3. What inhibits full direct realisation of our conscious nature as identical to universal consciousness as ground of all being is the sense of being a separate self, or 'I'. The self is a cognitive illusion that makes the nature of consciousness appear intrinsically confined to the focal perspective of a personal subject.
4. It is possible, via meditation techniques, to eliminate the illusion of self, such that one fully, directly and non-discursively realises one's fundamental grounding as universal consciousness. While post-realised perception continues to nominally operate via a subject/object framework, there is no longer an *identity* with the confines of a subject. The realisation involves a permanent transformative experience that axiologically and noetically forms the apex of human potential, unleashing native capacities for boundless happiness, benevolence and compassion.

Taken together these four tenets, expounding a form of idealism, would be extraordinary if true. Yet there has been no real investigation or defence of the Advaitic/Perennialist position within Western philosophy.[1] While a notion of universal consciousness was expressed through variants of sometimes theistic absolute idealism prevalent in the latter part of the 19th century (e.g. in Bradley), such consciousness was never linked to any radically transformative experience or methodology that would make it fully and non-discursively available to the human mind.[2] And while universal consciousness has found a recent revival in a non-pantheistic variant called 'cosmopsychism', the consciousness, bestowed to the cosmos, is again not generally touted as epistemically fully available to humans.[3] Cosmopsychism also differs from Perennialism by virtue of the fact that universal consciousness, as with many idealist predecessors, is usually cast as belonging to a fundamental cosmic mind or subject which directly experiences or somehow grounds our conscious lives as its objectual content.[4] (We can take 'subject' to mean 'conscious focal perspective'; and 'object' to broadly mean anything a subject can focus on within its perspective – more later). By contrast, Perennialism casts universal consciousness as (1) beyond any duality between subject and object – 'Advaita' literally means 'non-dual' – (2) not attributable to the cosmos; it grounds it, so is beyond space and time, and (3) fully and non-discursively available to the human mind via deep transformative experience.

While Western philosophy has developed notions of universal consciousness, the field has also independently harboured some excellent scholarly accounts of Advaita Vedanta, which sometimes compare it to the writings of other traditions and thinkers.[5] But to my knowledge there has yet to be a serious Western philosophical attempt to bring the ideas of Advaita Vedanta and universal consciousness together, through fully investigating or defending the four Perennialist pillars as a standalone metaphysical system.[6] By sketching a metaphysical outline for the Perennialist position, partly in response to difficulties raised by the cosmopsychic alternative, this chapter attempts to redress the balance.

As addressing all four tenets is well outside the scope of a single chapter, I will be endeavouring to sketch an outline for tenets 1 and 2 – that the world is grounded in a non-dual universal consciousness that forms the background to our own conscious experience. Tenets 3 and 4 will nevertheless serve to constrain the kind of outline that can be sketched. Universal consciousness must be construed in a way that makes it possible to be humanly experienced; the story has to make *psychological* as well as logical sense. With this in mind, the chapter will proceed as follows. Section 1 will set out what I think are some serious troubles for cosmopsychism and some of its idealist predecessors. I will close by suggesting that these troubles can be overcome by a Perennialist approach, which will bring its own challenges. Section 2 will attempt to make conceptual sense of a universal 'non-dual' consciousness. Section 3 will sketch the outline of a metaphysical model for how the appearance of concrete objects could be grounded in such consciousness. I will conclude with some cautionary remarks about the limits of discursive thought in relation to Perennialist claims about grounding.

2. Troubles for Cosmopsychism

This anthology is testament to the fact that panpsychism has made a revival. Its most prevalent version is the pluralist view that consciousness belongs fundamentally to the micro-physical ultimates, perhaps qualifying their categorical nature. The most intractable difficulty with the position, in what is known as the 'combination problem', asks how micro-subjects, in virtue of their conscious properties, could combine to form macro-subjects such as ourselves. Nothing about their individual phenomenal natures seems to necessitate the fact that, when combined in a particular way, they will form a larger unitary subject; it seems an utter mystery.[7] It is largely in response to this difficulty that a successor to absolute idealism has resurfaced in the form of cosmopsychism. Strictly speaking, cosmopsychism is not fully-fledged idealism, as consciousness does not ground the cosmos; rather, it characterises the deep intrinsic nature of this fundamental material entity (so is compatible with Russellian monism). The prevailing versions, like most of their predecessors, also take their fundament to be a *conscious subject of experience* that grounds our own conscious perspectives and their contents.

Two such recent proponents of cosmopsychism, Philip Goff (2017) and Itay Shani (2015), see a natural ally in Jonathan Schaffer's (2010) priority monism. For Schaffer, the cosmos exists as the sole fundamental concrete entity that grounds all other less basic entities, which can be considered parts of, or abstractions from, the unified whole. While grounding is a topic unto itself, it can for these purposes be thought of as a relation of metaphysical dependence between facts, whereby the grounded facts hold in virtue of the more fundamental grounding fact(s). According to Goff, when the inner nature of the cosmos is considered to be a conscious perspectival subject, it yields a grounding relation that solves the combination problem, or its reverse, which I think is best termed the 'decombination problem': how a whole conscious unity can coherently decombine into, or necessitate, smaller conscious unities.[8] Goff proposes that the fundamental cosmic subject contains within its unified conscious field each of our perspectives and their conscious experiences as its abstractable parts, just as our own conscious field contains various sensory experiences as parts. To take a toy example, if subject A experiences pain, and B experiences redness, and C has an experience of buzzing, then each of these subjects has their experience in virtue of fact that the fundamental cosmic subject S has a unified experience to its overarching perspective, involving pain-to-perspective-A, red-to-perspective-B and buzzing-to-perspective-C. This way of grounding each subject and all their experiences in the cosmic consciousness appears to satisfy what Goff, adapting Armstrong, calls the 'free lunch constraint' for a theory of fundamental reality, on which the less fundamental facts (in this case, those of the smaller subjects) are satisfactorily explained by the fundamental fact (the cosmic subject) – in this instance, by being intuitively nothing over and above it. Through each of us inheriting our subjecthood directly from the conscious field of the cosmic subject that contains them, the decombination problem is averted.

Central to this argument, as Goff notes, is the fact that even if we cannot actively imagine one conscious mind set up to subsume the perspectives of smaller conscious minds, the scenario reveals no contradiction or *a priori* incoherence. But I contend that further probing *does* reveal the scenario to be incoherent. The critique originates in two objections made by William James (1909) in *The Pluralistic Universe* towards the prevalent 19th-century idealism. While his objections target an absolute subject that is omniscient and eternal, I will suggest that they can be redirected, with dev-astating effect, towards Goff's position. The decombination problem that each objection exemplifies re-appears.

James's first objection, which I'll call the 'epistemic problem', is as follows:

> we experience ourselves ignorantly and in division. We indeed differ from the absolute not only by defect, but by excess. Our ignorances, for example, bring curiosities and doubts by which it cannot be troubled, for it owns eternally the solution of every problem. Our impotence entails pains, our imperfection sins, which its perfection keeps at a distance.
>
> (1909: Lecture V)

The epistemic problem arises from furnishing the 'absolute's' epistemically all-encompassing per-spective with content that also belongs to its smaller relatively ignorant perspectives. The ignorance owed to a subject's finite nature generates mental content, such as fear of mortality, that cannot be coherently ascribed to an absolute in the know. In reply, Goff is likely to point out that far from being omniscient, the conscious cosmos may well be a 'blobby mess' to which predicates like 'intel-ligent' or 'rational' don't apply. But the core of the epistemic problem does not disappear. Consider Fiona's intense and pervasive fear that she will be annihilated upon death, a fear whose first-personal character is partly owed to its mind-dominating nature. Goff's cosmic subject must directly experi-ence not only Fiona's intense fear of dying but also Fred's overwhelming excitement at his impend-ing reincarnation. Yet qualifying just a fraction of the cosmic mind, it's hard to envisage how each emotion could, from the personal cosmic perspective, retain their defining first-personal characters *as* intense and dominating, and hence as those particular emotions. It is also difficult to conceive of how the cosmic subject could first-personally harbour what would, to its singular conscious perspec-tive, be the mass of everyone's contradicting beliefs and identities, e.g. 'there is only one life', 'there is more than one life', 'I am Fiona', 'I am Fred'.[9] These epistemic considerations make Goff's subject-grounding scenario not only unimaginable, but I suggest, incoherent.

James's second objection, which I'll call the 'perspective problem' is as follows:

> It is impossible to reconcile the peculiarities of our experience with our being only the absolute's mental objects. . . . They are there only for their thinker, and only as he thinks them. How, then, can they become severally alive on their own accounts and think them-selves quite otherwise than as he [the absolute] thinks them? It is as if the characters in a novel were to get up from the pages, and walk away and transact business of their own outside of the author's story.
>
> (1909: Lecture V)

The perspective problem trades on the idea that the specific perspectival character and content of thoughts and experiences is determined by and available only to their thinker as they are thought up. But Goff's scenario requires that our seemingly unique perspectives also exist as mental objects for the conscious cosmos. The lurking incoherence is made more explicit in a version of the perspective objection by Sam Coleman (2014), discussed at length by Shani. Like James's version, it doubles as a variant of both the decombination and combination problem through insisting that perspectives cannot, as a matter of logical fact, survive being subsumed by a larger perspective. In summarising Coleman's objection, Shani writes:

> He asks us to imagine two micro-subjects, Red and Blue, such that Red sees only red, while Blue seems only blue. Red and Blue combine, in turn, to form a macro-subject, call it Mac, which integrates the phenomenal worlds into a single perspective. The problem,

says Coleman, is that Red's and Blue's perspective do not survive as *points of view* within Mac's unified perspective. For example, Red's take on the world is that of seeing red, to the exclusion of all else, but Mac's perspective defies this condition: it may contain seeing blue, in addition to seeing red, or it may simply consist of seeing purple ... the original perspectives have disappeared from sight.

(2015: 401)

While Goff's subject-grounding scenario seems clearly impaled on this objection, reinforcing its incoherence, Shani, whose cosmopsychism is also theoretically committed to Schaffer's priority monism, believes that he has a way out. He responds to the perspective problem by evoking a notion of partial grounding. If A only partially grounds B, A does not fully ground and thereby entail B, as it does on Goff's position; rather, B's features are intelligibly traceable, in part, to A (2015: 403–6). To see how this is employed to solve the problem, I need to say more about the outline of Shani's rich and nuanced position. The cosmic absolute is a vast conscious plenum that operates by what he calls the 'lateral duality principle', whereupon the absolute has a concealed as well as revealed nature. Concealed to our perspective is the absolute's subjective interiority – its first-person perspective – a dynamic and sentient sea of consciousness (or as he calls it, 'endo-phenomenological expanse') whose constant creative activity is revealed to us as its outer expressions in our familiar physical environment. Embedded in this environment are quasi-independent patterns that emerge and co-evolve like vortices on an oceanic plenum, some of which are subjects of experience (2015: 410–14).

Each such concrete perspective, although anchored in the absolute, has, as localised interference patterns, its own interiority (with perspectival thoughts, perceptions etc.) whose specific character is concealed from all other perspectives, including that of the absolute. Yet the global sentient and perspectival nature of the absolute's conscious field – its unifying 'light', as it were – imparts sentience (generalised what-it-is-likeness) and perspectivality (a first-personal perspective to whom the contents are presented) to the smaller subjects. So while these generic structural features of our conscious lives are, as on Goff's view, directly inherited from the shared medium of the absolute's conscious field, the specific hidden interiority to our conscious life is intelligibly explained, via partial grounding, as localised patterns in this sentient medium, avoiding the perspective (and epistemic) problem (2015: 425–7). The free lunch constraint appears to be met, and the decombination problem averted.

But if he avoids this problem, he falls into the trap of another. As with Goff's view, the absolute is stipulated by Shani to be a subject of experience who is aware of various contents as its objects. He correctly notes that part of what it means to *be* a conscious subject is for any contents within its field of consciousness to be disclosed to its first-personal perspective (2015: 426) – what Dan Zahavi (2005) calls their first-person givenness or for-me-ness. At the same time Shani wants to insist that the contents of our conscious fields, while embedded within the absolute's field of consciousness, are hidden to the absolute's perspective. But he cannot have it both ways. If our conscious perspectives and their contents are to be embedded within – and illuminated by the sentience of – the absolute's conscious field, then, given that the absolute is a subject, our contents (and perhaps perspectives) must also, by definition, be first-personally revealed to the absolute's perspective. This then either contradicts his claim about hidden contents, forcing his position back to what we can collectively call the 'incoherent contents objection' (with its epistemic and perspective problems) or it forces him to abandon the claim that the absolute is actually a subject of experience (that must be aware of what is in its field of consciousness).

A possible way out, following Freya Mathews (2011), might be to deploy a psychoanalytic analogy, insisting that those aspects of the cosmic subject that ground smaller conscious subjects are *as part of it* entirely unconscious and thus closed off to its perspective. But now it is not clear how Mathews meets the free lunch constraint, by which the generic *conscious* features of the smaller subjects are supposed to be adequately explained by their *unconscious* cosmic ground. Goff's and Shani's scenarios, assuming coherence of initial set-ups, did better in satisfying this constraint, our conscious subject-hood straight-forwardly inheriting its generic features, sentience and perspectivality, from the conscious cosmic field. By renouncing what might be called 'grounding by inheritance', cosmopsychists such as Mathews have to rely on what so far look to be far less obvious solutions to the decombination problem.[10]

The cosmopsychists (along with many of their idealist predecessors) are thus left in a fix. They can, as Goff and Shani do, initially avoid the decombination problem by proposing a variant of grounding by inheritance. But then they are forced to either give up on the cosmos being a subject of experience or have the decombination problem resurface in the form of incoherent contents, with its epistemic and perspective problems. Or, they can, as Mathews does, give up grounding by inheritance, thereby preserving the cosmos as a subject of coherent experiential content. But then lacking the free lunch delivered through grounding by inheritance (and short of plausible alternatives) they are back to the decombination problem. Could the cosmopsychist renounce the prevailing assumption that cosmic consciousness must qualify a subject – as Nagasawa and Wager (2016) do? They might, but without coherent exposition of what such consciousness could amount to, the position borders on vacuous.

It is here that Advaita Vedanta and other mystical traditions, rich in accounts of people having allegedly *experienced* subjectless consciousness, can offer a way forward. In its absolute form, this universal consciousness does not belong to any subject or the cosmos; it is beyond subject/object duality, and grounds all manifestation. As any contents that might arise within it are not presented as objects to a grand subjective perspective, incoherence of content (with its epistemic and perspective problems) is avoided. Indeed, insofar as it is not framed as a puzzle about how a universal *subject* could entail smaller subjects, the decombination problem does not arise. But the Perennialist is left with the formidable task of explaining just how such non-dual consciousness could coherently ground our individual conscious perspectives and their contents – as well as the objects that we take to be our mind-independent environment.

The goal of the remaining sections is thus twofold: first, to offer a conception of universal consciousness that could be an experienceable non-dual grounding-base, and then to schematically show how such consciousness could conceivably ground what appears to us as spatio-temporal objects – a task that may, in the end, stretch the notion of grounding beyond its normal range of application. Rather than a full-blown defence, the following should be seen as the preliminary but critical exercise of clarifying just what would, or could, be argued for, if one *were* to philosophically defend a Perennialist metaphysics.

3. Preparing the Ground With Non-Dual Consciousness

To be a non-dual grounding-base, universal consciousness must at the very least be (i) intrinsically unconfined to subject/object structuring and (ii) spatio-temporally unbound, while being (iii) humanly *experienceable* as such. What follows is the first step towards an exercise in its conceivability, with an account of how our experience could come to *seem* to partake in such consciousness.

I have already mentioned that a conscious subject is by definition the locus for a first-personal perspective on the world, such that its contents are disclosed to its viewpoint within a structured field of awareness. I will now draw upon my earlier work to say more about how the phenomenological structure of a subject can, arguably, be construed (Albahari 2006: 7–10, Albahari 2009). The conscious subject, I suggest, has two discernible components: (a) 'witness-consciousness' and (b) a focal perspective. Witness-consciousness denotes that aspect of consciousness which exemplifies a sense of present-moment being, and is sentiently luminous, knowing, intransitive and reflexive.[11] When directed at objects, witness-consciousness does not take a view from nowhere but appears from a focal, localised perspective whose circumscribed field, whether waking or dreaming, presents for humans as structured by psycho-physical and spatio-temporal parameters. Objects are witnessed attentively or inattentively, as they come and go from the field. An 'object', for these purposes, is broadly anything discrete that such a subject could pointedly attend to: physical objects, people, perceptions, thoughts, etc. While a subject's witness-consciousness can be intransitively aware of its own presence, it can never pointedly attend to itself as something discrete; it is not an object.

My strategy will be to suggest that perspectivality (component b) depends upon witness-consciousness (component a) being aware of objects, such that without the apprehension of objects there could be no subject (a+b): no perspectival lens through which witness-consciousness could form a focal point with a structured field of awareness. If we can conceive of a scenario where witness-consciousness, or something like it, is nevertheless present, perhaps as a sense of pure unstructured being, then this would give us a way in which to conceive of consciousness intransitively experiencing itself in its primal 'non-dual' mode, if it is indeed primal. I say 'something like it' as witness-consciousness normally presents as directional and object-oriented; without objects it would lack directedness. Yet while unfamiliar to most in this capacity, it would still exemplify pure intransitive awareness, and I'll refer to this mode as 'conscious awareness'.

To get a handle on how this may work, we need to first be clearer on how the presence of objects could *phenomenologically* furnish witness-consciousness with the psycho-physically, spatio-temporally structured field of a human perspectival subject. If we look to our current experience, we can begin to break it down in this way. Consider what directly cues us into the sense of being an embodied creature occupying a specific region in an external spatio-temporal world. It will involve awareness of an array of multi-modal perceptual cues – or perceptual-like cues if dreaming – visual, auditory, tactile, etc., setting external parameters on the boundaries of our experience. Without such cues could we have any inkling of such a world? Now consider what phenomenologically cues us into a thicker sense of ourselves as being in – and making sense of – this world. While harder to introspectively discern, cognitive objects are likely to play a central role. Thoughts, memories, emotions, intentions etc. conceivably help impart a sense of bounded coherence and identity around the embodied internal viewpoint *from which* all the various cues are experienced. (Note that it is not being claimed that these objectual cues tell the whole story about how we come to perceive the world; the idea is rather to make sense of what may be their immediate role in the phenomenological fabric of our experiencing the world right now).

Now imagine entering what I will call the 'Cognisensory Deprivation Tank'. Each conscious perceptual input – sight, sound, proprioception etc. – snuffs out one by one. Next, all conscious cognitive input, attentive or inattentive, goes too, eventually leaving no perceptions, thoughts, memories, imaginings, or emotions. But with the exit of each perceptual and cognitive input, it is conceivable that witness-consciousness, although increasingly less populated with objects, remains no less sharp or present. Extrapolating to the point whereupon all objects that cue us into a spatio-temporal, psycho-physical perspective vanish, it is conceivable that 'we' are left *not* in a coma-like vacuum, but rather with pure and unstructured conscious awareness. Beyond the scope of (structured) imagination, such awareness may amount to pure subjectivity: an undiluted sense of luminous being or presence – normally diluted and refracted through the structured filters of cognisensory experience. In the absence of any cues to create inner (self) or outer (world) boundaries, or to mark the passage of time, such objectless awareness, if actively present, could well be experienced as *boundless*, that is to say: non-dual, unbound by spatial or psychological parameters, and temporally unbounded – not coming or going. If, as Maharaj says in the opening passage, its default nature is in fact the unmanifest ground of all being, metaphysically prior to space, time and manifestation, then it might well *by default* apprehend its nature as such – intransitively, intuitively and non-discursively.

According to many mystical traditions, such a mode of non-dual (objectless and subjectless) consciousness, known in Advaita Vedanta as *nirvikalpa samadhi*, is not merely speculative, but attainable in highly advanced stages of meditation. Determining its psychological possibility is not the mission of this chapter, but it is encouraging to encounter what might turn out to be 'empirical' evidence. This is not to say that the thought (free) experiment, which sequentially and passively removes objects from the purview of witness-consciousness, is at all accurate in conveying the meditative methods that would elicit non-dual awareness, nor is it to say that there could in reality be such non-dual conscious experience (perhaps consciousness requires objects), or that if there were to be such experience it would be veridical. The thought experiment is rather meant to help us make sense of how non-dual consciousness, if indeed the ground of all being, might conceivably be experienced *as such* by humans, in its pure and native form.

Suppose that there *was* the genuinely direct apprehension of non-dual awareness, in say, a meditative mode. A return to bifurcated experience, I surmise, would elicit a profound alteration. The experient could never again harbour the sense – or, as the traditions say, the *illusion* – of consciousness being fundamentally restricted to the 'shape' of a subject, with each person's consciousness assumed numerically distinct. Having experienced pure consciousness as the ultimate ground of all being, they will have come to lose all identity as a solid, separate self, such that they now cognise the world very differently. It is as if a person were from birth to be confined to a square room, and having not experienced any different, assumed space to be fundamentally constricted to the dimensions of that room. Upon release into open air, they could never again view space in that confined way, even after a return to the room prompts its old appearance as square shaped.

A conception of universal non-dual consciousness as timeless ground of all manifestation can be reinforced via a further reflection. This locates within our experience what appear to be opposing intuitions about the present moment, suggesting that their full reconciliation requires those intuitions to be sourced in non-dual awareness. The first intuition invites us to consider those elements within experience that signal 'right now'. While it is common to think of *now* as dynamic and flowing (eliciting a moving spotlight analogy in the philosophy of time literature) there is also, I suggest, an element to our experience of *now* that seems unmoving, not arising or passing away, and in this sense conceivably *timeless* (incapable of coming or going) backing the intuition 'it's *always* now'.[12] To which aspect within experience does this element of unmoving nowness seem most naturally owed – subject or object? Clearly not the objects that come and go. It seems owed, rather, to *that which observes* the flow of objects – the subject – and in particular, its *modus operandi* of witness-consciousness. The conceivably timeless aspect within our experience of the present is *subjective*.

Turning to the second, opposing intuition: it is commonly supposed that the now or present moment we experience is not confined to our individual perspectives but is fundamentally *objective*. Were we – and indeed all organisms – to vanish, the present would continue to be. While we can think of this objective present as involving a flow of objects, is there a way to render objective that unmoving, subjective and conceivably timeless aspect of *now* that seems sourced in witness-consciousness? There is, but only if we allow that such consciousness is not intrinsically confined to subjects' perspectives but is essentially *non-dual*. Carried in our minds as an unmoving sense of presence, conscious awareness will be both subjective *and* objectively universal, grounding the arising of all objects as well as subjects. While not conclusive, such reflections help pave the way to conceiving of a universal non-dual consciousness as the timeless ground for all manifestation.

4. Grounding the World in Non-Dual Consciousness

It now remains to make sense of how non-dual universal consciousness *could* ground what appears to us as the spatio-temporal, psycho-physical world of objects, mental and physical. Taking the setup for the previous thought experiment as our first clue, 'mind-independent' objects are fittingly construed as complex arrays of sensory and cognitive imagery. But rather than being sourced purely from within an individual's private perspective, amounting to a form of solipsism, the cognisensory imagery that frames each subjective perspective will emanate from the non-dual conscious ground that can be considered its material cause. How might this emanation be construed in a way that both accounts for the appearance of multiplicity, while not 'conditioning' the unconditioned ground, such as by casting the appearances as temporal events efficiently caused by it? A promising tactic will be to treat all distinguishing aspects of the emanation somewhat analogously to how we would the projective contents of a dream, allowing that there is no *subject* who is dreamer. The conditioning descriptors (spatial, temporal, qualitative, efficiently causal, etc.) will be properly applied to the multi-perspectival content *within* the 'dreamscape' rather than to any relation between the ground and content. Our imagery-filled perspectives are thus somehow the contents of a timeless projective emanation from the non-dual ground of pure consciousness (further implications of which are visited in the conclusion).

The content of the projective emanation will manifest as numerous, inter-connecting subject-object poles: each a finite and unified conscious perspective that is furnished with structured intentional imagistic content, however simple or complex (e.g. atom or human). Following F. H. Bradley, I refer to these subjects as 'finite centres'.[13] The subjective character and content of each finite centre, besides partaking in unifying conscious awareness from the timeless absolute, will be determined by the subject's *own disposition* for other objects — themselves either subjects or aggregates of subjects — to appear to it in a particular way, along with the *dispositions of other objects* — subjects or aggregates — to appear to the subject in a particular way. In turn, that subject will be disposed to appear as a particular object (or aspect) to other finite centres.

I base my discussion of dispositionality upon the pioneering work of C. B. Martin (2008), on which I will present some bare bones before saying more about its adaptation to the Advaitic account. For Martin, objects are propertied regions of space-time, itself a substance. Each property is ontologically identical to both a disposition and a quality, which, like a duck-rabbit drawing, can be regarded with emphasis on one aspect or the other. A disposition can manifest in an infinite variety of ways, but how or whether it manifests will depend upon the co-presence of other 'reciprocal disposition partners' that it teams up with. For example, even if a sample of water were never to come into contact with salt, its properties have

> the directedness of a dispositionality as solvent *for* salt and *not* gold . . . for the *mutual* manifestation of a coming into a solution of salinity. And salt has a directedness and dispositionality as soluble in water and not *aqua regia*, even without the existence of water, for that same *mutual* manifestation of a coming into a solution of salinity.
>
> (2008: 88)

As well as being dispositional, a property such as wateriness is *qualitative*, itself the mutual manifestation of further reciprocal disposition partners such as the atomic properties of hydrogen and oxygen, which are, in turn, the manifestations of subatomic disposition partners. Qualities are either mental (e.g. sensory qualia) or non-mental (e.g. extensional), serving as the concrete side of a property that anchors the disposition to space-time. At any point, what manifests is "the tip of a disposition iceberg" (2008: 4), its deeply rooted lines of dispositionality or "power-net" always outrunning the manifestation. Causality occurs without time lag insofar as the co-presence of relevant disposition partners (e.g. match, striking, oxygen, etc.) involves an immediate manifestation (a bursting into flame).

For Martin, then, the double nature of a property is dispositional and qualitative, occurring in the mind-independent substratum of space-time. On the proposed Advaitic variant, the substratum, if we can call it that, is not space-time, but non-dual awareness, and each 'arising' is not a property, but a finite centre. Each centre, no matter how simple or complex, has a dispositional and *subjective* — as opposed to just *qualitative* — nature, the subjective nature being the appearance of objects to the perspective of a subject. The subject is not an empty perspective but must always co-arise with objects that lend to it a structured spatio-temporal viewpoint. Conversely, objects can never arise without the perspective of a subject that is aware of them; there are no purely mind-independent objects.

Filling in from before, the subjective character of each conscious projection will depend upon three factors, which are usefully emphasised rather than ontologically distinct. First, it will depend upon the native sense of conscious present-momentness bestowed by the common unifying ground. Second, upon its own disposition, as an arising subject, for other objects, whether themselves subjects or aggregates of subjects, to appear to it in a particular way. To the housecat, a book will appear very differently than to a literate human. If an atom is a subject, another atom will appear to it very differently, perhaps as primitive buzzing, than to a scientist peering at it through a microscope. Third, the internal subjective character will depend upon the manifesting dispositions of other objects – finite centres or their aggregates – that appear to it as various structured qualities. To the human perspective a housecat, a book and a magnified atom will be disposed to present very different appearances.

Each finite centre will in turn be disposed, in tandem with other finite centres, to appear as, or contribute to the appearance of, a variously qualitied object to other subjects; they will be reciprocal disposition partners for a mutual manifestation. While a given mutual manifestation is likely to involve a great many finite centres, it can be individuated by the unified appearance of various objects to a specific subject. Each object within that subject's purview will of course *itself* be either a finite centre or aggregate of such centres; the manifestations will thus intersect. An aggregate is an arbitrary grouping of finite centres into an object which, for pragmatic reasons, a subject may treat as a disposition partner. I have been supposing that atoms and animals are finite centres, while tables and toasters are not, and it will be a challenge to arbitrate the principles that sort finite centres from mere aggregates. But mutual manifestations will always be the *direct* upshot of finite centres, at whichever level of complexity they naturally occur.

The conference is ending. Each philosopher's complex perspective, which takes in the sight of a green table, will anchor a mutual manifestation that envelopes a wide array of finite centres. Continuing to suppose that atoms rather than tables are among the direct partnerings, when conference-goers exit the room they will not leave behind an 'Edenic' veridical mind-independent green table, nor a Lockean or Cartesian primary-qualitied substance, nor a watchful Berkeleian God (or Absolute) to keep the table existent in its mind, nor solipsistic nothingness, nor a Kantian noumenal something about which nothing can be said, nor a Martinian buzz of qualitative/dispositional properties arising from space-time, nor atomic particulars with inner conscious or qualitative natures. There will just be each of the inside perspectives of the dispositionally arising micro-subjects, appearing to one another as simple objects as they partake in the shared ground of non-dual awareness.

5. Conclusion

Much more needs saying on how the inter-connecting finite centres could help comprise the appearance of the spatio-temporal world with which we are familiar. But as indicated, care must be taken to not overstep boundaries of what can be said about the position. Readers may have noted that the absolute non-dual consciousness somewhat resembles Kant's noumenal 'subject' insofar as it is unconditioned by descriptors of space, time, quality and relation (see Kant 1787/1929: A404). A key difference is that the Perennialist/Advaitic noumenon is not just a transcendental ground for the possibility of experience, but can be humanly experienced in its pure unconditioned form as ground of all being. But just as with Kant's position, such descriptors can only be properly applied to the world as experienced or conceived of from *within* the inter-locking perspectives of each conscious centre, and from which those descriptors originate. A purely external 'objective' account of how the absolute consciousness grounds its projections, insofar as it would draw upon such descriptors, will never be possible. Aside from its most general statement as a bare transcendental fact, accounts of grounding will only be expressible as relative rather than ultimate truths, structured by perspectival limitations of the system. Perhaps paradoxically, it must be with this proviso that any defence of the Perennialist metaphysic is to make sense.[14]

Notes

1. Ken Wilber is an exception, although his emphasis is on developing a meta-theoretical 'neo-Perennialist' framework into which different disciplines (including philosophy) can be integrated and understood, rather than on explaining or justifying the Perennial Philosophy within the field of philosophy itself. For an example of his schema, see his (2006).
2. German idealists such as Schelling and Hegel might seem to have come close in the notion of intellectual intuition – acts of non-discursive apprehension that grasp an absolute that is beyond the subject/object distinction. But according to Frederick Beiser, their concept of the absolute "excludes its description as either subjective or objective" (2002: 5), and must be interpreted as something neutral, even though the subjective could be exemplified in its "highest *manifestation, expression* or *embodiment*" (2002: 6). While also beyond subject/object duality, the Perennialist absolute is nevertheless the nature of pure subjectivity whose apprehension involves not (merely) an act of intellectual intuition but a radically transformed mode of cognition.
3. Itay Shani has however recently defended a version of cosmopsychism which he says bears some resemblance to Vedic views of universal consciousness, claiming that view "leaves room for the idea that there are non-ordinary conditions under which this epistemic barrier breaks down, opening a gate to the realisation that one's own self is not as separate an entity as one would imagine" (2015: 427). Yet, as this paper will imply, in continuing to construe perspectivality as fundamental to both our own minds and universal consciousness, his model lacks the essential non-dual underpinning that could enable the barrier to break down.
4. An exception is Nagasawa and Wager (2016) whose cosmopsychism "does not assume that the cosmos is a subject of experience exemplifying experiential content". However, they provide little exposition of how they do construe the consciousness.
5. See for example Eliot Deutsch (1969), David Loy (1997), Bina Gupta (1998), and Wolfgang Fasching (2011). Advaita Vedanta sometimes alludes to the absolute as 'Self', but being aperspectival, it is not a subject of the sort described in this paper.
6. While Bernardo Kastrup presents an innovative metaphysics that goes beyond cosmopsychism, it still falls prey to subject/object dualism insofar as the fundamental universal consciousness ("That Which Experiences") forms a subjective perspective harbouring a "stream of inner experiences" as objects (2016: 4).
7. There are other versions of the combination problem, many alluded to in this volume. For a good survey, see also Chalmers (2015, 2017).
8. While the term 'combination problem' is owed to William Seager, the term 'decombination problem' has been used informally by Itay Shani and Luke Roelofs. There have been other terms, but I find this the most apt.
9. David Chalmers has suggested in conversation that the demonstratives could be experienced by the cosmos in a global non-contradictory manner ('this is Fred', 'this is Fiona', etc), which would ground the local indexical facts ('I am Fred', 'I am Fiona', etc). However, this departs from Goff's subject-grounding scenario, insofar as the cosmos no longer experiences the subsumed states in their original 'felt' format. It thus presents the mystery of how the cosmos would experience all the unfolding indexical facts embedded in its conscious field: would there be some mode of extrasensory perception?
10. Following Kastrup (2016), one might alternatively suggest that absolute consciousness, like a broken mirror, is fragmented into our separate conscious perspectives, a model of Dissociative Identity Disorder providing the story about ground. But then it is hard to retain any sense in which the Absolute *qua* conscious subject remains an all-encompassing conscious unity rather than plurality.
11. Evan Thompson (2015: 14, 17–18) has nicely expounded on most these aspects of consciousness, defining 'luminosity' as the "power to reveal, like a light", allowing objects to appear to it; 'knowing' as "the ability to apprehend whatever appears" and 'reflexiveness' as self-revealing. 'Intransitive' depicts its luminous, self-revealing character as non-objectual. For a more explicitly Advaitic take on witness-consciousness, see Gupta (1998: 17–18) and Fasching (2011).
12. What about dreamless sleep and anaesthesia, when consciousness seems suspended? Again it is arguably quite conceivable – and indeed part of Advaitic lore – that while the higher cognitive functions of our conscious lives go into repose, the pure knowing/being aspect remains present, so is conceivably timeless. For an excellent discussion of consciousness during dreamless sleep, see Thompson (2015: 231–71).
13. Bradley's 'finite centre' is the immediate and durationless locus for first-personal and bounded indexical experience – the raw data out of which we construct durational conceptions of ourselves and the world of

objects (Bradley 1914: 410–14; Mander 2011: 112–13). In this respect his notion comes close to what I wish to convey here.

14. Sincere thanks to Itay Shani, David Chalmers, Christian Lee, Luke Roelofs, Philip Goff, Nin Kirkham, Sam Baron, Sonia Albahari, Kieran Golby and the audience at Wollongong University for their helpful feedback. It should be noted that this paper was written in 2015 and the idealist metaphysic sketched in Section 3, that I now call 'Perennial Idealism', has been developed a lot further in Albahari (forthcoming).

References

Albahari, Miri (2006). *Analytical Buddhism: The Two-Tiered Illusion of Self*. Basingstoke: Macmillan.

Albahari, Miri (2009). 'Witness-Consciousness: Its Definition, Appearance and Reality'. *Journal of Consciousness Studies*, 16 (1): 62–84.

Albahari, Miri (forthcoming). 'Perennial Idealism: A Mystical Solution to the Mind-Body Problem', *Philosophers' Imprint*.

Beiser, Frederick (2002). *German Idealism: The Struggle Against Subjectivism*. Cambridge MA: Harvard University Press.

Bradley, F. H. (1914). *Essays on Truth and Reality*. Oxford: Clarendon Press, Oxford University Press.

Chalmers, D. J. (2015). 'Panpsychism and Panprotopsychism'. In T. Alter and Y. Nagasawa (eds.), *Consciousness in the Physical World: Essays on Russellian Monism*. Oxford: Oxford University Press, pp. 246–77.

Chalmers, D. J. (2017). 'The Combination Problem for Panpsychism'. In G. Brüntrup and L. Jaskolla (eds.), *Panpsychism: Contemporary Perspectives*. Oxford: Oxford University Press, pp. 179–214.

Coleman, S. (2014). 'The Real Combination Problem: Panpsychism, Micro-Subjects and Emergence'. *Erkenntnis*, 79: 19–44.

Deutsch, Eliot (1969). *Advaita Vedanta: A Philosophical Reconstruction*. Honolulu: University of Hawaii Press.

Fasching, Wolfgang (2011). '"I am the Nature of Seeing": Philosophical Reflections on the Indian Notion of Witness-Consciousness'. In M. Siderits, E. Thompson, and D. Zahavi (eds.), *Self, No Self? Perspectives and Analytical, Phenomenological, & Indian Traditions*. Oxford: Oxford University Press.

Goff, Philip (2017). *Consciousness and Fundamental Reality*. Oxford: Oxford University Press.

Gupta, Bina (1998). *The Disinterested Witness: A Fragment of Advaita Vedanta Phenomenology*. Evanston, IL: Northwestern University Press.

Huxley, Aldous (1946). *The Perennial Philosophy*. London: Fonatana Books.

James, William (1909). *A Pluralistic Universe: Hibbert Lectures at Manchester College on the Present Situation in Philosophy*. New York: Longmans, Green & Co. (Online edition produced by Felicia Urbanski, David Starner, Nicolas Hayes and the Online Distributed Proofreading Team. www.gutenberg.org/ebooks/11984.).

Kant, I. (1787/1929). *Critique of Pure Reason*. Trans. N. K. Smith. London: Macmillan.

Kastrup, Bernardo (2016). 'On Why Idealism Is Superior to Physicalism'. www.scribd.com/doc/295795222/On-Why-Idealism-is-Superior-to-Physicalism-Bernardo-Kastrup.

Loy, David (1997). *Non-Duality: A Study in Comparative Philosophy*. New York: Humanity Books.

Maharaj, Nisargadatta (1985). *Prior to Consciousness: Talks With Nisargadatta Maharaj*. Ed. J. Dunn. Durham, NC: The Acorn Press.

Maharaj, Nisargadatta (1994). *Consciousness and the Absolute: The Final Talks of Nisargadatta Maharaj*. Ed. J. Dunn. Durham, NC: Acorn Press.

Mander, W. J. (2011). *British Idealism: A History*. Oxford: Clarendon Press, Oxford University Press.

Martin, C. B. (2008). *The Mind in Nature*. Oxford: Oxford University Press.

Mathews, Freya (2011). 'Panpsychism as Paradigm'. In M. Blamauer (ed.), *The Mental as Fundamental*. Frankfurt: Ontos, pp. 141–55.

Nagasawa, Yujin, and Wager, Khai (2016). 'Panpsychism and Priority Cosmopsychism'. In G. Brüntrup and L. Jaskolla (eds.), *Panpsychism*. Oxford: Oxford University Press, pp. 113–29.

Schaffer, Jonathan (2010). 'Monism: The Priority of the Whole'. *Philosophical Review*, 119: 31–76.

Shani, Itay (2015). 'Cosmopsychism: A Holistic Approach to the Metaphysics of Experience'. *Philosophical Papers*, 44 (3): 389–437.

Thompson, Evan (2015). *Waking, Dreaming, Being: Self and Consciousness in Neuroscience, Meditation and Philosophy*. New York: Columbia University Press.

Wilber, Ken (2006). 'From the Great Chain of Being to Postmodernism'. www.kenwilber.com/writings/read_pdf/32.

Zahavi, D. (2005). *Subjectivity and Selfhood: Investigating the First-Person Perspective*. Cambridge, MA: MIT Press.

12

LIVING COSMOS PANPSYCHISM[1]

Freya Mathews

1. Introducing Panpsychism

According to the view that I am calling panpsychism, mind is a fundamental aspect of matter. That is to say, although mind cannot exist independently of matter, matter also cannot exist independently of mind. Mind is a part of what matter most fundamentally is. There is in this sense no 'brute matter'; the purely externalized 'stuff' proposed by classical physics has no correlate in reality. Whether the 'inner' properties hereby ascribed to matter are characterized in terms of intentionality, agency, teleology or more overtly psychological characteristics, such as consciousness, apperception, phenomenality, sentience, conativity, subjectivity or spirit, they cannot be captured in purely extensional terms. Such a view of the nature of reality may be theorized in a variety of very different ways, from Leibniz's monads, W. K. Clifford's 'mind stuff', Whitehead's 'prehending' particles and Williams James' 'mind dust' to the self-active universes of Spinoza, Schelling and David Bohm, to the intelligent life-systems of Gregory Bateson, or the scenario of nature-as-agent adopted by environmental philosophers such as Val Plumwood. (For a review of panpsychist streams in the history of ideas, see Skrbina 2005). All these philosophers argue that mentality, in some sense, is a fundamental aspect of materiality, and that the world around us has a depth dimension, inaccessible to observation, as well as an observable structure: it is a psychically textured terrain of embodied subjects or intelligences rather than a flat manifold of purely externalized entities.

This type of view has a long history, not only in Western thought but in many other traditions as well. In the West it was very much in abeyance throughout the 20th century, as metaphysics itself had fallen into disrepute as an academic discipline. But it has recently started popping up again in a variety of discursive contexts. Although one can distinguish between several different contemporary streams of panpsychist thought, my main aim here is to discuss the significance of panpsychism within environmental philosophy.

2. Environmental Philosophy

Over the last four decades, environmental philosophers have argued that the environmental crisis produced by industrial development on a global scale is the result of an anthropocentric outlook that permeates the Western tradition and in particular science and its epochal offshoot, modern civilization. Anthropocentrism is the expression, in the moral sphere, of the dichotomization of categories such as the human and the non-human, or culture and nature, where such dichotomization in turn rests on a strict dualism of mind and matter: mind is the province of the human; matter *sans* mind is the province of nature. Without mental attributes, material things or systems cannot matter to themselves and therefore it does not matter, morally speaking, what happens to them. If mentality is the exclusive province of humans, then only humans intrinsically matter – only humans are entitled to moral consideration in their own right. The non-human realm – the realm of mere matter – is valuable, and hence morally considerable, only insofar as it serves human purposes. We humans can accordingly use nature as we see fit.

Environmental philosophers mostly agreed that it would be necessary to restore mentality to nature if nature were to become a legitimate object of moral concern and consideration in its own right. They differed however in their various understandings of mind and also in the scope they assigned to the term, *nature*. For some, nature was understood in strictly biological terms; it was considered by others under its cosmological aspect. In the following section I shall review three versions of environmental panpsychism: the new animisms; mind-in-nature type views or panpsychism-without-consciousness; and cosmological or 'living cosmos' panpsychism.

3. Environmental Versions of Panpsychism

3.1. New Animisms

New animists tend to borrow their ontology from pre-scientific, often Indigenous, worldviews, attributing mental status to biological entities, such as organisms and populations, and to ecological systems, such as vegetation communities, in something like the way pre-scientific cultures often attributed spirit to trees, groves, springs, rivers, forests, animals and such like. In adopting the term animism, however, new animists are sometimes at pains to mark their difference from earlier, colonial conceptions of animism by pointing out that in Indigenous cultures conceptions of mentality were not drawn from a human paradigm but rather included the human as a minor subset of a prior realm of mind construed as co-extensive with nature (Rose 2013). Mind, in other words, was paradigmatically the kind of mentality distributed so variously, with such multi-functionality, right across nature rather than the kind of reflexive, language-centred consciousness we find in ourselves.

Rather than seeking to provide a theoretical account of this prior realm of mind however, new animists are generally happy to leave the actual metaphysical underpinnings of their position relatively unexamined, asserting that their goal is not to explain the world, via appeal to fully theorized metaphysical categories, but to institute new protocols for being in the world. These protocols are, again, generally inspired by modalities exemplified in Indigenous, often hunter-gatherer, societies. In terms used by Graham Harvey (2005), a prominent proponent of the new animism, we are to treat all things in the world as persons. To treat them as persons is not to impute dualistically conceived spirits or souls to them, as 19th-century anthropologists supposed that animists did, though it is indeed to see things as alive. Being alive, however, may be defined more in terms of due protocols than in terms of theoretical conditions that things must satisfy in order to count as alive. To treat things as persons is to treat them personally, where this means negotiating with them in matters that concern them. Harvey compares living in an animist world to walking down a crowded street: one does not simply plough through the crowd, mowing down whomever happens to be in the way; rather, one weaves in and out, giving way to someone here, being given way to by someone else there. One negotiates the crowd instinctively and pragmatically, without needing to deliberate. A principle of respect for the personhood of other people underlies this negotiation, though such respect need not in any way be sentimentalized: to respect the personhood of others in a crowd does not imply that one likes them or is obliged to care for them.

The new animist viewpoint provides a rich basis for ecological practice, and has been widely embraced by pagans, wiccans and other practitioners of nature spirituality. It has also inspired ecological philosophers and theorists such as David Abram, Patrick Curry and Deborah Bird Rose. Personally, I also find this new animism appealing and I acknowledge its contribution to ecological ethics in a contemporary context. I am happy to adopt and follow its protocols. However, from within the reference frame of the Western episteme, such animism does leave certain philosophical questions unaddressed: which entities can count as alive, in the animist sense? In many animist cultures rocks, for example, may count as inspirited but human artifacts, such as tables or cars, do not. Why so? And how can entities, such as hills, mountains, woods, streams or springs, which are often invested with an animist principle, count as living things when their identity is clearly nominal? Such things are often part of other, more extensive landforms or systems rather than clearly individuated entities or systems in their own right. In any case, what is it about animate things that entitles them to be treated with respect, as persons? Moreover, in animism there does seem to be a localism that, though a healthy counterpoint to the tendency of Western colonial thought to universalize its own self-serving assumptions, nevertheless perhaps overlooks the spiritual significance of the larger universe – a question to which I shall return later.

3.2. *Mind-in-Nature Views or Panpsychism-Without-Consciousness*

Not all environmental philosophers are content merely to borrow Indigenous protocols in the manner of the new animists. Some have tried to provide theoretical analyses of mind that could address the kinds of questions animism sets aside. While at least one of these philosophers, namely Val Plumwood (2009), does describe herself as a philosophical animist, others eschew both animism and panpsychism as labels while nevertheless developing outlooks that infuse nature with mind. The form of mentality attributed to nature however is often distinguished from consciousness, if consciousness is defined as experience in the inner, subjective, introspectively accessible or phenomenal mode that is the distinctive mode of mind in humans and certain animals.

I shall call such a view of mind-in-nature, *panpsychism-without-consciousness*, and in this section I shall examine Plumwood's version of it.[2]

Plumwood's panpsychism revolves around the logical category of intentionality. The roots of her account lie in a work she partly (though cryptically) co-authored with her then husband, Richard Routley, entitled *Exploring Meinong's Jungle and Beyond*, a thousand-page tome addressing the riddle of intensionality in logic.[3]

To track Plumwood's view, let us start with an explanation of this riddle. There are aspects of nature that, while not indicative of mind in the sense of consciousness, nevertheless express properties that are not, and cannot be, manifest to observers. These aspects are not, in other words, part of the extensional order of nature, accessible to ordinary empiricism; they cannot be fixed by ostensive reference. Such aspects include the causal powers and dispositions of things, where a disposition is the tendency of a thing to behave in a particular way in particular circumstances. Powers or dispositions cannot be observed in the way that ordinary empirical properties, such as shape, size and colour, can. At the level of appearance all that indicates the presence of a causal power is the fact that whenever event E1 occurs in certain specified circumstances, it is followed by event E2. It may be inferred from observations of this type that there is something in the first event – a certain power – that causes the second, since otherwise why would the second event invariably be predictable or even occur? This power itself however is not observable; it is not manifest in the appearances but is hidden and can only ever be inferred from the appearances, just as the presence of mind in sentient beings is hidden to observers and can only ever be inferred from appearances. Whatever is hidden but ascribable to things in this way, whether it pertains to thought or merely to matter, logically belongs to the realm of the intensional.

Intensionality is puzzling to logicians because it does not fit the extensionality of their semantical model, a semantics designed to corroborate an empiricist epistemology and a reductive materialist or mechanistic metaphysic. The semantical model in question is extensional in the sense that the meaning of a term is generally given by its extension, the class of referents the term picks out. So, for instance, the meaning of the term 'red' is given by the class of all red things. We learn what 'red' means by having red things pointed out to us. We cannot however learn what the expression 'the causal power of billiard balls to move other billiard balls' means by having such causal powers pointed out to us. Causal powers cannot be pointed out because they are not empirically manifest. Even the class of all instances of billiard balls moving other billiard balls does not constitute the extension of the expression, 'the causal power of billiard balls to move other billiard balls', because causality presumably involves an element of necessity: billiard balls do not just happen to set other billiard balls in motion; there is, or at least seems to be, a certain necessity in such causal sequences. Necessity, together with other modal properties, such as possibility and contingency, categorically goes beyond the appearances: we cannot directly observe the necessities, contingencies or possibilities of a thing's nature. The meaning of modal terms accordingly also cannot be given extensionally.

In order to explain how modal terms can be meaningful, given that they do not conform to the extensional approach, logicians resort to the apparatus of possible world theory. The meaning of modal concepts is then explained by reference to events not only in the actual world but also in possible worlds. So, to revert to billiard balls, when we say that billiard ball A possesses the causal power to move billiard ball B in specified circumstances, we mean that in all possible worlds in which A strikes B in the circumstances in question, B will be set in motion. It is the holding of this particular sequence of events across all worlds, or across all worlds in which the first event occurs, that indicates the presence of necessity. This is an example of the lengths to which logicians have to go to provide a semantical analysis of intensional concepts: the meaning of such concepts cannot be 'read off' the appearances in the way the meaning of straightforwardly empirical concepts can.

However, as Richard Routley pointed out, the hidden or non-manifest aspects of the world indicated by intensional terms are not rare and exceptional. Physics is full of them, inasmuch as many of its variables can only be defined dispositionally or via laws of nature which are implicitly modal. When we turn to the sphere of living organisms, the biosphere, such properties abound: telos, purpose and goal directedness; all these properties of living things and systems are hidden in the intensional sense (Routley 1980: 781–9).

Intensionality then afforded a way to affirm hidden aspects of nature that could not be accounted for by reference to the externalities exclusively countenanced by mechanism. But nor could this mysterious aspect of things be equated with full-fledged mentality, insofar as mentality was taken to connote the psychological capacity for consciousness. Intensionality, Routley argued, was an 'intermediate' category, situated in between the two Cartesian categories of mind and matter and permeating thought and nature indifferently (Routley 1980: 768).

Why intensional phenomena ought to be regarded as loci of moral considerability however remained a further question. The fact that sticks and bits of clay and old scraps of plastic are invested with causal powers, for instance, and fall under laws of nature, and that causal powers and laws of nature have modal and hence intensional properties does not on the face of it show why moral significance should attach to them. Plumwood (1993) clarified the argument when she shifted the emphasis from intensionality to intentionality.

Intentionality was a category originally introduced within phenomenology as the indicator of the mental: the occurrence of intentional phenomena served to mark the mental off from the non-mental or purely material. Intentionality was defined by Franz Brentano as the property of directedness, of pointing beyond what was given. This, Brentano explained, was a peculiar logical characteristic of psychological phenomena – they did not exist merely 'in themselves', as a lump of matter does, but were always 'about' something else, something beyond themselves. So in our psychological life we think *about*, say, cats or theories or the future or our own potential; we feel grudges *towards* people; we believe *in* gods or ghosts; we have percepts *of* sticks or stars.

For Brentano, it was this mysterious 'aboutness' or directedness-towards-something-beyond-itself, rather than awareness or consciousness per se, that distinguished the mental from the merely material. Intentionality is clearly an instance of intensionality, inasmuch as it shares in the hiddenness, the crypticness and the ungivenness, of the intensional, but it was understood by Brentano only to occur in mental contexts.

As a concept which is explicitly invoked as a marker of mind but which marks mind in a non-psychological way, intentionality served Plumwood's purpose very well. She pointed out that research in logic had attempted, by applying the test of intentionality, to demonstrate a categorical distinction between mental and merely material phenomena but had consistently failed to do so: intentional phenomena persistently turned up in nature as well. Properties such as growth, flourishing, function and self-directedness, for example, possess the quality of pointing beyond the given that Brentano had characterised as intentional; hence, they cannot be extensionally defined, any more than psychological phenomena can. In other words, the properties that characterise mind also turn up in nature, and these properties cannot be reductively analysed in terms of the purely extensional – despite the best efforts of logicians. The attempt to restrict analysis to extensional forms of discourse was, Plumwood observed – in line with Richard Routley's earlier argument – the corollary, in logic, of mechanism in science, and the failure of this program signaled the failure of mechanism. The mind-like cannot be dispelled from nature.

This argument, which delivered what Plumwood (1993) explicitly described as a weak form of panpsychism (weak in that it eschewed consciousness), went some way towards answering the question why intensional phenomena ought to be regarded as morally significant. Since intentional phenomena, as markers of mind, were morally significant, and since intentional phenomena could no longer be sharply distinguished from intensional ones, intensional phenomena might be seen as sharing in the moral significance of the intentional. But Plumwood strengthened the case for moral considerability by selecting a particular subset of the intentional, namely, the teleological – properties such as growth, flourishing, function and self- directedness – as the marker of moral status. All beings and systems with such teleological properties may be said to possess a good or interest of their own and a capacity to direct their own unfolding in response to the conditions of their life.

In finding a basis for moral significance in the teleological aspects of nature, Plumwood joined what was by then a host of other environmental philosophers (Taylor 1986; Johnson 1993; Rodman 1983). What made her approach distinctive was the way she arrived at teleology through intentionality, an argument for teleology more subtle and less dubious than most.

I have detailed Plumwood's argument here because it offers a careful account of how forms of mentality without consciousness are dispersed throughout nature. She insisted that panpsychism *must* take this 'weak' form based on intentionality rather than consciousness because 'strong' panpsychism, by which she meant the kinds of panpsychism that ascribe consciousness to everything, is still captive to mind-matter dualism (Plumwood 1993 and personal communication). It is captive to dualism, she thought, inasmuch as it uncritically accepts as universal the human-derived phenomenal notion of mind defined by dualism, and merely extends that outward into the rest of nature.

Teleocentric versions of panpsychism, such as Plumwood's, do indeed go a long way towards establishing strong foundations for environmental ethics. They generally emanate in a kind of multi-species ethic with which I personally am deeply in sympathy. But I am not sure that panpsychism-without-consciousness is as far as we can go in our investigation of mind in nature. When Plumwood points out that there is more even to basic physics than sheer externality, she is suggesting that the categories of physics are already more mysterious than a purely extensional approach allows. But she is not suggesting that our knowledge of reality can exceed physics. In this respect, her account of mind in nature, like versions of panpsychism found in contemporary philosophy of consciousness, fails ultimately to challenge the exclusive authority of Western science to set the parameters of our understanding of reality.

For a position that seeks to preserve consistency with science while nevertheless exceeding both the explanatory reach of science and the horizons of possible experience staked out by science, we need to move up to the cosmological level.

3.3. *Cosmological or Living-Cosmos Panpsychism*

The primary question addressed by cosmological panpsychism is simply the foundational question of metaphysics itself: what is the nature of reality at large and what is our relation to it – where this is arguably the primordial question of all philosophy. The history of cosmological panpsychism is thus interwoven, albeit in a minor key, with the entire history of philosophy. It is beyond the scope of the present chapter to detail this history; suffice it to say that the most notable exponents of the kind of tendency I am associating with cosmological panpsychism in the Western tradition include pre-Socratics such as Empedocles and Parmenides, and, in the modern era, Spinoza and certain of the German Romantics, such as Fichte, Schelling and Schopenhauer as well as 19th-century thinkers such as C. S. Peirce. One prominent cosmological panpsychist of the 20th century is David Bohm.

Philosophy in this grand style – addressed to ultimate questions about the nature of reality and our own place in the larger scheme of things – was radically out of fashion throughout much of the 20th century, both in analytical philosophy and in continental philosophy. If I may be permitted a quick personal aside, I can provide firsthand testimony to this historical fact. As a student in the 1970s, I was drawn to philosophy by a deep sense of affinity with Spinoza; I wanted to become a philosopher in the Spinozist tradition. But when it came time to embark on a doctoral thesis at the University of London, I found that my keenness to tackle the kinds of questions Spinoza had explored had to be filtered through an elaborate lens of logic and semantics. My thesis became a study of the metaphysical foundations of modal logic – the logic of possibility, contingency and necessity – and took the form of a critique of possible world theory, the then-fashionable semantic apparatus for the analysis of modal statements. (Shades of the Routleys' focus on the riddle of intensionality here!) Eventually I found a home for my metaphysical speculations in the new and still quite marginal discourse of environmental philosophy, in which, as I have mentioned, panpsychist tendencies were already in evidence.

Now that metaphysics has regained a certain respectability however, one can perhaps pursue the idea of cosmological panpsychism with a little more confidence. Excitingly, several new versions of this view have recently appeared within the context of philosophy of consciousness (Shani 2015; Jaskolla and Buck 2012; Nagasawa and Wager 2016). Here however I would like to outline and extend the view developed in my own earlier work as its implications for environmental thought were always core to its purpose: my premise was always that the malaise of modern civilization, as manifested in the environmental crisis, is, *au font*, a metaphysical one.

Cosmological panpsychism, as I understand it then, is a response to basic questions of metaphysics, including the following. Why does the universe – the observable world, as represented by physics – exist? Why is it a universe, a unity, i.e. why does it cohere, hang together, in the way that it does? Why is space – the frame of physics – unbounded yet unbroken, an indivisible wholeness, a field-like manifold? Why does it not break up, granulate, fragment, and hence cease to be the field that it is, the ground for physical existence?[4] Why is the frame of physics space? To such questions, physics of course has no answers. It cannot explain why there are laws that hold physical structures together and thereby guarantee the overall cohering of things. From the viewpoint of physics, this cohering is ad hoc, contingent; there is nothing in the nature of physicality per se that appears to underpin it.

Cosmological panpsychism, however, offers answers to these questions. As soon as an inner, subjectival dimension – the sense of self-presence accessible to introspection – is seen as integral to the nature not merely of matter but of physicality per se, which is to say, the entire field of spatio-temporal existence in its totality, then the necessity of this cohering of physical existence into a unity, a *universe*, an indivisible manifold such as that of space-in-time, is explained.[5] Subjectivity is itself, by its very nature, field-like, holistic, internally interpermeating, indivisible, unbounded. One's subjectivity cannot plausibly be constituted atomistically, as an aggregate of discrete units of experience or even as a continuum of point-like experiences. If mind is as primal as physicality in the overall scheme of things then, if it is immanent in physicality per se, and mind is understood as the innerness, the sense of self-presence or subjectivity subtending consciousness, then physicality must reflect the indivisible nature of mind. Physicality must exhibit the same field-like structure as mind.

Of course, the question might be pushed further back: we might ask why mind, in turn, is necessarily indivisible and field-like. Granted, if reality has an inner, subjectival dimension and subjectivity is field-like then reality must itself be field-like, but why is indivisibility or field-likeness inherent in the nature of subjectivity in the first place? In answer to this question, I would suggest that the field-likeness of mind is tied up with the self-evident field-likeness of *meaning* – the intrinsically interleaving and over-layering and interpermeating nature of meaning – and thereby with the constitution of experience through meaning. The kind of holistic internal indivisibility that confers unity on mind, in other words, is tied up with the necessary indivisibility of meaning. Subjectivity is the medium for a tissue of meanings that cannot be pulled apart without ceasing to be meaning – and without subjectivity thereby ceasing to exist. To the extent that meaning is the very stuff of mind then, the structure of mind must partake of the interpermeation and indivisibility that is characteristic of meaning. This is not to say that we might not identify or describe individual experiences by abstracting them from the field of experience – as this sense datum or that itch, this moment of elation or that insight into the nature of, say, number. It is just that such experiences cannot actually exist in isolation from the entire field of the subject's experience, and this field-like structure of subjectivity is a function of meaning.

In speaking of the field-like structure of subjectivity as a function of meaning, I am using the term 'meaning' not technically in a semantic or symbolic sense but in a more fundamental sense, to indicate the basic condition of things mattering – of things having relevance, significance, value. In other words, I am using 'meaning' in the sense of meaningfulness, the meaningfulness that we impute to life itself when we ponder 'the meaning of life'. And meaningfulness in this sense must ultimately be referenced to beings with an interest in their own existence. In my book, *The Ecological Self*, I termed such beings *selves*: a self is any entity, human or otherwise, that is systemically organised to maintain itself in existence by its own reflexive efforts.[6] Selves are thus defined by such interests: they have a constitutive interest in self-maintenance and self-increase. It is relative to the interests of such selves that things in the environment – particular objects, circumstances – assume significance, relevance, value. If there were no selves in the world, everything would just be what it is – nothing that occurred would matter more or less than anything else, so nothing would be meaningful. Specific meanings – the meanings of specific words or gestures, for instance – develop out of this underlying meaningfulness: 'I', 'you', 'dog', 'run', 'red' all develop, as discriminations, against this background of interests. If nothing mattered to us, there would be no reason to make the semantic discriminations we do make – or indeed any semantic or perceptual discriminations – in the first place. In the absence of beings with interests, it is hard to see how reality could be considered determinately differentiated in itself at all, since all possible discriminations would co-exist in a kind of *singularity*: in the absence of selves, and hence in the absence of discrimination, there could be no determinable entities nor hence could there be any fixed spatio-temporal intervals between entities. Without fixed spatio-temporal intervals, no metric for either space or time could even in principle be defined. It would follow that no extension in either space or time would exist. Might not then such a state of non-discrimination in fact be what the term 'singularity' implies? Not so much an originary state of infinite compression as simply reality considered logically under its undiscriminated aspect? But here I am jumping ahead – I shall return to this point later.

To see the universe as a whole as having a subjectival aspect inextricable from its physical aspect, then, is to see it as structured by meaning or meaningfulness in the present underlying sense. And to see it as structured by meaningfulness is to regard it as mattering to itself – as constituting a self-realizing system in its own right, with an interest in its own self-existence and indeed its self-increase. To regard the universe in this way is thus to view it too as a kind of self – a very special, *sui generis* self, indeed, but a self nonetheless, self-actualizing, self-preserving and self-expanding – a Self. (It is not hard to appreciate that a view of the universe as self-actualizing, self-preserving and self-expanding is by no means incongruent with contemporary cosmology.)

From the viewpoint of such a cosmological version of panpsychism, the empirical world, as charted by physics, is the outward appearance of an inner field of subjectivity, indeed of conativity, where by 'conativity' I mean precisely the will or impulse of a self to realize and increase its own existence.[7] Such a cosmological Self, being essentially conative, will be self-creating and in this sense its existence will be necessary. Panpsychism on a cosmological scale thus offers an answer to the question of why a universe exists. And, as a cosmological subject imbued with an inner, subjective sense of itself, this universe will, as I have already explained, cohere as an indivisible unity, where such unity and indivisibility will be manifested in the lawlikeness that ensures the spatiotemporal coherence of reality under its outer, physical aspect. However, although the universe, under both its outer and inner aspects, coheres as a unity, it also undergoes self-differentiation. In Spinozist and Einsteinian style, its field-like fabric ripples and folds locally to form a dynamic manifold of ever-changing, finite 'modes'; viewed from the outside, these modes appear as the empirical particulars observable by ourselves and described by physics; viewed from the inside, they constitute a texture of ever-unfolding impulse, will, felt force. This universe is thus both a psychophysical unity and a manifold of psychophysical differentia. Amongst its differentia, there are some which are themselves organized as nested self-realizing systems or selves. These include organisms and perhaps higher-order living systems, such as ecosystems and biospheres. This set of finite selves represents a tiny but significant subset of the wider, ever-changing set of differentia. Selves are significant, amidst the vast array of other differentia, because they represent real (because self-realizing) though relative (because not substantively discrete) loci of subjectivity and conativity in their own right. It is from the perspective of such finite selves that reality can be said to present an 'outward' appearance.

In sum, cosmological panpsychism may be articulated via a cluster of core categories: *selfhood*, defined as the status possessed by self-realizing systems; *conativity*, the impulse towards self-existence and self-increase that informs the self; *reflexivity*, the capacity of a system to reference itself; *subjectivity*, the felt sense of self-presence that underlies consciousness; and *meaningfulness*, the basis for making the discriminations that organize experience, where such discriminations in turn become the basis for thought and language in selves with the capacity for such modalities of consciousness. Selves are always relationally configured through ceaseless exchange with other selves and systems, up through indefinite levels of organization. In this sense, the impulse to reach out for 'the other' (where such reaching out may take the form of appetite, desire or communicativity) is always the flip side of the conative drive towards self-existence and self-increase.

Relative to the universe as a whole, qua ultimate Self or Self-realizing system, there are of course no exterior selves or systems via exchange with which it can relationally configure itself. It is this which occasions the need for cosmic Self-differentiation. Interaction with (real though relative) finite selves constellated through Self-differentiation on the part of the cosmic Self offers the only opportunity of exchange for such a Self. Since communication represents an essential horizon of self-realization and self-increase for any system structured *ab initio*, as this universe is, by meaning, exchange with finite selves may take communicative form. The cosmos as Self then is seen as capable of and as actively seeking communicative engagement with its finite modes, or at any rate with those of them capable of such engagement. It is the cosmos under this communicative aspect that I call the 'living cosmos'.

Though the living cosmos appears to its finite modes as extended in observable space, it does not experience itself as so extended. In itself, reality is prior to the discriminations of finite selves that select out from the flux of its self-actualizing activity those determinations that allow for metrics of both space and time to be established. Since this self-activity of reality is an expression of its conativity, it will be purposeful rather than arbitrary or merely chaotic in its felt form – its felt dynamics will cohere seamlessly around primal purpose. But from the perspectives of finite selves constellating within those felt dynamics – selves shaped by their own specific conativities but not necessarily attuned to the enfolding purpose of the whole – the self-activity of reality will appear vastly variegated and differentiated. Spinoza's distinction between *natura naturans* (nature as self-active and self-realizing, viewed under its undifferentiated, unitive, pre–spatially-extended aspect) and *natura naturata* (nature as the order of causally related finite modes organized deterministically in space) may serve to clarify this point. *Natura* is of course in both these instances one and the same; it is just nature viewed, in the case of *natura naturans*, from the perspective of itself as a whole; while in the case of *natura naturata*, it is nature viewed from the perspective of a finite mode. Spinoza illustrates this distinction by analogy with a circle also viewed under two different aspects (*The Ethics*, Part 2, Note to Prop VIII). Any circle formally contains an infinite number of equal rectangles. From the perspective of the figure as a whole, the set of infinite rectangles would appear as a simple unity – the circle: the rectangles would blend and cancel one another to describe a circumference. But if the figure is viewed from within, from the perspective of any one of the internal rectangles, it will appear not as a simple unity – which is to say, as a circle – but as a very large set of pointy particulars, because the rectangle from which the figure is viewed will not be observable to itself and hence the set of rectangles required for that figure to resolve into a circle will not be complete.

Similarly, from the viewpoint of the living cosmos itself, its own self-activity will be transparently suffused with its conative purpose, but from the viewpoint of finite modes this primal purpose may have become scattered, like light, into millions of points of individual conativity.

As a wellspring of the felt force of experience, unbounded and field-like in its quality, fired into coherence by self-purpose though in no way in itself located or extended in space, the living cosmos may be potentially subjectively present in its diffuse entirety to each of its finite modes. It may be for this reason that the universe can manifest locally, in instances of communicative engagement with individuals, wherever individuals with the capacity and inclination so to engage occur.

To see reality from this perspective is to take a step not merely from the descriptive realm of science but even from the realm of ethics (the province of teleocentric philosophies) to that of spirituality: as a responsive presence enfolding us, reality invites us not merely to recognize our moral obligation to all selves or life-systems but also to configure our existence in accordance with the larger meanings congruent with its own conativity. In other words, we may expect to discover in the fabric of reality a normative grain or intimation of how to live. Since reality owes its overall make-up to its conative ends – those pertaining to its self-realization and self-increase – patterns expressive of those ends will inevitably recur throughout the externalized realm of causally conditioned nature (*natura naturata*). In the context of life on earth, we find such patterns in the inexhaustible regenerativity and renewability of life, but also in a tendency towards ever-increasing differentiation and communicativity across and within all forms of life. Elsewhere I have identified the principle discernible in these patterns as that of conativity *modulated by a logic of least resistance*, where the latter may be understood as a logic of accommodation to our life-environment (Mathews 2011). If our own destinies are to be consistent with the primal conativity of the cosmos, we need to conform to these patterns of accommodation, regenerativity and communicativity.[8]

In pre-agrarian societies, in which peoples lived by hunting and gathering in close association with and attunement to ecological systems, this normative grain in the fabric of reality was readily discerned and enshrined as Law. Law was explicitly acknowledged – and is still acknowledged today by peoples who have managed to preserve Indigenous ways of life – as inhering in the land. As Hobbles Danaiyarri, a Mudbura man of Yarralin in the Northern Territory of Australia explained it to anthropologist, Deborah Bird Rose: 'Everything come up out of ground – language, people, emu, kangaroo, grass. That's Law' (1996: 9).

This Law is not merely the result of blind or mechanical natural selection, but emanates from the meanings, the stories, that underlie those natural processes. Aboriginal people refer to this meaning dimension that inheres in the manifest or empirical world as Dreaming, and stories that translate those meanings into the language of humans, as Dreamings. As another of Rose's informants, Mussolini Harvey, a Yanyuwa man from the Gulf of Carpentaria, told her:

> The Dreamings made our Law or narnu-Yuwa. This Law is the way we live, our rules. This Law is our ceremonies, our songs, our stories; all of these things came from the Dreaming . . . our Law is not like European [l]aw which is always changing – new government, new laws; but our Law cannot change, we did not make it. The Law was made by the Dreamings many, many years ago and given to our ancestors and they gave it to us. . . . The Dreamings are our ancestors, no matter if they are fish, birds, men, women, animals, wind or rain. It was these Dreamings that made our Law. All things in our country have Law, they have ceremony and song.
>
> (1996: 26)

Just as Law in this sense does not equate to man-made European laws so it in no way equates to the descriptive, quantitative 'laws of nature' encoded in science and strictly formulated on the 'fact' side of the presumed fact-value dichotomy in terms of which science so emphatically defines itself. Rather, Law consists of adaptive and prescriptive guidelines derived from close collaboration with living systems together with poetic attunement to narratives immanent, as Dreamings or as the very Dreaming itself, in the realm of matter.

In the context of Law, understood not as a rational postulate, in the manner of ethics, but as a palpable, enfolding normativity that makes itself felt to us as the very meaning of our existence, inextricable from our deepest attachments, 'environmental ethics' is transformed from a rational duty, external to our own interests, to a whole-hearted inclination to take care of the cosmos. Indeed it becomes our deepest taproot, a new dimension of love that turns us definitively on our metaphysical and motivational axis.

The religions that accompanied the rise of agrarian civilizations retain a memory of Law in this original sense – a law of accommodation to the needs of others in the interests of a larger whole. 'Do unto others' remains the moral touchstone of all major religions. But agrarianism, setting society as it did at a remove from nature, led to a new, ever-increasing reliance on human artifice and a new ethos of domestication and dominion with respect to the rest of life. The 'others' intended by the injunction, 'do unto others', progressively contracted to the exclusively human, till most religions eventually became arch vehicles of anthropocentrism. However, living-cosmos panpsychism, with its recognition of normativity in the fabric of reality, may be seen as a metaphysical underpinning for the centrality of this law of accommodation – whether in the form of Dharma, Covenant, Dao (Way) or Sharia (also Way) – in the configuration of religion, while also insisting upon its application to *all* living things.

The communicativity of reality, according to living-cosmos panpsychism, is not necessarily a given of our experience but may need to be activated via practices of address or invocation. Responses to such address may be manifested through serendipitous conjunctions or synchronistic arrangements of circumstances. From this perspective, the 'language' the world speaks, when it does speak, is a poetic – concretised and particularized – one. For example, in relevant invocational settings, it may take the form of a bush burning on a mountain, a raven participating discreetly in a funeral ceremony, a butterfly alighting on a dead woman's breast, a message bird appearing out of nowhere to show the way, lightning punctuating a ritual performance with apposite displays. All such 'signs', whether occurring in religious contexts or not, may be seen as instances of a vast poetic repertory, a repertory of imagery, of meaning conveyed through the symbolic resonance of things. It is in such language then that our invocations may need to be couched, since it is in such language that the world is able to respond: it is able to *speak things*. For things to acquire poetic resonance however, they generally need to be framed within a narrative context, which is why religious and spiritual traditions, and the liturgies which express them, generally rest on and are defined by founding narratives. In Indigenous societies, invocations are likewise shaped by Dreaming stories. But the efficacy of invocation need not necessarily be confined to either religious or Indigenous contexts.

When the living cosmos responds, in person as it were, to our poetic address, in terms referenced to the particular idiom of our invocation, we feel so intimately and extravagantly blessed, so moved and shaken on our metaphysical moorings, that our allegiance henceforth will be first and foremost to this cosmos itself, generally under its local aspect, the place or physical context which provides the lexicon of revelation. Love of world in this sense becomes our deepest attachment. It replaces self-love as the root of our motivation.

Wherever communicative engagement with reality is activated in this way, we might speak of a 'poetic order' – an order of poetic revelation – unfolding alongside the causal order ordained by science. Such a poetic order, or order of meaning, will exceed the causal order but in no way contradict it. We may call this poetic order, and the practice of participating in it, *ontopoetics*. Ontopoetics opens up a world of potential new meaning and experience hidden within the world already so familiar to us from science (Mathews 2017).

In closing, I would like to suggest that living-cosmos panpsychism makes sense of much religious experience without either acquiescing in supernatural ontologies on the one hand or contradicting science on the other. Indeed, it explains both the normative core of religion while also throwing light on certain of the questions that challenge the ultimacy of science. Why space? Why coherence? Why unity? Nonetheless, the prime affinity of living-cosmos panpsychism lies with neither religion nor science but with those Indigenous ontologies of Law and Land that religion and science left behind. In Australian Aboriginal thought, mind is, as it is in living-cosmos panpsychism, primordial; human consciousness is just a single mode of this universally distributed and diversely embodied mind (Viveiros de Castro 1998; Rose 2013; Mathews 2003). This stands in stark contrast to the way in which, in Western scientific and religious thought, mind has been seen as paradigmatically instantiated in humans, other entities being either devoid of it or attributed with it only to the degree they are perceived as resembling us (Rose 2013). From the viewpoint of living-cosmos panpsychism, the latter view gets things not merely wrong but precisely back to front, for this very property we claim so exclusively for ourselves is in fact the condition for spatiotemporal existence per se. In the form of primordial conativity, mind is the first property reality must possess if physics itself is to be possible. And in possessing it, the living cosmos also grounds a normative Law which is as immanent in its fabric as are space and time.

Although Kant has in no way figured in the development of the present account of living-cosmos panpsychism and does not usually find himself in the company of Indigenous thinkers, he may have approved. The quest of his life, etched on his tombstone, was to reconcile 'the starry heavens above' with 'the moral law within'. He intuited that the two were somehow fused at the root (along with beauty, figured in his *Third Critique* as forms of coherence). But his philosophical system allowed for no exploration of this mystery. Perhaps the 'singularity' I have here called the living cosmos is the noumenon in which the starry heavens and the moral law, and indeed the beauty that emanates from coherence, intelligibly inhere.

Notes

1. Several passages in this article have been adapted from Mathews (2015) and Mathews (2017).
2. Space forbids discussing a second thinker in this category worth mentioning: Gregory Bateson (see his 1979).
3. At that time Plumwood was writing under the name of Val Routley.
4. There are theories in physics which do ascribe a sub-particle foamlike or granular structure to space. For a recent discussion of these, see Ferreira 2014. But these are not inconsistent with the perfect macro-level cohering of space as the frame for physical processes.
5. I have elsewhere introduced a distinction between the two terms, 'subjective' and 'subjectival' (Mathews 1991). 'Subjective' refers to the felt quality of experience, 'subjectival' to the capacity for having such experience. An example might illustrate why the distinction is important. To speak of 'the subjective nature of reality' implies that reality is mind-dependent i.e. that it is 'in my mind', where this suggests idealism. To speak of 'the subjectival nature of reality', however, implies that reality itself has the capacity for experience, where this suggests panpsychism.
6. Self in this sense can be defined in terms of autopoietic theory, as it is in the work of Humberto Maturana and Francisco Varela; but this notion of self-realization as the essence of self goes back at least as far as Spinoza.
7. The notion of conativity thus represents a further articulation of teleology, but in the present context teleology is defined on a cosmological scale and in terms much more connotative of *feeling* than the versions of teleocentrism examined earlier.
8. To the question, how can finite selves depart from these patterns if they are themselves part of the conative unfolding of the living cosmos?, I would reply that the same faculty of reflexivity which enables us to communicate with reality in the ways I describe in this chapter – where such forms of communicativity do themselves contribute to the self unfolding of the cosmos – inevitably also enables us to reflect upon and hence deviate from our conditioned, ecological responses to life situations, where, in other species, such ecological responses exhibit patterns of cohering.

References

Bateson, Gregory (1979). *Mind and Nature: A Necessary Unity.* New York: Dutton.

Castro, Eduardo Viveiros de (1998). 'Cosmological Deixis and Amerindian Perspectivism'. *The Journal of the Royal Anthropological Institute*, 4 (3): 469–88.

Ferreira, Pedro G. (2014). *The Perfect Theory: A Century of Geniuses and the Battle Over General Relativity.* London: Little, Brown.

Harvey, Graham (2005). 'Animist Manifesto'. Accessed August 14, 2017. www.earthboundpeople.com/wp-content/uploads/2015/03/An-Animist-Manifesto-Graham-Harvey-2012.pdf.

Jaskolla, L. J., and Buck, A. J. (2012). 'Does Panexperiential Holism Solve the Combination Problem?' *Journal of Consciousness Studies*, 19: 190–9.

Johnson, Lawrence (1993). *A Morally Deep World: An Essay on Moral Significance and Environmental Ethics.* Cambridge: Cambridge University Press.

Mathews, Freya (1991). *The Ecological Self.* London: Routledge.

Mathews, Freya (2003). *For Love of Matter: A Contemporary Panpsychism.* Albany: SUNY Press.

Mathews, Freya (2011). 'Towards a Deeper Philosophy of Biomimicry'. *Organization and Environment*, 24 (4): 364–87.

Mathews, Freya (2015). 'Environmental Philosophy'. In N. Trakakis and G. Oppie (eds.), *A History of Philosophy in Australia and New Zealand.* Dordrecht: Springer Publishing, pp. 543–91.

Mathews, Freya (2017). 'Panpsychism: Position Statement', 'First Response' and 'Second Response'. In G. Oppie and N. Trakakis (eds.), *Philosophies of Religions: Multi-Faith Dialogues.* London: Routledge.

Nagasawa, Y., and Wager, K. (2016). 'Panpsychism and Priority Cosmopsychism'. In G. Brüntrup and L. Jaskola (eds.), *Panpsychism.* Oxford: Oxford University Press.

Plumwood, Val (1993). *Feminism and the Mastery of Nature.* London and New York: Routledge.

Plumwood, Val (2009). 'Nature in the Active Voice'. *Australian Humanities Review*, 46: 113–29.

Rodman, John (1983). 'Four Forms of Ecological Consciousness Reconsidered'. In D. Scherer and T. Attig (eds.), *Ethics and the Environment.* Englewood Cliffs, NJ: Prentice Hall, pp. 82–92.

Rose, Deborah Bird (1996). *Nourishing Terrains: Australian Aboriginal Views of Landscape and Wilderness.* Canberra: Australian Heritage Commission.

Rose, Deborah Bird (2013). 'Val Plumwood's Philosophical Animism: Attentive Interactions in the Sentient World'. *Environmental Humanities*, 3: 93–109.

Routley, Richard (1980). *Exploring Meinong's Jungle and Beyond.* Departmental Monograph 3. Canberra: Philosophy Department, Research School of Social Sciences, Australian National University.

Shani, Itay (2015). 'Cosmopsychism: A Holistic Approach to the Metaphysics of Experience'. *Philosophical Papers,* 44 (3): 389–437.

Skrbina, David (2005). *Panpsychism in the West.* Cambridge, MA: MIT Press.

Taylor, Paul (1986). *Respect for Nature.* Princeton: Princeton University Press.

13

COSMOPSYCHISM, MICROPSYCHISM AND THE GROUNDING RELATION

Philip Goff

Panpsychism is the view that consciousness is fundamental and ubiquitous. The most promising form of panpsychism is *constitutive panpsychism*, which we can define as follows:

> *Constitutive panpsychism* – O-consciousness (the 'ordinary' or 'organic' consciousness we pre-theoretically associate with humans and other animals) is *not* fundamental but is grounded in a more fundamental form of consciousness which is ubiquitous throughout nature.[1]

Constitutive panpsychism is most commonly construed as a 'bottom-up' view:

> *Constitutive Micropsychism* – All facts – including the facts about o-consciousness – are grounded in consciousness-involving facts at the micro-level.[2]

However, there is increasing attention being given to the 'top-down' version of constitutive panpsychism:

> *Constitutive Cosmopsychism* – All facts – including the facts about o-consciousness – are grounded in consciousness-involving facts concerning the universe.[3]

People still have a giggle when they hear about conscious electrons or the consciousness of the universe. But those who are genuinely interested in finding a place for consciousness in the natural world ought to appreciate that there is a case to be made for the view. We can see the contemporary mind-body problem as the following dilemma:

1. There are strong *empirical reasons* for doubting dualism: If there were fundamental mental properties in or associated with the brain that regularly impacted on the physical processes that govern behaviour, then this would show up in our neuroscience. We would find physical changes in the brain that have no physical cause. The fact that we don't find brain events that can't be explained in terms of physical laws constitutes a strong and ever-growing inductive case against dualism (Papineau 2001; Goff 2019).
2. There are strong *philosophical reasons* for doubting physicalism: The physical facts about my body and brain can wholly account for my conscious experience only if those physical facts necessitate the facts about my conscious experience. If the physical facts about my brain necessitate

144

the facts about my conscious experience, then there is no possible world in which there is a functioning body and brain physically identical to my own but in which there is no consciousness. And yet there is good reason to think that such a world is conceivable, in the sense of being rationally coherent, and this gives us good reason to think that such a world is possible (Chalmers 2009; Goff 2017, 2019).

By offering a non-physicalist reduction of human consciousness, constitutive panpsychism offers hope of avoiding this dilemma altogether. Of course, there are thoughtful and challenging objections to constitutive panpsychism but anyone who rejects the view simply because 'it's a bit weird' is not serious about the project of trying to find out what reality is really like.

A crucial element in the definition of constitutive panpsychism is the *grounding relation*. In this chapter I want to get clearer on what constitutive panpsychism is by examining what the grounding relation is. I will try to show that constitutive micropsychism and constitutive cosmopsychism involve very different conceptions of the grounding relation, and that as a result the constitutive micropsychist but not the constitutive cosmopsychist is committed to a deflationary view of o-consciousness. I conclude on the basis of this that cosmopsychism is the more plausible form of constitutive panpsychism. I will only be concerned here with constitutive forms of panpsychism, and so in what follows I will refer to constitutive micropsychism simply as 'micropsychism' and constitutive cosmopsychism simply as 'cosmopsychism'.

1. What Is Grounding?

From the 1930s onwards there was great deal of hostility to the project of metaphysics in analytic philosophy. At some point in the 1970s, with no explanation as to why it had become acceptable, people started doing metaphysics again, and today most departments in the analytic tradition have active engagement with the subject. More recently many analytic metaphysicians have gravitated towards the use of an extremely traditional vocabulary, involving primitive notions such as *essence* and *fundamental being* (Lewis 1983; Fine 1994; Sider 2012). One such primitive notion which has received a great deal of attention in the literature is the *grounding relation* (Schaffer 2009; Rosen 2010).

The grounding relation is taken to be a *non-causal explanatory relation* that holds between facts. The prima facie need for such a relation is given by reflection on examples:

- There is a party at Jane's *in virtue of* the fact that Rod, Jane and Freddy are reveling at Jane's.
- The rose is red *in virtue of* the fact that the rose is scarlet.
- There is a table at location L *in virtue of* the fact that atoms are arranged table-wise at L.

The italicised phrase in the preceding examples seems to express an explanatory relationship: the party exists *because* Rod, Jane and Freddy are revelling, the rose is red *because* it's scarlet. But this explanatory relationship is not causal: Rod, Jane and Freddy's revelling does not bring into being a new entity – the party – that floats above their heads; the scarlet colour does not secrete redness as the liver secretes bile. Hence we seem to have a non-causal but explanatory relationship; and this we call 'grounding'.

What more can we say about grounding relationships? Intuitively in cases of grounding the product is *nothing over and above* the producer: we want to say that there is 'nothing more' to the fact that there is a party than the fact that certain people are revelling, or that the former 'wholly consists' in the latter. Indeed, this seems to be what distinguishes grounding relationships from causal relations; for in causal relations new individuals and properties are brought into being, e.g. conception produces a child, match striking produces fire.

How can some fact X be 'nothing over and above' some other fact Y? A natural first thought would be that this is because X and Y are one and the same fact, i.e. they are identical. Thus, it is natural to try to analyse 'nothing over and above' talk in terms of identity:

> *The Identity Analysis (of 'nothing over and above' talk)* – X is nothing over and above Y iff X is identical with Y.

However, the previous examples of grounding are not plausibly construed as cases of identity, at least if we assume:

> *The Necessity of Identity* – If X is identical with Y then X could not possibly exist without Y.

The Necessity of Identity is extremely plausible. For X to be identical with Y is for X and Y to be one and the same thing; and nothing can exist without itself.

Why does the acceptance of the Necessity of Identity lead to the falsity of the Identity Analysis? Call the fact that there is a party at Jane's 'the party fact' and the fact that Rod, Jane and Freddy are revelling 'the RJF fact'. The party fact could exist without the RJF fact, e.g. if Rod and Freddy leave and their revelry is replaced by that of Ken and Clare. It follows by the Necessity of Identity that the party fact cannot be identical with the RJF fact. Hence the Identity Analysis fails, at least in this case and any other case in which the fact that is grounded could obtain in the absence of the fact that grounds it.

We now seem to be left with a prima facie paradox. It's hard to make sense of the idea that X is *not identical with* Y and yet X is *nothing over and above* Y. It seems almost tautological that if X is *not* Y then X is *something more than* Y. Thus, to make sense of the grounding relation we need to give some account that removes this prima facie paradox by clarifying how we can have nothing-over-and-above-ness obtaining between non-identical facts. I call this the 'free lunch constraint' on an adequate theory of grounding.[4]

There seem to me two options for satisfying the free lunch constraint, which lead to two distinct forms of the grounding relationship. I will consider each of these in turn in the following two sub-sections.

1.1. Grounding by Truthmaking

One influential way of making sense of 'nothing over and above' talk, developed by John Heil amongst others, focuses on truthmaking (Heil 2003; Cameron 2008, 2010; Horgan and Potrč 2008). In Heil's view, a great error in twentieth century metaphysics was the Quinean orthodoxy of reading off ontology from the entities quantified over in the sentences we take to be true. In this framework, avoiding an ontological commitment to Xs requires avoiding quantifying over Xs, or at least analysing sentences involving quantification over Xs into sentences not involving quantification over Xs. Contra this Quinean tradition, Heil thinks that ontology should focus not on the entities quantified over in our truths, but on the entities that serve as truthmakers for such truths. By holding for example that truths about tables are made true by states of affairs involving particles being arranged in certain ways – arranged 'table-wise' as philosophers tend to say – we avoid an ontological commitment to tables.

Proponents of the truthmaking approach often talk as though non-fundamental entities do not exist, saying for example that 'in reality' there are no tables, only table-wise arrangements of particles. But if the view is that table-wise arrangements of particles make it true that there are tables, we seem on the face of it to have a contradiction. If it is true that there are tables then there are tables, which is obviously inconsistent with there being no tables.

Suppose the truthmaker theorist avoids this contradiction by accepting that tables fully exist. It now becomes hard to see how truthmaking can help us to make sense of the thesis that the table is 'nothing over and above' the fact that particles are arranged table-wise (or whatever 'nothing over and above' thesis we happen to be focusing on). We are wanting clarification of the relationship between two facts in concrete reality – the fact that there is a table and the fact that particles are arranged table-wise – and it's not clear how mentioning a relationship between one of those facts and an abstract proposition (or a linguistic sentence) helps with this. Perhaps we could say that the fact that particles are arranged table-wise makes true the proposition <there is a table>, and that the existence of the table somehow arises from the truth of that proposition. But this gets the priority between being and truth the wrong way round: propositions are representations of reality, and hence their truth is dependent on what facts obtain in reality rather than vice versa.

The only way I can see around these difficulties for the truthmaker approach is to combine it with what we might call 'metaphysical elitism'. According to the metaphysical elitist, not all objects and properties are equals: some are *metaphysically privileged*, part of *Reality as it is in and of itself*. Theodore Sider is a prominent proponent of this view (Sider 2012). On his version the privileged structure of reality is captured in the 'Book of the World': the true and complete description involving only concepts which 'carve nature at the joints'. All other truths have 'metaphysical truth-conditions', i.e. specified in the metaphysically privileged language (i.e. the language involving only terms which carve nature at the joints) and satisfied by metaphysically privileged facts.

Combining the truthmaker account with metaphysical elitism provides a way of avoiding the contradiction of saying that tables don't exist even though <tables exist> is true: it is false in the metaphysically privileged language that 'tables exist' but it is true in a common or garden language like English that 'tables exist'. Tables exist, but they are not part of the metaphysically privileged structure of reality; tables are not part of Reality as it is in and of itself. This yields a clear sense in which tables are 'nothing over and above' facts about particles: facts about tables do not add to the metaphysically privileged structure of reality.

Some may be suspicious of the idea of a primitive notion of metaphysical privilege, and so I have provided an appendix in which I try to demystify the idea. To briefly summarise, it is plausible that we have a basic, simple notion of existence or reality – the notion we employ when we ask whether God exists, for example – and this is the notion we are ultimately interested in as theorists of reality. We can call this notion of existence 'basic' or 'privileged'. However, we use existence language for all kinds of purposes and these extended uses create a secondary notion of existence. Things that exist in this secondary sense are mere shadows cast by the structure of our language. Parties 'exist' in a sense, but only in the sense that we use talk of parties 'existing' to express facts about people revelling. Parties do not 'exist' in the sense of existence we are interested in when we are trying to find out what Reality is like.[5]

Thus, although truthmaker grounding gives us a good sense in which grounded facts are nothing over and above grounded facts, it does so at the cost of giving a deflationary account of non-fundamental individuals and properties. On the truthmaker + metaphysical elitism approach to grounding (which is in my view the only plausible version of truthmaker grounding) non-fundamental individuals and properties 'exist' in the lightweight sense that talk of their existing plays a role in ordinary language. But they do not 'exist' in the sense we are interested in when we conduct metaphysical enquiry into the nature of Reality.[6] At best talk of their existence plays the role of communicating facts about the privileged existence of some other kinds of thing.

1.2. Grounding by Subsumption

I turn now to the second way in which I believe we can make sense of 'nothing over and above' talk.

Philosophers tend to think that facts about big things are grounded in facts about little things: the table exists and is the way it is because its smallest bits exist and are the way they are. Sam Coleman calls this view 'smallism' (Coleman 2006). However, over the last decade or so Jonathan Schaffer has conducted a rigorous and wide-ranging defence of a view he calls 'priority monism', which turns smallism on its head. For the priority monist, facts about little things are grounded in facts about big things: the smallist bits of the table exist and are the way they are because the table as a whole exists and is the way it is. Ultimately all facts are grounded in facts about the biggest thing: the universe. According to priority monism the universe is the one and only fundamental thing.

A distinctive form of the grounding relation obtains in the context of priority monism. Schaffer characterises it as follows:

> the monist may offer a general conception of the partialia as abstract, in the etymologically correct sense of being a partial aspect. Wholes are complete and concrete unities. Parts may be conceived of as aspects of wholes, isolated through a process that Bradley describes as "onesided abstraction." The priority of the one whole to its many parts is thus of a piece with the priority of the substance to its modes, both being instances of the general priority of the concrete entity to its abstract aspects.
>
> (2010: 47)

I call this 'grounding by subsumption', which we can define as follows:

X grounds by subsumption Y iff Y is a partial aspect of X

This is not an incredibly helpful definition, as the notion of 'subsumption' and the notion of an 'aspect' are closely inter-defined. However, I think we can get a grip on the notion of grounding by subsumption by reflecting on instances of it. I will briefly outline three:

1.2.1. Grounding by Subsumption Between Experiences

Consider your total determinate conscious experience right now. In some sense it has 'parts': visual experience of colours, auditory experience of sounds, emotional experience of joy as you read this stimulating text. One might suppose that the whole experience is a bundle of these smaller experiences, tied together with the relation of co-consciousness. However, another option, to my mind more natural, is to suppose that the whole experience is more fundamental, subsuming the smaller experiences as aspects. Bayne and Chalmers (2003) defend such a view.

1.2.2. Grounding by Subsumption Between a Substance and Its Properties

In the previous quotation Schaffer alludes to the fact that grounding by subsumption offers an attractive model of the relationship between an object and its properties. There is an old and well-known difficulty, known in more recent philosophy as 'Bradley's regress', of how to account for the relationship between an object and its properties without involving oneself in vicious regress. Suppose we start with the aim of accounting for the connection between a ball and its red colour. A natural starting assumption is that we should explain the connection between the ball and redness in terms of the relation of *instantiation* that holds between them. But now the question is: what connects the ball to the instantiation relation? If we need a relation to connect the ball to redness, then surely we also need a relation instantiation★ to connect the ball to the instantiation relation that connects it to redness. And if we need a relation of instantiation★ to connect the ball to the instantiation relation that connects it to redness, surely we also need a relation of instantiation★★ to connect the ball to the relation of instantiation★ that connects it to the instantiation relation that connects it to redness.

And so on ad infinitum. The ultimate explanation of the connection between the ball and its colour is continually deferred and never given.

A promising way around this difficulty, defended by D. M. Armstrong and C. B. Martin among others, is to suppose that at the fundamental level we find not objects and properties somehow 'glued together', but rather *objects-having-properties* (you have to say it really quickly!), also known as states of affairs (Martin 1980; Armstrong 1997). The state of affairs of *the ball-being-red* is a unity more fundamental than either the ball or its redness; both the ball and its redness exist as aspects of that more fundamental unity. When God created the world, she didn't create electron E, an instance of negative charge, and then glue them together. Rather she created *e-having-negative-charge*; both the electron and the instance of negative charge being aspects of that more fundamental unity.

(Rather than thinking of the view in terms of states of affairs, I prefer to construe it in terms of *propertied objects*. On such a view, rather than creating the state of affairs of *electron-e-having negative charge*, God created a specific *negatively-charged-electron*, a fundamental unity that subsumes a given instance of negative charge.[7] Which view one goes for depends on whether one thinks the world is fundamentally made up of facts or things.)

1.2.3. *Grounding by Subsumption Between Substantival Space and Its Regions*

The central debate in the philosophy of space is between substantivalists and relationists. Substantivalists believe that space (or space-time) is a fundamental kind of thing in its own right: the great container in which all material objects are held. Relationists believe that at the fundamental level there are only material objects, related in various complex ways: facts about space are grounded in facts about material objects and the relationships they bear to each other.

How should the substantivalist construe the grounding relationship between space (or space-time) and its regions? I suppose one might adopt a kind of 'spatial atomism', according to which space as a whole is built up of its very small regions of space. But it is much more natural, or at least an option, to suppose that the whole of space is fundamental and that the regions of space are aspects subsumed within that unity.

Grounding by subsumption is a primitive notion but I think it is one that we can get a grip on through reflection on the preceding examples. And grounding by subsumption gives us a clear understanding of how it can be that (a) X is not identical with Y, and yet nonetheless (b) X is nothing over and above Y. My current red experience is nothing over and above my total conscious experience because my current red experience is one aspect of my total visual experience. The redness of the ball is nothing over and above the state of affairs of the ball's-being-red because the redness is one aspect of that state of affairs. A specific region of space is nothing over and above space as a whole because that region is one aspect of the whole of space. In each case, the reality of the whole subsumes the reality of the aspect.

We can now note a crucial difference between the two forms of grounding we have considered. Accounting for nothing-over-and-aboveness via grounding by truthmaking essentially involves committing to a deflationary view of non-fundamental entities or properties. For on the truthmaking account non-fundamental properties and entities are 'nothing over and above' fundamental properties and entities, in the sense that they do not add to the metaphysically privileged structure of reality; all and only fundamental entities are part of Reality as it is in and of itself. Non-fundamental objects and properties are mere shadows cast by the structure of our language.

In contrast, accounting for nothing-over-and-aboveness via grounding by subsumption need *not* involve a commitment to a deflationary view of non-fundamental entities or properties. My current red experience is 'nothing over and above' my current total experience in the sense that it is an aspect of that total experience; the total experience subsumes the red experience within its being. And therefore we do not need to deny that the red experience participates in the privileged structure of reality in order make sense of its 'not adding' to the total experience; we can consistently hold that both the total experience and its various aspects are parts of Reality as it is in and of itself.

There are other proposals in the literature for how to account for nothing-over-and-aboveness in the absence of identity; I have argued elsewhere that none is satisfactory.[8] And given the prima facie paradoxical character of nothing-over-and-aboveness in the absence of identity – how can X be *not* Y and yet *nothing more than* Y? – it does seem that some account is required which removes this paradoxical character. Thus, I will tentatively suppose in what follows that grounding must be one or other of the two forms I have outlined here.

2. Micropsychism and Cosmopsychism

Micropsychists attribute very basic consciousness to fundamental micro-level entities, perhaps electrons and quarks. They then take facts about o-consciousness, i.e. the kind of consciousness we associate with humans and other animals, to be nothing over and above facts about the basic consciousness of micro-level entities. Clearly we cannot make sense of this grounding claim in terms of grounding by subsumption: my mind and its consciousness are not aspects of the consciousness of any micro-level entity. Thus, this grounding claim must be made sense of in terms of grounding by truthmaking. I therefore interpret the micropsychist position as follows:

> *Truthmaker micropsychism* – The metaphysically privileged structure of reality consists entirely of facts involving micro-level entities instantiating very basic forms of consciousness, and perhaps certain other properties. These facts make true all other propositions, including propositions concerning o-consciousness, e.g. <Bill is feeling anxious>. Neither o-minds nor o-states of consciousness participate in the metaphysically privileged structure of reality. They are mere shadows cast by the structure of our discourse; just as sentences asserting the existence of parties merely communicate facts about people reveling, so sentences concerning how Bill is feeling and thinking merely serve to communicate facts about the consciousness of the micro-level entities in Bill's brain.

Micropsychism so construed is not a very plausible view. When I ask whether there is a party I am interested in whether people are reveling. But when I ask what it's like to be Bill I'm not interested in anything more fundamental than the o-subject that is Bill's conscious mind and its conscious states. This would be disputed by analytic behaviourists and functionalists, who hold that the function of propositions concerning consciousness is to convey information about behavioural functioning. Few people working on the mind-body problem these days accept this kind of view, and if you do accept this kind of view then you're going to have no motivation for trying to make sense of panpsychism. But once we deny analytic functionalism, there doesn't seem to be any other way of analyzing the truth-conditions of propositions concerning o-consciousness in more fundamental terms.

It could be claimed that the truth-conditions of propositions concerning o-consciousness are not *a priori* accessible, as the reference of concepts referring to conscious states is determined by facts outside of our grasp. This is roughly the view defended by physicalists who endorse the 'phenomenal concept strategy' (Loar 1990; Papineau 1998; Diaz-Leon 2010). However, as in the case of analytic functionalism, endorsing the phenomenal concept strategy entails losing the motivation for panpsychism. If the truth-conditions of propositions about consciousness are not *a priori* accessible, then there can be no *a priori* grounds for denying that those truth-conditions concern purely physical properties. Of course, I do not take myself here to have given any reason to doubt the phenomenal concept strategy – I have tried to do this at length elsewhere (Goff 2011, 2015, 2017). But panpsychism is a view one is attracted to because one is persuaded of the philosophical case against physicalism with which I started this chapter; such a philosopher has already rejected the phenomenal concept strategy.

Perhaps there is some way of construing micropsychism other than the truthmaking account I have given previously. However, this would require formulating some other account of grounding, an account that incorporates some other way of making sense of o-conscious minds being 'nothing over and above' facts about micro-level minds. I have found nothing like this in the literature so far, although to be fair the nature of the grounding relation has not thus far been much discussed in the panpsychism literature.

In the absence of some such alternative we should interpret micropsychism as I have construed it above. I submit that so construed it should be rejected. We can put the argument as follows.

The Absence of Analysis Argument:
1. The metaphysical truth-conditions of propositions about o-consciousness are *a priori* accessible.
2. If micropsychism is true, then the metaphysical truth-conditions of propositions about o-consciousness concern micro-level conscious entities.
3. It is not plausible that there are *a priori* accessible metaphysical truth-conditions of propositions about o-consciousness that concern micro-level conscious entities.
4. Therefore, micropsychism is false.

I turn now to cosmopsychism. Cosmopsychism (in its constitutive form) is a combination of priority monism – discussed previously – and panpsychism. On this view the universe considered as a whole is a conscious subject of some kind. All entities and properties, including o-conscious minds and their conscious experiences, are aspects of the conscious universe. The conscious universe subsumes all things in its being.

Thus, cosmopsychism entails the possibility of *subject-subsuming subjects*, i.e. conscious subjects that are aspects of other conscious subjects. Such a thing can seem hard to make sense of. Certainly we cannot imagine such a thing by using our perceptual and/or introspective faculties. But nor can we imagine in this way a four-dimensional object, and we nonetheless take four-dimensional objects to be coherent.

The cosmopsychist can plausibly attribute our difficulty positively conceiving of a subject-subsuming subject to the fact that we don't fully grasp the nature of conscious subjects. Contra Descartes, there is no reason to think that the essential nature of a subject of experience is entirely a matter of its being a subject of experience. And indeed we have a couple of reasons for thinking that there is more to the nature of a conscious subject than its consciousness:

- Conscious subjects have causal powers, and yet the categorical nature of a conscious state does not seem to essentially involve causal power, as evidenced by the fact that epiphenomenalism is coherent. Therefore, if conscious subjects are causally efficacious, they must instantiate some non-phenomenal categorical nature that is involved in grounding the subject's causal powers.[9]
- If conscious subjects are material, then they are spatially extended. Yet Descartes was arguably correct that we cannot conceive of a Cartesian ego (i.e. creature whose nature is exhausted by consciousness) extended in space. Mere consciousness doesn't seem to be the kind of property that can, on its own, be 'spread out' through space.[10] This gives us reason to think that there must be some other nature to the conscious subject that is involved in grounding its spatial extension, some nature that 'thickens out' the subject and its consciousness.

I don't think these considerations point us to the idea that a conscious subject has other properties – extension and causal powers – that are distinct from and, as it were, sit alongside its consciousness. For this would entail that consciousness itself was epiphenomenal and lacked extension. Rather I think they point us to the supposition that there is a more expansive property, call it consciousness+, that subsumes consciousness as one aspect, enfolding conscious and non-conscious aspects in a single unified property. If we grasped the nature of consciousness+ we would understand that it is an essentially extended, causally efficacious property; as it is we grasp only one aspect of that property.

Will we ever come to grasp the non-phenomenal aspects of consciousness+? I am cautiously pessimistic. We know about the causal structure of matter through the way it impacts on our senses, and we know about (some of) the phenomenal properties instantiated by matter through direct acquaintance (i.e. we acquainted with the phenomenal properties instantiated by our own brains). But we don't seem to have a faculty through which to access the non-phenomenal categorical nature of matter. Derk Pereboom (2011, 2015) has speculated that we might reach a conception of such properties through theoretical imagination. Whilst I don't have an argument to conclusively rule this out, it seems to me about as likely as the possibility of a blind scientist imagining her way to a positive conception of phenomenal red. Certainly such a thing has no precedent in natural science, which has no interest in the non-phenomenal categorical nature of matter.

It is frustrating to be stuck with a theory which entails our (probably permanent) partial ignorance of the nature of matter. But I don't think the fact that a theory has this implication gives us any reason to doubt its truth. If we are the products of natural selection rather than intelligent design, then we should not expect to be blessed with the capacity to discover the complete fundamental nature of reality. In fact, we should be surprised we've got as far as we have. The success of natural science in the last five hundred years has caused many to be optimistic concerning the human capacity to unearth the secrets of nature. Such optimism is dampened when one appreciates that, from Galileo onwards, the physical sciences have focused exclusively on mapping the causal structure of matter. The fact that we have had great success working out how matter *behaves* does not give us a reason to think that we will one day uncover its intrinsic nature.[11]

The crucial advantage of cosmopsychism, as opposed to micropsychism, is that it does not require a deflationary view of o-subjects and their experiences. According to cosmopsychism my consciousness is an aspect of the consciousness of the universe; this is consistent with supposing that my consciousness is part of the metaphysically privileged structure of reality. Similarly, the cosmopsychist claim that my conscious mind (the substance rather than the property) is an aspect of the cosmic mind is consistent with the claim that my conscious mind is part of Reality as it is in and of itself. There is no inconsistency in holding that both a whole and its aspects are privileged.

The micropsychist can account for the o-consciousness facts being nothing over and above the fundamental facts only if she holds that o-subjects and o-consciousness are mere shadows cast by the structure of our discourse. The cosmopsychist need not suppose this: facts about o-consciousness are subsumed within the fundamental facts about the conscious universe, and *this* accounts for the o-consciousness facts being nothing over and above the fundamental facts about the conscious universe.

In summary, I believe that micropsychism is, whilst cosmopsychism is not, reliant on a deflationary account of facts concerning human and animal experience, and that because of this the former is a much less plausible view than the latter. If we want to take advantage of the theoretical benefits of constitutive panpsychism, then we should embrace cosmopsychism.

3. Appendix: Demystifying Metaphysical Elitism

Some will be suspicious of the use of primitive notions in metaphysics which don't seem to have any analogue outside of metaphysics, such as the notion of 'metaphysical privilege' employed in this chapter. In response to this kind of worry, Sider tries to make the notion of metaphysical privilege 'earn its keep' by demonstrating its theoretical utility. However, Schaffer has persuasively argued that Sider fails to do this. Sider invests in a non-comparative notion of privilege – concepts either carve nature at the joints or they don't – whereas it is a comparative notion of privilege that seems to be needed for the theoretical uses to which Sider wants to put this notion, for example, in accounting for laws of nature and the determinacy of reference (Schaffer 2014).

In what follows, I will try to demystify the notion of a metaphysically privileged notion of existence. I start from the idea that we have a primitive notion of 'basic existence': the kind of existence at play when we ask whether God or Platonic entities exist, the kind of existence we predicate of the fundamental entities in our metaphysical system. This simple notion of existence cannot be defined in more fundamental terms: we can say that for something to exist in this sense is for it to be 'real' or to be 'part of the world', but these are just different ways of saying the same thing.

Some philosophers may be suspicious of simple concepts, preferring a holistic view in which all concepts are inter-defined. There is not space to properly defend this here, but I find the holistic view hard to make sense of, especially when we appreciate that the circle of definition must eventually loop back on itself. Imagine a simple language which contains only four terms 'X', 'Y', 'Z' and 'R', which are defined as follows:

1. Xs are not identical to Ys and Ys are not identical to Zs.
2. Xs are things that bear the R relation to Ys, Ys are things that bear the R relation to Zs, and Zs are things that bear the R relation to Xs.
3. The R relation is the relation that Xs bear to Ys, Ys bear to Zs, and Zs bear to Xs.

It seems clear that descriptions involving such terms could yield no positive understanding of reality beyond its bare structure. And the problem would not be addressed by expanding the number of terms. The language can yield no positive understanding of reality (beyond its structure) precisely because its terms are inter-defined. In order to understand what X, Ys and Zs are I need to know what relation R is; in order to understand what the R relation is I need to know what the Xs, Ys and Zs are. The cognitive buck is continually passed and nothing is ultimately grasped.

However, there are some primitive concepts involved in the preceding simple language: existence, numerical identity, negation, and the idea of a relation. It is because of the involvement of these concepts that the above language has the potential to provide information about the bare structure of a world. But now imagine that even these terms themselves are inter-defined. In so far as we can make sense of this, the result would be the elimination of any positive understanding of reality.

For these reasons I cannot see how we can avoid a foundationalist picture of our conceptual scheme. This does not mean returning to the dead end of logical atomism attempted in Wittgenstein's Tractatus. Most of our concepts are rough and ready, vague, and have extensions determined by factors outside of our cognitive grasp. However, in so far as we have positive understanding of reality, that understanding must be built up out of simple concepts. And there are many plausible candidates: the modal notions of possibility and necessity (understood in their unqualified senses), number, identity, property, relation, and perhaps nomic notions such as causation or law of nature. The most general such simple concept, without which any understanding of reality would be impossible, is the simple notion of existence itself. This simple property I call 'basic' or 'privileged' existence.

One use of the verb to be and related expressions in natural language is to express basic existence. However, existence language is used in a much broader way. Consider the sentence 'There is a party at John's.' We don't use this sentence to state that there is some entity – a party – that has basic existence. We don't want to say that there is something – a party – that 'exists' in the way God 'exists' (if she does) or fundamental particles 'exist' (if they do). Rather we use that sentence to state that certain people are revelling. This is not to deny that the fact that there are people revelling may involve things that do have basic existence; the point is simply that the sentence does not assert the basic existence of *a party*.

Why do we use existence language in this much broader way? Because it is extremely useful. Perhaps in a society of metaphysicians it would be good to restrict uses of the verb to be only to expressions of basic existence; we would then have the language Cian Dorr dubbed 'Ontologese' (Dorr 2005). But metaphysics is by no means our primary aim in communication, and hence it would be senseless (and indeed practically impossible) to limit the use of existence talk in this way.

The fact that we use existence talk in a way that is broader than the way a community of metaphysicians would use it entails that the meaning of the word 'existence' (and related terms) in ordinary English is much broader than the meaning of the word 'existence' in Ontologese. The Ontologese sentence 'There is a party' is a bad translation of the English sentence 'There is a party'. In Ontologese the word 'existence' expresses basic existence; in English 'existence' sometimes expresses basic existence – in sentences asserted the 'existence' of God and fundamental particles – and sometimes expresses another notion, let us call this other notion 'secondary existence' or 'existence$_S$'.

• We can understand what secondary existence is by reflecting on the use of existence talk in different contexts. We use the sentence 'There is a party' to express the fact that people are revelling; hence, for a party to exist$_S$ is for it to be the case that there are people revelling. We use the sentence 'There is a table at location L' to state that there is a certain table-ish pattern of penetration resistance among certain regions of space; hence, for a table to exist$_S$ is for the regions of space in question to instantiate a table-ish pattern of penetration resistance (resulting, for example, in my coffee cup not falling to the ground when I 'put it down on the table').[12] Reflection on such cases tells us all there is to know about what secondary existence is.

As metaphysicians we are not only interested in what things exist, but in their properties and relations. Things don't just *exist*, they exist *in ways*. And thus if we have a notion of basic existence, we also have a notion of *forms of basic existence*, or *the ways in which things basically exist* (both intrinsic and relational). I take the notion of a form of basic existence to be equivalent to what – following David Lewis (1983) – analytic philosophers call a 'natural property'.

Just as not all uses of existence language express basic existence, so not all predications express forms of basic existence. I am inclined to think that determinate forms of consciousness are forms of basic existence; if this is correct then predications of determinate consciousness express forms of basic existence. But the sentence 'Either Bill has determinate conscious state X or Bill has determinate conscious state Y' does not ascribe to Bill a form of basic existence; rather it claims that either Bill has form of basic existence X or he has form of basic existence Y. Just as extended uses of the language of existence create a secondary notion of 'existence', so extended uses of predication create a secondary notion of 'property'. As theorists of Reality we are interested not in properties per se, but in forms of basic existence.

By bringing together the metaphysically privileged sense of 'existence' and the metaphysically privileged sense of 'property' we reach a quite general notion of metaphysically privileged 'Reality' or the 'World-As-It-Is-In-And-Of-Itself'. Sometimes metaphysicians are interested in the shadows cast by our concepts, especially when those concepts hold deep significance for us (such as the concepts of knowledge, ethics or causation). But the primary focus of metaphysics is Reality itself.

Notes

1. The term 'constitutive panpsychism' is from Chalmers (2015), although I define it slightly differently here.
2. Galen Strawson (2006) defines 'micropsychism' in a slightly different way, in order to capture the difference between those who think that some micro-level entities are conscious and those who think all are. I am interested here in a different distinction – that between top-down and bottom-up conceptions of panpsychism – and my definition of 'micropsychism' reflects this.
3. Shani (2015), Nagasawa and Wager (2016), Goff (2017), Albahari (this volume).
4. The name is inspired by David Armstrong's term 'the ontological free lunch' (introduced in Armstrong 1997: 12–13).
5. My characterisation of the notion of privileged existence is not exactly the same as Sider's.
6. As metaphysicians we may also be interested in giving an account of things that have secondary existence. For example, Humean metaphysicians may want to give an account of causation, despite denying that causal

facts participate in the privileged structure of reality. The point of such activity is to analyse concepts that are significant to human beings and should be distinguished from the project of trying to understand Reality as it is in and of itself.

7. Lowe 2000 defends a view close to this.
8. Goff (2017: ch. 2). In fact I outline in that chapter a form of grounding – grounding by analysis – that sounds different from grounding by truthmaking. As I'm now thinking about these matters, the combination of truthmaking and metaphysical elitism is not inconsistent with grounding by analysis, rather the former offers us a deeper account of the latter. Why think a deeper account of grounding by analysis is required? I think there's a deep intuition that certain entities, e.g. parties, exist in a lightweight sense and metaphysical elitism captures this.
9. I am assuming that causal powers are grounded in categorical properties. I argue for this in Goff (2017: ch. 9).
10. This point is defended in more detail in McGinn (1995).
11. I have argued this point in more detail in Goff 2019: ch. 1).
12. I outline this analysis of macro-level material objects such as tables in more detail in 2.2.2 of Goff (2017). Strictly speaking, it is an analysis of table-shaped objects, as plausibly a material object can be a table only if it was designed to be one or is treated as one. I also offer in 2.2.2 a way of analysing higher-level physical natural kinds.

References

Albahari, M. (forthcoming). 'Beyond Cosmopsychism and the Great I Am: How the World Might Be Grounded in Universal "Advaitic" Consciousness'. In W. Seager (ed.), *Routledge Handbook of Panpsychism*.

Alter, T., and Nagasawa, N. (eds.) (2015). *Consciousness and the Physical World*. Oxford: Oxford University Press.

Armstrong, D. (1997). *A World of States of Affairs*. Cambridge: Cambridge University Press.

Bayne, T. J., and Chalmers, D. J. (2003). 'What Is the Unity of Consciousness?' In A. Cleeremans (ed.), *The Unity of Consciousness*. Oxford: Oxford University Press, pp. 23–58.

Cameron, R. (2008). 'Truthmakers and Ontological Commitment: Or, How to Deal with Complex Objects and Mathematical Ontology Without Getting into Trouble'. *Philosophical Studies*, 140: 1–18.

Cameron, R. (2010). 'Quantification, Naturalness and Ontology'. In A. Hazlett (ed.), *New Waves in Metaphysics*. New York: Macmillan, pp. 8–26.

Chalmers, D. J. (2009). 'The Two-Dimensional Argument Against Materialism'. In B. P. McLaughlin & S. Walter (eds.), *Oxford Handbook to the Philosophy of Mind*. Oxford: Oxford University Press.

Chalmers, D. J. (2015). 'Panpsychism and Panprotopsychism'. In Alter and Nagasawa, pp. 246–76.

Coleman, S. (2006). 'Being Realistic: Why Physicalism May Entail Panexperientialism'. *Journal of Consciousness Studies*, 13 (10–11): 40–52.

Diaz-Leon, E. (2010). 'Can Phenomenal Concepts Explain the Epistemic Gap?' *Mind*, 119 (476): 933–51.

Dorr, C. (2005). 'What We Disagree About When We Disagree About Ontology'. In M. E. Kaledron (ed.), *Fictionalism in Metaphysics*. Oxford: Oxford University Press, pp. 234–86.

Fine, K. (1994). 'Essence and Modality'. *Philosophical Perspectives*, 8: 1–16.

Goff, P. (2011). 'A Posteriori Physicalists Get Our Phenomenal Concepts Wrong'. *Australasian Journal of Philosophy*, 89 (2): 191–209.

Goff, P. (2015). 'Real Acquaintance and Physicalism'. In P. Coates and S. Coleman (eds.), *Phenomenal Qualities: Sense, Perception and Consciousness*. Oxford: Oxford University Press, pp. 121–46.

Goff, P. (2017). *Consciousness and Fundamental Reality*. Oxford: Oxford University Press.

Goff, P. (2019). *Galileo's Error: Foundations for a New Science of Consciousness*. New York: Pantheon, London: Rider.

Heil, J. (2003). *From an Ontological Point of View*. Oxford: Clarendon Press.

Horgan, T., and Potrč, M. (2008). *Austere Realism: Conceptual Semantics Meets Minimal Ontology*. Cambridge, MA: MIT Press.

Lewis, D. (1983). 'New Work for a Theory of Universals'. *Australasian Journal of Philosophy*, 61 (4): 343–77.

Loar, Brian (1990/1997). 'Phenomenal States'. Originally published in J. Tomberlin (ed.), *Philosophical Perspectives 4: Action Theory and Philosophy of Mind*. Atascadero, CA: Ridgeview, pp. 81–108. (Reprinted in substantially revised form in N. Block, O. Flanagan and G. Guüzeldere (eds.), *The Nature of Consciousness: Philosophical Debates*. Cambridge, MA: MIT Press, pp. 597–616).

Lowe, E. J. (2000). 'Locke, Martin and Substance'. *Philosophical Quarterly*, 50 (201): 499–514.

Martin, C. B. (1980). 'Substance Substantiated'. *Australasian Journal of Philosophy*, 58: 3–10.

McGinn, C. (1995). 'Consciousness and Space'. In T. Metzinger (ed.), *Conscious Experience*. Paderborn: Ferdinand Schöningh, pp. 149–64.

Nagasawa, Y., and Wager, K. (2016). 'Panpsychism and Priority Cosmopsychism'. In G. Brüntrup and L. Jaskolla (eds.), *Panpsychism*. Oxford: Oxford University Press, pp. 113–29.

Papineau, D. (1998). 'Mind the Gap'. *Philosophical Perspectives*, 12 (S12): 373–89.

Papineau, D. (2001). 'The Rise of Physicalism'. In C. Gillett and B. Loewer (eds.), *Physicalism and Its Discontents*. Cambridge: Cambridge University Press, pp. 3–36.

Pereboom, D. (2011). *Consciousness and the Prospects of Physicalism*. Oxford: Oxford University Press.

Pereboom, D. (2015). 'Consciousness, Physicalism and Absolutely Intrinsic Properties'. In Alter and Nagasawa, pp. 300–24.

Rosen, G. (2010). 'Metaphysical Dependence: Grounding and Reduction'. In B. Hale and A. Hoffman (eds.), *Modality: Metaphysics, Logic, and Epistemology*. Oxford: Oxford University Press, pp. 109–36.

Schaffer, J. (2009). 'On What Grounds What'. In D. Chalmers, D. Manley, and R. Wasserman (eds.), *Metametaphysics*. Oxford: Oxford University Press, pp. 347–83.

Schaffer, J. (2010). 'Monism: The Priority of the Whole'. *Philosophical Review*, 119 (1): 31–76. (Reprinted in P. Goff (ed.), *Spinoza on Monism*. New York: Macmillan, pp. 9–50, 2012).

Schaffer, J. (2014). 'Review of Sider's *Writing the Book of the World*'. *Philosophical Review*, 123: 125–9.

Shani, I. (2015). 'Cosmopsychism: A Holistic Approach to the Metaphysics of Experience'. *Philosophical Papers Volume*, 44 (3): 389–437.

Sider, T. (2012). *Writing the Book of the World*. Oxford: Oxford University Press.

Strawson, G. (2006). 'Realistic Materialism: Why Physicalism Entails Panpsychism'. *Journal of Consciousness Studies*, 13 (10–11): 3–31.

14

THE CRUX OF SUBJECTIVITY

The Subjective Dimension of Consciousness and Its Role in Panpsychism

Michael Blamauer

I will start this chapter with a confession: I am a panpsychist – a full-blown panpsychist who holds that consciousness is a fundamental as well as ubiquitous property of our universe. I believe that every concrete thing in our world has both mental and physical properties. However, even though I am a full-blown panpsychist, I am also a skeptical one and often worry about the problems of this meta-physical, far-from-common-sense, position. But whenever someone asks me why I am a panpsychist at all, I always give the same answer: It's because I am convinced that panpsychism is the best theory at hand to explain how subjective experience fits into the materialist metaphysics of our world.

The subjective dimension of consciousness plays a central role in the arguments for panpsychism, and most of the problems I think about, when I think about problems of panpsychism, relate to this issue. Curiously, it is this subjective nature of consciousness that not only constitutes the core of the arguments for panpsychism, but is also a source of support for the most prominent arguments against it. That is why I think focusing on the ambiguous role of subjectivity in the arguments for and against panpsychism will provide a good sketch of what I call "the crux of subjectivity". And I find this very conducive not only to deepening the understanding of the whole theory but also to opening new perspectives and thus helping lead to possible solutions for related problems. Everything I state in the following won't be particularly original or new to the mainstream discussion. I will simply shift the focus to a particular point that seems to me worth emphasizing when it comes to panpsychism.

In what follows, I outline the crux of subjectivity for panpsychism in four major steps followed by a summary at the end: (1) By exposing the mind-body problem I will pave the way to an anti-reductionist position on consciousness; (2) I will map the dimension of subjectivity; (3) I will sketch its role in two major arguments for panpsychism; (4) I will illustrate why subjectivity is also at the core of two hard problems for panpsychism; (5) I will give a short synopsis and present two attempts toward dealing with the concerns outlined in section 4.

1. Mind and Body: What's the Problem?

As previously mentioned, panpsychism is discussed mainly as a metaphysical theory about the relationship of mind and body. However, it is a theory about the nature of our universe as well. As I am primarily interested in questions within the Philosophy of Mind, and in the mind-body problem in particular, the focus of this chapter lies on the first, narrower meaning of panpsychism. To see its relevance as a valuable theory of the mind-body relationship it is necessary to provide a short sketch of the problem. So, what is the crux of the relationship of mind and body and why is panpsychism attractive at all?

The crux is easily stated: mind and body do not reduce to each other, which means that the existence of the one does not entail the existence of the other. However, we as human beings experience ourselves as a unity of both mind and body. But let me get a bit more technical. To me it is self-evident and unquestionable that consciousness exists, as is evidently warranted by everyday experience (which is the reason I ignore those philosophical positions that deny the existence of consciousness in general). If we take a look at the current discussion, we find – roughly speaking – two distinct positions that say something about the relationship of mind (or consciousness) and matter (or body). On the one hand, we have those who take consciousness to be a derivative phenomenon, who are mostly reductive materialists. And on the other hand, we have those who take it to be a fundamental phenomenon. The latter are in the majority of cases dualists, mostly property dualists.

Now, for reductive materialists the fundamental features of the world are physical features because even mental properties are identified with certain functional roles that logically supervene on physical states and are as such merely physical features.[1] In strict contrast, dualists, or non-reductionists in general, reject the possibility of reduction of the mind via identification, be it with functional roles or physical states or whatever. They argue that the ontology of physics (or any other ontology) does not entail the existence of consciousness or mental properties. To make their point they mostly use *a priori* strategies that reveal the independent variability of mental and physical properties, which should demonstrate their ontological distinction.[2] Now, if the facts of consciousness, or the mind, and the facts of physics, or the body, are ontologically distinct, then we have two fundamentally different ontologies, both irreducible to each other. Here we touch upon the crux: we have two fundamentally different kinds of phenomena, which nevertheless stand in a somewhat lawful relation to each other, as warranted by our everyday experience (e.g. when someone takes aspirin to cure her headache and it works, or when someone experiences the delicious, subtle flavor of this red physical substance called wine on her tongue). Of course, these laws must be fundamentally different to the yet-known natural laws of physics as they correlate not only physical to physical phenomena, but the fundamentally different phenomena of consciousness and the material world. Thus, these laws must be additional to the laws of physics and therefore expand our current physical worldview (see Chalmers 1996: ch. 4). In order to see how panpsychism comes into all this I will dig somewhat deeper into dualism.

For the sake of argument and because it is the most widely accepted version of dualism in the current debate, I will expose one serious problem with property dualism to get a better grip on the dynamics that will lead us to panpsychism. Dualists commonly rely on a basic set of three assumptions to which, more or less, all the major arguments against reductive materialism lead: (1) Physical properties are fundamental[3]; (2) Phenomenal properties are fundamental; and (3) Fundamental laws relate physical and phenomenal properties to each other.

Of course (nomen est omen) the dualist divides the universe into two fundamentally different kinds of things: One the one hand, there exist things which are definitely conscious and on the other hand, there are things which are definitely not conscious. She holds that only things with a specific physical (or functional) setup are able to instantiate consciousness, which is thereby taken to be an emergent property of certain, otherwise physical, systems. This is, I would say, essential to the dualist position since otherwise it would turn into a variety of panpsychism, since the fundamental mental properties would be ubiquitous in the same way physical properties are. This is of course what property dualists commonly tend to avoid. Now, if a phenomenon is fundamental in the aforementioned sense, it does not depend on (is not deducible from) other facts, say physical ones, which is why it is often referred to as the paradigmatic example of a "strongly emergent" phenomenon (cf. Chalmers 2006: 244).

Strongly emergent phenomena are obviously "brute facts" as there is no intelligible path which leads one from the underlying facts to the sudden coming-into-existence of the phenomenon. In his famous paper, Galen Strawson (2006) lengthily argued against the concept of strong, or brute emergence. He argued that it has no explanatory power whatsoever when it comes to the generation problem of consciousness. However, I will not now head into this argumentative direction, but rather focus on another aspect of the problem of emergence. I will argue that the strategy of restricting the range of consciousness leads to quite absurd consequences when it comes to the generation problem and the idea of an ontogenetically (as well as phylogenetically) smooth development of mental features, which makes it difficult to think of the phylogeny of human organisms, especially as conscious subjects, as a smooth process of insensible gradation.[4]

The crux lies – or so I will show – in the phenomenology of consciousness itself, which is why I find it highly productive to go into more detail about what we are talking about when we talk about consciousness. I do this in the following section in order to later pick up the central theme again and argue why the property dualist would be better of as a panpsychist.

2. What We Are Talking About When We Talk About Consciousness

Consciousness is generally a rather problematic term when it comes to philosophical positions because it naturally resists any attempt to precisely define it. The reason for this is consciousness's self-recursive structure. And it seems as if the situation gets even more confusing when we try to fix the meaning of the term regarding other species. For example, when we talk about a dog being aware of the bone in front of him or the cat being conscious of the mouse in the hole, we do so according to our "human" consciousness. However, in the debate of the last, say 30 years, a rather generally recognized characterization has established itself, following Nagel's (1974) original formulation that there is "something it is like" to be conscious. This formulation has succeeded in the discussion because it seems to catch some magical, unseizable aspect of conscious experience by not referring to any further capacities such as cognition or language, and hence it is not principally restricted to humans, but applicable to other species as well. Let me outline some essential characteristics of Nagel's formulation in order to gain a clearer picture of that notion before elaborating on what I take to be the intrinsic nature of consciousness, which I labeled the "subjective dimension".

When we use the formulation of "what it is like" as a kind of reference to what we mean, when we speak of "being conscious", we commonly equate this formulation with the special "phenomenal quality" of conscious experience, i.e. some exclusive feeling or quality that pervades every experiential episode. Thus, to say that the white rabbit is conscious is to say that there is a special phenomenal quality that characterizes the rabbit's current state of being. For example, if someone stabs the rabbit with a knife, the rabbit is conscious of it by feeling intense pain (paired with other feelings such as fear, maybe paired with internal visualizations as well). Referring to the phenomenal quality of an experiential episode when using the formulation of "what it is like" is state-of-the-art and it is widely held that the essence of consciousness lies in this phenomenal quality, exclusively accessible to only one point of view. However, holding that the essence of consciousness lies in this special and exclusive phenomenal quality is misleading and obscures the true nature of consciousness rather than elucidating it.

In the following I will try to expose why it is not so much the phenomenal quality of an experiential episode that renders it conscious, but rather the *subjective presence* of the quality as such. I will argue that this intrinsic subjective character, the subjective presence, is the essence of what qualifies an experiential episode as a conscious episode. If there is something it is like to be in a particular state of being, then there is something it is like (for a subject of experience) *to undergo, to live through* it. Thus, I will try to shift the focus from the particular quality of the experience to the unique "way" the experience is present, namely (taking the previous example), in the case of the white rabbit, uniquely as the white rabbit's one.

To get a better grip on the distinction between the two aforementioned fundamental aspects of conscious experience and to make my main point a little clearer, let me dive a little more deeply into the distinction between (a) the phenomenal quality of an experience (or its 'phenomenal character') and (b) its being-for-a-subject-of-experience (or its 'subjective character').[5]

The phenomenal quality of an experience characterizes it as just the experience it actually is (in contrast to qualitatively different experiences). For example, the rabbit which is stabbed with the knife will quite certainly feel pain. However, there may be rare cases in which the rabbit feels pleasure in such situations. It is not only that the rabbit's different experiential episodes can differ qualitatively, but that there will also be a difference between the rabbit's phenomenal quality and the ones of other subjects of experience. To provide a further example: While the wine tastes delicious to me, it may taste horrible to someone else (who e.g. has previously swallowed a mint). As already stated, most philosophers who use the phrase "what it is like" to characterize the nature of consciousness focus only on the subjectively given qualities (which are not objectively explainable or reducible), i.e. they focus primarily on the phenomenal character of consciousness. I have pointed out in other papers (2011a, 2011b, 2011c, 2012a, 2012b, 2013a, 2013b) that such a shortened and one-sided understanding of the nature of consciousness might easily lead someone to bark up the wrong tree when it comes to finding an appropriate theory of consciousness, which is why I have tried to stress that one should focus not so much on the phenomenal aspect of experiences, but rather on their subjective dimension.

By subjective dimension (or subjective character) of an experience I mean the "being-for-a-subject-of-experience" of the aforementioned phenomenal qualities. This "being-for-a-subject-of-experience" is the essence of what makes an experience an experience at all. For a start – I confess – I derive this fact from my experiences in the way I am acquainted with them in everyday life: If there is something it is like to be in a state of whatever (pain, pleasure, different experiences), then, necessarily, there is something it is like *for me* to be so. This is a rather strong claim – I know – and one which is widely rejected, because it is so difficult to grasp the meaning of "subject-of-experience", especially with respect to the universal applicability of the "what it is like" formulation. Being a "subject" is commonly associated with having complex cognitive abilities, which are generally restricted to human animals, maybe with the minor exceptions of chimpanzees, magpies, rats, pigs, and other "more intelligent" species. But, this cognitive conception of "subject" is not what I mean by "subject-of-experience".

Let emphasize once more the difference between the qualitative aspect, i.e. phenomenal qualities, vs. the subjective dimension of experience. First of all, and quite roughly put: The subjective dimension of experience is characterized not by any kind of contents of my experience; rather it touches the being of experience itself. Experiences can differ in various ways, depending on their particular contents: The feeling of pain is qualitatively different from the sensations you get while swallowing chocolate or having an orgasm or watching a movie or listening to Beethoven's Fifth Symphony or everything at once. However, there is an aspect of experience that is equal to all experiences, an aspect that unites rather than discriminates between the various experiences, namely that experiences have to manifest themselves first-personally in order to be experiences at all. I call this the "manifestation aspect (of experience)", which I will attempt to illustrate in the following.[6]

In contrast to physical facts, which are accessible not only and exclusively to one person, but to many persons, even at the same time, facts of consciousness are private. It is essential to experiences that there is something it is like to undergo them and this is only possible if they "manifest" themselves first-personally. Experiences have their very being in being exclusively present to one subject: their essential being is first and foremost their subjective manifestation. The following example will quite vividly illustrate what I mean by this. More or less everybody knows what it is like to feel pain, be it a toothache, headache, joint pain, or the pain you experience when you accidentally cut your finger with a knife. Now, imagine the rather bizarre situation of visiting a doctor, describing your symptoms, and having her reply that you should stop worrying because everything you've just told her about your pain is merely an illusion, and in truth you are not in a state of pain at all. I am pretty sure you would look for another physician.

This situation is so bizarre because of the impossibility of being wrong about myself feeling pain: what appears to me to be pain is pain. If I feel pain then there is pain present and it is impossible to be wrong about my own state of feeling. Vice versa, if someone denies feeling pain, then there is no pain present. Experiences have their very being in their appearing for/to a subject-of-experience: Their first-personal manifestation is likewise our direct acquaintance with them, which is why subjective experiences are generally indubitable. This special kind of direct acquaintance with our experiences, this being immediately conscious of our experiences, is the very aspect of experience that fundamentally separates the first-personal ontology of consciousness from the third-personal ontology of physics. And it provides the basis for most of the arguments against materialism, such as the zombie-argument or the explanatory-gap argument. For example, when I taste a cold, clear and transparent liquid, thinking it is water and am told afterwards that it is not H_2O but XYZ, I was wrong about the content's being (in this case, that I tasted water). But I definitely was not wrong about the experience's being: I tasted a cold, clear and transparent liquid because I was immediately and indubitably aware of it by having the experience. This is even more obvious in cases where the content's being is strictly tied to its appearance, as in the aforementioned case of pain. In this case, the subject cannot coherently deny the existence of the phenomenal quality due to its immediate and indubitable presence in her experience. It is simply impossible to err about the existence of an experience from a first-person perspective, irrespective of all other physical facts, because it is perfectly conceivable (and, I assume, therefore possible) that subjective awareness exists (I am in pain and I am certain of this fact) without the realization of the adequate physical state of the body. I think this is what the hard problem is all about.

Here is the point in a nutshell: If consciousness is primarily a dimension of experience with a first-person ontology, then its nature lies not so much in some kind of special phenomenal quality or qualities, but rather in the subjective, i.e. first-personal manifestation of the experience. By this I mean that talking about an exclusive kind of quality of experience only makes sense if we think of these qualities as being subjectively manifest: they have to be present to a subject-of-experience in order to exist. Without their subjective manifestation they lose their first-personal character and turn into third-person phenomena (see my 2013a). Thus, intrinsic subjectivity is essential to consciousness, because even if phenomena with a third-person ontology may or may not exist, regardless of whether they are present to anyone, experiences have to manifest themselves subjectively in order to be at all.

This, in the current debate, widely neglected aspect of consciousness is crucial to the arguments against a dualist position. Now, let me return once more to property dualism and point out some of its quite severe problems in order to establish the basis for arguing why panpsychism is a much more elegant and coherent theory of consciousness.

3. Problems With Property Dualism Revisited or: Why the Panpsychist Is Better Off

Dualists divide the world – roughly said – into two parties: conscious and non-conscious things. However, there are also a large number of things which are – following the dualist credo – both conscious, i.e. having experiences, and consisting of non-conscious parts. As mentioned previously, I think most of the dualists agree that not only do human beings have a body and a mind, but also a number of other species as well, such as primates, dogs, cats, horses, cows, pigs, etc. (the list would be quite long). However, at some particular point, dualists must define a border between conscious and non-conscious things.

As I see it, property dualists have just two possibilities of executing this division of the world: Either they accept a smooth transition from the non-conscious to the conscious sphere, a vague border so to speak, or they simply define a sharp border, a leap from the non-conscious to the conscious sphere. In the following I will provide a short sketch of both strategies in order to show at the end of the section that neither of them are adequate.

The common conception of the ontogenesis of a human being is a smooth process of insensible gradation. However, the conception is the same for the phylogenesis of the human (and other) species as a whole. As mentioned, there is quite a large set of beings for the dualist, consisting not only of non-conscious parts, but also having experiences, i.e. which are composites of both parties. Of course, dualists, in order to avoid the "threat of panpsychism" (see Chalmers 1996: 154) must claim that conscious beings gain the ability to experience at a later onto- or phylogenetic state of their development: The ability to experience depends on the complexity of the being's nervous system. They hold that consciousness – as a metaphysically fundamental feature – supervenes naturally on physical or functional states and at a certain stage of physical/functional complexity (seen from a phylogenetic as well as an ontogenetic perspective); consciousness "slowly", i.e. gradually, fades in.[7]

Now, the problem with this conception is that at some particular point of development, the being is in a borderline state between being conscious and being non-conscious, or rather, being conscious and not conscious at the same time. The reason for this is that there is at least one state in the development of the nervous system's architecture during which it is metaphysically indeterminate whether or not consciousness supervenes. Such fuzzy states of consciousness are of course impossible in view of its intrinsic subjective nature. In the previous section I put my finger on this point: Experiences, in order to be experiences, need to manifest themselves subjectively, i.e. first-personally. Obviously, the first-personal manifestation of an experience can never be indeterminate. It is impossible for a feeling to be present and not-present at the same time. Even the slightest feeling can only be coherently called a feeling if it manifests itself first-personally, i.e. is present to a subject-of-experience.

Another minor objection concerns the scientific status of the exposed considerations. Let me illustrate this objection with the following example: Imagine a system becoming more and more complex (like the aforementioned ontogenesis of a human being from the fertilization of the egg to the stage of a foetus in the third month). Let's assume that during this developmental process consciousness "fades in" at some particular point, starting with a very slight or dull feeling. However – as argued before – if it is a feeling, even a very dull one, it has to manifest itself subjectively in order to be one. Now, if the dualist tries to avoid a strong correlation (due to problems I will explain in the next section), she must abandon the idea of precise psychophysical laws governing the relation between the mind and the body. Thus, these laws cannot be precise in range because they describe only a fuzzy segment in the development of the foetus's nervous system at which point it randomly starts to feel and experience. This fuzzy segment contains a range of different states with (even only slightly) different functional complexity where consciousness is sometimes instantiated and sometimes not (we have already ruled out the possibility of both being the case). Such a scenario would of course turn property dualism into a non-theory in that it claims that consciousness is fundamental but allows pure randomness to decide which systems are conscious and which are not. This is the main reason why most of the dualists take consciousness to be the prime example of a strongly emergent phenomenon.

Let me address some problems with this account in the following. In order to avoid the aforementioned problems concerning impossible borderline-conscious states, dualists would have to define precise psychophysical laws governing the instantiation of consciousness. They would have to define one, and only one, particular condition of otherwise physical systems (i.e. a certain functional architecture of a system) at which consciousness is instantiated. In contrast, all other systems lacking this certain condition would not instantiate consciousness. Thus, they would have to define a sharp border between non-conscious systems and those which are able to experience. Of course, in that consciousness is a fundamental feature (i.e. not reducible to its non-conscious parts), it must be taken as an "strongly emergent" feature because both aspects of the system (being conscious and being physical) are fundamentally different.

Now, to make my point, let me present a case where the assumption of such precise psycho-physical laws leads to quite odd consequences regarding the claim that these laws should be consid-ered fundamental. Again, imagine the development of a foetus's brain from the first cell to exactly the degree of complexity at which consciousness arises. By reaching the required nervous system's architecture the foetus abruptly starts to experience, i.e. the first dull feeling manifests itself first-personally. Due to the requirement of precision of the psychophysical laws governing the instantia-tion of this first manifestation of experience, the slightest decrease of complexity of the nervous system e.g. substitution of a single isolated cell, makes it switch abruptly from being conscious to being non-conscious. Thus, whether or not the foetus is able to experience depends on the altera-tion of a single cell, which, of course, renders the psychophysical laws extremely arbitrary. This arbi-trariness of course makes consciousness quite an arbitrary feature as well, which otherwise stands in rather sharp contrast to the property dualist's claim that consciousness, as well as the laws governing its instantiation, should be considered fundamental.[8]

Now, if the considerations about the "manifestation aspect" of consciousness are correct, they present a problem for all those positions which hold that consciousness is a metaphysically funda-mental feature – and in light of the preceding, especially for property dualists. The reason is that all these positions distinguish things that are clearly conscious from things that are clearly not conscious. And – as I have tried to demonstrate – any attempt to precisely specify a system's state in order to meet the demands of such a sharp cut-off point would lead to highly arbitrary results. Now, to my mind, the only alternative position, which not only avoids the demonstrated problems by holding on to the fundamentality of consciousness, but which is also in line with a modest naturalistic worldview, would be a kind of panpsychistic monism. For now, I take the aforementioned problems of property dualism to be sufficient for even considering panpsychism as a viable doctrine. So why would the panpsychist be better off?

Panpsychists consider mental properties to be on par with physical properties, having similar characteristics. As such, they assume them to be ubiquitous in the same way as physical properties are. Besides their paradigmatic ubiquity, mental properties – like physical ones – are taken to be intrinsic properties, i.e. properties that are ontologically constitutive of higher-level properties of the same kind. This allows the panpsychist to sidestep the necessity of postulating arbitrarily defined leaps within the developmental process of beings from their non-conscious to their conscious stages. William Seager once suggested understanding mental properties as Lewisian, perfectly natural, prop-erties, i.e. as properties that have the feature of composing when they aggregate.[9] For example, if a thing has the property of carrying a particular charge, then this charge is the result of totalling the particular charges of all its components. The same is true of a being's property of having a particu-lar mass: this property is the result of the composition of the being's entire components having a particular mass. In this panpsychistic framework, higher-level forms of consciousness (instantiating not only dull feelings, but also specific cognitive features) are compositions of lower-level mental properties of elementary particles. This avoids the aforementioned problems of emergence and the definition of a sharp cut-off point, guarantees a smooth developmental process of a being's con-sciousness, and meshes perfectly well with a modest materialist framework. However, if it were that easy, then we would have found a rather elegant theory of consciousness with panpsychism – even though we would have to partly revise, or even reverse, our common scientific view of the world. But there are still two quite persistent problems for panpsychism, which I am going to discuss in the next section.

4. Panpsychism and Subjectivity: Again a Problem

As we have seen, dualists face problems that panpsychists are able to sidestep: in a panpsychistic framework, consciousness is a truly fundamental property (not an arbitrarily emergent one) and smooth progress in the development of conscious beings (beings which have both properties: mental and physical ones) is guaranteed. These problems of dualism are related to the nature of consciousness: the intrinsic subjective character of experience, i.e. the aspect of first-personal manifestation of experience. However, it is exactly the crux of subjectivity which causes not only the dualist quite a headache, but the panpsychist as well, which I will illustrate in the following paragraphs.

The first minor concern revolves around the principle of universal composition. If having an experience presupposes its first-personal manifestation (which means nothing but the "being present" of this experience for a subject-of-experience) then, necessarily, every composition of low-level mental properties entails a higher-level subject-of-experience. Of course, one can easily guess some of the bizarre consequences of such a scenario. The universal definition of the principle of composition implies that every composite thing is a subject of experience, be it a molecule, a table, a dog, or a human brain; or be it a composite of all these beings. For all of these composites their experiences manifest themselves first-personally in a way that it is somehow for this composite to be in this particular condition. Thus, following the universal character of composition, the number of subjects-of-experience would increase tremendously and in ways which are quite far away from our basic intuitions about what a subject-of-experience is. This of course poses no logical impossibility, but it would demand a rather radical revision of our current commonsense picture of the world and its inhabitants.

The second, more demanding, problem of panpsychism is also strongly related to the intrinsic subjective nature of experience. It is the well-known composition or combination problem. In a nutshell, it is based on the problem of making sense of higher-level subjects-of-experience, like you and me, in terms of compositions of lower-level subjects-of-experience. In contrast to the aforementioned concerns regarding the principle of universal composition, the composition problem is a logical one. In his critique of so-called "mind-dust"-theories, William James was one of the first philosophers to address this problem.[10] The crux lies in the logical incomprehensibility of the idea of subjects summing.

Given that panpsychism is true and that fundamental particles have experiences, we of course try to picture this by analogy to what it is like for us to experience. Even if we cannot simply impose our experiential life on a fundamental particle, and we nevertheless try to strip down the idea of experience to its fundamental, intrinsic nature, i.e. the properties that every experience has to satisfy in order to be an experience at all, then we are still bound to at least two aspects: (1) its phenomenology and (2) its first-personal manifestation. Now, if we take these two aspects of experience to be necessary properties, then the composition problem is quite obvious: how can single states of subjective experience (e.g. of the atoms of my body) be combined to result in a higher (and even more complex) state of consciousness (mine)? It is essential for an experience to manifest itself first-personally, which means that an experience must be present to a subject-of-experience. Thus experience implies a minimal kind of selfhood. Now, assuming that an atom has a specific sensation of its environment (very different from our own experience due to its lack of sense organs and fairly different functional complexity) then – in order to be a sensation or feeling at all – it must be subjectively manifest, which implies that even the atom has a minimal kind of selfhood. But how can it be that my own self is the result of a combination of quadrillions of selves, all having different manifestations of experiences? E.g. losing my arm in an accident might be a very painful and even life-altering experience, but it will not affect my own personal identity as a subject-of-experience. It will nevertheless be the same me, or rather I, having the experiences. And a quite similar point can be made for the qualitative character of experiences: When I have a terrible headache, this kind of severe pain is not entailed by some billions of atoms feeling slightly pained (see Goff 2006).

The combination problem also appears when we focus on the intentional character of experience, i.e. that experience is perspectival. Every conscious episode is a kind of temporal appearing and disappearing of qualitative contents to a subject-of-experience. If every atom of my body instantiates such a perspective, it is logically impossible that the streams of consciousness of every single atom combine to constitute my single perspective. The reason is that the perspective of the atom is determined by the relationship of self and content, which is different not only for each atom but also for all atoms with respect to my stream of consciousness.

Of course, given these considerations we have to ask whether Thomas Nagel wasn't right in his programmatic paper of 1979, where he said that panpsychism remains a rather problematic position, even though accepting the premises that lead to it in the first place is more coherent than negating them. In the following final section I will attempt to alleviate these concerns by offering two possible solutions to the aforementioned problems of panpsychism and outlining viable suggestions for future research.

5. Conclusion and Outlook

I began this chapter with the confession that I am a panpsychist. I am one because I am convinced that panpsychism is the best theory at hand concerning consciousness's place in nature. However, applying a cost-benefit analysis to what has been said, it seems as though we have a kind of standoff regarding the problems of both positions. So why should we accept panpsychism rather than another non-reductive materialist position, e.g. property dualism? My answer is: because the chances of solving the aforementioned problems of panpsychism are much greater than solving those of the dualist position. In the following, I will address the two mentioned problems of panpsychism once again, outlining two possible approaches toward their solution.

Let me start with some thoughts on the problem of universal composition. The problem is straightforward in that, with the concept of unrestricted composition, the number of subjects-of-experience would drastically increase, bringing with it some quite counterintuitive consequences, e.g. any possible combination of myself, my earring, my desk, and the door to my office, would entail a subject-of-experience. To mitigate these counterintuitive consequences, we have two possible strategies at hand. Either we revise our commonsense conception of subjects-of-experience, or we specify the principle of composition in a way that does not affect its universal character but rather reformulates it in a way that not in every case of composition does a new, higher-level subject of experience arise. I focus on the second strategy as there is not much to say about the first one.

William Seager (2010b: 175) has recently defended such a strategy of specifying the composition principle: A composition produces a subject-of-experience when, and only when, the parts compose themselves in a way where the subjective features become relevant. He gives a vivid analogy for such a composition: Even though charge is a perfectly natural property, it does not necessarily follow that every composed physical object is charged, "because positive and negative charge can cancel each other out." Obviously, this is quite a radical simplification. Regardless, it should merely serve as a suggestion for a direction it might be fruitful to head in order to solve the problem. Here, further intensive investigation of the phenomenology and structure (temporal structure, spatial structure, qualitative structure etc.) of consciousness, especially of those features related or bound to the intrinsic subjective nature of experience, seems promising. Thus, in order to deal with this objection, new ways of formulating panpsychism with respect to the subjective nature of consciousness is demanded.

Now, if we take a look at the second, more demanding, problem for panpsychism (the combination problem), research should head into the same direction. Contrary to what I have written in previous articles on this topic, I currently do not think this problem is unsolvable in principle, but is rather a question of deeper, phenomenological investigation into the nature and structure of consciousness itself. William Seager recently introduced a strategy in one of his articles, under the name of "combinatorial infusion". Combinatorial infusion is a principle with which to sidestep the "composition problem" by simply following the Leibnizian idea that consciousness is not an aggregate but rather a simple whole: Mental simples can enter a certain constellation or form a certain structure, which builds a "whole" (in contrast to a mere aggregate). In such cases, the subjective characteristics "infuse" into the mental whole which then absorbs and thereby effaces them. Due to the effacement of the subjective characteristics, the resulting mental whole becomes a large simple (rather than an aggregate of many). To illustrate his idea of combinatorial infusion, Seager (2010b) applies the analogies to phenomena of physics: "entanglement" in quantum mechanics and the classical black hole.

Of course, these are merely approaches toward solutions of the discussed problems. However, they point in a quite interesting direction. Despite the need for further investigation of the possible solutions to these problems of panpsychism, the latter seems to remain a viable candidate for a theory of consciousness, since it attempts to apply fundamental subjectivity to a moderately physicalist view of the world. And this is the overall prospect: How must we proceed in order to meet all the demands of panpsychist metaphysics by adhering to the fundamental characteristics of conscious experience? I think the challenge lies precisely in searching for a framework that can handle the tension between fundamental subjectivity and objectivity, unity and diversity, and which is likewise able to integrate and combine them with the facts of our material world. There will be progress – I am a believer.[11]

Notes

1. For a paradigmatic outline of such a "Reduction of Mind" see Lewis (1994).
2. A good synopsis of several arguments is offered by David Chalmers (1996). See also Seager (1999).
3. For a definition of "fundamental properties" see Chalmers (1996: 126): "Fundamental features cannot be explained in terms of more basic features, and fundamental laws cannot be explained in terms of more basic laws; they must simply be taken as primitive." I always found it necessary to expand this definition by adding "fundamental features do not ontologically depend on other, more fundamental features" in order to put an extra emphasis on the ontological dimension of fundamentality.
4. Armstrong (1968: 30–1) and Campbell (1984: 48–50) have made this point with respect to Ontogeny.
5. The conceptual distinction between "phenomenal character" and "subjective character" is taken from Kriegel (2009) and (2011).
6. I have already made this point in Blamauer (2013a) and (2013b), calling it the "manifestation thesis". By the idea of "manifestation" I roughly follow Zahavi (2005: 105 ff., 115 ff.) and Zahavi (2011: 324 ff.).
7. Chalmers (1996: 253–62) sketches such a fade-in / fade-out-scenario.
8. This point was made by William Seager against David Chalmers's "principle of organizational invariance", which can be interpreted as a principle to restrict the range of mental properties:

> It is disturbing that consciousness can be an absolutely fundamental feature of nature while being dependent upon particular systems satisfying purely functional descriptions. . . . No other fundamental feature of the world has this character, or a character even remotely like it. It is rather as if one declared that 'being a telephone' was a fundamental feature of the world, generated by a variety of physical systems agreeing only in fulfilling the relevant, highly abstract, behaviourally defined functional descriptions.
> *(Seager 1995: 275)*

9. Seager (2010a) therefore refers to them as "compositional properties".
10. James (1890/1998: 158, 160).
11. I am very grateful for Bill Seager's kind invitation to contribute to this volume – it is a great honour to me. Furthermore, I would like to thank Luke Roelofs for his helpful comments. And, of course, I would like to thank my good friend and all-time favourite interlocutor in philosophical matters, Wolfgang Fasching, for the fruitful discussions and amicable support.

References

Armstrong, D. M. (1968). *A Materialist Theory of the Mind*. London: Routledge.
Blamauer, M. (2011a). 'Wieviele Subjekte bin ich? Überlegungen zu einem Grundproblem des Panpsychism'. In T. Müller and H. Watzka (eds.), *Ein Universum voller Geiststaub? Der Panpsychismus in der aktuellen Geist-Gehirn Debatte*. Paderborn: Mentis, pp. 337–56.

Blamauer, M. (2011b). 'Taking the Hard Problem of Consciousness Seriously: Dualism, Panpsychism and the Origin of the Combination Problem'. In M. Blamauer (ed.), *The Mental as Fundamental: New Perspectives on Panpsychism*. Heusenstamm: Ontos, pp. 99–116.

Blamauer, M. (2011c). 'Is the Panpsychist Better Off as an Idealist? Some Leibnizian Remarks on Consciousness and Composition'. *EIDOS*, (15): 48–75.

Blamauer, M. (2012a). 'Does the Fundamentality of Consciousness Entail Its Ubiquity'. *Filozofia*, 67 (3): 243–53.

Blamauer, M. (2012b). 'Schelling's Real Materialism'. *Minerva – An Online Open Access Journal of Philosophy*, (16): 1–24.

Blamauer, M. (2013a). 'Panpsychism Without Subjectivity? – Brief Commentary on Sam Coleman's "Mental Chemistry" and "The Real Combination Problem"'. *Disputatio – International Journal of Philosophy*, V (37).

Blamauer, M. (2013b). 'The Role of Subjectivity in the Continuity-Argument for Panpsychism'. *Polish Journal of Philosophy*, 7 (1): 7–18.

Campbell, K. (1984). *Body and Mind*. Notre Dame, IN: University of Notre Dame Press.

Chalmers, D. J. (1996). *The Conscious Mind: In Search of a Fundamental Theory*. Oxford: Oxford University Press.

Chalmers, D. J. (2006). 'Strong and Weak Emergence'. In P. Clayton and P. Davies (eds.), *The Re-Emergence of Emergence*. Oxford: Oxford University Press, pp. 244–56.

Goff, P. (2006). 'Experiences Don't Sum'. In A. Freeman (ed.), *Consciousness and Its Place in Nature: Does Physicalism Entail Panpsychism?* Exeter: Imprint Academic, pp. 53–61.

James, W. (1890/1998). *The Principles of Psychology*, vol. I. Bristol: Thoemmes Press.

Lewis, D. (1994). 'Reduction of Mind'. In S. Guttenplan (ed.), *A Companion to Philosophy of Mind*. Oxford: Oxford University Press, pp. 412–30.

Kriegel, U. (2009). 'Self-Representationalism and Phenomenology'. *Philosophical Studies*, 143: 357–81.

Kriegel, U. (2011). 'Self-Representationalism and the Explanatory Gap'. In J. Liu and J. Perry (eds.), *Consciousness and the Self: New Essays*. Cambridge: Cambridge University Press, pp. 51–75.

Nagel, T. (1974). 'What Is It Like to Be a Bat?' *The Philosophical Review*, 83 (4): 435–50.

Nagel, T. (1979). 'Panpsychism'. In *Mortal Questions*. Cambridge: Cambridge University Press, pp. 181–95.

Seager, W. (1995). 'Consciousness, Information and Panpsychism'. *Journal of Consciousness Studies*, 2 (3): 272–88.

Seager, W. (1999). *Theories of Consciousness: An Introduction and Assessment*. London: Routledge.

Seager, W. (2010a). 'Concessionary Dualism and Physicalism'. *Royal Institute of Philosophy Supplement*, 85 (67): 217–37.

Seager, W. (2010b). 'Panpsychism, Aggregation and Combinatorial Infusion'. *Mind & Matter*, 8 (2): 167–84.

Strawson, G. (2006). 'Realistic Monism: Why Physicalism Entails Panpsychism'. In A. Freeman (ed.), *Consciousness and Its Place in Nature: Does Physicalism Entail Panpsychism?* Exeter: Imprint, pp. 3–31.

Zahavi, D. (2005). *Subjectivity and Selfhood: Investigating the First-Person Perspective*. Cambridge, MA: MIT Press.

Zahavi, D. (2011). 'Unity of Consciousness and the Problem of Self'. In S. Gallagher (ed.), *Oxford Handbook of the Self*. Oxford: Oxford University Press, pp. 314–33.

15

ANOMALOUS DUALISM

A New Approach to the Mind-Body Problem

David Bourget

A satisfactory solution to the mind-problem should answer the two following questions: (i) Are phenomenal properties, the properties that characterize states of consciousness, physical? (ii) How do phenomenal properties causally interact with physical properties? To a first approximation, physicalism and dualism are the two possible answers to the first question. Regarding (ii), there are three kinds of views on causal interactions between phenomenal and physical properties: nomism (they interact through deterministic laws), acausalism (they do not causally interact), and anomalism (they interact, but not through deterministic laws). In this chapter, I explore *anomalous dualism*, a combination of views that has not previously been explored. I suggest that a kind of anomalous dualism, *non-reductive anomalous panpsychism*, promises to offer the best overall answer to two pressing issues for dualism: the problem of mental causation and the mapping problem (the problem of predicting mind-body associations). I will start by charting the logical space around anomalous dualism.

1. The Logical Space

We can define *physical properties* as properties that fall under one of the following categories: (i) properties of roughly the kind that have so far been uncovered by biology, chemistry, and physics; (ii) properties that can be constituted by physical properties; and (iii) properties that actually constitute physical properties (if any). By *X constitutes Y,* I mean that X realizes Y, grounds Y, or stands in a determinate–determinable relationship to Y. This definition of physical properties corresponds roughly to Chalmers' (2015) definition of "broadly physical properties".

I take *physicalism* to be the view that everything, including phenomenal properties, is physical. *Anti-physicalism* is the negation of physicalism, whereas *dualism* is the view that phenomenal properties are instantiated but none is physical. Anti-physicalism without dualism is quite implausible, so the mind-body problem is typically conceived of as requiring us to choose between physicalism and dualism. Note that, since we understand "physical" broadly, Russellian monism and functionalism both count as kinds of physicalism.

Issues pertaining to mental causation figure centrally in the debate between physicalists and dualists. For present purposes, we can think of causation as a relation between events, and we can think of events as instantiations of properties by individuals at times. There are three possible views that one might take on any given alleged instance of causation between mental and physical events: *nomism* is the view that the instance of causation is subsumed under a deterministic law of nature; *anomalism* is the view that it is an instance of non-deterministic causation; *acausalism* is the view that denies that there is any

Table 15.1 Theories of consciousness

	Generalized nomism	*Generalized anomalism*
Physicalism	Standard physicalism	Anomalous monism
Dualism	Standard interactionism	Anomalous dualism

genuine causation. One can be a nomist (or an anomalist or an acausalist) about some alleged interactions and not others, but, plausibly, mind-to-matter interactions are either all nomic or all anomalous, and matter-to-mind interactions are either all nomic or all anomalous. I will refer to nomism about all mental-physical causation in both directions as *generalized nomism*, and likewise for the other views.

Physicalism and dualism can both be combined with each of nomism, anomalism, or acausalism about any given subset of alleged causal relations. If we consider only generalized versions of the views on causation and set aside acausalism as implausible, we have four options shown in Table 15.1.

Only one of these views has not been seriously considered: anomalous dualism. The aim of this chapter is to explore the viability of this view as an approach to the mind-body problem. More specifically, I am interested in finding out whether this view is promising *for a dualist view*.

For someone who is persuaded that physicalism is true, this might seem like a futile exercise, but I think there is something in this chapter even for convinced physicalists. Physicalism is largely motivated in opposition to dualism: dualism has too many problems (especially pertaining to mental causation), so physicalism must be true despite appearances (no one can deny that phenomenal properties really don't seem to be physical). If anomalous dualism turns out to avoid dualism's well-known difficulties, the motivation for physicalism will be weakened.

In the next two sections, I consider the two main problems that dualism faces: the problem of mental causation and the mapping problem. The latter has not been widely discussed, but it seems to me that it underlies much of the skepticism about dualism. I will suggest that anomalous dualism is the most promising dualist view as far as mental causation and the mapping problem are concerned. This is not to say that anomalous dualism does not have other problems. In section 4, I will consider various potential issues with anomalous dualism. I will suggest that a version of anomalous dualism that is also a version of panpsychism could conceivably solve many of anomalous dualism's apparent problems.

2. Mental Efficacy

Dualism has troubles with mental causation. The problem is that the physical world appears to be closed to causal influence from nonphysical factors, in the sense that nothing nonphysical can be causally relevant to physical events. If this is true, then either dualism is false or mental events are not causally relevant to physical events. Assuming that mental events are causally relevant to physical events, dualism must be false.

In order to see possible ways out of this argument, we need to get a little clearer on the justification for the claim that nothing nonphysical can influence physical events. This does not seem to be something that is revealed by physics or any other science.[1] To a first approximation, what physics seems to tell us is that every physical event is a deterministic effect of another physical event. This is what is generally referred to as the *completeness* of physics. For reasons that will become apparent shortly, I prefer to refer to this thesis as *physical determinism*.

Physical determinism: Every physical event is an immediate deterministic effect of a physical event.

By *immediate,* I mean that the effect is not mediated by another event.

It is not entirely obvious how to use physical determinism to argue against dualism, but there is at least one widely accepted way. Suppose first that mental events have physical effects.

Mental efficacy: Some phenomenal events have physical effects.

To complete the argument, we need to assume that the effects of mental events on physical events are not all overdetermined.

No systematic overdetermination: The immediate effects of phenomenal events on physical events are not all overdetermined.

An event is overdetermined when there are two wholly distinct events of which it is an immediate effect. By *wholly distinct,* I mean events that are nonidentical and not related through a relation of constitution (as defined above).[2]

Given mental efficacy and the no systematic overdetermination principle, we can infer that some phenomenal event M has an immediate physical effect P that is not overdetermined. P's not being overdetermined means that there is not a second event wholly distinct from M that also has P as immediate effect. But physical determinism requires that P is the immediate effect of a physical cause C. So M must not be wholly distinct from C. Given our definition of "physical", this means that M is a physical event. Assuming that events are instantiations of properties, it follows that some mental properties are physical properties. Therefore, dualism is false.

Since the no systematic overdetermination principle is not *a priori,* one might question it. The rationale behind it is that it is hard to see what plausible setup might guarantee the overdetermination of the effects of mental events on physical events. Overdetermination can happen, as in firing squad situations, but no one has made it plausible that the effects of mental events on physical events are systematically overdetermined. Without an independent justification, the hypothesis of systematic overdetermination is ad hoc and implausible.

One widely overlooked reason why denying the no systematic overdetermination principle is unattractive is that this premise is actually dispensable. It is dispensable on the assumption that mental efficacy entails *counterfactual dependence.*

Counterfactual dependence: Some physical event is counterfactually dependent on a mental event.

An event A is counterfactually dependent on an event B if and only if it is the case that A would not have occurred if B had not occurred. Even if mental efficacy didn't entail counterfactual dependence, counterfactual dependence is just as plausible as mental efficacy, so we can replace mental efficacy by counterfactual dependence in our argument. This yields the following argument against dualism. Take any physical event P that is counterfactually dependent on a phenomenal event M as required by counterfactual dependence. Physical determinism implies that P had an immediate sufficient physical cause C1, which itself had an immediate sufficient physical cause C2, and so on ad infinitum (or up to a first physical event if we make an exception to physical determinism for a first physical event). Take the event C along this chain that occurred at exactly the same time as M (we can slice the events of the chain in whatever way is necessary to delineate such an event). If dualism is true, C is wholly distinct from M. It follows from the standard, non-backtracking way of assessing counterfactuals that C would have occurred even if M had not occurred.[3] Since C is by hypothesis sufficient for a chain of events leading to P, this means that P would have occurred even if M had not occurred. This contradicts our assumption that P is counterfactually dependent on M. Therefore, one of physical determinism, counterfactual dependence, or dualism must be false.

Denying counterfactual dependence is an option for the dualist, but it comes with a huge cost: if counterfactual dependence is false, there is a clear sense in which the mental makes no difference to the physical. But if mental states made no difference to the physical, we wouldn't expect brains created through natural selection to involve any consciousness, much less for the phenomenal properties associated with physical properties to exhibit any sort of cohesion or "make sense". This seems to be a fatal objection to mind-to-matter acausalism however the relevant causal roles are understood exactly.[4]

This leaves a dualist with one possible response to the arguments from mental causation, which is to deny physical determinism. Unlike the other responses we have considered so far, this response has some initial plausibility. After all, physical determinism has been shown to be false by quantum mechanics. More specifically, quantum measurements are indeterministic in two ways: first, the outcomes of quantum measurements are probabilistic, following probability distributions fixed by quantum states; second, when a measurement occurs, and what the measured observable is, are not determined by anything within standard quantum theory.[5] These facts are typically ignored by philosophers of mind because the evidence from neuroscience seems to suggest that mental activity is implemented in macroscopic neural patterns, and it is generally thought that quantum effects are not relevant at this level of organization.[6] But our understanding of the brain remains fairly limited, and it is not hard to imagine how sub-neuronal conditions for consciousness might have gone unnoticed. So, let us not prejudge this empirical question. If we limit ourselves to assuming a limited completeness of physics that is consistent with quantum mechanics, the following is the principle that we should use as premise as part of arguments from mental causation against dualism:

Completeness: For every nonrandom physical event Y, some immediately prior physical event X is causally sufficient for Y.

A *random event* is an event whose occurrence was not determined by deterministic laws of nature, for example, the immediate outcome of a quantum measurement. I formulate the exception to determinism built into completeness in terms of randomness, and not specifically in term of quantum measurement, because I want to stay as close as possible to observation. We don't know whether a future, more complete physics might not drop "measurement" talk entirely in favor of a deeper characterization of what is going on. What we do know is that nature occasionally exhibits fundamentally indeterministic behavior that is correctly modeled by the mathematics of quantum mechanics.

Our qualified, scientifically correct completeness claim renders invalid the arguments sketched earlier. However, the dualist is not out of trouble yet, because the arguments can be fixed. To make our arguments valid again, we can add a further premise that specifies that the effects of mental events do not fall under the exception we have carved out for random physical events:

No-randomness: The immediately physical effects of mental events are not random events.

This might seem like a somewhat ad hoc claim, but it falls out of a slightly stronger claim that seems to be a natural, widely held view:

Mind-to-matter nomism: The effects of mental events on physical events fall under deterministic laws.

Given mental efficacy and no-randomness, we can infer that mental events have immediate, nonrandom physical effects. By the completeness principle, each of these effects has an immediate sufficient physical cause. Assuming that there is no systematic overdetermination, some of the physical causes of the effects of mental events are not wholly distinct from the mental events. This leads to the conclusion that dualism is false.

The argument from counterfactual dependence is slightly more complicated with completeness than with physical determinism. For simplicity, let us assume that time is discrete.[7] We must consider not just any counterfactual dependence relationship between mental and physical events, but a *direct* counterfactual relationship, one that is not the result of intermediary counterfactual dependence relationships. We can infer the existence of such relationships from counterfactual dependence: if there is a counterfactual dependence relationship between M and P, there must be a direct counterfactual dependence relationship between some mental event N and some physical event O, because the mental and the physical have to interface somewhere along the chain of dependent events. Now suppose that C is the physical event at the origin of (or far down) the chain of physical events leading to O. We know that C exists because of completeness and no-randomness. Either C occurred after N (the last mental event in the chain from M), or it did not. We can plausibly argue that C cannot have occurred after N because this would mean that it occurred in the time between N and O, but there cannot be any such time: if there was, we could discern intermediary events and counterfactual dependence relationships between N and O. If C did not occur after N, the argument proceeds as before: we can find a link in the chain C . . . O that is contemporaneous with N and argue from dualism that it would have occurred even if N had not occurred, which means that O (and P) would have occurred even if N (and M) had not occurred.

The versions of the argument from mental causation that appeal to completeness don't leave the dualist many options. Completeness is too well established scientifically to be questioned on the basis of *a posteriori* armchair considerations, and denying mental efficacy altogether seems absurd. As a result, denying mind-to-matter nomism seems to be the only potentially acceptable option. The thesis that mind-to-matter nomism is false has received some attention in the context of Davidson's (1970) defense of anomalous monism. There seems to be fairly widespread agreement that Davidson at least makes a good case for doubting the existence of strict laws connecting mental and physical events.[8] Many authors have raised doubts regarding the viability of anomalous monism as an account of mental causation, but anomalism remains fairly plausible independently of the rest of Davidson's view. In any case, it is far more plausible than denying completeness or denying mental causation altogether.

The dualist should not merely deny mind-to-matter nomism; she should also endorse mind-to-matter anomalism. First, this is required to escape the argument from counterfactual dependence, which only needs one instance of deterministic mind-to-matter causation. Second, if she took the position that some but not all effects of mental events on physical events are nonrandom, she would run the risk that some of the nonrandom events are also not overdetermined, which would allow her opponent to use our argument from no systematic overdetermination. Overdetermination plausibly can only occur by accident, so an "almost no overdetermination" principle is about as plausible as our no systematic overdetermination principle. As a result, the dualist has to at least endorse the view that deterministic causation from mental to physical events is rare. She might as well take the simpler, more principled view that it is the nature of such causation to involve some randomness (mind-to-matter anomalism).

Endorsing mind-to-matter anomalism seems to be the best strategy for the dualist, but one might worry that this response is merely an empty shell of a theory, and that it is not plausible unless there is some reasonable way of filling in the details, of explaining how the supposed random interface between the mental and the physical works.

A number of theorists have argued for a relationship between quantum randomness and consciousness. However, I am not aware of a "quantum theory of consciousness" that succeeds at giving a reasonably plausible account of mental causation that is consistent with completeness, mind-to-matter anomalism, and the totality of empirical evidence regarding the dynamics of physical systems.

Some theories allow mental states to deterministically cause physical states, claiming that such causation occurs under the cover of quantum randomness (cf. Eccles 1978), which is why we have not noticed it. This kind of view is ruled out by our arguments from completeness, as well as by empirical evidence (Bourget 2004). Other theories are consistent with completeness but not the totality of evidence regarding the dynamics of physical systems. According to Stapp's (1996) view, for example, the conscious mind acts on the body by selecting when a quantum measurement is performed and what observable is measured. Because of a phenomenon known as the "Zeno effect", this theoretically allows the conscious mind to control what the brain does. This is an example of a possible way of fleshing out mind-to-matter anomalism. However, this view turns out to be inconsistent with simple empirical observations (see Bourget 2004).

In order for the "quantum response" to the problem of mental causation for dualism to be plausible, it has to respect the constraint that quantum measurements have *very slight* effects on macroscopic systems as far as we can observe. To my knowledge, no theory that clearly respects this constraint has been offered. However, it remains that mind-to-matter anomalism seems to be the dualist's best possible solution to the problem of mental causation.

3. The Mapping Problem

The previous section motivated mind-to-matter anomalism. In this section, I present a motivation for matter-to-mind anomalism. While some authors have considered mind-to-matter anomalism, the combination of dualism and matter-to-mind anomalism has hardly been explored.[9] It seems to be almost universally assumed that if the mind is not physical, it arises via deterministic psychophysical laws. In this section, I want to point out that it is not obvious that this assumption is correct.

If dualism and matter-to-mind nomism were both true, the psychophysical laws that govern matter-to-mind causation would be fundamental laws of nature. As Chalmers (1996) points out, such a view would only be plausible if the psychophysical laws could be given a simple, general formulation (roughly, one that fits on a t-shirt). Otherwise, the relevant psychophysical laws would not be plausible candidate fundamental laws of nature. A canonical statement of the psychophysical laws should also explicitly relate mental states and physical states under their mental and physical descriptions, respectively. For example, it would not do to say simply that "a physical state gives rise to the mental state associated with it". A suitable statement of a psychophysical law would have to relate full descriptions of mental states as such with physical states under their full physical descriptions. Call a general, simple statement specifying which mental states (under a mental description) occur in any given physical condition (under a physical description) a *general psychophysical mapping*. Matter-to-mind nomic dualism seems to require the existence of a general psychophysical mapping, in the sense that the former would be quite implausible if we knew that there is no such mapping to be found. The problem of specifying a general psychophysical mapping (to the extent possible) is the *mapping problem*.

I want to suggest that we have fairly good evidence that there is no general psychophysical mapping. Note first that the existence of psychophysical correlations does not imply the existence of a general psychophysical mapping. It could be that there is a perfect correlation between phenomenal properties and physical properties, in the sense that the same phenomenal property is always instantiated along with the same physical property and vice versa, yet there is no general psychophysical mapping. Perfect correlation is even consistent with the absence of a finitely stable psychophysical mapping (a minimally demanding understanding of the requirement that a general psychophysical mapping be "simple").

Neuroscience has revealed numerous correlations between brain areas and types of conscious experience and other kinds of mental activity. It has also revealed what appear to be limited mappings between aspects of conscious experience and certain kinds of brain activity. For example, the phenomenological color space can plausibly be mapped in a relatively straightforward way to dimensions of activation in certain neural networks in the brain (see Churchland 1986). These are impressive findings, but they fall far short of a general psychophysical mapping. The associations that we know exist between phenomenal properties and physical properties don't seem to fall under a broad pattern that suggests a general psychophysical mapping. If we were to plot the known correlations between physical and phenomenal properties, we would see some local patterns (as in the case of color experience), but, aside from these local patterns, the points would jump all over the place, forming no recognizable curve that we can characterize. We have no idea how to extrapolate a general psychophysical mapping from what we have. Such a mapping has not even been *imagined*.[10]

I don't wish to diminish the accomplishments of neuroscience in any way: an extremely impressive number of correlations have been found. On the contrary, my point is that the vast quantity of correlational data that has been collected, together with the absence of a candidate general psychophysical mapping, makes it plausible that no psychophysical mapping is to be found. The more we find out about psychophysical correlations, the more non-generalizable they seem.

One philosophical theory initially seems to help with the mapping problem: representationalism. Representationalism is roughly the view that an experience of a quality Q is a mental state that phenomenally represents Q.[11] If we could give an account of the physical basis of phenomenal representation, then it seems that we would have a general psychophysical mapping. Suppose that physical relation R is the physical basis of phenomenal representation. Then it seems that we have the following general psychophysical mapping:

Representationalist mapping: An individual experiences quality Q just in case they stand in R to Q.

Suppose, for example, that R is the relation that one stands in to X just in case one has an internal state that is cognitively integrated and "tracks" the presence of X in the world. Call representationalism combined with this account of R *tracking representationalism*. Given tracking representationalism, it seems that we can predict what sort of experience one has in any given condition. For example, if one stands in R to redness, then one will experience redness.

Despite appearances, tracking representationalism does not provide a general psychophysical mapping. A general psychophysical mapping is supposed to relate phenomenal properties *under a phenomenal description* with physical properties *under a physical description*. Tracking representationalism does not specify such a mapping. The problem is that "experiencing Q" and "tracking Q" cannot at the same time be phenomenal and physical descriptions of phenomenal states and physical states, respectively, because "Q" is couched either in phenomenal language or in physical language.

To make the problem more vivid, consider how tracking representationalism might try to predict which mental state is associated with any given physical state. The idea is that we check which property is tracked. If an individual is tracking Q in the right way, we can predict that the individual is experiencing Q. The problem with this is that, when we identify what is tracked, we identify it under a physical description, for example, "the property of reflecting electromagnetic radiation of about 650 nm" (*R650*, for short). "Experiencing R650" is not a phenomenal description of the state of experiencing red – the proper phenomenal description of that state is "experiencing red". So the tracking representationalist account does not make any prediction about experiencing red under a phenomenal description. This fact is easily overlooked because we know, independently of tracking representationalism, that the experiences we have when looking at objects that have R650 are experiences of red, but this is knowledge we have above and beyond what tracking representationalism tells us. By itself, tracking representationalism does not give the phenomenal description of the state associated with tracking R650.

A parallel problem arises if we try to generate predictions in the mind-to-matter direction. If tracking representationalism is true, then experiencing red is associated with tracking redness. But "tracking redness" is not a physical description if "redness" is understood in a way that speaks to the phenomenology (if it means what it means as part of the phenomenal description "experiencing redness"). Without being given a physicalist theory of redness, which cannot be inferred from tracking representationalism, we don't know what is the correct physical description of redness or tracking redness.

The problem can be put slightly differently as follows. A solution to the mapping problem needs to specify a function that generates predictions such as this for all physically possible conditions that result in some conscious experience:

X experiences redness iff X stands in R to R650

Since phenomenal and physical descriptions are distinct, the representationalist schema does not have the right form to specify such a function. The following is the right form, where f is a function that maps physical descriptions of physical properties to phenomenal descriptions of experienced qualities:

An individual experiences f(Q) just in case they stand in R to Q.

Alternatively, the positions of "Q" and "f(Q)" could be swapped and the inverse of f used. Only a theory that fits this schema could possibly relate phenomenal descriptions with (distinct) physical descriptions, but I am not aware of any proposed non-trivial specification of f. So far, tracking representationalists have effectively assumed that it is the identity function.

There are other relational views of experience that might seem to specify a general psychophysical mapping of the form of the representationalist mapping, for example, naïve realism. The very form of that mapping guarantees that these theories do not supply a general psychophysical mapping.

It turns out, then, that tracking representationalism and other relational theories of consciousness do not specify a general psychophysical mapping. This is why I said earlier that a general psychophysical mapping has not even been *imagined*. What we have imagined is a theory that *seems* to specify a general psychophysical mapping.

Once the apparent solution to the mapping problem offered by tracking representationalism and similar views is set aside, the problem seems completely hopeless for matter-to-mind nomic dualism. There is simply no discernible suitably general pattern in the known phenomenal-physical correlations revealed by neuroscience or everyday observation, and there is little hope of finding any.

This leaves the dualist with two choices regarding causation in the matter-to-mind direction: acausalism and anomalism. Matter-to-mind acausalism would require something like a preestablished harmony to keep mental states and physical state in sync, which is extremely implausible (especially without theism as a supporting hypothesis). Matter-to-mind anomalism, however, effectively dissolves the mapping problem. On this view, there is no deterministic causation from the physical to the mental, so we should not expect there to be a general psychophysical mapping.

4. Anomalous Panpsychism

In section 2, we saw that, despite obvious difficulties, the most reasonable approach to the problem of mental causation for the dualist is to reject mind-to-matter nomism in favor of mind-to-matter anomalism. The mapping problem discussed in section 3 is a challenge for dualism combined with matter-to-mind nomism, and we have seen that matter-to-mind anomalism may be the best way out of this problem for the dualist. Taken together, these considerations make a case for considering anomalous dualism, the kind of dualism that endorses anomalism about both mind-to-matter and matter-to-mind causation. As far as the considerations pertaining to mental causation and the mapping problem are concerned, anomalous dualism seems to be the most promising dualist view.

Even if anomalous dualism combines the best answers to the arguments from completeness and the mapping problem, this does not mean that the view is plausible. In particular, a number of objections need to be addressed. I will consider the following objections:

First, even if anomalous dualism is technically speaking consistent with mental efficacy, does it not give up on a truly significant causal role for consciousness? As we noted in our discussion of quantum theories of mental causation, quantum mechanics and the total body of evidence concerning the dynamics of physical systems do not seem to leave much room for mind-caused random effects to make much of a difference to the course of physical events. For this reason, it seems that mind-to-matter anomalism is inconsistent with macroscopic mind-to-matter causal connections. For example, it seems inconsistent with the fact that my conscious intention to raise my arm causes my arm to raise. I will refer to the claim that there is macroscopic mind-to-matter causation but hardly any observable macroscopic random events as *causation without randomness*.

Second, anomalous dualism seems in tension with the existence of psychophysical correlations. Even if neuroscience has not solved the mapping problem, it has uncovered numerous correlations between brain activity and conscious activity: the same brain activity is always accompanied by the same conscious activity. Call this fact *the mind-brain correlation observation*. It is not clear that anomalous dualism is consistent with the mind-brain correlation observation.

Third, if mind and matter were only randomly associated, wouldn't our experience be a mere "blooming, buzzing confusion"? Instead, our conscious minds seem to have some sort of internal cohesion. Call this fact *phenomenal cohesion*.

Lastly, anomalous dualism might not have the problem of specifying a general psychophysical mapping, but is this not simply because it gives up on explaining consciousness altogether? How could anomalous dualism explain consciousness and shed light on its place in nature without giving us psychophysical laws that explain how phenomenal states arise and what effects they have?

Despite appearances, anomalous dualism is at least in principle consistent with causation without randomness, mind-brain correlations, and phenomenal cohesion. It is also easy to see how it can be genuinely explanatory. The following picture can serve as a kind of proof of concept, though its details are somewhat implausible. Suppose that physical and phenomenal properties are wholly distinct, but that every physical property is "linked" to a randomly selected phenomenal property (within certain constraints) the first time it occurs in the history of universe.[12] As an example, suppose that the following two constraints apply to this random linking: (i) if physical properties P and Q are both instantiated at the time of the linking, they are linked to consistent phenomenal properties (assuming representationalism, we can say that two phenomenal properties are consistent when their contents are consistent); and (ii) if physical property P necessitates physical property Q, then P's phenomenal property necessitates Q's. Once linked, phenomenal and physical properties forever co-occur across the universe. Suppose also that the phenomenal properties of a physical system can in some circumstances have a random effect on the dynamics of the system. Say, for example, that any physical system about to enter a total physical state involving physical properties associated with inconsistent phenomenal properties randomly jumps to another physical state with a probability determined by the physical state of the system. (Such an event could be modeled as a measurement by quantum mechanics, but it doesn't have to be something that we would intuitively describe as a measurement and, conversely, events that we describe as measurements don't have to occur in this way). These suppositions together specify a view I am going to refer to as *the random theory*. This view is a kind of non-reductive anomalous panpsychism: it combines dualism (non-reductionism) with generalized anomalism and *panpsychism*, the view that phenomenal properties pervade the physical universe. I am going to refer to this kind of view more simply as *anomalous panpsychism*.

The random theory is quite implausible on its face, and seriously vague and underspecified, but it is useful to consider as a first step into the largely unexplored conceptual space of anomalous dualism and anomalous panpsychism. I want to suggest that its principles could potentially be precisified in a way that might yield an explanation of consciousness consistent with the mind-brain correlation observation, phenomenal cohesion, causation without randomness, completeness, and the overall body of evidence regarding the dynamics of physical systems.

The mind-brain correlation observation is easiest: it only requires that the same phenomenal and physical properties tend to occur together. The random theory is not only consistent with this fact, but its linking principle offers an explanation for it (however intrinsically implausible it might seem as stated).

Phenomenal cohesion requires us to think about what would have happened over time if the random theory were true. Let us assume that there is some principled way of delineating the physical systems to which the random theory refers that counts properly functioning animal brains, or at least big parts of animal brains, as whole systems.[13] Under this assumption, we would expect the brains of organisms to have evolved so that they barely ever enter physical states that have been linked to inconsistent phenomenal properties (or at least not macroscopic states linked to inconsistent properties). Unless they had so evolved, they would be suffering from the disruptive effects of random jumps, which would make them unstable, hence not prone to survive. Regarding simpler physical systems (including, in the limit case, isolated particles), their having fewer phenomenal properties (in virtue of having fewer physical properties) might explain their stability: they are not very likely to enter inconsistent states. The final result, then, should be brains and other macroscopic physical systems in which the potential random effects due to consciousness are largely absent, which is what we find. We should also expect the resulting stream of experiences supported by human brains to be generally coherent, which is what we find (phenomenal cohesion).

In addition to predicting a certain orderliness that is consistent with what we find, the random theory also predicts that phenomenal-physical associations should appear essentially random except for any structure implied by the linking principle. Again, this is roughly consistent with what we find. This is particularly interesting because no other theory even begins to explain the apparent randomness of mind-body correlations. Our half-baked anomalous panpsychism seems to provide not only a proof of concept for an explanation of the ways in which consciousness is organized, but it seems that a story along these lines could also potentially explain the ways in which it is *disorganized*. This might answer the charge that anomalous dualism gives up on explanation.

We have yet to show that anomalous dualism, anomalous panpsychism, or the random theory is consistent with causation without randomness, which one might say is the main problem with these views.

There is one important way in which the random theory illustrates the possibility of macroscopic effects consistent with completeness and a general lack of macroscopic quantum effects. If this theory is true, consciousness might have played a role in structuring physical systems in the past, progressively weeding out complex systems whose tendency to generate inconsistent experiences makes them unstable. This requires that there were many macroscopic random events triggered by consciousness in the past, but not that such events be common *today*. In this way, the random theory illustrates the possibility that consciousness played an important causal role in the course of evolution without making a detectable difference today.

This addresses the need for some efficacy throughout natural evolution, but this does not fully address the objection that consciousness has macroscopic effects that are not simply random effects. In particular, this does not accommodate alleged causal connections such as a mental state causing a bodily movement.

The first thing to note here is that it is almost certain that no mental state is nomologically sufficient for a bodily movement. The most that we can ask for is causal *relevance,* not strictly speaking *causation.*

Without giving an analysis of causal relevance, it is plausible that events that stand in counter-factual dependence relationships are *in some sense* causally relevant to each other. For example, had there not been a spark, the fire would not have started. This seems to make the presence of the spark causally relevant to the fire.

A view along the lines of the random theory could potentially deliver just this kind of causal relevance between mental events and bodily movements in a manner that is entirely consistent with completeness and the general absence of macroscopic random events. To illustrate, take the following counterfactual claim:

> **Chocolate:** Had you not consciously thought that there was a chocolate bar in front of you, you would not have reached out in the way you did at the time you did.

If Chocolate were true, your conscious thought that there was a chocolate bar in front of you would be causally relevant to your reaching in the way you did, just like the spark is causally relevant to the fire. The random theory can potentially be precisified in such a way as to be consistent with, and explain, facts such as Chocolate consistently with all evidence on hand. Suppose, for example, that your perceptual systems were rigged in such a way that, given their input at t (a retinal image of a chocolate bar), they will trigger a conscious thought to the effect that there is a chocolate bar in front of you at a specific location L if you are not having such a thought at t. At the same time, suppose that your cognitive system was poised to theorize about what is in front of you in such a way that if you don't consciously think that there is a chocolate bar in front of you at t, you will quickly form a conscious thought to the effect that there is a certain non-chocolate desert, say, lemon pie, in front of you at L. In sum, your brain is in such a state that, as a matter of nomologically necessity, if you are not having a thought that there is a chocolate bar at L at t, it will, at $t+1$, produce both a conscious thought that there is a chocolate bar at L *and* a conscious thought that there is lemon pie at L. Given that these thoughts have inconsistent contents, this setup makes the following counterfactual true: had you not consciously thought that there was a chocolate bar in front of you, you would have formed inconsistent conscious thoughts. On the random theory, inconsistent phenomenal states trigger random disruptions. In principle, we could flesh out the details of the case and the random theory in such a way that this would have prevented you from reaching at just the time you did. This would make Chocolate true. Of course, this example is highly contrived (I am only trying to make a point of principle), but, for all we know, it could be that the brain's massively redundant architecture ensures that many phenomenal states cannot be altered without generating an inconsistency, which would underpin a kind of causal relevance for these states on the random theory.

This kind of causal relevance could be pervasive consistently with completeness and a general absence of detectable macroscopic random events. This is because counterfactuals make no observable difference. For example, the truth of Chocolate makes no observable difference to the course of physical events. If the physical universe and the organisms it contains had evolved to keep consciousness-caused random events to a minimum as the random theory seems to predict, we would expect numerous counterfactuals like Chocolate to be true, which would give consciousness widespread causal relevance that makes no detectable difference today.

While anomalous dualism is consistent with two important causal roles for mental events, there are also causal roles that it is not consistent with: it does not allow mental events to be nomologically necessary nor sufficient for physical events, and, intuitively, it does not allow causal *oomph* to pass from mental events to physical events in a deterministic way. One might say that these are important shortcomings of the view. They are perhaps shortcomings, but anomalous dualism at least succeeds in accommodating the core evidence regarding mental causation. We don't have very strong reasons to think that causal *oomph* passes between mental and physical events, much less to think that the two kinds of event are subsumed under nomological principles. Such claims are simply not apparent to ordinary or scientific observation. The key reason mental causation must be accommodated is not that it is directly observable, but that it seems necessary in order to make sense of the place of consciousness in the mind and nature, in particular, of the fact that brains seem to have evolved to make use of conscious states in some way (as noted in section 2). Anomalous dualism promises to satisfy on this score.

Our exploration of the random theory suggests that a view along these lines can in principle explain the apparent arbitrariness of phenomenal-physical associations while being consistent with macroscopic mental efficacy, an evolutionary role for consciousness, the existence of numerous mind-brain correlations, phenomenal cohesion, the completeness of physics, and a general lack of observed macroscopic randomness. As a kind of dualism, the random theory is also consistent with arguments against all types of physicalism (including those of Chalmers (1996) and Goff (2009)). This makes anomalous panpsychism the only position on the mind-body problem that is not currently open to principled objections (that I know of). Of course, the random theory is implausibly vague and almost certainly not entirely correct. It is an open empirical question whether or not a more precise anomalous panpsychic theory can be specified that retains the theoretical virtues of the random theory and is consistent with everything we know or may find out in physics and neuroscience. My goal in this chapter was only to try to open some new conceptual space. Even though the random theory itself is implausible, its many virtues suggest that the overall approach of anomalous panpsychism might deserve more investigation.[14]

Notes

1. Papineau (2001) makes this point and offers an excellent overview of the history of the closure problem for dualism. The first argument discussed below is adapted from Papineau's discussion.
2. The "wholly distinct" qualification makes the no systematic overdetermination principle consistent with non-reductive physicalism and Russellian monism.
3. In assessing counterfactuals of the form "had A been the case, B would have been the case", we must check whether B is the case at the nearest possible worlds at which A is the case. Importantly, the nearest worlds need not be worlds that are physically possible: we don't look for worlds that have histories that explain A through laws like ours (this would typically require us to "backtrack" into the history of the world). Rather, we allow A to be the case at a world just like ours, without a suitable history, as if by miracle (Lewis 1973, 1979). As a result, any contemporaneous or earlier fact at the actual world that is metaphysically compatible with A is also a fact at the nearest A worlds. In our case C is contemporaneous with M and metaphysically independent of it (in virtue of dualism), so the nearest M-less world is a C world.
4. One might also argue from everyday experience that phenomenal states have bodily effects. For example, conscious intentions seem to cause bodily movements. Some considerations in section 4 throw some doubt on this, but they leave untouched the argument that consciousness must do something for our brains to have evolved to produce cohesive streams of experience.
5. There are developments of the theory that attempt to give a physical explanation of measurement, but none is widely accepted.
6. Sometimes, allowances are made for quantum randomness by formulating completeness as follows: the objective probability of every physical event is determined by a prior physical event (Yablo 1992; Bennett 2007). This is still too strong because *that* a measurement will occur at any given time in a quantum system is not physically determined on standard interpretations. Events that could occur as a result of measurement don't have any objective probability *until* a measurement is "decided". If measurement is not decided by a physical state (which is not the case on standard QM), not every physical event has a probability fixed by a prior physical event.
7. We can make do without this assumption, but it requires thinking of infinite sets of events occurring within intervals of time rather than discrete events, which complicates parts of the argument.
8. Seager (1981) offers a rigorous defense of anomalism that refines Davidson's arguments.
9. One notable exception is Seager (1991: 328–33).
10. Chalmers' (1996) information-theoretic proposal might be the closest that we have come.
11. For defenses of representationalism, see Byrne (2001), Crane (2003), Chalmers (2004), Pautz (2009), Bourget and Mendelovici (2014), and Bourget (2019). Some representationalists suggest that a further ingredient

might be required in addition to phenomenal representation of a content: an intentional mode or representational manner (see Crane 2003; Chalmers 2004; Speaks 2010, 2015). I argue against such extra ingredients in Bourget (2015, 2017a, 2017b).

12. This principle might require a sparse understanding of the relevant physical properties, for example, as natural physical properties in Lewis' sense.

13. Someone attracted to something like the random theory might speculate that quantum entanglement is what delineates systems. A number of authors have explored entanglement-based explanations of the fact that consciousness seems to unify contributions from different parts of a physical system (e.g. Lockwood 1989; Penrose 1994; Seager 1995). There is a widespread misconception (among philosophers) that "decoherence" virtually eliminates entanglement from the macroscopic world, but in fact the theory only predicts that decoherence makes entanglement unnoticeable by making the results of quantum measurement statistically like those of classical measurements. See Schlosshauer 2005 for a relatively non-technical explanation of decoherence.

14. Thanks to Angela Mendelovici for her extensive feedback.

References

Bennett, K. (2007). 'Mental Causation'. *Philosophy Compass*, 2 (2): 316–37.

Bourget, D. (2004). 'Quantum Leaps in Philosophy of Mind'. *Journal of Consciousness Studies*, 11 (12): 17–42.

Bourget, D. (2015). 'Representationalism, Perceptual Distortion and the Limits of Phenomenal Concepts'. *Canadian Journal of Philosophy*, 45 (1): 16–36.

Bourget, D. (2017a). 'Representationalism and Sensory Modalities: An Argument for Intermodal Representationalism'. *American Philosophical Quarterly*, 53: 251–67.

Bourget, D. (2017b). 'Why Are Some Experience "Vivid" and Others "Faint"? Representationalism, Imagery, and Cognitive Phenomenology'. *Australasian Journal of Philosophy*, 95 (4): 673–87.

Bourget, D. (2019). 'Implications of Intensional Perceptual Ascriptions for Relationalism, Disjunctivism, and Representationalism About Perceptual Experience'. *Erkenntnis*, 84 (2): 381–408.

Bourget, D., and Mendelovici, A. (2014). 'Tracking Representationalism'. In A. Bailey (ed.), *Philosophy of Mind: The Key Thinkers*. New York: Continuum, pp. 209–35.

Byrne, A. (2001). 'Intentionalism Defended'. *Philosophical Review*, 110 (2): 199–240.

Chalmers, D. J. (1996). *The Conscious Mind: In Search of a Fundamental Theory*. Oxford: Oxford University Press.

Chalmers, D. J. (2004). 'The Representational Character of Experience'. In B. Leiter (ed.), *The Future for Philosophy*. Oxford: Oxford University Press, pp. 153–81.

Chalmers, D. J. (2015). 'Panpsychism and Panprotopsychism'. In T. Alter and Y. Nagasawa (eds.), *Consciousness in the Physical World: Essays on Russellian Monism*. Oxford: Oxford University Press, pp. 246–76.

Churchland, P. S. (1986). *Neurophilosophy: Toward a Unified Science of the Mind-Brain*. Cambridge, MA: MIT Press.

Crane, T. (2003). 'The Intentional Structure of Consciousness'. In Q. Smith and A. Jokic (eds.), *Consciousness: New Philosophical Perspectives*. Oxford: Oxford University Press, pp. 33–56.

Davidson, D. (1970). 'Mental Events'. In *Essays on Actions and Events*. Oxford: Clarendon Press, pp. 207–24.

Eccles, J. C. (1978). *Mind and Brain*. Saint Paul, MN: Paragon House.

Goff, P. (2009). 'Why Panpsychism Doesn't Help Us Explain Consciousness'. *Dialectica*, 63 (3): 289–311.

Lewis, D. K. (1979). 'Counterfactual Dependence and Time's Arrow'. *Noûs*, 13 (4): 455–76.

Lewis, D. K. (1973). *Counterfactuals*. Oxford: Blackwell.

Lockwood, M. (1989). *Mind, Brain, and the Quantum*. Oxford: Oxford University Press.

Papineau, D. (2001). 'The Rise of Physicalism'. In C. Gillett and B. Loewer (eds.), *Physicalism and Its Discontents*. Cambridge: Cambridge University Press.

Pautz, A. (2009). 'A Simple View of Consciousness'. In R. Koons and G. Bealer (eds.), *The Waning of Materialism: New Essays*. Oxford: Oxford University Press, pp. 25–66.

Penrose, R. (1994). *Shadows of the Mind*. Oxford: Oxford University Press.

Schlosshauer, M. (2005). 'Decoherence, the Measurement Problem, and Interpretations of Quantum Mechanics'. *Review of Modern Physics*, 76: 1267–305.

Seager, William (1981). 'The Anomalousness of the Mental'. *Southern Journal of Philosophy*, 19 (3): 389–401.

Seager, William (1991). *The Metaphysics of Consciousness*. London: Routledge.

Seager, William (1995). 'Consciousness, Information, and Panpsychism'. *Journal of Consciousness Studies*, 2 (3): 272–88.

Speaks, J. (2010). 'Attention and Intentionalism'. *Philosophical Quarterly*, 60 (239): 325–42.

Speaks, J. (2015). *The Phenomenal and the Representational*. Oxford: Oxford University Press.

Stapp, H. P. (1996). 'The Hard Problem: A Quantum Approach'. *Journal of Consciousness Studies*, 3 (3): 194–210.

Yablo, S. (1992). 'Mental Causation'. *Philosophical Review*, 101 (2): 245–80.

PART III

Comparative Alternatives

16

SUBJECTIVE PHYSICALISM AND PANPSYCHISM

Robert J. Howell

The past fifty or so years have had philosophers of mind talking about bats, zombies and experientially deprived geniuses (Nagel 1974; Jackson 1982; Chalmers 1996). These flights of fancy have resurrected the mind-body problem by helping us see what was so intractable about it in the first place. Put simply, it is hard to understand how the pushings and pullings described by physics, or even the pumpings, squishings and zaps described by biology and neuroscience, could ultimately, at some level of description, be the same thing as the feeling of pain or the experience of redness. The natural move, of course, is to say that pending some inconceivable revelation we should be dualists. We should believe that the properties and states that constitute phenomenal conscious experience escape the net of physics and therefore physicalism. There are two worries that complicate that move, though. One is that dualism is apt to make phenomenal states epiphenomenal. Those pale pushings and pullings explain an awful lot. It's arguable that they explain all of the physical events there are – including the many brain processes that underly our cognitive processes. If so, there seems to be no unique work for phenomenal states to do. It's a sad ontology that expands to include features of the world that don't do anything.

This problem, the problem of the causal relevance of the phenomenal, is why many non-zombies like myself nevertheless want to hold on to physicalism. Fortunately, I think, we can do so given the second hasty move to the conclusion that physicalism is false. This move involves the inference from the incompleteness of physics (or the physical sciences in general) to the falsity of physicalism. Physicalism is a metaphysical position, about what properties and things there are in the world. The view that physics and related sciences are incomplete is ultimately an epistemic point about the ability of those sciences to convey, via their theories, a complete grasp of the world. This opens space for a physicalism that is immune to the traditional antimaterialist arguments

1. The Missing Option

An objective to the knowledge argument can help us see the space for our new physicalism. According to that argument we learn that physicalism is false – and presumably that there are extra, non-physical properties in the world – because of the limits of what one can know by studying the physical sciences alone. So, as the story goes, brilliant Mary has learned all the truths of physics and the physical sciences from within a black and white room, yet she learns something new when she goes out and sees red for the first time (Jackson 1982). Most of us find this intuitive. But, can we really conclude that there are properties that Mary needs to add to her ontology once she leaves this room? In a famous objection, Paul Churchland thought not.

> if Jackson's argument were sound, it would prove far too much. Suppose Jackson were arguing not against materialism, but against dualism: against the view that there exists a non-material substance – call it "ectoplasm" – whose hidden constitution and nomic intricacies ground all mental phenomena. Let our cloistered Mary be an "ectoplasmologist" this time, and let her know everything there is to know about the ectoplasmic processes underlying vision. There would still be something she did not know: what it is like to see red. Dualism is therefore inadequate to account for all mental phenomena!
>
> (Churchland 1985: 24–5)

Churchland is rightly pointing out that merely substituting some sort of psychic goo for the more conventional physical stuff will do nothing to satisfy the intuitions behind the knowledge argument. Churchland is wrong to think, however, that the knowledge argument would show that dualism is false. It would only show that if the dualist held that phenomenal states could be fully grasped objectively, in the sort of terms that could be conveyed to Mary by scientific textbooks. That is, it only shows that a sort of "objective dualism" is false. Unfortunately for Churchland, no one holds that view. The dualist admits that these special mental properties can only be known in a certain way, namely by having them and (perhaps) being acquainted with them. Still, this response to Churchland's point helps us see that traditional dualism is really a two-sided position. On the one hand it is a metaphysical view, that there are properties other than physical ones. On the other, though, is an epistemological view about how those properties can be known. Traditional dualism is subjective dualism. Objective dualism is a coherent view, but Churchland is right that the knowledge argument could never establish it.

The conclusion of the knowledge argument is the truth of subjective dualism, but its target is objective physicalism. Objective physicalism is again a hybrid of a metaphysical view – that all properties are physical – and an epistemological view – that physical properties can be completely grasped by objective methods. But just as the response to Churchland's *tu quoque* involves pointing out the nature of subjective dualism, it seems there is a view in logical space that evades the knowledge argument: subjective physicalism (Howell 2013).

Subjective physicalism is, like the other views mentioned, a hybrid view. Metaphysically it is physicalist: everything in the world is physical. But the epistemological side is subjectivist: not all physical states can be fully grasped or known by objective approaches like those employed by physics. The knowledge argument fails to challenge subjective physicalism for the same reason it fails to challenge subjective dualism.

This sounds simple enough, and even intuitive, but it's fair to say things are not as simple as they appear. For one thing, there are really a number of very different positions that could rally behind this subjective physicalist thesis. A lot will depend on what one is willing to call "physicalism." Panpsychism or Russelian Monism could both be considered "subjective physicalist" given a certain notion of the physical. If, for example, one said that a property is physical iff it is the sort of property had by paradigmatically physical things like rocks and carbon atoms, then many forms of panpsychism will turn out to be versions of subjective physicalism (Stoljar 2001 presents a similar view). Everything might well be made up of the same stuff and have the same properties as paradigmatically physical things, yet because the roots of phenomenality are ubiquitous that stuff cannot be fully described by objective methods. Granted, this is not your grandfather's physicalism (unless your grandfather is Grover Maxwell), but it shouldn't be rejected out of hand for that reason.[1]

It's tempting to think that this sort of subjective physicalism, at least, only avoids dualism by semantic slight of hand. This is a real worry, and it is important to be clear on what we mean by "physical," while simultaneously being clear about what hangs in the balance.[2] What, in other words, should determine what counts as "physical" in this debate? This is a difficult question, but my own inclination is to think we should keep an eye on two different guidelines for a definition of "physical." The first is that we need to be aware of how the term has been used in philosophical debates. My own inclination is to say that the question of whether or not everything is physical hasn't been about whether there is a way to stretch our notion of the physical to cover phenomenal states. It has been about whether phenomenal states are in some sense grounded in the sort of states and properties described by physics.[3] (Note – just because physics is describing states that as a matter of fact involve phenomenal properties doesn't mean physics is describing those properties.) So there is a certain historical precedent that recommends against considering things like panpsychism "subjective physicalism." Perhaps more important, though, is that we keep an eye on the reason it seemed important to be a physicalist in the first place. It's not because "physical" is such a lovely word or that "dualism" causes secular humanists to blush. It's rather that it looks as though dualism has a difficult time giving phenomenal properties a causal role in the world. If the new physical properties don't have a role to play in the world, not much has been gained. We can hardly be proud that phenomenal properties are allowed into the physicalist club if they still have to huddle together silently in the coatroom.

These two criteria, or perhaps warnings, shouldn't keep us from looking at surprising physicalist theses. But once we have a few on the table, they might give us a means of determining if they are really what we are looking for. To get a handle on the different possible theses, we can look a little more closely at the structure of a definition of physicalism. It's helpful to think about a definition of physicalism as involving three parts: a microphysical part, a macro-physical part, and an account of the relation between the two (see Stoljar 2010). The microphysical part of the definition provides the criteria for what makes basic or fundamental stuff physical. But, of course, not everything is fundamental and it might be a mistake to think that the non-fundamental should be considered physical in precisely the same sense. The macro-physical definition tries to provide a criterion for non-fundamental physicality. Finally, the relation between the two should attempt to explain what relation the macro-phenomena must have to the micro-phenomena to count as physical.

A full exploration of subjective physicalism would need to say more about just how the micro-physical and the macro-physical are defined and just what makes them physical. For our purposes, though, perhaps it will suffice to work with intuitive notions – the microphysical base is the type of stuff described by basic physics (leaving open whether or not physics completely describes it) and the macro-physical is what is composed by that stuff – tables, chairs, people and planets.[4]

2. Varieties of Subjective Physicalism

Given the fact that physicalism can be defined distinctly for the micro and the macro, we can come up with at least two varieties of subjective physicalism:

> *Subjective Micro-Physicalism*: Although all of the properties in the world, fundamental and otherwise, are physical, some of those fundamental properties cannot be completely grasped except by beings constituted by those properties.
> *Subjective Macro-Physicalism*: All of the properties in the world, fundamental and otherwise, are physical, and all of the fundamental physical things can be completely grasped by objective methods of inquiry, but there are, nonetheless, macro-physical properties that cannot be completely grasped except by beings who instantiate those properties.

On the face of it, subjective micro-physicalism is apt to be a form of panpsychism. (It really depends on how widespread these objectively ungraspable fundamental properties are and how "pan" panpsychism must be.) Similarly, on the face of it, subjective macro-physicalism looks like a form of emergentism. On this view, the base is just as physics describes it but things composed by the elements of that base have properties that have to be experienced to be fully grasped.

The situation gets more complicated, though, when one looks into what is involved in "fully grasping," an admittedly slippery notion. On the one hand, one might think that if one only partially grasps a property, there is another property, which is part of the original property, that one doesn't grasp at all. Though this sounds paradoxical, it is actually a pretty natural line of thought that issues in part from the analogy of "grasping." If one doesn't touch all of something, mustn't there be some part of that thing that one doesn't touch? If one doesn't fully grasp or understand something, surely there is something that one doesn't understand. That thing totally eludes ones understanding, even if it forms a whole with something that is partially understood. One might, however, deny this. The line of thinking I've just spelled out relies on a principle that one can doubt. We can call it the epistemic exclusion theorem:

> *Epistemic Exclusion Theorem*: If one doesn't fully grasp some property F, there is necessarily some property G that is a part of F that one doesn't grasp at all.

Though this seems natural enough, based on an analogy with the physical grasping of objects, I think it should be questioned when it comes to properties.[5] Properties might not divide as finely as our understanding. I pursue this sort of view elsewhere (see Howell 2013), but the important point here is that the different stances one can take on the epistemic exclusion theorem generates a further disambiguation of subjective physicalism that runs orthogonal to the micro-macro division. There can be subjective physicalisms that accept subjective properties, and those that don't.

> *Subjective Property Physicalism*: All of the properties in the world are physical, but there are some physical properties that cannot be grasped except by beings instantiating those properties.
>
> *Subjective Aspect Physicalism*: All of the properties in the world are physical, and can be given physical description, but some of those properties cannot be fully grasped except by beings instantiating those properties.[6]

The difference between Subjective Property Physicalism (SPP) and Subjective Aspect Physicalism (SAP) is essentially whether it can be said that there is some property that physics or the objective ways of knowing "leave out." SPP says yes, while SAP says no. One's stance here will be determined by one's acceptance of epistemic exclusion.

One can adopt property and aspect versions of both subjective micro-physicalism and subjective macro-physicalism, depending on whether one thinks that there are or are not properties that escape objective description on either the micro or the macro level.

In what follows I will sketch what I believe to be the most promising form of subjective physicalism, macro subjective aspect physicalism.

3. Subjective Physicalism Without Emergent Properties

One way to put the difference between macro-SAP and macro-SPP is that according to macro-SPP there really is a new property that supervenes upon the pure physical base. It is, in a sense, emergent – only necessarily so. I personally have some question about the coherence of necessary emergence, but I won't rehearse them here (see Howell 2009). Macro-SAP rejects such new properties. It accepts instead new "aspects" of properties that only appear at the macro level. Making sense of this view, in my opinion, primarily requires discharging three dialectical responsibilities. The first is to motivate the rejection of the epistemic exclusion thesis. The second is to explain what aspects are. The third is to explain how this view is not merely a terminological variant of emergentist dualism. Achieving this third goal, in my opinion, will require explaining how it avoids dualism's problems with emergent causation.

3.1. Rejecting the Epistemic Exclusion Theorem

The epistemic exclusion theorem (EET), again, holds that if one doesn't fully grasp some property F, there is necessarily some property G that is a part of F that one doesn't grasp at all. Denying this theorem, therefore, requires that some properties can have conceptually distinguishable but metaphysically inseparable parts that make an epistemic difference for subjects. Since these parts are not metaphysically separable, they should not be called different properties. One might say, for example, that equilateral-triangularity and equilangular-triangularity are two aspects of a single property. Some features of the world that we can distinguish in language and thought nonetheless occur together by necessity.

It's not easy to get one's head around rejecting EET for properties. This is because, I think, we tend to associate properties and concepts in such a way that the latter come to define the former. So, for example, on what I call an intensionalist framework for individuating properties, two distinct concepts can't have the same properties as their extensions.[7] The subjective physicalist should reject this picture, however. Instead she should embrace an extensionalist framework for property individuation, according to which properties are individuated in ways that are completely independent of the way they appear to subjects. My preferred view is that they are individuated by causal powers (following Shoemaker 1979). Though I think there are other possible extensionalist views, this is a promising one that will be helpful as a sample view in what follows. According to this view, then, no two properties completely share causal powers. If one adopts this sort of view, it isn't obvious why one should accept EET. Why think that our ability to conceive of the world in different ways, or our ability to group things by similarities that strike the mind, corresponds to similarities and differences between causal powers? The extensionalist picture doesn't contradict EET, but it no longer makes it seem like an obvious feature of properties. If there are other reasons to reject it, we should feel free to do so.

3.2. Explaining Aspects

What, then, are aspects of properties? For the extensionalist they are those features of properties that can be distinguished by the mind but do not possess an independent causal power. A bent plane has a concave aspect and a convex aspect. For the intensionalist about properties, aspects are simply properties – though perhaps properties without their own causal powers, or properties that are necessarily bound to other properties. But the intensionalist owes us a story about why we should think the world is carved up so neatly in line with the way we think about the world. That it often seems to do so isn't really much of an argument, since the same argument can be given for the extensionalist picture. The argument would only work if in the disputed cases – the cases the intensionalist calls properties and the extensionalist does not – the intensionalist picture comes out ahead. But in fact there are reasons to think the extensionalist comes out ahead here, for the simple reason that in many of the disputed cases the alleged properties wind up being theoretical danglers that are difficult to integrate into a picture of the causal world.

3.3 Aspects, Properties and Causal Exclusion

The extensionalist way of individuating properties, and the subjective aspect physicalism that results from it, has the advantage when it comes to explaining how mental properties integrate with the world as described by physics. For the intensionalist, there are mental properties independent of the physical properties. Since the physical properties have the causal powers, though, the extra mental properties are left without any causal efficacy. It's not a coincidence that this is precisely what we find in the debate over phenomenal consciousness. There is no work left for phenomenal properties to do because all of the work is done by the physical properties. This not only makes it hard to see how phenomenal properties cause our flinchings and gasps. It also makes it difficult to see how we could know of and speak of such properties.[8] The extensionalist's verdict isn't that there are no phenomenal properties or that phenomenal properties are epiphenomenal, but rather that the exclusion problem is a result of double counting. This double counting is the result of adopting an intensionalist framework of property individuation. The extensionalist picture, however, embraces the fact that properties – individuated by their causal powers – have phenomenal aspects, but those aspects should no more be considered additional properties than the convexity of a plane should be considered a different property from its concavity.

4. Subjective Physicalism and Mental Causation

So, the subjective aspect macro-physicalist's picture is that all properties are physical, but some supervenient properties have certain aspects that are only graspable by being a subject partly constituted by those properties. Properties in general are associated with causal powers. These causal powers provide their individuation conditions, and they constitute the descriptive domain of the physical sciences. Those sciences are, however, incomplete – as any objective science would have to be. They are incomplete not because they leave out properties, but because their theories cannot convey the "what-it's-like" aspect of things.

How does this view fare with respect to the problem of mental causation? Every property in this view has a causal role to play because properties are individuated by the causal powers they bestow. The phenomenal properties are physical properties, but when we think of them as phenomenal properties we are considering them under their phenomenal aspect. But those phenomenal properties have plenty of causal powers – they have whatever causal powers their physical aspects have.

It is tempting to say that this way of carving things up has merely swept the problem under the rug. Just as we could ask about Davidsonian mental events whether they were causing things in virtue of their mental properties or their physical properties, it seems we can ask of the subjective physicalist's physical/phenomenal properties whether they cause things in virtue of their physical or phenomenal aspects.[9] And, it seems, the answer must be obvious: the physical aspects do all the work and the phenomenal is left again without a role to play in the world.

This is, however, too quick. Unlike the various properties that constitute Davidson's thick events, aspects of properties are necessarily co-instantiated. Because one feature does not come without the other, we can't give metaphysical heft to the "in virtue of" question that asks which aspect of the property is the reason it causes what it does. In a typical case in which one asks which of two co-instantiated properties does the work, one can give an answer because of the truth of various counterfactuals. The mass of the red brick, rather than its redness, is the reason the scale tips. This truth is grounded in the counterfactuals that were the brick black the scale would still tip, and were the red thing a feather the scale would not. In cases of necessary co-instantiation these sorts of counterfactuals aren't available. This doesn't merely prevent us from recognizing which property is the real cause; the epistemic point is parasitic on the metaphysical point. In such a case there is no fact of the matter about which is the real cause since the two features are inseparable.[10] Despite the somewhat abstract foregoing argument, the point is really quite intuitive. If the distinction between two features F and G is merely conceptual, and whether or not something causes something else in virtue of one property or another is a mind-independent metaphysical fact, something cannot cause something else in virtue of F rather than G (or *vice versa*).

This, then, completes the basic case for subjective aspect macro-physicalism. It recognizes the epistemic gains provided by phenomenal consciousness while maintaining that everything is physical. Phenomenal properties are aspects of physical properties that must be possessed to be fully grasped, but they are physical nonetheless and thus have all the causal powers of the physical properties they are aspects of.

5. Panpsychism Without Micro-Physical Phenomenal Properties

Though this case, and the more developed case in Howell (2013), is in support of exclusive macro-subjective physicalism, it seems likely that a similar – and perhaps even better – case can be made in support of Micro-SAP. On this view, again, the micro-physical properties are physical, but are nonetheless objective science would leave out their ability to compose subjects with phenomenal states. This ability is an overlooked aspect of that microphysical property. If the preceding arguments against property intensionalism are good, then the resultant picture of properties allows us to embrace micro-physical aspects just as easily as we embrace macro-physical aspects. Given this, there is a compelling form of subjective physicalism that is really rather close to panpsychism.

Micro-subjective physicalism will embrace much of the story offered by macro-subjective physicalism. On the microphysical level there are not independent phenomenal or protophenomenal properties. There are phenomenal or protophenomenal aspects. These are the features of physical properties that give rise, under appropriate combinations, to macro-phenomenal aspects. These aspects are necessarily bound with the causal powers that define the fundamental properties they are aspects of. The objective sciences, then, do not fully describe even the micro-physical or fundamental properties of our universe. There are some aspects of those properties that can only be grasped by subjects who are composed of those properties.

There might seem to be a drawback to this micro-subjective physicalism in that we can't be said to grasp these aspects of micro-physical aspects in the same way that we grasp macro-physical aspects. We are, after all, confronted with phenomenal experience in quite an obvious way, and we are not confronted with anything like that when it comes to micro-physical properties. What does it mean, then, to say that there are these subjective aspects to micro-physical properties?

I think the right thing to say here is that though we are not acquainted with subjective micro-physical aspects directly, we can nevertheless know of them indirectly as those aspects that give rise to the macro aspects. The micro-physical properties don't have feels, precisely because there are no micro-physical subjects. But they do have subjective aspects, or proto-feels, in virtue of composing subjects who have phenomenal experiences. Considered objectively, in terms of properties and causal powers, physics really isn't missing anything. Considered as a part of a system that composes a subject, though, we have to recognize that there are features of micro-physical properties that give rise to phenomenal experience. Focusing only on the causal powers of micro-physical properties and how they sum won't reveal that. Only the subjective perspective forces the protophenomenal upon us.

6. Is There Really a Difference Between These Two Views?

Though micro-SAP and macro-SAP appear to be different views, it is likely that they are really just the same view considered in two different ways. They are, I think, mutually entailing.

According to subjective aspect macro-physicalism there are aspects to properties of physical systems that cannot be fully grasped except by the systems – i.e. the subjects – that have those properties. But these properties and the systems that have them are physical because they supervene upon the microphysical state of things. So, the microphysical particles and the way they are necessitate the way the subjects are. Properties are partly defined by what they necessitate. If properties F and G, for example, necessitate the existence of property H when they are in a certain configuration, this is because of some feature of F and/or G. Put crudely, F and G have some form of proto-H-ness in that they give rise, with necessity, to H. If one fully described the causal powers of F and G, and left out the fact that they gave rise to H, one would be missing an important fact about F and G.[11] So, if the microphysical properties give rise with necessity to properties with a subjective aspect, it is partly due to their natures. Those aspects of their natures that are relevant to phenomenality, unlike their causal aspects, can only be grasped from the top-down. If microphysical properties have part of their nature that can only be grasped from the top down, and by subjects who have to grasp experiences from the inside by having them, subjective micro-physicalism is true. Thus subjective aspect micro-physicalism seems to be entailed by subjective aspect macro-physicalism. And, of course, the entailment must go the other way as well since part of what it means to say that microphysical properties have subjective aspects is that they compose subjects who have properties with subjective aspects. Subjective aspect micro-physicalism and subjective aspect macro-physicalism are just two different ways of describing the same view.

7. Conclusion

If the foregoing is true, subjective physicalism bears a family resemblance to panpsychism. Both views recognize that there is something about the microphysical that cannot be grasped except by a subject, and what can't be grasped is relevant to explaining phenomenal consciousness. The difference, though, is that subjective physicalism – at least exclusive subjective physicalism – denies that these features are properties distinct from the physical properties. Subjective physicalism views the phenomenal aspect of things as only separable conceptually, as what might be called an epistemic feature of the world. More traditional panpsychism, on the other hand, typically views phenomenal or protophenomenal properties as properties in their own right that, in some way distinct from the physical properties, constitute the building blocks of the world.

It is worth noting one other way that subjective physicalisms (and views in their neighborhood) more broadly resemble panpsychism. Panpsychism often gets labeled as crazy because it seems to imply that things like rocks could be conscious. (Perhaps they aren't; perhaps the particular combination of fundamental psychic properties that compose consciousness doesn't occur in rocks, but nothing in principle says that it couldn't be.) But in actuality, views that put a more epistemic spin on the nature of phenomenal knowledge – what Chalmers (2003) calls type-B physicalism, which roughly lines up with *a posteriori* physicalism – have a similar commitment. These views ultimately claim that something about the subject's epistemic perspective – be it the phenomenal concepts they deploy, the acquaintance they have, or what have you – provides a certain form of knowledge of the physical stuff that is not provided by objective science. This is what knowledge of qualitative nature of things involves. We have this perspective on our brain states. But what in principle says that this perspective can only be taken on brain states? Why couldn't it in principle be taken on rocks? If there are aspects of the physical properties that are phenomenal, why think that is limited to the physical properties that make us up? Perhaps for various reasons we can't take such a perspective on rocks, but in principle there doesn't seem to be anything special about brains when it comes to supporting phenomenal aspects of things. If this is the case, the subjective physicalist and the panpsychist are in similar boats once again. Since both of them agree that there is such a thing as phenomenal consciousness and the stuff that makes it happen in humans is the same stuff that makes up other physical objects, they both open up the possibility that the world has more consciousness in it than it first appeared. The panpsychist thinks that is because everything is made up of stuff that has phenomenal properties, and the subjective physicalist thinks that is because of an epistemic perspective that can be adopted in certain circumstances, but in the end there might be less difference between these two views than it first appears.

Notes

1. Maxwell (1978) pointed out the viability of this strategy.
2. See Stoljar (2010) for a more detailed discussion of the difficulties facing definitions of physicalism, and what hangs in the balance.
3. Alter (2009) can be seen as arguing something similar. Others, who recommend a "via negativa" definition of physicalism, think similarly; see, for example, Montero (2001), Wilson (2006).
4. See Howell (2013, Part I) for a deeper account of the story I prefer.
5. Though if there are extended simples I suspect some object versions of this would have to be rejected as well.
6. In previous work, such as Howell (2013), I called these views exclusive and inclusive subjective physicalism. Since I myself couldn't remember which was which, I thought a name change was in order.
7. A better, more regimented intensionalism would hold that two concepts whose coextension could not be determined *a priori* are not coextensive (see Howell 2013: ch. 5).
8. Chalmers (1996) makes this point clearly in discussing the paradox of phenomenal judgment.
9. See Davidson (1970), and responses by Kim (1989, 1993) and Sosa (1993).
10. This response derives from that given by Bennett (2003).
11. One wouldn't be describing F and G at all, really, since giving rise to H is a necessary feature of them. One would be describing F★ and G★, perhaps, but not F and G (see Howell 2009).

Bibliography

Alter, Torin (2009). 'Does the Ignorance Hypothesis Undermine the Conceivability and Knowledge Arguments?' *Philosophy and Phenomenological Research*, 79 (3): 756–65.
Bennett, Karen (2003). 'Why the Exclusion Problem Seems Intractable and How, Just Maybe, to Tract It'. *Noûs*, 37 (3): 471–97.
Chalmers, David J. (1996). *The Conscious Mind: In Search of a Fundamental Theory*. Oxford: Oxford University Press.
Chalmers, David J. (2003). 'Consciousness and Its Place in Nature'. In S. Stich and T. Warfield (eds.), *Blackwell Guide to the Philosophy of Mind*. Oxford: Blackwell, pp. 102–42.
Churchland, Paul M. (1985). 'Reduction, Qualia and the Direct Introspection of Brain States'. *Journal of Philosophy*, 82: 8–28, January.
Davidson, Donald (1970). 'Mental Events'. In L. Foster and J. Swanson (eds.), *Experience and Theory*. Amherst: University of Massachusetts Press, pp. 79–101.
Howell, Robert J. (2009). 'Emergentism and Supervenience Physicalism'. *Australasian Journal of Philosophy*, 87 (1): 83–98.
Howell, Robert J. (2013). *Consciousness and the Limits of Objectivity: The Case for Subjective Physicalism*. Oxford: Oxford University Press.
Jackson, Frank (1982). 'Epiphenomenal Qualia'. *Philosophical Quarterly*, 32: 127–36, April.
Kim, Jaegwon (1989). 'The Myth of Non-Reductive Materialism'. *Proceedings and Addresses of the American Philosophical Association*, 63 (3): 31–47.
Kim, Jaegwon (1993). 'Can Supervenience and "Non-Strict Laws" Save Anomalous Monism?' In J. Heil and A. Mele (eds.), *Mental Causation*. Oxford: Oxford University Press, pp. 19–26.
Maxwell, Grover (1978). 'Rigid Designators and Mind-Brain Identity'. In W. Savage (ed.), *Minnesota Studies in the Philosophy of Science*, vol. 9. Minneapolis: University of Minnesota Press, pp. 365–403.
Montero, Barbara (2001). 'Post-Physicalism'. *Journal of Consciousness Studies*, 8 (2): 61–80.
Nagel, Thomas (1974). "What Is It Like to Be a Bat?" *Philosophical Review*, 83: 435–50, October.
Papineau, David (2002). *Thinking About Consciousness*. Oxford: Oxford University Press.
Shoemaker, Sydney (1979). 'Identity, Properties, and Causality'. *Midwest Studies in Philosophy*, 4 (1): 321–42.
Sosa, Ernest (1993). 'Davidson's Thinking Causes'. In J. Heil and A. Mele (eds.), *Mental Causation*. Oxford: Oxford University Press, pp. 41–50.
Stoljar, Daniel (2001). 'Two Conceptions of the Physical'. *Philosophy and Phenomenological Research*, 62 (2): 253–81.
Stoljar, Daniel (2010). *Physicalism*. London: Routledge.
Wilson, Jessica M. (2006). 'On Characterizing the Physical'. *Philosophical Studies*, 131 (1): 61–99.

17

PANPSYCHISM

A Cognitive Pluralist Perspective

Steven Horst

The aim of this chapter is to reflect upon panpsychism from the standpoint of a view I have developed elsewhere (Horst 2007, 2011, 2014, 2016) called cognitive pluralism, which is first and foremost a thesis about the nature of understanding, but also has implications for epistemology, semantics, and metaphysics. Many readers will be unfamiliar with cognitive pluralism, though they may be familiar with other philosophical views that bear some similarities to it – transcendental idealism, pragmatism, perspectival and internal realism – and so it will be necessary to introduce it at some length in section 2. But the word 'panpsychism' has also served as the name of a number of otherwise very different philosophical doctrines. The Stanford Encyclopedia of Philosophy article on panpsychism begins by characterizing it as "the doctrine that mind is a fundamental feature of the world which exists throughout the universe," (Seager and Allen-Hermanson 2015) and goes on to describe a number of historically important variations upon it. In this chapter, I shall focus on three particular strands: (1) The view, common to animism and some forms of philosophical and scientific panpsychism, that a wide range of *specific* phenomena (particularly those involving self-initiated motion and active causal powers) are best understood in mentalistic terms, (2) Leibniz's more general and foundational claim that we need a fundamental ontology framed in the intentionalist terms of "perceptions and appetitions" to account for active causal powers, and (3) Chalmers' (2015) argument that an ontology that includes "microexperiential" properties at a fundamental level is our most promising candidate for a fundamental metaphysics.

1. Positive and Critical Ontologies

Panpsychism is not the only philosophy that accords minds *some type* of fundamental metaphysical role. Cartesian dualism, of course, treats minds as a distinctive type of substance characterized by irreducibly mentalistic properties.

Cognitivist, pragmatist, and social constructionist philosophies also accord thinking beings special roles in the division of the world into objects, kinds, properties, and processes. Their claims, however, are not about the *inventory* of the world, nor about which portions of that inventory are fundamental. Rather they consist in distinctive ways of cashing out *what it is to be* an object, to have a property, etc. In Kant's transcendental idealism, what it is to be a (phenomenal) object is to be a possible object of cognition for a thinking being with faculties of sensibility and understanding more or less like our own. Phenomenal objects (with the exception of human beings) are not taken to be thinking things in their own right or composed of mind-like parts. Nor, generally, is their existence causally dependent upon activities of minds. What Kant's transcendental story provides is more on the order of a gloss upon the *status* of the notion of a (phenomenal) object – one that does not rest content to treat posits about the *inventory* of the world as bedrock metaphysics. I have elsewhere (2007) called this type of metaphysics and ontology, which addresses what it is to be an object (property, relation, etc.), *critical metaphysics* and *critical ontology*, in distinction with metaphysical approaches that are concerned only with the inventory of the world, which I called *positive* or *inventory metaphysics/ontology*.

Positive ontology may further be divided into two varieties. *Inclusive positive ontology* is concerned with identifying *all* of the objects, kinds, properties, relations, and processes that are *real*, regardless of whether they are composed of or derivative from something else. *Fundamental* positive ontology is concerned with the further question of which elements of this ontological inventory are in some sense *fundamental* – for example, by being irreducible or not having a more basic supervenience base.

Panpsychism, like materialism and dualism, is a thesis about fundamental positive ontology: a thesis about what sorts of phenomena are real and not reducible to or supervenient upon something else. Perhaps some animists believe that every real thing has a mind of its own, but philosophical panpsychists generally claim only that some sorts of mentalistic phenomena (perhaps quite unlike those we experience) are fundamental. But whereas the dualist holds that only a special class of things have mentalistic properties, the panpsychist claims that they are to be found in all, or at least some, of the simplest constituents of the universe.

The distinction between positive and critical metaphysics is of a different sort. Critical ontology examines the *status* of objects and properties, and also of unifying strategies like reduction, generally holding that we cannot simply take ontological posits at face value, but must see how their status is tied to the ways minds like ours conceive of the world (cognitivism) or interact with it (pragmatism). Doing this can lead to a different perspective on the nature and prospects of fundamental positive metaphysics, either in the form of an outright suspicion that the project of fundamental metaphysics is problematic or at least in the form of a reconception of what the fundamental metaphysician is actually doing.

I shall now turn to one such approach to critical metaphysics. In the next section I shall introduce cognitive pluralism's core commitments as an account of how we understand the world. I shall then discuss how such an account of understanding might shape an approach to critical metaphysics, laying the groundwork for a discussion of panpsychism from a cognitive pluralist standpoint.

2. What Is Cognitive Pluralism?

Cognitive Pluralists believe that we understand the world through the use of many mental models of different content domains, rather than (a) through an even larger number of distinct and independent propositional beliefs or (b) through a comprehensive and holistic worldview. The concepts and beliefs we have about a particular domain, such as chess, are constitutively interrelated with other concepts, beliefs, and inference patterns involved in our mental model of that domain but are comparatively independent of those of other models. This model-based view of cognition is first and foremost an account of cognitive architecture and of the basic units of understanding. The basic unit of understanding is a mental model, and concepts and the semantic inferences associated with them are derivative from models in which they appear. One has not fully understood a concept like CHESS_KNIGHT or the movement rules for knights unless one has mastered a model of the entire game of chess; but one can master chess quite independently of how one understands other domains, like gravitation or the etiquette of restaurant dining. A model of a domain provides ways of representing objects, states of affairs, and processes within the domain, and a framework for perceiving, reasoning about, and interacting with them.

Models provide *idealized* ways of representing their domains which are generally well suited to perception, belief formation, inference, and the guidance of action in particular circumstances; and in such circumstances, the model is considered "apt". One way that models are idealized (a *bracketing idealization*) is that they characterize objects in terms of a subset of their actual properties – e.g., a gravitational model deals with mass but not charge. Models can also employ *distorting idealizations*, such as treating bodies as point-masses or subjects as ideally rational decision-theoretic agents. Idealization can place limits upon how well a model can be used to describe and predict real-world behavior, which in turn has implications for which classes of cases they are aptly applied to.

Even our best fundamental models in physics bracket aspects of the world covered by other models. Moreover, models, including scientific models, can fail to play well together by being formally incommensurable, making incompatible assumptions, and generating divergent predictions. I have argued (2007, 2011, 2014, 2016) that such disunities of science – and more generally of disunities understanding, of which scientific disunities are a special case – are predictable consequences of a cognitive architecture that provides understanding through a large number of idealized special-purpose mental models, each employing a representational system well-suited to efficient cognition about its target domain, but not optimized for a single comprehensive understanding of everything. As a result, it is possible (perhaps even likely) that minds like ours may be incapable of remolding the understanding we have of many distinct domains through many different models into a single self-consistent system that retains all of the epistemic probity, practical utility, and explanatory power that a set of distinct models affords.

I have argued as well (2016) that model-based understanding also stands in a complementary relationship with another distinct element of thinking, which I call "object-oriented cognition". We frame our thoughts about objects using concepts that are embedded in models, and this allows us to make swift domain-specific inferences about them. But to think of something as an object is not simply to think of it as the tokening of a property signified by a concept. It is to posit a mind-transcendent *thing* to which that concept might aptly be applied. There is thus a kind of purely ostensive component to our thinking that operates together with the application of sense-giving models and concepts. This object-oriented component of thinking has the function of tracking particulars through changes they might undergo and changes in the ways we conceive of them.

As a result, when we think of a thing in some concrete way – say, as a man who is sitting – there is always a great deal more that is implicit in our thought. For example: that the selfsame thing might change its attributes (e.g., by standing), that we might be mistaken in how we are thinking of it (e.g., that it is a statue and not a man), that there are indefinitely many other apt ways of thinking of it (that he is thinking, a husband, an Athenian, or weighs 180 pounds), and even that the concepts and models we are using might prove to require adjustment or wholesale change. Moreover, we hold ourselves normatively accountable to the object as a mind-transcendent reality in updating, expanding, and revising our beliefs about it and the concepts and models we use to frame our thoughts about it. To think of something as a real object is to think of it as having indefinitely more to it than is contained in the content of any particular thought about it; and indeed even the sum total of ways we are in principle capable of *conceiving* it do not capture the "pure that-ness" of the purely ostensive component of object-oriented thinking.

3. Cognitive Pluralism, Metaphysics, and Ontology

Cognitive pluralism is first and foremost a theory about cognitive architecture. As such, it may be compatible with a number of different positive metaphysical positions. It is, however, possible to pursue a metaphysics driven by its cognitivist and pluralist commitments (Cf. Horst 2007: ch. 9). This would, first and foremost, be an exercise in *critical* metaphysics in the cognitivist style, sharing some aspects of Kantianism, but also differing in some crucial respects: The cognitive pluralist cannot assume that there are universal principles, like Kant's categories and forms of sensibility, that are guaranteed to apply to all objects of cognition, and this deprives him of the transcendental high road to synthetic *a priori* knowledge about mathematics, substance, and causation. Cognitive pluralism also countenances the possibility that the posits of our best models may not be susceptible to integration into a single system that is at once comprehensive and consistent. Its approach to the transcendence of objects – cast in terms of the complementarity of model-based and object-oriented systems – may have significantly different implications from the Kantian division between phenomena and noumena. And positing a cognitive architecture based in many idealized mental models that form the basis for intuitive judgments opens the doors to types of cognitive illusion beyond those described in the transcendental dialectic (Horst 2016).

For the cognitive pluralist, *inclusive* ontology is driven first and foremost by the commitments of models that prove apt. Each model has its own "internal ontology": the types of objects, kinds, properties, etc., provided by the concepts bound up in the model. And where a model proves apt, this suggests a *prima facie* commitment to the reality of its posits, and thus to accommodating them in our inclusive positive ontology. Our starting point in inclusive positive ontology is more or less a commitment to the sum of the kinds of phenomena posited by the models we take to be apt. Such commitments are, of course, defeasible. We may discover that a model is not truly apt at all and cease to be committed to its posits. And conflicts between models may call into question our commitments to the posits of the models involved, and this sometimes (but not always) leads to the rejection of one model and its posits or to a reevaluation of what its aptness really commits us to.

But even when there are not outright conflicts between models, our inclusive ontological commitments can be messy. Different models may divide up the world in different ways. This object is a chess bishop, a carved piece of wood, a body with shape and mass, etc. We are committed to there being such kinds of things as chess bishops, game pieces, games, rules of games, people who can play games, thoughts about states of play and movements, diagonal movements, wood, artifacts, bodies, shapes, masses, etc. Our inclusive ontology seems to come in the form of many overlapping classes of things – what Cartwright (1999) calls a "dappled world". A particular individual or event may fall into several such classes, but the classes themselves are not co-extensive.

One of the tasks to which fundamental positive metaphysics sets itself is to try to bring some order to this. Any project in fundamental positive metaphysics is subject to the pulls of two opposing norms: to do justice to the posits of all of the models that seem to have proven apt, and the pursuit of some kind of unifying strategy as a regulative ideal. Philosophers have weighed these against each other in very different ways. Some have enshrined common sense or intuition as a litmus against which any philosophical theory must be tested, others have assumed that the availability of some parsimonious fundamental ontology is something on the order of a truth of reason and been willing to deny the ontological *bona fides* of common sense and even scientific commitments in order to have a tidy theory, and perhaps most fall somewhere in between.

What attitude should the cognitive pluralist take towards such projects? I think that she should respect the pursuit of regulative ideals for unification, but should also presume in favor of the inclusive ontological commitments of models that have proven apt. There are, to be sure, often reasons to conclude that a model is not apt after all, or that its aptness does not in fact commit us to the ontological posits we might at first have assumed. For the most part, these take place at the level of assessing individual models and their relations to one another, and the implications of this for inclusive ontology. By contrast, it does not seem like a good strategy to conclude, say, that there are no intentional states, numbers, or moral facts simply on the grounds that we can get a simpler fundamental theory by denying them. For one thing, to the extent that we still *use* models framed in such terms, we still *do* have some kind of commitment to their posits. If we embrace a fundamental theory that does them injustice, we do a kind of epistemic violence to ourselves. But there is also another reason: we have reason to believe that when models produced by learning or evolution afford epistemic and practical grip, they do so because they have latched onto something real, even if the ways we conceive of their domains also carry traces of, or even reflect limits of, our cognitive architecture. As Dennett (1981) suggests, empirical and practical success are good indicators that we have hit upon real patterns that are not simply artifacts of the mind. By contrast, the fact that we have an impulse to seek unifications in more fundamental theories does not provide any reason to assume that the project can be fully carried out so far as to produce a comprehensive, well-integrated fundamental metaphysics.

This raises questions about what implications the aptness of a model should have for positive ontology beyond a defeasible *prima facie* commitment to the posits of its internal ontology, and what we should do when there is more than one apt model for what is in some sense the same phenomenon. To take the case of mentalistic models, if there are apt mentalistic models for every phenomenon, is this in itself enough to provide a case for a panpsychist conclusion? If there are both mentalistic and non-mentalistic models available, does this undercut the warrant for panpsychist claims in favor of an alternative positive metaphysics?

There may be no single answer that will serve for all cases. In some cases, two models might both preserve the same phenomena, but in different terms. In others, they might provide only partially overlapping insights, all of which seem legitimate. In still others, it might prove possible to reduce one model to another. While cognitive pluralism raises a distinctive set of potential issues about reduction, and I believe the prospects of reduction of the mental to the physical or vice versa to be slim, the cognitive pluralist should not be opposed to *seeking* reductions where they are to be found. She simply believes that *whether* they are there to be found is a second-order empirical question, and one involving not only how the world is, but what minds like ours are capable of achieving. And with such questions left open, we also leave open the question of whether the pursuit of a fundamental positive metaphysics may prove to be impossible to fulfill, even if it has a certain normative status as a regulative principle of reasoning.

4. Panpsychism From a Cognitive Standpoint

One thing that a cognitivist approach can shed light upon is why mentalistic models can be appealing for such a broad range of phenomena. Contemporary readers probably underestimate the range of phenomena for which such models have been proposed and taken seriously. It is no surprise that members of an advanced social species would have special-purpose ways of predicting one another's behavior via models of species-typical mental processes, nor that these might be readily applied to other species with physiological and behavioral similarities. But for much of our intellectual history, many of the best thinkers also found their most promising explanations of self-initiated motion, the development of organisms, and even forces like gravitation and electromagnetism in models that posited either internal teleological principles or the activity of internal or external souls. Even early modern mechanists agreed, for the most part, that matter was by nature "passive", spurring Descartes to attribute the cohesion and initial motion of matter to divine action, Leibniz to adopt panpsychism, and Newton to search for a separate set of "active" principles in alchemy.

Why is the mind so readily disposed to use mentalistic models to understand things that, upon reflection, we might have qualms about deeming to really be mental? The answer to this question, I think, is that (a) our minds are strongly biased to find *some* model that allows us to track patterns found in experience, (b) intentional stance models are part of the developmentally normal cognitive toolkit of human beings, (c) they are readily applied to phenomena that seem to exhibit self-generated activity, and (d) without a great deal of specialized theory of a form that was not developed until early modernity, intentional stance models are often the *only* resources we have that provide such an epistemic grip.

I say "intentional stance models" in the plural because I regard the "intentional stance" (Dennett 1981) as a characteristic *style* of model, which can appear in various forms and degrees of sophistication. Developmental psychologists have argued that human infants already have distinct and dissociable "core systems" for thinking about "objects" and "agents" (see Spelke and Kinzler 2007). The "rules" for the core object and core agency systems are different, and indeed incompatible: Core agents, but not core objects, are understood as being capable of self-initiated motion; core objects, but not core agents, are understood to be constrained to move only through continuous paths; and only core agents are represented as having goals. A richer understanding of beliefs and desires is developed through early childhood into what is sometimes called "folk psychology". At the same time, the child also develops a "folk physics" and "folk biology", and we can learn more sophisticated scientific models of roughly the same domains. Even when we have learned scientific models, however, core and folk models are still *persistent* and we tend to revert to them under pressure and cognitive load. And it is quite possible that many of our more sophisticated models are developed by a bootstrapping process (Carey 2011) that begins with earlier-appearing models, and which retains some of their features by default.

Folk physics is quite apt for understanding a wide range of simple mechanical phenomena we encounter in everyday life. Because we use it automatically, it seems intuitively necessary that solid objects resist interpenetration, fall when dropped, and can cause changes in motion when they collide, because these principles are already encoded in models acquired in normal development. But processes involving self-initiated motion, self-organization, or behavior suited to an end are beyond the resources of folk physics, or indeed of scientific physics until comparatively recently. As a result, ancient, medieval, and early modern philosophers and scientists were drawn to mentalistic and teleological models, and not unreasonably so, as arguably such models provided at least limited ways of understanding and predicting phenomena for which there were no alternative models, and thus were, to some extent, apt.

It is a further question, however, just what ontological posits the use of an apt model commits us to. We might be tempted to say that such mentalistic descriptions are "merely metaphorical." And in a sense this is right. Their formation does involve a process of metaphorical transposition: taking an existing model of a source domain and using it as a ready-made scaffolding for a model of a new target domain. But the word 'merely' does not do justice to the complexities of metaphorical transposition, which Lakoff and Johnson (2003) have argued to be a powerful and ubiquitous cognitive strategy for understanding new domains. The *success* of a newly formed model of the target domain in picking out real patterns and licensing predictions does not tell us which of the ontological commitments of the source model should be carried over. The model might work simply because the two domains exhibit isomorphic functional or dynamic patterns. Or it might work because both the source and the target domain really involve exactly the same sorts of entities and properties. And there is also a range of possibilities in between, in which we might discover that the familiar cases of the source domain (say, our own mental states) are actually special cases of broader classes of phenomena. Even attributing mental states to non-human animals requires us to broaden our notion of "mental states" beyond states exactly like our own, and in ways that are difficult or impossible to spell out in detail. Perhaps Leibniz was correct that there is an even broader class, of which human mental states are a very special case, that can really be found ubiquitously.

The status of such models can also change as we develop different types of models that are not cast in mentalistic terms. One crucial question here is whether the newer models capture all of the legitimate explanatory insights of the older ones. Does a model of the mechanisms underlying phototropism really explain the goal-directed character of the growth of plants? And if not, should we reject teleological descriptions as inapt, or regard teleology as emergent from or supervenient upon other types of processes? Teleological characterizations still seem to pick out real patterns; yet at the same time, developmental and evolutionary models help us understand how goal-directed processes operate in particular cases, and each type of case requires its own microexplanation. At least at the level of inclusive ontology, models seem to cross-classify and pick out different regularities, even though we gain greater explanatory insight by looking at the relations between multiple models of the same particular cases. If respecting the integrity of apt models and their inclusive ontological commitments were to drive *fundamental* ontology, this would seem to point to a richly pluralistic fundamental ontology. If there is a reason to prefer a more unified and parsimonious fundamental ontology, it must come from other sources, such as treating unification as an overriding regulative ideal, or perhaps an intuition that fundamental properties must be ones that can be found at the level of the simplest entities – say, those of fundamental physics.

5. Two Roads to Panpsychism

The previous section discussed why, from a cognitive standpoint, mentalistic models of various phenomena have seemed attractive in their own right, on a one by one basis, and the status of the inclusive positive ontological commitments such models might carry. The most influential developments of panpsychism in philosophy, however, have been concerned with *fundamental* positive ontology. Consider Leibniz's panpsychist monadology and Chalmers' Russellian panpsychism. These theories differ from one another in two significant ways. Most palpably, Leibniz's framework of monads with perceptions and appetitions would seem to be a pan*intentionalist* view, while Chalmers' view is pan*experientialist*. But there is also an important difference in how they reach their panpsychist conclusions. Leibniz's approach, which we can find in his works on mechanics as well as the more metaphysical *Monadology*, involves an argument that we can make sense of active dynamic powers only in mentalistic terms. It is thus a generalization of the type of *direct* case for panpsychism we have already explored with respect to mentalistic models of *particular* phenomena. On my interpretation of Leibniz, we need a mentalistic framework to make metaphysical sense of any natural phenomena with active causal powers, even in physics. Chalmers' approach, by contrast, is more *hypothetical* in character. Our best physical models are not mentalistic but mathematical and metaphysically neutral, and positing "microexperiential" properties that are possessed by at least some fundamental physical entities does not provide better physical models. What it does, rather, is provide a framework for explaining the "macroexperiential" properties of our own mental life in a fashion that is consistent with mental causation and the causal closure of the universe under physical laws.

6. Leibniz's Direct Approach

Leibniz's route to panpsychism was based in a combination of assumptions about metaphysics and mechanics. Leibniz accepted something very close to the Cartesian *notions* of thinking substance and extended substance as the clear *candidates* for a fundamental positive ontology. Cartesian mechanics, based in the idea that extension is the *only* essential property of matter and that all of the modes of bodies can be cashed out in purely extensive terms, had ways of characterizing *motion*. But it had no way of incorporating *dynamic* powers such as gravitational force or magnetism. Only God and souls could be sources of dynamic powers. Like Newton, Leibniz was convinced that physics needed such dynamic principles, and that matter must be purely passive. But whereas Newton's lifelong interest in the source of active dynamic powers led him to explore alchemy and theology, Leibniz turned to the other side of the Cartesian dichotomy, thinking substances. If our notion of thinking substance already supplies a way of understanding the origins of dynamic powers in intentional agency, and indeed is the only option we possess for understanding them, we must understand the objects studied by mechanics to be (or be composed of) substances whose essential properties are mentalistic. If one reads only Leibniz's scientific works, one might well conclude that the talk of "perceptions and appetitions" is merely a vivid but misleading way of talking about passive and active causal capacities – in cognitive terms, that models of our own mental states can be transposed into the domain of mechanics, but without any ontological commitment to states that are of the same metaphysical kind as intentional states. But it is clear that Leibniz takes "perceptions" and "appetitions" to be broad and basic metaphysical kinds of which our own mental states are but particularly sophisticated examples (see Leibniz 1989).

I classify Leibniz as a proponent of the direct route to panpsychism because he seems to be arguing (1) that any viable metaphysics must posit entities with active powers as fundamental and essential properties, (2) that mentalistic models are apt for characterizing such entities and their powers, and (3) that *only* mentalistic models can be suited to this task. Even if we don't know *exactly* what sorts of properties monads other than our own souls have, they must have intrinsic capacities that must be characterized as some sorts of perceptions and appetitions. And Leibniz assumed that the apparent logical/conceptual necessity involved in (3) amounted to a metaphysical necessity rather than an artifact or limitation of our cognitive architecture. Clearly, from a cognitive standpoint, we are not entitled to this assumption. If indeed we "must" view phenomena in mentalistic terms, this may simply be an artifact of the modeling resources human minds possess – a psychological necessity, not a fact about the world.

But even the case for psychological necessity was to come under attack. By the end of the eighteenth century Kant would challenge his predecessors' assumption that matter must be regarded as passive. In both the pre-critical *Physical Monadology* (1756/1986) and the late *Metaphysical Foundations of Natural Science* (1786/2004), Kant argued that the basic commitments of mechanics are neither to Cartesian extended substance nor to atomism, but to bodies exerting attractive and repulsive forces. These forces were not to be understood in the mentalistic terms of Cartesian psychology, but as a unique kind of posit required by mechanics and amounting to a reconceptualization of the philosophical notion of matter. Not only are mentalistic models *not* the only way we possess of understanding dynamic matter, our mechanics in fact already commits us to something quite different.

But when we turn to physics as we find it since the early twentieth century, we must note, along with Russell (1927), that its models have become primarily *mathematical* in character. In the seventeenth century, a metaphysical notion of matter was also doing some scientific work. But today the word 'matter', as used by scientists, is really more of an inclusive placeholder for various sorts of entities that appear in the theories of physicists. Our understanding of electrons and quarks is supplied by the mathematics of theories that describe their behavior and interactions, but those theories leave open questions about any deeper natures they might have. Perhaps in contemporary physics we have reached a level at which the human mind is ill-suited to metaphysical thinking altogether. At very least, the characterizations of mathematical physics leave us agnostic as to the underlying metaphysics.

7. Chalmers' Hypothetical Strategy

The idea that contemporary physical theories are primarily mathematical is one of the starting points for Chalmers' (2015) explorations of types of panpsychism (and panprotopsychism) he classifies as "Russellian". Chalmers' argument, however, is of the hypothetical variety:

> we can understand panpsychism as the thesis that some fundamental physical entities have mental states. For example, if quarks or photons have mental states, that suffices for panpsychism to be true, even if rocks and numbers do not have mental states ... we can read the definition as requiring that all members of some fundamental physical types ... have mental states.
> (Chalmers 2015: 246)

The kinds of mental states Chalmers is concerned with are not intentional states but conscious experiences: "that there is something it is like to be a quark or a photon or a member of some other fundamental physical type" (2015: 246–7). These "microexperiences" – with "microphenomenal properties" – are probably not much like the "macroexperiences" we undergo, and we are probably not in a position to have a clear idea of what they are like (2015: 252).

Chalmers develops an argument for panpsychism dialectically: materialism and dualism each face a serious problem in accounting for mental states. Materialism cannot account for the phenomenal character of experience, while dualism cannot account for mental causation. A resolution can be found if the fundamental entities that play the causal roles in physics also have microphenomenal properties and these properties ground macrophenomenal properties. Here that we can see a crucial role for Russell's insight

> that physics reveals the relational structure of matter but not its intrinsic nature. According to this view, classical physics tells us a lot about what mass does – it resists acceleration, attracts other masses, and so on – but it tells us nothing about what mass intrinsically is. We might say that physics tells us what the mass role is, but it does not tell us what property plays this role.
>
> (Chalmers 2015: 253–4)

The error of the materialist is to assume that fundamental physical theories either stipulate the entire nature of the entities they posit or that we are obliged to read a non-mentalistic metaphysics onto them. The Russellian view of scientific theories allows for the possibility that the functional/ dynamic roles essential to the aptness of the theories are the result of some underlying natures – what Chalmers calls "quiddities" – that are not fully specified by the theories. The terms of the theories specify *roles*, while quiddities are the properties that *play* these roles.

Nothing about our physical theories prevents us from supposing that at least some fundamental entities identified in the theories (and hence having causal powers) also have microphenomenal properties (and hence might ground macroexperience), avoiding the problems that plague materialism and dualism and thus providing one reason to prefer panpsychism over these alternative metaphysical views.

On this view, we come to know about the basic building blocks of reality through the models supplied by the physicists. There is nothing overtly mentalistic about these models; and even if we were to recast them in mentalistic terms (*à la* Leibniz), this would not provide any advantages in prediction or explanation of the phenomena in their domain, because what they are designed to capture are causal regularities, and the role-describing mathematical formulas capture those quite well on their own, without metaphysical commitments. Mentalistic quiddities are postulated solely in order to account for the macroexperiential properties we experience, and in a fashion that renders psychophysical causation consistent with causal closure under microphysical laws. As we have no concrete knowledge of mentalistic quiddities, this is really only a *schema* for such an account – a sketch of how our understanding of macroexperiential properties might, in principle, be integrated with an understanding of properties of the basic constituents of the universe *if* we had the right sorts of models of those properties, and if those models would allow us to derive macroexperiential properties as "*a priori* entailments" – and the chief thing that recommends it is that it seems to avoid the kinds of principled problems that have long beset materialist and dualist alternatives.

Cognitivism takes no issue with hypotheses in general. Indeed, many models are hypothetical in character, and the main reason for commitment to their posits lies in the fact that such models would explain phenomena with which we are more directly acquainted. Likewise, the cognitivist can acknowledge that it is a powerful regulative ideal to seek to unite different domains in ways that integrate understanding.

The peculiarity in this case is that we "have a hypothesis" only in a very schematic form. A concrete hypothesis would involve a concrete model of the underlying properties (microexperiences), with which we could see how much about the things they are to account for (macroexperiences) could be derived through something like a reduction. But in this case, not only do we not in fact know what microexperiential properties are in their own right, we might be incapable of such knowledge. And without such knowledge, we might be permanently debarred from knowing whether there are, in fact, such *a priori* entailments.

In one sense, this is an *epistemological* problem: we can *posit* a panpsychist fundamental metaphysics, but we cannot know exactly what we are positing or test whether the posits would explain the phenomena they are posited to explain. The cognitivist should ask:

1. What are we doing when we posit properties we not only do not understand but potentially could not understand?
2. What are we doing when we posit that there might be "*a priori* entailments" from these to other properties, even though they are not *a priori* for us?
3. What are we doing when we move from the epistemic level of talking about apt models and entailment relations between them to the metaphysical level of positing principles of fundamental metaphysics?

The cognitive *pluralist* should additionally ask how features found in human cognition – particularly, understanding through many idealized models and the problems about uniting these through reduction – affect this kind of project in fundamental metaphysics.

On the cognitive pluralist story there is nothing odd in supposing that there are things about the world that we do not understand. Indeed, our normative beholdenness to the object as something that transcends our ways of representing it amounts to a tacit recognition that there might be indefinitely more to any object than we have ways of modeling. For the cognitivist, a "property" may be what we posit in the world corresponding to a concept in a model, but the cognitivist recognizes that we now know about properties we once had no models of, and that there are presumably properties we do not have models of now, but could develop in the future. The properties are and were in some sense "always there", whether we understand them or not. Moreover, she does not assume that our minds are suited to understanding everything, and hence the notion of an "object or property we are incapable of understanding" should not be regarded as sheer grammatical nonsense.

What is potentially more problematic is speaking of and reasoning about the "*a priori* entailments" of such properties. First, *a priori* entailments are not relations that hold between properties or states of affairs, but between ways properties and states of affairs are represented using concepts, propositions, and models. Second, such derivations can take place only when we have concrete models of the two domains in their own right. This does not mean that we cannot speak of the potential for such entailment relations until we have the models in hand – we can perfectly well pose the possibility that, *when* we have adequate models of A and B in their own right, we will be able to derive features of B from our model of A. But when the A-phenomena are something we are unable to understand in their own right, we are no longer talking about something *we* might someday be able to do.

Here, I have two worries, one specific to this case, the other more general. First, many philosophers who have discussed phenomenological properties have held that what it is like to have a particular type of experience is knowable only to the sort of being that has them. If there is something it is like to be a quark, it is not clear that even God (not being a quark) could know what that was like. So there is a special problem, perhaps unique to experiential properties, about the possibility of *any* being having the sort of understanding of all of them it would require to be in a position to work out their *a priori* entailments.

The second and more general worry is that this strategy involves a kind of speculative projection, not only of an ideal mind, but of what sorts of understanding such a mind would be capable of. There is a way of doing this that may be comparatively innocent: projecting a mind that has the familiar sorts of cognitive *competences* we ourselves possess but freed from *performance limitations*. But if the cognitive pluralist is right, the kind of "ideal mind" envisaged here has to be *unlike* the kinds of minds we know about in more fundamental ways. Our understanding comes in the form of idealized models of particular domains, and these have not yielded to the sorts of comprehensive reductive integration that philosophers from Descartes to Carnap hoped for. Cognitive *Pluralism* was initially introduced as a way of explaining how such disunities of knowledge could be products of a cognitive architecture built around idealized domain-centered models, rather than a result of performance limitations or a puzzling metaphysical feature of the world itself. If this is correct, to posit an "ideal mind" that does not have such limitations is to posit a mind whose basic forms of cognition are quite unlike our own. The problem is that we really have no idea what a mind so different from our own would be like, or what it would be capable of. There is a danger that, in positing a mind specifically in terms of its being able to possess such a comprehensive and integrated understanding, we are drawn into an *illusory* conviction that such a mind is really possible.

8. Cognitivism, Rationalism, and Realism

In the end, both direct and hypothetical approaches to panpsychism seem to depend upon rationalist and realist assumptions which the cognitive pluralist ought to hold in suspicion. Both involve the realist assumption that the world divides itself in ways that yield a canonical and mind-independent set of properties. Leibniz's direct approach involves a more conventional rationalist assumption that *minds like ours* have the resources to understand the essential nature of these properties, at least in the very broad terms of "perceptions and appetitions". Chalmers' hypothetical approach acknowledges that these might be unknowable to us, but assumes that they are ideally knowable, and that an ideal mind would be able to see how they imply macroscopic properties through *a priori* entailments. It is certainly not the sort of rationalism that holds that we can know the real and fundamental natures of things *through innate ideas* or *without empirical investigation*, and indeed Chalmers seems pessimistic about the prospects of *our* having concrete understanding of quiddities. Rather, it projects a vision of an ideal form of rational understanding, and one which lacks what the cognitive pluralist regards as vitally important: the division of understanding into idealized models that do not seem to be susceptible to unification through reduction into something like an axiomatic deductive system based in fundamental properties. This, of course, is a feature shared with other fundamental positive metaphysical positions such as reductive physicalism, and such views are similarly suspect to the cognitive pluralist.

From a cognitive standpoint, the road to this sort of fundamental metaphysics looks something like this. We are familiar with a powerful way in which particular things we understand can (sometimes) be unified – through a part-whole reduction in which the properties of complex things can exhaustively be derived from those of the simplest parts. The power of such unifications is so great that *seeking* such reductions serves as a kind of regulative ideal. It is an empirical question just which portions of our understanding can be thus unified, and the empirical questions are not just about the world, but also about our mental capabilities. Even before there had been serious attempts to find even local reductions, philosophers were able to project what the ideal completion of such a project might look like: an understanding of the simplest entities from which everything else we understand could be derived. This supplied a further regulative ideal of *comprehensive* unification, though again one whose feasibility depends upon empirical questions about both world and mind. And this, in turn, allows for a schematic vision for a metaphysics in which the properties of the simplest entities determine those of everything else. This is the kind of metaphysics that must be correct *if the project of integrating understanding in this particularly powerful and comprehensive way could be carried out to its ideal conclusion.*

This, however, gives us little reason to believe either that some version of this schematic metaphysical picture is correct or that the epistemological project can be carried out. In fact, disunities of science (as well as the apparent irreducibility of mind, normativity, and mathematics) seem to suggest that *we* cannot carry it out. But the advocate of fundamental metaphysics responds that this may be due to limitations of our own minds, and projects the kind of ideal mind that would be needed precisely in order to have the requisite forms of understanding. In short, what we start from is a real strategy for unifying things we understand, and from there we project the kind of world and the kind of mind that would be needed to carry out this strategy to its ideal conclusion. There is nothing wrong with this kind of speculation, so long as we keep track of what we are doing. The danger is more or less the danger Kant pointed out with respect to his dialectical illusions: we come to mistake the "necessity" of *what would have to be the case to ideally complete the strategy* for a kind of metaphysical necessity in its own right, and mistake the intuitive appeal of an idealized and speculative picture of how knowledge might be unified for a trustworthy intuition about fundamental metaphysics.

References

Carey, S. (2011). *The Origin of Concepts*. New York: Oxford University Press.

Cartwright, N. (1999). *The Dappled World: A Study in the Boundaries of Science*. New York: Cambridge University Press.

Chalmers, D. J. (2015). 'Panpsychism and Panprotopsychism'. In T. Alter and Y. Nagasawa (eds.), *Consciousness in the Physical World*. Oxford and New York: Oxford University Press, pp. 246–76.

Dennett, D. C. (1981/1997). 'True Believers: The Intentional Strategy and Why It Works'. In J. Haugeland (ed.), *Mind Design II*. Cambridge, MA: MIT Press.

Horst, S. (2007). *Beyond Reduction: Philosophy of Mind and Post-Reductionist Philosophy of Science*. New York: Oxford University Press.

Horst, S. (2011). *Laws, Mind and Freedom*. Cambridge, MA: MIT Press.

Horst, S. (2014). 'Beyond Reduction: From Naturalism to Cognitive Pluralism'. *Mind and Matter*, 12 (2): 197–244.

Horst, S. (2016). *Cognitive Pluralism*. Cambridge, MA: MIT Press.

Kant, I. (1756/1986). 'The Employment in Natural Philosophy of Metaphysics Combined with Geometry, of Which Sample I Contains the Physical Monadology'. In L. W. Beck (ed.), *Kant's Latin Writings, Translations, Commentaries, and Notes*. New York: P. Lang, pp. 115–32.

Kant, I. (1786/2004). *Metaphysical Foundations of Natural Science*. Trans. M. Friedman. Cambridge: Cambridge University Press.

Lakoff, G., and Johnson, M. (2003). *Metaphors We Live By*. Chicago: University of Chicago Press.

Leibniz, G. W. (1989). *Leibniz: Philosophical Essays*. Trans. R. Ariew and D. Garber. New York: Hackett.

Russell, B. (1927). *The Analysis of Matter*. London: Kegan Paul.

Seager, W., and Allen-Hermanson, S. (2015). 'Panpsychism'. In E. N. Zalta (ed.), *The Stanford Encyclopedia of Philosophy*. http://plato.stanford.edu/archives/fall2015/entries/ panpsychism/.

Spelke, E. S., and Kinzler, K. D. (2007). 'Core Knowledge'. *Developmental Science*, 10 (1): 89–96.

18

NEUTRAL MONISM REBORN

Breaking the Gridlock Between Emergence and Inherence

Michael Silberstein

1. Introduction

As this volume attests, radical emergence, panpsychism and neutral monism seem to be making something of a comeback; why might this be? Presumably it is because the prospects of 'biological naturalism' are dimming even among many of its former proponents. Biological naturalism says that consciousness or subjectivity is a biological phenomena generated by the brain in the way that liquidity is a global emergent property of a certain molecular structure. Conscious experience then, like liquidity, is a weakly emergent property of the whole brain. John Searle (2004, 146 ff.) asserts that given biological naturalism, the scientific study of consciousness requires two steps: first, discover the neural correlate (NCC) of the entire field of conscious experience, and second, go from this NCC to a discovery of its actual biological causal mechanisms.

However, at least in certain quarters of the cognitive neuroscience of consciousness and consciousness studies more generally, Searle's program did not come to pass. Cristof Koch writes:

> Yet the mental is too radically different for it to arise gradually from the physical. This emergence of subjective feelings from physical stuff appears inconceivable and is at odds with a basic precept of physical thinking, the Ur-conservation law – *ex nihilo nihil fit.*
>
> (2014, 2)

What exactly led to Koch's change of heart is debatable but in the preceding passage he seems to have had the epiphany that for conscious experience to be caused by brains and their purely biological properties would require *radical* emergence, not weak emergence as Searle suggests. And Koch seems to have sided with fans of panpsychism such as Galen Strawson (2006) who claim that radical emergence is impossible.

This chapter has two primary purposes – to argue against radical emergence and panpsychism, and for an alternative: neutral monism. In the next section the 'generation problem' will be defined because it is that problem that drives both radical emergence and panpsychism. And then radical emergence and panpsychism will be defined in terms of their respective reactions to this problem. In the following section it will be argued that both radical emergence and panpsychism are untenable. In the final section it will be argued that only neutral monism truly defeats the generation problem by deflating it and has many other virtues as well. The overall thrust is that we are apparently driven to radical emergence or panpsychism because of the standard physicalist/materialist assumptions shared by both, that matter is fundamental, the nature of reality is therefore compositional and therefore that material and mental features are essentially different and distinct. Radical emergence and panpsychism are therefore just 'patches' for physicalism, whereas neutral monism is the cure.

2. The Generation Problem: Radical Emergence Versus Panpsychism

The generation problem (GP) or hard problem is this: assuming that matter is fundamental then how does mere insensate matter generate consciousness? For this problem to be as devastating as David Chalmers (1996) and others allege one has to assume something like: matter is *essentially* non-mental. As Barbara Montero puts it:

> Instead of construing the mind/body problem as finding a place for mentality in a fundamentally physical world, we should think of it as the problem of finding a place for mentality in a fundamentally non-mental world.
>
> (2010, 210)

If we take GP seriously then consciousness must be fundamental *in some sense*.

Radical (or strong) emergence is the view which claims, for example, that there are brute psycho-physical bridge laws in the actual world. Such brute bridge laws are supposed to involve nomological necessity and pertain to the actual world only.

Radical emergence attempts to answer GP in terms of some brute fundamental psycho-physical bridge law or causal process. A stand-alone, one of a kind brute/fundamental law/cause is a Deus ex Machina – 'and then a miracle occurred' kind of affair. That is, if matter is fundamental and essentially non-mental then radical emergence must be like some sort of occasionalism that replaces God with a miraculous law of nature. For those who want unity, the primary motivation for believing in physicalism or ontological reductionism in the first place, such psycho-physical bridge laws are deeply disunifying no matter how you construe them. Again, such laws/causes are a very strange thing to have the status of fundamental facts: given the right physical, functional, informational structure, etc., and POOF conscious experience appears! This may be explanatory for some, but it isn't a natural or scientific explanation, nor is it a law of nature like any other law; it's a brute law of meta-nature, surprising to not only the Mathematical Archangel but perhaps to God herself. This is a law that would have to be tacked onto a theory of everything or quantum gravity were those ever to be achieved.

Panpsychism also takes GP at face value and proposes the following resolution:

Whatever matter is most fundamental such as particles, fields or the quantum wave function is the basic 'building block' of reality, but itself has no intrinsic physical properties (fundamental physical properties are relational).

The physical world is 'composed' of or otherwise determined by basic physical entities and such fundamental physical entities have (however proto) an intrinsic psychical-conscious or subjective aspect.

Therefore, there is a sense in which all physical composites have a psychical/subjective nature however attenuated.

Therefore, the purely physical description of the world is incomplete – consciousness or subjectivity is co-fundamental with matter.

According to panpsychism there can be no consciousness without matter (and perhaps the reverse as well) but consciousness is an intrinsic property of matter. And the latter claim is just an axiomatic fact about the universe, it is not explained by anything else.

3. Why Both Radical Emergence and Panpsychism Fail

Radical emergence would have us believe that physicalism or ontological reductionism is true for everything except consciousness, that everything else in the universe is a nomological, causal, logical or metaphysical consequence of the fundamental physical facts. Admittedly, science is in no position to absolutely rule out the possibility of radical emergence; the doctrine is certainly not incoherent. However, by the lights of science given the stipulated nature of the rest of the universe, radical emergence posits *weird* laws. Such psycho-physical bridge laws are for all practical purposes, supernatural.

Does panpsychism fare any better than radical emergence? No. The best arguments for panpsychism are generally taken to be what Seager (2009, 500) calls the 'argument from analogy', the 'genetic argument' and the 'argument from the dispositional nature of fundamental physical properties.' The first argument claims there is some feature of fundamental matter that is mind-like. The second argument is really just the claim that radical emergence is impossible. The third argument claims that fundamental physical properties are not intrinsic, that they must nevertheless possess intrinsic properties and the only intrinsic properties are mental. Needless to say, none of these arguments is decisive and they have all been heavily attacked (see Silberstein (2010), (2014) and Silberstein, Stuckey and McDevitt (2018)).

The standard arguments against panpsychism are as follows (Seager 2016, ch. 13):

1. Combination problems.
2. No sign and not-mental problems.
3. Unconscious mentality problem – pan(proto).
4. Causal completeness problem

Panpsychism may not have a generation problem but it does have several combination problems (Chalmers 2016), namely, how do all those simple minds combine to make conscious agents such as ourselves? If you think fundamental physical entities possess free-floating qualia then how do all those very tiny discretized quales come together to make one of us? If you think subjective experience requires an experiencer then how do those very tiny conscious beings combine to make one human conscious agent with a unified experiential field? The second problem says that contrary to the argument from analogy there is absolutely no evidence that fundamental physical entities have mental properties or minds and therefore panpsychism is simply unjustified. The third problem says that pan(proto)psychism only makes the first problem worse because now we can't even conceive of what proto-mentality might be or if it's even coherent. So it threatens to turn the combination problem back into the generation problem. The fourth problem is that causal closure of the physical would seem to render mental properties epiphenomenal. The point is that we *never* have to bring mental properties to bear to explain the behavior of purely physical, chemical or biological systems.

To many of us, any one of these problems is enough to reject panpsychism. Space permits presenting only a very general argument against any form of panpsychism here which is that panpsychism is not a logically consistent position. According to panpsychism the only intrinsic properties of fundamental physical entities are psychical. But here is the problem: most theorists hold that essential properties must be intrinsic properties because those are the only non-relational and non-contingent properties an individual possesses. According to Robertson and Atkins (2016):

> *P* is an *essential property* of an object *o* just in case (1) it is necessary that *o* has *P* if *o* exists, and (2) *P* is an intrinsic property.
>
> Roughly, an intrinsic property is a property that an object possesses *in isolation*, while an extrinsic property is a property that an object possesses *only in relation to other objects*.

So if the intrinsic and thus essential properties of matter are mental as panpsychism claims then it just isn't true as panpsychism asserts that matter is the fundamental building blocks of reality and the physical world is composed of or otherwise determined by basic physical entities. You cannot consistently assert that matter is fundamental or co-fundamental and that its essential properties are mental. In short, panpsychism is not a stable position; it reduces to idealism or dualism of some sort.

Before we move on to neutral monism let us summarize what we have learned thus far. Regarding radical emergence, it is hard to see how it could be true and the GP is real. If matter is essentially non-mental and yet there is some basic physical law that says under the right configurations of matter that consciousness arises from it then such a law must be either impossible per the GP or beyond naturalistic explanation. That is, if matter is fundamental and essentially non-mental then radical emergence must be some sort of occasionalism-like view that replaces God with a miraculous law of nature. Again, there is no other law/cause like this, making conscious experience the radically unique exception. As for panpsychism, it is, as noted, fraught with several well-known problems, none of which are easily discharged. Further, in the service of explaining conscious experience on the length and time scales of embodied creatures on Earth with at least some sort of sensory apparatus and some sort of central nervous system, panpsychists have appealed to the very small (quantum systems) and the very large (the universe itself), but *everything* we have *ever* experienced tells us that only the 'middle porridge' is 'Ahhh, just right' when it comes to the processes associated with conscious experience.[1]

The best argument for either radical emergence or panpsychism seems to be the claim that they are the lesser of evils with respect to the other, but there are alternatives. One thing we know for sure, on pain of contradiction, panpsychism cannot invoke radical emergence to get out of its various combination problems and radical emergence cannot invoke panpsychism to resolve the GP. So what assumptions led to us to this absurd situation where we think it's either one or the other? The assumptions are as follows:

1. The generation problem is real (matter is essentially non-mental and it's fundamental).
2. All fundamental entities must have intrinsic properties.
3. Fundamental physical entities don't have intrinsic physical properties.
4. Consciousness is an intrinsic property and by elimination must be the intrinsic aspect of fundamental physical entities.

Where does this leave us? Given the problems with both radical emergence and panpsychism it's high time to question at least some of their shared assumptions.

4. Neutral Monism to the Rescue

Both radical emergence and panpsychism agree to (1) above and therefore both attempt to answer the generation problem directly. To *deflate* the GP and get around the master arguments for radical emergence and panpsychism we need another alternative. As long as matter is conceived as essentially non-mental and experience is conceived as intrinsic qualia we are stuck with these problematic views. So the alternative must reconceive matter and mind. This is exactly what, properly understood, neutral monism does. Given that the key defenders of neutral monism such as William James and Bertrand Russell also defended panpsychism at various points and given that 'the avowed neutrality of neutral monism tends to slides towards some kind of panpsychism or idealism' (Seager 2007, 28), people can certainly be forgiven for thinking that neutral monism and panpsychism may not be completely distinct doctrines, but it is very important to see that they are distinct. As James saw very clearly, we need to *deflate* the GP, not answer it directly. We need to deny that everyday conscious experience is an entity – it isn't qualia-like, it's not intrinsic. As James notes, it is 'intellectualism' or rationalism that got us into this mess in the first place and that's what we must reject:

> Intellectualism in the vicious sense began when Socrates and Plato taught that what a thing really is, is told by its *definition*. Ever since Socrates we have been taught that reality consists of essences, not of appearances, and that the essences of things are known whenever we know their definitions. So we first identify the thing with a concept and then we identify the concept with a definition, and only then, inasmuch as the thing *is* whatever the definition expresses, are we sure of apprehending the real essence of it or the full truth about it. . . . Intellectualism does not stop till sensible reality lies entirely disintegrated at the feet of 'reason'.
>
> (1912, 218)

Let's start with what we actually know: everyday conscious experience appears to be intimately related to embodied organisms with certain complex internal structures maneuvering an environment. This much radical emergence has right. As James puts it:

> The individualized self, which I believe to be the only thing properly called self, is a part of the content of the world experienced. The world experienced (otherwise called the 'field of consciousness') comes at all times with our body as its centre, centre of vision, centre of action, centre of interest. Where the body is is 'here', where the body acts is 'now'; what the body touches is 'this'; all other things are 'there', and 'then' and 'that'.
>
> (1912, 380)

James is defending neutral monism, which, following Stubenberg (2014), holds the following:

1. Mental and material features are real but in some specified sense, reducible to or constructable from a neutral basis in a non-eliminative sense of reduction.
2. The neutral basis is generally not conceived as substance.
3. Mental and material features are not separable or merely correlated, they are *non-dual*; indeed, they are *not essentially different and distinct aspects*.

Quoting James himself, here is how Stubenberg (2014) characterizes his neutral monism:

> Prior to any further categorization, pure experience is, according to James, neutral – neither mental nor material: 'The instant field of the present is at all times what I call the 'pure' experience. It is only virtually or potentially either object or subject as yet. For the time being, it is plain, unqualified actuality, or existence, a simple *that*' (James 1904b, 23). Mind and matter, knower and known, thought and thing, representation and represented are then interpreted as resulting from different groupings of pure experience.

Let us then adopt the neutral monism of William James and Bertrand Russell as characterized herein:

> Just so, I maintain, does a given undivided portion of experience, taken in one context of associates, play the part of the knower, or a state of mind, or 'consciousness'; while in a different context the same undivided bit of experience plays the part of a thing known, of an objective 'content'. In a word, in one group it figures as a thought, in another group as a thing.
>
> (James 1904, 480)

The whole duality of mind and matter . . . is a mistake; there is only one kind of stuff out of which the world is made, and this stuff is called mental in one arrangement, physical in the other.

(Russell 1913/1993, 15)

Things and thoughts are not fundamentally heterogeneous; they are made of one and the same stuff, stuff which cannot be defined as such but only experienced; and which one can call, if one wishes, the stuff of experience in general. . . . 'Subjects' knowing 'things' known are 'roles' played, not 'ontological' facts.

(James 1905/2005, 63)

On this view, conscious experience (subjectivity) is not an 'add-on', it is as much a part of the fabric of the universe as so-called matter. The GP is a cognitive illusion generated by the inference or projection that experience is inherently or essentially mental and the 'external' world is inherently non-mental. The claim that the world is carved at the joints a la physical/mental; inner/outer; subject/object, etc., is not a datum, but rather an inductive projection.

One way to interpret James or at least amend his view is as follows:

1. There is no conscious experience without a subject.
2. Where there are perceptions there is a perceiver and vice versa.
3. No subject/self without an object/world and vice versa.

So experience is inherently relational in the following sense: a conceptual or projected cut is made in 'the stuff of experience' between the subject and the object. In the Buddhist tradition (and in some Hindu traditions as well) it happens when the 'I am' thought arises, e.g., the individual thought 'I am in pain now.' In keeping with the suggested amendment to James it helps to look at a possible way of understanding neutral monism that is inspired by Kant (1998), Husserl (2001), Heidegger (1996), Merleau-Ponty (1962), Schopenhauer (1969), and a variety of Asian traditions such as Advaita Vedānta (Gupta 1998). This is not the place for historical details, and important differences between these thinkers will be glossed over. Most of them do not necessarily self-identify as neutral monists, but following Zahavi (2005) who is writing about Husserl, Merleau-Ponty and others, we can say that for all these traditions of thought, the minimal subject and the external world (the minimal object) self-consistently co-exist, you cannot have one without the other. There is a self-consistency relation such that the subject and the external world are both necessary and sufficient for the other. Following Kant's unity of apperception and Schopenhauer's will and representation, we can go a step further: It is only when the subject/object cut exists that one gets a world in space and time – the phenomenal experience of being a subject in an external world in which time is passing. So subject/object and world in space/time are both necessary and sufficient for one another. One can of course find similar ideas in the works of Husserl and Merleau-Ponty in their respective accounts of temporal experience. One can also find excellent expressions of this idea in Advaita Vedānta as illustrated by the following passage from Gupta (1998), which again echoes neutral monism:

The goal of Advaita Vedānta is to show the ultimate non-reality of all distinctions; reality is not constituted of parts.

(1)

When pure consciousness individuates itself into subject and object, there results knowledge – the distinction between 'knower and known'. . . . In talking about Brahman [pure consciousness], it is not a subject or an object, but neither and both; the distinction is not real.

Because reality is non-dual, the known and the knower come to be recognized as one: brahman and atman, the objective and subjective poles of experience, are nondifferent.

(31)

Atman is pure distinctionless, self-shining consciousness, which is non-different from brahman. It is that state of being in which all subject-object distinction is obliterated. It does not have a beginning or an end; it is eternal and timeless. Time only arises within it.

(34)

That is, in the Vedic view time is merely the separation of *rishi* (knower), *devata* (knowing) and *chandas* (object). In transcendence, the three become one: the knower *is* the object and *is* the process of knowing. If one has a certain analytic or Western philosophical bias, it is easy to be put off by the Advaita Vedānta terminology, but we urge the reader to set aside that reaction and think of such claims from a purely phenomenological perspective.

Many of the aforementioned Western thinkers, however, make a mistake that neutral monism corrects. Namely, they place the explanation for this grand self-consistency relation between subject/world in space and time, in the head of individual experiencers. For Schopenhauer it is his 'representations', for Kant it is his 'categories', and for Husserl it is his 'inner representations' or presentations of temporal experience. Kant famously argues that the unity of experience in time and space requires a unity of self and vice versa, otherwise there is no manifold of successive representations. This means that the dynamical character of thought and the world are two sides of the same coin. Kant and the others are right that we do not experience things in time and space, but rather we experience them temporally and spatially. But, they are wrong to say that this is an imposition of individual minds and their categories.

The mistake, in one form or another, which we find in both the analytic and continental tradition, is representationalism. Once we take neutral monism on board we can immediately see that there is no need for (and no sense to) representationalism to explain the experience of space or time (Silberstein and Chemero 2015). The point here is that subject and object co-dependently exist as a subject-in-a-world-in-space-and-time; they are two sides of the same coin, so the agent is not trapped behind 'a veil of perception' but is directly part of the world, and the external world is not some external container onto which the subject projects a virtual reality. Given neutral monism, (transcendental) phenomenology cannot be and should not be divorced from natural science, and experience cannot be separated from the natural world. There is not space enough here to repeat the argument but in Silberstein and Chemero (2012, 2015) the claim is made that enactivism, radically embodied and extended cognitive science in the dynamical systems tradition and other related traditions goes hand-in-hand with neutral monism, i.e., mind-brain-body-environment constitute non-linearly coupled aspects of one system. If this is true then unlike panpsychism, neutral monism is not scientifically moribund.

In other words, we are talking about direct realism. Again, we must take the brackets off phenomenology and let it be unbound. The experience of time's passage for example (a key focus of Husserl and perhaps the very essence of everyday conscious experience) is neither in the head (the subject) nor the external world (the object); the experience is fundamentally relational in that it requires that subject/object cut be made in the neutral 'field of pure experience' as James calls it. It is the self-consistency relation between subject and object that allows for the experience of time. This relation or structure is not in anything nor located anywhere; rather it why there are things in time and space as experienced. Given neutral monism, self/world are two sides of the same coin, therefore the dynamical character of thought and the world are two sides of the same coin.

Martin Heidegger wrote, 'Human life does not happen in time but rather is time itself' (2002, 169) – time is interwoven with consciousness. Henri Bergson, who very famously debated Einstein about the nature of time, was deeply bothered by the implication of relativity theory that time was just all in the mind. His claim, much like Heidegger's, was that 'We are time'. Further, 'Bergson . . . believed this distinction could never be absolute; that we could never establish a fixed boundary between matter and mind' (Canales 2015, 340). Here is the point: neutral monism does what Bergson wanted, 'to turn subjective time into something objective'. Neutral monism tells us that Einstein's 'time of the universe' and Bergson's 'lived time' are one.

If these ideas about the unity of subject-object-world-in-space and-time, strike you as little more than phenomenology with no naturalistic grounding in science, think again. The question of how to explain the experience of time has now taken center stage in cognitive science and in physics (Arstila and Lloyd 2014; Callender 2010, 2017). There are primarily two aspects of the experience of time that science wants to explain: (1) the flow, passage or 'woosh' (constant change in the future direction) and (2) the specialness of the present moment or 'nowness'. The suggestions made here about the explanation for the experience of time are not merely phenomenology, they also have grounding in both the recent cognitive science of time perception and in recent speculations in physics about time. For example, the cognitive neuroscientist Marc Wittmann who studies time perception writes:

> Because I have a body, I perceive the passing of time.
>
> (2016, 133)

> Temporal experience, self-consciousness, and the perception of bodily states and feelings are tightly bound to each other; they cannot be experienced separately.
>
> (2016, 135)

> Research on consciousness inevitably shows that our concepts of self, time and body are interrelated. Presence means becoming aware of a physical and psychic self that is temporally extended. To be self-conscious is to recognize oneself as something that persists through time and is embodied.
>
> (2016, 104)

Jennifer Windt (2015) notes that even in dreams phenomenal selfhood requires the experience of a self-world boundary and phenomenal selves are always spatiotemporally situated.

As for the physics, there are speculations about the experience of time that would support the thinking that there is no hard and fast division between subjective and objective time. As philosopher of physics Craig Callender notes, philosophers such as Merleau-Ponty were already onto to this idea:

> Merleau-Ponty argued that time itself does not really flow and that its apparent flow is a product of our 'surreptitiously putting into the river a witness of its course'. That is, the tendency to believe time flows is a result of forgetting to put ourselves and our connections to the world into the picture. Merleau-Ponty was speaking of our subjective experience of time, and until recently no one ever guessed that objective time might itself be explained as a result of those connections. Time may exist only by breaking the world into subsystems and looking at what ties them together. In this picture, physical time emerges by virtue of our thinking ourselves as separate from everything else.
>
> (2010, 65)

Callender goes on to note that this idea is taking shape as a concrete research project in quantum gravity:

> The universe may be timeless, but if you imagine breaking it into pieces, some of the pieces can serve as clocks for the others. Time emerges from timelessness. We perceive time

because we are, by our very natures, one of those pieces. . . . Historically, physicists began with the highly structured time of experience, the time of a fixed past, present and future. They gradually dismantled this structure, and little, if any, of it remains. Researchers must now reverse this train of thought and reconstruct the time of experience from the time of nonfundamental physics, which itself may need to be reconstructed from a network of correlations among pieces of a fundamental static world.

(2010, 65)

We have sketched out how one might explain the 'woosh' or experience of the passage of time, but what about the 'nowness', the specialness of the present moment or the 'presence' James alluded to earlier? It turns out that neutral monism has us covered there as well:

Neutral monism has to accept a notion of 'presence in experience' (what James called 'pure experience'). This presence is not labeled as 'consciousness' by the neutral monists, since they regard consciousness, and its subject, as a very sophisticated feature of the constructed mental realm. Nonetheless, presence is, I believe, what funds the hard problem of consciousness. Presence is what constitutes the 'what it is like' of conscious experience. This is quite explicit in the neutral monist's alignment of the neutral with the qualities of experience, and especially perceptual experience.

(Seager 2016, 326)

One way of interpreting James is that 'being', 'pure being' or 'being thus' is nowness or presentness, what some might call presence. Presentness, i.e., 'being', in the Western traditions of phenomenology and existentialism is typically thought of as either bracketed experience in the phenomenological tradition or merely a qualitative experience to ultimately be explained by neuroscience in the analytic tradition. In the traditions of existentialism, pragmatism and phenomenology, one can find varying expressions of the idea that the 'lived present', 'lived experience' or 'living present' are among the most fundamental aspects of reality. Also, as we saw, in some Hindu and Buddhist texts, presence is neither bracketed nor just a brain state, it is fundamental. When all qualitative and intentional states have ceased, what remains is presence (nirvikalpa samadhi). There is also savikalpa samadhi, in which there is still a residual sense of subject and object, whereas in nirvikalpa samadhi, even that relation goes, and there is only what might be called 'pure presence'. Given that presence is fundamental, it cannot be defined in terms of other concepts, of either a material or mental nature:

Advaita Vedānta centrally posits the existence of a permanent 'self' (atman). The self is characterized as the 'witness' (saksin) of the experiences, that is as that which is conscious of them – yet not in the sense of some substantial entity that performs the witnessing, but rather as nothing but the taking place of witnessing (consciousness) itself. . . . Synchronically and diachronically, manifold experiences are presented in one and the same consciousness, whose oneness is not reducible to some unifying relations between the experiences, but rather forms the dimension in which they, together with all their interrelations, have their existence in the first place. This *presence-dimension* is [my emphasis] . . . what is called atman (qua witness) in Advaita.

(Fasching 2010, 20)

Savikalpa samadhi would be direct awareness of presence. Nirvikalpa samadhi would be pure presence. Can the latter be 'known'? If it is known, it is experienced as an object. But then it is not pure presence. It can, though, be experienced. That is nirvikalpa samadhi. This is not awareness of, or consciousness of presence, this is nowness/presence itself. Whereas we generally experience time as an endless succession of point-like 'nows' as a result of that subject/object cut, the idea here is that presence is actually relatively fundamental, universal, unmoved and unchanging. To ask, 'where is presence' is to miss the point that presence or pure being is a precondition for all spatiotemporal experience, including the localization of objects and properties. Presence or nowness is the backdrop against which change is perceived.

Presence/pure being/pure experience/nowness/etc. may open a response to Stephen Hawking's question:

> Even if there is only one possible unified theory, it is just a set of rules and equations. What is it that breathes fire into the equations and makes a universe for them to describe? The usual approach of science of constructing a mathematical model cannot answer the questions of why there should be a universe for the model to describe. Why does the universe go to all the bother of existing?
>
> (1998, 2)

Here Hawking is playing off of John Wheeler's famous question, 'how come existence'? Wheeler's infamous answer does invoke the observations of conscious entities such as ourselves as part (only part) of the resolution to that question. He calls this the 'participatory universe' hypothesis (1977). A physicist's observations such as their decisions about what to measure in a quantum experiment like the ordinary twin-slit setup determine whether quantum systems manifest wave-like or particle-like behavior, for example. Think of Wheeler's cosmic delayed-choice thought experiment in which a single photon emitted from a distant quasar can simultaneously follow two paths to Earth, even if those paths are separated by many light-years. One photon travels past two different galaxies, with both routes deflected by the gravitational pull of the galaxies. The real kicker is that, as Wheeler notes, the observations astronomers make on Earth in the present decide the path the photon took billions of years ago. The wider implication of the 'participatory universe' is that the universe is a giant feedback loop with the following counterintuitive properties:

> Wheeler's idea was more radical. He claimed that the existence of life and observers in the universe today can help bring the very circumstances needed for life to emerge by reaching back to the past through acts of quantum observation. It is an attempt to explain the Goldilocks factor by appealing to cosmic self-consistency: the bio-friendly universe explains life even as life explains the bio-friendly universe.
>
> (Leslie and Kuhn 2013, 168)

Wheeler acknowledges that the universe looks as if it existed in a definite state before we started observing it but argues that quantum mechanics suggests otherwise. There are a number of things to note here. Wheeler seems to say that such observations need not be made by conscious observers but could be made by measuring devices, so consciousness as such isn't essential. Otherwise Wheeler's suggestion would seem to be a variant of idealism – there is a sense here in which 'to be is to be perceived or observed'. Wheeler's idealism or any other brand of subjective idealism raises the question of how the universe evolved or appeared to evolve in those past spatio-temporal regions in which it seems there were no conscious observers. For example, it certainly looks as if the Big Bang and cosmic microwave background radiation was there even when astronomers were not looking for it or at it. If we are good naturalists, then unlike Berkeley we cannot invoke God to answer this question. The vast majority of people writing about quantum mechanics do not want conscious observers to be essential to the theory. Wheeler's idea seems to imply some sort of anthropic principle, perhaps even the strong one (see Barrow and Tipler 1986).

Furthermore, there are interpretations of quantum mechanics such as Bohmian mechanics with its point particles with definite position that do not license Wheeler's inference about future events determining a particle's past trajectories.

So maybe we do not want to adopt Wheeler's particular suggestion about how individual human observation (or that of other such conscious agents) puts the fire in the equations. It is definitely the case that if neutral monism as described herein is true, then there is no external (objective) world without a self or subject; indeed, the very distinction does not ultimately hold up – the 'field of experience' is neutral and depending on how it's cut or 'foliated', it includes both subject and object. Given neutral monism it just isn't true that one can strip the world of space, time and matter of subjectivity and still discuss it in sensible terms. But this is not because the external world somehow arises from the minds of humans or God, nor because an individual conscious mind must 'lay eyes' on something in some causal sense before it can be real. The subject and the external world co-arise in a transcendental sense; the external world is not born of temporally or causally prior observation, perception or mentation, e.g., the things that make up the external world are not ideas in the mind of God.

In terms of the question of how 'witnessing' could be behind reality when the universe allegedly existed for billions of years before individual conscious beings came along, it's important to disentangle the witness consciousness (in the language of Advaita Vedānta) – which we could also call consciousness or subjectivity as such – from the consciousness of individual beings. As described previously, in Western philosophical terms the witness consciousness could be seen as the transcendental condition for the existence of any *thing or individual* – for the world as experienced perhaps not for existence simpliciter. This is not to invoke noumenal mind; given direct realism there is only the-world-as-experienced. The fact that any particular individual becomes conscious in the conventional sense, and becomes aware of this witness consciousness (perhaps through introspection, reasoned argument or meditative practice) does not create this witness consciousness. It is an objective reality that is taken to be transcendentally prior. Just as the physical world, on a conventional understanding, existed before any individual was there to perceive it, similarly the witness consciousness was also always already 'there', transcendentally prior to conscious individuals as we understand them today. In other words, the witness consciousness is a different kind of thing from individual consciousness as conventionally understood. It is not emergent, but logically prior and transcendental. The same argument for a self/world cut at the level of individual consciousness can be made for the world at large. Perceiver (subject) and perceived (object) co-exist in a self-consistent fashion as a single aspect of the witness consciousness. So the point is that while subject and object are co-dependent and thus relational, presence is the only remaining intrinsic feature and it also is a neutral feature that spans both the 'physical' and the 'mental', with all that those terms imply. The poisonous ontological dichotomies of mind/matter; inner/outer; subject/world, subjective/objective, etc., have infected traditions as diverse as metaphysical realism, physicalism and phenomenology. Neutral monism is the conceptual antidote.

'Witnessing' is neutral in three important respects. First, there are no qualia, no fundamental self or I, and no categorical distinction between the mental (the subjective) and the physical (the objective). Therefore, there is also no dualism between the qualitative and the intentional, they are all non-dual. Second, the subject/object cut is a self-consistency relation; there is only one reality, just 'foliated' and characterized in certain ways, as it were. Third, there is no ontic priority of the 'witnessing' over the external world – they are co-fundamental. In other words, while it has been emphasized that there can be no worldly phenomenal experience without the 'witnessing', it is also true that there can be no 'witnessing' (no minimal subject) without the object, i.e., a world in space and time. It is not as if the minimal subject exists prior in time to the external world of minds and physical objects and the latter arises out of the minimal subject in some causal or dynamical process.

However, one might argue that once again the problem of how to keep neutral monism from sliding into idealism looms large. 'To be is to be witnessed' sounds a lot like 'to be is to be perceived', the very essence of subjective idealism. We have already suggested several ways to resist this analogy but if for the sake of discussion one is willing to take Advaita Vedānta or certain Western traditions seriously as a possible expression of neutral monism, then perhaps there is another worthwhile reply. It is important to understand that in the Advaita tradition and in such Western traditions as phenomenology and existentialism, what is ultimately fundamental is not the witness consciousness or pure subjectivity, but rather pure being – being itself or being thus. It is pure being that is to be identified with the now, nowness or pure presence. For example, in the Advaita Vedānta tradition the everyday individual conscious being such as ourselves can merge into the witness consciousness-subjectivity itself, which in turn can merge into pure being or being itself. 'Witness' is a relative term for pure presence inasmuch as it is related to something called 'world'. However, 'World' and 'witness', 'object' and 'subject' are really just pure presence aware of itself.

Here is the point: the Advaita Vedānta tradition of Hinduism provides us with another alternative for what the neutral might be. In this tradition, while brahman is equated with the witness consciousness (sakshi), there are varying degrees of subtlety of the witness consciousness. The blanket term for the experience of such states is samadhi (absorption). In savikalpa samadhi, there remains some residual sense of a distinction between witness and witnessed. But in nirvikalpa samadhi that slips away, so there is nothing but the witness. It is no longer really 'witnessing' itself, it is simply being itself (Deutsch 1969, 62 ff.). This being itself is beyond all description, concepts and predication, 'free from distinctions of all kinds'. The claim is that brahman is nirguna, i.e., without qualities. It is hard to imagine anything more neutral! In the Advaita Vedānta texts it is often said therefore that brahman is one with yet beyond the world of space and time. Brahman is beyond the world, but it also *is* the world.

The English word 'witness' (especially if followed by the English word 'consciousness') implies something observing something else. That concept of observation clearly implies something like consciousness (in the conventional sense), so asserting that it is fundamental sounds like idealism. However, if we take seriously the phenomenology of meditative states, the shift from savikalpa samadhi to nirvikalpa samadhi entails that the sense of 'observer-hood' passes away, and one is not so much 'witnessing' as 'being'. Think of this state as a kind of coalescence of mentality and materiality – and hence as 'neutral' in this sense. Here the claim is that 'being', 'pure being' or 'being thus' *is* nowness or presentness, what some might call presence. Again, when all qualitative and intentional states have ceased, what remains is presence (nirvikalpa samadhi). Given that presence is fundamental, it cannot be defined in terms of other concepts of either a material or mental nature. Again, this is not awareness of, or consciousness of, presence – this is nowness/presence itself. Perceiver (subject) and perceived (object) co-arise in a self-consistent fashion from presence. And again, do not think of this co-arising as a causal process in time. From the perspectiveless (and experienceless experience) 'perspective' of pure being, there is no subject, nor a world in space and time, only being itself. Only from the perspective of the witness consciousness and individual manifestations of it such as ourselves does the world exist. This sounds plausibly like neutral monism. Again, the point here is that space-time and matter cannot be stripped of subjectivity; the existence of our world cannot exist without the subject, but not in the sense of subjective idealism; the subject cannot exist without the world either.

It is understandable that some readers will be put off by the invocation of analytic, continental and Eastern traditions of thought. It is also understandable that some readers will find the view sketched here too much to accept, they would rather struggle with trying to patch Western physicalism or materialism. Two points. First, we have seen that radical emergence and panpsychism are fatally flawed, so if we accept that we are going to have to look elsewhere and face new challenges and new questions. Second, once one does accept something like the view sketched herein and acquires sympathy for it, it is quite alright to take advantage of the fact that certain Eastern and continental traditions have understood that pure being and subjectivity are fundamental and have been trying to work out the consequences of that for some time. As Seager said, neutral monism 'knocks the physical, as scientifically understood, from its perch of ontological preeminence' (2016, 326). Perhaps it's time to stop patching physicalism and begin to explore the new world.[2]

Notes

1. Of course, both strong emergence and panpsychism have responses to all these concerns and they deserve more critical attention. For a fully developed critique of these positions see Silberstein, Stuckey and McDevitt (2018).
2. I would like to thank William Seager for his invaluable comments and editing.

References

Arstila, V., and Lloyd, D. (eds.) (2014). *Subjective Time: The Philosophy, Psychology and Neuroscience of Temporality*. Cambridge, MA: MIT Press.
Barrow, J., and Tipler, F. (1986). *The Anthropic Cosmological Principle*. Oxford: Oxford University Press.
Callender C. (2010). 'Is Time an Illusion?' *Scientific American*, 302 (6): 58–65.
Canales, J. (2015). *The Physicist and the Philosopher: Einstein, Bergson, and the Debate That Changed Our Understanding of Time*. Princeton: Princeton University Press.
Chalmers, D. (1996). *The Conscious Mind: In Search of a Fundamental Theory*. Oxford: Oxford University Press.
Chalmers, D. (2016). 'The Combination Problem for Panpsychism'. In G. Brüntrup and L. Jaskolla (eds.), *Panpsychism*. Oxford: Oxford University Press, pp. 229–48.
Deutsch, E. (1969). *Advaita Vedānta: A Philosophical Reconstruction*. Honolulu: University of Hawaii Press.
Fasching, W. (2010). 'I am of the Nature of Seeing: Phenomenological Reflections on the Indian Notion of Witness-Consciousness'. In M. Siderits, E. Thompson, and D. Zahavi (eds.), *Self, No Self? Perspectives from Analytical, Phenomenological, and Indian Traditions*. Oxford: Oxford University Press, pp. 193–216.
Gupta, B. (1998). *The Disinterested Witness: A Fragment of Advaita Vedānta Phenomenology*. Evanston: Northwestern University Press.
Hawking, S. (1998). *A Brief History of Time*. New York: Bantam Books.
Heidegger, M. (1996). *Being and Time*. Trans. J. Stambaugh. Albany: SUNY Press.
Heidegger, M. (2002). *Supplements: From the Earliest Essays to Being and Time and Beyond*. Ed. J. van Buren. Albany: SUNY Press.
Husserl, E. (2001). *Logical Investigations*. Trans. J. N. Findlay. London: Routledge.
James, William (1904). 'Does "Consciousness' Exist?' *Journal of Philosophy, Psychology, and Scientific Methods*, 1: 477–91. (Reprinted in *Mind and Matter*, 8: 131–44, 2010).
James, William (1905/2005). 'The Notion of Consciousness'. *The Journal of Consciousness Studies*, 12 (7): 55–64. (Translation by J. Bricklin of James's Communication made (in French) at the 5th International Congress of Psychology, Rome.).
James, William (1912). *A Pluralistic Universe*. New York: Longmans, Green and Co.
Kant, I. (1998). *The Critique of Pure Reason*. Trans. P. Gruyer and A. Wood. Cambridge: Cambridge University Press.
Koch, C. (2014). 'Ubiquitous Minds'. *Scientific American Mind*: 26–9, January–February.
Leslie, J., and Kuhn, L. (eds.) (2013). *The Mystery of Existence: Why Is There Anything at All?* Chichester: Wiley-Blackwell.
Merleau-Ponty, M. (1962). *Phenomenology of Perception*. London: Routledge.
Montero, B. (2010). A Russellian response to the structural argument against physicalism. *Journal of Consciousness Studies*, 17(3–4): 70–83.
Robertson, T., and Atkins, P. (2016). 'Essential vs. Accidental Properties'. In E. Zalta (ed.) *The Stanford Encyclopedia of Philosophy*, Summer edition. http://plato.stanford.edu/archives/sum2016/entries/essential-accidental/.
Russell, B. (1913/1993). 'Theory of Knowledge'. In E. Eames and K. Blackwell (eds.), *The Collected Papers of Bertrand Russell*, vol. 7. London: Routledge.
Schopenhauer, A. (1969). *The World as Will and Representation*. New York: Dover.
Seager, W. (2007). A brief history of the philosophical problem of consciousness. In P. Zelazo, M. Moscovitch, and E. Thompson (eds.), *The Cambridge Handbook of Consciousness*. Cambridge: Cambridge University Press, pp. 9–34.
Seager, W. (2009). 'Panpsychism'. In T. Bayne, A. Cleeremans, and P. Wilken (eds.), *The Oxford Companion to Consciousness*. Oxford: Oxford University Press, pp. 500–2.
Seager, W. (2016). *Theories of Consciousness: An Introduction and Assessment*, 2nd edition. London: Routledge.

Searle, John R. (2004). *Mind: A Brief Introduction*. New York: Oxford University Press.

Silberstein M. (2010). 'Why Neutral Monism Is Superior to Panpsychism'. *Mind and Matter*, 7 (2): 239–48.

Silberstein, M. (2014). 'Experience Unbound: Neutral Monism, Contextual Emergence and Extended Cognitive Science'. *Mind and Matter* (special issue entitled *Naturalizing the Mind*), 12 (2): 289–339.

Silberstein, M., and Chemero, A. (2012). 'Complexity and Extended Phenomenological-Cognitive Systems'. *Topics in Cognitive Science*, 4 (1): 35–50.

Silberstein, M., and Chemero, A. (2015). 'Extending Neutral Monism to the Hard Problem'. *Journal of Consciousness Studies* (special issue on Embodied and Extended Theories of Conscious Experience entitled *Consciousness Unbound: Going Beyond the Brain*), 22 (3–4): 181–94.

Silberstein, M., Stuckey, W. M., and McDevitt, T. (2018). *Beyond the Dynamical Universe: Unifying Block Universe Physics and Time as Experienced*. Oxford: Oxford University Press.

Strawson, G. (2006). 'Realistic Monism: Why Physicalism Entails Panpsychism'. In A. Freeman (ed.), *Consciousness and Its Place in Nature*. Exeter: Imprint Academic, pp. 3–31.

Stubenberg, L. (2009). 'Neutral Monism'. In E. Zalta (ed.), *The Stanford Encyclopedia of Philosophy*, Fall 2014 edition. http://plato.stanford.edu/archives/fall2014/entries/neutral-monism/.

Wheeler, J. A. (1977). 'Genesis and Observership'. In R. Butts and J. Hintikka (eds.), *Foundational Problems in the Special Sciences*. Dordrecht: Reidel, pp. 3–34.

Windt, J. M. (2015). *Dreaming: A Conceptual Framework for Philosophy of Mind and Empirical Research*. Cambridge, MA: The MIT Press.

Wittmann, M. (2016). *Felt Time: The Psychology of How We Perceive Time*. Cambridge, MA: MIT Press.

Zahavi, D. (2005). *Subjectivity and Selfhood: Investigating the First-Person Perspective*. Cambridge, MA: MIT Press.

19

PANPSYCHISM AND NON-STANDARD MATERIALISM
Some Comparative Remarks

Daniel Stoljar

1. Introduction

Much of contemporary philosophy of mind is marked by a dissatisfaction with the two main positions in the field, standard materialism and standard dualism, and hence with the search for alternatives. My concern in this chapter is with two such alternatives. The first, which I will call *non-standard materialism*, is a position I have defended in a number of places, and which may take various forms.[1] The second, *panpsychism*, has been defended and explored by a number of recent writers.[2] My main goals are: (a) to explain the differences between these positions; and (b) to suggest that non-standard materialism is more plausible than panpsychism.

I will begin by reviewing briefly why the standard views are unsatisfactory. I will then turn to our main business, the comparison of non-standard materialism and panpsychism.

2. Standard Materialism

The project of transforming the impressionistic idea of materialism into something more tractable is a large and surprisingly complex one. Here I will work with a formulation due to David Lewis that starts from the assumption that any possible world, and so the actual world in particular, instantiates a relatively small class of fundamental properties, where 'fundamental' or 'perfectly natural' properties are (among other things) "not at all disjunctive, or determinable, or negative. They render their instances perfectly similar in some respect. They are intrinsic; and all other intrinsic properties supervene on them" (2009: 204; see also Lewis 1994: 291). This assumption is certainly non-trivial, but it is not important for us to evaluate it here. The important point is rather that if we make this assumption, we have a natural way of stating the basic idea of materialism, as follows:

Materialism (basic idea): all instantiated fundamental properties are physical properties.

Understood this way, materialism does not entail that all instantiated properties whatsoever are physical. It permits that many instantiated properties are non-physical, so long as those properties are not fundamental but instead supervene on, or are necessitated by, the fundamental properties.

If this is the basic idea of materialism, what is 'standard' materialism? Standard materialism (at least as I will understand it) takes this basic idea and adds that the physical properties in question are standard, where by a 'standard physical property' I mean a property of the kind expressed by the physical theories we currently have:

> *Standard Materialism:* all instantiated fundamental properties are standard physical properties.

For the standard materialist, therefore, "materialism is metaphysics built to endorse the truth and descriptive completeness of physics more or less as we know it" (Lewis 1986a: x).

Standard materialism faces a number of challenges but the most prominent of these is the conceivability argument and similar arguments. The conceivability argument – to put it roughly but serviceably for present purposes – proceeds from two premises. The first premise is that it is conceivable that there is a world identical to the actual world in respect of fundamental physical properties, and yet different from it in terms of the nature and distribution of certain psychological properties, in particular those associated with phenomenal consciousness. The second premise is that if this is conceivable it is possible. These two premises entail that standard materialism is false, since standard materialism entails that such properties supervene on or are necessitated by the fundamental physical properties, a claim which rules out the possible world in question. Of course there are many things to be said about the conceivability argument, but I will not go into the details here. Instead, I will assume that, whether it is successful or not, it at least motivates the search for an alternative to standard materialism.

3. Standard Dualism

Turning now to dualism, the basic idea here too may be formulated in the framework we have taken over from Lewis:

> *Dualism (basic idea):* (a) some instantiated fundamental properties are psychological properties; and (b) all instantiated non-psychological fundamental properties are physical properties.

Understood this way, dualism agrees with materialism about all instantiated properties apart from psychological ones.

If this is the basic idea of dualism, what is 'standard' dualism? Well, standard dualism takes this basic idea and adds both that physical properties are standard (in the way indicated previously) and that the psychological properties in question are standard too, where by a 'standard psychological property' I mean a property of the kind expressed by folk psychological theories of the sort we currently have; hence a standard psychological property is for example having an itch in your toe, seeing a cup, believing that snow is white, or wondering about your financial position:

> *Standard Dualism:* (a) some instantiated fundamental properties are standard psychological properties; and (b) all instantiated non-psychological fundamental properties are standard physical properties.

For the standard dualist, therefore, dualism is metaphysics built to endorse the near truth and near descriptive completeness of physics more or less as we know it – the only exceptions are standard psychological properties.

Like standard materialism, standard dualism has a number of challenges, but perhaps the most prominent is the exclusion argument and related arguments. The exclusion argument – to put it again roughly but serviceably for present purposes – proceeds from two premises. The first premise – the closure premise – is that for every physical event that has cause, there are physical properties that are causally efficacious in the production of that event. The second premise – the exclusion premise – is that if some property F is causally efficacious in the production of an event, then no property metaphysically distinct from F is also causally efficacious in the production of that event. These two premises entail that standard dualism is false, at least if we assume (reasonably) that psychological properties are causally efficacious in the production of behaviour, for the events involved in the behaviour of people and animals are physical events. And physical events, according to the closure premise, are such that physical properties are causally efficacious for their production. But then if standard dualism is true, psychological properties are not causally efficacious – for if they were they would have to be so in addition to physical properties, and this is something ruled out by the exclusion premise. There is much to say also about the exclusion argument, but again here I will assume that, whether or not it is successful, it at least motivates the search for an alternative to standard dualism.

What then might these alternatives be? As I said earlier, I will be concerned with non-standard materialism and panpsychism, and it is to these that I now turn.

4. Non-Standard Materialism

Non-standard materialism takes the general idea of materialism and adds that the physical properties in question can be *either* standard *or* non-standard:

> *Non-Standard Materialism:* all instantiated fundamental properties are either standard physical properties or non-standard physical properties

So non-standard materialism is logically weaker than standard materialism; it does not require that the fundamental properties are standard physical properties.

What is a non-standard physical property? There are two main strategies of approaching this question.[3] The first, which I will call the Nagelian strategy, contrasts physical theories we currently have with the physical theories that we will (or might) have in the ideal limit, or equivalently for present purposes, with the physical theories (whatever they are) that are true and complete. If we assume that the theories that we currently have are either not true or not complete, there is a difference between the properties expressed by current theories (i.e. standard physical properties) and those expressed by ideal theories (i.e. non-standard physical properties). Correlatively, we have a Nagelian version of non-standard materialism, according to which all fundamental properties are either standard or non-standard physical properties (in the Nagelian sense).

The second strategy, which I will call the Russellian strategy, appeals to the idea that standard physical properties are structural or dispositional properties and then suggests that there must be non-structural or non-dispositional properties that ground the standard properties in question. If we assume that these non-structural or non-dispositional properties are not expressed by physical theories of the kind we currently have, we have a distinction between dispositional or structural properties expressed by those theories (i.e. standard physical properties) and non-dispositional or non-structural properties which ground such properties (i.e. non-standard physical properties). Correlatively, we have a Russellian version of non-standard materialism, according to which all fundamental properties are either standard or non-standard physical properties (in the Russellian sense).

There is a lot to say about the contrast between the Nagelian and Russellian versions of non-standard materialism. This contrast is not our focus here, although I will say a little about it later. But why should we adopt a version of non-standard materialism of any sort in the first place?

Well, non-standard materialism has two apparent advantages. First, unlike standard materialism, it does not face the conceivability argument. The reason is that our epistemic relation to the non-standard properties (on either the Russellian or the Nagelian version of non-standard material-ism) is quite unlike our epistemic relation to standard properties; in particular, while we can *describe* non-standard properties, we don't know what they are, and since we don't know what they are, we cannot reason about them in the way that the conceivability argument requires. Second, unlike standard dualism, non-standard materialism does not entail that standard psychological properties are fundamental; hence it does not face the exclusion argument about these properties.

5. Non-Standard Dualism

Turning now to panpsychism, it is helpful here first to formulate a more general position I will call non-standard dualism. Non-standard dualism takes the basic idea of dualism and replaces 'standard psychological property' with 'non-standard psychological property':

> *Non-Standard Dualism:* (a) some instantiated fundamental properties are non-standard psychologi-cal properties; and (b) all instantiated non-psychological fundamental properties are standard physical properties.

So non-standard dualism, unlike standard dualism, and like all the forms of materialism we have considered, entails (at least with trivial further assumptions) that standard psychological properties are not fundamental.

What is a non-standard psychological property? As will emerge as we proceed, this is a difficult question for any sort of non-standard dualism. But to a first approximation (I will consider further proposals in a moment) we may assume that a non-standard psychological property is a psychological property like any other except that it has (or may have) a non-standard bearer. Standard (i.e. usual) bearers of psychological properties are objects such as people or animals, and an important feature of these objects is that they do not themselves instantiate fundamental physical properties. Non-standard psychological properties are instantiated in such objects, but also in other objects; in par-ticular, in the bearers of fundamental physical properties. So for example, if some electron – a bearer of a fundamental physical property – has some psychological property *F*, then, *F* is a non-standard psychological property in this sense.

6. From Non-Standard Dualism to Panpsychism

Non-standard dualism is not yet panpsychism. If you let etymology be your guide, the basic idea of panpsychism is that everything *whatsoever* has psychological properties. And if you let the recent lit-erature be your guide, as I will here, the basic idea is that everything *that is fundamental* – that is, every bearer of a fundamental property – has psychological properties. By itself non-standard dualism is not committed to these claims. It is consistent with non-standard dualism, for example, that only some, or indeed only one, bearer of a fundamental property has a psychological property.

However, while this is true, it is possible to add a further requirement to non-standard dualism, and so obtain the version of panpsychism we will be interested in, as follows:

> *Panpsychist Non-Standard Dualism:* (a) some instantiated fundamental properties are non-standard psychological properties; (b) all instantiated non-psychological fundamental properties are standard physical properties; and (c) everything that bears a fundamental physical property bears a fundamental property that is a non-standard psychological property.

The requirement formulated in (c) is an optional extra for non-standard dualism. If we add it, we get a panpsychist version of non-standard dualism; if we do not, we get a version of non-standard dualism that may not be panpsychist. I will come back later to whether the panpsychist version of the view is preferable to the non-panpsychist version. But first, why adopt non-standard dualism of any sort?

Well, like non-standard materialism, non-standard dualism has two apparent advantages as well. First, unlike standard dualism, it does not entail that standard psychological properties are fundamental; hence it avoids the exclusion argument about such properties. Second, unlike standard materialism, it does not entail that standard psychological properties supervene on standard physical properties, and so avoids the conceivability argument about such properties.

7. Three Problems for Panpsychism

Whatever its attractions, panpsychist non-standard dualism (hereafter 'panpsychism') faces at least three big problems.

> *Big Problem 1* is that it provokes an incredulous stare.[4] Surely electrons do not think and feel! That suggestion is on the face of it offensive to common sense in a very basic way.
>
> *Big Problem 2* is that, while panpsychism does not face the modal challenge in the form of the conceivability argument formulated earlier, it nevertheless faces an analogous argument; indeed this point is extremely prominent in the recent literature.[5] According to this argument, it is conceivable, and so possible, that there is possible world identical to the actual world in respect of fundamental physical properties and fundamental non-standard psychological properties, and yet different from it in terms of the nature and distribution of certain standard psychological properties, in particular those associated with phenomenal consciousness. If this is possible then panpsychism is false, for the same reason that standard materialism is false in the analogous situation.
>
> *Big Problem 3* is that, while panpsychism does not face the exclusion argument about standard psychological properties, it nevertheless faces an analogous challenge. Consider some electron α, and suppose, in accordance with panpsychism, that α has both psychological and physical properties. If we assume, as we should, that α behaves in various ways, we can mount an argument about it just as we did earlier about people and animals. For the events involved in the behaviour of α are physical events. And physical events, according to the closure premise mentioned above, are such that physical properties are causally efficacious for their production. But then if panpsychism is true, psychological properties of α are not causally efficacious – for if they were they would have to be so in addition to physical properties, and this is something ruled out by the exclusion premise. To adapt a phrase of Mark Johnston's, we face a mind-body problem at the fundamental level, a problem that looks in essence the same as the problem we originally faced at the non-fundamental level (Johnston 1996).

Taken individually these three problems (hereafter, BP1–3) present major challenges to panpsychism. But it is perhaps taken collectively that they have most force. What we wanted was a theory that avoided the problems of standard dualism and standard materialism. But what we have is a theory that faces both problems (suitably adjusted) and in addition provokes an incredulous stare.

8. Unimaginable Properties

How might the panpsychist respond to these problems? Of course there are a number of possible avenues to consider; however, *if* one's concern is with the comparison between panpsychism and non-standard materialism, perhaps the most obvious thing to do here is to point out that we have so far operated with a somewhat limited idea of what a non-standard psychological property is.

Such properties are non-standard, we said, only in so far as they have non-standard bearers. But it is open to the panpsychist to insist that, while they may be non-standard in this limited sense, they are also non-standard in a more dramatic way as well; indeed, it is open to them to suppose that these properties are quite unimaginable for us. After all, it is not implausible that other creatures instantiate psychological states that are unimaginable for us; so too, one might say for the psychological properties, if any, that are instantiated by electrons.

This 'unimaginable property' reply is, I think, most plausible when it is focused on BP1 and BP2, so let us concentrate on them first. As regards BP1, the panpsychist can say that while it may be offensive to common sense to say that electrons think and feel in ways familiar to us, it is not offensive to common sense (for example, because common sense has no view on the matter) that they think and feel in ways that are unimaginable to us. As regards BP2, if non-standard psychological properties had by the bearers of fundamental properties are unimaginable to us, then it is possible for the panpsychist to respond to the conceivability argument in the same way as the non-standard materialist. In particular (they might say) it is not possible for us to conceive (in the relevant sense) a situation in which they along with other properties are instantiated and yet standard psychological properties are not.

9. Essential Features of Psychological Properties

The unimaginable properties response is attractive on the surface, but it also faces two objections. The first starts from the point that, while it may be true that there are psychological properties unimaginable to us, it is also true that psychological properties, whether imaginable or not, have certain essential features. Moreover, when we focus on these features, what emerges is that they themselves are sufficient to generate BP1 and BP2. Hence the possibility of unimaginable properties does not alter the dialectical situation.

What are these essential features of psychological properties? One good candidate here is that psychological properties essentially consist in (or at least partially consist in) awareness of properties.[6] For example, feeling a pain in your toe is or entails being aware of some property or properties that your toe apparently instantiates. Likewise seeing a lemon is or entails being aware of certain properties that the lemon apparently instantiates, e.g. its colour, shape or position. On the assumption that these examples are typical, it is an essential feature of any phenomenal property that it consists in awareness of a property.

However, if this is an essential feature of any phenomenal property, the unimaginable property reply to BP1 and BP2 is no good. To see this, consider again BP1. If any phenomenal property essentially involves being aware of some property, then panpsychism is committed to the view that electrons and other bearers of fundamental properties are themselves aware of various properties. But this idea will surely provoke an incredulous stare just as much as the original suggestion that electrons think and feel in the way that we do. And here of course, it makes no difference that we cannot imagine what these states of awareness are like.

Or consider again BP2, the problem that panpsychism faces an argument analogous to the original conceivability argument against standard materialism. The reply we formulated before to this analogous argument is that if non-standard psychological properties are unimaginable, what this argument claims to be conceivable is not so, or anyway is not in the relevant sense. But the problem with this reply is that, if any non-standard psychological properties, imaginable or not, consist in awareness of properties, it is hard to argue that the relevant claim is *not* conceivable. For it certainly does seem conceivable that all the bearers of fundamental properties are aware of certain properties, then the non-fundamental objects which are composed of these bearers – objects such as people and animals – are not themselves aware of anything; at any rate, from the fact that the parts of a thing are aware of something, it scarcely follows that the complex made out of those things is likewise aware of some other property. And if that is so, appealing to unimaginable properties does not after all provide the panpsychist with the materials to respond to BP2.

10. The Threat of Collapse

A panpsychist might respond to this objection by denying that psychological properties have the essential feature we have been looking at; at the limit, they might even say that phenomenal properties have no essential features at all. However, any move of this sort leads only to the second objection to the unimaginable properties reply.

The second objection is that the unimaginable properties reply threatens to remove the difference between panpsychism and non-standard materialism. After all, if we literally know nothing about non-standard psychological properties, it is hard to see why they should be called 'psychological properties' in the first place. And if they are not psychological properties, then this 'panpsychist' position stands revealed as no different to non-standard materialism.

One might object that, as far as the threat of collapse goes, the panpsychist and the non-standard materialist are in the same boat. After all, if we literally know nothing about non-standard physical properties, it is hard to see why they should be called 'physical properties' either. However, while this is certainly a natural line of thought, it remains the case that the issue of collapse causes more trouble for the panpsychist than for the non-standard materialist, for two main reasons. First, the non-standard materialist begins from the claim that there are non-standard physical properties whose nature we do not know; that is the initial and defining claim of the position. But the panpsychist by contrast does not start from this position; rather it is forced on them when the most obvious way to spell out the view becomes untenable. Second, the idea that there are physical properties whose nature is completely unknown to us is relatively easily tolerated by our contemporary understanding of a physical property in a way that the analogous claim is not tolerated by our understanding of a mental property. According to our contemporary understanding of a physical property, a physical property (very roughly) is either a property distinctive of ordinary physical objects or else is a property that explains the properties distinctive of ordinary physical objects. The second clause here is forced on us by empirical developments, and in particular by the fact that contemporary physics talks about properties quite distinct from the distinctive properties of ordinary physical objects. But in view of this second clause, our understanding of the physical is very open ended. Hence while we might be able to say in the case of mental properties that they have various essential features, this is not at all clear in the case of physical properties.

11. A Mind-Body Problem at the Fundamental Level

I have been looking at the first two problems of the three set out earlier, BP1 and BP2. What now of BP3, the objection that the panpsychist faces the integration problem just as the standard dualist does?

In this case the most promising avenue is for the panpsychist to adopt a Russellian version of panpsychism. As we saw previously, a Russellian version of non-standard materialism holds (a) that standard physical properties are dispositional or structural properties, and (b) that non-standard physical properties are the non-dispositional or non-structural properties that ground standard physical properties. A Russellian version of panpsychism agrees with this with the exception that it is non-standard psychological properties, rather than non-standard physical properties, that ground standard physical properties.[7]

How does a position of this sort answer BP3? Well consider again the second premise of the exclusion argument, namely, that if some property F is causally efficacious in the production of an event, then no property metaphysically distinct from F is also causally efficacious in the production of that event. However exactly this premise is to be interpreted, one might argue that it should not apply in the case of structural or dispositional properties and the non-structural or non-dispositional properties that ground them. After all, if the solubility of a tablet may cause the water you put it in to fizz, so too does its chemical composition. In this case it seems mistaken to view the chemical composition as being in competition with the solubility. If so, it would appear that a Russellian version of panpsychism can withstand the exclusion argument, even when that argument is targeted at the fundamental level rather than the non-fundamental level.

12. Essential Features Again

Earlier we noted that it is possible to be a non-standard dualist but not a panpsychist; what we have just noted is that it is possible to be a panpsychist but not Russellian panpsychist. On the other hand, it appears that when faced with BP3, the best thing for the non-standard dualist to do is to become both a panpsychist and a Russellian panpsychist. It is for this reason that this is the most common form of non-standard dualism.

However, while this may be the best thing to do in the face of BP3, it too has a downside, and the problem again has to do with the essential features of psychological properties. For suppose that the psychological properties in question consist in being aware of some properties. Then what is being claimed of fundamental objects such as electrons is not merely that they are aware of various properties, but that they play their normal physical roles in virtue of being aware of various properties. But it seems to be quite unobvious why this should be so. Suppose, for example that some electron has rest mass, and in consequence is disposed to exert gravitational attraction on other elementary particles. Off hand it is reasonable to ask what it is about the electron that grounds its ability to do this. According to the Russellian panpsychist the answer is that that the electron is aware of certain properties. But this I think is an extremely peculiar answer. For one thing, that you aware of a property does not usually make you attractive to others! More generally, there seems no reason at all why the fact (assuming it to be a fact) that the electron is aware of something should make it have the dispositions electrons do when they have rest mass.

13. Does Non-Standard Materialism Face These Problems?

I have been suggesting that BP1–3 present difficulties for panpsychism that are very considerable indeed. But at this point one might wonder whether non-standard materialism faces the same problems, perhaps suitably adjusted. If that were the case, nothing we have said constitutes a reason to favour non-standard materialism over panpsychism.

However, I think it is clear that this is not the case. Consider BP1, the incredulous stare. The non-standard materialist does not face this problem. For saying that there are fundamental properties whose nature we do not know is one thing, saying that every bearer of a fundamental property instantiates a psychological fundamental property is quite another.

Consider BP1, that panpsychism faces a conceivability argument that is very similar to the one faced by standard materialism. The non-standard materialist does not face this problem. For suppose we formulate a third conceivability argument, similar to the two already on the table; according to this argument, it is conceivable, and so possible, that there is a possible world identical to the actual world in respect of fundamental standard and non-standard physical properties, and yet different from it in terms of the nature and distribution of certain standard psychological properties, in particular those associated with phenomenal consciousness. This argument is unpersuasive and the reason is the one noted previously, viz., that while we can describe these non-standard physical properties, we don't know what they are. Notoriously, the notion of 'conceivability' that is in operation in these arguments is epistemically demanding: you cannot conceive a situation in which various properties are instantiated unless you know, at least in outline, what those properties are.

Since we don't know what they are we can't conceive of them in the way required by a conceivability argument.

Finally, consider BP3, the mind-body problem at the fundamental level. The non-standard materialist does not face this problem. For the non-standard materialist who is a Russellian, there is the same reply as the one I considered earlier, but in this case there is no problem of the sort I described. And for the non-standard materialist who is a Nagelian, there is every reason to reject the closure premise when it is formulated in terms of standard physical properties, and so the exclusion argument has no purchase. Admittedly it remains the case that for the non-standard materialist there is some story to be told about the integration of the standard physical properties and non-standard physical properties. But this is conceived of by the non-standard materialist as a standard case of integration in science, something like the integration of gravity and electromagnetism. We may have no idea now how the story goes, and, human life being what it is, we may never have much of an idea. But there is no reason in principle that the problem cannot be solved.

14. Other Problems for Non-Standard Materialism

Even if it does not face BP1–3, non-standard materialism faces problems of its own. I have tried to respond to these problem elsewhere, and will not try to provide a comprehensive treatment here (see Stoljar 2006). However, *if* our concern is with the contrast between panpsychism and non-standard materialism, two problems are perhaps most prominent.

First, the panpsychist might object that claims about unknown properties do not alter the dialectical situation: "Unknown properties bear deep theoretical similarities to the properties we already know about and so the dualism-materialism issue will persist in a recognizable form." But this view hasn't fully absorbed the key point of non-standard materialism. The whole idea of that view is that the known is no guide to the unknown and so there is no deep theoretical similarity here. You can deny that if you like but doing so is just to deny the non-standard materialism without offering an argument for doing so. Alternatively one might try to support this idea by appealing to the conceivability argument. But as we have seen, that style of argument is no good against the non-standard materialist.

Second, the panpsychist might object (in an exasperated tone of voice) that speculations about unknown properties are useless: "Surely we are interested ultimately in building a theory and building theories requires known parts to build them from." But this objection confuses different questions you could ask about consciousness. True, if you want to know *exactly* what the relation is between physical and phenomenal properties, non-standard materialism is no help; indeed, the view itself predicts that you can't (now) answer that question. But many of the most interesting questions about consciousness can be pursued without answering that question. What is it that makes a mental state conscious? Are you always aware of your conscious states? How do those states interact with other psychological features? How do they evolve over time? What is their epistemological and rational role? In what ways, if any, are they valuable? What neural and computational structures are associated with them? There is nothing in non-standard materialism that says you can't answer these questions. On the contrary, they have often seemed so hard precisely because they are entangled with metaphysical debates about dualism and materialism. If we get over that debate in the way the new model suggests, we will be likely to make more progress, not less, on these very real questions about consciousness.

Indeed, at this point we can make a more general remark about the comparison between non-standard materialism and panpsychism, and the way in which they depart from the standard views we began with. An important feature of standard materialism is that it is, as Frank Jackson once pointed out, excessively optimistic: "it is not sufficiently appreciated that physicalism is an extremely optimistic view of our epistemic powers. If it is true . . . in principle we have it all" (Jackson 1982: 135).

The same is true of standard dualism since even if standard psychological properties are an exception to materialism, they are not an exception to an extremely optimistic view of our powers, since the dualist typically supposes that the subjects who are in these states know that they are in what Lewis later called an "uncommonly demanding sense" (Lewis 1995).

Now both panpsychism and non-standard materialism depart from these standard views as we have seen. But do they also depart from excessive optimism? In the case of non-standard materialist, it is clear that it does. That view is designed to emphasize the limitations of our knowledge of nature; indeed, it is plausible also that this feature of the view is precisely what prompts the two objections just considered and what permits it to respond to those objections in the way that it does. In the case of panpsychism, however, it is clear it does not. Just as is it is not sufficiently appreciated that physicalism is an extremely optimistic view of our epistemic powers, so too is it not appreciated in the case of panpsychism. Panpsychists present themselves as radical and are sometimes dismissed for that reason. But from the point of view of non-standard materialism, the key feature of panpsychism is not that it is too radical (though it may be) but that it is too conservative. What we need are unknown elements, the non-standard materialist says, not non-standard arrangements of known ones.

15. Russellian Non-Standard Materialism Versus Russellian Panpsychism

I have argued that non-standard materialism is distinct from, and more plausible than, panpsychism. Let me turn finally to a question that has been in the background all along but has not be brought to the surface, viz., if they are distinct, why are non-standard materialism and panpsychism so often assimilated?

I think the answer to this is these views look similar only if we focus on their Russellian incarnations. As we have seen, both views can be presented in Russellian form, and if they are presented in this way, it is plausible that they are structurally equivalent – that is, they have exactly the same consequences for which structural or dispositional properties are instantiated. Hence if one counts theories by whether they are structurally equivalent, one will be inclined to think that we have one theory here rather than two.

However, it is a mistake to think that theories that are structurally equivalent in this sense are equivalent *simpliciter*. First, it remains the case both that there are non-Russellian versions of these views and these non-Russellian versions are very different from each other. For example, Russellian versions of panpsychism are akin to the non-Russellian versions of panpsychism; we miss this fact if we concentrate simply on the Russellian version of the view.

Second, while the Russellian versions of non-standard materialism and panpsychism are structurally equivalent, there are many other theories that likewise have Russellian versions, and these other theories are naturally thought of as distinct from either non-standard materialism or panpsychism. Take the view, advocated at one time by D. M. Armstrong, that colours are the non-structural properties that fundamental objects instantiate (Armstrong 1961; see also Chalmers 2016). This view might be thought of as a sort of pan-colour-ism. The Russellian version of this view is likewise structurally equivalent to the Russellian version of panpsychism and non-standard materialism. But we would not think on that ground that it is the same view.

16. Conclusion

The results of our comparison of non-standard materialism and panpsychism may now be summarized briefly: (a) Both theories are well motivated in that both are responses to well-known problems with the standard versions of dualism and materialism. (b) Panpsychism faces three big problems that non-standard materialism does not. (c) An initially promising way the panpsychist has to respond to the first two of these problems is confounded by the point that phenomenal properties have essential features, e.g., that they consist in awareness of properties, and moreover threaten to collapse panpsychism into non-standard materialism. (d) An initially promising way the panpsychist has to respond to the third of these problems is also confounded by the point that phenomenal properties have essential features. (e) Non-standard materialism faces problems of its own but on reflection these problems are much less serious than those faced by the panpsychist, in part because they are generated by precisely the sort of optimism that non-standard materialists are trying to reject. Finally, (f) while it may be true that Russellian versions of panpsychism and non-standard materialism are structurally equivalent, that is no reason to think they are equivalent *simpliciter*.

Notes

1. See, e.g., Stoljar (2001, 2006, 2014, 2015). For further discussion see Pereboom (2011, 2014). Three terminological points: (a) I will use 'materialism' and 'physicalism' interchangeably here. (b) In other work I have argued that, strictly speaking, there is no thesis at all which is true and deserves the name 'physicalism'; see Stoljar (2010). In this paper, as is in fact common in philosophy of mind, I will ignore this and use the notion informally. (c) Both positions I will discuss in this paper have versions that are called 'Russellian Monism', but I will ignore that phrase in this paper.
2. See, e.g., Strawson (2006), Chalmers (2016), Goff (2017), Mørch (2014, 2018), Roelofs (2015), Seager and Allen-Hermanson (2015).
3. For some discussion of these two strategies see Stoljar (2015).
4. This phrase is borrowed, of course, from Lewis (see 1986b: 133).
5. I have in mind here the recent literature on the so-called combination problem (see Seager and Allen-Hermanson (2015); also Chalmers (2016), Coleman (2012, 2013), Goff (2006, 2009, 2016, 2018), Mørch (2014, 2018), Roelofs (2015, forthcoming)).
6. Might there be other candidate features? One possibility is that phenomenal properties are essentially systemic or holistic, i.e., if you instantiate one of them you instantiate a whole system of them. So when you feel a pain in your toe, you are aware of various different properties of your leg and indeed of your surrounds. A different possibility is that phenomenal properties essentially play rational roles, for example, in that being in the property justifies you in believing certain things – e.g., if the property is being aware of F, then being in it justifies you in believing something is F. It would be interesting to develop the point against the unimaginable properties focusing on these features, but I will concentrate here on the feature mentioned in the text.
7. There are some complications for the Russellian panpsychist here which concern the classification of dispositional physical properties, which the position assumes to be standard physical properties. Are these properties fundamental? If you say yes, you are committed to the view that fundamental properties can be grounded in other fundamental properties, which is something Lewis, whose views about fundamental properties were our starting point, would have denied. If you say no, you are committed to the view that the only fundamental properties are phenomenal, which looks more like idealism than panpsychism. I will not try to clear up this complication here, however.

References

Armstrong, D. (1961). *Perception and the Physical World*. London: Routledge.
Chalmers, D. (2016). 'The Combination Problem for Panpsychism'. In G. Brüntrup and L. Jaskolla (eds.), *Panpsychism*. Oxford: Oxford University Press, pp. 229–48.
Coleman, S. (2012). 'Mental Chemistry: Combination for Panpsychists'. *Dialectica*, V66 (1): 137–66.
Coleman, S. (2013). 'The Real Combination Problem: Panpsychism, Micro-Subjects, and Emergence'. *Erkenntnis*, 79 (1): 19–44.
Goff, P. (2006). 'Experiences Don't Sum'. *Journal of Consciousness Studies*, 13 (10–11): 53–61.
Goff, P. (2009). 'Why Panpsychism Doesn't Help Us Explain Consciousness'. *Dialectica*, 63 (3): 289–311.
Goff, P. (2016). 'The Phenomenal Bonding Solution to the Combination Problem'. In G. Brüntrup and L. Jaskolla (eds.), *Panpsychism*. Oxford: Oxford University Press, pp. 283–304.
Goff, P. (2017). *Consciousness and Fundamental Reality*. New York: Oxford University Press.
Jackson, F. (1982). 'Epiphenomenal Qualia'. *Philosophical Quarterly* (32): 127–136.

Johnston, M. (1996). 'A Mind–Body Problem at the Surface of Objects'. *Philosophical Issues 7: Perception*: 219–29.

Lewis, D. (1986a). *Philosophical Papers Vol II*. Oxford: Blackwell.

Lewis, D. (1986b). *On the Plurality of Worlds*. Oxford: Blackwell.

Lewis, D. (1994). 'Reduction of Mind'. In S. Guttenplan (ed.), *A Companion to the Philosophy of Mind*. Oxford: Blackwell,1994, pp. 412–431. repr. in his Papers in Metaphysics and Epistemology. Cambridge: Cambridge University Press, 1999, pp. 291–224. All references are to the reprinted version.

Lewis, D. (1995). 'Should a Materialist Believe in Qualia?' *Australasian Journal of Philosophy*, 73: 140–4.

Lewis, D. (2009). 'Ramseyan Humility'. In D. Braddon-Mitchell and R. Nola (eds.), *Conceptual Analysis and Philosophical Naturalism*. Cambridge, MA: MIT Press, pp. 203–22.

Mørch, H. H. (2014). *Panpsychism and Causation: A New Argument and a Solution to the Combination Problem*. Doctoral Dissertation, University of Oslo. https://philpapers.org/archive/HASPAC-2.pdf.

Mørch, H. H. (2018). 'Does Dispositionalism Entail Panpsychism?' *Topoi* https://doi.org/10.1007/s11245-018-9604-y

Pereboom, D. (2011). *Consciousness and the Prospects of Physicalism*. New York: Oxford University Press.

Pereboom, D. (2014). 'Russellian Monism and Absolutely Intrinsic Properties'. In U. Kriegel (ed.), *Current Controversies in Philosophy of Mind*. London: Routledge, pp. 40–69.

Roelofs, L. (2015). *Combining Minds: A Defence of the Possibility of Experiential Combination*. Doctoral Dissertation, University of Toronto. https://tspace.library.utoronto.ca/handle/1807/69449.

Roelofs, L. (forthcoming). 'Can We Sum Subjects: Evaluating Panpsychism's Hard Problem'. In W. Seager (ed.), *The Routledge Handbook of Panpsychism*. London: Routledge.

Seager, William, and Allen-Hermanson, Sean (2015). 'Panpsychism'. In E. Zalta (ed.), *The Stanford Encyclopedia of Philosophy*, Fall 2015 edition. http://plato.stanford.edu/archives/fall2015/entries/panpsychism/.

Stoljar, D. (2001). 'Two Conceptions of the Physical'. *Philosophy and Phenomenological Research*, 62 (2): 253–81.

Stoljar, D. (2006). *Ignorance and Imagination: The Epistemic Origin of the Problem of Consciousness*. New York: Oxford University Press.

Stoljar, D. (2010). *Physicalism*. London: Routledge.

Stoljar, D. (2014). 'Four Kinds of Russellian Monism'. In U. Kriegel (ed.), *Current Controversies in Philosophy of Mind*. London: Routledge, pp. 17–35.

Stoljar, D. (2015). 'Russellian Monism or Nagelian Monism'. In T. Alter and Y. Nagasawa (eds.), *Consciousness in the Physical World: Essays on Russellian Monism*. Oxford: Oxford University Press, pp. 324–45.

Strawson, G. (2006). 'Realistic Monism: Why Physicalism Entails Panpsychism'. In A. Freeman (ed.), *Consciousness and Its Place in Nature: Does Physicalism Entail Panpsychism?* Exeter: Imprint Academic.

20

PANPSYCHISM AND RUSSELLIAN MONISM

Torin Alter and Sam Coleman

Panpsychism has recently gained interest among analytic philosophers of mind. This is due largely to the view's close relationship with Russellian monism, according to which consciousness is constituted at least partly by intrinsic properties that serve as categorical grounds of dispositional properties posited by fundamental physics.[1] On a leading version of this view, those intrinsic properties are phenomenal, that is, experiential: properties that constitute what it is like to have an experience (Chalmers 1996, 2013; Goff 2017; Rosenberg 2004). Panpsychism seems to follow. Interest in Russellian monism has therefore led to interest in panpsychism.[2]

But what explains the recent interest in Russellian monism? Part of the explanation runs as follows. Over the last half-century or so, discussions of consciousness in analytic philosophy have focused largely on materialism/physicalism (we use the terms interchangeably) and dualism. But many are unsatisfied with traditional forms of these views. Traditional materialist views seem to either disregard or distort the distinctive features of consciousness, and traditional dualist views have trouble integrating consciousness adequately into the natural, causal order. Russellian monism seems to avoid both problems. Russellian monists reject the doctrine that they believe leads to the problem with traditional materialism: the doctrine that phenomenal properties are nothing over and above the properties physics reveals. On panpsychist Russellian monism, phenomenal properties are taken to be no less fundamental than physical properties. Dualism says that too. But unlike traditional dualist views, panpsychist Russellian monism is designed to accord consciousness a crucial role in (or closely related to) physical causation: the role of categorically grounding physical, dispositional properties.

In this chapter, we will discuss two significant challenges to these supposed virtues of Russellian monism: one by Robert Howell (2015) and one by Amy Kind (2015). Howell argues that Jaegwon Kim's exclusion argument can be modified to show that Russellian monism is untenable. And Kind argues that it is "simply an illusion" that Russellian monism "transcend[s] the dualist/physicalist divide" (2015: 417). We will argue that neither challenge is insurmountable.

1. Russellian Panpsychism

Following David Chalmers, we understand panpsychism as the thesis that all members of some fundamental physical types have conscious experiences. On this view, "there is something it is like to be a quark or a photon or a member of some other fundamental physical type" (2013: 246–7).

We understand Russellian monism to be the view that consciousness is constituted at least partly by intrinsic properties that serve as categorical grounds of the dispositional properties posited by fundamental physics. Panpsychist Russellian monism, or *Russellian panpsychism* for short, results from combining this view with the thesis that those intrinsic properties are phenomenal.

Not all versions of Russellian monism entail panpsychism. There is also pan*proto*psychist Russellian monism, which results from identifying the intrinsic properties that ground physical, dispositional properties with what Chalmers calls *protophenomenal* properties. He writes,

> [L]et us say that *protophenomenal* properties are special properties that are not phenomenal (there is nothing it is like to have a single protophenomenal property) but that can collectively constitute phenomenal properties, perhaps when arranged in the right structure.
>
> (2013: 259)

Because of this volume's panpsychist theme, we will focus mostly on Russellian panpsychism. But much of what we will say applies equally to panprotopsychist Russellian monism, *mutatis mutandis*.

1.1. The Conceivability Argument

To better appreciate why Russellian panpsychism might compare favorably to traditional materialism and traditional dualism, consider how Russellian panpsychists can respond to influential anti-materialist and anti-dualist arguments. For example, consider a basic version of the anti-materialist conceivability argument involving a zombie world, that is, a minimal physical duplicate of the actual world but without consciousness. The argument begins with the premise that such a world is ideally conceivable – that is, such a world cannot be ruled out by *a priori* reasoning – and ends with the conclusion that materialism is false. The argument's main steps can be summarized as follows:

1. A zombie world is ideally conceivable.
2. If a zombie world is ideally conceivable, then a zombie world is metaphysically possible.
3. If a zombie world is metaphysically possible, then materialism is false.
4. Therefore, materialism is false.

Materialists have responded in myriad ways, but many find their responses inadequate (Alter and Howell 2012). Russellian panpsychists can respond to the aforementioned conceivability argument in at least three ways.

First, Russellian panpsychists can reject premise 1. This premise, they might argue, seems true only if we conflate the physical with the dispositional: we recognize that a consciousness-free dispositional duplicate of the actual world, or a *dispositional zombie world*, is ideally conceivable, and we infer that a zombie world is ideally conceivable. But that inference is questionable. A dispositional zombie world would resemble the actual world in all dispositional respects but, unlike a zombie world, perhaps not in all physical respects. Here is why. Arguably, a complete physical duplicate of the actual world would also have to include instantiations of any properties that, in the actual world, ground the dispositional properties that physics describes. And if the grounding properties are phenomenal, Russelian panpsychists might argue, then it follows that such a duplicate world would have to contain consciousness.

Alternatively, Russellian panpsychists can reject premise 2. On this response, although there is no *a priori* entailment from the physical to the phenomenal, there is an *a posteriori* entailment: a zombie world is ideally conceivable but metaphysically impossible. The Russellian panpsychist might base this move on a semantic view about terms in physics such as "mass" and "charge": a view on which such terms refer rigidly to the intrinsic, categorical phenomenal properties that ground dispositional properties and consciousness, but in a way that cannot be discovered by *a priori* reflection.[3]

As a third alternative, Russellian panpsychists can accept the argument's anti-materialist conclusion. They can argue that phenomenal properties are nonphysical properties that nevertheless categorically ground physical dispositional properties. But the core idea underlying this third response is the same as that which underlies the first: because Russellian panpsychists reject the traditional materialist doctrine that the phenomenal is nothing over and above the dispositional, their view does not entail the sorts of claims that anti-materialist arguments such as the conceivability argument threaten to undermine.[4] Here are three examples of such claims: there are no phenomenal properties (a claim associated with eliminativist materialism); phenomenal properties are functionally analyzable (a claim associated with analytic functionalism); and the complete dispositional truth *a posteriori* necessitates and is ontologically prior to all phenomenal truths (a claim associated with nonreductionist materialism). Russellian panpsychists reject all such claims.

1.2. The Exclusion Argument

Influential anti-dualist arguments fault dualism for inadequately integrating consciousness into the natural, causal order. We will focus on one of these arguments, known as the exclusion argument. The exclusion argument says that nonphysical mental properties have no work to do in bringing about physical events: all physical effects have entirely physical sufficient causes (Kim 1989, 2000). We will summarize the exclusion argument's main steps as follows:

1.   Mental distinctness: no mental events are identical to physical events.
2.   Physical adequacy: all physical events have sufficient physical causes (if they are caused at all).
3.   Therefore, no physical events are uniquely caused by mental events.[5]

The exclusion argument is often adduced against interactionist dualism, on which mental events are said to help bring about physical events, and against nonreductionist forms of materialism, on which the mental and physical are numerically distinct but materialism is true nonetheless. Dualists and nonreductionist materialists have responded in myriad ways, but many find their responses inadequate.[6]

Russellian panpsychism is sometimes construed as a form of dualism and sometimes as a form of nonreductionist materialism. But it provides resources for responding to anti-materialist arguments that traditional versions of those views do not. Russellian panpsychists can respond to the exclusion argument in at least three ways (Howell 2015: 26–8).

First, Russellian panpsychists can deny premise 1, mental distinctness, arguing that phenomenal properties are not distinct from the dispositional properties they ground – and thus that events in which instantiations of phenomenal and dispositional properties figure need not be distinct. Suppose R is a categorical phenomenal property that grounds negative charge. On this first strategy, Russellian panpsychists deny that there are two properties here, R and negative charge. Instead, there is one property and a law governing how things with that property behave. So, there is no competition among properties for causal efficacy: there is just a single property, which can be construed in different ways.

Alternatively, Russellian panpsychists can deny premise 2, physical adequacy. They can argue that the properties physics describes cause nothing on their own: such properties would not even exist (or be instantiated) without their phenomenal grounds. Interactionist dualists too deny physical adequacy. But they do so in a way many find unacceptable. They posit causal gaps among physical events as described by the physical sciences: gaps filled by nonphysical, mental events. Russellian panpsychists need not posit any such gaps. Rather, this view enriches the basis of the complete physical causal chain already posited by the physical sciences.

Finally, Russellian panpsychists can deny that the argument is valid. That is, they can argue that it does not follow from mental distinctness and physical adequacy that mental events do not help cause physical events. Here Russellian panpsychists would follow a well-trodden path. Several philosophers (who do not commit to Russellian panpsychism) reject the argument's validity, often on the basis that some mental-physical relations can be modeled on the relation between determinables and determinates (Yablo 1992; Bennett 2003; Shoemaker 2007; Ehring 2011; Wilson 2011). Russellian panpsychists can offer a distinctive version of that sort of strategy. Plausibly, just as there is in general no competition between determinable and determinate properties such as being red and being scarlet, there is in general no competition between categorical properties and the dispositions they ground: both make unique contributions to the causal process. So, Russellian panpsychists can argue, since phenomenal properties categorically ground physical, dispositional properties, the contribution of the latter properties in causing physical events does not compete with the contribution of the former. On this model, neither sort of property is causally redundant in the bringing about of physical events.

There is a common thread running through these three responses: Russellian panpsychism provides a principled basis for rejecting the idea that dispositional and phenomenal properties compete in the way the exclusion argument requires. More generally, Russellian panpsychism does not seem to be threatened in the way traditional dualism is by the problem of finding a role for consciousness in the causation of physical events.

Thus, Russellian panpsychism might seem to have considerable advantages over traditional materialism and traditional dualism. But appearances can be deceiving. Howell and Kind each argue that in this case they are. We will now turn to their arguments, starting with Howell's, and explain some ways Russellian panpsychists might respond.

2. Can Russellian Panpsychists Answer the Exclusion Argument?

In Howell's view, although the original exclusion argument does not undermine Russellian panpsychism, a modified formulation does. He writes "[m]y general argument will be that even if phenomenal properties cause things on the Russellian Monism picture, they do not cause things in virtue of their phenomenal nature" (2015: 28). If his modified exclusion argument is sound, then on Russellian panpsychism phenomenality makes no unique contribution to the causation of physical events, despite initial appearances to the contrary.

2.1. The Modified Exclusion Argument

According to the original exclusion argument, physical and mental properties compete for causal influence. Howell argues that the Russellian panpsychist's responses to that argument merely relocate this problem. The competition is no longer between properties, but rather between aspects of the properties in virtue of which the properties do causal work. But there is still causal competition and, he argues, the phenomenal aspects lose.

Howell illustrates the problem by describing three worlds:

> Consider a world w1 in which R, phenomenal redness, grounds the property of negative charge given the causal laws governing R in w1. Now consider world w2 where G, phenomenal greenness, is covered by those same laws so that G grounds the causal powers associated with negative charge and R instead grounds the powers associated with negative spin. Finally, consider a third world, w3, in which the laws are such that either R or G can ground the powers of negative charge – R and G are governed by exactly the same laws in exactly the same ways.
>
> (2015: 28)[7]

Howell then compares R as instantiated in w1 with R as instantiated in w2, noting that, "They are similar in one respect, their phenomenal character, but different in another, their causal profile"

(2015: 29). Next compare R as instantiated in w1 with G as instantiated in w2. These properties differ in phenomenal character while being similar in causal role. And the same point applies to R compared with G as both are instantiated in w3.

Howell writes,

> In all cases . . . some similarities are grounded in the phenomenal character and others are grounded in the causal profile. Even given the ontology of Russellian Monism, therefore, there must be different relationships of grounding in virtue of which the different resemblance relations hold.
>
> (2015: 29)

So, *RM properties*, as Howell calls them, have two aspects: one that grounds phenomenal resemblance relations and another that grounds causal resemblance relations. If so, the question arises, in virtue of which of these two aspects do RM properties have physical effects?

According to Howell, the answer is clear: physical effects occur in virtue of the latter aspect and not the former:

> In the case of phenomenal causation, we want phenomenal properties to have causal power in virtue of their phenomenality. That means that we want the properties to cause things in virtue of that which grounds the similarity between R in w1 and R in w2. But that doesn't appear to be the case since R in w1 and R in w2 are causally quite dissimilar. The point can be made within a world as well. We want the properties in w3 to cause things in virtue of that which grounds the similarity between R and G (in that world). It cannot be the phenomenal character because they are quite dissimilar phenomenally. It thus appears that these properties do not, after all, cause things in virtue of their phenomenal character.
>
> (2015: 29)

Howell states his modified exclusion argument as follows, where "an RM property is a property that has a phenomenal categorical ground and some causal dispositions" (2015: 32):

1. [T]here are two distinct and separable aspects of RM properties, those that ground phenomenal resemblance relations and those that ground resemblances between causal profiles.
2. [A]ll physical events have sufficient causes in virtue of those aspects that ground resemblances between the causal profiles of RM properties.
3. Therefore, the aspects of RM properties that ground phenomenal resemblances make no unique causal contribution to the physical world (2015: 32).

If that argument is sound, Howell suggests, then Russellian monism fares no better than dualism at integrating consciousness into the natural, causal order.

In the previous section, we described three ways the Russellian monist could respond to the original exclusion argument. According to Howell, none of those responses succeeds against the modified version. On the first response (denying the original premise 1, mental distinctness), there is a single RM property rather than two properties, one categorical and one dispositional, that compete for causal influence. But that claim is consistent with the modified exclusion argument, which locates the competition within a single RM property: aspects of that property compete.

On the second response (denying the original premise 2, physical adequacy), physical, dispositional properties would not exist (or be instantiated) were it not for the categorical RM properties in which they are grounded. But it does not follow from that claim that the phenomenal aspects of

RM properties contribute to physical causation. And, Howell argues, the modal separability of the phenomenal and dispositional aspects suggests that the former do not so contribute:

> The fact that both R and G can ground certain causal dispositions within a world despite their phenomenal dissimilarity suggests again that it is not the phenomenality of the ground that is really doing the work. It is whatever it is in virtue of which they fall under the relevant laws.
>
> (2015: 31)

Similar considerations, Howell argues, undermine the third response, denying the validity of the original argument. On that response, "the dispositional properties and the categorical grounds don't causally compete because they enjoy such a tight metaphysical relationship" (2015: 31). According to Howell, the relationship is not tight enough to undermine the argument's validity if the two aspects of RM properties can come apart, as they would in w1 compared with w2 and in w3.

However, there are other ways Russellian panpsychists could respond to Howell's modified exclusion argument. For one thing, they could accept his causal inefficacy conclusion and argue that this does not show that Russellian panpsychism fares no better than dualism at integrating consciousness into the natural, causal order. Phenomenality, Russellian panpsychists might argue, achieves the desired integration not in virtue of helping to cause physical events but rather in virtue of grounding physical properties. Causation is one thing. Grounding is another (Lange 2017). If phenomenality grounds physical, dispositional properties then, Russellian panpsychists might argue, that is integration enough.

To some, that first response, if successful, would blunt the force of the modified exclusion argument. But others might find the causal inefficacy conclusion itself a significant strike against Russellian panpsychism. For that reason, we will leave the first response aside and focus on two other responses, which are ways to avoid the causal inefficacy conclusion. One of those ways is to deny that the modal separability of the dispositional and phenomenal aspects of an RM property shows that the latter aspect does no causal work. Call that *the compatibilist strategy* or *compatibilism* for short. The other way is to deny that the two aspects are modally separable in the way that Howell's argument requires. Call that *the necessitarian strategy*. We will discuss these strategies in turn.

2.2. The Compatibilist Strategy

In the actual world, chlorophyll plays a causal role in photosynthesis: it enables plants to absorb energy from light. Suppose that there is a possible world in which the same role is played by a biomolecule that is chemically distinct from chlorophyll. It would be a mistake to infer that in the actual world chlorophyll makes no unique causal contribution to photosynthesis. According to the compatibilist strategy, the modified exclusion argument makes an analogous mistake.

According to compatibilism, in w1 negative charge has physical effects partly in virtue of R (phenomenal redness) even though in w2 negative charge has those same effects partly in virtue of G (phenomenal greenness). This is so, say compatibilists, because the grounding laws in w1 differ from those in w2: they differ with respect to which phenomenal property plays which grounding role. Or consider w3, in which each of R and G ground negative charge. According to compatibilism, w3's grounding laws entail that, in that world, both R and G help produce the effects of negatively charged particles. In general, the assumption that the same grounding role can be played by two different categorical properties (either across or within worlds) does not entail that those categorical properties are causally inefficacious. The grounding laws may be contingent. But they determine which (if any) categorical properties in a given world do the grounding work. And it is precisely such grounding work that constitutes the unique contribution phenomenal properties make to physical causation.

Compatibilists could challenge premise 2 of the modified exclusion argument: "[A]ll physical events have sufficient causes in virtue of those aspects that ground resemblances between the causal profiles of RM properties." Arguably, the aspects that ground resemblances between the causal profiles of RM properties are not phenomenal properties. For example, R and G are phenomenally distinct and yet the causal profiles associated with R in w1 and G in w2 are exactly alike. Nonetheless, the compatibilist might argue, in w1 negative charge has the effects it does partly because it is grounded by R. In that world, given its contingent grounding laws, negative charge would have no physical effects if not for R's playing the grounding role it plays. That fact, say compatibilists, is compatible with a distinct property G playing that same role in worlds with different grounding laws, such as w2. Thus, the compatibilist might argue that premise 2 of the modified exclusion argument is false.

Compatibilism faces objections. For one thing, the photosynthesis analogy is inexact. When we described chlorophyll as playing a causal role in photosynthesis, we said that it enables plants to absorb energy from light. That description is fairly coarse grained, and one might argue that this explains why the possibility of something else playing that role does not threaten the causal efficacy of chlorophyll in the actual world. But such coarse-grained descriptions are not relevant to the modified exclusion argument. For example, describing the causal profiles associated with R in w1 and G in w2 in a maximally fine-grained way would reveal no difference whatsoever between those profiles (that is true by stipulation). By contrast, causal differences would be revealed when comparing chlorophyll to its role-filler in another possible world, if both are described in a maximally fine-grained way. So, analogies to the photosynthesis case and similar examples are of limited use in supporting the compatibilist strategy.

Additionally, Howell might object that the compatibilist strategy leaves a Russellian panpsychist in essentially the same position as the interactionist dualist vis-à-vis integrating phenomenality into physical causation. Instead of the interactionist's contingent psychophysical laws, the Russellian panpsychist posits contingent phenomenal-dispositional grounding laws. But that, Howell might argue, is no improvement. If so, Russellian panpsychism still loses its alleged advantage over traditional dualism and the compatibilist strategy fails.

That objection is partly correct. The Russellian panpsychist's grounding laws can seem arbitrary in the way that, to many, the interactionist dualist's psychophysical laws do. For example, the Russellian panpsychist might seem to have no good explanation of why in w1 R rather than G grounds negative charge. But there is a difference. The interactionist dualist rejects the causal closure of the physical, positing gaps in scientific explanations – gaps filled by nonphysical, mental events. The Russellian panpsychist needs posit no such gaps. Her grounding laws are, in that sense, compatible with the causal closure of the physical. That difference gives Russellian panpsychism what might be regarded as a significant advantage over interactionist dualism.

2.3. The Necessitarian Strategy

The compatibilist strategy is to reject Howell's inference from the modal separability of the phenomenal and dispositional aspects of RM properties to the conclusion that the former aspects are causally inefficacious. Russellian panpsychists might instead reject his premise that those aspects are modally separable in the way the modified exclusion argument requires. They might, for example, argue that the three worlds Howell imagines are not metaphysically possible. More specifically, they might deny that w1 and w2 are compossible and that w3 is possible in its own right. This is the necessitarian strategy.[8]

Howell considers the necessitarian strategy:

> Such a 'necessitarian' Russellian Monism might in fact dodge the [modified] exclusion argument. Whether or not the base is phenomenal or protophenomenal, if the relationship between the causal and phenomenal features of the base is intimate enough – and metaphysical necessitation from the phenomenal to the causal probably qualifies – the [modified] exclusion argument doesn't succeed.
>
> (2015: 35–6)

Actually, "metaphysical necessitation from the phenomenal to the causal" would seem to only partly qualify as supplying the requisite intimacy: that between phenomenal and dispositional features needed in order to answer the modified exclusion argument. Granted, such metaphysical necessitation would guarantee that if R (phenomenal redness) grounds negative charge in w1, then there is no possible world w2 in which R does not ground negative charge – and thus that w1 and w2 are not jointly possible, sparing the Russellian panpsychist that part of Howell's exclusion challenge.

But what about w3, in which R and G (phenomenal greenness) have the same causal profiles? Metaphysical necessitation from the phenomenal to the dispositional does not seem to rule out that world as impossible. It rules out only that R or G should exist in *another* world without grounding negative charge. Yet the metaphysical possibility of w3 alone might be enough to motivate the modified exclusion argument. In w3, the phenomenal dissimilarity between R and G does not correspond to a causal difference. Regarding w3, Howell writes, "it is not the phenomenality of the ground that is really doing the work" (2015: 31).

So, to completely dodge the modified exclusion argument, the necessitarian Russellian panpsychist might also have to defend metaphysical necessitation in the other direction, from the dispositional to the phenomenal. With both entailments in place, from phenomenal aspect to dispositional aspect and *vice versa*, necessitarian Russellian panpsychism pairs causal roles with phenomenal aspects one-to-one with metaphysical necessity.

Howell rejects the necessitarian strategy as dialectically unacceptable. Adopting necessitarianism, he suggests, conflicts with the Russellian panpsychist's "acceptance of . . . zombie-style conceivability arguments that pushed her to Russellian Monism in the first place" (2015: 36–7). That concern is natural enough. Necessitarian Russellian panpsychism rules out premises that those arguments typically invoke. For example, if the view includes a necessary entailment from the dispositional to the phenomenal then necessitarianism would rule out the premise that a zombie world is metaphysically possible.

However, Russellian panpsychists (necessitarian and otherwise) need not accept zombie-style conceivability arguments without qualification. These philosophers take those arguments to (i) refute the traditional materialist view that the phenomenal is nothing over and above the dispositional and (ii) support their view that consciousness consists at least partly in intrinsic, phenomenal properties that categorically ground physical, dispositional properties (Alter 2016). But (i) and (ii) are consistent with necessitarianism: they do not entail that the phenomenal and the dispositional are modally separable.

Howell raises another dialectical problem for the necessitarian strategy: the strategy would undercut the Russellian panpsychist's advantages over traditional views. If she argues that zombie worlds are only prima facie and not ideally conceivable, "then she appears to be making the same sort of move as the type A physicalist with no more plausibility" (Howell (2015: 37).[9] If she posits "necessities that hold despite conceivability," then "she has to allow the same answer for the type B physicalist and the property dualist" (2015: 37). Thus, he concludes, "Given this, necessitarian Russellian Monism might be conceptually coherent, but it is unmotivated" (2015: 37). Adopting necessitarianism, he suggests, would result in sacrificing the advantages over traditional positions that Russellian panpsychism is often presented as having.

But that complaint could also be questioned. For example, consider the Russellian panpsychist who accepts the conclusion of zombie-style conceivability arguments, that materialism is false. As we have seen, her doing so does not require positing gaps in physical explanations. That is what is thought to make her reaction more plausible than the traditional interactionist dualist's way of accepting the arguments. Adopting necessitarianism would not seem to threaten the Russellian panpsychist's ability to react in that way.

3. Does Russellian Monism Transcend the Dualist/Physicalist Divide?

Like Howell, Kind (2015) challenges the idea that Russellian monism[10] has certain advantages over traditional views. But her argument is different. She targets the claim that Russellian monism "transcend[s] the dualist/physicalist divide," arguing that "this is simply an illusion" (2015: 417). What exactly she means by "transcend[ing] the dualist/physicalist divide" is not entirely clear, as we will shortly explain. One point she emphasizes is that Russellian monism leaves unresolved at least some of the main issues over which dualists and physicalist disagree. She is right about that. But she seems to infer that Russellian monism lacks the advantages it is supposed to have over traditional views. And that inference, we will argue, is not justified.

3.1. Kind's Argument

Kind distinguishes between *phenomenal* Russellian monism and *physical* Russellian monism, or *phenomenal monism* and *physical monism* for short. These two views differ over the nature of the intrinsic properties that categorically ground dispositional properties. Following Montero (2010), she calls those intrinsic properties *inscrutables*. Phenomenal monism construes inscrutables as phenomenal properties, and physical monism construes them as physical properties. She notes that, for the purposes of her main argument, what ultimately matters is that on physical monism the inscrutables are nonphenomenal. So, phenomenal and physical monism correspond at least roughly to what we call panpsychist and panprotopsychist Russellian monism.

Kind writes:

> [T]here are really only two possibilities for the nature of inscrutables: they must be either phenomenal or physical. That means that a Russellian monist must endorse either phenomenal monism [or] physical monism. To my mind, these two views are as different from one another as traditional dualism and traditional physicalism are. Any attempt to adjudicate between them will have to settle the question as to whether consciousness is a fundamental part of nature – the same question that needs to be adjudicated in the debate between dualism and physicalism.
>
> (2015: 418)

Call the question as to whether consciousness is a fundamental part of nature *the fundamentality question*. Kind's argument can then be summarized as follows:

1. Russellian monism transcends the dualist/physicalist divide only if it settles the fundamentality question.
2. Russellian monism is neutral between phenomenal monism and physical monism.
3. If Russellian monism is neutral between phenomenal monism and physical monism, then Russellian monism does not settle the fundamentality question.
4. Therefore, Russellian monism does not transcend the dualist/physicalist divide.

3.2. *What Kind's Argument Does and Does Not Show*

Note that Kind does not conclude that no specific version of Russellian monism transcends the dualist/physicalist divide. Her conclusion is rather that Russellian monism as such, the generic form, fails in that regard. Bearing that in mind, let us assess her argument.

Premises 2 and 3 are plausible, and we grant them. The argument is valid. That leaves premise 1. This premise, along with the conclusion, could be understood in at least two different ways, depending on what it means to transcend the dualist/physicalist divide.

Perhaps what it means to transcend the dualist/physicalist divide is to settle the fundamentality question. Call this *the pleonastic interpretation*. On the pleonastic interpretation, premise 1 is pleonastic and the argument's conclusion seems unobjectionable. Unobjectionable but not insignificant: if anyone believes that (generic) Russellian monism settles whether consciousness is a fundamental part of nature, then Kind's argument (on the pleonastic interpretation) should convince him that he is mistaken. Note, however, that settling the fundamentality question is not among the advantages that (generic) Russellian monism is typically presented as having. On the contrary, Russellian monists argue among themselves as to the best form for the inscrutables to take. So, on the pleonastic interpretation, Kind's argument does not show that Russellian monism lacks any of its advertised advantages.

On an alternative interpretation, to transcend the dualist/physicalist divide would be to move the discussion forward: to achieve relevant things that have eluded traditional views. Kind's discussion of her argument's implications could be read as supporting this interpretation. For example, she suggests that her argument shows that Russellian monism is over-hyped: that "the excitement about Russellian monism is misplaced" (2015: 402). But on this alternative interpretation, premise 1 is questionable. Russellian monism is touted as providing precisely what traditional views have arguably failed to provide: a way to integrate consciousness adequately into the natural, causal order without disregarding or distorting consciousness's distinctive features. If the view achieves that result, it does so by how it applies the dispositional/categorical distinction to the mind-body problem: (proto)phenomenal properties are said to figure into physical causation by categorically grounding physical dispositional properties. Applying the dispositional/categorical distinction in this way does not require taking a stand on whether the categorical grounding properties are phenomenal or nonphenomenal. Indeed, panpsychist and panprotopsychist Russellian monists, who differ over precisely that issue, lay equal claim to the desired result. Thus, the advance that Russellian monism promises seems not to depend on settling the fundamentality question, *contra* Kind's premise 1 (on the alternative interpretation of "transcending the dualist/physicalist divide").

Kind allows that Russellian monism might make "*some* progress." (2015: 420; original italics). She concedes that phenomenal monism might improve upon traditional dualism and that physical monism might improve upon traditional materialism. Yet, she suggests, the fact that Russellian monism does not settle the fundamentality question implies that, with respect to the debate between dualism and physicalism, Russellian monism leaves us "essentially back where we started" (2015: 420). But that does not follow.

Arguably, where we started was with traditional dualism having no adequate way to integrate consciousness into nature (no way that evades causal arguments such as the exclusion argument) and traditional materialism having no plausible way to answer the anti-materialist arguments (no response that avoids disregarding or distorting consciousness's distinctive features). By construing (proto)phenomenal properties as categorical grounds of physical dispositional properties, Russellian monism provides a framework for developing a view that has neither of those shortcomings: a view that adequately integrates consciousness into nature without denying or distorting consciousness's distinctive features. In that sense, Russellian monism takes us to a different place. The generic form of this view does not take us to the final destination, if that means settling the fundamentality question. But neither does it purport to do so.

To be sure, Russellian monists will ultimately want to settle the fundamentality question. For them, this will involve deciding between (what Kind calls) phenomenal and physical monism. But the progress achieved by the generic form should not be underestimated. Adopting the generic form implies reconceiving of the framework within which the fundamentality question is to be addressed. That is no mean feat.

4. Conclusion

Only a decade or two ago, it would have been fair to say that panpsychism was not taken seriously by most analytic philosophers of mind. *Reductio ad panpsychism* would widely have passed as a valid form of argument, a special case of *reductio ad absurdum*. Recent interest in Russellian panpsychism has changed all that. We believe this is a change for the better, especially given the longstanding interest in panpsychism from a global, historical perspective. Old questions are being recast in new ways, and there appears to be hope for resolving a lamented impasse between materialism and dualism.

It is not all sweetness and light for those with panpsychist sympathies. While leading versions of Russellian monism imply panpsychism, there is also a panprotopsychist version that seems no less viable. And Russellian panpsychism faces serious objections.[11] We have tried to address two of these, one by Howell and one by Kind. We have argued that neither is decisive. In our view, Russellian panpsychism remains a contender position: one that is well worth investigating and developing. In particular, compatibilist and necessitarian versions of the view seem worthy of further attention.[12]

Notes

1. This characterization of Russellian monism will suffice for present purposes, but see Alter and Nagasawa (2012). Chalmers (1997) introduced the term "Russellian monism."
2. There are other reasons for the recent interest in panpsychism among analytic philosophers. A closely related reason is the influence of Galen Strawson's work (e.g. 2006a, 2006b).
3. However, this second response seems susceptible to the same sorts of objections often brought against parallel appeals to *a posteriori* necessity made by traditional materialists (Chalmers 2013: 253). This does not appear to be true of the other two alternative Russellian monist responses we describe.
4. Here we use "traditional materialism" (and "traditional physicalism") to name those (and only those) versions committed to the doctrine the (proto)phenomenal is nothing over and above the dispositional. We use the unqualified "materialism" (and "physicalism") for the broader view, which also includes versions lacking that commitment.
5. This formulation, which closely follows Howell (2015: 23–4), ignores various complications that are not directly relevant, for example, in omitting a premise ruling out the possibility of rampant overdetermination.
6. For a dualist response, see List and Stoljar (2017). For a nonreductionist materialist response, see Pereboom (2011).
7. We assume that "phenomenal redness" and "phenomenal greenness" are proxies for microphenomenal properties, which presumably differ from phenomenal redness and phenomenal greenness.
8. For necessitarian versions of Russellian monism, see Mørch 2014 and Coleman 2017. Carruth's (2016) view of dispositions suggests a roughly similar doctrine, but he contrasts his view with Russellian monism.
9. The alphabetic taxonomy comes from Chalmers (1996, 2003a). Type-A materialism says roughly that all phenomenal truths are *a priori* entailed by the complete physical truth. Type-B materialism says roughly that though some phenomenal truths are not *a priori* entailed by the complete physical truth, all phenomenal truths are metaphysically necessitated by the complete physical truth.
10. In this section, we refer to both the panpsychist and panprotopsychist versions of Russellian monism because of the central role they play in Kind's argument.
11. For example, in addition to Kind (2015) and Howell (2015), see Seager (1995), Chalmers (2013, 2017), Coleman (2014), Ney (2015), Robinson (2015), Stoljar (2015), Pautz (n.d.), Ebbers, (n.d.).
12. For helpful comments and discussions, we thank Robert J. Howell, Amy Kind, Galen Strawson, and William Seager.

References

Alter, T. (2016). 'The Structure and Dynamics Argument Against Materialism'. *Nous*, 50: 794–815.

Alter, T., and Howell, R. J. (eds.) (2012). *Consciousness and the Mind-Body Problem: A Reader*. New York: Oxford University Press.

Alter, T., and Nagasawa, Y. (2012). 'What Is Russellian Monism?' *Journal of Consciousness Studies*, 19: 67–95.

Bennett, K. (2003). 'Why the Exclusion Problem Seems Intractable and How, Just Maybe, to Tract It'. *Nous*, 37: 471–97.

Carruth, A. (2016). 'Powerful Qualities, Zombies, and Inconceivability'. *Philosophical Quarterly*, 66 (262): 25–46.

Chalmers, D. J. (1996). *The Conscious Mind: In Search of a Fundamental Theory*. New York: Oxford University Press.

Chalmers, D. J. (1997). 'Moving Forward on the Problem of Consciousness'. *Journal of Consciousness Studies*, 4: 3–46.

Chalmers, D. J. (2003). 'Consciousness and Its Place in Nature'. In S. Stich and T. Warfield (eds.), *Blackwell Guide to the Philosophy of Mind*. Cambridge: Blackwell. (Reprinted in D. J. Chalmers (ed.), *Philosophy of Mind: Classical and Contemporary Readings*. New York: Oxford University Press, 2002, pp. 247–72).

Chalmers, D. J. (2013). 'Panpsychism and Panprotopsychism'. Amherst Lecture in Philosophy. www.amherstlecture.org/index.html. (Also in T. Alter and Y. Nagasawa (eds.) *Consciousness in the Physical World: Perspectives on Russellian Monism*. New York: Oxford University Press, 2015, pp. 246–76).

Chalmers, D. J. (2017). 'The Combination Problem for Panpsychism'. In G. Brüntrop and L. Jaskolla (eds.), *Panpsychism*. New York: Oxford University Press, pp. 179–214.

Coleman, S. (2014). 'The Real Combination Problem: Panpsychism, Microsubjects, and Emergence'. *Erkenntnis*, 79(1): 19–44.

Coleman, S. (2017). 'Panpsychism and Neutral Monism: How to Make Up One's Mind'. In G. Brüntrup and L. Jaskolla (eds.), *Panpsychism: Contemporary Perspectives*. New York: Oxford University Press, pp. 249–82.

Ebbers, M. (n.d.). 'A Priori Entailment and the Reference-Fixing Problem'. Unpublished ms.

Ehring, D. (2011). *Tropes: Properties, Objects, and Mental Causation*. Oxford: Oxford University Press.

Fine, K. (2012). 'The Pure Logic of Ground'. *Review of Symbolic Logic*, 5: 1–25.

Goff, P. (2017). *Consciousness and Fundamental Reality*. New York: Oxford University Press.

Howell, R. J. (2015). 'The Russellian Monist's Problems with Mental Causation'. *Philosophical Quarterly*, 65: 22–39.

Kim, J. (1989). 'The Myth of Non-Reductive Materialism'. *Proceedings and Addresses of the American Philosophical Association*, 63: 31–47.

Kim, J. (2000). *Mind in a Physical World: An Essay on the Mind-Body Problem and Mental Causation*. Cambridge: MIT Press.

Kind, A. (2015). 'Pessimism About Russellian Monism'. In T. Alter and Y. Nagasawa (eds.), *Consciousness in the Physical World: Perspectives on Russellian Monism*. New York: Oxford University Press, pp. 401–21.

Lange, Marc (2017). *Because Without Cause: Non-Causal Explanation in Science and Mathematics*. New York: Oxford University Press.

List, C., and Stoljar, D. (2017). 'Does the Exclusion Argument Put Any Pressure on Dualism?' *Australasian Journal of Philosophy*, 95 (1): 96–108.

Montero, B. G. (2010) 'A Russellian Response to the Structural Argument Against Physicalism,' *Journal of Consciousness Studies* 17: 70–83.

Mørch, H. (2014). *Panpsychism and Causation: A New Argument and a Solution to the Combination Problem*. Dissertation, University of Oslo. https://philpapers.org/archive/HASPAC-2.pdf.

Ney, A. (2015). 'A Physicalist Critique of Russellian Monism'. In T. Alter and Y. Nagasawa (eds.), *Consciousness in the Physical World: Perspectives on Russellian Monism*. New York: Oxford University Press, pp. 346–69.

Pautz, A. (n.d.). 'A Dilemma for Russellian Monists About Consciousness'. ms.

Pereboom, D. (2011). *Consciousness and the Prospects of Physicalism*. New York: Oxford University Press.

Robinson, W. S. (2015). 'Russellian Monism and Epiphenomenalism'. *Pacific Philosophical Quarterly*, 98 (on-line version; DOI:10.1111/papq.12138).

Rosenberg, G. (2004). *A Place for Consciousness: Probing the Deep Structure of the Natural World*. New York: Oxford University Press.

Seager, W. E. (1995). 'Consciousness, Information, and Panpsychism'. *Journal of Consciousness Studies*, 2: 272–88.

Shoemaker, S. (2007). *Physical Realization*. Oxford: Oxford University Press.

Stoljar, D. (2015). 'Russellian Monism or Nagelian Monism?' In T. Alter and Y. Nagasawa (eds.), *Consciousness in the Physical World: Perspectives on Russellian Monism*. New York: Oxford University Press, pp. 324–45.

Strawson, G. (2006a). 'Realistic Monism: Why Physicalism Entails Panpsychism'. In A. Freeman (ed.), *Consciousness and Its Place in Nature*. Exeter: Imprint Academic, pp. 3–31.

Strawson, G. (2006b). 'Panpsychism? Reply to Commentators with a Celebration of Descartes'. In A. Freeman (ed.), *Consciousness and Its Place in Nature*. Exeter: Imprint Academic, pp. 184–280.

Wilson, J. M. (2011). 'Non-Reductive Realization and the Powers-Based Subset Strategy'. *The Monist (issue on powers)*, 94: 121–54.

Yablo, S. (1992). 'Mental Causation'. *Philosophical Review*, 101: 245–80.

PART IV

How Does Panpsychism Work?

21

CAN WE SUM SUBJECTS? EVALUATING PANPSYCHISM'S HARD PROBLEM

Luke Roelofs

Panpsychist accounts of consciousness hold that humans are conscious because matter itself is conscious. One widespread motivation for panpsychism is dissatisfaction with physicalist explanations of consciousness (Nagel 1979; Seager 1995; Chalmers 1995; Strawson 2006). If a non-mental understanding of physical matter leaves an 'explanatory gap' between physics and consciousness, and all physicalistic attempts to 'close the gap' fail, perhaps we should make consciousness itself fundamental, governed by some set of psychophysical laws of nature. Since the laws of physics seem to derive much of their appeal from being simple and general, with a multitude of forms building up gradually from a small set of widespread basic elements, let us suppose similarly general psychophysical laws, with consciousness throughout the material universe.

But what if we accept fundamental, omnipresent, consciousness but find our explanatory situation unchanged: human consciousness stills seems like an unexplained mystery? This is the impasse to which many critics have accused panpsychism of leading. Since panpsychism aims to add new fundamental laws *only* at the basic level, it still needs to explain how complex things like human minds are 'built up' from the basic experientiality of matter. And it needs to offer a more satisfying explanation than either physicalism, which denies the fundamentality of consciousness, or emergentism, which denies its omnipresence.[1] And there is a concern, widely voiced by both opponents of and sympathisers with panpsychism,[2] that this cannot be done: minds simply do not combine in the necessary way. This has been labelled the 'combination problem' (Seager 1995: 283).

Different panpsychists respond differently to the combination problem, and different components of it demand different responses. This chapter focuses on the very possibility of explanatory relations between distinct subjects; in section 1 I explain why this is the principal 'hard problem' of combination. Section 2 covers the standards for an adequate solution, section 3 reviews three proposals, evaluating them in light of these standards, and section 4 cautiously recommends a mixture of two of these proposals.

1. Hard and Easy Problems of Combination

Much work has been done to classify the components of the combination problem. Coleman distinguishes 'internal' and 'bridging' problems (2017: 3 ff.), Goff distinguishes 'from above' and 'from below' (2017b: chs. 7–8), and Chalmers distinguishes problems around subjecthood, qualities, and structure (2017). I will suggest another division, modelled on Chalmers' division between the 'hard problem' and 'easy problems' of consciousness (1995: 1 ff.). I believe there is a 'hard problem of combination', interestingly different from several 'easy problems of combination'.

Neither Chalmers' distinction nor mine is about *degree* of difficulty, but rather about *type* of difficulty. Chalmers says: 'The easy problems of consciousness are those that seem directly susceptible to the standard methods of cognitive science. . . . The hard problems are those that seem to resist those methods' (1995: 201).

Even if it is very difficult to say, for instance, how the brain produces words matching the stimuli its sense organs are exposed to, we at least have methods for approaching the task: those of psychology, neuroscience, and other empirical sciences of the mind. By contrast, the problem of subjective experience is 'hard' precisely in that those methods seem inappropriate. They just don't make contact with the problem, since for any neural mechanism or functional architecture, it still makes sense to ask 'But why does that *feel like anything?*'

My distinction between 'hard' and 'easy' problems of combination is meant to exhibit an analogous contrast between difficulties in applying an appropriate method, and difficulties where we seem to lack a method which would even address the issue. But the methods in question are different – the easy problems of consciousness are those which are tractable by the methods of the cognitive sciences, but the easy problems of combination are those which are tractable by the methods of *phenomenological analysis*. The hard problems of combination are whatever problems are not thus tractable: I believe the main, and perhaps only, example is what has become known as 'the subject-summing problem'.

By 'phenomenological analysis' I simply mean the inward-looking sort of attention to one's own experience which we routinely use to address questions about whether one type of experience is necessary or sufficient for another. When we ask, for instance, whether the experience of mathematical reasoning is fully accounted for by the experience of entertaining the associated images, or whether an experience of something as objectively existing might require certain kinds of imaginative capacities, we are exploring relations among types of experience by analysing them as they occur within our own mind. While some question the trustworthiness of such methods (e.g. Dennett 1991; Blackmore 2002), they are a well-established part of how philosophers approach questions about experience, not an *ad hoc* invention of panpsychists.

So what are 'hard' and 'easy' problems of combination? Consider the subject-summing problem. This problem is very simple to express: no facts about one subject's consciousness seem to directly explain facts about another's. Or at least, it is not clear how they would, and many people find it implausible that they ever could – in particular, many feel that subjects are in some sense 'metaphysically insulated', 'cut off' from each other (e.g. James 1890: 226; Coleman 2012: 146; Blamauer this volume). Since my parts are not identical with me, their consciousness is cut off from explaining mine. Note that this worry is immune to any resolution based simply in phenomenological analysis of experience, for in phenomenological analysis the experiences I analyse *are all mine*: I cannot do phenomenological analysis on your experience. All I can find is that when certain experiences are had together *by the same subject*, another sort of experience is had *by that subject* – which is irrelevant to explanatory relations among different subjects. Just like the hard problem of consciousness, the subject-summing problem is methodologically distinctive in a way that makes it obscure how to even approach it.

To see the contrast with other problems of combination, imagine we fully satisfied ourselves that given a certain configuration of microsubjects, the whole they compose must be a subject of experience. Many problems remain, but all concern explaining particular kinds of experience – why is the macrosubject's experience unified, qualitatively diverse, coarse-grained, epistemically bounded, and so on? And for these questions, phenomenological analysis is entirely relevant, since phenomenological analysis is how we decide what sorts of experience might give rise to what other sorts. For example, for the 'palette problem', of how a few basic ingredients can yield the diverse qualities we experience, it is relevant to analyse the relations among different experienced qualities, to ask whether some are blends of others, and so on (see Mizrahi 2009). So for addressing these other problems, panpsychists can draw on and extend existing phenomenological work – work which on each occasion is done within a single subject's mind. This is the sense in which I call them 'easy'.

There might be other hard problems of combination, apart from that of subject-summing. But that is my primary example, and it is to this hard problem that I devote the rest of this chapter.

2. Explanation and Explanatory Gaps

To solve the subject-summing problem, microsubjects must 'explain' macrosubjects. But what is it for one thing (*x*) to 'explain' another (*y*)? One answer is that an idealised reasoner, given complete knowledge of *x*, could deduce everything about *y*. Moreover, they need no additional *a posteriori* premises: if some additional *a posteriori* premise *z* is needed to deduce *y*, then what explains *y* is '*x* and *z* together', not just *x*. Call this the '*a priori* deduction' standard of explanation. It follows that *x* fails to explain *y* if '*x*-without-*y*' is conceivable, for deduction just rules out what cannot be consistently conceived. Hence anti-physicalists argue for an explanatory gap from the conceivability of any physical facts without consciousness.

Applying the same standard, we ask: given a complete account of the microsubjects, is it conceivable that there be no consciousness in the whole? Note that 'a complete account of the microsubjects' covers not only their experiential properties, but also the relations among them, their physical properties, and the micro-level laws that govern them. This includes psychic or psychophysical laws, *if they operate at the micro-level*, but not if they are 'cross-level' laws, connecting facts at one mereological level with facts at another (as 'emergence laws' do).

A priori deduction is not a universally accepted standard for explanation. If we have compelling empirical and theoretical reason to identify A with B, why should it matter if our concept of B gives us no grasp of A? Plausibly, the right model of explanation is whichever best accounts for the explanatory power of natural science (see esp. Block and Stalnaker 1999; Chalmers and Jackson 2001; Diaz-Leon 2011; McQueen 2015), and there can be reasonable disagreement here. We should thus ask whether panpsychists could retreat from the demanding standard of *a priori* deduction, and maintain that microsubjects explain macrosubjects in some other way. But we must recall the panpsychist's dialectical positioning: if physicalism and emergentism are rejected for their explanatory failures, panpsychism needs to deliver more.[3]

So if panpsychists say that microsubjects ground macrosubjects in an 'opaque' but necessary way, without giving any *a priori* insight, then physicalists will reply that their purely physical explanatory base can 'explain' consciousness in that sense (cf. Block and Stalnaker 1999; Levine 1983; Loar 1990). On the other hand, if panpsychists accept the possibility of microsubjects without macrosubjects, and postulate a cross-level emergence law to produce the latter out from former, then emergentists will reply that since we need the law to generate macrosubjects, the microsubjects are pointless.

Are there ways for panpsychists to accept explanatory opacity, or cross-level laws, while retaining an explanatory advantage over physicalism and emergentism? Perhaps. Consider physicalism first. Classic anti-physicalist arguments, such as the 'absent qualia' and 'inverted qualia' thought experiments, are often treated as establishing the same result (the physical does not fix the experiential), but we can actually distinguish two issues. To have no explanatory gap at all, the physical facts need to explain why certain systems are *conscious at all*, and the 'absent qualia' thought experiment seems to undermine this. But they also need to explain why any conscious system has the *particular sort of experiences* that it has, and the 'inverted qualia' thought experiment seems to undermine this too. To explain consciousness means both to 'explain-that' some systems have consciousness, and also to 'explain-what' sorts of consciousness they have.

Explaining-what and explaining-that might come apart. Given *x* we might be able to deduce that *some* sort of *y* must appear, and yet not know which specific *y*. Those who accept the conceivability of inverted qualia but not absent qualia hold this view of the physical and experiential facts (cf. Shoe-maker 1975). On the other hand, *x* might show clearly what sort of *y* there would be *if* there was some sort but leave open that there be none. For instance, suppose we encounter a robotic system of unknown internal structure that seems to converse with us intelligently. Its behaviour might not tell us whether to regard its apparent propositional attitudes as genuine or illusory, but still tell us that *if* it has genuine propositional attitudes, then it has those which it seems to express.

Physicalism seems to neither explain-that nor explain-what, so any view which achieves one or the other would be an explanatory advance. This sense of complete mystery is evoked by Huxley's remark that '[H]ow it is that anything so remarkable as a state of consciousness comes about as a result of irritating nervous tissue, is just as unaccountable as the appearance of the Djinn, when Aladdin rubbed his lamp' (1986: 193). If the panpsychist can either explain-that macrosubjects have experi-ence, or explain-what sort of experience they have, they will have made human consciousness *less* mysterious than Aladdin's Djinn.

What about maintaining an advantage over emergentism? There are ways to claim partial explan-atoriness here as well. One might insist that it is just more intelligible for things of one fundamental type to emerge from each other, than for fundamentally different things to emerge from each other (e.g. Strawson 2006: 16–19), though this may seem question-begging to emergentist opponents. A more neutral way is to focus on theoretical virtues. Why is (non-panpsychist) emergentism unat-tractive? Not simply because it holds that some of the fundamental laws of nature connect things at different mereological levels, but because doing so compromises its theoretical virtue. This involves three specific problems.

One problem concerns causal exclusion and arises somewhat as follows. If the panpsychist, or the physicalist, could claim that macrosubjects are intelligibly grounded in micro-level entities (identical to them, composed of them, realised by them, etc.) they could maintain that macro- and micro-entities are *not in causal competition*: both can be causally efficacious without their effects being 'overdetermined' like the death of someone shot by two members of a firing squad. But if the micro-level entities need the aid of a special emergence law to generate macrosubjects, it seems like macrosubjects are something ontologically independent of them, and so if both cause some effect that really does look like over-determination. Insofar as rampant overdetermination is theoretically vicious, this drives emergentists towards either epiphenomenalism about macrosubjects, or denying the causal closure of microphysics. Neither of these is attractive: one attraction of panpsychism is that it seemed to offer anti-physicalists an escape from this dilemma, but re-introducing (strong) emergence will remove this advantage.

Of course, avoiding causal competition between micro and macro is little consolation if there is still competition between micro-experience and microphysics. To avoid this, many panpsychists present their view as a form of 'Russellian monism' (traced to Russell 1927, cf. Eddington 1929; Lockwood 1981; Alter and Nagasawa 2015), on which micro-experience provides the basis for microphysics. On this view, physical descriptions are in some sense 'structural' (cf. Stoljar 2014), saying how matter behaves but leaving unspecified what it actually is that behaves that way. This allows the panpsychist to posit micro-experience as that unspecified inner nature, thereby giving experience a central role in physical causation and avoiding causal competition. But this commits them to a thorough-going isomorphism of mental and physical (relating to the third criticism of emergentism, below), which they cannot violate without risking the loss of their apparent advantage on the causal score.

A second problem is that non-panpsychist emergence laws may offend very heavily against the ideal of 'simplicity'. To preserve the intuition that only human beings and some animals are con-scious, the fundamental laws must connect consciousness with a specification – in wholly fundamen-tal terms – of what it takes to be one of the relevant sorts of animal, and this specification would be many orders of magnitude longer than any of the mathematical terms appearing in the laws currently recognised by physics, with many more 'brute facts' about which precise values the many variables must take (Cf. Feigl 1958: 428; Smart 1959: 142–3; Rosenberg 2004: 107–10).

A third issue is the desire to keep the mental and the physical 'in line' with one another as much as possible. Overwhelming empirical evidence seems to show that they are closely intertwined, and even if a theory recognises them as fundamentally distinct aspects, it should not let them 'drift out of sync' (Cf. Mørch 2014: 10, 50). Consequently if the brain's physical profile is just what we would predict, given its parts and their arrangement, we should prefer a theory with a similar sort of continuity in the mental realm. Certainly we should be reluctant to accept a radical change on the mental side if the relevant physical processes are all fully continuous (Cf. James 1890: 147–8; Mørch 2014: 161–3).

If the problem with emergentism is these three threats (to macroexperiential causal efficacy, to theoretical simplicity, and to mental-physical correspondence), then a theory that postulated cross-level laws but avoided these problems would be a comparative explanatory success. And if this theory's microsubjects were crucial to avoiding these results, we would have good reason to prefer panpsychist emergentism to non-panpsychist emergentism.

So if an account of subject combination secures *a priori* entailment of macrosubjects without cross-level laws, it meets the 'gold standard'. Other accounts can be partially successful by doing two things: *explaining more than physicalism* (e.g. by either explaining-that or explaining-what), while being *more theoretically virtuous than emergentism* (in causal non-competition, structural simplicity, and mental-physical correspondence).

3. How to Sum Subjects

This section reviews three approaches to the subject-summing problem that have appeared:

- The 'experience-sharing' approach, on which token experiences belong simultaneously both to parts and whole.
- The 'fusion' approach, in which microsubjects predate macrosubjects rather than co-existing with them.
- The 'phenomenal bonding' approach, on which the crucial explanatory ingredient is a special relation among subjects.

Each approach has strengths and weaknesses: experience-sharing secures theoretical virtue at the expense of revising pre-theoretical notions of subjecthood, fusion sacrifices theoretical virtue almost as much as strong emergentism, and phenomenal bonding rests its explanation on a posit of which we have no positive conception.

Two approaches that I will not discuss here abandon the assumption that elementary particles are the fundamental conscious subjects: 'panprotopsychism' holds that they are fundamental, but not subjects (see Coleman 2012, 2014, cf. Chadha this volume), while 'cosmopsychism' holds that they are not fundamental, but merely the smallest fragments of what is fundamental, namely the conscious cosmos itself (see Jaskolla and Buck 2012; Shani 2015; Goff this volume, cf. Albahari this volume). Rather than trying to solve the subject-summing problem, these approaches seek to re-frame it by changing the starting point. In my view, both struggle to get beyond 'moving the bump under the rug', with the basic difficulty of explaining human-sized subjects always reappearing in a different guise, and with the same basic moves available to address it.

3.1. Experience-Sharing

Why are physical wholes so readily explicable through their parts? One plausible answer is that they have no properties (whether universal types or particular instances) that don't, in some fashion, 'come from' their parts. For example, a physical whole with a red spot shares an instance of redness with a part of its surface; if dented or ripped, it likewise shares an instance of dentedness or rippedness with a part. And, significantly, physical wholes often share token causal powers and responsibilities with their parts, so that both can cause one effect without overdetermination. Of course not all properties of a whole are shared with its parts: you can build a circle out of square parts. But as long as unshared properties are themselves grounded in by some pattern of shared properties – as the shape of a circle is accounted for by the location properties it shares with its many square parts – then we need no 'further reality' to make the whole: it simply shares the reality of its parts.

What I call the 'experience-sharing' approach hopes that something similar is true of macrosubjects: each of their primitive experiential properties belongs both to the whole and to one of its parts, and their other experiential properties are simply patterns of these shared primitive experiences. This changes the shape of the subject-summing problem. If token experiences are not shared, we need to explain not just a new subject, but a whole new stream of consciousness. But if the whole shares token experiences with its parts, we already have our stream of consciousness. And if we take human subjects to be identical with certain physical systems (brains), we already have our candidate macrosubject. So given this composite entity, and this collection of experiences in its parts, the subject-summing problem shrinks to: why is this entity related to these experiences suitably to be (one of) their subject(s)? This does not remove the problem but might make it seem less insuperable.

Consider three challenges to experience-sharing: that it intensifies the 'easy problems' of combination, that it is incompatible with the nature of subjectivity, and that it does not explain subject-summing. The first concern is that if the whole has the very same experiences as its parts, it becomes harder to explain apparent discrepancies between human experience and what we can reasonably posit at the micro-level. For instance, the micro-level is fantastically fine-grained, but qualitatively homogeneous, while human experience is comparatively coarse-grained, but qualitatively diverse. Panpsychists who deny experience-sharing might dodge this problem by saying that macro-experience is dependent on, but still entirely distinct from, micro-experience. But no such move is available to the experience-sharer. These problems may still be soluble, but experience-sharing makes them harder.

A second concern is that experience-sharing may contradict something basic about subjecthood. For instance, we might think that conscious experience is essentially 'private', directly knowable by only one subject, in contrast to the 'public' world of physical things. Since *having* an experience seems closely linked to being able to know it directly, privacy seems to rule out experience-sharing. But perhaps the experience-sharer can say that our intuitive idea of privacy is correct, but only when applied to *discrete* (non-overlapping) subjects, rather than to *distinct* (non-identical) subjects. Since my parts are distinct from me but not discrete from me, their sharing my experiences is compatible with this qualified form of privacy (cf. Roelofs 2019: 121 ff).

A related worry, articulated in different forms by Basile (2010) and Coleman (2012, 2014), is that experience-sharing conflicts with the holistic, perspectival, character of consciousness. Even if some sort of 'element' were shared between two consciousnesses, this element will be experienced differently from their two perspectives, due to the other contents of their respective consciousnesses. And if they experience it differently, surely we should count it as a different experience: hence a single experience cannot be shared. To put it another way, for experience-sharing to explain macro-subjects, we must be able to build up a single conscious field from individual experiences with some degree of independent existence, which is what this line of objection denies. Against this, the experience-sharer could accept that consciousness is holistic, but analyse this in terms of mutual influence among elements, so that the parts are fundamental but also heavily affected by each other. This would imply that the total experience of one component subject will depend on the experiences of the *others*: its phenomenology somehow reflects theirs (see Roelofs 2016, 2019).

A third worry: even if the experience-sharing approach changes the explanandum ('why do physical composites bear the 'being-a-subject-of' relation to their parts' experiences?'), does it actually explain that? It at least does better than physicalism. Recall section 2's distinction between explaining-what and explaining-that: experience-sharing at least accomplishes explaining-what. If we knew that the parts of me had certain experiences, and knew that I had *some* experiences, it seems we could deduce which experiences I would have – namely, those of my parts (and whatever other more complex experiences those might underlie).[4]

But why does the macrosubject have *any* experiences – why are there macrosubjects at all? If there is no contradiction in a composite of microsubjects lacking experience, we still need an explanation for why we do not inhabit a world of microsubjects without macrosubjects. One possibility is that it is somehow in the nature of *composition in general* that wholes 'inherit' properties from their parts, for at least some range of properties (this makes most sense if composition is something like identity, cf. Baxter 1988; Lewis 1991, 1993; Sider 2007; Cotnoir 2013; Baxter and Cotnoir 2014). Or it might be the nature of *subjects* that all their properties are reducible to certain patterns of resemblance, representation, or causation among experiences (as on NeoLockean accounts of personhood, cf. Parfit 1984, 1999; Shoemaker 1997). In both these cases (both explored in Roelofs 2019), the explanation would be *a priori*, but would require defending a contentious position on an independent metaphysical question.

Alternatively, the experience-sharing theorist might posit a cross-level law of nature that wholes (conditionally or unconditionally) share the experiences of their parts. This means accepting the possibility of a 'panpsychic zombie world', where experiences were not shared: we know we are not in such a world, because we know ourselves to be conscious, but this knowledge is *a posteriori*. This implies a sort of 'emergentism', in that macrosubjects do not follow *a priori* from even the fullest account of their parts. However, *a posteriori* experience-sharing lacks the theoretical vices which I discussed in section 2. It does not generate causal competition between microsubjects and macrosubjects, if causal responsibility is tied to particular shareable properties. It does not drive a wedge between mental and physical structure – indeed, it posits a law of nature to make the mental realm behave the same way as the physical realm. And because the posited law does not apply specifically to humans and other animals, it lacks the ungainly complication required to specify such a narrow range of application.

Overall, experience-sharing offers a high-risk, high-reward strategy for panpsychists. It is the approach most open to refutation – on grounds of privacy, perspectival holism, and the intensified 'easy problems'. But if these objections can be resolved, panpsychists get a better explanation than either emergentists (for simplicity, mental-physical correspondence, and causal non-competition) or physicalists (for explaining-*what* the macrosubject experiences), whether or not the fact that macrosubjects experience anything is explained by the metaphysics of subjecthood, or of composition, or by a cross-level law.

3.2. *Diachronic Fusion*

Could the challenges facing experience-sharing show a problem with the whole idea of two co-existing levels of experience? This thought leads some panpsychists (e.g. Seager 2010, 2017; Mørch 2014, cf. Humphreys 1997) to theorise combination as the 'fusing' of many subjects into one, so that as soon as the macrosubject exists the microsubjects are gone. There are first some parts and no whole, and then a whole and no parts, and the explanatory relation between them is diachronic, not synchronic.

Part of the appeal of the fusion approach is that in a sense there is no emergence at all, because everything goes on 'at the micro-level'. All subjects become 'micro-subjects', since none is composed of any others. The laws governing fusion, therefore, are 'micro-level' laws – or rather, they are laws operating on the most basic level, rather than 'inter-level' emergence laws. Thus human consciousness is entailed *a priori* by a full specification of 'micro-level' facts and laws, meeting our 'gold standard' for explanation. Yet this arguably satisfies the letter while violating the spirit: the human subject may be synchronically simple but its complexity and causal powers are macro-scale, and so in our intuitive sense of 'micro-level', the fusion approach denies the adequacy of the micro-level. To properly evaluate it, we must look to the criteria outlined in section 2. Does it offer theoretical simplicity, isomorphism with physics, and causal harmony?

Seager (2010, 2017) argues that we should find fusion unproblematic, since there are examples available in physical science. His first example (also used by Humphreys 1997: 15ff) is quantum entanglement: when particles become entangled, they 'form a new state whose mathematical representation cannot be decomposed into a product of the representations of the constituents' (Seager 2017: 12). His second example is black holes, which may satisfy a 'no-hair' conjecture according to which all details of the matter which enters them are permanently abolished, leaving the hole with only three features: mass, charge, and angular momentum. Two black holes of the same mass, charge, and angular momentum are identical in all respects, lacking any 'hair' that might distinguish them.

If either of these provided a good model for the human mind, we really would have a good micro-level explanation. For in both cases, the laws governing the fusion of many entities into one are simply the general laws of physics, not laws tailored to specific complex cases. However, examining how these two examples differ reveals a dilemma for the fusion approach. Consider the problem of 'basal loss', identified by Wong in his critique of Humphreys:

> The basal properties giving rise to [an emergent property] also constitute myriad non-emergent, structural properties. . . . If these lower level properties literally ceased to be in fusing . . . then so, it seems, would those structural properties.
>
> (Wong 2006: 355)

Suppose, for instance, that certain of my neurone-states vanish into a fused mental state; what becomes of the non-emergent total neural state that they composed? If it vanishes also, it will deprive the brain of its mass, volume, shape, visible appearance, etc. Yet clearly brains do retain these non-emergent physical properties, suggesting that they retain the underlying neurone-states.

Note that for 'hairless' black holes, basal loss makes sense. What interested us in them is that the specific features of what enters them really do seem to be *lost*. This makes it both an excellent model of fusion, and a bad model for anything supposed to happen in the brain. Quantum entanglement fits the brain better, but quantum entanglement is very different from black hole formation. Entangled systems retain all the features of their 'parts'; rather than losing anything, they add something, namely lawlike relations between these features. Consequently, Wong's point about basal loss seems to count against treating entanglement as fusion.

Note that although the properties of an entangled system cannot be explained just by the individual properties of its parts, this does not mean that they cannot be explained by those individual properties, along with the 'entanglement relations' between them. These relations are certainly odd, connecting the properties of disparate objects but not behaving like other 'causal' interactions described by physics (in particular, ignoring the speed-of-light time limit). But any account of quantum phenomena must be odd, and there need be nothing offensive to reductionistic scruples about relations among parts being essential to a whole's behaviour, as long as those relations follow from the micro-level laws.

The fact that we *can* treat entangled systems as composites does not show that we cannot or should not treat them as a sort of emergent simple. So the holistic treatment might still be the *model* for the mental case. But there is something problematic about treating them as fusion, which the black hole example brings out. Consider two particles which become entangled with respect to certain of their properties (e.g. spin) but not with respect to all (e.g. charge). The resultant entangled system still has a certain total charge and has portions of that charge at certain locations. Why does it have these charge properties? Surely because the particles that entered into it had those charge properties. But why should the properties of non-existent particles explain the properties of this system, unless they are in some sense still around? The charge was not involved in the interaction that entangled them, so it need not be mentioned in any sort of 'fusion law' of the form 'when property X and property Y interact, they form a new property Z' (see Humphreys 1997 for details of the 'fusion operation'). The entangled system might have simply *not had* any charge properties, as the example of the hairless black hole illustrates. So it seems we need extra laws, or extra clauses in the laws, saying that unless otherwise specified, the charge of an entangled system is inherited from the now-vanished particles that brought it into existence. But this seems like an unattractive multiplication of laws just to account for what seem like trivial results. It seems more efficient to see the entangled system as composed of the original particles, now differently related – or else to be thoroughly holistic, denying the fundamental existence of individual particles either before or after entanglement. But in neither of these cases is there really any fusion going on.[5]

This poses a dilemma when considering the brain. If the panpsychist's fusion law specifies that microsubjects displaying (say) a certain functional organisation fuse into a brain-sized subject, this leaves open that all their properties irrelevant to functional organisation simply vanish, leaving behind a macrosubject which 'has no hair'. Yet the brain seems to retain all the physical features of its parts, including the incredibly specific (though functionally irrelevant) distribution of features across microscopically small locations. But fundamental laws specifying that this one thing, quite distinct from the many things which go into it, should nevertheless match them exactly in trillions of respects, are, as Mørch admits, 'not very simple and elegant' (2014: 190).

We could avoid these worries about basal loss by letting mental and physical drift apart. Perhaps the experiential parts of the brain fuse into a single macrosubject, but the physical parts do not correspondingly fuse into a single physical entity (Seager 2017: 15). But this runs into causal exclusion – not between between macrosubjects and microsubjects, but between macrosubjects and micro*physics*. If the many particles account for everything the brain causes, the distinct single macrosubject faces epiphenomenalism. Certainly, it is hard to see how to retain isomorphism between mental and physical, let alone the Russellian identification of one as the categorical basis of the other.

The fusion approach deduces human subjects *a priori* from facts that can be called 'micro-level', but risks losing the structural advantages associated with panpsychism. Mental fusion without physical fusion threatens causal harmony and mental-physical isomorphism; fusion that is both mental and physical requires unparsimonious fusion laws. Perhaps the approach can somehow avoid both problems, but it is hard to see how.

3.3. *Phenomenal Bonding*

Micro-physical explanations typically make essential reference to relations among components – few macroscopic phenomena are explained by microphysics if we ignore causal, spatial, and other relations. So maybe the subject-summing problem results from not conceiving component subjects *as properly related*.

Of course, we can imagine subjects standing in many relations – resembling each other, acting on each other, communicating with each other, etc. But these familiar relations don't seem to help: indeed, a classic way to dramatise the subject-summing problem is to imagine human subjects so related (interacting, talking, touching, etc.) and observe how easily conceivable it is that there be no further consciousness belonging to the group (see Plotinus 1956: 346; Brentano 1987: 293; James 1890: 160). But even if familiar relations cannot do the job, perhaps some relation previously unrecognised does better. Following Goff (2017a, 2017b) I will call this relation 'phenomenal bonding'.

But what is phenomenal bonding, beyond 'the relation that solves the subject-summing problem'? Goff maintains that its nature actually precludes our understanding it, because we cannot learn about it either introspectively or perceptually. We cannot understand inter-subject relations introspectively, for introspection reveals only one subject, not many. And we cannot understand it perceptually, because it is essentially subjective, or 'inner', and perception shows us only what is objective and 'outer' (2017a: 293–294). Thus Goff admits this approach 'leads to a kind of mysterianism' (2017a: 294).[6]

So while the monadic properties of microsubjects do not explain the consciousness of macrosubjects, those properties *together with phenomenal bonding relations* do. If we had a proper conception of those relations, we would find it inconceivable that subjects standing in them *not* compose a subject. The subject-summing problem arises because we lack, and cannot acquire, a proper conception of the bonding relations.

Goff suggests we can indirectly characterise the bonding relation as the 'deep nature' of spatial relations (2017: ch. 7). This talk of 'deep natures' assumes Russellian monism: physics describes only the abstract structure of things, not their intrinsic nature. Russellian panpsychists say that the deep nature of physical properties is consciousness; Goff extends this by saying that the deep nature of physical relations is a phenomenal relation.

How to evaluate the phenomenal bonding approach? In one sense, it explains macrosubjects: it postulates something whose nature entails them, and it provides a principled reason why we cannot grasp this something. But in another sense it explains nothing: lacking a grasp of the explanatory base, we gain no illumination as to why there are macrosubjects with any particular features.

For one thing, we have no idea when and where the bonding relation obtains. Suppose we identify it with space or causation: does it hold wherever there is any degree of these (in which case it probably connects every subject in the universe to every other), or does it require some threshold of proximity or intensity, or does it itself come in degrees? This makes it hard to judge parsimony. Perhaps, given our ignorance, we should suppose the most parsimonious distribution possible, such as an entirely thorough-going one (as in Goff 2013). But this seems problematic, posing what Rosenberg (1998, 2004) calls the 'boundary problem': it is easy to see how a universally distributed bonding relation could yield a single cosmic mind, or an infinity of overlapping subjects. But why exactly do we get the specific human subjects that we wanted to explain, or at least why do they in particular have such prominence, being the only ones that get recognised as such? Perhaps this challenge can be met, but without any insight into the bonding relation, the particular size and shape of the human subject starts to seem mysterious.

Moreover, when two microsubjects get phenomenally bonded, thereby forming a composite subject, we are told basically nothing about what this subject's experience will be like. Perhaps its experiences will be type-identical to those of some or all of its parts, or perhaps token-identical, or perhaps quite different. Goff insists that *constituting* an experience need not mean *characterising* it (2017: 189 ff). But this invites the question: what *does* characterise the macrosubject's experience? The phenomenal bonding approach does not seem to tell us.

Overall, I think phenomenal bonding provides a good fall-back position for the panpsychist, if all other approaches fail. The bonding approach can claim narrow advantages both over physicalism (because while it does not *provide* an explanation of consciousness, it postulates a suitable explanatory base, as opposed to the knowably insufficient physicalist base) and over emergentism (because while it does not avoid positing an epistemically brute 'factor X', this factor is simple, general, and already operative at the micro-level). It may however have trouble showing an advantage over non-standard forms of physicalism (see Stoljar this volume), which postulate unknowable features of physical reality but not fundamental consciousness. But if the subject-summing problem cannot otherwise be solved, phenomenal bonding may be the best panpsychists can do.

4. A Combined Proposal

I think the best approach for Russellian panpsychists combines experience-sharing and phenomenal bonding. If we hold *both* that token experiences can belong to multiple subjects, *and* that the formation of macrosubjects depends crucially on distinctively phenomenal relations, we mitigate some of the shortcomings of each approach. Moreover, we get a productive direction for future research: extrapolating intra-subject phenomenal relations into inter-subject phenomenal relations.

First, experience-sharing makes phenomenal bonding less mysterian. If the bonding relations obtain between our own component subjects, and pertain specifically to their experiences, and if we ourselves share those experiences, we do have access to the relations after all. We know them as structural relations among our own experiences, such as phenomenal unification, composition of content, mutual reference or accessibility, or whatever else phenomenology reveals. On this approach, Goff is wrong to say that introspection reveals only one subject: introspection shows us at least some of our component subjects as well as ourselves. Second, phenomenal bonding helps stop experience-sharing from 'making the easy problems harder'. If experiences change each other's phenomenal character through being bonded, and if moreover not all parts of me, or not all of their experiences, are bonded, that might explain why our experience is sensitive to certain features of our brain and not others.

Neither of these advantages is a completed result: the easy problems are still quite hard, and we still need a fuller account of the bonding relations. But this combined proposal suggests a methodology to address these challenges. First, find distinctively phenomenal relations within human experience. Then, evaluate them as potential bonding relations, asking if they are suitably basic and explanatory. If they seem promising, work out how those relations could hold inter-subjectively, between experiences of distinct subjects. This means both identifying any problems that follow from such a supposition and finding points of contact between our chosen intra-subjective relations and our inter-subjective relations with each other. This methodology, which I pursue in other work (Roelofs 2016, 2017, 2019), is not guaranteed to succeed: but hopefully it will be illuminating, whether it succeeds or fails.

Notes

1. When I speak of 'emergentists', I mean 'strong' emergentism, on which some property of a complex could not be predicted from its emergence base even with the most complete knowledge of the relevant properties of that base. Instead, it arises from a *sui generis* law. Moreover, I will assume that (strong) emergentists are not panpsychists. 'Weak' emergentists, who hold emergent phenomena to be predictable in principle, even if not in practice, I count as physicalists or panpsychists, depending on the features of their emergence base (see Broad 1925; Chalmers 2006; Wilson 2016).
2. See James (1890: 147–61), Nagel (1986: 50), Van Cleve (1990: 219), Rosenberg (1998, 2004), Strawson (2006), Goff (2006, 2009a, 2009b), Basile (2010), Shani (2010), Seager (2010, 2017), Coleman (2012, 2014), Sebastián (2015), Mørch (2014), Roelofs 2014, 2016, 2019), and Mendelovici (this volume).
3. Of course, not all panpsychists rest their position on the explanatory gap faced by physicalism. There are other arguments for panpsychism available, most especially the 'intrinsic natures' argument that seems to show all non-panpsychist views to be unparsimonious and borderline unintelligible (e.g. Seager 2006; Coleman 2009). But since much of the recent interest in panpsychism does derive from explanatory concerns, we should consider what panpsychists have to do to maintain their claim of explanatory superiority.
4. Note that in order to deduce this we would have to rule out that I had some other experiences, unrelated to those of my parts. But we are perfectly entitled to rule this out, according to the most prominent models of how explanatory deductions proceed in the physical realm (Chalmers and Jackson 2001; Chalmers 2012), which explicitly requires a 'that's-all' clause in any micro-level explanation.
5. Will it help to say that the entangled system is not really *partless*, but simply holistic in the sense of being more fundamental than its parts (cf. Mørch 2014: 167–75, 191)? We can still say that at the fundamental level, the parts are replaced by a simple whole. And it is not clear that this provides any *genuine* persistence of the parts,

because it is not clear whether there can be genuine identity between a fundamental entity at one time and a non-fundamental entity at a later time.

6. Chalmers (2017), following Dainton (2011), offers a less mysterian proposal: that the phenomenal bonding relation is 'co-consciousness', the relation studied in the literature of the unity of consciousness. I think this version of the bonding approach is stronger than the mysterian one, and have defended a version of it myself (Roelofs 2016, 2019).

References

Albahari, M. (this volume). 'Abhidharma Panprotopsychist Metaphysics of Consciousness'. In W. Seager (ed.), *The Routledge Handbook of Panpsychism*. London: Routledge.

Alter, T., and Nagasawa, Y. (eds.) (2015). *Consciousness in the Physical World: Perspectives on Russellian Monism*. Oxford: Oxford University Press.

Basile, P. (2010). 'It Must Be True – But How Can It Be? Some Remarks on Panpsychism and Mental Composition'. *Royal Institute of Philosophy Supplement*, 67: 93–112.

Baxter, D. (1988). 'Many-One Identity'. *Philosophical Papers*, 17 (3): 193–216.

Baxter, D., and Cotnoir, A. (eds.) (2014). *Composition as Identity*. Oxford: Oxford University Press.

Blackmore, S. (2002). 'There Is No Stream of Consciousness'. *Journal of Consciousness Studies*, 9 (5–6): 17–28.

Blamauer, M. (this volume). 'The Crux of Subjectivity the Subjective Dimension of Consciousness and Its Role in the Arguments for and Against Panpsychism'. In W. Seager (ed.), *The Routledge Handbook of Panpsychism*. London: Routledge.

Block, N., and Stalnaker, R. (1999). 'Conceptual Analysis, Dualism, and the Explanatory Gap'. *Philosophical Review*, 108: 1–46.

Brentano, F. (1987). *The Existence of God: Lectures Given at the Universities of Worzburg and Vienna, 1868–1891*. Ed. and Trans. S. Krantz. Nijhoff International Philosophy Series. Dordrecht: Nijhoff.

Broad, C. D. (1925). *The Mind and Its Place in Nature*. London: Kegan Paul.

Chadha, M. (this volume). 'Abhidharma Panprotopsychist Metaphysics of Consciousness'. In W. Seager (ed.), *The Routledge Handbook of Panpsychism*. London: Routledge.

Chalmers, D. (1995). 'Facing Up to the Problem of Consciousness'. *Journal of Consciousness Studies*, 2 (3): 200–19.

Chalmers, D. (2006). 'Strong and Weak Emergence'. In P. Clayton and P. Davies (eds.), *The Re-Emergence of Emergence: The Emergentist Hypothesis from Science to Religion*. Oxford: Oxford University Press, pp. 244–56.

Chalmers, D. (2012). *Constructing the World*. Oxford: Oxford University Press.

Chalmers, D. (2017). 'The Combination Problem for Panpsychism'. In G. Brüntrup and L. Jaskolla (eds.), *Panpsychism: Contemporary Perspectives*. Oxford: Oxford University Press, pp. 179–214.

Chalmers, D., and Jackson, F. (2001). 'Conceptual Analysis and Reductive Explanation'. *The Philosophical Review*, 110 (13): 315–61.

Coleman, S. (2009). 'Mind Under Matter'. In D. Skrbina (ed.), *Mind That Abides*. Amsterdam: Benjamins, pp. 83–107.

Coleman, S. (2012). 'Mental Chemistry: Combination for Panpsychists'. *Dialectica*, 66 (1): 137–66.

Coleman, S. (2014). 'The Real Combination Problem: Panpsychism, Micro-Subjects, and Emergence'. *Erkenntnis*, 79: 19–44.

Coleman, S. (2017). 'Panpsychism and Neutral Monism: How to Make Up One's Mind'. In G. Brüntrup and L. Jaskolla (eds.), *Panpsychism: Contemporary Perspectives*. Oxford: Oxford University Press, pp. 249–82.

Cotnoir, A. (2013). 'Composition as General Identity'. In K. Bennett and D. Zimmerman (eds.), *Oxford Studies in Metaphysics*, vol. 8. Oxford: Oxford University Press, pp. 295–322.

Dainton, B. (2011). 'Review of *Consciousness and Its Place in Nature*'. *Philosophy and Phenomenological Research*, 83 (1): 238–61.

Dennett, D. (1991). *Consciousness Explained*. Boston: Little, Brown and Co.

Diaz-Leon, E. (2011). 'Reductive Explanation, Concepts, and a Priori Entailment'. *Philosophical Studies*, 155: 99–116.

Eddington, A. (1929). *The Nature of the Physical World*. Cambridge: Cambridge University Press [1927 Gifford Lectures. First edition published in 1928].

Feigl, H. (1958). 'The "Mental" and the "Physical"'. In H. Feigl, M. Scriven, and G. Maxwell (eds.), *Minnesota Studies in the Philosophy of Science, vol. 2: Concepts, Theories and the Mind-Body Problem*, Minneapolis: University of Minnesota Press, pp. 370–497.

Goff, P. (2006). 'Experiences Don't Sum'. *Journal of Consciousness Studies*, 13 (10–11): 53–61.

Goff, P. (2009a). 'Why Panpsychism Doesn't Help Us Explain Consciousness'. *Dialectica*, 63 (3): 289–311.

Goff, P. (2009b). 'Can the Panpsychist Get Round the Combination Problem?' In D. Skrbina (ed.), *Mind That Abides: Panpsychism in the New Millennium.* Amsterdam: John Benjamins.

Goff, P. (2012). 'There Is More Than One Thing'. In P. Goff (ed.), *Spinoza on Monism.* New York: Macmillan, pp. 113–22.

Goff, P. (2013). 'Orthodox Property Dualism + Linguistic Theory of Vagueness = Panpsychism'. In R. Brown (ed.), *Consciousness Inside and Out: Phenomenology, Neuroscience, and the Nature of Experience.* Dordrecht: Springer, pp. 75–91.

Goff, P. (2017a). 'The Phenomenal Bonding Solution to the Combination Problem'. In G. Brüntrup and L. Jaskolla (eds.), *Panpsychism: Contemporary Perspectives.* Oxford: Oxford University Press, pp. 283–304.

Goff, P. (2017b). *Consciousness and Fundamental Reality.* Oxford: Oxford University Press.

Goff, P. (this volume). 'From Russellian Monism to Cosmopsychism'. In W. Seager (ed.), *The Routledge Handbook of Panpsychism.* London: Routledge.

Humphreys, N. (1997). 'How Properties Emerge'. *Philosophy of Science,* 64: 1–17.

Huxley, T. H. (1986). *Lessons in Elementary Physiology.* London: Macmillan (originally published 1866).

James, W. (1890). *The Principles of Psychology.* Cambridge, MA: Harvard University Press.

Jaskolla, L., and Buck, A. (2012). 'Does Panexperiential Holism Solve the Combination Problem?' *Journal of Consciousness Studies,* 19: 190–9.

Levine, J. (1983). 'Materialism and Qualia: The Explanatory Gap'. *Pacific Philosophical Quarterly,* 64: 354–61.

Lewis, D. (1991). *Parts of Classes.* Oxford: Blackwell.

Lewis, D. (1993). 'Many, But Almost One'. In J. Bacon, K. Campbell and L. Reinhardt (eds.), *Ontology, Causality, and Mind: Essays in Honour of D. M. Armstrong.* Cambridge: Cambridge University Press, pp. 23–45.

Loar, B. (1990). 'Phenomenal States'. *Philosophical Perspectives,* 4: 81–108.

Lockwood, M. (1981). 'What Was Russell's Neutral Monism?' *Midwest Studies in Philosophy (The Foundations of Analytic Philosophy),* VI: 143–58.

McQueen, K. (2015). 'Mass Additivity and A Priori Entailment'. *Synthese,* 192 (5): 1373–1392.

Mendelovici, A. (this volume). 'Panpsychism's Combination Problem Is a Problem for Everyone'. In W. Seager (ed.), *The Routledge Handbook of Panpsychism.* London: Routledge.

Mizrahi, V. (2009). 'Is Colour Composition Phenomenal?' In D. Skusevich and P. Matikas (eds.), *Color Perception: Physiology, Processes and Analysis.* Hauppauge: Nova Science Publishers, pp. 185–202.

Mørch, H. H. (2014). *Panpsychism and Causation: A New Argument and a Solution to the Combination Problem.* Doctoral Dissertation, University of Oslo. https://philpapers.org/archive/HASPAC-2.pdf.

Nagel, T. (1979). 'Panpsychism'. In T. Nagel (ed.), *Mortal Questions.* Cambridge: Cambridge University Press, pp 181–195.

Nagel, T. (1986). *The View from Nowhere.* Oxford: Oxford University Press.

Parfit, D. (1984). *Reasons and Persons.* Oxford: Oxford University Press.

Parfit, D. (1999). 'Experiences, Subjects, and, Conceptual Schemes'. *Philosophical Topics,* 26: 217–70.

Plotinus. (1956). *Enneads.* Ed. and Trans. S. MacKenna and B. Page. London: Faber and Faber. Accessed July 2013. http://archive.org/stream/plotinustheennea033190mbp#page/n11/mode/2up.

Roelofs, L. (2014). 'Phenomenal Blending and the Palette Problem'. *Thought,* 3 (1): 59–70.

Roelofs, L. (2016). 'The Unity of Consciousness, Within and Between Subjects'. *Philosophical Studies,* 173 (12): 3199–221.

Roelofs, L. (2017). "Rational Agency without Self-Knowledge: Could 'We' Replace 'I'?" *Dialectica* 71 (1): 3–33.

Roelofs, L. (2019). *Combining Minds.* New York: Oxford University Press.

Rosenberg, G. (1998). 'The Boundary Problem for Phenomenal Individuals'. In S. Hameroff, A. Kaszniak, and A. Scott (eds.), *Toward a Science of Consciousness: The First Tucson Discussions and Debates (Complex Adaptive Systems).* Cambridge, MA: MIT Press, pp. 149–56.

Rosenberg, G. (2004). *A Place for Consciousness: Probing the Deep Structure of the Natural World.* Oxford: Oxford University Press.

Russell, B. (1927). *The Analysis of Matter.* London: Kegan Paul.

Seager, W. (1995). 'Consciousness, Information and Panpsychism'. *Journal of Consciousness Studies,* 2–3: 272–88.

Seager, W. (2006). 'The Intrinsic Nature Argument for Panpsychism'. *Journal of Consciousness Studies,* 13 (10–11): 129–45.

Seager, W. (2010). 'Panpsychism, Aggregation and Combinatorial Infusion'. *Mind and Matter,* 8 (2): 167–84.

Seager, W. (2017). 'Panpsychist Infusion'. In G. Brüntrup and L. Jaskolla (eds.), *Panpsychism: Contemporary Perspectives.* Oxford: Oxford University Press, pp. 229–48.

Sebastián, M. A. (2015). "What panpsychists should reject: on the incompatibility of panpsychism and organizational invariantism." *Philosophical Studies* 172 (7):1833–1846.

Shani, I. (2010). "Mind Stuffed with Red Herrings: Why William James' Critique of the Mind-Stuff Theory Does Not Substantiate a Combination Problem for Panpsychism." *Acta Analytica* 25 (4): 413–434.

Shani, I. (2015). 'Cosmopsychism: A Holistic Approach to the Metaphysics of Experience'. *Philosophical Papers*, 44 (3): 389–437.

Shoemaker, S. (1975). 'Functionalism and Qualia'. *Philosophical Studies*, 27: 291–315.

Shoemaker, S. (1997). 'Parfit on Identity'. In J. Dancy (ed.), *Reading Parfit*. Oxford: Blackwell, pp. 135–48.

Sider, T. (2007). 'Parthood'. *Philosophical Review*, 116: 51–91.

Smart, J. J. C. (1959). 'Sensations and Brain Processes'. *The Philosophical Review*, 68 (2): 141–56.

Stoljar, D. (2014). 'Four Kinds of Russellian Monism'. In U. Kriegel (ed.), *Current Controversies in Philosophy of Mind*. London: Routledge, pp. 17–39.

Stoljar, D. (this volume). 'Panpsychism and Nonstandard Materialism: Some Comparative Remarks'. In W. Seager (ed.), *The Routledge Handbook of Panpsychism*. London: Routledge.

Strawson, G. (2006). 'Realistic Monism: Why Physicalism Entails Panpsychism'. In A. Freeman (ed.), *Consciousness and Its Place in Nature*. Exeter: Imprint Academic, pp. 3–31.

Van Cleve, J. (1990). "Mind-Dust or Magic? Panpsychism versus Emergence." *Philosophical Perspectives* 4: 215–226.

Wilson, J. (2016). 'Metaphysical Emergence: Weak and Strong'. In T. Bigaj and C. Wüthrich (eds.), *Metaphysics in Contemporary Physics* (Poznan Studies in the Philosophy of the Sciences and the Humanities). Leiden: Brill Rodopi, pp. 251–306.

Wong, H. Y. (2006). "Emergents from Fusion." *Philosophy of Science*, 73: 345–367.

22

PANPSYCHISM VERSUS PANTHEISM, POLYTHEISM, AND COSMOPSYCHISM

Yujin Nagasawa

1. Introduction

Philosophers of mind have long debated the relationship between the mind and the body. Philosophers of religion have long debated the relationship between God and the cosmos. On the face of it, there is no link between these debates in two distinct areas of philosophy. However, at a certain level they are structurally parallel and the contrast between them can be useful for making philosophical progress.[1] In this chapter, I discuss and utilise these parallel debates by reference to four views: panpsychism and cosmopsychism in the philosophy of mind, and polytheism and pantheism in the philosophy of religion.

Panpsychism says that phenomenality is everywhere. Pantheism says that divinity is everywhere. These views appear parallel initially and that is why they are often contrasted or conflated. I argue, however, that panpsychism is not exactly parallel to pantheism. We cannot derive pantheism merely by replacing phenomenality in panpsychism with divinity in pantheism. I argue that what we can derive by replacing phenomenality with divinity is (an extreme form of) polytheism. I argue that if, on the other hand, we replace divinity with phenomenality in pantheism we can derive cosmopsychism. I analyse the relationships between these four views in detail. I argue based on the analysis that we can develop a new way of undercutting the combination problem, which is widely considered the greatest challenge for panpsychism.

2. Relationships Between Pantheism, Panpsychism, Polytheism and Cosmopsychism

Exactly how panpsychism should be defined is disputed. Some define it as a version of physicalism while others define it as a version of dualism or nonphysicalist monism such as Russellian monism. Yet others define it as a form of idealism.[2] I will not attempt to develop a precise definition of panpsychism or specify necessary and sufficient conditions for it in this chapter. It does not make much difference here which form of panpsychism is correct because our discussion applies equally to most versions of panpsychism. We can start our discussion with the following broad formulation of panpsychism:

Panpsychism: Phenomenality is everywhere throughout the cosmos.

Classical panpsychists hold the radical view that mentality in general, which includes a broad range of items such as thought, cognition, emotion and consciousness, is everywhere throughout the cosmos. Yet many contemporary panpsychists hold a more modest thesis that *phenomenal properties* are everywhere throughout the cosmos. For our purposes in this chapter it suffices to adopt the preceding formulation in terms of phenomenality rather than mentality in general.

Panpsychism is often compared or conflated with pantheism, which can be formulated as follows:

Pantheism: Divinity is everywhere throughout the cosmos.

One might wonder exactly what 'divinity' means here. I do not address this question in detail in this chapter as it is a major question which philosophers of religion and theologians have disputed for centuries. It suffices for our purposes to assume somewhat imprecisely that something is divine if it is considered God or a god (but not another being – such as an angel – or the result of an act of God or a god).

The term 'panpsychism' originates from 'panpsychia', which the sixteenth-century Italian philosopher Francesco Patrizi applied to his view that God's phenomenality is present throughout the cosmos. Hence, the first view that was labelled 'panpsychism' seems to be a version of pantheism. This is understandable given how similar panpsychism and pantheism initially appear. In Greek 'pan' means 'all', 'psyche' means 'soul' or 'mind', and 'theos' means 'God'. Hence, panpsychism is the view that all is mind while pantheism is the view that all is God. If we replace 'psyche' with 'theo' in 'panpsychism' we obtain 'pantheism'. Conversely, if we replace 'theo' with 'psych' in 'pantheism' we obtain 'panpsychism'.

The relationship between panpsychism and pantheism has not been carefully discussed in the literature but, as we have seen, it is commonly assumed that panpsychism and pantheism are at least structurally parallel. I argue, however, that this is not correct. In what follows, I try to establish the following six relevant theses:

(i) Panpsychism is not parallel to pantheism.
(ii) Panpsychism is parallel to polytheism.
(iii) Pantheism is parallel to cosmopsychism.
(iv) Cosmopsychism is not parallel to polytheism.
(v) Pantheism entails cosmopsychism but not vice versa.
(vi) Polytheism entails panpsychism but not vice versa.

The relationships between these six theses are illustrated in Figure 22.1.

(i) Panpsychism is not Parallel to Pantheism

Again, panpsychism and pantheism are often thought to be parallel because panpsychism says that phenomenality is everywhere and pantheism says that divinity is everywhere. I submit, however, that they are radically distinct metaphysical views because the reason that panpsychism says that phenomenality is everywhere is fundamentally different from the reason that pantheism says that divinity is everywhere. Panpsychism says that phenomenality is everywhere throughout the cosmos because *everything in the cosmos* is phenomenal. On the other hand, pantheism says that divinity is everywhere throughout the cosmos because *the cosmos as a whole* is divine. In other words, while the focus of panpsychism is on individual things in the cosmos the focus of pantheism is on the cosmos as an entity in its own right. Panpsychism says that phenomenality is immanent and pantheism says that divinity is immanent but they reach these conclusions from different directions – indeed from the exact opposite directions.

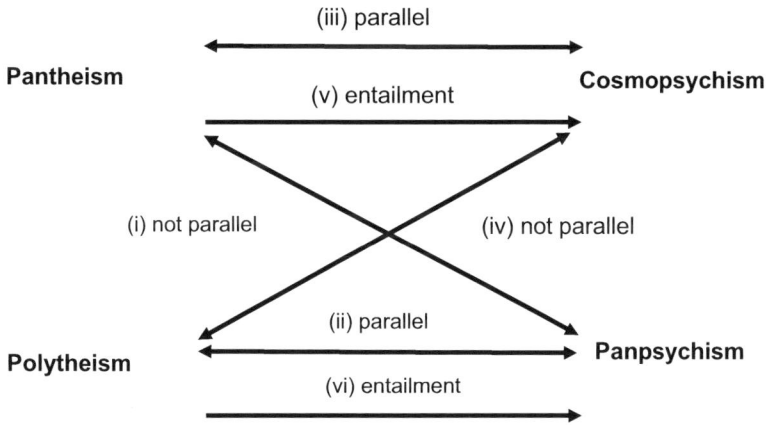

Figure 22.1   Relationships between panpsychism, pantheism, polytheism and cosmopsychism

(ii) Panpsychism Is Parallel to Polytheism

If pantheism is not parallel to panpsychism, which view of divinity is parallel to panpsychism? Again, panpsychism says that phenomenality is everywhere throughout the cosmos because *everything in the cosmos* is phenomenal. This means that a parallel view of divinity would hold the following: Divinity is everywhere throughout the cosmos because *everything in the cosmos* is divine. This is an extreme form of polytheism.

Polytheism is the view that there is more than one god. This means that polytheism negates the following two views: (a) atheism, according to which the number of gods is exactly zero; and (b) monotheism, according to which the number of gods is exactly one. Polytheism says that the number of gods is two or more. Monotheism is accepted in such Abrahamic traditions as Christianity, Islam and Judaism, while polytheism is accepted in such Eastern traditions as Hinduism and Shinto. Polytheism in principle subsumes infinitely many views because it covers all views that hold that the number of God/gods is anything between two and infinity. The form of polytheism that we address here is an extreme one which says that everything in the cosmos is divine. If there are infinitely many things in the cosmos, according to this view, there are infinitely many gods. This extreme form of polytheism is structurally parallel to panpsychism. It holds that everything is divine in the same way as panpsychism holds that everything is phenomenal.

There can be more nuanced forms of panpsychism. For example, some panpsychists might narrow their focus and hold that only individual things in the cosmos that have specific properties are phenomenal rather than that absolutely everything in the cosmos is phenomenal. This, however, does not undermine my claim that panpsychism and pantheism are structurally parallel because we can narrow (or widen) the scope of polytheism in the same way that we can narrow (or widen) the scope of panpsychism. For example, pantheists can hold the parallel thesis that only individual things in the cosmos that have specific properties are divine rather than that absolutely everything in the cosmos is divine. Having said that, in what follows, for the sake of simplicity, by the term 'polytheism' I refer to the extreme form of polytheism according to which everything in the cosmos is divine.

(iii) Pantheism Is Parallel to Cosmopsychism

We have seen that panpsychism is not parallel to pantheism despite the apparent similarity. Which view of phenomenality then is parallel to pantheism? I submit that it is cosmopsychism. Pantheism says that divinity is everywhere throughout the cosmos because the cosmos as a whole is divine. We can obtain cosmopsychism by replacing divinity in this thesis with phenomenality: phenomenality is everywhere throughout the cosmos because the cosmos as a whole is phenomenal. These two theses are clearly parallel. Among the four views that we address in this chapter, cosmopsychism is probably the one that is least discussed in philosophy.

It is important to grasp what cosmopsychism is *not* because many views may seem similar to cosmopsychism. First, cosmopsychism is distinct from the 'Gaia hypothesis', which regards the Earth as a single organic living system (Lovelock 1979). While the focus of the Gaia hypothesis is on a specific planet, the Earth, the focus of cosmopsychism is on the cosmos as a whole. Moreover, while the Gaia hypothesis is formulated in terms of life, cosmopsychism is formulated in terms of consciousness. Cosmopsychism is also distinct from Richard Maruce Bucke's theory of 'cosmic consciousness' (Bucke 1901). Bucke maintains that cosmic consciousness is a form of consciousness which is higher than the consciousness of ordinary people but appears in some specific people of 'good intellect', such as Buddha and Christ. Contrary to cosmopsychists, Bucke does not attribute cosmic consciousness to the cosmos as a whole. Perhaps Bucke's view is comparable to John Hick's thesis of the Real, which I address ahead. Cosmopsychism is also distinct from Émile Durkheim's view of 'collective consciousness' (Durkheim 1893/1997). Collective consciousness is, according to Durkheim, a set of shared beliefs and sentiments that are common to people in a given society. Collective consciousness is broader than ordinary consciousness in its scope but it is not attributed to the cosmos as a whole. Perhaps cosmopsychism is most closely related to the theory of *anima mundi*, or the 'world soul', discussed in ancient Greek philosophy. In *Timaeus* 30b, Plato considers the world as a 'living Creature endowed with soul and reason owing to the providence of God'. A version of cosmopsychism we discuss in this chapter is formulated in terms of consciousness rather than soul and reason, but the attribution of mentality to the world as a whole in the theory of *anima mundi* is analogous to the attribution of phenomenality to the cosmos in cosmopsychism.

(iv) Cosmopsychism Is Not Parallel to Polytheism

I argued previously that panpsychism is not parallel to pantheism because while the focus of panpsychism is on individual things in the cosmos the focus of pantheism is on the cosmos as a whole. Similarly, cosmopsychism is not parallel to polytheism because while the focus of cosmopsychism is on the cosmos as a whole the focus of polytheism is on individual things in the cosmos.

(v) Pantheism Entails Cosmopsychism but not Vice Versa

Again, pantheism holds that divinity is everywhere throughout the cosmos because the cosmos as a whole is divine. Assuming that God has mental states with phenomenal properties, or, more simply put, assuming that divinity entails phenomenality, pantheism entails the cosmopsychist thesis that the cosmos as a whole is phenomenal. It makes sense in this respect that Patrizi calls his pantheistic view panpsychism. This does not necessarily, however, mean that pantheism entails all versions of cosmopsychism because there can be a disagreement about the nature of the phenomenality in question. Pantheism is a form of theism, so pantheists are likely to identify the phenomenality of the cosmos with the phenomenality of God.[3] That is, they are likely to hold that the phenomenality in question corresponds to the consciousness or phenomenal states of the higher self. Yet some cosmopsychists might reject the existence of a higher self and postulate the phenomenality of the cosmos as a whole without assuming the self as its bearer. For example, some cosmopsychists might choose to attribute to the cosmos as a whole what Gregg Rosenberg calls 'protoconsciousness', which does not require a specific cognitive bearer, instead of full-blown consciousness, which does require it. According to Rosenberg, properties of protoconsciousness are, contrary to what Chalmers calls 'protophenomenal properties', themselves phenomenal. Rosenberg remarks, "In contrast with protophenomenal properties, the properties of protoconsciousness are phenomenal properties properly considered phenomenal, but they do not require an associated cognitive engine to be experienced" (Rosenberg 2004: 97). That is, according to Rosenberg, while properties of protoconsciousness are phenomenal on their own, they are not cognised by any subject. Having said that, we can set aside these details because they do not affect my overall argument.

It should be noted that while pantheism entails cosmopsychism, cosmopsychism does not seem to entail pantheism. Even if, as cosmopsychism says, the cosmos as a whole is phenomenal it does not immediately follow from the pantheistic thesis that the cosmos as a whole is divine (unless there is a valid reason to think that the cosmos cannot be phenomenal without also being divine). It seems possible that the phenomenality in question is not divine.

(vi) Polytheism Entails Panpsychism but not Vice Versa

To the extent that pantheism entails cosmopsychism, polytheism entails panpsychism. Polytheism says that divinity is everywhere throughout the cosmos because everything in the cosmos is divine. Assuming that gods have mental states with phenomenal properties, or, more simply put, assuming that divinity entails phenomenality, polytheism entails the panpsychist thesis that everything in the cosmos is phenomenal. This does not, however, necessarily mean that polytheism entails all versions of panpsychism because there can be a disagreement about what the phenomenality in question is. Polytheism is a form of theism so polytheists are likely to identify the phenomenality of individual things in the cosmos with the phenomenality of gods. That is, they are likely to hold that the phenomenality in question corresponds to the consciousness or phenomenal states of selves. Yet some panpsychists might reject the existence of selves in everything and postulate the phenomenality of individual things in the cosmos without assuming selves as its bearers. For example, some panpsychists might choose to attribute to individual things in the cosmos the aforementioned protoconsciousness instead of full-blown consciousness. Having said that, we can once again set aside these details because they do not affect my overall argument.

It should be noted that while polytheism entails panpsychism, panpsychism does not seem to entail polytheism. (This is comparable to the fact that cosmopsychism does not seem to entail pantheism.) Even if, as panpsychism says, everything in the cosmos is phenomenal it does not immediately follow from the polytheistic thesis that everything in the cosmos is divine (unless there is a valid reason to think that individual things in the cosmos cannot be phenomenal without also being divine). It seems possible that the phenomenality in question is not divine.

3. Are Pantheism and Polytheism Compatible?

Let us set aside the philosophy of mind for a moment and focus on the relationship between the two views in the philosophy of religion: pantheism and polytheism.

Again, pantheism says that divinity is everywhere throughout the cosmos because the cosmos as a whole is divine, and polytheism says that divinity is everywhere throughout the cosmos because everything in the cosmos is divine. These two views seem completely distinct. While the focus of pantheism is on the cosmos as a whole the focus of polytheism is on individual things in the cosmos. Moreover, these two views appear to be incompatible. Pantheism is normally construed as a form of monotheism as it postulates the cosmos as a sole God. Polytheism, on the other hand, postulates more than one god, possibly infinitely many gods. It seems, therefore, that we cannot hold pantheism and polytheism simultaneously.

One might attempt to show that they are actually compatible. For example, one might purport to derive the pantheist thesis that the cosmos as a whole is divine from the polytheist thesis that everything in the cosmos is divine. Such a derivation, however, seems to commit the fallacy of composition. It seems to assume erroneously that we can always derive something that is true of the whole from something that is true of its parts. (Parallel example: It is fallacious to derive that the cosmos as a whole is small from the fact that parts of the cosmos are small.) Similarly, one might attempt to derive the polytheist thesis that everything in the cosmos is divine from the pantheist thesis that the cosmos as a whole is divine. Such a derivation, however, seems to commit a fallacy of decomposition. It seems to assume erroneously that we can always derive something that is true of parts from something that is true of the whole. (Parallel example: it is fallacious to derive that parts of the cosmos are massive from the fact that the cosmos as a whole is massive.) With my philosopher-of-religion hat on, I am interested in discovering if there is a way to show that pantheism and polytheism are compatible.

John Hick's (2004) strategy for defending religious pluralism can be construed as an attempt to resolve the apparent incompatibility between pantheism (or monotheism more generally) and polytheism. Hick tries to resolve the apparent incompatibility by appealing to the notion of the 'Real', transcendental reality. He distinguishes 'the Real in itself' and 'the Real as humanly experienced' (or manifested within the intellectual and phenomenal purview of a certain tradition). Hick says that the Real in itself is 'transcategorial' or ineffable. That is, our limited human language and thought cannot grasp its true nature. Therefore, for example, number does not apply to the Real. Yet people from divergent religious or cultural traditions perceive the Real differently due to human limitations; people in a monotheistic tradition see the Real as a single divine being and call it God while people in a polytheistic tradition see it as many divine beings and call them gods. This does not mean that polytheism and monotheism (like pantheism) are fundamentally incompatible; their incompatibility is merely epistemic, not ontological.

I propose a new strategy to establish the compatibility between pantheism and polytheism. This strategy is distinct from Hick's strategy because, unlike Hick's, it is purely ontological. I mentioned earlier the claim that it is fallacious to derive properties of the whole from properties of its individual parts and to derive properties of individual parts from properties of the whole. But such derivations are not *always* fallacious. Suppose, for example, that there is a car that consists solely of parts that are thoroughly red. It is then right to infer that the car as a whole is thoroughly red. Suppose, to take another example, that there is a car that is thoroughly red. It is then right to infer that every individual part of the car is thoroughly red. These inferences about the car and its parts are valid and do not commit the fallacies of composition or decomposition because we have added a premise in each case – that a car consists solely of parts that are thoroughly red in the first case and that a car is thoroughly red in the second case. Similarly, we can show that polytheism can entail pantheism or that pantheism can entail polytheism by introducing extra assumptions. In this way, we can avoid the fallacy of composition and the fallacy of decomposition. Again, pantheism says that the cosmos as a whole is divine and polytheism says that everything in the cosmos is divine. In order to show that polytheism and pantheism are compatible, we can add an extra assumption that the cosmos as a whole is divine *in virtue of everything in the cosmos being divine*. Here, the divinity of individual things in the cosmos is considered ontologically prior to the divinity of the cosmos as a whole. Let us call this approach the 'bottom–up approach' because it starts with the divinity of individual things in the cosmos and we derive the divinity of the cosmos as a whole from it. There can also be a 'top–down approach': In order to show that pantheism and polytheism are compatible, we can add an extra assumption that everything in the cosmos is divine *in virtue of the cosmos as a whole being divine*. Here, the divinity of the cosmos as a whole is considered ontologically prior to the divinity of individual things in the cosmos.

I do not have space to discuss whether either of the approaches ultimately succeeds. Nevertheless, they hint at a novel way of tackling an intractable problem in the philosophy of mind, which initially appears irrelevant to these approaches. The problem in question is the combination problem, which is widely considered the greatest challenge for panpsychism. I introduce the combination problem in the next section, and explain in section 5 how we can utilise the previous observation of the apparent incompatibility between pantheism and polytheism to undercut the combination problem.

4. The Combination Problem

The main reason for holding panpsychism is that it avoids the problem of strong emergence, which physicalism faces. This problem arises from the 'unexpectedness' of phenomenal properties: phenomenal properties are instantiated by physical things in the cosmos such as aggregates of neurons. This is unexpected and surprising because neurons seem to be fundamentally non-phenomenal. It seems impossible to explain how something that is phenomenal can be instantiated by an aggregate of something that is fundamentally non-phenomenal. Galen Strawson claims that the instantiation of phenomenal properties by wholly non-phenomenal properties is as implausible as the instantiation of spatial properties by wholly non-spatial properties (Strawson 2008: 64–5).

Panpsychism avoids the problem of strong emergence by postulating that all physical things in the cosmos, or at least physical ultimates, are themselves phenomenal. That is, according to panpsychism, it is not surprising that phenomenal properties are instantiated by aggregates of neurons because physical ultimates, which constitute neurons and other relevant physical entities, are already phenomenal. That is, phenomenal properties of physical ultimates are fundamental phenomenal building blocks. According to panpsychism, therefore, 'smaller' phenomenal properties realised by physical ultimates are more fundamental than 'larger' phenomenal properties realised by the brain. (I use the terms 'larger' and 'smaller' metaphorically here.) Panpsychism is comparable to the aforementioned bottom-up approach for deriving pantheism from panpsychism. Panpsychism says that, because physical ultimates are phenomenal, certain larger objects constituted by them, such as an aggregate of neurons, if not the cosmos as a whole, are also phenomenal.

Panpsychism may succeed in responding to the problem of strong emergence but it pays a price. That is, it faces a difficult problem of its own: the combination problem. The combination problem arises from the apparent discrepancy between, on the one hand, a highly complex, structured aggregate of neurons and, on the other hand, a smooth, uniform phenomenal experience such as a visual experience. The problem can be formulated as the following objection to panpsychism: ordinary phenomenal experiences realised by the brain present themselves as smooth, continuous, and unified. They do have distinct aspects but they have an underlying homogeneity. According to panpsychism, however, all neurons instantiate phenomenal properties and our ordinary phenomenal experiences result from combinations of these properties. It is hard to see, however, how 'smaller' phenomenal properties of neurons could add up to manifest the homogeneous character of 'larger' phenomenal properties instantiated by the brain.[4]

The combination problem is widely recognised as the most intractable problem for panpsychism. David Chalmers, for example, contends that it "is certainly the hardest problem for any sort of Russellian view [which includes a version of panpsychism]" (1996: 307). William Seager regards it as "the most difficult problem facing any panpsychist theory of consciousness" (Seager 1995: 280). In the next section, I argue that the combination problem can be avoided by replacing panpsychism with cosmopsychism.

5. Cosmopsychism as a Way of Undercutting the Combination Problem

The combination problem arises because panpsychism is a bottom-up view. It regards 'smaller' phenomenal properties instantiated by physical ultimates to be ontologically prior to 'larger' phenomenal properties instantiated by the brain. The smoothness, uniformity and homogeneity of the 'larger' phenomenal properties are lost on the panpsychist assumption that they are aggregates of 'smaller' consciousnesses instantiated by physical ultimates.

The combination problem does not arise, however, if we adopt cosmopsychism because it is a top-down view. Recall the top-down approach to deriving polytheism from pantheism discussed earlier. According to this approach, we can derive the divinity of individual things in the cosmos from the divinity of the cosmos as a whole by holding that the divinity of the cosmos as a whole is ontologically prior to the divinity of individual things in the cosmos. Similarly, we can adopt cosmopsychism and contend that the phenomenality of the cosmos as a whole entails the phenomenality of individual things in the cosmos by holding that the phenomenality of the cosmos as a whole is ontologically prior to the phenomenality of individual things in the cosmos.[5] In the bottom-up approach of panpsychism, the 'smaller' consciousnesses are the more fundamental they are. The consciousnesses of physical ultimates are the 'smallest' and most fundamental, and any 'larger' consciousnesses are compositions of them. In the top-down approach of cosmopsychism, on the other hand, the 'larger' consciousnesses are the more fundamental they are. The consciousness of the cosmos is the 'largest' and most fundamental, and any 'smaller' consciousnesses are derivatives of it.

We can illustrate these points with an analogy. Suppose, *per impossibile*, there is an absolutely perfectly smooth painting, which is analogous to a smooth, homogeneous phenomenal experience instantiated by the brain. Such a painting cannot be an aggregate of small dots, which are analogous to phenomenal properties of physical ultimates. Yet it can well be a segment of a larger painting that is equally smooth and homogeneous, which is analogous to phenomenal properties of the cosmos as a whole. We face the combination problem in the bottom-up approach of panpsychism because we try to derive the 'larger' consciousness instantiated by the brain (an absolutely perfectly smooth painting) from the 'smaller' consciousness of physical ultimates (small dots). But we do not face the same problem if we try to derive the consciousness instantiated by the brain (an absolutely perfectly smooth painting) from the 'larger' consciousness of the cosmos as a whole (a larger painting that is equally perfectly smooth).

One might claim, however, that cosmopsychism still fails to respond to the following problem, which I call the 'derivation problem': How could the consciousnesses of individuals like us be derived from the consciousness of the cosmos as a whole? It is not easy to respond to the derivation problem because we do not know the exact nature of the consciousness of the cosmos. Yet we can speculate about how we might be able to respond to the problem. It is reasonable to assume that the consciousness of the cosmos is somewhat comparable to the consciousnesses of individuals because, after all, it is a form of consciousness. If we can then show that the consciousnesses of individuals can be divided into 'smaller', less fundamental segments, then we have reason to think that the consciousness of the cosmos can also be divided into 'smaller', less fundamental segments. And it seems indeed possible to divide the consciousnesses of individuals into 'smaller' segments.

Consider, for example, a visual experience. A visual experience can be considered a unity which may be segmented into distinguishable colour experiences (e.g., experiences corresponding to red and green hues) or experiences of separable regions in space (e.g., experiences corresponding to the right-hand side and the left-hand side of the visual field). Yet the whole visual experience is considered a unity which is ontologically prior to the segments. Perhaps the consciousness of the cosmos relates itself to 'smaller' consciousnesses, such as consciousnesses instantiated by the brain, in a comparable way. The consciousness of the cosmos is ontologically prior to the consciousnesses of individuals, so it is not the case that the consciousnesses of individuals are building blocks of the consciousness of the cosmos. On the contrary, smooth, continuous and unified consciousnesses of individuals are derived or segmented from the smooth, continuous and unified consciousness of the cosmos. Hence, it seems reasonable to think that cosmopsychism can answer the derivation problem.[6]

Cosmopsychism would not be attractive if it entailed that we have to give up the virtues of panpsychism. As mentioned earlier, the main virtue of panpsychism is that it provides a successful answer to the problem of strong emergence confronting physicalism. Again, the problem is concerned with the difficulty, if not the impossibility, of explaining how phenomenal properties can be instantiated by aggregates of neurons, which are fundamentally non-phenomenal. The problem arises for physicalism because physicalism adopts the bottom-up approach and holds that things on the fundamental, bottom level are physical, that is, non-phenomenal. While panpsychism adopts the bottom-up approach too, it avoids the problem by holding that things on the fundamental, bottom level are phenomenal rather than physical. Panpsychism says that it is not surprising that the brain can instantiate phenomenal properties because neurons, which are ontologically prior to the brain according to the bottom-up approach, are already phenomenal. Cosmopsychism avoids the problem of strong emergence in a unique way. It puts everything upside down and adopts the top-down, rather than bottom-up, approach. It holds that the problem does not arise because things on the fundamental, *top* level are phenomenal. According to cosmopsychism, it is not surprising that the brain can instantiate phenomenal properties because the cosmos as a whole, which is ontologically prior to the brain according to the top-down approach, is already phenomenal. Whether the fundamental level is on the top or bottom of reality, if things on the fundamental level are phenomenal the problem of strong emergence does not arise.

In sum: Physicalism faces the problem of strong emergence. Panpsychism avoids the problem of strong emergence but it faces the combination problem. Cosmopsychism is an attractive alternative because it avoids both the problem of strong emergence and the combination problem.

6. Conclusion

We have compared and discussed the relationships between four views: panpsychism, cosmopsychism, polytheism and cosmopsychism. The relationship between panpsychism and cosmopsychism is comparable to the relationship between polytheism and pantheism. I have argued that polytheism and pantheism can be compatible because there is a way to derive polytheism from pantheism and vice versa. By utilising the top-down approach to derive polytheism from pantheism I have developed a way of avoiding the combination problem. I have argued that we can avoid the combination problem if we endorse cosmopsychism in conjunction with the top-down approach, according to which the consciousness of the cosmos is ontologically prior to the consciousnesses of individuals like us. I have also argued that cosmopsychism does not sacrifice the main virtue of panpsychism; it undermines the problem of strong emergence to the same extent that panpsychism does.[7]

Notes

1. For another attempt to bridge debates in the philosophy of mind and the philosophy of religion by considering their parallel structures see Nagasawa (2008). There I develop new responses to Thomas Nagel's bat argument and Frank Jackson's Mary argument in the philosophy of mind, both of which are directed against physicalism, by contrasting them with arguments against the existence of God in the philosophy of religion.
2. For a variety of formulations of panpsychism see this volume and Brüntrup and Jaskolla (2016).
3. By the claim that pantheism is a form of theism I mean that it postulates the existence of God, whether or not the pantheistic God is radically different from the God according to traditional theism. In characterising the uniqueness of pantheism in comparison with traditional theism, Michael Levine calls pantheism 'nontheistic theism' (Levine 1994: 3).
4. This problem is sometimes called the 'grain problem' or the 'structural mismatch problem'. Some claim that there are several other versions of the combination problem. See Chalmers (2016).
5. Similar points are made or anticipated by Philip Goff (2017), Ludwig Jaskolla and Alexander Buck (2012), Freya Mathews (2011) and Nagasawa and Wager (2016) but the metaphysical grounds of their views differ radically from each other.
6. See Nagasawa and Wager (2016) for a more thorough defence of this idea.
7. I would like to thank Philip Goff, Nino Kadić and Khai Wager for helpful comments on an earlier version of this essay. This publication was made possible through the generous support of a grant from the John Templeton Foundation. I would particularly like to thank Alex Arnold, John Churchill and Michael Murray from the Foundation for their help. The opinions expressed in this publication are those of the author and do not necessarily reflect the views of the Foundation.

References

Brüntrup, Godehard, and Jaskolla, Ludwig (eds.) (2016). *Panpsychism*. New York: Oxford University Press.

Bucke, Richard Maruce (1901). *Cosmic Consciousness: A Study in the Evolution of the Human Mind*. New York: E.P. Dutton and Company.

Chalmers, David (1996). *The Conscious Mind: In Search of a Fundamental Theory*. Oxford: Oxford University Press.

Chalmers, David (2016). 'The Combination Problem for Panpsychism'. In G. Brüntrup and L. Jaskolla (eds.), *Panpsychism*. New York: Oxford University Press, pp. 179–214.

Durkheim, Émile (1893/1997). *The Division of Labour in Society*. Trans. W. D. Hallas. New York: Free Press.

Goff, Philip (2017). *Consciousness and Fundamental Reality*. Oxford: Oxford University Press.

Hick, John (2004). *An Interpretation of Religion: Human Responses to the Transcendent*. Basingstoke: Macmillan.

Jaskolla, Ludwig J., and Buck, Alexander J. (2012). 'Does Panexperiential Holism Solve the Combination Problem?' *Journal of Consciousness Studies*, 19: 190–9.

Levine, Michael (1994). *Pantheism*. London: Routledge.

Lovelock, James (1979). *Gaia: A New Look at Life on Earth*. Oxford: Oxford University Press.

Mathews, Freya (2011). 'Panpsychism as Paradigm'. In M. Blamauer (ed.), *The Mental as Fundamental*. Frankfurt: Ontos, pp. 141–55.

Nagasawa, Yujin (2008). *God and Phenomenal Consciousness: A Novel Approach to Knowledge Arguments*. Cambridge: Cambridge University Press.

Nagasawa, Yujin, and Wager, Khai (2016). 'Priority Cosmopsychism'. In G. Brüntrup and L. Jaskolla (eds.), *Panpsychism*. New York: Oxford University Press, pp. 113–29.

Rosenberg, Gregg (2004). *A Place for Consciousness*. New York: Oxford University Press.

Seager, William (1995). 'Consciousness, Information and Panpsychism'. *Journal of Consciousness Studies*, 2–3: 272–88.

Strawson, Galen (2008). *Real Materialism and Other Essays*. Oxford: Oxford University Press.

23

THE ARGUMENT FOR PANPSYCHISM FROM EXPERIENCE OF CAUSATION

Hedda Hassel Mørch

1. Introduction

Panpsychism is the view that all things are associated with some form of consciousness or phenomenal experience. In recent literature, panpsychism has been defended by appeal to two main arguments: first, an argument from philosophy of mind, according to which panpsychism is the only view which successfully integrates consciousness into the physical world (Strawson 2006; Chalmers 2013); second, an argument from categorical properties, according to which panpsychism offers the only positive account of the categorical or intrinsic nature of physical reality (Seager 2006; Adams 2007; Alter and Nagasawa 2012).[1]

Historically, however, panpsychism has also been defended by appeal to a third argument based on considerations about the nature and observability of causation. This argument has not been much discussed in recent times. Here is a concise version from William James:

> The concrete perceptual flux, taken just as it comes, offers in our own activity-situations perfectly comprehensible instances of causal agency . . . If we took these experiences as the type of what actual causation is, we should have to ascribe to cases of causation outside of our life, to physical cases also, an inwardly experiential nature. In other words, we should have to espouse a so-called "pan-psychic" philosophy.
>
> (James 1911: 218)

James here suggests that we have direct experience of causation in our own agency. He thereby directly contradicts David Hume, who famously denied that we have any experience of causation. James goes on to claim that if this experience is representative of causation in general, it follows that all causation is mental, and that panpsychism is true.

This kind of argument for panpsychism can be called the argument from (experience of) causation. This chapter offers, first, a history of this argument and arguments closely related to it, and second, an analysis of the argument – is it valid, are its premises in any way defensible, and how does it relate to the other, more popular arguments for panpsychism from philosophy of mind and categorical properties?

2. Historical Proponents of the Argument

2.1. Leibniz

G. W. Leibniz held that reality ultimately consists of mind-like substances called monads. Among his arguments for this view is the argument from causation:[2]

> The clearest idea of active power comes to us from the mind. So active power occurs only in things which are analogous to minds, that is, in entelechies; for strictly matter exhibits only passive power.
>
> (Leibniz 1704/1981: 171)

> I found then that [the nature of all substances] consists in force, and that from this there follows something analogous to sensation and appetite, so that we must conceive them on the model of the notion we have of souls.
>
> (Leibniz 1695/1989: 139)

Active power, for Leibniz, is the power to affect other substances, while passive power is the power to be affected. He holds that active power must belong to all substances, because, echoing Plato's Eleatic Stranger, "what does not act does not exist" (1691/1965: 470).[3] He finds it self-evident that we experience active power in our own thinking and willing. To the suggestion that this might be denied, he responds that "nothing in the world appears to be more contrary to reason" (Leibniz 1698/1908: 126). He thinks we should not posit non-mental active power in other substances because we do not have as clear an idea (perhaps no idea at all) of non-mental power. He also adheres to the principle that nature does not make leaps, i.e., is everywhere continuous. We know from our own case that mental powers exist, but not that non-mental powers do, and there would be a discontinuity between mental and non-mental powers; therefore, he holds, we should not posit non-mental powers.

2.2. Schopenhauer

Arthur Schopenhauer held a dual-aspect panpsychist view, according to which from the outside, the world appears as representation (*Vorstellung*), but from the inside, it appears as will (*Wille*).[4] The will is both mental and causal in nature. Like Leibniz, Schopenhauer holds that all things must have causal powers or be animated by forces. Furthermore, the only way to understand these powers or forces is by analogy with our own power to act. Specifically, Schopenhauer argues, all causation must be driven by a kind of motivation:

> Only from a comparison with what goes on within me when my body performs an action from a motive that moves me, with what is the inner nature of my own changes determined by external grounds or reasons, can I obtain an insight into the way in which those inanimate bodies change under the influence of causes, and thus understand what is their inner nature.
>
> (Schopenhauer 1859/1966a: 125)

> from the law of motivation I must learn to understand the law of causality in its inner significance. Spinoza (*Epist.* 62) says that if a stone projected through the air had consciousness, it would imagine it was flying of its own will. I add merely that the stone would be right.
>
> (Schopenhauer 1859/1966a: 126)

2.3. James

William James was committed to panpsychism throughout large parts of his career. As we saw previously, James claims that if we experience causation in agency, then panpsychism may follow. In other work, he explicitly endorses that we really have such as experience:

> the recesses of feeling, the darker, blinder strata of character, are the only places in the world in which we catch real fact in the making, and directly perceive how events happen, and how work is actually done.
>
> (James 1902/1987: 448–9)

He continues:

> Hume's criticism has banished causation from the world of physical objects, and "Science" is absolutely satisfied to define cause in terms of concomitant change. . . . The "original" of the notion of causation is in our inner personal experience, and only there can causes in the old-fashioned sense be directly observed and described.
>
> (James 1902/1987: 449, footnote 1)

In this passage, James explicitly points to the experience of agency as a response to Hume's famous query as to whether we have any impression (or experience) that matches our commonsense idea (or concept) of causal power. In later work, we find an elaborate discussion how this idea leads into the "region of panpsychic . . . speculation" (1912: 189).

2.4. Whitehead, Hartshorne and Others

A. N. Whitehead developed a distinctive process-ontological version of panpsychism, according to which the fundamental components of reality are "occasions", i.e., events or instantiations, of experience. He argues that:

> in so far as we apply notions of causation to the understanding of events in nature, we must conceive these events under the general notions which apply to occasions of experience. For we can only understand causation in terms of our observations of these occasions.
>
> (Whitehead 1933/1967: 184).

Unlike other proponents of the argument, Whitehead does not focus on volition or motivation as the basis of our experience of causation, but rather on the relation between memories and perceptions and the events remembered or perceived. In this, he is followed by Charles Hartshorne, a subsequent process philosopher:

> Psychicalism [i.e., panpsychism] has the signal advantage, hinted at by Francis Bacon,[5] that it can construe causal connectedness of events in terms of generalized concepts of memory and perception. Materialism and dualism lack these resources and are in Hume's predicament about causality. Memory and perception are effects whose causes are intrinsically given to them. These are our only clues to the intelligible connectedness of events.
>
> (Hartshorne 1977: ch. 3; see also Hartshorne 1954, 1973)

Other philosophers who have endorsed versions of the argument from causation include James Ward (1915: 172–173), G. F. Stout (1931, 1935) and Friedrich Schiller (1906, 1907). These philosophers mainly base their arguments on volition or motivation.

A similar argument for a weaker conclusion can be found with Isaac Newton. Newton often engaged in metaphysical speculation about the origin of the laws of motion and gravity and the nature of force. On the one hand, he considered whether they might originate directly from God. But he also considered whether laws and forces could be grounded in the powers we experience as underlying our own motion: "We find in ourselves a power of moving our bodies by our thoughts". From this, he infers: "we cannot say that all nature is not alive" (Newton in a draft of *Opticks*, transcribed in McGuire 1968: 171; see also Gabbey 2002). In other words, from the fact that we seem to experience causation in agency, Newton concludes that panpsychism is *possibly* true.

3. Historical Proponents of the *Reductio*

3.1. Hume

Historically, several philosophers have also put forth a *modus tollens*, or *reductio ad absurdum*, version of the argument – according to which one of the premises must be rejected because the panpsychist conclusion is unacceptable. One example is Hume himself:

> It may be pretended, that the resistance which we meet with in bodies, obliging us frequently to exert our force, and call up all our power, this gives us the idea of force and power. It is this *nisus*, or strong endeavour, of which we are conscious, that is the original impression from which this idea is copied. But . . . we attribute power to a vast number of objects, where we never can suppose this resistance or exertion of force to take place; . . . to inanimate matter, which is not capable of this sentiment. . . . It must, however, be confessed, that the animal *nisus*, which we experience, though it can afford no accurate precise idea of power, enters very much into that vulgar, inaccurate idea, which is formed of it.
>
> (Hume 1748/1999: 139, footnote 13, emphasis original)

Somewhat surprisingly, Hume here admits that we do have an impression to match our idea of causation. Yet, he claims that this impression does not match any *accurate* and *precise* idea. One of Hume's reasons for dismissing the impression is that it would lead to a conflict with the assumption that matter is not capable of sentiment; or in other words, that if the impression were accurate, it would entail panpsychism. He thereby affirms the validity of the argument from causation but opts to reject the premise that things have (knowable) causal powers rather than accepting the conclusion.[6]

This shows that, from the very beginning, reductionism about causation was not solely motivated by empiricism, as is often claimed, but also by resistance to panpsychism.

3.2. Reid

Thomas Reid was one of the earliest critics of Hume's view of causation. Reid argues that we know causal powers from the experience of agency, and furthermore, that only conscious beings could have them:

> of the manner in which a cause may exert its active power, we can have no conception, but from consciousness of the manner in which our own active power is exerted.
>
> (Reid 1788: 37)

Every thing we can discover in our own constitution leads us to think, that active power cannot be exerted without will and intelligence.

(Reid 1788: 40–1)

One might think this would lead Reid to accept panpsychism, but this he considers primitive and unscientific (1788: 282–3). Instead, he rejects the premise that purely physical, non-conscious things have causal powers. How does he think purely physical things get by without their own causal powers? Reid concludes that they must be governed by the active power of God – another conscious being. In other words, he adopts a form of occasionalism with respect to the inanimate world.

3.3. Newtonians

In the days of Newtonian science, many scientists were dissatisfied with Newton's concept of force. As mentioned, Newton himself understood force in partially metaphysical terms. Many of his readers also engaged in extensive metaphysical speculation about the true nature of force (see Jammer 1957: ch. 8). On the other hand, many scientists came to see the concept as essentially anthropomorphic. They were therefore motivated to pursue a purely relational, mathematical definition of force – effectively endorsing the *reductio* (see Jammer 1957: ch. 11).

3.4. Mach

The scientist and philosopher Ernst Mach played an important role in the development of a relational reduction of force. He held that the concept of causation, which is linked to the metaphysically suggestive, unreduced concept of force, should be eliminated altogether, partly on the basis of its inherent anthropomorphism:[7]

I hope that the science of the future will discard the idea of cause and effect, as being formally obscure, and in my feeling that these ideas contain a strong tincture of fetishism [i.e., animism, panpsychism], I am certainly not alone. The more proper course is, to regard the abstract determinative elements of a fact as interdependent, in a purely logical way, as the mathematician or geometer does. True, by comparison with the will, forces are brought nearer to our feeling; but it may be that ultimately the will itself will be made clearer by comparison with the accelerations of masses.[8]

(Mach 1897: 253–4)

3.5. Collingwood

Another eliminativist about causation is R. G. Collingwood. In his article "On the So-Called Idea of Causation", Collingwood claims:

In the first sense of the word cause, that which is caused is the free and deliberate act of a conscious and responsible agent, and "causing" him to do it means affording him a motive for doing it.

(Collingwood 1937: 86)

This is "historically the original sense [of the word 'cause' . . .] and remains strictly speaking the one and only 'proper' sense" (1937: 85). From this he concludes that Newton, with his distinction between caused (forced) and uncaused (inertial) motions, effectively advocated a "reduction of physics to social psychology" (1937: 105). Accordingly, he recommends that the concept of causation should be outright eliminated.

3.6. Russell

Bertrand Russell, in his "On the Notion of Cause", argues:

> the word "cause" is so inextricably bound up with misleading associations as to make its complete extrusion from the philosophical vocabulary desirable. . . . The law of causality, I believe, like much that passes muster among philosophers, is a relic of a bygone age, surviving, like the monarchy, only because it is erroneously supposed to do no harm.
>
> (Russell 1912: 1)

Part of the reason why the concept of causation is harmful is its connection with agency:

> The importance of these considerations lies partly in the fact that they lead to a more correct account of scientific procedure, partly in the fact that they remove the analogy with human volition which makes the conception of cause such a fruitful source of fallacies.
>
> (Russell 1912: 9)

Russell does not explicitly claim that panpsychism constitutes or is involved in the fallacies in question, but it is a natural interpretation.[9]

4. Recent Proponents of the *Reductio*

The argument from causation has not found many contemporary defenders, but the *reductio* has found quite a few. Since the decline of the anti-metaphysical influence of logical empiricism, non-reductionism about causation has been on the rise. Edward Madden and Peter Hare were early proponents of the revival of non-reductive causal powers metaphysics. They argue that we should reject the view that causation can only be experienced in agency because it leads to panpsychism:

> It is most crucial to avoid what we like to call the "inferential predicament," because getting involved in it forces one inevitably into pan-psychism and animism, an unmitigated disaster in the eyes of a great majority of contemporary philosophers. . . . The inferential predicament arises by taking volitional contexts as the only ones in which causal power is directly perceived, and then projecting such experienced power onto objects and events in order to make sense of causal necessities in the physical world.
>
> (Madden and Hare 1971: 23)

> The best, and perhaps only, way to avoid the inferential predicament and its pan-psychical consequence is to reject the premise that one is directly aware of causal power only in volitional situations.
>
> (Madden and Hare 1971: 25)

They proceed to argue that we are rather directly aware of causal power in the physical world.

David Armstrong is known for developing the view that causation is grounded in irreducible universal laws, as opposed to causal powers. He also endorses a version of the *reductio*, but takes it to indicate only the falsity of dispositionalism, i.e., realism about causal powers, as opposed to realism about irreducible laws:

a disposition as conceived by a Dispositionalist is like a congealed hypothetical fact or state of affairs: 'If this object is suitably struck, then it is caused (or there is a certain objective probability of its being caused) to shatter.' It is, as it were, an inference ticket (as Ryle said), but one that exists in nature (as Ryle would hardly have allowed). That is all there is to a particular disposition. Consider, then, the critical case where the disposition is not manifested. *The object still has within itself, essentially, a reference to the manifestation that did not occur.* It points to a thing that does not exist. This must remind us of the *intentionality* of mental states and processes, the characteristic that Brentano held was the distinguishing mark of the mental, that is, their being directed upon objects or states of affairs that need not exist. This intentionality of the mental undoubtedly exists. But for physicalists such as myself it presents a *prima facie* problem. If the mental has intentionality, and if, as Brentano thought, it is also *ontologically irreducible*, then there is something here that would appear to falsify Physicalism. Physicalists about the mind are therefore found trying to give some ontologically reductive account of the intentionality of the mental. But if irreducible dispositions and powers are admitted for *physical* things, then intentionality, irreducible intentionality, has turned up in everything there is.

Is this not objectionable? Does it not assimilate the physical to the mental, rather than the other way around?

(Armstrong 1997: 79, emphasis original)

Intentionality is the manner in which thoughts, actions and other mental phenomena can be about or directed toward other things. Armstrong observes that dispositions must also be conceived as directed toward something. Fragility, he says, refers or points to shattering. Similarly, we could think of electrons with the power of charge as referring, pointing, or perhaps aiming, toward repelling other electrons. Armstrong claims that if dispositions and powers are irreducible, they can only be understood as intentional and therefore mental, which he finds unacceptable. He concludes that dispositions and powers must be reducible to laws, which, on his view, have nothing to do with intentionality.

C. B. Martin and Karl Pfeifer consider a similar *reductio* based on the similarities between causation and intentionality. They argue:

the most typical characterizations of intentionality . . . all fail to distinguish intentional mental states from non-intentional dispositional physical states. Accepting any of these current accounts will be to take a quick road to panpsychism!

(Martin and Pfeifer 1986: 531)

After surveying various accounts of intentionality, they assert:

Somewhat ironically, if we were to leave our discussion at this point, someone might interpret it as an argument for panpsychism, in that the characterizations of intentionality that we have discussed apply to anything (mental or physical) that has causal dispositions. For some, this may be a happy result – for us it is a *reductio ad absurdum* and an invitation to look elsewhere for an account of the intentional.

(Martin and Pfeifer 1986: 551)

Martin and Pfeifer only take this as a *reductio* of a certain kind of account of intentionality. They think dispositionalism can be made compatible with physicalism by revising our account of intentionality.

5. An Analysis of the Argument

The argument from causation can be understood as having the following general form:

I. *Non-reductionism:* All physical things have causal powers.
II. *Mental causation:* The only causal powers whose nature we can know, or positively conceive of, are mental.
III. *Non-skeptical realism:* The nature of the causal powers of physical things is knowable, or positively conceivable.

Therefore,

IV. *Panpsychism:* All physical things have mental properties.

This argument seems valid. But are the premises defensible? Let us consider them one by one.

5.1. Premise I: Non-Reductionism

Causal powers can be roughly defined as intrinsic properties in virtue of which causes *produce* or *bring about* their effects, or *make* them happen, and thereby metaphysically *necessitate* them.[10] Note that causal necessitation is defeasible, not absolute: causes only necessitate their effects in the absence of interference from other causes, i.e., *ceteris paribus*.

On Hume's view, there is no such thing as causal powers (at least not as far as we know). On the Humean regularity view of causation, to say that one thing causes another is merely to say that things of the first kind happen to be regularly *followed* by the things of the second kind. Or in other words, causal regularities are metaphysically contingent, not necessary.

According to Premise I of the argument from causation, all physical things have causal powers. There are many different arguments that could support this view, but there is one which is especially relevant for the argument from causation. This is the very basic argument from appearances: causation appears (in our experience) to involve causal powers and we have no good reason to distrust this appearance.

Most reductionists and skeptics about causation, including Hume, agree that causes pre-theoretically appear to necessitate their effects, but take this appearance to be illusory. According to Hume, all appearances of causal power are based on our own habits or subjective expectations that certain kinds of events always go together. Hume supports this via a link between conceivability and possibility. On Hume's view, if we really experience necessary connections between objects or events themselves, i.e., something in virtue of which it would be *impossible* for an effect not to occur given the cause (in the absence of interference), then it should also be *inconceivable* for the effect not to occur given the cause (in the absence of interference). But, Hume argues, we can conceive of any cause with or without any effect, which shows that we experience nothing in virtue of which their connection is necessary.

How can Premise I be defended against this Humean view? Some argue that we really do experience causal powers in the external, physical world (Michotte 1963; Anscombe 1971). But if Premise I is defended on this basis, there is a risk of undermining Premise II, according to which the *only* causal powers we can know, or positively conceive of, are mental.

Another option, that avoids this problem, is to rather defend Premise I on the basis of Premise II. Assuming we really experience our own causal powers in agency, as suggested by many philosophers discussed so far, this would show that some physical things, human beings, have causal powers. It does not follow from this that all physical things have them, as Premise I asserts. But it would be natural to suppose that all causation is of the same general metaphysical kind. It therefore seems arguable that if some causes necessitate their effects in virtue of causal powers, as per Premise II, then all causes do, as per Premise I.

Another way of defending Premise I would be to appeal to additional, more general arguments against the regularity theory. One such argument is that if causation is contingent, it would be great "cosmic coincidence" that the world is regular, which seems highly implausible for various reasons (see, e.g., Armstrong 1983; Strawson 1987). Note, however, that these arguments leave it open whether causes necessitate their effects in virtue of intrinsic causal powers of in virtue of extrinsic governing laws *a la* Armstrong.

5.2. *Premise II:* Mental Causation

Premise II says that the only kinds of causal powers whose nature we can know, or positively conceive of, are mental. This is the most central premise of the argument from causation, and also the most controversial. As noted, Hume takes inconceivability as a criterion of necessity. Taking this as a starting point, there are two available strategies for defending Premise II: (1) to argue that some mental properties, but no non-mental properties, are truly inconceivable without their effects; (2) to argue that Hume's criterion is too strong, and that we should rather adopt another criterion, which only mental properties can meet.

Several proponents of the argument from causation hold that in voluntary action, we experience ourselves as exerting will, and to exert will is to exert power. Several philosophers who would not support the panpsychist conclusion also hold a similar view (Locke 1689/1975: I.XXI.4, Searle 1983; Strawson 1992: ch. 9; Armstrong 1997).

Hume considers this view, but objects that we can easily conceive of willing, intending or trying to do something but where no action follows. This seems correct. In the case of physical action, it seems conceivable that someone tries to move their limbs, but their limbs refuse to move, in the absence of any interference from other causes. The same holds for mental action: for example, it seems conceivable that someone tries to solve a simple math problem, or tries to remember something, but the right solution or memory just fails to come to mind, without any interference. It therefore seems that willing, intending or trying cannot be defended as experiences of causal power via strategy (1); that is, they do not meet the inconceivability criterion.

But they could perhaps be defended by strategy (2); that is, by showing that they meet a weaker criterion. Even if we do not experience a strictly necessary connection between will and action, the experience of will might still seem to give a more direct experience of causal power than the experience of external, physical causation. Many philosophers have noted that our own actions are directly experienced as events that do not just passively happen to us; rather, it feels as though we actively bring them about (Ginet 1997; Bayne and Levy 2006; Horgan 2011). We do not inductively infer that some bodily events are actions caused by us (e.g., walking, raising an arm) while others are not (e.g., stumbling, having one's arm lifted by someone else); rather, it seems we can directly feel the difference.

Some would argue that we can also sometimes non-inferentially detect physical causation, for example, there is a sense in which many mechanical interactions such as collisions just *look* causal (Michotte 1963). Such interactions could clearly conceivably be different, but if the conceivability criterion is relaxed for volition, it should arguably also be relaxed for physical causation. But the case for volition might still be stronger than the case for physical causes. Our ability to detect physical, non-volitional causation seems mostly limited to specific kinds of mechanical cases (such as solid objects colliding). In other contexts, it often goes wrong (for example, concerning action at a distance). It is also not highly reliable within the mechanical context: sequences that are not really causal can easily be set up to look causal. In contrast, our ability to distinguish our own actions from mere happenings seems much more general and reliable (that is to say, we are often wrong about the results of our actions, but not about whether or not we are acting at all), which suggests that we have a more immediate awareness of volitional causation. In further support of this, some empirical research suggests that our phenomenology of effort tends to accurately track our actual, physically measurable energy expenditure (Bayne and Levy 2006). We do not seem to have a similar ability to directly track external, physical energy transfer.

Some philosophers, notably Schopenhauer, hold that we experience causation in motivation. This proposal is different from the proposal just considered. Whereas will or agency can be understood as how agents exert causal power on the world, motives appear to exert causal power on the will or the agent. Motives appear to *make* us (try to) do things. Elsewhere, (Mørch 2014, 2017, 2018, 2019) I have elaborated on this idea and argued that we experience necessary connections between motives such as pain and pleasure and efforts to avoid or pursue them. This is a connection which Hume did not consider and which may have a chance of passing his conceivability requirement, i.e., it might be defensible on the basis of strategy (1). It is hard to conceive of someone experiencing strong pain, but where this does not make them at least try to avoid it[11] – assuming the complete absence of interfering motives to endure the pain.

Other philosophers, including Whitehead and Hartshorne, argue that we experience causal powers via perception and memory. They claim that perceptions and memories present themselves not as causes, but rather as effects of the events they are perceptions and memories of. It is hard to see how this suggestion can be defended via strategy (1), because seems clearly conceivable that perceptions and memories can be non-veridical. Whitehead and Hartshorne rather defend it via a version of strategy (2): they endorse a distinctive indeterministic metaphysics of causation, according to which the inconceivability criterion would not seem to apply (see Hartshorne 1973).

Even if it is granted that we really experience causal powers through our phenomenology of will, agency or motivation (from here I will set the proposal of memory and perception aside), it could be objected that it does not follow that the causal powers we experience are mental. Perhaps our experiences of causal powers can be viewed as analogous to ordinary perception. In perception, we represent properties such as the color and size of an apple by means of mental, perceptual phenomenology. This does not mean that color and size are mental properties of the apple, and that all things with size and colors must have minds. Why should we not regard our phenomenology of will, agency or motivation in the same way; that is, as mental representations of non-mental causal powers?

One response is that the reason we take will and motivation to be mental is not because we represent them by mental phenomenology; rather, it is because will and motivation are mental in and of themselves. Will essentially involves intentionality, which, as noted previously, is widely regarded as a mark of the mental. Motives such as pain and pleasure, on the other hand, seem to affect our will in virtue of how they feel or what they are like for a conscious subject. If there is such a thing as unconscious or unfelt pain or pleasure, it would not affect the will in the same direct way. If this is correct, then the causal powers of will and motives cannot be separated from mentality in the way physical properties can be separated from our mental perceptual representations of them (Mørch 2014, 2018).

Another objection to Premise II is that even if the only causal powers we *experience* are mental properties, we can still *conceive* of non-mental causal powers. As mentioned, Armstrong holds that causal powers, while not reducible to contingent regularities, are fundamentally grounded in irreducible governing laws of nature. Can this give the basis for a non-mental conception of causal powers?

Etymologically, the concept of a law of nature is closely connected to both mental agency and causal powers. The concept of a law of nature was originally a legal metaphor – before the scientific revolution, the only concept of law was the concept of a rule imposed by human or divine agents, who would have the *power* to impose laws. But of course, the etymology of a concept does not necessarily determine its meaning. Armstrong proposes that that laws are to be understood as "relations between universals" (Armstrong 1978, 1983), a notion which does not seem to have any connection with the notion of agent-imposed laws. But one might wonder how Armstrong's view should be more precisely understood. Somewhat surprisingly, in view of his criticism of dispositionalism cited earlier, to clarify his concept of causation Armstrong at one point appeals to the experience of agency as well:

> we have – in certain favourable cases – perception of forces acting on our bodies or our body exerting force on things, and perhaps also introspective awareness of the successful application of the will – direct or non-inferential, awareness of singular . . . causation. In Humean terms, there is an impression from which we derive the idea of causality.
>
> (Armstrong 1997: 216–17)

He then claims that the concept of a law comes from bringing together this experience of causation and our experience of regularity. But if we experience our own will as mental, it is not clear how this could yield a wholly non-mental concept of a law.

Perhaps we can conceive of non-mental powers or laws on the basis of mental powers? One might think that from the concept of a mental power we can abstract away a general, non-mental concept of causal power (or law, but from here I will set the notion of irreducible laws aside). These kinds of causal powers could be posited throughout the physical world.

In response to this, panpsychists may argue that by abstracting away from the mental aspects of power we are left with no *positive* conception of power (Mørch 2014, 2018). It seems that all we can know about non-mental powers on this basis is that they are just like mental powers, but not mental. But if we take away the mental aspect of will and motivation, then arguably not much is left to conceive of: do we have any idea of what non-mental will or non-mental motives would be like, or how they may enforce necessary connections or make things happen? Non-panpsychists must respond either by explicating the positive content of their conception of non-mental power, or by arguing that there is nothing wrong with positing non-mental powers of whose nature we have no positive conception. The latter option may seem more promising. But this option is ruled out by Premise III of the argument from causation, to which we now turn.

5.3. *Premise III:* Non-Skeptical Realism

Premise III says that the nature of the causal powers of physical things is knowable, or positively conceivable. This premise is denied by proponents of skeptical realism about causation, i.e., the view that all physical things have irreducible causal powers, but we are completely ignorant about the nature of these powers. That is to say, all we know (roughly) about causal powers is that they ground necessary connections between causes and effects, but we have no positive grasp of how they do so or what they are otherwise like. Someone who accepts Premises I (all physical things have causal powers) and II (only mental causal powers can be positively conceived of) of the argument from causation could nevertheless avoid panpsychism by adopting skeptical realism about physical causal powers.

How can the panpsychist respond to the skeptical realist? It would be hard to defend the general thesis that if things have causal powers, then their nature must be conceivable by us. There is no clear reason why reality should be limited to what we humans can know and conceive of. Hume and James both (at times) expound meaning empiricism, the view that concepts without positive content derived from concrete experiences are meaningless.[12] Given meaning empiricism, it would be meaningless to assert Premise I, i.e. that all things have causal powers, while denying Premise III, i.e., that we have a positive concept of causal powers from experience. However, meaning empiricism is a highly controversial view, and perhaps something panpsychists especially should be wary of accepting anyway, as it risks undermining a whole host of metaphysical concepts that may be necessary for articulating other aspects of the view.

Yet, if Premise II is already granted, i.e., that some things have mental causal powers whose nature we do know, there is a case to be made for Premise III which does not presuppose meaning empiricism. As we saw earlier, Leibniz invokes a principle of the continuity of nature. Given such a principle, we should not posit non-mental, but otherwise unknown, powers because they would be discontinuous with mental powers. Another helpful principle is the principle of qualitative parsimony: do not posit more fundamental kinds of properties and entities than you need in order to account for your observations. Given this principle, we should not posit two kinds of powers, mental and non-mental, when we can make do with only mental ones to account for our observations (recall, according to Premise II, there are no observations of non-mental powers).

But the best option may be to appeal another, general methodological principle: we should never reject adequate, positive theories *merely* because there are other theories in terms of unknowable, inconceivable properties which cannot be ruled out. For example, we cannot rule out that there is some theory that no human could ever positively grasp that explains gravity much better than general relativity theory. This does not seem like a good reason to reject the theory of general relativity. In the same way, one might argue, panpsychism gives us an adequate, positive theory of causation which should not be rejected in favor of the purely negative theory that there are unknowable powers.

6. Other Arguments for Panpsychism

How does the argument from causation fit with the other, more commonly discussed arguments for panpsychism from philosophy of mind and categorical properties?

The argument from causation seems fully compatible with the argument from philosophy of mind. In philosophy of mind, it has been argued that panpsychism can avoid the main problems of both physicalism and dualism at once (Alter and Nagasawa 2012; Chalmers 2013). The argument from causation can be regarded as further supporting the claim that it avoids the problem of dualism is particular. Dualism's main problem is the problem of mental causation: how can mental properties be causally relevant to the physical? The argument from causation further assures us that panpsychism does not face this problem by providing a more detailed picture of how panpsychist mental causation would work. According to the argument, physical properties can only be causally efficacious in virtue of mental powers, and these mental powers relate to physical relations in a way analogous to how our will and motivation relate to our physical behavior.

The argument from causation may seem less compatible with the argument from categorical properties (Seager 2006; Alter and Nagasawa 2012). This argument can be construed as follows:

I. *Categoricalism*: All physical things have categorical properties.
II. *Mental categoricity*: The only categorical properties whose nature we can know, or positively conceive of, are mental.
III. *Non-skeptical realism:* The nature of the categorical properties of physical things is knowable or positively conceivable.

Therefore,

IV. *Panpsychism*: All physical things have mental properties.

Categorical properties are often understood as the opposite of dispositional properties, such as causal powers. Proponents of the argument from categorical properties often argue that all mental properties are categorical, and if categorical and dispositional properties are indeed opposites, this would rule out that any mental properties, such as motivational or volitional properties, are dispositional, as per the argument from causation.

One way to resolve this conflict would be to deny that all mental properties are categorical, i.e., to claim that motivational or volitional properties are purely dispositional and not categorical, whereas other mental properties (such as sensory phenomenology) are purely categorical. But it might be hard to defend that different kinds of phenomenal properties are that radically metaphysically discontinuous. A better alternative would be to reject the assumption that categorical and dispositional properties are opposite fundamental kinds. Some philosophers (Martin and Heil 1999; Strawson 2008) defend the view that all properties necessarily have both dispositional and categorical aspects, and that categorical and dispositional properties are actually identical. By assuming the identity view, the argument from categorical properties and the argument from causation can be reconciled in a more elegant and plausible way.

Given the identity view, the argument from causation will appear very similar to the argument from categorical properties, and one might worry it would therefore be dialectically superfluous. But the argument has at least one distinct dialectical advantage. Premise 1 of the argument from categorical properties, according to which all physical things have categorical properties, is often defended by appeal to the principle that dispositions need categorical grounds. But this principle is rejected by the aforementioned dispositionalists, according to whom all properties are irreducibly dispositional and do not need categorical grounds (Mumford 2006). It is not clear how panpsychists can defend Premise 1 of the argument from categorical properties against this claim. However, given the argument from causation, no such defense is needed. If the argument is sound, dispositionalism entails panpsychism.

7. Conclusion

The argument from causation is important both for the history of panpsychism and, in its *reductio* version, the history of reductionism about causation. Now might be the right time for its revival. In the current debate, panpsychism can no longer be dismissed as absurd, so the *reductio* in support of reductionism (or the denial of some other aspects of the premises) can be turned on its head in order to further support panpsychism.

As we have seen, the argument can be construed as having a valid form. The premises are all highly controversial, but still defensible. The most controversial premise is the premise that the only kinds of causal powers whose nature we can know, or positively conceive of, are mental. This can be defended by appeal to unique features of our phenomenology of will, agency and motivation. But more work is still needed to fully develop and assess this idea.

The argument makes a distinctive contribution to the debate about panpsychism, especially as a response to the challenge from dispositionalism to the argument from categorical properties. It may also contribute to debates within the metaphysics of causation, where non-reductionism about causal powers is a widespread view, but no clear response is to be found to Hume's challenge of how to positively conceive of their nature. The argument from causation shows that a strong and straightforward response may be found with panpsychism.[13]

Notes

1. Historical defenders of the first type of argument include Leibniz (Monadology §17) and James (1890/1981: 151–2); see also Skrbina (2005) on the arguments from non-emergence and continuity for others. Historical defenders of the second kind of argument include Leibniz (see Pereboom 2015), Schopenhauer (see 1859/1966a: §24; 1859/1966b: ch. XVIII) and Eddington (see Strawson 2006).
2. Leibniz may have been the first philosopher to explicitly put forth the argument from causation. Giordano Bruno and Francis Bacon also connect causation to mentality, but their reasoning is less explicit – see Skrbina (2005).
3. One might be surprised to hear this from Leibniz, who is known for his view that monads cannot be causally influenced by other monads. But Leibniz only denies the existence of *transeunt* or inter-substantial

causation, i.e., causation between distinct monads. *Immanent* or intra-substantial causation, whereby one state of same the monad causes the next, is real and essential to his system.

4. Schopenhauer repeatedly states that the will is not necessarily conscious, which may seem to show that he is at best a panprotopsychist and not a panpsychist. One reason to nevertheless interpret him as a panpsychist is that he does not seem to use the term consciousness (*Bewusstseyn*) to mean *phenomenal* consciousness, but rather to denote a mode of knowledge (see Schopenhauer 1859/1966b: 199).

5. For Bacon's hint, see Skrbina (2005: 83).

6. Many scholars regard Hume as an eliminativist about irreducible causal powers. But some, such as Strawson (1989) regard him as a skeptical realist, i.e., as affirming the (possible) existence of irreducible causal powers but denying that we can form any positive conception of their nature.

7. This is somewhat curious, given that Mach endorsed a type of neutral monism that bordered on panpsychism (he took the neutral substrate to be pure experience). Perhaps it was only the kind of panpsychism that takes causation to be related to agency that he found objectionable.

8. Interestingly, Schopenhauer takes the exact opposite view: "if we refer the concept of force to that of will, we have, in fact, referred something more unknown to something infinitely better known, indeed to the one thing really known to us immediately and completely; and we have very greatly extended our knowledge. If, on the other hand, we subsume the concept of will under that of force, as has been done hitherto, we renounce the only immediate knowledge of the inner nature of the world that we have, since we let it disappear in a concept abstracted from the phenomenon, with which therefore we can never pass beyond the phenomenon" (Schopenhauer 1859/1966a: 111–112).

9. At least at this point of Russell's career. Like Mach, Russell later endorsed neutral monism, a view very close to panpsychism. But the time of the publication of "On the Notion of Cause", he was one of neutral monism's staunchest critics.

10. Given indeterminism, one might say causes necessitate some objective probability of their effects. I will set indeterminism aside here for the sake of simplicity.

11. Note that it might still be conceivable that these tryings or efforts do not lead to successful avoidance, as per Hume's objections discussed previously. In other words, the claim is that there is a necessary connection between motives (such as pain) and efforts (such as effort towards avoidance) understood as mental events, not between motives and successful physical actions.

12. As Hume claims: "If we have really no idea of a power or efficacy in any object, or of any real connexion betwixt causes and effects, it will be to little purpose to prove, that an efficacy is necessary in all operations. We do not understand our own meaning in talking so" (Hume 1739–40/2000). This is echoed by James:

> Everything real must be experienceable somewhere, and every kind of thing experienced must somewhere be real. . . . By the principle of pure experience, either the word "activity" must have no meaning at all, or else the original type and model of what it means must lie in some concrete kind of experience that can be definitely pointed out.
>
> (James 1912: 160)

He continues:

> If we suppose activities to go on outside of our experience, it is in forms like these that we must suppose them, or else give them some other name; for the word "activity" has no imaginable content whatever save these experiences of process, obstruction, striving, strain, or release, ultimate qualia as they are of the life given us to be known.
>
> (James 1912: 167)

13. I would like to thank John Morrison and Galen Strawson for helpful comments on this chapter.

References

Adams, Robert (2007). 'Idealism Vindicated'. In D. Zimmerman and P. van Inwagen (eds.), *Persons: Human and Divine*. Oxford: Oxford University Press, pp. 35–54.

Alter, Torin, and Nagasawa, Yujin (2012). 'What Is Russellian Monism?' *Journal of Consciousness Studies*, 19 (9–10): 67–95.

Anscombe, G. E. M. (1971). *Causality and Determination: An Inaugural Lecture*. Cambridge: Cambridge University Press.

Armstrong, David M. (1978). *A Theory of Universals, Universals and Scientific Realism, Vol. II*. Cambridge: Cambridge University Press.

Armstrong, David M. (1983). *What Is a Law of Nature?* Cambridge: Cambridge University Press.

Armstrong, David M. (1997). *A World of States of Affairs*. Cambridge: Cambridge University Press.

Bayne, Tim, and Neil Levy (2006). 'The Feeling of Doing: Deconstructing the Phenomenology of Agency'. In N. Sebanz and W. Prinz (eds.), *Disorders of Volition*. Cambridge, MA: MIT Press.

Chalmers, David J. (2013). 'Panpsychism and Panprotopsychism'. *The Amherst Lecture in Philosophy* 8 (1–35). www.amherstlecture.org/chalmers2013. (Reprinted in G. Brüntrup and L. Jaskolla (eds.), *Panpsychism*. Oxford: Oxford University Press, pp. 19–47).

Collingwood, R. G. (1937). 'On the So-Called Idea of Causation'. *Proceedings of the Aristotelian Society, New Series*, 38: 85–112.

Gabbey, Alan (2002). 'Newton, Active Powers, and the Mechanical Philosophy'. In I. B. Cohen and G. E. Smith (eds.), *The Cambridge Companion to Newton*. Cambridge: Cambridge University Press.

Ginet, Carl (1997). 'Freedom, Responsibility, and Agency'. *The Journal of Ethics*, 1 (1): 85–98.

Hartshorne, Charles (1954). 'Causal Necessities: An Alternative to Hume'. *The Philosophical Review*, 63 (4): 479–99.

Hartshorne, Charles (1973). 'Creativity and the Deductive Logic of Causality'. *Review of Metaphysics*, 27 (1): 62–74.

Hartshorne, Charles (1977). 'Physics and Psychics: The Place of Mind in Nature'. In J. B. Cobb and D. R. Griffin (eds.), *Mind in Nature: The Interface of Science and Philosophy*. New York: University Press of America.

Horgan, Terry (2011). 'The Phenomenology of Agency and Freedom: Lessons from Introspection and Lessons from Its Limits'. *Humana Mente*, 15: 77–97.

Hume, David (1739–40/2000). *A Treatise of Human Nature*. Ed. J. Cottingham. Oxford Philosophical Texts. Oxford: Oxford University Press.

Hume, David (1748/1999). An Enquiry Concerning Human Understanding. Ed. T. L. Beauchamp. Oxford: Oxford University Press.

James, William (1890/1981). 'The Principles of Psychology, vol. 1'. In F. H. Burkhardt, F. Bowers, and I. K. Skrupskelis (eds.), *The Works of William James*, vol. 8. Cambridge, MA and London: Harvard University Press.

James, William (1902/1987). 'The Varieties of Religious Experience'. In B. Kuklick (ed.), *William James: Writings 1902–1910*. New York: Library of America.

James, William (1911). *Some Problems of Philosophy: A Beginning of an Introduction to Philosophy*. New York, London, Bombay and Calcutta: Longmans, Green & Co.

James, William (1912). 'The Experience of Activity'. In James's *Essays in Radical Empiricism*. New York, London, Bombay and Calcutta: Longmans, Green & Co.

Jammer, Max (1957). *Concepts of Force: A Study in the Foundations of Dynamics*. Cambridge, MA: Harvard University Press.

Leibniz, Gottfried Wilhelm (1691/1965). 'De Primae Philosophiae Emendatione, Et De Notione Substantiae'. In C. I. Gerhardt (ed.), *Die Philosophischen Schriften*. Hildesheim: G. Olms.

Leibniz, Gottfried Wilhelm (1695/1989). 'A New System of the Nature and Communication of Substances, and of the Union of the Soul and Body'. In R. Ariew and D. Garber (eds.), *Philosophical Essays*. Indianapolis: Hackett Publishing Company.

Leibniz, Gottfried Wilhelm (1698/1908). 'On Nature in Itself'. In G. M. Duncan (ed.), *Philosophical Works of Leibniz*. New Haven: The Tuttle, Morehouse & Taylor Company.

Leibniz, Gottfried Wilhelm (1704/1981). *New Essays on Human Understanding*. Ed. and Trans. P. Remnant and J. Bennett. Cambridge and New York: Cambridge University Press.

Locke, John (1689/1975). *An Essay Concerning Human Understanding*. Ed. P. H. Nidditch. Oxford: Clarendon Press.

Mach, Ernst (1897). *Popular Scientific Lectures*. Trans. T. J. McCormack. Chicago: The Open Court Publishing Company.

Madden, Edward H., and Hare, Peter H. (1971). 'The Powers That Be'. *Dialogue*, 10 (1): 12–31.

Martin, C. B., and Heil, John (1999). 'The Ontological Turn'. *Midwest Studies in Philosophy*, 23 (1): 34–60.

Martin, C. B., and Pfeifer, Karl (1986). 'Intentionality and the Non-Psychological'. *Philosophy and Phenomenological Research*, 46 (4): 531–54.

McGuire, James E. (1968). 'Force, Active Principles, and Newton's Invisible Realm'. *Ambix*, 15 (3): 154–208.

Michotte, Albert (1963). *The Perception of Causality*. Oxford: Basic Books.

Mørch, Hedda Hassel (2014). *Panpsychism and Causation: A New Argument and a Solution to the Combination Problem*. Doctoral Dissertation, Department of Philosophy, Classics, History of Art and Ideas, University of Oslo, Oslo.

Mørch, Hedda Hassel (2017). 'The Evolutionary Argument for Phenomenal Powers'. *Philosophical Perspectives*, 31 (1): 293–316.

Mørch, Hedda Hassel (2018). 'Does Dispositionalism Entail Panpsychism?' *Topoi*, https://doi.org/10.1007/s11245-018-9604-y

Mørch, Hedda Hassel (2019). 'Phenomenal Knowledge Why: The Explanatory Knowledge Argument Against Physicalism'. In S. Coleman (ed.), *The Knowledge Argument*. Cambridge: Cambridge University Press.

Mumford, Stephen (2006). 'The Ungrounded Argument'. *Synthese*, 149 (3): 471–89.

Pereboom, Derk (2015). 'Consciousness, Physicalism, and Absolutely Intrinsic Properties'. In T. Alter and Y. Nagasawa (eds.), *Consciousness in the Physical World: Perspectives on Russellian Monism*. Oxford: Oxford University Press.

Reid, Thomas (1788). *Essays on the Active Powers of Man*. Edinburgh: John Bell and London: G. G. J. & J. Robinson.

Russell, Bertrand (1912). 'On the Notion of Cause'. *Proceedings of the Aristotelian Society*, 13: 1–26.

Schopenhauer, Arthur (1859/1966a). *The World as Will and Representation*. Trans. E. F. J. Payne, vol. 1. New York: Dover.

Schopenhauer, Arthur (1859/1966b). *The World as Will and Representation*. Trans. E. F. J. Payne, vol. 2. New York: Dover.

Seager, William (2006). 'The "Intrinsic Nature" Argument for Panpsychism'. *Journal of Consciousness Studies*, 13 (10–11): 129–45.

Searle, John R. (1983). *Intentionality: An Essay in the Philosophy of Mind*. Cambridge: Cambridge University Press.

Skrbina, David (2005). *Panpsychism in the West*. Cambridge, MA: MIT Press.

Stout, G. F. (1935). 'Mechanical and Teleological Causation'. *Proceedings of the Aristotelian Society, Supplementary Volume*, 14 (1): 46–65.

Strawson, Galen (1987). 'Realism and Causation'. *The Philosophical Quarterly*, 37 (148): 253–77.

Strawson, Galen (1989). *The Secret Connexion: Causation, Realism and David Hume*. Oxford: Oxford University Press.

Strawson, Galen (2006). 'Realistic Monism: Why Physicalism Entails Panpsychism'. *Journal of Consciousness Studies*, 13 (10–11): 3–31.

Strawson, Galen (2008). 'The Identity of the Categorical and the Dispositional'. *Analysis*, 68 (4): 271–82.

Strawson, P. F. (1992). *Analysis and Metaphysics: An Introduction to Philosophy*. Oxford: Oxford University Press.

Whitehead, Alfred North (1933/1967). *Adventures of Ideas*. New York: The Free Press.

24

A QUANTUM CURE
FOR PANPHOBIA

Paavo Pylkkänen

"What reason have we to suppose that the hoped for revolution in our understanding of matter at the most fundamental level will involve ascribing essentially *mentalistic* properties to it?"

(Seager and Allen-Hermanson 2015: 31)

1. Introduction

When I was doing my PhD in the early 1990s, I was amused by Jerry Fodor writing about "epiphobia" – which he defined as the fear that one is turning into an epiphenomenalist (Fodor 1989: 59). The philosophers suffering from epiphobia were physicalists who did not want to deny the existence of intentional (understood as non-physical) states. The worry of epiphenomenalism was there because if one accepted the causal closure of the physical domain, there seemed to be no way that the intentional states *qua* intentional could be causally responsible for behavioural outcomes – which amounts to epiphenomenalism. But epiphobia is not the only worry a philosopher of mind can suffer from.

In his essay "Panpsychism" Thomas Nagel (1979) proposed that a set of reasonable assumptions, commonly held by philosophers, imply *panpsychism* – the view that the basic elements of matter ("physical ultimates") have mental properties. Nagel saw this option (which he took as a sign that something may not be quite right) as arising out of the assumptions that we ought to take conscious experience seriously, while denying psychophysical reductionism and radical emergence (for discussion, see Pylkkänen 1996). More recently Galen Strawson (2006) has with great force argued toward a similar conclusion, suggesting that the basic elements of matter even involve experience (Strawson 2006: 25). For him the idea arises as a result of assuming that everything concrete is physical; that everything physical is constituted out of physical ultimates, and that experience is part of concrete reality (2006: 25). Note especially that he considers "micropsychism" as the only reasonable option, not merely as something one arrives at via inference to the best explanation.

Those who find these arguments compelling may find themselves overcome by a worry, *panphobia*, which we can define, following Fodor, as the fear that one is turning into a panpsychist. Why should one be afraid of turning into a panpsychist? Strawson himself admits having felt abashed about arguing for panpsychism (2006: 186) and acknowledges that it is not easy to accept in the current intellectual climate (2006: 25). Nagel has remarked that "panpsychism has the faintly sick-ening odor of something put together in a metaphysical laboratory" (1986: 49), while Seager and Allen-Hermanson note that panpsychism has come to seem an implausible view, given our immense scientific knowledge of the physical world and the corresponding desire to explain everything in physical terms (2015: 1). Peter Simons summarizes more bluntly how many feel about this issue:

"Panpsychism, at least in caricature, is one of the most immediately counterintuitive and off-putting of metaphysical positions. The idea of electrons making decisions about how to spin, nuclei harbouring intentions to split, or photons with existential Angst, makes ideal-ism seem positively sane."

(Simons 2006: 146-7)

Colin McGinn provides a more sympathetic and yet critical characterization:

"Panpsychism is surely one of the loveliest and most tempting views of reality ever devised; and it is not without its respectable motivations either. There are good arguments for it, and it would be wonderful if it were true – theoretically, aesthetically, humanly. Any reflective person must feel the pull of panpsychism once in a while. It's almost as good as pantheism! The trouble is that it's a complete myth, a comforting piece of utter balderdash."

(McGinn 2006: 93)

If panpsychism is taken to mean that the elementary particles of physics (physical "ultimates") have proto-mental properties (Nagel 1986: 49), or even involve experience (Strawson 2006: 25), the doc-trine seems very implausible. Nagel himself notes this:

"What kind of properties could atoms have (even when they are part of a rock) that could qualify as proto-mental; and how could *any* properties of the chemical constituents of a brain combine to form a mental life?"

(Nagel 1986, p. 49)

Lycan underlines the lack of scientific evidence for panpsychism:

". . . there is nothing I can exhibit to show decisively that a muon or a quark is not a locus of experience. But neither is there any scientific evidence for panpsychism; there is no sci-entific reason, as opposed to philosophical argument, for believing it."

(Lycan 2006: 66)

He goes on to spell out the absurdity of the notion:

". . . if every ultimate particle has mental properties, what sorts of mental properties in par-ticular do the particles have? It seems ludicrous to think that a photon has either sensory experiences or intentional states. (It does not even have mass.) How could it see, hear or smell anything? And if it has experiential properties, then presumably it also has rudimen-tary propositional attitudes. What would be the contents of its beliefs or desires? Perhaps it wishes it were a **u** quark."

(Lycan 2006: 70)

More technically, McGinn worries about the causal inefficacy of the micro-experiential that seems to be implicit in panpsychism (cf. epiphobia!):

"Do the E [experiental] properties of elementary particles (or molecules or cells) contribute to their causal powers? If so, how come physics (and chemistry and biology) never have to take account of their contribution? . . . if they are agreed not to have any causal powers – and so are entirely epiphenomenal – how can they blossom into properties that do have such powers once they take up residence inside brains?"

(McGinn 2006: 94)

One apparent advantage of panpsychism is that it seems to solve the problem of how the experientality of an organism can emerge from its parts. McGinn however sees problems even here:

"What kinds of E [experiental] properties do particles have? . . . This is a game without rules and without consequences. Is it really to be supposed that a particle can enjoy these kinds of experiences – say, feeling depressed at its monotonous life of orbiting a nucleus but occasionally cheered up by its experience of musical notes? [. . .] Even the faint and blurry is phenomenology too much for the humble electron. The problem is that we can solve the emergence problem only if we credit the ultimates with a rich enough phenomenology to form an adequate basis for a full-bodied human mind . . ."

(McGinn 2006: 95)

So, on the one hand we have excellent philosophers arguing that panpsychism is the only reasonable option, while equally excellent philosophers argue that the doctrine is just very implausible. Note in particular how the arguments against panpsychism appeal to our intuitions about elementary particles. It is assumed to be obvious that electrons cannot make decisions, nuclei cannot harbour intentions, photons cannot have sensory experiences, intentional states or existential Angst, and atoms cannot have proto-mental properties. Thus, anyone who feels the pull of panpsychism but also shares these common anti-panpsychist intuitions is likely to experience bouts of panphobia.

The story we will tell in this chapter does not go all the way to claim that elementary particles have all the properties that are ridiculed in the above quotes. However, we will propose that our best physics implies that elementary particles are far more complex than what is commonly supposed by contemporary materialist or physicalist philosophers of mind. Not only that, we will also show how some leading physicists have suggested that it is even reasonable to interpret some novel properties of elementary particles as protomental and that these protomental properties are causally efficacious. This, then, opens up the possibility for a scientific argument for panpsychism – or at least panprotopsychism, the weaker doctrine according to which the ultimates have proto-mental properties, rather than mental properties in a full sense.

Epiphobia and panphobia lie at the opposite ends of a spectrum in philosophy of mind. An epiphobic worries that one's mind-matter theory gives too weak a role for mind, while a panphobic worries that it gives too strong a role. In this chapter we will explore whether a cure for *both* epiphobia *and* panphobia might be found in quantum theory.

2. The Ontological Interpretation of Quantum Theory

Quantum phenomena exhibit a curious combination of wave and particle behavior. For example, in the famous two-slit experiment, electrons arrive one by one at the detecting screen at localized points, suggesting that they are particles. Yet as we keep on watching, the individual spots gradually build up an interference pattern typical of wave behavior, suggesting that each individual electron ALSO has wave properties. The usual interpretation of quantum theory describes the electron with a wave function. In the minimalist (Bohr's) version, the wave function only allows us to calculate probabilities for finding the electron (as a localized particle) at a given location. In other words, the wave function is seen as a part of a mathematical algorithm and is not given an ontological interpretation. However, following von Neumann, many physicists assumed that the wave function provides a complete description of an individual quantum object. This gives rise to the many infamous puzzles of quantum theory, such as the claim that a single electron is in two (or more) places at once; that a cat is alive and dead at the same time; that the world at the macroscopic level is constantly branching into copies ("many worlds"); and that to solve such problems we must assume an *ad hoc* collapse of the wave function, or assume that the non-physical consciousness of the observer plays an active role (for some of the problems with von Neumann's approach, see Bohm and Hiley 1993, ch 2). Thus, it seems that quantum theory forces us to choose between Bohrian instrumentalism/antirealism or some very counterintuitive realist interpretation. (For a brief introduction to quantum theory, see Polkinghorne 2002; Pylkkänen 2018; see also Lewis 2016; for Bohr's views see Plotnitsky 2010)

An apparently more sober realist version of quantum theory was discovered by Louis de Broglie in 1927 and independently rediscovered and further developed by David Bohm in 1952 and in subsequent research. In this theory the electron is seen as a particle AND a wave. In the two-slit experiment the particle goes through one of the slits. The wave goes through both slits, interferes and guides the particle in such a way that an interference pattern is gradually formed, spot by spot, as many electrons pass through the slit system (thus the theory has also been called the pilot wave theory). It thus seems that we can have a realist or ontological interpretation of the quantum theory, without the usual puzzles, such as Schrödinger's cat, many worlds, collapse of the wave function, or the consciousness of the observer producing physical reality (see Bacciagaluppi and Valentini 2009; Bohm 1952a and 1952b; Bohm and Hiley 1987, 1993; Bricmont 2016; for latest developments, see Walleczek et al. (eds.) 2018; Pylkkänen et al. 2016)).

However, the Bohm theory, too, has exotic features. For one thing it implies a non-local interaction between particles at a quantum level, creating a tension with relativity. Note however that this non-locality is characteristic of quantum theory in general and consistent with the experimental results (see Walleczek and Grössing 2016). Also, the wave function for a many-body system lives in a multidimensional configuration space, making it difficult to assume that it describes an ordinary physical field in a 3-dimensional space (see Ney and Albert (eds.) 2013). To alleviate this problem (and for other reasons) Bohm and Hiley (1987, 1993) proposed the radically new notion that the wave function describes not an ordinary physical field, but rather a field of information, which literally in-forms the energy of the particle. Bohm (1990) further proposed that such "active information" can be seen as a primitive mind-like quality of elementary particles. Here, then, opens up the possibility for scientific (rather than merely philosophical) support for panprotopsychism. Let us thus examine the Bohm theory in more detail.

While it is common in the usual interpretation of quantum theory to say that a quantum object (such as an electron) is a particle OR a wave (depending on the context), the Bohm theory, as we already mentioned, says less ambiguously that an electron is always a particle AND a wave. More precisely, it assumes that every particle has a well-defined position and momentum and is accompanied by a new type of field, described by the wave function ψ which satisfies the Schrödinger equation. The field affects the particle via a new potential, *the quantum potential* Q (eq. 1):

$$Q = -\frac{\hbar^2}{2m} \frac{\nabla^2 R}{R}$$

This suggests a model of, say, an electron as a particle which moves along a trajectory and which is influenced not just by classical potentials but also by the new quantum potential. The quantum potential accounts for all (non-relativistic) quantum behavior, and in situations where the quantum potential is negligible, classical physics provides a good approximation. From the perspective of the Bohm theory we can call the physical world "an overall quantum world". Within this world there is a classical sub-world – that is, a domain where the quantum potential has a negligible effect (e.g. due to temperature), and Newton's laws provide a good approximate description for how a macroscopic object (e.g. a chair) behaves. But in circumstances where the quantum potential is not negligible (e.g. in quantum experiments), the behavior of particles can be radically non-classical,

Figures 24.1 and 24.2 provide well-known visualizations for the two-slit experiment (from Philippidis et al. 1979). In Figure 24.1 we are looking toward a partition with two slits in it. The electrons are moving toward us (one by one) and as they go through one of slits they encounter a quantum potential. One can think of a potential as a bit analogous to a mountain, so that the quantum potential will, for example, keep the electrons away from areas where it has a high value.

The electrons have their source in a hot filament, which means that there is a random statistical variation in their initial positions. This means that each particle typically enters the slit system in a different place. Figure 24.2 shows possible trajectories than an electron can take after it goes through

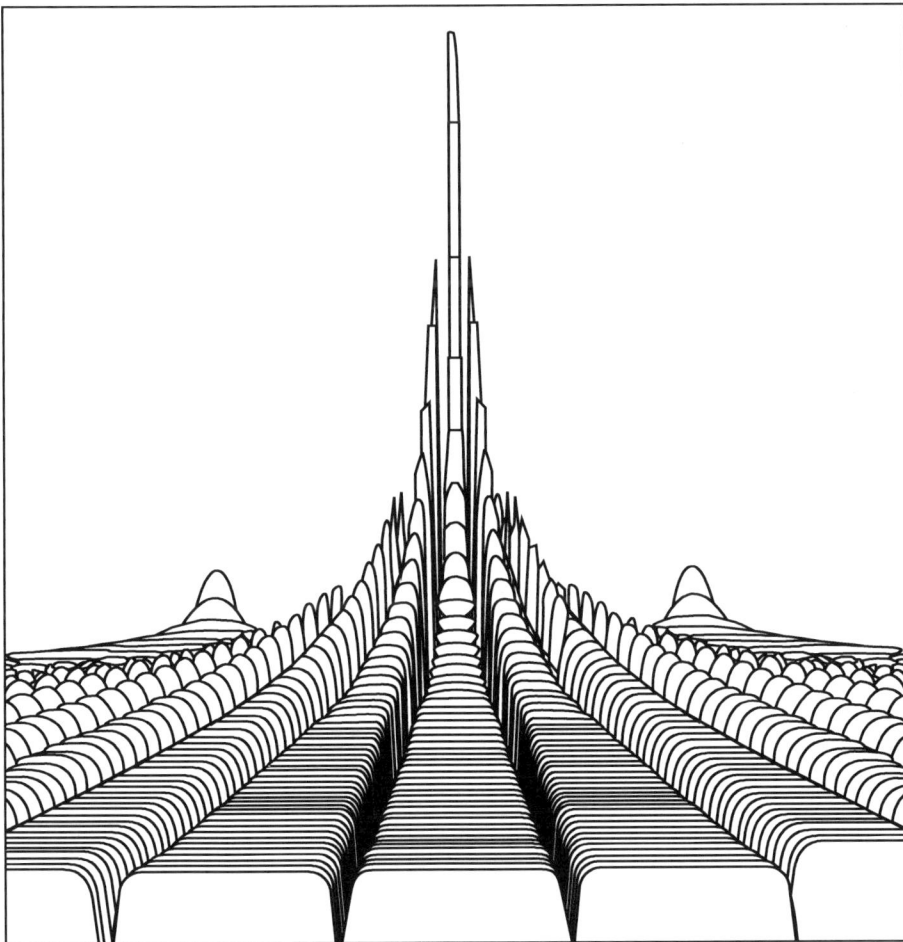

Figure 24.1   Quantum potential for two Gaussian slits

Reprinted with kind permission of Società Italiana di Fisica, copyright (1979) by the Italian Physical Society

Figure 24.2 Trajectories for two Gaussian slits

Reprinted with kind permission of Società Italiana di Fisica, copyright (1979) by the Italian Physical Society

the slits. Which trajectory it takes depends, of course, on which place it happens to enter the slit system.

Note that the trajectories should be seen as a *hypothesis* about what may be going on in the two-slit experiment. Because of the uncertainty principle it is not possible to measure the initial conditions (position and momentum) of a particle simultaneously with an accuracy that would enable us to predict which trajectory a given individual electron will follow (however, measurements of so-called weak values allow us to calculate average trajectories, see Flack et al. 2018).

3. The Interpretation of the Quantum Field as Active Information

In the 1970s Bohm and Hiley (1975) began to re-examine the de Broglie–Bohm theory, partly as a result of the interest their research students were showing in this approach, as well as the new attention to the question of non-locality due to John Bell's work (see Bell 1987). They considered the mathematical expression of the quantum potential, which describes the way the quantum wave field affects the particle (eq. 1):

$$Q = -\frac{\hbar^2}{2m} \frac{\nabla^2 R}{R}$$

Here ħ-bar is Planck's constant divided by 2π, m is the mass of the particle, R is the amplitude of the quantum wave and ∇^2 is a differential operator which takes the second spatial derivative of R. The term $\nabla^2 R$ reflects how R changes, i.e., the shape or form of the quantum wave. In classical physics (e.g. with the classical electromagnetic field), a potential depends on the amplitude of the field (somewhat like the size of a water wave determines the effect the wave has on a floating object). However, Bohm realized that the quantum potential, and thus the effect of the quantum field upon the particle, depends *only* on the form or shape of the field, not on its size or amplitude R. This is so because R appears both in the nominator and the denumerator in the right hand side of equation 1, and so can be multiplied by an arbitrary constant without changing the quantum potential; a wave of small amplitude thus has the same effect as a wave of large amplitude, as long as the waves have the same form. Bohm was thereby led to suggest that the quantum field is not pushing and pulling the particle mechanically, but rather the quantum field literally puts form into or "in-forms" the particle to behave in a certain way. The idea is that the electron is moving under its own energy that is being in-formed by the quantum field.

Bohm proposed that this is an instance of a general feature of *active information* that we see operating at many levels of nature (for discussion, see Seager 2018). The basic idea of active information is that a low-energy form enters a greater energy and as a result the form of the greater energy becomes the same as that of the smaller energy. If you consider a ship on autopilot guided by radar waves, the waves are not pushing and pulling the ship. Rather, the form of the waves is taken up by the autopilot device and is used to direct the ship. Analogously the quantum field contains information about the environment of the particle (e.g. slits) and this information, along with the classical forces, then determines the movement of the particle. Note, however, that there are important differences between the ship analogy and the electron. It is important to emphasize that with the electron we encounter holistic active information (with non-locality and irreducible wholeness), as opposed to the more (classical) mechanical active information we encounter in the ship analogy (Pylkkänen 1992: 95–6; Dickson 1996: 234).

Bohm also realized that the idea that the essential nature of the quantum field is that it is information, rather than an ordinary physical field, enables one to make sense of the notorious multidimensionality of the many-body quantum field. With information, multidimensionality is a natural concept in the sense that information can be organized into as many dimensions as may be needed. As we will see later, the many-body quantum field can be seen as a *common pool of information* for the two particles.

One important potential criticism of the active information approach has to do with the notion of information that is presupposed. Is it really justified to use the term "information" to describe the sorts of processes connected to the quantum field? One can examine this question in the light of recent developments in the philosophy of information (e.g. Floridi 2015). Floridi distinguishes between semantic and environmental information. Semantic information involves factual semantic contents (i.e. information as meaningful data that represents facts correctly or incorrectly). Environmental information sees information as mere correlation, e.g. the way tree rings carry information about age. Semantic information can be further distinguished into factual and instructional information. The quantum active information is *about* something (the environment, slits, etc.), it is *for* the particle and it helps to *bring about* something (a certain movement of the particle). This suggests that it is not merely correlational but is also (proto)semantic and has both factual and instructional aspects (see Pylkkänen 1992: 96–8). Also, Maleeh and Amani (2012) have usefully considered active information in relation to Roederer's (2005) notion of pragmatic information, suggesting that only biological systems are capable of "genuine" information processing. I think one can argue that Bohmian quantum information potential involves genuine information processing (indeed, the most fundamental kind of genuine information processing science has thus far discovered).

While the notion of active information in quantum theory has not been widely accepted (for criticism see Riggs 2008), some leading thinkers do take it seriously (e.g. Smith 2003). Also, an interesting adaptation of the active information scheme to neuroscience has been proposed by Thomas Filk (2012). In the field of the social sciences, Andrei Khrennikov (2004) has made imaginative use of the proposal and the Bohm theory – as an analogical model – has also been applied to financial processes by Olga Choustova (2007) and Emmanuel Haven (2005). For other ways of using the mathematical and conceptual tools of quantum theory to model cognition, see Wang et al. (2013). Of course, the notion of "quantum information" has been extensively discussed in recent years (e.g. Bouwmeester et al. 2000). The advantages of the concept of active information over quantum information are explored in Maroney (2002) and Maroney and Hiley (1999). Note finally that the Bohm theory can be presented in a more minimalist way without giving the quantum potential (and active information) a key role (see Goldstein 2013). Bohm, however, felt that at least something like the notion of active information is needed if we want to give an intelligible ontological interpretation of quantum theory (Bohm and Hiley 1993: 60; see also Holland 1995: 90-1).

4. Is information a Mind-Like Quality?

So let us assume, for the sake of the argument, that it is a reasonable hypothesis that the quantum field encodes information. What reasons do we have to think that such information is a "primitive mind-like quality", as Bohm suggested? The idea that cognition is information processing has, of course, been a central notion in cognitive psychology and cognitive science (Velmans 2009: 64–79). Note also that some other researchers in philosophy of mind and consciousness studies have made use of the concept of information in their theories of mind and consciousness. For example, Dretske (1981) and Barwise and Seligman (1997) have explored the possibility that information in the sense of factual semantic contents can be grounded in environmental information. For Dretske this was an important part of his attempts to give a naturalistic account of sensory experiences, qualia and consciousness. During recent years the notion of information has been used to explain consciousness most notably by David Chalmers (1996), as well as by Giulio Tononi and his co-workers (Tononi and Koch 2014; Oizumi et al. 2014); see also Velmans (1991a, 1991b). The relation of Bohm's active information to Chalmers's views has been discussed in Pylkkänen (2007: 244–6), while its relation to Tononi's views is discussed in Pylkkänen (2016). While Bohm's notion of information differs from the notions of information mentioned above, there are some relevant similarities. For example, both Bohm's and Tononi's notions of information differ from Shannon information in that they refer to the literal meaning of information as "in-forming", albeit in different ways.

The preceding indicates that the idea that information is a mind-like quality is one of the key options in contemporary discussions about the nature of mental states. In the light of this, Bohm's proposal that quantum theoretical active information is a primitive mind-like quality of elementary particles seems not too unreasonable. The proposal implies that electrons have "proto-cognition" (because of the information aspect) and "proto-will" (because the information is fundamentally active) (cf. Wendt 2015: 139). Whether it also implies that electrons have proto-phenomenal properties is a more tricky question. But one could claim that the electron is in some sense "perceiving" or monitoring its environment via its information field, and that such "perceiving" involves proto-phenomenality.

5. Active Information and the Relation of Mind and Matter

Bohm also thought that the idea of active information at the quantum level opened up a way to tackle a perennial problem in philosophy, namely that of the relationship between mind and matter (1989, 1990). First of all, he suggested that mental states involve a hierarchy of levels of active information. We do not merely think about objects in the external world, but we can also become aware of our thinking. He suggested that such meta-level awareness typically gives rise to a higher level of information. This higher level gathers information about the lower level. But because its essential nature is active information, it does not merely make a passive representation of the lower level. Rather, the higher level also acts to organize the lower level, a bit analogously to the way the active information in the pilot wave acts to organize the movement of the particle. And of course, we can become aware of this higher level of information from a yet higher level, and so on.

How then does mind, understood as a hierarchy of levels of active information, connect with matter in the Bohmian scheme? First of all, he suggested that it is natural to extend the quantum ontology. So just as there is a pilot wave that guides the particle, there can be a super-pilot wave that can organize the first-order pilot wave, and so on. He claimed that such an extension is "natural" from the mathematical point of view (Bohm and Hiley (1993: 378–81, 385) discuss such extensions in the context of quantum field theory). Now it seems that we have two hierarchies, one for mind and another for matter. Bohm's next step was to postulate that these are the same hierarchy, so that there is only one hierarchy. This then allows, at least in principle, for a new way of understanding how mind and body can affect each other. The meaning of information at a given level in the mind can act downwards, all the way to the active information in the pilot waves of particles in, say, the synapses or neural microtubules, and this influence can then be amplified to signals in motor cortex, leading to a physical movement of the body (see Hiley and Pylkkänen 2005). In a reverse process, perception can carry information about the external world and the inner state of the body to higher levels, where the meaning of the information is apprehended, and can unfold again to organize the more manifest levels. (For criticisms see Kieseppä (1997a, 1997b), Chrisley (1997); for replies, see Hiley and Pylkkänen (1997, 2001) and Pylkkänen (1992: 96)). Bohm's discussion fits well with the idea of the mind-brain as a self-organizing system. Jenann Ismael (2016) has emphasized that the human mind also essentially includes a self-governing system which is capable of deliberative reasoning and self-conscious thought. In the Bohmian scheme one can say that even conscious reflection in thought happens according to the total meaning that prevails in a situation (see Bohm 1990: 282). This weakens the distinction between self-organizing and self-governing systems.

6. Quantum Ballet: The Priority of the Whole

As has already been hinted previously, the ontological interpretation also brings into focus the "undivided wholeness" characteristic of the quantum world, implying a monistic metaphysics (cf. Schaffer 2010). This wholeness can be seen already when considering a single particle, for because the quantum potential only depends upon the form of the field, it does not necessarily fall off with distance even if the intensity of the field becomes weak as the field spreads out. Thus even distant features (e.g. slits) of the environment of the particle can have a strong effect upon the particle, implying that there can be a strong context-dependence in the behaviour of the particle. In the two-body system there is wholeness also in the sense that the quantum potential depends on the position of both particles in a way that does not necessarily fall off with the distance, implying the possibility of a non-local interaction between the two particles. And we can generalize this to the N-body system where the behaviour of each particle may depend non-locally on all the others, regardless of how far away they may be (Bohm and Hiley 1987: 330).

Nonlocality is an important new feature of the quantum theory, but Bohm emphasized that there is yet another feature that is even more radical, namely that the quantum potential Q depends on the quantum state of the whole system in a way that cannot be defined simply as a pre-assigned interaction between all the particles. This underlines the priority of the whole that is typical of quantum systems (cf. Schaffer 2010). For example, in the Hydrogen atom the interaction of the electron and the proton depends on the quantum state of the whole system in a way that cannot be expressed in terms of the relationships of the particles alone. In this sense the whole is prior to its parts in the quantum domain (see Bohm and Hiley 1987: 331-2; see also Holland 1995: 281-2).

In Bohmian terms the quantum state can be seen as a *common pool of information* that is guiding the particles in the system. Note also that the quantum state is evolving in time according to Schrödinger's equation, so it is a dynamic whole that is guiding the particles. Bohm thus thought that quantum theory was primarily about dynamical wholeness that is not reducible to the interactions between individuals. As Max Jammer has pointed out, this means that the individuals are not "constitutive" to the whole but rather depend on the state of the whole (1988: 696).

However, the physical world we find in everyday experience can be approximately described in terms of classical physics, characterized by relatively independent and separable objects. How do we get from quantum wholeness to classical separability? The answer is that in certain circumstances the wave function (i.e. the quantum field) of a system *factorizes* into two parts, and the corresponding subsystems will then behave independently. These factorized parts of the wave functions represent independent pools of information. The subsystems will cease to be guided by a common pool of information and will instead respond to independent pools.

An example that illustrates the preceding is provided by superconductivity where electrons at low temperatures are able to move without resistance in a wire. In terms of the Bohm theory this happens because the electrons are guided by a common wave function (or common pool of information) to move in such a way that they do not scatter from obstacles but rather go around them in a coordinated way. This is like a "ballet dance" where the wave function is the score and the particles are the dancers. At higher temperatures the property of superconductivity disappears. This is because the wave function factorizes into independent pools of information, and the particles behave independently and scatter from obstacles. The particles are no longer like ballet dancers but are now like an unorganized crowd of people who are acting independently and get in each other's way (1993: 71).

The key point is that the quantum potential arising under certain conditions can organize the activity of an entire set of particles in a way that depends directly on the state of the whole. Bohm and Hiley think it is plausible that such an organization can be carried to higher and higher levels and eventually may become relevant to living beings. Indeed, given the recent advances in quantum biology (Ball 2011, Marais et al. 2018)), it is tempting to speculate that the quantum potential (or some higher-order quantum-like "biological potential") plays a relevant role in determining whether a system is "living" or "non-living". The idea is that when the quantum potential within a biological system has a non-negligible effect, it provides the organic unity characteristic of a living system. Death, on the other hand, would correspond to a situation when the wave function factorizes and the system loses its organic unity (cf. Pylkkänen 1992: 55).

Mental states, too, can be seen as involving common pools of information which guide and coordinate spatially distinct neural activities. Taken as a literal quantum model of the brain, a Bohmian common pool of quantum information in the brain would imply that there can be non-local correlations between particles in spatially separate brain areas. This, of course, is a speculative idea, but recent advances in quantum brain theory (see Hameroff and Penrose 2014) make such a radical idea at least conceivable.

Note also that the idea of a common pool of information is interestingly similar to Baars's (2007) idea of a global workspace in consciousness studies. If we assume that consciousness would correspond to a situation where a common pool of mental information is having a global effect on distinct neural modules, then we could say that the transition from conscious to non-conscious state corresponds to some kind of factorization of such a conscious common pool of information to non-conscious independent pools. However, as Rosenthal (2009) has pointed out, while consciousness is sometimes connected with the global effects of a workspace, there also seem to be situations where there are conscious states without such global effects (e.g. conscious peripheral perceptions), and non-conscious states with global effects (e.g. non-conscious thoughts as steps in problem solving). Thus it does not seem reasonable to identify consciousness with the operation of a global workspace or common pools of information in connection with neural processes, even though these may often be correlated (for discussion, see Velmans 2009: 274-81). We will return to the issue of consciousness later.

7. The Ontological Interpretation and the History of Panpsychism

The ontological interpretation resonates with many panpsychist approaches in the history of philosophy. We saw previously that this interpretation involves a top-down approach in the sense that the basic law (which involves active information) refers to the whole universe, and that through factorization we get relatively independent sub-wholes, each guided by their pools of information. We can even imagine a wide range of situations where the quantum potential (and thus the influence of active information) upon an elementary particle becomes negligibly small, in which case classical physics provides a good approximate description of the behaviour of the particle (and aggregates of such particles, such as tables and chairs). In this sense any Bohmian panpsychism is top down − a mind-like quality (active information) is an essential part of the basic law that applies to the universe as a whole, but it is not necessary to always attribute mind-like qualities to the ultimate constituents of matter. The Bohmian scheme thus allows us to make a distinction between things with mind-like qualities and things lacking mind-like qualities. At the level of fundamental physics, particles for which the quantum potential is negligible lack (for all practical purposes) mind-like qualities, while particles for which the quantum potential is non-negligible have mind-like qualities. Similarly, at the macroscopic level we can make a distinction between systems where some kind of active information is having a non-negligible effect (and the system [e.g., a living organism] has mind-like qualities) and systems where such effect is negligibly small (and the system [e.g., a chair] has no mind-like qualities). This view is reminiscent of Fechner's endorsement of a "world-mind" of which everything is a part. Fechner's view did not require that every thing in the world be itself enminded (Seager and Allen-Hermanson 2015: 5).

Bohm's way of thinking fits particularly well with Leibniz's panpsychism. Leibniz's idea that each monad carries within it complete information about the entire universe is captured by Bohm's general notion of the implicate order, according to which each part of the universe enfolds information about the universe as a whole in a holographic manner (Bohm 1980; see also Pylkkänen 2007, Seager 2013). For Leibniz space and time emerge from sets of relations amongst the monads (Seager and Allen-Hermanson 2015: 11). This again fits with the idea that the implicate order describes a kind of pre-space out of which the ordinary 3-dimensional space unfolds (Bohm and Hiley 1984). Seager and Allen-Hermanson note that the only model Leibniz found adequate to describe his monads was one of perception and spontaneous activity. This is analogous with the Bohmian electron, if we assume there is a sense in which the electron "perceives" its environment via the quantum field, and that the flexibility allowed by the hierarchy of quantum fields of information makes possible a kind of spontaneity on the activity of the electron (cf. Bohm and Peat 2000: 183–4; 202–4). A further similarity between the Leibnizian and Bohmian panpsychist schemes is that both can make a distinction between things that have mental attributes from those who do not. Leibniz held that there is a difference between a "mere aggregate" (e.g. a heap of sand) and the "organic unity" of an organism. In Bohmian terms a "mere aggregate" corresponds to a situation where the wave function of a system of particles has factorized in such a way that each particle is guided only by its own pool of information (and when the quantum potential of a particle has a negligible effect, so that classical laws prevail), while "organic unity" corresponds to a situation where particles are guided by a common pool of information, with a non-negligible quantum potential.

8. An analogical argument for panpsychism based on the ontological interpretation

Seager and Allen-Hermanson (2015: 26) characterize a typical argument from analogy for panpsychism as follows: "if we look closely, with an open mind, we see that even the simplest forms of matter actually exhibit behavior which is akin to that we associate with mentality in animals and human beings." They note that one fairly promising analogy is provided by the indeterminism of quantum mechanics, and draw attention to how Whitehead wanted to see this indeterminacy "... as an expression not of blind chance but spontaneous *freedom* in response to a kind of *informational inclination* rather than mechanical causation." This general idea fits quite well with the way Bohm made use of notions such as active information and "generative order" to characterize freedom and causation (Bohm and Peat 2000). While it is usually assumed that quantum indeterminacy is pure randomness and as such remote from deliberation, decision and indecision (Seager and Allen-Hermanson 2015: 27), reasonable extensions of quantum theory (e.g. Penrose 1994; Bohm and Hiley 1993: 378-381) can go towards capturing the kind of interplay of spontaneity, contingency and determination that is characteristic of human deliberation and decision.

Seager and Allen-Hermanson think that a more promising quantum theory related analogical argument for panpsychism has to do with the relation between consciousness and information. The idea is that an important function of consciousness is to integrate information and to monitor external and internal states. This idea can be developed into a view that monitoring and integrated information actually make for consciousness (Lycan 1996: 40, quoted in Seager and Allen-Hermanson 2015: 27). Seager and Allen-Hermanson note: "... it follows from this view that *if* information monitoring is a fundamental and pervasive feature of the world at even the most basic levels, then consciousness too should appear at those levels" (2015: 27-8). There is a sense in which quantum theoretical active information involves information monitoring, so in case the ontological interpretation is correct, philosophers who emphasize the link between monitoring and consciousness, such as Lycan, may be closer to panpsychism than they realize (cf. Lycan's remarks about the lack of scientific evidence for panpsychism that we cited in the Introduction). Also, Seager and Allen-Hermanson suggest that already according to the usual interpretation of quantum theory, experiments on entangled photons imply that two entangled photons are effectively monitoring each other's state of polarization (2015: 28). Thus, regardless of whether we are using Bohm and Hiley's ontological interpretation, or the usual interpretation of quantum theory, it can be argued that quantum theory implies that some kind of superluminal informational monitoring is taking place at a fundamental level of the physical world (it is likely, however, that this does not involve superluminal signaling or communication, see Walleczek and Grössing (2016)).

If one accepts that monitoring and integrated information make for consciousness then, if Seager and Allen-Hermanson are correct, the quantum theory implies that there is at least elementary consciousness associated with quantum phenomena. However, as we have seen, Bohm for one thought that it is obvious that elementary particles are not conscious. We will return to this issue later.

9. The Combination Problem

Bohm and Hiley's interpretation provides a novel way of approaching the combination problem of panpsychism, i.e. the problem of explaining how the (primitive) consciousness of the elements of a system could possibly combine into the full consciousness of the system. Nagel, for example, worries about not only what the proto-mental properties of atoms could possibly be but also about how they could "combine to form the mental life that we are all familiar" and "how could any properties of the chemical constituents of a brain combine to form a mental life?" (1986: 49–50).

We have seen already that quantum theory challenges some key assumptions on the basis of which the combination problem has traditionally been formulated in the first place. For while the problem typically presupposes in a bottom-up fashion that the properties of the whole have to be explained in terms of the properties of the parts, quantum theory strongly points to a monistic ontology, in the sense that the whole is prior to its parts (cf. Schaffer 2010). This does not deny the existence of the parts, nor does it deny that some aspects of the whole can be conveniently understood in terms of the properties of the parts. But, as we have seen earlier, there are quite generally instances in quantum theory (brought out especially clearly by the ontological interpretation) where the whole is prior to parts in the sense that the behaviour of individual particles cannot be understood in terms of their spatial relationships only. So we do not explain the behaviour of the whole in a bottom-up way in terms of the behaviour of the parts, but rather explain the behaviour of the parts in a top-down way partly in terms of the properties of the whole.

We also saw that in terms of the ontological interpretation, the particles in a many-body quantum system are guided by a "common pool" of information that cannot be reduced to the "private pools" of individual particles. On the contrary, the whole is prior to the parts in the sense that these private pools arise from the common pool in certain circumstances through factorization. Thus quantum reality seems to provide a powerful holistic principle of combination, which in the ontological interpretation can be understood in terms of a quantum potential, a new kind of non-local, holistic organizing factor. Regarding the combination problem, the ontological interpretation provides one way of understanding, at least as an analogy, how a subsystem (such as a human being) can have properties (e.g. consciousness) that need not be accounted for entirely by the properties of the parts of the subsystem (e.g. elementary consciousness of the parts). Thus, while the ontological interpretation has a panpsychist flavour in postulating that elementary particles have mind-like qualities (when the quantum potential for a particle is non-negligible), its emphasis on the priority of the whole goes against the spirit of the bottom-up way of explaining consciousness characteristic of traditional panpsychism. This can be seen as a deflationary approach to the combination problem (Ilpo Hirvonen, private communication).

10. Active Information and Conscious Experience

The preceding gives rise to the question of what the origin of conscious experience is in the Bohmian scheme. We have noted that in this scheme the whole is primary, in the sense that active information associated with an elementary particle derives from a common pool of information, ultimately that of the universe as a whole. However, if we think of the quantum field of the universe in the light of the ontological interpretation, there seems to be no reason to think that the active information encoded in this vastly multidimensional quantum field is conscious. Indeed, while Bohm saw nature as a dynamic process where information and meaning play a key dynamic role, he assumed that "99.99 per cent "of our meanings are not conscious (see Weber 1987: 439). But how can one then address the problem of consciousness in this scheme? In other words, why is there sometimes conscious experience associated with the activity of information? Why doesn't all the activity of information in humans proceed "in the dark", as it seems to do in physical and biological processes in general?

Given that Bohm's mind-matter scheme has a hierarchical structure, one natural possibility to explore is whether some version of a higher-order theory of consciousness could be applied here. Alternatively one could try to apply Tononi's integrated information theory of consciousness (Oizumi et al. 2014) to active information, or consider the relationship of the active information scheme (with its emphasis on common pools of information) to Baars's (2007) global workspace theory of consciousness. Or perhaps a suitable combination and modification of these theories would do the job of accounting for consciousness in the active information scheme? One thing to consider here is that Tononi's theory has been subject to severe criticisms by Scott Aaronson, who argues that according to Tononi's theory a simple Reed-Solomon decoding circuit would, if scaled to a large enough size, bring into being a consciousness vastly exceeding our own – something Aaronson thinks is simply absurd (for the debate, see Aaronson 2014a & 2014b). If we postulate that consciousness requires the activity Bohmian quantum information (or something analogous to it), such simple counterexamples will not work. In order for the system to be conscious, non-trivial quantum effects have to play a role in it.

A simple possibility would be to postulate that what makes a given mental state (or level of information or mental activity) conscious is that there exists a higher level of (typically) unconscious information, which has the content that one is in the first order mental state or activity (cf. Rosenthal 1997; Gennaro 2012). Note also that David Chalmers (1996) famously suggested that we tackle the hard problem of consciousness with a double-aspect theory of information. The idea is that information is a fundamental feature of the world, which always has both a phenomenal and a physical aspect. Now, we could take this idea to the Bohm scheme and postulate that active information, too, has phenomenal properties. This then raises the question about what we should think about the active information in the pilot wave of an electron. Does it, too, have phenomenal properties in some sense? We have seen that Bohm himself went as far as to say that an electron has a "primitive mind-like quality", but by "mind" he was here referring to the "activity of form", rather than conscious phenomenal experience in any full sense.

I think that it is reasonable to combine Chalmers's hypothesis with active information, but we need to restrict the hypothesis. For example, we could say that a certain kind of active information (for example, holistic active information that is analogous to quantum active information) has the potentiality for phenomenal properties, but this potentiality is actualized only in suitable circumstances (for example, when a given level of active information is the intentional target of a higher level of active information; or if we want to follow a Tononian-Baarsian approach, we could say that suitably integrated active information which can act as a global workspace is conscious). Of course, this also opens up the possibility for genuine artificial consciousness. If we could implement suitably integrated quantum-like active information in an artificial system and set up suitable higher-order relationships between levels and a global workspace in the system, phenomenal properties should actualize themselves, according to this type of hypothesis.

One advantage is that while Chalmers's double-aspect theory suffers from epiphenomenalism, Bohm's scheme, when modified, opens up the possibility of a genuine causal efficacy of phenomenal properties upon the physical domain (see Pylkkänen 2007: 244–6; Pylkkänen 2017). Also, Chalmers thinks it an interesting possibility that some sort of activity is required for experience, and that static information (e.g. information in a thermostat in a constant state) thus is not likely to have experience associated with it (1996: 298). If we say that phenomenal properties are always properties of some kind of Bohmian active information, we could do justice to the intuition that activity is required for experience.

11. Conclusion

We started off by noting that, given the *prima facie* absurdity of the notion that physical ultimates have mental or even experiential properties, those who find panpsychist arguments convincing may find themselves overcome by panphobia. We then examined in some detail Bohm and Hiley's proposal that elementary particles have mind-like qualities. Thus, panpsychism is not as anti-scientific as it may seem, and perhaps a cure or at least alleviation of panphobia is here available. However, there is one important point we need to consider. Bohm's idea that elementary particles (or physical ultimates) are not conscious (and that the quantum field of the universe as a whole is not conscious) means that one needs to appeal to some kind of emergence to account for consciousness; and emergentism and panpsychism are often seen as competing doctrines (Seager and Allen-Hermanson 2015: 3). Thus some panpsychists would not see the active information scheme – at least in the form I have presented it here – as a genuinely panpsychist one, but rather as a form of emergentism. If so, I suggest that the active information scheme makes emergentism a more plausible doctrine. It is easier to see how a mind-like state can become conscious, than how a "purely physical" state can become conscious. This intuition is shared by some higher-order theorists (see e.g. Lycan's (1996: 24) answer to the so-called problem of the rock for higher order theories). By postulating that mind-like qualities are a fundamental aspect of the universe, Bohm's active information and implicate order schemes make the emergence of conscious experience more intelligible.

Acknowledgements

I would like to thank Valtteri Arstila, Ilpo Hirvonen, Kristjan Loorits and William Seager for their valuable comments on this chapter. The work for this chapter was partially funded by the Fetzer Franklin Fund of the John E. Fetzer Memorial Trust.

References

Aaronson, S. (2014a) 'Why I Am Not An Integrated Information Theorist (or, The Unconscious Expander)', *Shtetl Optimized: The Blog of Scott Aaronson*. https://www.scottaaronson.com/blog/?p=1799
Aaronson, S. (2014b)'Giulio Tononi and Me: A Phi-nal Exchange', *Shtetl Optimized: The Blog of Scott Aaronson*. https://www.scottaaronson.com/blog/?p=1823
Baars, B. (2007). 'The Global Workspace Theory of Consciousness'. In M. Velmans and S. Schneider (eds.), *The Blackwell Companion to Consciousness*. Malden, MA: Blackwell, pp. 236–46.
Bacciagaluppi, G., and Valentini, A. (2009). *Quantum Theory at a Crossroads: Reconsidering the 1927 Solvay Conference*. Cambridge: Cambridge University Press.
Ball, P. (2011). 'The Dawn of Quantum Biology'. *Nature* 474, pp. 272-4.
Barwise, J., and Seligman, J. (1997). *Information Flow: The Logic of Distributed Systems*. Cambridge: Cambridge University Press.
Bell, J. (1987). *Speakable and Unspeakable in Quantum Mechanics*. Cambridge: Cambridge University Press.
Bohm, D. (1952a). 'A Suggested Interpretation of the Quantum Theory in Terms of "Hidden Variables I"'. *Physical Review*, 85 (2): 166–79.
Bohm, D. (1952b). 'A Suggested Interpretation of the Quantum Theory in Terms of "Hidden Variables II"'. *Physical Review*, 85 (2): 180–93.
Bohm, D. (1980). *Wholeness and the Implicate Order*. London: Routledge.
Bohm, D. (1989). 'Meaning and Information'. In P. Pylkkänen (ed.), *The Search for Meaning*. Wellingborough: Crucible, pp. 43–62.
Bohm, D. (1990).'A New Theory of the Relationship of Mind and Matter'. *Philosophical Psychology*, 3: 271–86.
Bohm, D., and Hiley, B. J. (1975). 'On the Intuitive Understanding of Non-Locality as Implied by Quantum Theory'. *Foundations of Physics*, 5: 93–109.
Bohm, D., and Hiley, B.J. (1984). 'Generalization of the Twistor to Clifford Algebras as a Basis for Geometry'. *Revista Brasileira de Fisica, Vol. Esp. Os 70 anos de Mário Schönberg*, pp. 1-26.

Bohm, D., and Hiley, B. J. (1987). 'An Ontological Basis for Quantum Theory: I. Non-Relativistic Particle Systems'. *Physics Reports*, 144 (6): 323–48.

Bohm, D., and Hiley, B. J. (1993). *The Undivided Universe: An Ontological Interpretation of Quantum Theory*. London: Routledge.

Bouwmeester, D., Ekert, A., and Zeilinger, A. K. (eds.) (2000). *The Physics of Quantum Information: Quantum Cryptography, Quantum Teleportation, Quantum Computation*. Heidelberg and Berlin: Spinger.

Bricmont, J. (2016). *Making Sense of Quantum Mechanics*. Heidelberg: Springer.

Chalmers, D. (1996). *The Conscious Mind: In Search of a Fundamental Theory*. Oxford: Oxford University Press.

Choustova, O. (2007). 'Toward Quantum-Like Modeling of Financial Processes'. *Journal of Physics: Conference Series*, 70: 012006.

Chrisley, R. C. (1997). 'Learning in Non-Superpositional Quantum Neurocomputers'. In Pylkkänen et al. (eds.) (1997), pp. 126–39.

Dickson, M. (1996). 'Antidote or Theory?' *Studies in History and Philosophy of Modern Physics*, 27 (2): 229–38.

Dretske, F. (1981). *Knowledge and the Flow of Information*. Cambridge, MA: MIT Press.

Filk, T. (2012). 'Quantum-Like Behavior of Classical Systems'. In J. Busemeyer, F. Dubois, A. Lambert-Mogiliansky, and M. Melucci (eds.), *Quantum Interaction (Lecture Notes in Computer Science)*, vol. 7620. Berlin: Springer, pp. 196–206.

Flack, R., Monachello, V., Hiley, B.J. and Barker, P. (2018) 'A Method for Mesuring the Weak Value of Spin for Metastable Atoms' *Entropy* 20, 566. Republished in Walleczek et al. (eds.) (2018).

Floridi, Luciano (2015). 'Semantic Conceptions of Information'. In E. N. Zalta (ed.), *The Stanford Encyclopedia of Philosophy*, Spring 2015 edition. http://plato.stanford.edu/archives/spr2015/entries/information-semantic/.

Fodor, J. (1989). 'Making Mind Matter More'. *Philosophical Topics*, XVII (1): 59–79.

Gennaro, R. (2012). *The Consciousness Paradox*. Cambridge, MA: MIT Press.

Goldstein, Sheldon (2013). 'Bohmian Mechanics'. In E. Zalta (ed.), *The Stanford Encyclopedia of Philosophy*. http://plato.stanford.edu/archives/spr2013/entries/qm-bohm/.

Hameroff, S., and Penrose, R. (2014). 'Consciousness in the Universe: A Review of the "Orch OR theory"'. *Physics of Life Reviews*, 11 (1): 39–78.

Haven, E. (2005). 'Pilot-Wave Theory and Financial Option Pricing'. *International Journal of Theoretical Physics*, 44: 1957–62.

Hiley, B.J. and Pylkkänen, P. (1997). 'Active Information and Cognitive Science: A Reply to Kieseppä'. In Pylkkänen et al. (eds.) (1997), pp. 64–85.

Hiley, B. J., and Pylkkänen, P. (2001). 'Naturalizing the Mind in a Quantum Framework'. In P. Pylkkänen and T. Vadén (eds.), *Dimensions of Conscious Experience*. Amsterdam: John Benjamins, pp. 119–44.

Hiley, B.J., and Pylkkänen, P. (2005) 'Can Mind Affect Matter Via Active Information'. *Mind and Matter* 3 (2): 7-26, URL = http://www.mindmatter.de/resources/pdf/hileywww.pdf

Holland, P. (1995). *The Quantum Theory of Motion. An Account of the de Broglie – Bohm Causal Interpretation of Quantum Mechanics*. Cambridge: Cambridge University Press.

Holland, P. (2011). 'A Quantum of History'. *Contemporary Physics*, 52 (4): 355–8.

Ismael, J.T. (2016). *How Physics Makes Us Free*. Oxford: Oxford University Press.

Jammer, M. (1998). 'David Bohm and His Work: On the Occasion of His Seventieth Birthday'. *Foundations of Physics*, 18: 691–9.

Khrennikov, A. (2004). *Information Dynamics in Cognitive, Psychological and Anomalous Phenomena*. Series: Fundamental Theories of Physics, vol. 138. Dordrecht: Kluwer.

Kieseppä, I. A. (1997a). 'Is David Bohm's Notion of Active Information Useful in Cognitive Science?' In Pylkkänen et al. (eds.) (1997), pp. 54–63.

Kieseppä, I. A. (1997b). 'On the Difference Between Quantum and Classical Potentials – A Reply to Hiley and Pylkkänen'. In Pylkkänen et al. (eds.) (1997), pp. 86–99.

Lewis. P. (2016). *Quantum Ontology. A Guide to the Metaphysics of Quantum Mechanics*. Oxford: Oxford University Press.

Lycan, W. G.(1996). *Consciousness and Experience*. Cambridge, MA: MIT Press.

Lycan, W.G. (2006). 'Resisting ?-ism'. *Journal of Consciousness Studies* 13 (10-11): 65-71.

Maleeh, R., and Amani, P. (2012). 'Bohm's Theory of the Relationship of Mind and Matter Revisited'. *Neuroquantology*, 10: 150–63.

Marais, A., et al. (2018) 'The Future of Quantum Biology'. *J. R. Soc. Interface* 15: 20180640.

Maroney, O. (2002). *Information and Entropy in Quantum Theory*. Ph D thesis, Birkbeck College, University of London. www.bbk.ac.uk/tpru/OwenMaroney/thesis/thesis.html.

Maroney, O., and Hiley, B. J. (1999). 'Quantum State Teleportation Understood Through the Bohm Interpretation'. *Foundations of Physics*, 29 (9): 1403–15.

McGinn, C. (2006). 'Hard questions'. *Journal of Consciousness Studies* 13 (10–11): 90–99.

Nagel, T. (1979). 'Panpsychism'. In *Mortal Questions*. Cambridge: Cambridge University Press, pp. 181–95.

Nagel, T. (1986). *The View from Nowhere*. Oxford: Oxford University Press.

Ney, A., and Albert, D. (2013). *The Wave Function: Essays on th Metaphysics of Quantum Mechanics*. Oxford: Oxford University Press.

Oizumi, M., Albantakis, L., and Tononi, G. (2014). 'From the Phenomenology to the Mechanisms of Consciousness: Integrated Information Theory 3.0'. *PLoS Computational Biology*, 10 (5): e1003588.

Penrose, R. (1994). *Shadows of the Mind*. Oxford: Oxford University Press.

Philippidis, C., Dewdney, C., and Hiley, B. J. (1979). 'Quantum Interference and the Quantum Potential'. *Il Nuovo Cimento*, 52 (1): 15–28.

Plotnitsky, A. (2010). *Epistemology and Probability. Bohr, Heisenberg, Schrödinger and the Nature of Quantum-Theoretical Thinking*. Heidelberg and New York: Springer.

Polkinghorne, J. (2002) *Quantum Theory: A Very Short Introduction*. Oxford: Oxford University Press.

Pylkkänen, P. (1992). *Mind, Matter and Active Information*. Reports from the Department of Philosophy No. 2, University of Helsinki. Helsinki: Yliopistopaino.

Pylkkänen, P. (1996). 'On Baking Conscious Cake with Quantum Yeast and Flour'. In J. Shawe-Taylor (ed.), *Consciousness at a Crossroads of Cognitive Science and Phenomenology*. Thorverton: Imprint Academic.

Pylkkänen, P. (2007). *Mind, Matter and the Implicate Order*. Berlin and New York: Springer (Frontiers Collection).

Pylkkänen. P. (2016). 'Can Bohmian Quantum Information Help Us to Understand Consciousness?' In H. Atmanspacher, T. Filk, and E. Pothos (eds.), *Quantum Interaction 2015: 9th International Conference, Revised Selected Papers*. Heidelberg: Springer, pp. 76–87.

Pylkkänen, P. (2017). 'Is There Room in Quantum Ontology for a Genuine Causal Role of Consciousness?' In A. Khrennikov and E. Haven (eds.), *The Palgrave Handbook of Quantum Models in Social Science*. London: Macmillan, pp. 293–318.

Pylkkänen, P. (2018). 'Quantum Theories of Consciousness'. In R. J. Gennaro (ed.) *The Routledge Handbook of Consciousness*. New York and London: Routledge, pp. 216–231.

Pylkkänen, P., Hiley, B. J. and Pättiniemi, I. (2016). 'Bohm's Approach and Individuality'. In A. Guay and T. Pradeu (eds.), *Individuals Across the Sciences*. Oxford: Oxford University Press, pp. 226–49. http://arxiv.org/abs/1405.4772.

Pylkkänen, P., Pylkkö, P. and Hautamäki, A. (eds.), *Brain, Mind and Physics*. Amsterdam: IOS Press

Riggs, P. (2008). 'Reflections on the de Broglie – Bohm Quantum Potential'. *Erkenntnis*, 68: 21–39.

Roederer, J. G. (2005). *Information and Its Role in Nature*. Berlin: Springer.

Rosenthal, D. (1997). 'A Theory of Consciousness'. In N. Block, O. Flanagan, and G. Güzeldere (eds.), *The Nature of Consciousness: Philosophical Debates*. Cambridge, MA: MIT Press, pp. 729–53.

Rosenthal, D. (2009). 'Concepts and Definitions of Consciousness'. In W. Banks (ed.), *Encyclopedia of Consciousness*. New York: Elsevier.

Schaffer, J. (2010). 'Monism: The Priority of the Whole'. *Philosophical Review*, 119 (1): 31–76.

Seager, W. (2013). 'Classical Levels, Russellian Monism and the Implicate Order'. *Foundations of Physics*, 43: 548–67.

Seager, W. (2018). 'The Philosophical and Scientific Metaphysics of David Bohm'. *Entropy* 20, 493. Republished in Walleczek et al. eds (2018).

Seager, W., and Allen-Hermanson, S. (2015). 'Panpsychism'. In E. Zalta (ed.), *The Stanford Encyclopedia of Philosophy*, Fall 2015 edition. https://plato.stanford.edu/archives/fall2015/entries/panpsychism/.

Simons, P. (2006). 'The seeds of experience'. *Journal of Consciousness Studies* 13 (10–11): 146–50.

Smith, Q. (2003). 'Why Cognitive Scientists Cannot Ignore Quantum Mechanics?' In Q. Smith and A. Jokic (eds.), *Consciousness: New Philosophical Perspectives*. Oxford: Oxford University Press, pp. 409–46.

Strawson, Galen (2006). 'Realistic Monism – Why Physicalism Entails Panpsychism'. *Journal of Consciousness Studies*, 13 (10–11): 3–31.

Tononi, G., and Koch, C. (2014). 'Consciousness: Here, There but Not Everywhere'. https://arxiv.org/abs/1405.7089v1. (Published as 'Consciousness: Here, There and Everywhere?' *Philosophical Transactions of the Royal Society B*, 370: 20140167.).

Velmans, M. (1991a). 'Is Human Information Processing Conscious?' *Behavioral and Brain Sciences* 14 (4): 651–69.

Velmans, M. (1991b). 'Consciousness from a First-Person Perspective'. *Behavioral and Brain Sciences*, 14 (4): 702–26.

Velmans, M. (2009). *Understanding Consciousness*, 2nd edition. London: Routledge.

Walleczek, J., and Grössing, G. (2016). 'Nonlocal Quantum Information Transfer Without Superluminal Signalling and Communication'. *Foundations of Physics*, 46 (9): 1208–28.

Walleczek, J., Grössing, G., Pylkkänen, P., and Hiley B.J. (2018). *Emergent Quantum Mechanics: David Bohm Centennial Perspectives*. Printed Edition of the Special Issue Published in *Entropy*. Basel: MDPI. Free download: https://www.mdpi.com/1099-4300/21/2/113

Wang, Z., Busemeyer, J. R., Atmanspacher, H., and Pothos, E. M. (2013). 'The Potential of Using Quantum Theory to Build Models of Cognition'. *Topics in Cognitive Science*, 5: 672–88.

Weber, R. (1987). 'Meaning as Being in the Implicate Order Philosophy of David Bohm: A Conversation'. In B. Hiley and F. Peat (eds.), *Quantum Implications: Essays in Honour of David Bohm*. London: Routledge, pp. 436–50.

Wendt, A. (2015). *Quantum Mind and Social Science: Unifying Physical and Social Ontology*. Cambridge: Cambridge University Press.

25

PANPSYCHISM'S COMBINATION PROBLEM IS A PROBLEM FOR EVERYONE

Angela Mendelovici

1. Introduction

Panpsychism is the view that the phenomenal experiences of macrophysical items, like ourselves, are nothing over and above combinations of phenomenal experiences of microphysical items, where the relevant modes of combination might involve physical properties and relations.[1] Most versions of the view can be seen as being motivated by the perceived failure of *physicalism* – the view that consciousness is nothing over and above some arrangement of (non-experiential) physical items – to provide an intelligible explanation of phenomenal consciousness, together with a desire to explain at least our own experiences in more fundamental terms. Physicalist attempts at explaining consciousness in terms of fundamental non-experiential physical reality are subject to explanatory gap worries (Levine 1983), the conceivability argument (Chalmers 1996), and the knowledge argument (Jackson 1982), all of which arguably arise from physicalism's failure to render intelligible the putative connection between phenomenal consciousness and physical reality. *Dualism*, which takes phenomenal experiences such as our own to be fundamental, avoids such worries by denying that phenomenal experiences can be explained in terms of something else, but gives up on the reductive spirit of physicalism, taking our phenomenal experiences to be primitive, and perhaps brute and inexplicable, features of reality.

Panpsychism attempts to get the best of both worlds, combining physicalism's reductive spirit with dualism's skepticism about explaining consciousness in non-experiential terms. Like physicalism, panpsychism aims to explain our phenomenal experiences in terms of something else, though it denies that this something else is wholly non-experiential. Like dualism, panpsychism takes at least some instances of phenomenal consciousness to be fundamental. *Our* experiences may not be fundamental, but they are made up of experiences that are.

Unfortunately, it is not clear that panpsychism can offer an intelligible explanation of the phenomenal experiences of macrophysical entities like ourselves at all, and so it is not clear that panpsychism is any better off than physicalism with respect to explaining our experiences. The problem is that it is not clear how fundamental experiences can come together to form experiences such as our own. This problem is the combination problem, and it has been discussed at length by James (1890), Seager (1995), Goff (2006), Stoljar (2006), Basile (2010), Coleman (2012), Roelofs (2014), Chalmers (2016), Mørch (2014), and others.

The aim of this chapter is to clarify the combination problem, assess the extent to which problems of mental combination are unique to panpsychism, and consider the implications for arguments against panpsychism. I will argue that the panpsychist's combination problem might not be hers alone and that this suggests an "epistemic" reply to objections to panpsychism from the combination problem.

2. Panpsychism and the Combination Problem

Panpsychism is a theory of *phenomenal consciousness*, the felt, qualitative, subjective, or "what it's like" (Nagel 1974) aspect of mental life. Particular instances of phenomenal consciousness are *(phenomenal) experiences*, and the specific "what it's like" or felt quality of an experience is its *phenomenal character*. For example, an experience of redness might be said to have a "reddish" phenomenal character.

According to panpsychism, the fundamental physical constituents of reality (*microphysical* entities) have experiences, and the experiences of non-fundamental physical items (*macrophysical* entities) are constituted by the experiences of microphysical entities, perhaps combined in a certain way, where the relevant mode of combination might involve functional and physical properties and relations. We can call the experiences of microphysical items *microexperiences* and the experiences of macrophysical items *macroexperiences*. For panpsychism, phenomenal consciousness is both a posit and an explanandum: panpsychism aims to explain macroexperiences such as our own and it does so by positing microexperiences.

Given that a central motivation for panpsychism is the failure of physicalism to provide an intelligible explanation of phenomenal consciousness, I will assume that panpsychists aim to provide an explanation of macroexperience that is *intelligible*. I will take this to require that the macroexperiential facts are *a priori* entailed by the facts about microexperiences and how they are combined. I will not assume, however, that panpsychism requires that we can ever *know* such a theory, and I will eventually suggest that such a theory might not be knowable by us.

Perhaps the most pressing worry for panpsychism is the *combination problem*, the problem of explaining how the hypothesized microexperiences combine to form macroexperiences, such as our own observed experiences. We can sharpen the worry with some assumptions:

(A1) Macroexperiences are not identical to any one of their constituent microexperiences.

(A2) The subjects of macroexperiences are not identical to any one of the subjects of their constituent microexperiences.

(A3) Macroexperiences have phenomenal characters that are not had by any of their constituent microexperiences.

Given these three assumptions, the combination problem becomes that of explaining how groups of microexperiences come together to constitute (1) *new experiences*, which belong to (2) *new subjects*, and have (3) *new phenomenal characters*. We can thus tease apart three combination problems for panpsychism:

(CP1) The new experience problem
(CP2) The new subject problem
(CP3) The new phenomenal characters problem

Note that, given our definition of panpsychism, none of the assumptions that give rise to the combination problems form a definitional part of panpsychism, and so a panpsychist solution to these problems might coherently deny any one of them.

Problems (CP1) and (CP2) are sometimes lumped together under the heading of "the subject combination problem" and taken to be the central or most difficult part of the combination problem (see Roelofs' contribution to this volume). As we will soon see, (CP1) and (CP2) are distinct problems, though they interact with one another in interesting ways.

The remainder of this section elaborates upon the combination problems for panpsychism and suggests that what makes them particularly challenging is that they require mental things to come together to form more than a mere collection of their parts.

The New Experience Problem

The *new experience problem* is the problem of explaining how microexperiences combine to form distinct macroexperiences. For example, according to panpsychism, two microexperiences, e1 and e2, when combined in the right way, might give rise to a distinct macroexperience, E. The problem is that of explaining how this new experience arises. What makes the new experience problem challenging is that it is not clearly intelligible why a collection of experiences, however organized, should result in a *further* experience.

The new experience problem can be avoided by rejecting assumption (A1), the assumption that microexperiences combine to form *distinct* macroexperiences, and instead claiming that each macroexperience is identical to a constituent microexperience. On such a view, macroexperiences are present at the fundamental level, and so there are no "new" experiences to account for. Leibniz's (1714/1989) monadology is such a version of panpsychism. One worry with this general approach is that it seems there would be a surprising structural mismatch between the microphysical properties of the dominant monad and its corresponding experience (see Chalmers 2016). Another reason to disfavor such a view is that taking our own experiences to be fundamental foregoes one of the main advantages of panpsychism over ordinary dualism, which is that it promises to offer an explanation of our own experiences in terms of something else. For these reasons, the panpsychist probably should not try to avoid the new experience problem by rejecting (A1).

The New Subject Problem

The *new subject problem* is the problem of explaining how subjects of microexperience combine to form distinct subjects of macroexperience. Suppose s1 and s2 are the subjects of experiences e1 and e2, respectively. On most natural versions of panpsychism, when e1 and e2 combine to form the new experience E, this experience is an experience of a new subject, S, which is distinct from s1 and s2. The new subject problem is that of explaining how S arises from a combination of s1 and s2. The problem is challenging because it is not clearly intelligible why a mere collection of subjects, however organized, should yield a new subject (see, e.g. Goff 2006, 2009).

The new subject problem can be avoided by rejecting (A2), the assumption that the subjects of macroexperiences are distinct from the subjects of any one of their constituent microexperiences, and instead claiming that the subjects of macroexperiences are simply the subjects of one or more of the constituent microexperiences. In the preceding example, we could say that E is an experience of s1, s2, or both s1 and s2, taken severally. Of these options, the first two seem arbitrary (why should E be an experience of s1 rather than s2?), which leaves us with the last option: s1 experiences E, and s2 also experiences E. But such a view, on which, presumably, every macroexperience is had by all the subjects of all its constituent microexperiences, seems a bit excessive. It also faces the same structural mismatch problem as the Leibnizian view discussed previously. For these reasons, the panpsychist probably should not try to avoid the new subject problem by rejecting (A2).

The New Phenomenal Character Problem

The *new phenomenal character problem* is the problem of explaining how the phenomenal characters of microexperiences combine to form the phenomenal characters of macroexperiences. The problem arises from (A3), according to which macroexperiences have phenomenal characters that their constituent microexperiences do not have. For example, we experience colors, shapes, and feelings of déjà vu, but microphysical items presumably do not have all these kinds of experiences.

We can distinguish between two types of new phenomenal characters the panpsychist might want to accommodate: *complex* phenomenal characters, which are phenomenal characters that have parts that are also phenomenal characters, and *simple* phenomenal characters, which are phenomenal characters that are not complex. For example, the phenomenal character of an experience of a red square might be complex in that it involves as parts both reddish and squarish phenomenal characters, but the phenomenal character of an experience of redness might be simple, not involving other phenomenal characters as parts.

The panpsychist faces challenges in accommodating both simple and complex new phenomenal characters. Suppose a macroexperience E has a complex reddish-squarish phenomenal character. According to panpsychism, E's complex phenomenal character is a result of the phenomenal characters of its constituent experiences. Perhaps E is a combination of two experiences, e1 and e2, where e1 has a reddish phenomenal character and e2 has a squarish phenomenal character. The problem is that it is not clear why E should have a reddish-squarish phenomenal character, rather than a reddish phenomenal character alongside a squarish phenomenal character. In other words, it is not clear why e1 and e2's phenomenal characters should combine in E to yield a complex whole, a reddish-squarish phenomenal character, rather than simply co-exist as two unrelated simple (or simpler) phenomenal characters. It is even less clear how new simple phenomenal characters could arise from the phenomenal characters of microexperiences, since they do not even have constituent parts that are phenomenal characters. There aren't any candidate phenomenal characters to be combined, let alone a way of intelligibly combining them into a new whole.

The problems can be avoided by rejecting (A3): If microphysical items do have the full range of experiences found in macrophysical items, then there need be no combined phenomenal characters. But it is implausible that the full range of experiences found at the macrolevel is found at the microlevel. Many of the phenomenal characters of macroexperiences appear to be too sophisticated to be found at the microlevel, such as feelings of jealousy or cognitive experiences of suddenly grasping a difficult concept. Additionally, and perhaps more persuasively, it is implausible that there are enough kinds of microexperiences to correspond to all the kinds of macroexperiences we can have. For these reasons, the panpsychist probably should not try to avoid the new phenomenal characters problem by denying (A3).

3. Combination Problems for Everyone

Panpsychism's combination problems are challenging (see especially Goff 2006, 2009; Chalmers 2016), but the panpsychist does not face them alone. They are of the same kind as the problems of explaining phenomenal unity, mental structure, and changes in quality spaces, which are problems for anyone holding certain plausible assumptions.

3.1. The New Experience Problem Is Not Special to Panpsychism

This subsection argues that the new experience problem is the same in kind as two other well-known problems, the problems of explaining phenomenal unity and mental structure. The phenomena of phenomenal unity and mental structure arguably involve experiences coming together to form new experiences in much the same way that panpsychism requires microexperiences to come together to form new macroexperiences.

The Problem of Phenomenal Unity

You might now be enjoying various visual, auditory, and cognitive experiences. These experiences are in some sense experienced *together*. In contrast, your experiences and the experiences of other people are not experienced together. *Phenomenal unity* is the phenomenon of experiences being experienced together that is present in the former kinds of cases and absent in the latter.

The *problem of phenomenal unity* is the problem of explaining how and why some experiences are phenomenally unified while others are not. Solving this problem is particularly difficult because it seems that what is required for a group of experiences to be phenomenally unified is something more than their co-occurrence. Something like this is assumed by two influential characterizations of phenomenal unity.

On Bayne and Chalmers' (Bayne 2012; Bayne and Chalmers 2003) characterization, experiences are phenomenally unified when they are subsumed by a single conscious state; phenomenal unity involves a *new* experience, one that subsumes the unified experiences.

Similarly, Dainton (2000: 4) characterizes phenomenal unity in terms of co-consciousness, where co-consciousness is not merely a matter of experiences occurring at the same time or place, or even in the same subject, but rather "consists in a relationship between experiences that is itself experienced." On this characterization, the phenomenal unity of e1 and e2 involves an experienced relation between e1 and e2, and the experience of this relation is a new experience, distinct from e1 and e2.

The Problem of Mental Structure

Our mental states do not form an undifferentiated whole, or a set of isolated states, but are instead related and structured in various ways. For example, a visual experience of a red circle does not only involve an experience of redness and an experience of a circle, but also involves these experiences being related in a certain way: The experienced redness qualifies the experienced circle. The *problem of mental structure* is that of explaining how mental states come to be structured in this and other ways.

One instance of the problem of mental structure is a version of the binding problem, the *experience binding problem*, which is the problem of explaining how distinct experiences that are subserved by distinct neural areas are experienced as pertaining to the same consciously represented object. Another instance of the problem of mental structure concerns intentional structure. *Intentional contents* – what mental states "say," are directed at, or represent – can be structured in various ways. The *problem of intentional structure* is that of explaining how intentional states representing a content's constituent contents come together to form a complex structured intentional state rather than, say, a mere set of contentful states.

Mental structure quite plausibly involves *new* mental states, mental states involving but distinct from the mental states that compose them. For example, suppose M1 and M2 are bound to the same represented object. Then there is a mental state distinct from M1 and M2, consisting of M1 and M2 together and organized in a certain way, i.e., as bound to the same represented object. For example, a thought that Lisa loves Sally involves not only the representation of the contents <Lisa>, <Sally>, and <loves>, but also a distinct state representing <Lisa loves Sally>.

If the preceding claims about the problems of phenomenal unity and mental structure are right, then the problem of explaining how experiences combine to form new experiences may not be special to panpsychism. On the reasonable assumption that certain kinds of holism are not true, an assumption that we will consider shortly, phenomenal unity involves experiences coming together to form new unified experiences, and mental structure involves experiences or intentional states coming together to form new complex experiences or intentional states, respectively. Of course, panpsychism requires that *micro*experiences combine to form new experiences, whereas phenomenal unity and mental structure only require *macro*experiences to combine to form new experiences. But it is not clear that what is required is different in kind.

One might object that there is a way out of this commitment in the case of the problems of phenomenal unity and mental structure that is not available in the case of the panpsychist's new experience problem, so the problems are different in kind. The way out is to reject the assumption that when we experience a phenomenally unified or mentally structured whole, we also experience its parts. A holistic view of this sort (see, e.g., James 1890) avoids commitment to new experiences by denying that macroexperiences ever combine in the relevant way. What appear to be separable parts of our experiences are in fact mere aspects of the experiences, having no distinct and independent existence, but instead having an existence that depends on the whole of which they are an aspect.

However, the panpsychist might similarly avail herself to a "holistic" solution to the new experience problem, maintaining that the ultimate constituents of reality are not "small" things, but rather the world as a whole, which has one single experience (at least at a time) with many aspects corresponding to what we take to be our experiences (see Goff 2017). Alternatively, she might maintain that the ultimate constituents of reality are or include subjects like ourselves. Like the way out of the problems of phenomenal unity and mental structure, this strategy involves denying that the relevant sort of mental combination occurs. Such a view still qualifies as panpsychist on our definition, since it still maintains that macroexperiences are nothing over and above microexperiences combined in a certain way – it's just that every macroexperience is identical to a single microexperience. Unless there is good reason to think that the problems of phenomenal unity and mental structure are particularly amenable to the holistic strategy while the new experience problem is not, the availability of this strategy in their case does not suggest that the new experience problem is different in kind from the problems of phenomenal unity and mental structure.

Another objection to the claim that the new experience problem is the same in kind as the problems of phenomenal unity and mental structure is that in the case of new experiences arising from phenomenal unity and mental structure, the new experiences are experiences of the *same* subjects that experience the combined experiences, whereas in the case of the panpsychist's new experiences, the new experiences are experiences of *new* subjects. This suggests that perhaps the way in which microexperiences combine to form new macroexperiences is different from the way in which macroexperiences combine to form new macroexperiences, which would mean that the panpsychist's new experience problem is indeed special to panpsychism. We will return to this objection shortly.

3.2. The New Subject Problem Is Not Special to Panpsychism

Consider first a fairly thin notion of subjects on which subjects are sets of phenomenally unified experiences. On this notion, when mental combination results in a new experience, that experience automatically has a subject. For example, once phenomenal unity results in a new experience subsuming or including the unified experiences, that experience thereby automatically has a subject.

On the thin notion of subjects, there is no mystery as to why phenomenally unified experiences have subjects: they have subjects simply because they are phenomenally unified and subjects are sets of phenomenally unified experiences. It might seem that the panpsychist can solve the new subject problem in the same way: when the experiences of microsubjects are phenomenally unified, a new macrosubject comes to exist and experiences the phenomenally unified experiences. The new subject problem, then, can be solved by adopting a thin view of subjects and solving the new experience problem, which is a problem for everyone.

There is a worry, however, which brings us back to the worry raised at the end of the previous subsection: The way subjects combine to form new subjects according to panpsychism and the way phenomenally unified experiences come to form subjects of experiences in the case of phenomenal unity are importantly disanalogous. In a case of panpsychist subject combination, a new subject, S, experiences microexperiences m1 and m2 combined (i.e., a macroexperience M), but, it is natural to assume, m1 and m2 are each *also* experienced by a subject distinct from S. In contrast, in a case of phenomenal unity, when experiences e1 and e2 are phenomenally unified to form experience E, it is natural to assume that there is only a single subject of experience, which experiences e1 and e2 together (i.e., E). So, what's responsible for the arising of new subjects on panpsychism cannot be the same thing as what's responsible for phenomenally unified experiences having subjects. The problem is not so much to do with how the new subject arises but rather with what happens to the "old" subjects once combined. In the case of phenomenal unity, the old subjects cease to exist or are subsumed by the new subject. In the case of panpsychist subject combination, the old subjects continue to exist. When microexperiences m1 and m2 combine into M, there are three subjects, whereas when experiences e1 and e2 are phenomenally unified to form E, there is only one.

This worry arises from two assumptions, the first of which is natural on panpsychism, and the second of which is natural on any picture of phenomenal unity:

(A) When microexperiences (or macroexperiences) combine to form macroexperiences, they are experienced both together and in isolation.
(B) When macroexperiences are phenomenally unified, they are experienced together but not in isolation.

We can avoid the worry described above by rejecting either of these assumptions. On (A), when m1 and m2 are combined to form M, there is an experience of m1 in isolation, an experience of m2 in isolation, and an experience of m1 and m2 combined (M). On a thin notion of subjects, this means that there are three subjects of experience, a subject of m1, a subject of m2, and a subject of M. The panpsychist might choose to deny (A) and instead claim that when m1 and m2 are combined, they are experienced together but not in isolation.

The *combinatorial infusion view* (Seager 2010, 2016; Mørch 2014) makes precisely such claims. On this view, when microexperiences combine to yield macroexperiences, they fuse together and cease to exist independently. As Seager (2010) puts it, they are "absorbed" or "superseded" by the macroexperience they come to constitute. On this picture, when microexperiences combine, the result is only one subject that experiences the combined microexperiences.

The combinatorial infusion view, and any other panpsychist view that rejects the first assumption, avoids the worry that the problems of explaining subject unity and phenomenal unity are different in kind because they yield different treatments of the old subjects of experience. Indeed, Seager suggests that the combinatorial infusion view might help solve the problem of phenomenal unity (2010: 184).

We can also avoid the worry by rejecting (B). Perhaps when e1 and e2 are phenomenally unified, e1 and e2 are experienced both together *and* severally. There is an experience of e1 together with e2 (E), an experience of e1 in isolation, and an experience of e2 in isolation. This option might seem unlikely, since we have no phenomenological evidence that phenomenally unified experiences are also experienced in isolation. But note that there is also no phenomenological evidence against this possibility: It is entirely compatible with an experience of E that there exist isolated experiences of e1 and e2. On the thin notion of subjects, there would then be three subjects of experience: the subject of e1, the subject of e2, and the subject of e1 and e2 together. Indeed, Roelofs (2016) suggests that such a view is true and helpful to panpsychism, helping us make sense of how experiences can be shared between distinct microphysical and macrophysical entities.

In sum, if we adopt a thin notion of subjects and reject one of (A) or (B), the panpsychist's subject combination is plausibly of the same kind as whatever results in phenomenally unified experiences having subjects. The claim that panpsychism faces a *special* problem of subject combination depends on both assumptions being true.

The rejection of either (A) or (B) also allows us to respond to the worry described at the end of section 3.1 that there is an important difference between the new experiences required by panpsychism and those required by phenomenal unity and mental structure. The alleged difference is that in the case of new experiences arising from phenomenal unity and mental structure, the new experiences are experiences of the *same* subjects that experience the combined experiences, whereas in the case of the panpsychist's new experiences, the new experiences are experiences of *new* subjects. But if we adopt a thin notion of subjects and reject (A), then, in both cases, the combined experience is an experience of a single subject that is distinct from the subject of the experiences that form the experience's parts. And if we adopt a thin view of subjects and instead reject (B), then, in both cases, the combined experience is an experience of a single subject that is also the subject of the experiences that form the experience's parts. So, the cases are not disanalogous. Again, the worry that panpsychism faces a *special* problem of mental combination concerning new experiences depends on both assumptions being true.

I have argued that the panpsychist faces no special problem in accounting for new thin subjects of macroexperience. But what if we think that there are such things as subjects on a thicker notion of subjecthood, perhaps one that builds in criteria for identity over time? If the panpsychist accepts that there are such thick subjects and that they can combine to form new thick subjects, then, depending on what exactly they are supposed to be, she might face special problems in accounting for the required kinds of combinations. But even if the panpsychist accepts that macroexperiences have thick subjects, she need not accept that microexperiences have thick subjects that combine to form them. It is enough for the panpsychist to say that microexperiences have thin subjects, and that thick subjects, if there are any, arise in some other way at the macro level. The problem of explaining how they arise at the macro level, of course, is a problem for anyone who accepts them.

3.3. The New Phenomenal Characters Problem Is Not Special to Panpsychism

If the preceding arguments are sound, the new experience and new subject problems are not special to panpsychism. Things are less clear in the case of the new phenomenal characters problem. Recall that there are two types of new phenomenal characters that our macroexperiences seem to exhibit that we need to explain: complex and simple phenomenal characters.

To explain how macroexperiences can have new complex phenomenal characters we must explain how complex phenomenal characters arise from their simpler parts. If the phenomenal characters of the simplest parts are those of microphysical entities, then that is all we must do. If it is not, then there is the further problem of explaining how these simple parts arise from the phenomenal characters of microphysical entities, which calls for an explanation of how macroexperiences can come to have new simple phenomenal characters, the second type of new phenomenal character the panpsychist should accommodate.

Let us start with the problem of explaining how complex phenomenal characters arise from their simpler parts. This problem is of the same kind as the problem of mental structure, the problem of explaining how phenomenal and intentional mental features come to be structured. Structured experiences and intentional states have complex phenomenal characters and intentional contents, respectively, which presumably are combinations of their constituent phenomenal characters or intentional contents.

Of course, since the panpsychist but not the non-panpsychist requires that there be microexperiences that combine in the relevant ways, she might require that there be more instances of mental structure than the non-panpsychist, and so her problem might be wider in scope. Still, the problems are of the same kind.

The situation is less clear when it comes to accounting for the combination of phenomenal characters into new *simple* phenomenal characters. The problem of explaining simple combined phenomenal characters is arguably the hard nut, and perhaps the special nut, of the combination problem. The problem seems *hard* because what it seems to require, simple yet combined items, seems incoherent. The problem seems *special* to panpsychism since the non-panpsychist appears not to be committed to such simple yet combined phenomenal characters. She might accept that the simple phenomenal characters in question exist but deny that they are the results of combinations of other phenomenal characters.

The panpsychist might attempt to sidestep this problem of accounting for the combination of phenomenal characters into new *simple* phenomenal characters by denying that macroexperiences have simple phenomenal characters. Roelofs (2014) considers such a view, suggesting that our apparently simple phenomenal characters might be blends of the "alien" phenomenal characters of microexperiences.

In defense of this view, Roelofs points to examples of macroexperiences that appear simple but plausibly are complex blends of other macroexperiences, such as the apparently simple phenomenal characters of color experiences. An orangish phenomenal character might appear simple, but, he claims, it is in fact a blend of a reddish and a yellowish phenomenal character. Roelofs suggests that such examples show that it is possible for phenomenal characters to blend, and, further, that we are bad at recognizing such blends. In the case of color experience, the reason we can come to appreciate the relevant blends is that we can come to have experiences with the constituent phenomenal characters on separate occasions. For example, we can have experiences with reddish phenomenal characters, and by comparing our reddish experiences with our orangish experiences, we can come to appreciate that "there's a little bit of red in orange." In the case of the alien phenomenal characters of microexperiences that blend to form the phenomenal characters of macroexperiences, we are not able to experience the alien phenomenal characters in isolation, so we are not in a position to appreciate that the phenomenal characters of our macroexperiences are blends of them.

However, it is not clear that Roelofs' examples are effective. An orangish phenomenal character is similar to reddish and yellowish phenomenal characters, but the reason for this similarity isn't that it is *composed* of them. The phenomenal characters of color experiences might be simple but have various properties that are related to those of other phenomenal characters and that account for the similarities between them, namely their values on dimensions of hue, saturation, and brightness. If this is right, then it is not clear that the panpsychist can avoid commitment to new simple phenomenal characters, and the new phenomenal characters problem remains.

I want to suggest that the problem may not be special to panpsychism. There is a nearby problem facing everyone, that of explaining how we can come to have macroexperiences with new simple phenomenal characters that in some sense "build on" the phenomenal characters of other macroexperiences:

As we develop and learn, we acquire abilities to have new experiences. For example, a budding wine taster might gradually acquire new abilities to have new wine tasting experiences, such as experiences with fruity, oily, and tannin-ish phenomenal characters. The new phenomenal characters we are able to have in such cases are not wholly unrelated to the phenomenal characters we were previously able to have, but, instead, are similar and different to them in certain ways. We can perspicuously model such relationships of similarity and difference between phenomenal characters using *quality spaces*, abstract spaces with one or more dimensions corresponding to the dimensions of possible variation in a system of phenomenal characters, where different phenomenal characters are represented by different positions in the space. For example, since colors vary in hue, saturation, and brightness, a quality space with axes corresponding to hue, saturation, and brightness is a perspicuous way of modeling them and their similarity relations. We can think of learning and development as building upon or expanding our pre-existing quality spaces. For example, the wine taster's quality space for wine-related experiences might expand to include new dimensions. In this way, newly acquired abilities to experience new phenomenal characters might be thought to build upon pre-existing abilities. Call the problem of explaining how exactly the quality spaces characterizing our abilities to have experiences change in such ways the *changing quality space problem*.

On the face of it, the panpsychist's problem of explaining new simple phenomenal characters and the changing quality space problem seem quite alike: they both require explaining how we can come to experience (at least sometimes) simple phenomenal characters that are not present in our other concommitant or past experiences but that are nonetheless importantly related to them. Perhaps, then, both problems involve the same kind of mental combination.

Against this, one might suggest that only the panpsychist's problem is a problem of mental combination. The panpsychist assumes that an experience's new simple phenomenal characters are a matter of the combination of the phenomenal characters of some constituent experiences, but a solution to the changing quality space problem need not make such an assumption. One non-combinatorial solution to the changing quality space problem maintains that it is macroexperiences' functional roles that determine their specific phenomenal characters. Perhaps, for instance, the functional roles of color experiences fix their phenomenal characters, and when we acquire new concepts, their functional roles, including those in relation to old experiences, alter our quality spaces, allowing for experiences with new phenomenal characters.

Even if such a functionalist solution to the changing quality space problem can succeed, this is not automatically a problem for the claim that the panpsychist does not face a special problem in accounting for new simple phenomenal characters, since she can co-opt the functionalist's solution. The panpsychist wants to explain new simple experiences in terms of mental combination, but the relevant modes of combination can include functional properties. Where the non-panpsychist might say that macroexperience E has a new simple phenomenal character C in virtue of playing a certain functional role, R, the panpsychist can say that macroexperience E has a new simple phenomenal character C in virtue of being constituted by experiences e1 and e2, which, together, play functional role R. In effect, the panpsychist can turn the functionalist's non-combinatorial solution to the changing quality space problem into a combinatorial solution for the problem of explaining new simple phenomenal characters. In the same way, other non-combinatorial solutions to the changing quality space problem might be co-opted by the panpsychist. (Of course, this takes some of the bite out of panpsychism, but the view still qualifies as a version of panpsychism.)

I am doubtful, however, that the functionalist solution to the changing quality space problem can succeed. Functionalism faces well-known indeterminacy worries. For instance, a set of states that implements a symmetrical system of functional roles could equally well be said to realize at least two quality spaces (Block 1978; Palmer 1999). More generally, even if functional roles can determine the relations between phenomenal characters, it is far from clear that there is only one set of phenomenal characters whose members can bear those relations to one another.[2]

The functionalist might attempt to avoid indeterminacy worries by taking at least some functional states to be broad, involving relations beyond the experiencing individual, as on some versions of representationalism, but this would result in externalism about phenomenal consciousness, the view that a subject's experiences are at least partly determined by environmental features, which is arguably implausible (see Gertler 2001 for a defense of phenomenal internalism). Another problem with this view is that it makes the wrong predictions in certain cases, since the phenomenal characters of many phenomenal states do not match any items in the external environment (see Bourget and Mendelovici 2014; Pautz 2006b, 2013b; Mendelovici 2013, 2016, 2018: chs. 3–4). A second strategy is to throw phenomenal characters into the mix. If at least some positions in a quality space have their phenomenal characters independently of their functional roles, then they can serve as "anchor points" (Graham et al. 2007: 479), helping to constrain the possible phenomenal character assignments to the rest of the space.[3] However, it is not clear that this is enough to solve indeterminacy worries (see Bourget MS).

If there are no viable non-combinatorial solutions to the changing quality space problem, then it might just turn out that *everyone* should accept a combinatorial solution, one that takes the new phenomenal characters of macroexperiences to be a matter of the combination of other constituent phenomenal characters, had either by the macroexperience itself or by constituent experiences.

The upshot of this discussion is that the panpsychist's problem of explaining new simple phenomenal characters might be the same in kind as the problem of explaining changing quality spaces, a problem facing everyone. While it might seem that the two problems admit of different solutions, I have suggested that the panpsychist can co-opt non-combinatorial solutions to the changing quality space problem, if such solutions can succeed, but that the changing quality space problem might have to be solved by appeal to mental combination anyways.

4. Implications for Panpsychism

I have argued that panpsychism's combination problems are problems for everyone. This section considers the implications of this claim for objections to panpsychism based on the combination problem. I want to suggest that the fact that the combination problem is a problem for everyone suggests the *ignorance hypothesis*, on which we are ignorant of certain key facts about mental combination, similar to Stoljar's (2006) "ignorance hypothesis" used to defend (broad) physicalism. The ignorance hypothesis allows us to respond to two important objections to panpsychism based on the combination problem.

One objection to panpsychism based on the combination problem is that the combination problem undercuts one of the key motivations for panpsychism over physicalism, the argument from physicalism's perceived failure at offering an intelligible explanation of our experiences (see Strawson 2003). If the panpsychist cannot offer an intelligible explanation of our experiences either, then panpsychism is no better off than physicalism in this regard (see Goff 2009).

The second objection is that the combination problem shows that panpsychism is false. If the facts about microexperiences and how they are combined do not *a priori* entail the macroexperiential facts, then macroexperiences are not nothing over and above combinations of microexperiences, and panpsychism is false. Goff (2009) and Chalmers (2016) consider a conceivability argument against panpsychism along such lines, which is analogous to Chalmers' (1996) conceivability argument against physicalism.

The ignorance hypothesis allows the panpsychist to respond to these objections. We might argue for the ignorance hypothesis as follows: Everyone should agree that mental combination of the kinds the panpsychist requires *does* occur, so we know that there exists an intelligible explanation of mental combination, whether or not we do or can know it. This explanation might make reference to physical, functional, phenomenal, or other kinds of facts, or it might even take certain forms of mental combination to be primitive – for present purposes, it doesn't matter. But we don't currently have such an explanation. This suggests the ignorance hypothesis: we are ignorant of certain key facts about mental combination.

The ignorance hypothesis allows us to respond to the second objection: We simply are not able to conclude that the facts about microexperiences and how they are combined do not *a priori* entail the macroexperiential facts. For all we know, the facts about mental combination that we are ignorant of secure the required entailment. So, conceivability arguments fail to show that panpsychism is false.[4]

The first objection can also be avoided so long as the physicalist cannot similarly avail herself to an appeal to ignorance. If an appeal to ignorance is equally available to the physicalist and the panpsychist, then the panpsychist's intelligibility-based argument for panpsychism over physicalism still fails. I want to suggest that the panpsychist's ignorance hypothesis is more plausible than an analogous physicalist ignorance hypothesis: The classic arguments against physicalism (the conceivability argument, the knowledge argument, and explanatory gap worries) show not only that the physicalist has not offered an intelligible explanation of consciousness in terms of the physical, but, further, that there is no such explanation to be had. Given a certain conception of physical facts (e.g. Chalmers' (1996) conception as facts concerning the structure and dynamics of physical processes), we can see that no set of physical facts can *a priori* entail the phenomenal facts, and so, that not only do current physical theories fail to intelligibly explain consciousness, but so too would *any* other possible physicalist theories. If this is right, then an appeal to ignorance cannot help the physicalist: We may be ignorant of many physical facts, but we know enough about what physical facts look like in order to see that they cannot result in phenomenal consciousness. In contrast, we have less of a clear idea of what a plausible account of mental combination might look like. As a result, we simply do not know that there is no possible account of mental combination that renders panpsychist explanations of macroexperiences intelligible. Our epistemic situation rules out a physicalist account of macroexperience but leaves open a panpsychist account.

5. Concluding Remarks

I have argued that the panpsychist's combination problems are problems for everyone and suggested that this alleviates the panpsychist's worries concerning intelligibility. Before concluding, it is worth emphasizing that combination problems afflict our very understanding of the mind largely independently of any particular metaphysical theories of mind. These problems are pervasive and multi-faceted, arising for many different kinds of mental states and under many guises. And they are largely underappreciated. For example, much discussion of phenomenal unity focuses on simply characterizing the phenomenon rather than explaining it.[5] Similarly, much discussion of intentional structure focuses on determining rules for when simpler contents combine to form more complex contents rather than explaining how mental structure is possible at all.[6]

Given the pervasiveness and apparent intractability of combination problems, it is worth considering the possibility that we not only *have not* solved them, but that we simply *cannot* solve them. Perhaps we are "cognitively closed" (McGinn 1989) to them in that our minds simply cannot grasp how mental things can combine. It at least seems that we can intuitively understand items being spatially, causally, or temporally related in various ways, that we can understand them piling up, bumping each other around, and existing and changing through time (whether or not this is enough to understand physical combination). But mental combination arguably requires something more than that. It requires a new mode of interaction whereby mental things merge, blend, or otherwise become more than a spatiotemporally and causally integrated sum of their parts. Perhaps this is something we are simply not equipped to grasp, making the mind impossible for us to completely understand, and giving rise to an unbridgeable (by us) explanatory gap between mental combinations and their uncombined parts that faces physicalists, dualists, and panpsychists alike.[7]

Notes

1. This is what Chalmers (2016) calls "constitutive panpsychism." "Panpsychism" is sometimes more generally defined as the view that consciousness is fundamental and ubiquitous.
2. One way to put the worry is that there are reasons for thinking that functionalism cannot solve what Bourget (this volume) calls the "mapping problem." The worry mirrors undetermination worries with functionalism about semantic properties; see, e.g. Kripke (1982), BonJour (1998), Putnam (1977), Mendelovici and Bourget (forthcoming), and Mendelovici (2018).
3. Such a strategy is employed by several phenomenal intentionality theorists, who take some intentional states to be determined by phenomenal states while others are determined by their functional relations to phenomenal states. See Graham et al. (2007), Horgan and Graham (2009), Loar (2003), Bourget (2010), and Pautz (2006a, 2013a).
4. Such a response, in effect, casts doubt on the conceivability argument's conceivability premise, e.g., that it is conceivable for there to exist microexperiential zombies, understood as creatures having the same microexperiences combined in the same ways as the panpsychist stipulates are found in us but lacking macroexperience. (Goff's (2009) and Chalmers' (2016) arguments against panpsychism understand microexperiential zombies as having the same microexperiences (and sometimes physical properties) as us but not necessarily involving the same modes of combination. However, these alternative characterizations of panpsychist

zombies would yield conceivability arguments only effective against versions of panpsychism on which the relevant modes of combination are entailed by the microexperiential (or perhaps physical) facts, and not versions that take mental combination to involve extra ingredients).

5. For instance, both Dainton (2000) and Bayne and Chalmers (2003) mainly aim to characterize phenomenal unity rather than to offer an explanation of how it arises.
6. King (2007) provides an explanation of intentional structure in language, appealing to complex linguistic facts and the mental acts of "ascription," and Soames (2010) offers an explanation appealing to mental acts of "predication." These explanations only pass the buck to an explanation of *mental* structure.
7. Many thanks to David Bourget, Luke Roelofs, and Bill Seager for helpful comments on earlier drafts of this paper.

References

Basile, P. (2010). 'It Must Be True – But How Can It Be? Some Remarks on Panpsychism and Mental Composition'. *Royal Institute of Philosophy Supplement*, 85 (67): 93–112.

Bayne, T. J. (2012). *The Unity of Consciousness*. Oxford: Oxford University Press.

Bayne, T. J., and Chalmers, D. J. (2003). 'What Is the Unity of Consciousness?' In A. Cleeremans (ed.), *The Unity of Consciousness*. Oxford: Oxford University Press, pp. 23–58.

Block, N. (1978). 'Troubles with Functionalism'. *Minnesota Studies in the Philosophy of Science*, 9: 261–325.

Bonjour, L. (1998). *In Defense of Pure Reason*. Cambridge: Cambridge University Press.

Bourget, D. (2010). 'Consciousness Is Underived Intentionality'. *Noûs*, 44 (1): 32–58.

Bourget, D. (MS). 'The Underdetermination Problem for Conceptual Role Semantics and Phenomenal Functionalism'.

Bourget, D., and Mendelovici, A. (2014). 'Tracking Representationalism'. In A. Bailey (ed.), *Philosophy of Mind: The Key Thinkers*. London: Continuum, pp. 209–35.

Chalmers, D. J. (1996). *The Conscious Mind*. Oxford: Oxford University Press.

Chalmers, D. J. (2016). 'The Combination Problem for Panpsychism'. In L. Jaskolla and G. Brüntrup (eds.), *Panpsychism*. Oxford: Oxford University Press, pp. 179–214.

Coleman, S. (2012). 'Mental Chemistry: Combination for Panpsychists'. *Dialectica*, 66 (1): 137–66.

Dainton, B. F. (2000). *Stream of Consciousness: Unity and Continuity in Conscious Experience*. London: Routledge.

Gertler, B. (2001). 'Introspecting Phenomenal States'. *Philosophy and Phenomenological Research*, 63 (2): 305–28.

Goff, P. (2006). 'Experiences Don't Sum'. *Journal of Consciousness Studies*, 13 (10–11): 53–61.

Goff, P. (2009). 'Why Panpsychism Doesn't Help Us Explain Consciousness'. *Dialectica*, 63 (3): 289–311.

Goff, P. (2017). *Consciousness and Fundamental Reality*. Oxford: Oxford University Press.

Graham, G., Horgan, T. E., and Tienson, J. L. (2007). 'Consciousness and Intentionality'. In S. Schneider and M. Velmans (eds.), *The Blackwell Companion to Consciousness*. Oxford: Blackwell, pp. 468–84.

Horgan, T., and Graham, G. (2009). 'Phenomenal Intentionality and Content Determinacy'. In R. Schantz (ed.), *Prospects for Meaning*. Amsterdam: De Gruyter, pp. 321–44.

Jackson, F. (1982). 'Epiphenomenal Qualia'. *Philosophical Quarterly*, 32: 127–36, April.

James, W. (1890). *The Principles of Psychology*. New York: Dover Publications.

King, J. C. (2007). *The Nature and Structure of Content*. Oxford: Oxford University Press.

Kripke, S. A. (1982). *Wittgenstein on Rules and Private Language*. Cambridge, MA: Harvard University Press.

Leibniz, G. W. (1714/1989). 'The Principles of Philosophy, or, Monadology'. In R. Ariew and D. Garber (eds.), *G. W. Leibniz: Philosophical Essays*. Indianapolis: Hackett, pp. 213–24.

Levine, J. (1983). 'Materialism and Qualia: The Explanatory Gap'. *Pacific Philosophical Quarterly*: 356–61.

Loar, B. (2003). 'Phenomenal Intentionality as the Basis of Mental Content'. In M. Hahn and B. Ramberg (eds.), *Reflections and Replies: Essays on the Philosophy of Tyler Burge*. Cambridge, MA: MIT Press, pp. 229–58.

McGinn, C. (1989). 'Can We Solve the Mind-Body Problem?' *Mind*, 98: 349–66, July.

Mendelovici, A. (2013). 'Reliable Misrepresentation and Tracking Theories of Mental Representation'. *Philosophical Studies*, 165 (2): 421–43.

Mendelovici, A. (2016). 'Why Tracking Theories Should Allow for Clean Cases of Reliable Misrepresentation'. *Disputatio*, 8 (42): 57–92.

Mendelovici, A. (2018). *The Phenomenal Basis of Intentionality*. Oxford: Oxford University Press.

Mendelovici, A., and Bourget, D. (forthcoming). 'Consciousness and Intentionality'. In U. Kriegel (ed.), *The Oxford Handbook of the Philosophy of Consciousness*. Oxford: Oxford University Press.

Mørch, H. H. (2014). *Panpsychism and Causation: A New Argument and a Solution to the Combination Problem*. Doctoral Dissertation, Department of Philosophy, Classics, History of Art and Ideas, University of Oslo, Oslo. https://philpapers.org/archive/HASPAC-2.pdf.

Nagel, T. (1974). 'What Is It Like to Be a Bat?' *The Philosophical Review*, 83 (4): 435–50.

Palmer, S. (1999). 'Color, Consciousness, and the Isomorphism Constraint'. *Behavioral and Brain Sciences*, 22 (6): 923–43.

Pautz, A. (2006a). 'Can the Physicalist Explain Colour Structure in Terms of Colour Experience?' *Australasian Journal of Philosophy*, 84 (4): 535–64.

Pautz, A. (2006b). 'Sensory Awareness Is Not a Wide Physical Relation: An Empirical Argument Against Externalist Intentionalism'. *Noûs*, 40 (2): 205–40.

Pautz, A. (2013a). 'Does Phenomenology Ground Mental Content?' In U. Kriegel (ed.), *Phenomenal Intentionality*. Oxford: Oxford University Press, pp. 194–234.

Pautz, A. (2013b). 'The Real Trouble for Phenomenal Externalists: New Empirical Evidence for a Brain-Based Theory of Consciousness'. In R. Brown (ed.), *Consciousness Inside and Out: Phenomenology, Neuroscience, and the Nature of Experience*. Berlin: Springer, pp. 237–98.

Putnam, H. (1977). 'Realism and Reason'. *Proceedings and Addresses of the American Philosophical Association*, 50 (6): 483–98.

Roelofs, L. (2014). 'Phenomenal Blending and the Palette Problem'. *Thought: A Journal of Philosophy*, 3 (1): 59–70.

Roelofs, L. (2016). 'The Unity of Consciousness, Within Subjects and Between Subjects'. *Philosophical Studies*, 173 (12): 3199–221.

Roelofs, L. (forthcoming). 'Can We Sum Subjects? Evaluating Panpsychism's Hard Problem'. In W. Seager (ed.), *The Routledge Handbook of Panpsychism*. London: Routledge.

Seager, W. (1995). 'Consciousness, Information, and Panpsychism'. *Journal of Consciousness Studies*, 2 (3): 272–88.

Seager, W. (2010). 'Panpsychism, Aggregation and Combinatorial Infusion'. *Mind and Matter*, 8 (2): 167–84.

Seager, W. (2016). 'Panpsychist Infusion'. In L. Jaskolla and G. Brüntrup (eds.), *Panpsychism*. Oxford: Oxford University Press, pp. 229–48.

Soames, S. (2010). *What Is Meaning?* Princeton: Princeton University Press.

Stoljar, D. (2006). *Ignorance and Imagination: The Epistemic Origin of the Problem of Consciousness*. Oxford: Oxford University Press.

Strawson, G. (2003). 'Real Materialism'. In L. Antony and N. Hornstein (eds.), *Chomsky and His Critics*. Oxford: Blackwell, pp. 49–88.

26

WHAT DOES "PHYSICAL" MEAN? A PROLEGOMENON TO PHYSICALIST PANPSYCHISM

Galen Strawson

'Panpsychism must be considered a species of naturalism.'

(Sellars 1927: 218)[1]

1. Introduction

Philosophy is plagued by the fact that different people use the same words in very different ways. The misunderstandings that result are often calamitous, for a reason clearly stated by Mary Shepherd:

> every one must be conscious that the particular forms of expression, in which thoughts of an abstruse and subtle nature are introduced to the imagination, and grow familiar there, are so intimately associated with them, as to appear their just and accurate representative. But these forms of expression, though clear and satisfactory to the person in whose mind they are so associated, may yet fail in conveying the same ideas with sufficient precision to the understandings of others.
>
> (1824: vi)

All too often, philosopher A can't hear what philosopher B is saying because A can't help hearing B's words as meaning something different from what B is using them to mean. Many of us have had the experience of re-reading a piece of philosophy and realizing that the reason we disagreed with it the first time we read it was simply that we were closed to the way its author was using certain words.

It's widely agreed that terminological problems are acute when it comes to the discussion of mind. I'm going to make some proposals about how we may best use certain words, proposals that will constantly raise substantive matters.

2. Panpsychism and Psychism

Panpsychism is the view that mind or consciousness (*psyche*) is present in all (*pan*) reality. In its strongest form, *pure* panpsychism, it's the view that mind is all there is to reality: mind is the stuff of reality, the ('categorical') *stuff being* of reality. Eddington puts it plainly: 'the stuff of the world is mind-stuff' (1928b: 276). Drake says the same:

> psychic stuff is the very stuff of which the world is made; and while everything is subject to physical law, everything is made of the very stuff of which we ourselves – with our inner mental being – are composed.
>
> (1925: 89)

According to the *panexperientialist* version of pure panpsychism, consciousness, or experience, or experiencing, or experientiality, is all there is to reality (it is all there is to mind).[2] Whitehead puts it plainly: 'apart from the experiences of subjects there is nothing, nothing, nothing, bare nothingness'.[3]

It's worth saying straight away that there's no conflict between panexperientialism and anything true in physics. For while physics tells us a great deal about structural-relational features of reality, it has little to say about the intrinsic structure-transcendent nature of the stuff that has the structure (see section 10) – where by 'stuff' I simply mean whatever it is (however insubstantial-seeming or fundamentally processual in nature) that gives the structural-relational features of reality their concrete existence. Physics is wholly open to the possibility that the intrinsic nature of the shimmering stuff it posits is consciousness or experientiality.[4] Panexperientialism is accordingly wholly compatible with physicalism, when physicalism is properly understood (see section 4).

This point was well understood in the first half of the last century. Since then it has been largely lost from sight, partly (or largely) for terminological reasons of the sort I aim to address in this chapter – to the point where many now find it preposterous, in a way that Mary Shepherd would find wholly unsurprising. It is a cast-iron point, but it has become very hard for some to see.

A weaker form of panpsychism holds that while mind or consciousness – experience or experiencing or experientiality – is present in all of reality, it isn't all there is. The *Oxford English Dictionary* defines panpsychism in this weaker way as the view that 'there is an element of consciousness in all matter'.

There's good reason to think that panpsychism is the most plausible view of the fundamental nature of reality – where by 'reality' I mean concrete reality, everything that exists in the universe.[5] What's the next most plausible view? One might call it *psychism*, although the name isn't ideal. Psychism is panpsychism without the 'pan'. It's the view that while mind/consciousness/experience/experientiality is one of the *fundamental* features of reality (like electric charge), it isn't all there is.

I won't go on repeating 'mind or consciousness or experience or . . .'. From now on I'll often simply use 'experience', by which I'll always mean conscious experience (I take it that there isn't any other kind), although I'll also use 'consciousness' or 'experientiality'.

3. Physicalist Pure Panpsychism

What do I mean by '(conscious) experience' or 'consciousness'? I mean what most people mean in the current debate. I'll say more in section 7. Before that I want to note one of the most *im*plausible views of the fundamental nature of reality. This is the view held by many (I think most) in the West today, the view that psychism (and *a fortiori* panpsychism) is certainly false – that experience certainly isn't one of the fundamental features of reality.

Those who endorse this last view have to hold either that

(i) experience doesn't really exist at all – that it is an illusion –

or

(ii) experience somehow 'emerges' from stuff that is in its fundamental nature wholly and utterly non-experiential.

Like many, I don't think (ii) is tenable, because it requires that something known as *radical emergence* takes place in nature. Few, however, will deny that it looks preferable to (i). So it's striking that many philosophers, unable to accept panpsychism or psychism, have in the last sixty years or so chosen (i) over (ii).

These philosophers standardly deny that they've chosen (i), even as they commit themselves to claims that do in fact entail (i), and this denial, at least, is not surprising, because (i) – which is also known as *eliminativism* about experience or consciousness – is I believe the silliest view that has ever been held by any human being.

You may wonder who these philosophers are. They include (for a start) all genuine *philosophical behaviourists*, all those who genuinely endorse *functionalism* in the philosophy of mind, and some if not all of those who now call themselves 'strong representationalists'. Nearly all of them deny that they're eliminativists about consciousness, as remarked; they say that they offer 'reductions' of the experiential to the non-experiential, and that reduction is not elimination. But reduction *is* elimination in certain cases. All these so-called 'reductions' of experience amount to the denial of its existence, in any honest accounting, simply because they propose to reduce experience to something that it obviously is not (see Strawson 2018).

I need to say more about radical emergence, and about words like 'mind' and 'experience'. First, though – this topic is like a jigsaw puzzle – let me specify the kind of panpsychism I'll focus on. I'll call it *physicalist pure panpsychism*, and concentrate on its *panexperientialist* version: *physicalist panexperientialism* – *PP* for short. According to PP, the physical world is wholly constituted of experience (even subjects of experience are nothing ontologically over and above experiences). As far as I can see, Strong, Drake and Eddington are physicalist pure panpsychists, along with Whitehead, Sprigge, and many others, including, arguably, James (see e.g. Strong 1918, 1930; Drake 1925; Whitehead 1925; Eddington 1928b; Sprigge 1983; James 1909). Russell is open to the idea that it is true, and constantly stresses the point that there must be a fundamental continuity of nature between the conscious experience with which we have immediate acquaintance and the rest of concrete reality (1927a, 1927b, 1948, 1956, 1959). More recently, Sprigge (1983) and Griffin (1998) stand out among pure panexperientialist panpsychists.[6]

4. Stuff

To be a *physicalist* or *materialist*[7] is simply to hold that everything that concretely exists is wholly physical (I start trying to say what it is to be physical in section 9). PP is physicalist by definition, and it's straight-up realist about everything that comprises what we ordinarily think of as the physical world: clouds, brains, chairs, mountains, and all the entities and qualities whose existence physics is right to recognize, quarks, say, or charge, or fields.[8] It has nothing to do with idealism in the Berkeleyan sense of the term (Berkeley 1710), according to which 'physical objects' are ideas in minds. PP leaves the universe wholly independent of our minds – except for those parts of it that are our minds. So too it leaves everything true in physics wholly in place, as remarked. Panpsychism has no quarrel with physics because it offers an answer to a question about concrete reality about which physics, strictly interpreted, has little or nothing to say. (Quine makes the key point: when it comes to the denoting terms of physics, he says, 'reference [can] be wildly reinterpreted without violence to evidence' (1992: 9).) The question is

> What is the ultimate, intrinsic, categorical nature of the stuff that exemplifies the structures that physics discerns and captures in its equations?

PP answers: the ultimate, intrinsic, categorical nature of physical stuff is experience, experientiality.[9] Most present-day physicalists assume that the ultimate intrinsic nature of physical stuff is non-experiential, and they further assume that this assumption is an essential part of physicalism. The first assumption has no obvious warrant in physics, and the second is therefore doubtful.

If one puts aside the standard use of the term 'energy' in physics to denote the power of doing work possessed by a body or system of bodies, one can adopt Heisenberg's large metaphysical use of the term when he says that 'energy is a substance', and that 'all particles are made of the same substance: energy' (Heisenberg 1958: 63, 71). On this view, concrete stuff isn't well thought of as something that is distinct from energy and that *has* energy. Rather concrete physical stuff *is* energy. This is one way to make a first step towards PP.[10]

Given that concrete physical stuff = energy, we can ask the following question: What is the fundamental intrinsic structure-transcendent nature of this energy, this energy stuff? Physics doesn't say (section 10). We face the question whether it is non-experiential or experiential. PP points out (1) that we know for certain that there is experientiality, (2) that we don't know for certain that there is any non-experiential reality, (3) that we have very strong reason to expect *fundamental continuity of being* or nature between the experiential reality we know for certain to exist and any other concrete reality there is, and (4) that to suppose that the fundamental intrinsic nature of reality is wholly non-experiential requires one to posit 'radical' emergence of the experiential from the non-experiential. In the light of this it proposes that the most natural and parsimonious hypothesis is that all concrete reality is experiential.

On this view, then, experientiality is a kind of stuff: stuff = energy = experientiality. If reality is indeed spatio-temporal, then experientiality is spatio-temporal in exactly the same way as we ordinarily suppose non-experiential stuff to be. It may be said that a thing has to have some sort of non-experiential stuff being in order to be spatial, and hence spatio-temporal. This is one potent source of resistance to PP. In section 11 I'll argue that it's misguided.

As with any stuff, one can wonder how much experientiality there is. We know there's a lot on this planet – human, elephantine, leonine, canine, feline. We may wonder how much more there is in the universe. Most people think there isn't any on the moon. They're wrong if any form of panpsychism or psychism is true, but they're probably right that there isn't any *biologically evolved* experientiality on the moon.[11] If experientiality is the whole stuff of reality, as PP proposes, or even if it is only one fundamental feature of reality, as psychism proposes, then almost none of it is biological (I'll use 'biological' to cover all forms of evolved experientiality). When evolution gets going it works physical stuff (= energy = experientiality) into wonderfully complex experiential forms, e.g. animal vision, smell, and hearing, just as it works physical stuff (= energy = experientiality) into wonderful spatial forms, e.g. the eagle spatial form or the human spatial form (opposable thumbs and all).

Another potent source of resistance to PP may be expressed as follows. (1) The *power being* of stuff is (as Locke says) wholly grounded in – in fact nothing over and above – the *categorical being* of stuff.[12] (2) It seems natural at first to think that there is far more difficulty in supposing that all the power being that we find in concrete reality is grounded in experiential categorical stuff than in non-experiential categorical stuff. The principal reason for this, perhaps, is that (3) we find it extraordinarily difficult, when we think of these things, to factor in a proper appreciation of the extent to which what we apprehend as the physical world is an *appearance* – not only in our everyday life but also when we are doing physics and taking it (as we naturally and mistakenly do) that in doing physics we are apprehending the nature of physical stuff in some way that goes beyond our apprehension of the equations of physics. We have forgotten Kant, or if you like, the neo-Kantian correction of Kant. We are as Russell said, constantly 'guilty, unconsciously and in spite of explicit disavowals, of a confusion in [our] imaginative picture of matter' (1927a: 382). The problem is compounded by the fact that we (many of us) tend to think we know what experientiality is in such a way that we know that it couldn't possibly ground all the power being that we see running the world, alive in the world (as it were).[13]

Kant makes point (1) as follows in a 'pre-critical' text –

> every substance, including even a simple element of matter, must . . . have some kind of inner activity as the ground of its producing an external effect, and that in spite of the fact that I cannot specify in what that inner activity consists
>
> (1766: 315, Ak. 2.328)

– and adds an intriguing footnote about point (2):

> Leibniz said that this inner ground of all its external relations and their changes was a *power of representation* [*nb* this power is an inner *activity*]. This thought . . . was greeted with laughter by later philosophers. They would, however, have been better advised to have first considered the question whether a substance, such as a simple part of matter, would be possible in the complete absence of any inner state. And, if they had, perhaps, been unwilling to rule out such an inner state, then it would have been incumbent on them to invent some other possible inner state as an alternative to that of representations and the activities dependent on representations.
>
> (ibid.)

The point is simple: it's not clear that we have any good reason to think we know anything about concrete reality that favours the view that non-experiential stuff is better than experiential stuff as (a ground for) the power being of the world. It's quite unclear that *physics* favours this view (sections 10 and 12).

It's worth adding this. When we think of the physical world in the standard non-experiential way, we easily allow that leptons and quarks jointly constitute larger things that have intrinsic, natural, categorical properties that are essentially more and other than the intrinsic, natural, categorical properties of leptons and quarks. So too, when we switch to thinking of the physical world in a non-standard, panpsychist way as constituted of experientiality, we may allow that non-biological experiential entities like leptons and quarks jointly constitute larger things (e.g. biologically evolved experiences) that have properties that are essentially more and other than the (experiential) properties of leptons and quarks.

5. Unity

We may do this even if we continue to conceive of leptons and quarks in a crude 'smallist' way as genuine individuals of some sort. It seems, though, that we do better to conceive of them in a quantum-field-theoretic way, as features or aspects of the various 'fields' that jointly constitute the universe in a way that is profoundly mysterious to us, or (perhaps better still) as features or aspects of the single complex field that constitutes – is – the universe, and is perhaps not ultimately ontologically distinct from space-time.[14]

A further point in this vein. It seems we must allow the interconnection of everything ('pick a flower on Earth and you move the farthest star' – a remark attributed to Paul Dirac) and the deep (non-trivial) sense in which the universe is a single thing. At the same time, quantum field theory has no difficulty with the fact that things like animals, stones, bottles, and aeroplanes present as individual entities that are in some very fundamental manner ontologically distinct from other such entities – even though they're all wholly constituted by changing energy levels in the set of vibratory motions in fields – and I can see no good reason to think that quantum field theory will have any more difficulty with the fact that subjects of experience like ourselves present as individual entities that are in some fundamental manner ontologically distinct from, closed off from, other such entities.[15]

'No. The cases are quite different. The distinctness or individuality of the bottles and aeroplanes is really just an appearance, an appearance to a subject of experience whose distinctness or individuality can't be just a matter of appearance – appearance to itself.'

There is, I think, no real difficulty here. First, it seems that the unity of a planet orbiting a star – an aeroplane in flight, a person walking along a road – must be allowed to be a genuine functional unity in some sense given which the unity is not just a matter of appearance; even if there is a respect in which it's true to say that all there are in the end are vibratory motions in fields. Second, there's no reason to suppose that the seeming individuality of a single experience or single mind is not something of the same sort, a genuine functional unity that is, as such, not just a unity-*appearance*. Suppose we represent the various fields (or the single complex field) that arguably wholly constitute (or constitutes) concrete reality pictorially, as a great flexible grid. Human (and other biological) subjects of experience may then be depicted as local peaks or bulges in the grid. To be an experiential peak of this sort is to experience one's consciousness as essentially bounded or isolated even though it's essentially part of the great interconnected weave. It is in fact essential to one's biologically evolved consciousness having the adaptive function it does that it have the character of being experience from a single point of view.

There is more to say. Many accounts have been given of how individual biological experiential fields like our own may have the closed character they do even if they are in some sense just aspects or 'modes', in Spinoza's terminology (Spinoza 1677), of some larger field. The present aim is simply to propose that there is no fundamentally greater difficulty in what one might call the singleness or unity phenomena of subjects of experience than there is in the singleness or unity phenomena of things like planets and bottles.[16]

6. Why *Physicalist* Panpsychism?

'Look, I understand that you might perhaps want to defend *panpsychism*, even *pure* panpsychism, but why on earth do you want to defend *physicalist* pure panpsychism, PP? How can one possibly claim to be both a physicalist (or materialist) and a panpsychist?'

Well, this is an attempt to explain how one can do this and why one might want to. David Lewis and Bertrand Russell are immediately helpful. Lewis points out that

> a thesis that says [that] panpsychistic materialism . . . is impossible . . . is more than just materialism
>
> (1983: 36)

rebuking those who think that materialism (or physicalism) and panpsychism are mutually incompatible. Russell makes a related point when he notes that

> common sense leaves us completely in the dark as to the true intrinsic nature of physical objects, and if there were good reason to regard them as mental, we could not legitimately reject this opinion merely because it strikes us as strange. The truth about physical objects *must* be strange.
>
> (1912: 19)

In later writings he adds that science – physics – also leaves us in the dark in this way:

> physics is mathematical, not because we know so much about the physical world, but because we know so little.
>
> (1927b: 125)

So far, then, and as already remarked, the way is wide open to PP – a point that was widely understood in the first half of the twentieth century.

7. Terminology 1: 'Experience', 'Experientiality'

I'm now going to define and comment on a few terms and declare some assumptions. I'll continue to shunt certain details into footnotes designed for those who already have some familiarity with these issues. I can't hope to defend all the philosophically controversial things I will say in doing this – even putting aside the fact that everything is controversial in philosophy. This chapter is at best a prolegomenon to PP. Most of the work it aims to do lies in the following definitions and comments.

So to begin. By 'experience' (used as a mass term with no plural) or 'experientiality' I mean what many today in philosophy mean by 'consciousness'. In more complicated vocabulary, I mean concretely occurring experiential 'what-it-is-likeness', phenomenological 'what-it-is-likeness', however simple or primitive, considered just as such. I mean subjective experience with a certain qualitative character that is private in the straightforward and unexceptionable sense that it is directly known only to the creature that is having it. Our own experience affords us clear examples of this sort of 'what-it-is-likeness': colour experience, thought experience, pain, fear, anxiety, amusement, and so on. These examples suffice to convey the idea of what experience is in a completely general manner that allows us to grasp the thought that there may be (and surely are) forms of experience that we cannot imagine, including, perhaps, or no doubt, the most primitive forms of experience. It also gives us the resources to suppose (in the way sketched at the end of section 4) that our own complex biologically evolved experiences may be manifestations or effects or fusions of other experiential phenomena of which we have no from-the-inside knowledge.[17]

'Phenomenological what-it-is-likeness considered just as such': the words 'considered just as such' are important. They're designed to limit the meaning or reference of the words 'experience' and 'experientiality' strictly to the *concretely occurring experiential character – the immediately given phenomenological*[18] *content or character – of conscious mental episodes*, while excluding any reference to anything else that may exist, including anything else on which the existence of such character or content may be thought to depend.[19]

Experience is always and necessarily experience *of* or *about* something, simply because it necessarily has some experiential/phenomenological content or 'what-it-is-likeness' or other, and it is always (and trivially) experience of that, whatever else it is or isn't experience of. In the limiting case it isn't experience of anything else at all. There needn't, for example, be anything red in concrete reality, over and above the kind of redness that may be truly said to be instantiated in the conscious occurrence of the red-experience itself, in order to for there to be red-experience.[20]

I'm an all-out, out-and-out realist about experience, a *real* realist about experience. I take it that we know what experience is simply in having it, because *the having is the knowing*. (This may help some to understand what I mean by 'experience': it's that of which it is true to say that the having is the knowing.) We not only know exactly what particular kinds of experience are, simply in having them. We also know what experience is quite generally considered, simply in having experience of certain sorts, because, again, the having is the knowing. A five-year-old child knows as well as anyone else what it is.

Suppose five-year-old Lucy is facing the sun with her eyes closed and eating a sweet. If we ask her whether she likes the taste, and what colour she is experiencing, she'll know exactly what we mean and find it easy to answer. In the last century philosophers managed to turn this simple matter into a conceptual Mordor, but we can ignore them. The real 'mind – body problem' begins only when one endorses real, out-and-out, everyday realism about experience.

To do anything else is to refuse to face the problem, as many who call themselves 'physicalists' do today.[21] All serious materialists or physicalists, all *real* or *genuine* materialists or physicalists, as I like to say, are realistic materialists or physicalists. They are in other words materialists or physicalists who, like almost all materialists or physicalists for well over two thousand years (until about 1960 – or perhaps 1920), are *real realists* about experience. The idea that materialism or physicalism might or does lead to the denial (covert or overt) of the existence of consciousness or experience is very recent. As far as I know, no one before the twentieth century was foolish enough to entertain it.

8. Terminology 2: 'Mental', 'Mind'

I take the words 'mental' and 'mind' to cover the whole range of things that are ordinarily taken to be mental, from the most complicated thoughts about algebraic topology to the simplest possible feeling experience, the simplest occurrence of which it is true to say that there's 'something it is like', experientially, to have it.

According to this definition all experience is mental, and my concern in this chapter is only with the experiential. It is, however, important to be aware that some philosophers use 'mind' and 'mental' in an essentially narrower and more exclusive sense, according to which 'mere' or 'bare' feeling, primitive experiential what-it-is-likeness, *does not count as mental*. Russell, for example, standardly takes it that some sort of cognitive and mnemic (memory) capacity is a necessary condition of mind or mentality, and accordingly classifies mere or bare feeling/sentience as not intrinsically mental. This allows him to say that he is a *neutral monist*, someone who thinks that the fundamental stuff of reality is stuff of a single kind that is neither mental nor physical, even as he proposes that 'sensations' are the fundamental stuff of reality – things that we today ordinarily classify as paradigmatically mental. Something similar is true of James when he declares himself to be a neutral monist while holding that the fundamental stuff is 'pure experience' – something that we today ordinarily classify as paradigmatically mental.[22] Drake also holds that mind entails cognition, and takes it accordingly that there can be essentially 'psychic stuff' (1925: 91) without mind.

There's a parallel point to be made about the word 'conscious(ness)'. I use it here in a standard inclusive way according to which any sort of feeling or experiential what-it-is-likeness, however primitive, is conscious. Russell, James, Drake, and many others use 'consciousness' to mean something essentially more complex, something that is essentially intentionally of something other than its immediately given phenomenological character, and essentially cognitive in that sense.

It is, to repeat, very important to be aware of these different usages, especially when reading earlier twentieth-century work. The terminological landscape is treacherous. Here I'll continue to use 'mind', 'mental', and 'conscious' in the inclusive way according to which any sort of experiential what-it-is-likeness, however primitive, is correctly called 'mental' and 'conscious'. Unlike James and Russell, therefore, I accept [feeling → conscious] and [experiential → mental].[23] We all accept [conscious → mind], but for different reasons: they because they have more restrictive notions of both mind and consciousness, as just described, I because I have more inclusive notions of both. One has to learn to navigate these differences.

9. Terminology 3: 'Physical', 'Physicalism'

The definition of the words 'physical' and 'physicalism' is particularly important. Much of the confusion in the current discussion of the 'mind – body problem' stems from the fact that different philosophers use these words in a number of different ways. (I suspect that this problem will never be remedied, as succeeding generations pile enthusiastically into the debate and lock on to one use or another.)

I take it, to begin, and entirely uncontroversially, that

[a] [x is physical → x is concrete]

and

[b] [x is physical → x is the subject matter of physics].

[b] states that the physical is what physics is actually talking about, what is actually *referred* to in or by physics, however wrong physics is about the physical, and however limited the *descriptive* powers of physics are when it comes to the physical. There is as already remarked a fundamental respect in which these descriptive powers are extremely limited (see further in the following).

As a physicalist or materialist, I also take it that

[c] [x is found in our universe → x is physical]

and that

[d] [x is physical → x is physics-tractable]

where by saying that something x is 'physics-tractable' I mean something quite rich — roughly that our physics doesn't just talk about x but is capable of getting quite a lot right about its nature and does in fact get quite a lot right about its nature.[24]

I take it that [b] and [c] are enough to *fix the reference* of the term 'physical' while (rightly) leaving fundamental questions about the nature of the physical as yet undetermined.

I will also take it that

[e] [x is physical → x is a spatio-temporal entity]

and indeed that

[f] [x is physical ↔ x is spatio-temporal]

while noting, first, that a number of physicists think that space-time is not a truly fundamental feature of reality, and, second, that there appear to be fundamental things that we don't understand about the nature of space-time.

Given these two points, I'm going to treat 'space-time' as a *proper name* for whatever is in fact the fundamental dimensionality of concrete reality. I take it as given — *a priori* — that concrete reality must have some dimensionality or 'existence-room' (*Existenzraum*) or other. At the same time, I take it — along with certain leading cosmologists — that there may be no real distinction between what the existence of the (stuff of the) universe consists in and what the existence of (what we think of as) its dimensionality consists in. Steven Weinberg's characterization of a version of string theory is one vivid illustration of this idea: on this view the fundamental entities currently recognized in the standard model of physics are not strictly speaking fundamental and are to be explained as 'various modes of vibration of tiny one-dimensional rips in space-time known as strings' (1997: 20).[25]

With these provisions, 'space-time' and its adjective 'spatio-temporal' denote the actual dimensionality of concrete reality even if (even though) we are in various ways wrong about or ignorant of its nature. [e] and [f] emerge as trivially true given this ruling, but there's no harm in that — no harm in having [f] listed as an explicit condition of physicality. (One could simply name the actual dimensionality of our universe 'D', and to use 'D' as adjective and noun to replace 'spatio-temporal' and 'space-time'.)

Plainly to be a physicalist is also to hold that

[g] [x is experience and is in this universe → x is physical],

and to be a real physicalist, in my present terms, is to be a real realist (a five-year-old Lucy realist) about experience. It's to hold that 'the heady luxuriance of experience', 'experience in all its richness', in Quine's robustly realist words (1981: 185),[26] is wholly physical in nature. Let me say it again: when I claim that experience (considered just as such — see p. 6) is physical, I'm not saying that it is *in any way* other than what we ordinarily take it to be (unlike most philosophers when they say that experience is physical). I'm saying that it's experience exactly as we ordinarily and generally understand it that is wholly physical if physicalism is true.

This simple point already conflicts directly with many uses of the terms 'physical' and 'physicalist'. It's one of the most unfortunate – stickiest – sticking points of the debate. Physicalism is by definition the view that everything in this universe is physical. It accordingly entails that the experiential – *the experiential as ordinarily and correctly understood, which we know for certain to exist* – is physical. No clear-headed physicalist can think that there is a fundamental distinction between the physical on the one hand and the experiential/mental on the other hand, a distinction of such a kind that physical and experiential/mental stand in some sort of opposition.[27]

So far, perhaps, so good. I also take it to be part of the meaning of 'physical' that everything physical has a *single fundamental metaphysical nature* – a single fundamental metaphysical *stuff-nature* that we denote by the word 'physical'.[28]

I'll call this single fundamental metaphysical stuff-nature 'φ', so that I can refer to it without using the word 'physical'. All physical stuff is φ stuff by definition:

[h] [x is physical $\leftrightarrow$ x is φ].

It follows immediately that physicalism is a *monist* view, a *stuff-monist* view, according to which there is only one fundamental kind of stuff in reality.[29] What it is to be φ is still very largely undetermined.

It may be said that [h] is a redundant move. 'Of course it's part of the meaning of "physical" that all physical things share the same fundamental-kind nature or stuff-nature. Why introduce a new fundamental-kind term, "φ", and then say that it's coextensive with "physical"'?

Reply: It seems conceivable that that there are in fact three fundamentally different kinds of stuff or substance in our world – ζ stuff, ξ stuff and χ stuff – that interact smoothly and are all equally part of the subject matter of our science of physics. To rule out this possibility, we need something like [h] in addition to [b] and [c].[30]

'No. In this imagined case, ζ stuff, ξ stuff, and χ stuff are all correctly called 'physical' simply because they're all 'physics-tractable' in such a way that they can all be treated in an integrated fashion by a single theory: our physics. That's just what it is to be physical. So [h] isn't necessary after all.'

This response fits with the (anti-metaphysical, instrumentalist) way some philosophers think about the meaning of 'physical', but it simply overrides the core metaphysical idea that all physical phenomena share a single fundamental stuff-nature. The single-naturedness of the stuff of our world is not guaranteed by its physics-tractability.

Another seeming possibility, after all, is that two different fundamental kinds of stuff, not only φ stuff but also π stuff, satisfy all the equations of our physics. There may be a π stuff universe distinct from our own. Perhaps there may be a planet made entirely of π stuff, existing inside a π bubble in our otherwise wholly φ universe. If we examine it we'll take the π planet to be physical stuff, and the cheerful anti-metaphysicalists will say we're right; but we'll be wrong.

To be physical, then, is not just to be physics-tractable; it's not just to be tractable for any theory formally identical to physics.[31] It's also to be φ, where φ refers to a certain ultimate intrinsic stuff-nature – the stuff-nature of the stuff that is in fact the only fundamental kind of stuff in our universe. According to PP, experience is the ultimate intrinsic nature of the stuff of our universe.

It may now be said that the notion of fundamental same substancehood has little content unless one can offer some account of how we might possibly decide whether or not smoothly interacting entities are of the same or different fundamental stuffs. This kind of move is sometimes appropriate in philosophy, but not here. Metaphysics is not subject to epistemic constraints of this sort; the notion of same fundamental stuff is sufficiently robust for present purposes (if necessary, we can anchor it in the idea that an omniscient being could tell whether there is one or more substance in play). We can't assume that physics-tractability is a sufficient condition of fundamental same substancehood.

Is the $\zeta - \xi - \chi$ case really possible? Is it possible given that it requires that there be genuine causal interaction between the three different fundamental kinds of stuff?[32] I think it has to be allowed to be possible by anyone who thinks that standard (Cartesian) substance dualism is coherent – even if they think it is false. For when standard substance dualism allows that different fundamental substances may possibly interact causally, it opens up the general possibility that the causal interactions captured by the equations of physics are in fact interactions between different fundamental substances. I'm inclined to take ability to interact causally to be a sufficient condition of same substancehood, directly contrary to the spirit of the $\zeta - \xi - \chi$ story (see Strawson 2003: 50). This, however, rules out standard Cartesian dualism, and many think that Cartesian dualism is at least a coherent position.

10. Terminology 4: 'Physics'

I haven't finished with 'physical', but I want now to say something about the word 'physics', and indeed physics itself, in support of the claim that one has gone badly wrong if one is a physicalist and thinks that there is a basic opposition between the physical and the experiential.

There is of course an everyday use of 'physical' given which the opposition claim comes naturally. But this is precisely the problem: the present claim is that this use is shatteringly unhelpful in philosophy and – at the limit – plain wrong. Certainly we shouldn't use 'physical' in philosophy in such a way that Russell, Whitehead, and Eddington and many others are simply contradicting themselves when they say (for example) that

> from the standpoint of philosophy the distinction between physical and mental is superficial and unreal
>
> (Russell 1927a: 402)

or that

> we do not know enough of the intrinsic character of events outside us to say whether it does or does not differ from that of 'mental' events
> (Russell 1927b: 221; see also the quotation in §4 above)

or that

> science has nothing to say as to the intrinsic nature of the atom. [From the point of view of physics] the physical atom is, like everything else in physics, a schedule of pointer readings. The schedule is, we agree, attached to some unknown background [the actual physical stuff]. Why not then attach it to something of spiritual [i.e. mental] nature of which a prominent characteristic is *thought* [in Descartes's sense of 'thought', i.e. consciousness]?
> (Eddington 1928b: 259)

I agree completely with Maxwell when he says that

> *the physical* is, very roughly, the subject matter of physics. By 'subject matter' I mean *not* the *theories, laws, principles*, etc., of physics, but rather **what the theories and laws are about**. *The physical* thus includes tables, stars, human bodies and brains, and whatever the constituents of these may be.
> (1978: 366; my emphasis in bold)[33]

So what about physics? It's widely agreed that it can tell us a great deal about structural-relational aspects of φ, the stuff in our universe (consider the inverse square laws, the mass–energy equivalence equation, the Dirac equation, the Schrödinger equation, etc.). It is at the same time a commonplace that physics is incapable – *essentially* incapable – of revealing the ultimate structure-transcendent nature of φ, i.e. the nature of the stuff that has to be there given that the structural relations expressed in the equations of physics are actually exemplified by something concretely real. Physics is silent on this aspect of the nature of φ. Why? Because physics is as Hawking says 'just a set of rules and equations' (1988: 174). It can't tell us anything that can't be expressed in such rules and equations. This is why Eddington says that 'if you want a *concrete* definition of matter it is no use looking to physics' (1928a: 95); physics can't access 'its inner un–get–atable nature' (1928b: 257). 'Science ignores what anything is in itself', Whitehead observes: 'its entities are merely considered in respect to their extrinsic reality, that is to say, in respect to their aspects to other things' (1925: 153). 'Physics is mathematical', says Russell in a passage already quoted, 'not because we know so much about the physical world, but because we know so little' (1927b: 125). This isn't any sort of failure on the part of physics; it's just not its job. 'Physical science has reduced nature to activity, and has discovered abstract mathematical formulae which are illustrated in these activities of nature. But the fundamental question remains, How do we add content to the notion of bare activity?' (Whitehead 1938: 166).

It doesn't follow, in Kantian fashion, that we can't know anything at all about the non-structural or structure-transcendent nature of φ – I'll call this 'φ_{ST}' ('ST' for 'structure-transcendent'). Physics does indeed go beyond purely logico-mathematical structural description in asserting that the universe has specifically *spatio-temporal* structure and *causal* structure, and in taking these to be the fundamental concrete 'real relations' or 'generating relations' (Newman 1928: 145–6) that the purely logico-mathematical structural descriptions of physics cotton onto. That said, to describe something as causally structured is still to give a highly abstract description of it, a description that is silent on its stuff-nature (causation is simply the 'because something is, something else must be' relation; Kant 1781–7: B288). The same goes for the description of something as spatio-temporally structured, to the extent that we remain ignorant of the intrinsic nature of space-time. I will for this reason include attribution of causal and spatio-temporal structure under the general heading of structural description, even though it is not purely logico-mathematical structural description.

That's one point. The next point is that if physicalism is true, as we're supposing it is, then we do know something utterly fundamental about φ_{ST}. This is because we're directly acquainted with it, at least in certain respects. We're directly acquainted with φ_{ST} whenever we're caught up in the concrete process of having conscious experience, as we so very often are. This is because conscious experience is part of concrete reality, hence a part of physical reality, given physicalism; and because, when it comes to conscious experience – and as already remarked – the having is the knowing. As Russell says, using 'intrinsic' loosely[34] to mean 'structure-transcendent':

> we know nothing about the intrinsic quality of physical events *except when* these are mental events that we directly experience.
>
> (1956: 153, my emphasis)

When the physical events are mental events that we directly experience, we do know something about their intrinsic structure-transcendent quality. So when Peter Lewis says that quantum mechanics 'is a theory in which we have no idea what we are talking about, because we have no idea what (if anything) the basic mathematical structures of the theory represent' (Lewis 2016: 23) we need to make one correction: we do have some idea what we are talking about because sometimes we're talking about our experiences, whatever else we may or may not be talking about, and we know their intrinsic structure-transcendent nature in certain very fundamental respects. We may then ask whether physical events possess any other, radically different kind of intrinsic structure-transcendent quality. PP answers No, and (backed up by Occam) challenges dissenters to give good reason to think otherwise.

11. Terminology 5: 'Physical', 'Physicalism' Continued

This raises a point about our epistemological limits – a point about the respect in which we will only ever be able to form one kind of *descriptively contentful general conception of* φ_{ST} that we can know to cotton on (even if only partially) to the intrinsic nature of φ_{ST}. Which conception is this? It's the conception just mentioned, the conception we form of it in having experience and knowing its nature in having it because the having is the knowing.

Suppose we let '$\varphi\star_{ST}$' stand for the structure-transcendent stuff-nature of concrete reality without carrying any implication that there is only one fundamental kind of stuff. Suppose we somehow gain access to two different and compelling modes of description of $\varphi\star_{ST}$, and are able to know that both of them cotton on (even if only partially) to the intrinsic nature of $\varphi\star_{ST}$. And suppose we continue to have good reason to think that reality as it is in itself forms a causally interconnected whole. In that case, the two modes of description might be so different that we feel we have good reason to suppose that there are two different substances in causal interaction. I take it that that is not our actual case, but many dualists have supposed that it is: that there is, first, the access to the essentially experiential nature of $\varphi\star_{ST}$ that we have simply in having conscious experience, and, secondly, the access to the essentially non-experiential nature of $\varphi\star_{ST}$ that we have not only when we engage in science but also in our everyday experience of moving round in the world.

But now we encounter one of the points that supports the panpsychist position: the fact that we do not in fact have the second sort of access. We do not in fact have good reason to think that there is any non-experiential stuff, or that we know its nature in any fundamental non-structural respect.

Some may now say that we're taking $\varphi\star_{ST}$ to be spatio-temporal stuff whatever else is or is not the case

[e] [x is physical $\rightarrow$ x is a spatio-temporal entity]

and that anything spatio-temporal must be spatially extended

[i] [x is a spatio-temporal entity $\rightarrow$ x is spatially extended]

and that anything spatio-temporally extended must have some sort of non-experiential stuff-nature

[j] [x is spatially extended $\rightarrow$ x has non-experiential stuff being],

and therefore that

[k] [x is physical $\rightarrow$ x has non-experiential stuff being].

And this may seem to settle the case against PP. But [k] isn't warranted. First, we don't know that we know the nature of space-time (see §9), or whether it is indeed a genuinely fundamental feature of $\varphi\star_{ST}$.[35] Secondly, it's not at all obvious that space-occupation requires non-experiential stuff being, even if it seems so at first.[36]

Some philosophers and physicists seem to think that a concretely real thing can exist in a spatio-temporal universe and have no spatial extension at all. I think that's incoherent, so I'm prepared to agree that

[l] [x is physical $\rightarrow$ x is spatially extended]

– always assuming that concrete reality is indeed fundamentally spatio-temporal. I'm also prepared to put aside the view that we may be (surely are) deeply ignorant of the intrinsic nature of space, although it already supplies grounds for rejecting the objection to PP in the last paragraph, and to take it that we really do have a reasonably good if partial positive intuitive (more than merely structural) grasp of its nature. For, even then, when I go on to think of the (Heisenbergian) energy that wholly constitutes everything that we think of as spatially extended (and even, perhaps, space-time itself), and then go on to raise the question of the intrinsic stuff-nature of this energy, and then go on to consider the current hypothesis that it is wholly a matter of experientiality – the active, live occurrent phenomenon that we know experience to be – I can see no good reason to think that something consisting of wholly experiential stuff cannot be spatial in just the same way as the way in which something thought of as non-experiential is supposed to be; so I reject [j], which was used in conjunction with [e] and [i] to argue for [k], even as I accept [l].

This leads to an important related point. Wholly experiential stuff can certainly be said to have numerical and structural properties, and numerical and structural properties, considered specifi-cally as such, are indeed correctly called *non-experiential* properties. It does not, however, follow from this that there is any non-experiential *stuff*; it doesn't follow that there are any non-expe-riential *stuff-properties*. So one can't refute PP simply by showing that one can correctly ascribe properties to concrete reality that are correctly or naturally said to be non-experiential proper-ties. Failure to appreciate this point is likely to be another potent source of misunderstanding.[37] 'Non-experiential' is not the name of a positive type of stuff being; to say that a thing has non-experiential properties is not *ipso facto* to say that it has any non-experiential stuff being.[38] More generally, one can say this: whatever the dimensionality of the concrete real, a panpsychist may take it that its nature is such that it fits smoothly with the nature of the concrete real conceived of as nothing but experientiality in exactly the same way as the way in which the dimensionality of the concrete real understood as spatial in the conventional way is seen to fit smoothly with the nature of the concrete real understood as good old fashioned non-experientially propertied physical stuff.

'But you must retain the idea of dimensional *position*, even when you take the dimensionality of the concrete real to fit smoothly with the view of the concrete real as wholly experiential, because the idea of position and difference of position is essentially built into the idea of dimensionality. And the property of having some dimensional position is essentially non-experiential.' True, but the reply is the same as before; this raises no difficulty for the idea that the stuff-nature of the concrete real is experientiality. (Note also that non-pure physicalist panpsychism remains an option even if one continues to think that spatio-temporality entails non-experientiality.)

12. Terminology 6: 'Physical', 'Physicalism' Continued

So: to be a *physicalist* is simply to hold [c] that all the stuff in this universe, including of course [g] all experientiality, is wholly physical in every respect and feature. To be a serious or *realistic* physicalist is to be (with Russell and almost all if not all materialists until some time in the twentieth century) a real five-year-old-Lucy realist about experience. It's also to hold (again with Russell) that in having experience we know something about the intrinsic nature of the physical.

What is it to be *physical*? It is (at least) to be [a] concrete, [b] what physics talks about, in its own strictly limited way, [d] physics-tractable, [e] spatio-temporal and hence [l] spatially extended, and [h] of a single kind of fundamental stuff φ whose single-kindhood must be allowed to transcend physics-tractability by anyone who allows that the story of ζ stuff, ξ stuff and χ stuff is coherent. On this view, leptons and quarks, fermions or bosons, matter and antimatter, charged and chargeless particles (these are familiar classificatory distinctions made within the realm of the physical) are all of the same fundamental kind of stuff, although they are importantly different types of things. They are as one might say all *made of* the same fundamental kind of stuff.

Don't ask me how we might identify and distinguish fundamental kinds of stuff. I don't have access to *Concretics*, God's great textbook of concrete reality, in which all possible types of concrete stuff are specified. I'm simply expounding a way of understanding 'physical' according to which 'physical' carries an implication of sameness of fundamental nature that goes beyond being treatable by a single theory, mathematical physics. [h] is (among other things) a dramatization of the point that 'physical' is a natural-kind term of a special kind.[39]

Some may think that the above characterization of 'physical' is still radically incomplete, because it's part of the core or fundamental meaning of 'physical' that

[m] [x is physical → x is at least partly constituted of non-experiential stuff].

Many endorse the stronger view that

[n] [x is physical → x is wholly constituted of non-experiential stuff].

Russell and many others disagree, as I do. Nothing in physics provides compelling reason to endorse [m] or [n]. They may certainly be allowed to be part of the meaning of 'physical' (or 'material') in everyday use, but no one who uses 'physical' when engaged in metaphysical speculation about the nature of things – using it to mean *the stuff of which the world is in fact constituted*, or *the stuff that physics is in fact concerned with and (so we believe) says many true things about* – should accept this feature of the ordinary meaning of 'physical' as a constraint on the theoretical employment of the term. It's not just that physics radically undermined the everyday conception of the nature of matter long ago. The deeper point is that physics itself rules against this constraint by its very nature. This is the silence of physics. It used to be well known: 'the materialist, holding that the world is matter, is not wedded to any one doctrine of the nature of matter' (Williams 1944: 425). 'Physical' is not a term that carries or contains any determinate positive descriptive non-structural characterization of a kind of stuff.

Some philosophers may now say that the characterization of the word 'physical' (or 'material') proposed here is bad because it's incompatible with the terminology of the traditional debate about the 'mind-body problem', which has matter (the physical) firmly and comfortably on one side, and mind and conscious experience (the mental, the experiential), firmly and comfortably opposed to matter, on the other. I think this is the opposite of the truth. This incompatibility is perhaps the key virtue of the current characterization of 'physical'. The traditional debate is a dead end, full of seductive patterns of confusion, many of which revolve principally around the use of the word 'physical'. We know experience is real, so we know that experience is physical if physicalism is true, and the fundamental metaphysical question, given that we know that there is experiential physical stuff, is whether there is any respectable reason to posit any non-experiential physical stuff. I think that the best (and Occamical) answer may be No. And now Quine and Nietzsche turn up at my side. Nietzsche points out, correctly, that the view that 'substance is experienceless is only a hypothesis! Not based on experience!' (1882–4: KSA 10, 24[10]). Quine (using 'physical' in the standard sense that implies having non-experiential being) observes that physical objects are 'posits comparable, epistemologically, to the gods of Homer' (1951: 44).

13. Terminology 7: 'Radical Emergence'

I want now to say briefly what I mean by 'radical emergence' (also called 'strong emergence', see e.g. Wilson 2015) and then conclude.

In a case of radical emergence, at least as I understand it, some concrete stuff develops into or produces or comes to constitute some concrete stuff that belongs, intuitively, and presumably also in fact, to a wholly, radically different order of being. In the present case the first stuff is by hypothesis non-experiential, so I'll call it NE. The second stuff is experientiality, experiential stuff, so I'll call it E. E being is held to *emerge* – wholly naturally – from NE being that is quite radically different from it: either constitutively (E being emerges from NE being as a result of some NE being's coming to constitute some E being) or causally (some E being emerges from some NE being inasmuch as some NE being causes some E being to come into existence).

One way to illustrate the force of 'radical' is to observe that one can transform or develop any form of matter into any other (steel into marshmallow, water into diamond), given sufficient force. No such transformation will be a case of radical emergence, because all matter is made of the same stuff (leptons and quarks, on one account). In fact the same goes for transforming matter into anti-matter. This may sound as if it must be a case of radical emergence, but all this shows is that the terms 'matter' and 'antimatter' are potentially misleading. The only difference between an electron and an antimatter electron (a positron) is that their charges are reversed.

These are not cases of radical emergence. The transformation of wholly and utterly NE stuff into E stuff – experiencing, experientiality – would, by contrast, be a case of radical emergence; so I claim. I have no argument for this widely held view, nor anything to add to the kinds of intuitive considerations I've given before (Strawson 2006a, 2006b). I'm not claiming that radical emergence is provably impossible. I don't think it is, although I think that the postulation of radical emergence must always be a huge black mark against a theory.

14. Radical Emergence

The principal objection to taking it that E exists in our universe by virtue of radical emergence from wholly and utterly NE can be put as follows. I'll use 'E' (italic capital) to refer to all theories that suppose that the fundamental stuff is wholly experiential, 'NE' to refer to all theories that suppose that the fundamental stuff is wholly non-experiential, and 'RE' to refer to the view that radical emergence exists.

[1] We know for certain that E exists (biological E, at the very least). [2] We don't know for certain that any NE exists. So right from the start, [3] the burden of proof is on those who believe that NE exists. [4] There is, to begin, a burden on them to prove that it exists at all.

This burden is very heavy; in fact it can't be lifted. It's a very old and familiar point that [5] it can't be proved that NE exists.

The point [5] that it's impossible to prove that there is any NE being is weighty. But let us put it aside. Even when we put it aside it remains true that [6] there is a burden on those who believe that NE exists to show that there is at least good reason to posit NE. It looks, however, as if [7] E and $NE+RE$ are empirically equivalent (theories are empirically equivalent if no empirical test can decide between them). This is because it seems that [8] our best and most fundamental science of the nature of reality – physics – can't decide between them. Why not? Because of the silence of physics on the question of the intrinsic structure-transcendent nature of reality. The reference of the terms that refer to the structure-transcendent reality can as Quine says 'be wildly reinterpreted without violence to evidence' (1992: 9). If this is right, [9] it won't be possible to find good reason to posit NE in addition to E (E which we know for certain to exist).

At this point I think that there's only one thing left for the advocates of NE to do. They need to try to show that [10] even if $NE+RE$ and E are empirically equivalent, still $NE+RE$ is theoretically superior to E. Their first and very large difficulty is immediate: there appears to be no reason to posit radical emergence anywhere else in science. It is to that extent sorely *ad hoc* to posit it just and only in the case of experience. It's directly contrary to the dictates of sound methodological naturalism.

Suppose the advocates of NE press on, in spite of this, and turn to perceived problems for E in the hope that they can show at least one of them to be insuperable. They are likely to turn to the most popular perceived problem for E – the problem of how we account for the existence of biological experience like our own given the postulation of non-biological experience – and argue more or less as follows.

Suppose first that [11] we assume an irreducibly plural ontological setup in concrete reality. Suppose for example that we take the language of particle physics more or less literally, if only for purposes of argument. In this case, say the advocates of NE, [12] we face the 'combination problem'.[40] Experience can't exist without an experiencer of some sort, and it appears to follow that (non-biological) particle-like microexperiences entail the existence of (non-biological) particle-like microexperiencers. But how can non-biological microsubjects combine to constitute biological macrosubjects like ourselves? The combination problem is so acute, they say, that [13] it's more plausible to suppose that biological E arises from or consists in the activity of a multiplicity of NE microelements than a multiplicity of non-biological E microelements.

Suppose alternatively that [14] we think of the universe in the way a considerable number of present-day cosmologists and philosophers think best, i.e. as ultimately a single thing structured or indeed constituted by a number of fields, or perhaps one complex field. Even then (say the advocates of *NE*) [15] it's more plausible to suppose that biological E arises from or consists in some sort of activity-complexity in fields that have a fundamentally NE intrinsic nature than to think that it arises from or consists in some sort of activity-complexity in fields that have a fundamentally E intrinsic nature.

I can see no force in [15]. There does seem to be some initial force to [12], given [11], but, first, even if it's very difficult, when we think in a simple particle-physics way, to conceive of how biological E arises from or consists in the activity of a multiplicity of non-biological E elements, and hardly less difficult, when we think in the field-theoretic way, to conceive of how biological E arises from or consists in some sort of activity-complexity in a non-biological E field, it's most unclear that it's easier to imagine that biological E arises from or consists in the activity of a multiplicity of NE elements, or some sort of activity-complexity in an otherwise fundamentally NE field.

Many have said that there is a special and overwhelming difficulty in the idea that a multitude of subjects can combine into a larger single subject, including, famously, William James in *The Principles of Psychology* (1890: 160). But this leads directly to a second reply to those who wish to argue that *E* faces such acute problems that it's reasonable to suppose that *NE+RE* is theoretically superior to *E*.

The point is simple and has wide implications when to comes to the general discussion of idealist theories, panpsychist or not. Almost all those who have argued that the combination problem is insuperable for panpsychism have used *a priori* argument in support of their case. This is why they've supposed that the arguments are decisive. It is, however, foolish to suppose that *a priori* argument can have any decisive role to play in this matter. A hundred years ago someone might have argued, with supreme confidence, and on purely *a priori* grounds, that wave-particle duality or quantum entanglement or quantum superposition was provably impossible. That would have been a mistake. We have daily proof from physics that there are fundamental things about the nature of concrete reality, and in particular the structural-relational-combinatorial nature of concrete reality, that we don't understand and have no prospect of understanding.

William James anticipates this general point beautifully, I believe, when in *A Pluralistic Universe* (1909) he simply abandons his earlier *a-priori*-argument based endorsement of the view that the combination problem is insuperable. He understands our ignorance. Kant also anticipates this point – shows a suitable grasp of our ignorance – when he considers one of the standard 'rationalist' or immaterialist objections to the materialists: if someone rejects materialism (or equally micropsychism, the idea that there are many small non-biological E elements) and argues for a simple non-material soul

> merely on the ground that the unity of apperception in thought does not allow of its being explained [as arising] out of the composite, instead of admitting, as he ought to do that he is [quite generally] unable to explain the possibility of a thinking nature (*einer denkender Natur*), why should not the *materialist* [or equally the micropsychist], though he can as little appeal to experience in support of his possibilities, be justified in being equally daring, and in using his principle to establish the opposite conclusion?
>
> (Kant 1787: B417–18, my emphasis)[41]

We just don't know enough to reach conclusions of the 'rationalist' sort.

James and Kant aside, I think that the general doubt about the use of *a priori* argument in this domain (a doubt strongly supported by physics) is enough to establish that we have no good reason to pay much attention to standard formulations of the combination problem.[42] We have to remember and respect our ignorance, however much it galls us. We have to remember Orgel's Second Rule: 'Evolution is cleverer than you are'. If it's adaptive for a portion of matter that moves around under its own steam as a single unit to have an environment-representing experiential perspective that corresponds to that singleness, evolution will make it happen, even if (and this is far from obvious) it has to conjure that perspective out of many experiential perspectives. We have to remember the silence of physics, and the fact that even when we limit ourselves to the limited sorts of things that physics can tell us about, nature appears to be more puzzling than we are likely to be able to understand. After acknowledging all the known unknowns, we have to remember the unknown unknowns, not to mention the unknowable unknowns, not to mention the knowably unknowable unknowns.[43]

15. Conclusion

This chapter has gone on long enough, and there are plenty of other expositions of the virtues of panpsychism in this book.[44] I want to conclude with an apparent difficulty. I'm attracted to the thing-monist view according to which the universe is a single thing in some non-trivial sense and is indeed space-time (i.e. not ultimately ontologically distinct from what we think of as its dimensionality). On this view space-time itself is a substantial something, a stuffy something, a plenum, a weave of fields, or rather perhaps a single complex field – which is in fact an experientiality field (Weinberg's characterization of a version of string theory, noted in §9 above, is one way among many of giving colour to the thing-monist idea).

This picture raises a large question. For if the universe is space-time, and if space-time is stuff, and if it is experiential stuff, and if it is also, in a fundamental sense, a unity, and if the existence of an experience entails an experiencer, in some fundamental and ineliminable sense, as I believe it does, then – so it seems – we must not only suppose that the universe is itself a subject, but must also (unless considerations about the nature of time show this to be a mistake) suppose that it is experiencing all the disparate and often mutually incompatible thoughts and feelings of all sentient beings.

I'm not sure what to say about this. Certainly there are ways of conceiving of what we are, and of why it is that we experience ourselves as radically bounded subjects that don't clash irreconcilably with the seemingly extraordinary idea of a cosmic subject. On the terms of section 5, we're local peaks in the great experiential weave. We're not in fact radically isolated experiential units, but we are sweetly tuned by evolution to experience ourselves as such.

One possible solution is to give up thing monism. Some think that thing monism is the best or only way to avoid the combination problem (see e.g. Goff 2017); but I can't feel worried by the combination problem, for reasons given in the previous section. Another possibility, perhaps, is that the experientiality field (weave of fields) is a unity in some way that doesn't require the universe to be itself a single subject of experience. Goff engagingly suggests that the universe is indeed conscious, but that 'the consciousness of the universe is simply a mess. It may be hard for us to *imagine* a single mental state involving such wildly conflicting contents, but I see no reason to think that such a thing is impossible' (2017: 243).

As a passionate physicalist naturalist atheist, I think the thing to do is to relax. *Die Welt ist tief* – as Nietzsche observed (1883–92: 264). The general case for favouring panpsychism over other theories of the fundamental nature of reality is close to being overwhelming, independently of issues like this one. I can't at present see that a conception of the universe that posits a cosmic subject is worse off than other conceptions.

If there were such a subject, it wouldn't, I think, be any sort of agent. The universe is a vast, magnificent, and from some perspectives terrifying unfolding of being, but I don't think anyone or anything can do anything about how it goes.[45]

Notes

1. When I cite a work I give the date of first publication, or sometimes the date of composition, while the page reference is to the edition listed in the bibliography. In the case of quotations from languages other than English I give a reference to a standard translation but do not always use precisely that translation.
2. The term 'panexperiential' was introduced by Griffin (1977). See also Shields (2001).
3. 1927–8: 167. Note that to say this is *not* to say or imply that subjects are ontologically distinct from experiences.
4. By one estimate, 700 billion solar neutrinos pass through one's brain every second.
5. 'Concrete reality' contrasts with 'abstract reality': some hold that numbers and concepts are real things, part of reality, but are abstract entities rather than concrete entities. One quick way to characterize concrete reality is to say that to be concretely real is to be capable of entering into causal relations. Here I put aside questions about abstract reality and usually speak simply of 'reality'.
6. See also Hartshorne (1936, 1942). For some more recent discussion, see Nagel (1979, 2012: 54–8), Seager (1995, 2016), McHenry and Shields (2016). For a survey, see Skrbina (2005). I endorse psychism, although not under that name, in Strawson 1994 (e.g. pp. 60–2).
7. I follow D. C. Williams (1944: 418) and David Lewis (1994: 293) in treating these two terms as equivalent, although there is more to the physical than matter.
8. 'Fundamental particle' is a misleading term given quantum field theory; but terms like 'quark' and 'electron' do pick out concretely real somethings, and it's often useful to talk in terms of particles.
9. I'm hoping to avoid a nest of disputes by piling the terms 'ultimate', 'intrinsic' and 'categorical' on top of each other. I should say that I take it (contrary to some widespread terminological habits) that there's a fundamental sense in which potencies or power properties are correctly said to be categorical properties, i.e. actual properties, properties that are always there, constitutive of the being of the thing whose potencies they are (they do not have a 'merely dispositional' existence). As Cavendish says: 'body cannot quit power, nor power the body, being all one thing' (1664: 98). See also Locke (1689–1700: §2.8), Heil and Martin (1998), Strawson (2008), Heil (2012: ch. 4).
10. So too, concrete physical stuff isn't well thought of as something that is in some way distinct from process, in which processes go on or occur; it is process. So too, concrete stuff isn't something that possesses certain natural, categorical, concretely instantiated intrinsic qualities while being in some manner irreducibly ontologically distinct from them; its existence is nothing ontologically over and above the instantiation of those qualities. It is, however, hard for us to hold this point steadily in mind given the deep object-property/subject-predicate structure of our thought and language.
11. In this case there is no *mind* on the moon, in the Russell-James sense to be explained in section 8 – even if there is *experientiality* or *feeling/sentience* or *consciousness* in the most common present-day sense of 'consciousness'. This distinction between *mind* and *consciousness*, which is found in some of the principal writings on this topic, is a major terminological pitfall, because we take it today that consciousness entails mind. Another lies in the essentially cognitive-relational sense of 'consciousness' favoured by many in the early twentieth century, which has the consequence (directly contrary to standard present-day use) that *sentience*, in the maximally general sense of feeling of any sort (which does not presuppose sense organs), is not sufficient for *consciousness*.
12. Locke expresses this basic metaphysical point, which he shares with Descartes, and which is now sometimes called the 'powerful qualities' view, in an exemplary fashion (1689–1700: §2.8). Its occlusion is one of the catastrophes of modern metaphysics. One mistake (see note 7 above) is to think of power being as 'merely dispositional' in a way that forces one to oppose it to categorical being. In fact, power being is essentially something live, active, categorical. (It's because 'particles' are essentially dynamic entities, always humming away, as it were, that they can and do do what they do). Another mistake is to think of the categorical being of stuff in a 'staticist' and 'separatist' manner – as if it could be what it is independently of the laws of nature that are in fact essentially constitutive of its nature.
13. It is perhaps the sense that experientiality just hasn't got the resources (clout, oomph) to ground all the power being of the world that leads Goff to argue for a version of panpsychism in which there is 'consciousness+' in addition to basic consciousness = experientiality (see Goff 2017: 179ff). Compare Sellars 1932: 420: 'a brain-state is for me conscious content *plus*'. Although I think this way of putting things is useful,

I don't think we have good reason to suppose that we know enough about experiential stuff to know that it is less well fitted than non-experiential stuff to ground, or rather be, the power being of the world. To know the nature of experience just in having it is not *ipso facto* to know its power being, in the sense of the effects it is disposed to have on other things.

14. What we have are particle-like *appearances*, produced by changing energy levels in the set of vibratory motions in fields, that are not well thought of as persisting things. 'Particles . . . are emergent entities in modern physics . . . the popular impression of particle physics as about the behavior of lots of little point particles whizzing about bears about as much relation to real particle physics as the earth/air/fire/water theory of matter bears to the Periodic Table' (Wallace 2013: 220).

15. 'The breaches between [experiences] belonging to different . . . minds', in James's words, 'are the most absolute breaches in nature' (1890: 1. 226).

16. I take it that planets and bottles are not also subjects of experience, and I know of no panpsychist who thinks that all collocations of subjects of experience are subjects of experience. Football teams aren't subjects of experience any more than bottles are.

17. There are various ways of sketching how this comes about. See e.g. Seager (2010, 2016); see also Mørch (2014), Turausky (MS). See also Drake (1925: 98–100).

18. What is immediately phenomenologically given may be highly complex and conceptually rich, as it usually is in our own case. See e.g. Montague (2016), Siegel (2017).

19. This is another point at which misunderstanding is possible – and likely, given a hostile reader. Suppose that someone takes experientiality as just defined to be an intrinsic feature of a complex event *e* that also essentially has *non*-experiential intrinsic features. (Many think in this way when they suppose that experiences are neural goings-on.) The point is then that the words 'experience' and 'experientiality' as used in this paper refer *only* to the experientiality of *e* and do not refer even indirectly to any supposed non-experiential being. This ruling may be felt to clash with a picture of things according to which the experiential and the non-experiential are somehow identical. It does, but this is a good thing, because the picture is incoherent – a simple point that explains why Sprigge says that 'anything going for the identity theory', i.e. the mind-brain identity theory, 'is evidence for the truth of panpsychism, as was realized long ago by philosophers such as Josiah Royce' (Sprigge 1983: 102). There is a deep thought-bog here (I speak from painful past experience of embogment).

20. There is as Pautz has remarked a primordial sense in which 'colors live only in the contents of our experiences' (2009: 60). To this extent, the old and confident protest that experiences of red aren't themselves red is too quick. We can give a good account of the sense in which redness as we ordinarily and naively conceive of it is an essentially experiential matter.

21. For an account of how Lewis does this, see Strawson 2019: §4.

22. I think this is the best way to take Russell's and James's neutral monism *if* one reads them in a more or less straightforwardly metaphysical way. There is, however, disagreement about how to read them (see in particular Wishon 2015; Stubenberg 2016), and one must never forget that both are strongly driven by epistemological considerations of a radical empiricist kind. These lead Russell to say that both mental and physical entities are 'constructions', 'logical constructions' out of sensations, and, as constructions, can't be the basic stuff (James holds a similar view but substitutes 'pure experience' for 'sensations'). The fact remains that the 'material' out of which the mental and physical is constructed ('sensation' or 'pure experience') counts as mental on most views, as do the 'raw feels' Tolman uses to characterize Russell's view: 'raw feels may be the way physical realities are intrinsically, i.e., in and for themselves' Tolman (1932: 427).

23. I use '→' to mean 'metaphysically entails'.

24. Note for philosophers of science: I take it that physics gets quite a lot right in a way that is not only compatible with the truth of PP but also with Laudan's 'pessimistic induction' (Laudan 1981).

25. In the classic debate about space and time between 'substantivalists' and 'relationalists', some 'substantivalists' think of space as a pure container of stuff that is in itself stuffless, relative to the stuff it contains, so they're not substantivalists in the present sense.

26. Quine the great naturalist never denied the existence of (real) experience, as some self-styled 'naturalists' now feel they need to do. Compare Maxwell, when he characterizes his own physicalism

> as a *nonmaterialist physicalism*. It is nonmaterialist in that it does not attempt to eliminate or in any way deemphasize the importance of the 'truly mental'. On the contrary, it accords central roles to *consciousness,* 'private experience', subjectivity, 'raw feels', 'what it's like to be something', to thoughts, pains, feelings, emotions, etc., as we live through them in all of their qualitative richness. The theory also claims, however, that all of these genuinely mental entities are also genuinely physical, from which it follows that some genuinely physical entities are genuinely mental. This should occasion no shock, for it is a consequence of any authentic mental-physical identity thesis. Of course, some call themselves identity

theorists and, at the same time, deny the existence of the genuinely mental (in my sense); but the result of this is always some kind of physical-physical identity thesis rather than a genuine mental-physical identity claim.

(1978: 365)

27. On this point see Strawson 1994: 57–8. A good number of philosophers seem to be trapped in the terminology that allows the opposition. See further ahead.

28. This allows that physical stuff may be found in other universes: [c] doesn't state a necessary condition of being physical.

29. Stuff dualism holds that there are two fundamental kinds of stuff. Stuff monism contrasts with *thing monism*, the view (held for example by Spinoza) that there is at bottom only one thing (substance, entity) in reality. Schaffer (2010) calls thing monism and stuff monism 'existence monism' and 'substance monism' respectively. In this chapter I take the notion of stuff or substance monism to be viable although it's not entirely clear what it amounts to: see e.g. Strawson (2003: §15); see also the discussion of 'fungibility' in Strawson (2017).

30. In this case, spatio-temporality isn't a sufficient condition of same substancehood, nor of physicality (assuming our world is indeed spatio-temporal).

31. Physics can be seen as a formal structure which can be given different interpretations or models.

32. I'm assuming that there is such causal interaction and therefore putting aside a 'Leibnizian' variant of the case.

33. See also Drake (1925: 243), Strong (1930: 327), and Lewis in section 6, this chapter.

34. It's loose insofar as it's natural to think that the structural properties of the physical are also part of its intrinsic nature.

35. Many physicists now doubt that it is. Kant rides again.

36. See e.g. Strawson (2017: 382–3) for an argument that it does not. It's a tricky issue.

37. We might equally well take it that the property of having temporal duration is in itself an entirely non-experiential *property*. If so, it is again a property which may be exemplified without there being any non-experiential *stuff*.

38. I try to clarify this issue in Strawson 2016: 87–90, where I introduce 'hylal' as a positive term for a specific type of non-experiential stuff being distinct from experiential being.

39. It's special because we do know something for sure about the intrinsic nature of the physical if physicalism is true, because (once again) we know that our experience is concretely real, and hence physical if physicalism is true, and there is a fundamental respect in which we know its nature in having it. (This claim that 'we know its nature' is likely to be misunderstood by anyone who hasn't taken in note 19 and the paragraph to which it is attached.)

40. See e.g. Lucretius (c50 BCE), Clarke (1707–18), Kant (1781–7), James (1890: ch. 6), Goff (2006), Chalmers (2015); I'm going to take general familiarity with the combination problem for granted, and stick to the 'subject combination problem'.

41. I.e. that the unity of apperception does arise from the composite. Kant undermines the view that we can know that the mind or soul or thinking subject is a single substance in his discussion of the Second Paralogism. He grants – stresses – the sense in which the thinking subject is something that is necessarily single in the activity of thought or experience, and points out that we cannot infer its ultimate metaphysical simplicity from this fact.

42. I like to think (hope) that this general line of thought applies to all the problems listed in Chalmers (2015).

43. See further Stoljar 2006a, 2006b.

44. I offer a direct four-stage argument that PP is the most plausible theory of concrete reality in Strawson (2017: 386–7).

45. My thanks to Peter Lewis, Bill Seager, Jim Weatherall, and members of the Shanghai workshop on idealism held in June 2017.

References

Berkeley, G. (1710/1998). *A Treatise Concerning the Principles of Human Knowledge*. Ed. J. Dancy. Oxford: Oxford University Press.

Cavendish, M. (1664/1994). 'Letter 30' of *Philosophical Letters: Or, Modest Reflections Upon Some Opinions in Natural Philosophy*. In M. Atherton (ed.), *Women Philosophers of the Early Modern Period*. Indianapolis: Hackett, pp. 24–9.

Chalmers, D. (2015). 'Panpsychism and Panprotopsychism'. In T. Alter and Y. Nagasawa (eds.), *Consciousness in the Physical World: Perspectives on Russellian Monism*. New York: Oxford University Press.

Clarke, S., and Collins, A. (1707–1718/2011). *The Clarke-Collins Correspondence of 1707–18*. Ed. W. Uzgalis. Peterborough, ON: Broadview Press.

Drake, D. (1925). *Mind and Its Place in Nature*. New York: Macmillan.

Eddington, A. (1928a). 'Review of *The Analysis of Matter*'. *Journal of Philosophical Studies*, 3 (9): 93–5.

Eddington, A. (1928b). *The Nature of the Physical World*. New York: Macmillan.

Goff, P. (2006). 'Experiences Don't Sum'. In A. Freeman (ed.), *Consciousness and Its Place in Nature*. Thorverton: Imprint Academic, pp. 53–61.

Goff, P. (2017). *Consciousness and Fundamental Reality*. Oxford: Oxford University Press.

Griffin, D. (1977). 'Some Whiteheadian Comments on the Discussion'. In John B. Cobb and David Ray Griffin (eds.), *Mind in Nature: Essays on the Interface of Science and Philosophy*. Lanham, MD: University Press of America, pp. 97–100.

Griffin, D. (1998). *Unsnarling the World-Knot: Consciousness, Freedom, and the Mind-Body Problem*. Berkeley, CA: University of California Press.

Hartshorne, C. (1936). 'The Compound Individual'. In O. Lee (ed.), *Essays for Alfred North Whitehead*. London: Longmans, Green, pp. 193–220.

Hartshorne, C. (1942). 'Organic and Inorganic Wholes'. *Philosophy and Phenomenological Research*, 3 (2): 127–36.

Hawking, S. (1988). *A Brief History of Time*. New York: Bantam Books.

Heil, J. (2012). *The Universe as We Find It*. Oxford: Oxford University Press.

Heil, J., and Martin, C. B. (1998). 'Rules and Powers'. *Philosophical Perspectives*, 12: 283–312.

Heisenberg, W. (1958). *Physics and Philosophy*. New York: Harper and Brothers.

James, W. (1890/1950). *The Principles of Psychology*. New York: Dover.

James, W. (1909/1996). *A Pluralistic Universe*. Lincoln, Nebraska: University of Nebraska Press.

Kant, I. (1766/1992). 'Dreams of a Spirit-Seer'. In D. Walford (ed.), *Theoretical Philosophy 1755–1770*. New York: Cambridge University Press, pp. 301–60.

Kant, I. (1781–7/1933). *Critique of Pure Reason*. Trans. N. Kemp Smith. London: Macmillan.

Laudan, L. (1981). 'A Confutation of Convergent Realism'. *Philosophy of Science* 48 (1): 19–49.

Lewis, D. (1983/1999). 'New Work for a Theory of Universals'. In *Papers in Metaphysics and Epistemology*. Cambridge: Cambridge University Press, pp. 8–55.

Lewis, D. (1994). 'Reduction of Mind'. In S. Guttenplan (ed.), *A Companion to the Philosophy of Mind*. Oxford: Blackwell.

Lewis, P. (2016). *Quantum Ontology: A Guide to the Metaphysics of Quantum Mechanics*. Oxford: Oxford University Press.

Locke, J. (1689–1700/1975). *An Essay Concerning Human Understanding*. Ed. P. Nidditch. Oxford: Clarendon Press.

Lucretius. (c50 BCE/2007). *The Nature of Things*. Trans. A. Stallings. London: Penguin.

Maxwell, G. (1978). 'Rigid Designators and Mind-Brain Identity'. In C. Wade Savage (ed.), *Perception and Cognition: Issues in the Foundations of Psychology*. Minneapolis: University of Minnesota Press, pp. 365–403.

McHenry, L., and Shields, G. (2016). 'Analytical Critiques of Whitehead's Metaphysics'. *Journal of the American Philosophical Association*, CJO 2016. DOI:10.1017/apa.2016.21.

Montague, M. (2016). *The Given*. Oxford: Oxford University Press.

Mørch, H. H. (2014). *Panpsychism and Causation: A New Argument and a Solution to the Combination Problem*. University of Oslo, PhD dissertation. https://philpapers.org/archive/HASPAC-2.pdf.

Nagel, T. (1979). 'Panpsychism'. In *Mortal Questions*. New York: Cambridge University Press, pp. 181–95.

Nagel, T. (2012). *Mind and Cosmos: Why the Materialist Neo-Darwinian Conception of Nature Is Almost Certainly False*. Oxford: Oxford University Press.

Newman, M. (1928). 'Mr. Russell's "Causal Theory of Perception"'. *Mind*, 37: 137–48.

Nietzsche, F. (1882–1884). *Nachgelassene Fragmente 1882–1884: Sämtliche Werke 10*. Berlin: de Gruyter.

Nietzsche, F. (1883–1892/2006). *Thus Spoke Zarathustra: A Book for All and None*. Trans. A. del Caro. Cambridge: Cambridge University Press.

Pautz, A. (2009). 'A Simple View of Consciousness'. In R. Koons and G. Bealer (eds.), *The Waning of Materialism: New Essays*. Oxford: Oxford University Press, pp. 25–66.

Quine, W. V. (1951). 'Two Dogmas of Empiricism'. *The Philosophical Review*, 60: 20–43.

Quine, W. V. (1981). *Theories and Things*. Cambridge, MA: Harvard University Press.

Quine, W. V. (1992). 'Structure and Nature'. *The Journal of Philosophy*, 89 (1): 5–9.

Russell, B. (1912/1959). *The Problems of Philosophy*. Oxford: Oxford University Press.

Russell, B. (1927a/1992). *The Analysis of Matter*. London: Routledge.

Russell, B. (1927b). *An Outline of Philosophy*. London Allen & Unwin.

Russell, B. (1948/1992). *Human Knowledge: Its Scope and Limits*. London: Routledge.

Russell, B. (1956/1995). 'Mind and Matter'. In *Portraits from Memory*. Nottingham: Spokesman, pp. 135–53.

Russell, B. (1959). *My Philosophical Development*. New York: Simon and Schuster.

Schaffer, J. (2010). 'Monism: The Priority of the Whole'. *Philosophical Review*, 119: 31–76.

Seager, W. (1995). 'Consciousness, Information and Panpsychism'. *Journal of Consciousness Studies*, 2–3: 272–88.

Seager, W. (2010). 'Panpsychism, Aggregation and Combinatorial Infusion'. *Mind & Matter*, 8 (2): 167–84.

Seager, W. (2016). 'Panpsychist Infusion'. In G. Brüntrup and L. Jaskolla (eds.), *Panpsychism: Contemporary Perspectives*. New York: Oxford University Press, pp. 229–48.

Sellars, R. W. (1927). 'Why Naturalism and Not Materialism?' *Philosophical Review*, 36: 216–25.

Sellars, R. W. (1932). *The Philosophy of Physical Realism*. New York: Macmillan.

Shields, G. (2001). 'Physicalist panexperientialism and the mind-body problem'. *American Journal of Theology & Philosophy*, 2: 133–154.

Shepherd, M. (1824). *An Essay Upon the Relation of Cause and Effect, &c.* London: Hookham.

Siegel, S. (2017). *The Rationality of Perception*. Oxford: Oxford University Press.

Skrbina, D. (2005). *Panpsychism in the West*. Cambridge, MA: MIT Press.

Spinoza, B. de (1677/1985). 'Ethics'. In E. Curley (ed. and trans.), *The Collected Works of Spinoza*. Princeton: Princeton University Press.

Sprigge, T. L. S. (1983). *The Vindication of Absolute Idealism*. Edinburgh: Edinburgh University Press.

Stoljar, D. (2006a). *Ignorance and Imagination: On the Epistemic Origin of the Problem of Consciousness*. Oxford: Oxford University Press.

Stoljar, D. (2006b). 'Comments on Galen Strawson'. In A. Freeman (ed.), *Consciousness and Its Place in Nature*. Thorverton: Imprint Academic, pp. 170–6.

Strawson, G. (1994). *Mental Reality*. Cambridge, MA: MIT Press.

Strawson, G. (2003/2008). 'Real Materialism'. In *Real Materialism and Other Essays*. Oxford: Oxford University Press, pp. 19–52.

Strawson, G. (2006a). 'Realistic Monism: Why Physicalism Entails Panpsychism'. In A. Freeman (ed.), *Consciousness and Its Place in Nature*. Thorverton: Imprint Academic, pp. 3–31.

Strawson, G. (2006b). 'Reply to Commentators, with a Celebration of Descartes'. In A. Freeman (ed.), *Consciousness and Its Place in Nature*. Thorverton: Imprint Academic, pp. 184–280.

Strawson, G. (2008). 'The Identity of the Categorical and the Dispositional'. *Analysis*, 68: 271–82.

Strawson, G. (2016). 'Mind and Being: The Primacy of Panpsychism'. In G. Brüntrup and L. Jaskolla (eds.), *Panpsychism: Philosophical Essays*. New York: Oxford University Press, pp. 75–112.

Strawson, G. (2017). 'Physicalist Panpsychism'. In S. Schneider and M. Velmans (eds.), *The Blackwell Companion to Consciousness*, 2nd edition. New York: Wiley-Blackwell, pp. 374–90.

Strawson, G. (2018). 'The Silliest Claim'. In *Things That Bother Me*. New York: New York Review Books.

Strawson, G. (2019). 'A Hundred Years of Consciousness: A Long Training in Absurdity'. *Estudios de Filosofía*, 59: 9–45.

Strong, C. A. (1918). *The Origin of Consciousness: An Attempt to Conceive the Mind as a Product of Evolution*. London: Macmillan.

Strong, C. A. (1930). 'Nature and Mind'. In G. P. Adams and W. P. Montague (eds.), *Contemporary American Philosophy: Personal Statements*, vol. 2. London: George Allen and Unwin, pp. 313–32.

Stubenberg, L. (2016). 'Neutral Monism'. In Edward N. Zalta (ed.), *The Stanford Encyclopedia of Philosophy*, Winter 2016 edition. https://plato.stanford.edu/archives/win2016/entries/neutral-monism/.

Tolman, E. C. (1932). *Purposive Behaviour in Animals and Men*. New York: Century.

Turausky, K. (MS). 'Picturing Panpsychism: New Approaches to the Combination Problem(s)'.

Wallace, D. (2013). 'A Prolegomenon to the Ontology of the Everett Interpretation'. In A. Ney and D. Albert (eds.), *The Wave Function: Essays on the Metaphysics of Quantum Mechanics*. Oxford: Oxford University Press, pp. 203–22.

Weinberg, S. (1997). 'Before the Big Bang'. *The New York Review of Books*, 44 (10), June 12.

Whitehead, A. (1925/1967). *Science and the Modern World*. New York: The Free Press.

Whitehead, A. (1927–8/1978). *Process and Reality: An Essay in Cosmology*. Ed. D. Griffin and D. Sherburne, corrected edition. New York: Free Press.

Whitehead, A. (1938/1969). *Modes of Thought*. New York: The Free Press.

Williams, D. C. (1944). 'Naturalism and the Nature of Things'. *The Philosophical Review*, 43: 417–43.

Wilson, J. (2015). 'Metaphysical Emergence: Weak and Strong'. In T. Bigaj and C. Wüthrich (eds.), *Metaphysics in Contemporary Physics*. Amsterdam and New York: Rodopi, Brill.

Wishon, D. (2015). 'Russell on Russellian Monism'. In T. Alter and Y. Nagasawa (eds.), *Consciousness in the Physical World: Perspectives on Russellian Monism*. Oxford: Oxford University Press, pp. 91–118.

27

STRAWSON ON PANPSYCHISM

Terry Horgan

Galen Strawson's case for panpsychism has caused me to regard that metaphysical position as more plausible than I did formerly. As of now, however, I find myself incapable of believing panpsychism, or of coming close to believing it – even though I do appreciate its theoretical virtues, which Strawson is very good at articulating. Here I will explain why I remain unconvinced, focusing mainly on two of his papers, Strawson (2016) and Strawson (this volume). Then I will situate my attitude toward panpsychism in a wider context, by briefly rehearsing and motivating my comparative-plausibility ordering regarding a range of alternative positions concerning the metaphysics of mentality. Finally, I will say how I see the relation between "blobjectivsm," a version of ontological monism I favor concerning concrete particulars, and the form of panpsychism known as "cosmopsychism."

1. I begin by commenting on several passages in Strawson (2016). Consider first the following passage[1]:

> (A) *Objection*: But still – why suppose that the basic nature of concrete reality is experiential? . . . I reply . . . with another question – 'Why suppose that it's nonexperiential – either in its basic nature or in any respect at all?' What evidence is there for the existence of nonexperiential reality, as opposed to experiential reality? None. There is zero evidence for the existence of nonexperiential reality – even after we allow in a standard realist way that each of us encounters a great deal in concrete reality that is not his or her own experience. Nor will there ever be any. All there is, is one great big wholly ungrounded wholly question-begging theoretical intuition or conviction.
>
> (2016: 94)

It seems to me that claiming that there is zero observational evidence for the existence of non-experiential reality, over and above experiential reality, is very much like claiming that there is zero observational evidence that here's one hand and here is another. (After all, I could be a lifelong envatted brain.) In both cases, the underlying thought seems to be this: since all my experience would be exactly the same even if the given existence claim were false, I have zero observational evidence for the existence claim.

Admittedly, there is the following fact to consider, regarding my belief that here's one hand and here's another. The intentional content of my sensory-perceptual experience *itself* is as-of here being one hand and here being another. Arguably, the ongoing numerous occurrences of sensory-perceptual experiences with various presentational contents constitute constantly increasing observational

340

evidence for my *beliefs* with those same contents – all the more so because the ongoing sensory-perceptual experiences all cohere so well with one another, and with my ongoing expectations about how these experiences will unfold in the short-term future.

What about my many beliefs about the non-experientiality of numerous portions of reality – e.g., the non-experientiality of tables, chairs, H20 molecules, black holes, and electromagnetic radiation? Since on matters of epistemology I lean toward some version of experiential evidentialism, I myself would look toward *experience* as providing justification for these beliefs. Now, is the non-experientiality of tables, for example, part of the direct *presentational content* of my experiences as-of tables? Probably not – which, admittedly, is a potentially pertinent difference from how my sensory-perceptual experience is evidentially related to my belief that here's one hand and here's another. However, it's certainly the case that my experiences as-of tables, chairs, rocks, mountains, and trees do not present such entities to me *as experiential*. Also, it's certainly the case that the perceptible features of such entities do not provide me with any evidence from which I can confidently abductively *infer* that such entities (and/or their parts) are experiential – although I do have such evidence in the case of the behaviors of other humans, non-human animals, birds, and so on. And it seems to me that this *pervasive absence* of evidence for the experientiality of such entities constitutes good – indeed, very good – evidence for the contention these entities (and their component parts) are *not* experiential. I am strongly abductively warranted, on the basis of my *experiences* as-of such entities, in believing of them that they are non-experiential.

Consider next this passage:

(B) [P]hysics is silent about the intrinsic nonstructural nature of reality. The question is then this (it's an ancient question, but I'll give it again in Hawking's words): "What is it that breathes fire into the equations and makes a universe for them to describe?" (Hawking 1988: 174). What is it that the equations are true of? What is the fundamental, intrinsic, nonstructural nature or stuff being of the concrete reality that the true statements of physics are true of?

(2016: 85)

I'm not persuaded. An intrinsic feature, as I understand the notion of intrinsicness, is (roughly, at least) a categorical feature whose presence does not depend constitutively on how the thing that possesses the feature is related to other things that do not overlap with the given thing. Why aren't determinates of the determinable *mass* intrinsic features, especially since physics treats mass as a feature that does not vary depending on the local strength of gravitation? Aren't mass–determinates construed in physics as intrinsic *categorical* properties underlying the dispositions systematized in laws of motion? Why isn't *propagating at 186,000 miles per second* an intrinsic feature of electromagnetic radiation? True enough, our knowledge about the intrinsic features posited in physics ultimately depends on experience. And perhaps, as seems plausible, our positive conceptions of such intrinsic features often partly (or even largely) involve their varying experiential effects – e.g., the varying experiences associated with lifting different dumbells, some weighing more than others. But for all that, it seems to me that we do have some positive non-structural conception of certain intrinsic features posited by physics, features like determinate masses or the speed of light.

Here is a third passage from Strawson:

(C) Let me now add a version of an old metaphysical thesis. . . :

(7) *natura non facit saltum*
i.e. (roughly) there are no absolute or radical qualitative discontinuities in nature. I take
(7) – No Jumps – to be a solid part of any sound naturalism, and from (7), as

I understand it, one can derive the No Radical Emergence thesis as I understand it, that is,

(8) there is no radical emergence

(some may think that (8) is effectively the same as (7)). And from (8), I submit, we can derive

(9) the experiential (experiential being) can't emerge from the wholly and utterly nonexperiential (wholly and utterly nonexperiential being)

– because any such emergence would have to be radical in an impossible way.

I'm not going to argue for (8) and (9). The general idea is simple. "Emergence – e-mergence", no less – can't be brute. In all genuine (nonradical) cases of emergence of one thing from another there's a fundamental sense in which the emergent phenomenon, say Y, is wholly dependent on – somehow wholly flows from – that which it emerges from, say X. Otherwise it simply won't be true after all to say that Y is emergent from X, for some part or aspect of Y will have come from somewhere else. . . .

Many will agree. Others won't. Two things seem worth saying straight away. The first is that it's metaphysically far more extravagant and antinaturalistic to reject (7) the No Jumps thesis, and postulate radical emergence of the human or biological experiential from the nonhuman or nonbiological experiential – whatever difficulties the second idea might seem to raise (e.g., the 'combination problem').

Secondly, and more importantly, one doesn't need to meet those who don't agree with No Radical Emergence with an argument to support it. All one has to do is ask them politely why they think anything nonexperiential exists; especially when this belief forces them to endorse radical emergence, given that they're realists about experience. (2016: 82–3)

As a prelude to commenting on this passage, let me distinguish several pertinent theses. First is what I will call *gradualism*, by which I mean the following. As evolution gradually produced creatures with increasingly sophisticated forms of intentionality, thereby it gradually produced creatures with increasingly more subtle and sophisticated forms of phenomenal consciousness – with phenomenally conscious states being (1) inherently intentional (with phenomenal intentionality being the *basic* kind of intentionality in nature), and (2) the categorical basis of the systematically content-appropriate functional roles that intentional mental states play in creatures that undergo such states. Entities in nature whose behavior is not explainable in terms of mental intentionality, not even very primitive forms of mental intentionality, *don't undergo* states with mental intentionality – and thus don't undergo phenomenally conscious states, which are themselves inherently intentional. And the most primitive forms of mental intentionality are very simple – in phenomenal character, in content, and in terms of associated, content-appropriate, causal role. Consciousness emerged gradually from there, in the course of evolution.

Second is what I will call *weak metaphysical emergentism*, which goes as follows. (1) There are metaphysically brute, explanatorily basic, supervenience relations between (i) certain complex physical properties instantiable by sufficiently complex creatures, and (ii) phenomenal-intentional mental properties. Furthermore, (2) the supervenient experiential properties are not fundamental force-generating properties with causal efficacy over and above the causal efficacy of the physical properties upon which they supervene; rather, they are only efficacious "superveniently" (so to speak), via the causal efficacy of those subvenient physical properties. I call this position *metaphysical* emergentism because it posits metaphysically brute, unexplainable, physical-to-experiential supervenience relations. And I call it *weak* metaphysical emergentism because it does not deny the nomological completeness of the physical; i.e., it does not treat emergent experiential properties as fundamental force-generating properties.

There are two different versions of weak metaphysical emergentism, which I call, respectively, *nomic* and *Moorean*. The nomic version asserts that the pertinent physical-to-experiential supervenience connections are (fundamental) laws of nature; i.e., they obtain with nomic necessity. The Moorean version asserts instead that these supervenience connections obtain with (synthetic) metaphysical necessity, rather than with merely-nomic necessity. (G.E. Moore held that supervenience relations with this latter kind of modal strength obtain between certain natural properties and moral properties like intrinsic goodness.)

Third is *strong* metaphysical emergentism. This position embraces claim (1) of weak metaphysical emergentism, while also asserting that experiential properties are fundamental force-generating properties with causal efficacy over and above the causal efficacy of the physical properties upon which they supervene. This position too has two different versions, nomic and Moorean.

With the three-way distinction in hand between gradualism, weak metaphysical emergentism, and strong metaphysical emergentism, I have several things to say concerning passage (C). First, I submit that gradualism is enormously plausible, and moreover that gradualism constitutes one important respect in which it is true that there is no "radical emergence" in nature.

Second, gradualism is compatible with both versions of weak metaphysical emergentism, and likewise is compatible with both versions of strong metaphysical emergentism.

Third, I think that both versions of weak metaphysical emergentism are seriously viable metaphysical positions, with two notably attractive features. First, they explain why there is an apparent "hard problem" of phenomenal consciousness – an apparent "explanatory gap" regarding questions of the form "Why is physical property P a supervenience-base property of phenomenal-mental property M, rather than being a supervenience-base property of some other phenomenal-mental property or of none at all?" The explanation of the existence of this apparent hard problem is that those physical-to-experiential supervenience relations are *metaphysically brute necessitation relations*, and hence that they therefore are not themselves explainable. (The apparent explanatory gap is a *genuine*, unfillable, explanatory gap.) Second, weak metaphysical emergentism is entirely compatible with the thesis – central to any broadly materialist metaphysic of mind – that the physical domain is nomologically complete in itself (and thus that there are no non-physical fundamental-force–generating properties in nature). For more on this theme, see Horgan (2010).

Fourth, although both versions of weak metaphysical emergentism look seriously viable to me, and although I think that weak emergentism deserves to be called a form of metaphysical naturalism, in my view it should not count as a *materialist* metaphysical position, even in a broad sense that distinguishes between "reductive" and "nonreductive" versions of materialism. In my view, any form of metaphysical materialism should maintain that all supervenience relations in nature are explainable rather than brute (cf. Horgan 1993).

Fifth, consider now Strawson's claim, in passage (C), that "it's metaphysically far more extravagant and antinaturalistic to reject (7) the No Jumps thesis, than it is to postulate radical emergence of the human or biological experiential from the nonhuman or nonbiological experiential." To me the tradeoff between panpsychism and (either version of) weak metaphysical emergentism is a much closer call. Weak emergentism, after all, (i) not only acknowledges the hard problem but also explains its existence, (ii) fully comports with gradualism, (iii) fully comports with the nomological completeness of the physical, and (iv) eschews the radical-seeming suggestion that everything – all of concrete reality – is mind or consciousness. (I am not prepared to reject materialism and embrace weak emergentism, however. I call myself a "wannabe materialist"; more on this to follow.)

Sixth, consider Strawson's remark in passage (C) regarding those who don't agree with No Radical Emergence (understood as the denial of both weak and strong *metaphysical* emergentism): "All one has to do is ask them politely why they think anything nonexperiential exists; especially when this belief forces them to endorse radical emergence, given that they're realists about experience." Well, as I said earlier in this section when commenting on passage (A), I maintain that the pervasive absence of evidence for the experientiality of such things as tables, mountains, trees, or molecules constitutes very good evidence for the contention that these entities (and their component parts) are not experiential. In correspondence, however, Strawson has questioned this contention of mine. So I turn next to some elaboration and defense of it.

2. Under what epistemic circumstances does absence of evidence for a hypothesis H count as evidence in favor of the proposition $\sim H$? Roughly, at least, this is so under circumstances in which H is a *bold* hypothesis – and one that not knowable *a priori*. That is certainly the case in science. Epistemically, bold scientific hypotheses are "guilty until proven innocent"; i.e., they need to "show their mettle," so to speak. One way to do this is abductively, via "inference to the best explanation": the hypothesis constitutes, or significantly contributes to, a good explanation of various phenomena to which it pertains – and a better explanation than available competing alternatives. Another way is empirically, for instance by generating specific empirical predictions that subsequently are borne out by means of observational testing. Ideally, H will show its mettle in both ways.

Bold metaphysical hypotheses too are epistemically guilty until proven innocent; they too must show their mettle in order to be credible. Things often are trickier here than in science, in the following important respect: very often in metaphysics, competing hypotheses do not generate alternative, observationally testable, empirical predictions. Nonetheless, bold metaphysical hypotheses should positively advance the broad project of philosophy, a project famously described by Wilfrid Sellars (1962: 35) this way: "The aim of philosophy, abstractly formulated, is to understand how things in the broadest possible sense of the term hang together in the broadest possible sense of the term." Bold metaphysical hypotheses can show their mettle in this respect by contributing to the overall simplicity, and/or the overall unity and cohesiveness, and/or the overall explanatory power, of one's large-scale, science-respecting, worldview. They can do so even when they do not generate specific empirical predictions and hence are not susceptible to observational tests.

Panpsychism is certainly a bold hypothesis. But just what *kind* of hypothesis is it? There are two perspectives from which one might regard it. First is what I'll call the *empirical* perspective. Here one expects attributions of mentality to provide fairly specific explanations of fairly specific observable phenomena. Certain beings in nature exhibit patterns of behavior that are susceptible to explanation in terms of sensory-perceptual states, goals, beliefs, desires, intentions, emotional states like fear or aggression, and so on. Humans and many other earthly creatures exhibit such behavioral patterns, and the susceptibility of those patterns to psychological explanation constitutes positive observational evidence in support of attributions of mentality to these creatures. Many entities, however – both ones encountered in ordinary life and ones posited in science – exhibit no known or hypothesized behavioral patterns that are susceptible in any plausible way to psychological explanation. From the empirical perspective, therefore, the hypothesis that mentality is pervasive in nature fails to show its mettle – and fails *dramatically*. Absence of empirical evidence in favor of pervasive mentality thereby constitutes strong empirical evidence in favor of widespread non-mentality.

But there is a second perspective too, which I'll call the *metaphysical* perspective. Here one first concedes – or anyway, *should* concede – that the hypothesis of pervasive mentality does not show its mettle from within the empirical perspective. One then proceeds to argue that despite this fact, the pervasive-mentality hypothesis contributes very substantially to the philosophical aim of understanding how things in the broadest sense of the term hang together in the broadest sense of the term. Providing such an argument is a substantial dialectical burden, especially given how things stand epistemically from the empirical perspective alone. But perhaps it can be done nonetheless.

In the next two sections I say more about the prospects for successful-metaphysical perspective argumentation in favor of panpsychism. But before doing that, let me briefly revisit passage (A). There Strawson claims that "there is zero evidence for the existence of nonexperiential reality – even after we allow in a standard realist way that each of us encounters a great deal in reality that is not his or her own experience." I say, on the contrary, that there is plenty of evidence for the existence of nonexperiential reality – viz., the fact that so much of reality as we know it does not exhibit behavior patterns that are plausibly susceptible to psychological explanation. I.e., there is plenty of ordinary *empirical* evidence for the existence of nonexperiential reality.

3. Earlier I mentioned what David Chalmers calls the "hard problem" of consciousness, which I glossed as involving questions of this form: "Why is physical property P a supervenience-base property of phenomenal property M, rather than being a supervenience-base property of some other phenomenal-mental property or of none at all?" One might think that panpsychism can somehow solve or dissolve the hard problem, and that this would go a long way toward showing its mettle metaphysically.

As far as I can see, however, the hard problem still arises within the framework of panpsychism, under the guise of the so-called "combination problem." Relative to a version of panpsychism embracing what Strawson (2016: 86) calls "smallism" – viz., the doctrine that "there are a great many ultimate constituents of reality" – the problem is expressible by questions of the following kind.

> Why is complex property P of organism O – where O comprises such-and-such ultimate constituents that are related to one another in thus-and-such ways and respectively instantiate so-and-so respective kinds of consciousness themselves – a supervenience-base property for phenomenal property M of organism O, rather than being a supervenience-base property of some other phenomemal-mental property of O or of none at all?

I myself see no clear progress, with respect to metaphysical understanding, from replacing the original hard problem with the combination problem. I have as little idea about what could constitute answers to the replacement-questions as I have about what could constitute answers to the original hard problem questions. And, insofar as the combination problem has no clear solution and remains just as prima facie puzzling as does the original hard problem, no discernible metaphysical insight is gained from the proposed replacement.

Suppose that one addresses the combination problem by positing brute supervenience relations – possessing perhaps nomic necessity, or perhaps metaphysical necessity – linking (i) certain complex combinations of primitively conscious ultimate constituents with (ii) certain high-level consciousness-properties instantiable by complex organisms that are constituted by those primitively conscious ultimate constituents as thus physically combined with one another. Well then, I see no significant gain in metaphysical understanding, above and beyond the comparable kind of gain that results from weak emergentism – viz., the theoretical advantage of treating the apparent explanatory gaps as genuine explanatory gaps, ones that cannot be closed because the supervenience relations at issue are just metaphysically brute. Also, if I was right when I claimed in Horgan (1993) that any metaphysical position worthy of the label 'materialism' must eschew brute supervenience relations, then the now-envisioned approach to the combination problem would be no less a departure from materialism than weak metaphysical emergentism.

What I have been saying in this section ties in closely with my remarks in section 1 about Strawson's passage (C). In one plausible and unproblematic-looking way, nature surely does conform to his slogan No Jumps: viz., gradualism is very likely true. But panpsychism offers no clear metaphysical advantage with respect to accommodating problematic-looking "jumps" in nature, because it still confronts the issue of combination-problem-style "jumps." So, insofar as the hard problem of consciousness is concerned, the bold hypothesis of panpsychism remains unmotivated from the metaphysical perspective, while meanwhile encountering ample evidence against it from the empirical perspective.

4. Are there perhaps other ways in which panpsychism can show its mettle from the metaphysical perspective? I turn next to another metaphysical argument I find in Strawson (2016) and, more prominently, in Strawson (this volume). The central line of thought, as I understand it, goes as

follows. The only kind of concrete reality whose intrinsic, fundamental "stuff-nature" we know or can know is experience. If there is only one kind of fundamental stuff in reality, then "everything in physics remains in place, and physics continues to be a theory about the nature of concrete reality" (this volume: 16). Therefore, "genuine, realistic, monistic naturalists ought to favour panpsychism above all other theories of the nature of concrete reality, on grounds of theoretical simplicity and ontological parsimony (one can add in "Occam's Razor" as a further premiss)" (this volume: 16).

Two considerations leave me unpersuaded by this argument. First, although I am happy to grant that all one knows *directly and by acquaintance*, and all one can know in this way, is the intrinsic phenomenal character of (one's own) experience, this leaves open the possibility of knowing *in other ways* facts about the intrinsic, fundamental, "stuff-nature" of various kinds of concrete reality. For instance, one can know the masses of various kinds of concrete entities, e.g., stars, planets, subatomic particles. And, arguably, mass is an intrinsic characteristic of these entities. The general point here is that there is no reason in principle why one cannot know – for instance, via abductive scientific theorizing, accompanied by suitable observational hypothesis-testing – about intrinsic, fundamental, stuff-natures of various concrete entities that lack mentality altogether.

Second, the contention that we know the intrinsic, fundamental, stuff-nature of experience seems to me highly questionable, because it seems to presuppose several bold metaphysical hypotheses none of which I find very credible. The apparent presuppositions include (1) the claim that experience is a kind of stuff (indeed, a fundamental kind of stuff), and (2) the claim that subjects of experience are not concrete beings in their own right, distinct from concrete experiences themselves. (See the opening section of Strawson (this volume), including in particular the theses he labels [3], [4], and [5] and his remarks there about them.)

Prima facie, a better way to construe the ontology of experience goes as follows. Subjects of experience are concrete beings distinct from experiences themselves. A concrete experience consists in the instantiation, by a subject of experience, of a phenomenal mental property. By undergoing an experience, the experiencer thereby comes to know, directly and by acquaintance, the intrinsic phenomenal character of that property itself. But subjects of experience do not know *directly and by acquaintance* the fundamental stuff-nature of anything in concrete reality.

If this alternative construal is right, then claims (1) and (2) are both mistaken. Strawson clearly holds that the construal is not right. Indeed, he explicitly embraces not only (1) and (2) but also yet another bold metaphysical hypothesis, which seems to me to be functioning as an additional presupposition of his contention that we know the fundamental stuff-nature of experience, viz., (3) the claim that the right ontology (i) does not involve distinct categories of *object* and *property* and hence (ii) also does not involve *instantiations* of properties by objects. (See section 3.4 of Strawson 2016).

I favor the ontological construal of experience described two paragraphs ago. Admittedly, this construal is best regarded as a metaphysical hypothesis itself, rather than as something knowable directly and by acquaintance. (What one knows directly and by acquaintance is the intrinsic phenomenal character of one's current experience – which leaves open how experience is best construed ontologically.) And if this construal is correct, then each of the bold metaphysical hypotheses (1)–(3) is false – which in turn falsifies Strawson's contention that we know the (putative) fundamental stuff-nature of experience. Before I could come to believe this contention, I would first need to be persuaded of all three of those dubious-seeming presuppositions, each of which is itself a (very) bold metaphysical hypothesis.

5. Let me now situate my own attitude toward panpsychism within a broader perspective, by saying something about my attitude toward various other competing positions in philosophy of mind. To begin with, I have long called myself a "wannabe materialist," a label by which I mean that I lean strongly toward a materialist metaphysic of mind but I know of no form of materialism that I find plausible enough to believe. (I literally don't know *what* to believe about the metaphysics of conscious experience.) I will describe a range of alternative positions, ordered progressively from

the one I find least plausible to the one I find most plausible. And I will briefly explain why each of these positions leaves me unsatisfied.

First is the view, embraced most clearly and explicitly by Daniel Dennett (e.g. 1988, 1991), that there is no such thing as phenomenal consciousness – no mental states such that there is "something it is like" to undergo them, with this aspect (often called *phenomenal character*) being intrinsic to these states, qua mental. I agree wholeheartedly with Strawson (2003), who calls this view The Great Silliness. As Strawson rightly stresses, nothing is more epistemically secure, or more certain, than the phenomenal character of one's present experience; the intrinsic phenomenal character of experience is known directly, and by acquaintance. The Great Silliness therefore ranks dead last on my own plausibility scale and is not a philosophical position I can take seriously.

Second is functionalism, which in one version or another has been the dominant generic position in philosophy of mind for the past half-century. What I call *second-order* functionalism (sometimes called *role* functionalism) holds that the complete essence of any mental property – any mental state-type – is its typical causal role in a creature's cognitive architecture vis-à-vis sensory/perceptual states, behavior, and other mental state-types whose full essences likewise comprises their own distinctive typical causal roles. What I call *first-order* functionalism (sometimes called *filler* functionalism) holds (i) that every mental property-name is definable via typical-cause connections to sensory/perceptual states, behavior, and other mental state-names that also are thus definable, and (ii) that these state-names are population-relative nonrigid designators of certain first-order physical properties, viz., whichever physical properties actually *fill* the pertinent causal roles in the creatures belonging to a specific creature-population. Second-order functionalism was first articulated by Hilary Putnam (1960), and versions of it have since been embraced by many in philosophy of mind. First-order functionalism, which combines a functionalist account of mental *concepts* with a form of the psychophysical identity theory for mental *properties*, was advocated most forcefully and explicitly by David Lewis (1966, 1980) and David Armstrong (1968).

In my view, second-order and first-order functionalism both suffer the same fatal flaw: they wrongly contend that the full essence of mental properties, qua mental, is entirely non-intrinsic and relational – entirely a matter of mental property's typical-cause connections to *other* state-types. (First-order functionalism can allow that mental properties do have intrinsic physical aspects, but cannot allow that these aspects accrue to these properties *qua mental*.) Both kinds of functionalism thereby fail to acknowledge the fact that phenomenally conscious mental state-types have intrinsic aspects, qua mental – viz., their phenomenal character, i.e., their intrinsic "what-it-is-like-ness." And in my view, as an advocate of both cognitive phenomenology and agentive phenomenology, virtually all mental state-types that are conscious-as-opposed to unconscious are also phenomenally conscious, with their own phenomenal character that is distinctive, proprietary, and individuative. So the flaw I am complaining about is extensive and pervasive, rather than applying only to a proper subset of the full range of conscious mental state-types such as sensory-perceptual experiences. Functionalism too is therefore a position that I cannot take seriously – although at least it is more plausible than the Great Silliness.

Turning now to philosophical approaches to conscious mentality that I do take seriously (and in ascending order of how plausible I find them), next on the list is panpsychism. To me this position certainly deserves to be taken seriously, because (i) it acknowledges the intrinsic phenomenal character of conscious experience, qua mental, and (ii) it purports to be fully compatible with physics and with all of the sciences. Nonetheless, I find it implausible for the kinds of reasons I have set out in earlier sections of this chapter. From the empirical perspective, not only is there significant lack of positive evidence for panpsychism, but (as explained in section 2), the systematic lack of positive evidence counts as strong empirical evidence *against* this bold hypothesis. And from the metaphysical perspective (as explained in sections 3 and 4), panpsychism does not do enough theoretically to render itself credible by virtue of contributing to the philosophical project of understanding how things in the widest sense of the term hang together in the widest sense of the term.

Next on my list of successively more plausible metaphysical construals of mentality is weak metaphysical emergentism, with slight preference for the Moorean version over the nomic version because I think the former has somewhat better prospects than the former for fending off epiphenomenalism (see Horgan 1987). A major theoretical advantage of metaphysical emergentism, as I emphasized earlier, is that it explains why there seems to be intractable explanatory gap concerning the ways phenomenal properties supervene on phenomenal properties. According to weak emergentism, this gap is real and irremedial, because the pertinent physical-to-phenomenal supervenience relations are metaphysically brute necessitation relations – brute relations of either nomic necessity or metaphysical necessity.

Despite this significant theoretical advantage, however, I find myself unable to believe in such brute inter-level necessitation relations, especially insofar as they involve subvenient physical properties that are physically non-basic and are instantiable only by entities which themselves are physically non-fundamental and are composed of vastly many fundamental physical constituents. I hanker after a metaphysic of conscious mentality under which any and all supervenience relations involving subvenient physical properties are *explainable* rather than being brute and sui generis. And in my view, nothing less than this deserves to count as a *materialist* metaphysic of mind (cf. Horgan 1993). So I am unable to believe metaphysical emergentism, even though I do regard it as both seriously viable and, from the metaphysical perspective, theoretically attractive.

In some moods, slightly higher on my plausibility ordering than either kind of weak metaphysical emergentism is the view sometimes called "mysterianism," associated most notably with Coin McGinn (1989). This view, as I understand it, is a version of materialism: it treats physical-to-phenomenal supervenience relations as explainable in some materialistically kosher way, rather than as being metaphysically brute. It also asserts, however, that humans are constitutionally incapable of formulating or understanding the pertinent explanations; by our very natures, we just aren't smart enough. To me the principal theoretical attraction of this view is that it manages to embrace materialism while also explaining why, try as I might, I find myself unable to comfortably regard the apparent "hard problem" of phenomenal consciousness as just a pseudo-problem. But the theoretical downside is that it offers a counsel of despair, at least as far as phenomenal consciousness is concerned, about the prospects for the philosophical project of understanding how things in the widest sense of the term hang together in the widest sense of the term. I am unable to believe that such understanding is impossible for humans.

At the top of my current plausibility ranking is a position of a kind that, as far as I know, has been most clearly and most explicitly advocated in the philosophical literature by Brian McLaughlin (2007, 2010, 2012). The key ideas in the version most attractive to me are the following. First, each phenomenal mental property is identical to some intrinsic, categorical, physical property. Second, phenomenal properties are instantiable only by physical entities that are physically complex rather than physically fundamental. Third (and largely because of the preceding point), phenomenal properties are identical to physically non-fundamental properties – properties which, by their very nature, probably require enormous physical complexity in any entities that could potentially instantiate them. (Physical specifications of these properties would then require specifying requisite structural complexity features of entities capable of realizing these properties.) Fourth, the intrinsic phenomenal character of phenomenal properties is not something distinct from – something "over and above" – the intrinsic categorical physical nature of the physical properties to which the phenomenal properties are identical; rather, phenomenal what-it's-like-ness consists in fact that the intrinsic categorical physical nature of the phenomenal properties is *directly presented* experientially to the entities that instantiate such properties, presented in such a way that those entities thereby know this intrinsic categorical physical nature directly and by immediate experiential acquaintance. Fifth, physical-phenomenal properties that are experientially directly presented in this way give rise, at least in creatures as cognitively sophisticated as humans, to corresponding phenomenal *concepts*; these concepts deploy those very properties – or mental images of them – as what, in Fregean language, can be called *self-presenting modes of presentation*. I.e., the experientially directly presented physical-phenomenal properties – or mental images thereof – get redeployed in thought as modes of presentation of themselves. Sixth, "knowing what it's like" is thus a matter of direct-acquaintance knowledge of an intrinsic physical property that one either is currently experiencing or mentally images experiencing. Seventh, knowing in this way the intrinsic categorical nature of a physical property does not constitute knowing that property's intrinsic categorical nature "qua physical"; rather, the latter consists of knowing that same nature *under a concept of physics*, which is a different matter entirely. Eighth, the complex, non-fundamental, categorical physical properties to which phenomenal properties are identical might well be "multiply realizable" by more finely specified physical properties – perhaps in such a way that these non-fundamental physical properties are realizable by physically complex creatures quite different in their fine-grained physical composition than earthly creatures (e.g., by being composed of silicon rather than organic molecules). (By way of analogy, think of *mean molecular kinetic energy*, as a property of gases that is arguably identical with *temperature*. It doesn't matter what kinds of molecules compose the gas, and there are innumerable different fine-grained inter-molecular states each of which instantiate the very same temperature property.)

Among the theoretical advantages of this position are the following. First, it acknowledges that phenomenal mental state-types have an intrinsic nature, qua mental – something that functionalism, for instance, fails to do. Second, as a type-type identity theory, it is a materialist metaphysic of mind, thoroughly eschewing metaphysically brute supervenience relations between physical properties and mental properties. Third, as a type-type identity theory, it also firmly avoids the threat of epiphenomenalism about mental properties (a threat that looms over any metaphysical position that fails to identify mental properties with certain physical properties). Fourth, it has resources to accommodate familiar "multiple realization" arguments against type-type identity theories – viz., by identifying phenomenal mental properties with physical properties that are complex and non-basic, it can allow (i) that such physical properties might well be instantiable by a variety of different kinds of physically complex creatures that differ significantly from one another in physical fine-grained ways (e.g., in the kinds of molecules they are composed of), and also (ii) that such physical properties might well be instantiable, within a single creature at a certain moment in its history, in a variety of different physically fine-grained ways (e.g., by a variety of different specific neural firing-patterns). (The second possibility is what elsewhere I have called *strong* multiple realization.) Fifth, by distinguishing between phenomenal concepts of physical-phenomenal state-types and physics-involving concepts of those same physical-phenomenal state-types, it has resources to explain the existence of the apparent "hard problem" of phenomenal consciousness – viz., a phenomenal concept and the corresponding, co-referring, physics-involving concept are conceptually independent because of the different modes of presentation they deploy. Sixth, it purports to eliminate any genuine hard problem, by treating a phenomenal concept and the corresponding physics-involving concept as deploying respective non-contingent modes of presentation which, despite being distinct (and, indeed, conceptually independent), nevertheless are modes of presentation of a single physical property.

Despite these theoretical advantages, however, the lately described position also is one that I find myself unable to believe. For me the principal stumbling block is that the apparent hard problem continues to strike me as a *genuine* explanatory problem – even though I have to admit that have no clear conception of what could even count as a solution. Here is one way to express the quandary I feel. I see no reason in principle why there couldn't be physically possible zombie-creatures that (i) are quite different from humans in their fine-grained physical composition (e.g., are not composed of organic molecules), (ii) have all the same *functional* cognitive architecture as humans, and yet (iii) have no phenomenal consciousness at all. But if indeed such creatures are physically possible, then recalcitrant hard-problem questions of the following kind seem to arise: Why do the intrinsic physical properties that are the categorical bases of the pertinent cognitive-architectural functional roles in the zombie-creatures have no phenomenal character, whereas the intrinsic physical properties that play those same disposition-subserving roles in humans do have phenomenal character? Why are the latter properties (the ones instantiated in humans) experientially presented what-it's-like physical properties, whereas the former properties (the ones instantiated in zombie-creatures, and subserving the very same cognitive-architectural functional roles) are phenomenally blank?

So I remain a "wannabe materialist." If someone could persuade me that panpsychism is a form of materialism that can effectively assuage my persistent hard-problem philosophical worries, then panpsychism might then move into first place in my priority ordering – or it might then even become a position that I could believe. (Strawson's own case for panpsychism, although worthy of serious philosophical respect, leaves me unpersuaded for the reasons explained earlier.)

6. For some years Matjaž Potrč and I have been defending and articulating a large-scale metaphysical-cum-semantic position we call "blobjectivism" (2000, 2002, 2008). Concerning metaphysics, this view asserts that there is really just one concrete particular in the right ontology – viz., the whole cosmos (the *blobject*, as we call it). Although the blobject is nonhomogenous and enormously structurally complex, these features do not involve a multiplicity of part-entities that also belong to the correct ontology; rather, they are a matter of how various properties and relations are instantiated, in various specific spatio-temporally local *manners of instantiation*, by the one concrete particular – the blobject. Blobjectivism is a version of what Jonathan Schaffer (2010) calls "existence monism." (Schaffer himself defends a less austere position that he calls "priority monism," which asserts (i) that the right ontology includes a multiplicity of concrete particulars over and above the whole cosmos, and yet (ii) that the whole cosmos is ontologically prior to any of its proper parts.)

In ordinary thought and discourse, and also in science, numerous thoughts and statements commonly regarded as true posit concrete entities other than the blobject. According to the semantic aspect of the Horgan/Potrc version of blobjectivism – *contextual semantics*, as we call it – typically such thoughts and statements are indeed true, despite blobjectivism's severe ontological austerity. This is because (i) we construe truth as correct affirmability under contextually operative affirmability norms, and (ii) we maintain that in most contexts of thought and discourse (including scientific contexts), the contextually operative affirmability norms operate in such a way that truth is an *indirect* form of thought/world and language/world correspondence that is consistent with the claim that the blobject is the only concrete particular in the correct ontology. On this view, true statements attributing specific kinds of mentality to specific individuals are made true by the way that phenomenally determinate mental properties are instantiated, in different local manners of instantiation, by the blobject.

A version of panpsychism called *cosmopsychism* has recently begun to be discussed and taken seriously in the panpsychism literature (e.g., Nagasawa and Wager 2016). On this view (as I understand it), the ontologically most fundamental kinds of consciousness accrue not to metaphysically fundamental micro-entities like subatomic particles, but rather to the entire cosmos. As a form of panpsychism, cosmopsychism fits naturally with Schaffer's priority monism, as Nagasawa and Wager emphasize. Indeed, they call their own version "priority cosmopsychism."

A priority monist need not embrace cosmopsychism but could instead contend that mental properties are instantiable only by fairly complex creatures that themselves are ontologically dependent upon the ontologically prior concrete particular – the whole cosmos. Blobjectivism, on the other hand, advocates an ontology that eschews ontologically dependent concrete particulars. So the question naturally arises: Since, according to blobjectivism, mental properties only get instantiated by the entire cosmos, does blobjectivism thereby qualify as a form of cosmopsychism – and hence as a species of panpsychism?

Well, one could *choose*, stipulatively, to call blobjectivism a form of cosmopsychism, on the grounds that this view asserts that the blobject is the sole concrete particular in the right ontology and therefore is the sole instantiator of mental properties. However, it seems to me that this would be contrary to the spirit of the metaphysical position which has recently been labeled cosmopsychism. That position (as I understand it) asserts (i) that the ontologically fundamental kinds of consciousness occur in a single, experientially unified mind (the cosmic mind), and (ii) that ordinary human forms of consciousness are ontologically less basic that this unified cosmic consciousness. (There thus arises, for cosmopsychism, a problem that is the logical dual of traditional panpsychism's "combination problem" – viz., the "decombination problem," as one might say.) By contrast, the blobjectivist metaphysic of mind that I favor does not posit an experientially unified cosmic consciousness; rather, it only posits various specific instantiations of mentality by the blobject in various distinct and diverse spatio-temporally local manners of instantiation. Those spatio-temporally disjoint instantiations do not collectively constitute a single unified cosmic consciousness, and I doubt that there is one. So, in reply to the question "Is blobjectivism a form of cosmopsychism?", my answer is No.[2]

Notes

1. I will label passages I quote with capital letters, to facilitate subsequent cross-references.
2. This paper is based on my commentary on Strawson (2016) in a symposium session on that paper at the 2015 Pacific Division meeting of the American Philosophical Association in Vancouver. My thanks to William Seager for inviting me to contribute to the present volume, and to Phillip Goff, Mark Timmons, and especially Galen Strawson for helpful interaction and feedback.

References

Armstrong, D. M. (1968). *A Materialist Theory of the Mind*. London: Routledge.

Dennett, D. (1988). 'Quining Qualia'. In A. Marcel and E. Bisiach (eds.), *Consciousness in Modern Science*. Oxford: Oxford University Press, pp. 42–77.

Dennett, D. (1991). *Consciousness Explained*. London: Penguin.

Hawking, S. (1988). *A Brief History of Time*. New York: Bantam Books.

Horgan, T. (1987). 'Supervenient Qualia'. *Philosophical Review*, 96: 491–520.

Horgan, T. (1993). 'From Supervenience to Superdupervenience: Meeting the Demands of a Material World'. *Mind*, 102: 555–86.

Horgan, T. (2010). 'Materialism, Minimal Emergentism, and the Hard Problem of Consciousness'. In G. Bealer and R. Koons (eds.), *The Waning of Materialism*. Oxford: Oxford University Press, pp. 309–30.

Horgan, T., and Potrč, M. (2000). 'Blobjectivism and Indirect Correspondence'. *Facta Philosophica*, 2: 249–70.

Horgan, T., and Potrč, M. (2002). 'Addressing Questions for Blobjectivism'. *Facta Philosophica*, 4: 311–21.

Horgan, T., and Potrč, M. (2008). *Austere Realism: Contextual Semantics Meets Minimal Ontology*. Cambridge, MA: MIT Press.

Lewis, D. (1966). 'An Argument for the Identity Theory'. *Journal of Philosophy*, 63: 17–25.

Lewis, D. (1980). 'Mad Pain and Martian Pain'. In N. Block (ed.), *Readings in the Philosophy of Psychology*, vol. 1. Cambridge, MA: Harvard University Press, pp. 216–22.

Putnam, H. (1960). 'Minds and Machines'. In S. Hook (ed.), *Dimensions of Mind*. New York: New York University Press, pp. 148–79.

McGinn, C. (1989). 'Can We Solve the Mind Body Problem?' *Mind*, 98: 349–66.

McLaughlin, B. (2007). 'Type Materialism for Phenomenal Consciousness'. In M. Velemans and S. Schneider (eds.), *The Blackwell Companion to Consciousness*. Oxford: Blackwell, pp. 431–444.

McLaughlin, B. (2010). 'Consciousness, Type Physicalism, and Inference to the Best Explanation'. *Philosophical Issues*, 20: 266–304.

McLaughlin, B. (2012). 'Phenomenal Concepts and the Defense of Materialism'. *Philosophy and Phenomenological Research*, 84: 206–214.

Nagasawa, Y., and Wager, K. (2016). 'Panpsychism and Priority Cosmopsychism'. In G. Brüntrup and L. Jaskolla (eds.), *Panpsychism: Contemporary Perspectives*. Oxford: Oxford University Press, pp. 113–29.

Schaffer, J. (2010). 'Monism: The Priority of the Whole'. *Philosophical Review*, 119: 31–76.

Sellars, Wilfrid (1962). 'Philosophy and the Scientific Image of Man'. In R. Colodny (ed.), *Frontiers of Science and Philosophy*. Pittsburgh: University of Pittsburgh Press, pp. 35–78.

Strawson, G. (2003). 'Real Materialism'. In L. Antony (ed.), *Chomsky and His Critics*. Oxford: Blackwell, pp. 49–88.

Strawson, G. (2016). 'Mind and Being: The Primacy of Panpsychism'. In G. Brüntrup and L. Jaskolla (eds.), *Panpsychism: Contemporary Perspectives*. Oxford: Oxford University Press, pp. 75–112.

Strawson, G. (this volume). 'What Does "physical" Mean? A Prolegomenon to Physicalist Panpsychism'. In W. Seager (ed.), *The Routledge Handbook of Panpsychism*. London: Routledge.

28

IDEALISM AND THE MIND-BODY PROBLEM[1]

David Chalmers

When I was in graduate school, I recall hearing "One starts as a materialist, then one becomes a dualist, then a panpsychist, and one ends up as an idealist".[2] I don't know where this comes from, but I think the idea was something like this. First, one is impressed by the successes of science, endorsing materialism about everything and so about the mind. Second, one is moved by the problem of consciousness to see a gap between physics and consciousness, thereby endorsing dualism, where both matter and consciousness are fundamental. Third, one is moved by the inscrutability of matter to realize that science reveals at most the structure of matter and not its underlying nature, and to speculate that this nature may involve consciousness, thereby endorsing panpsychism. Fourth, one comes to think that there is little reason to believe in anything beyond consciousness and that the physical world is wholly constituted by consciousness, thereby endorsing idealism.

Some recent strands in philosophical discussion of the mind – body problem have recapitulated this progression: the rise of materialism in the 1950s and 1960s, the dualist response in the 1980s and 1990s, the festival of panpsychism in the 2000s, and some recent stirrings of idealism.[3] In my own work, I have taken the first two steps and have flirted heavily with the third. In this chapter I want to examine the prospects for the fourth step: the move to idealism.

1. Varieties of Idealism

I will understand idealism broadly, as the thesis that the universe is fundamentally mental, or perhaps that all concrete facts are grounded in mental facts. As such it is meant as a global metaphysical thesis analogous to physicalism, the thesis that the universe is fundamentally physical, or perhaps that all concrete facts are grounded in physical facts. The only difference is that "physical" is replaced by "mental".

We can understand mental facts as facts wholly about the instantiation of mental properties.[4] Later we will examine possible versions of idealism that loosen this constraint. My focus is largely on conscious experience as opposed to non-conscious mental states, so the mental states and properties I will focus on are largely experiential states and properties, but in principle the definition includes views on which other sorts of mental states play a role. As for concreteness: this excludes truths about abstract domains, such as mathematics. In practice most physicalists and idealists are not committed to the strong claim that mathematical truths are grounded in physical or mental truths, and the restriction to concrete domains helps to avoid the issue.

Although it is common to define idealism as a global metaphysical thesis analogous to materialism, in practice idealism is often understood more narrowly as a version of Berkeley's "esse est percipi" thesis, holding that appearance constitutes reality. This sort of idealism is typically seen as a paradigm of anti-realism, in that it holds that there is no concrete reality external to how things appear: all concrete non-mental truths p are grounded in or constituted by appearances that p, or in closely related truths involving appearances. If we understand appearances as experiences had by observers (most naturally as perceptual experiences, though thoughts about the external world are also sometimes understood as appearances in a broad sense), it follows that the physical world is fully grounded in the experiences as of a physical world had by observers.

Anti-realist idealism entails idealism in the broad sense, but the reverse is not the case. For example, there are panpsychist versions of idealism where fundamental microphysical entities are conscious subjects, and on which matter is realized by these conscious subjects and their relations. There are also cosmopsychist versions of idealism where the whole universe is conscious, and on which the complex physical states of the cosmos are realized by structurally isomorphic cosmic mental states. Whether or not these views are plausible, they need have no commitment to "esse est percipi" or to other anti-realist doctrines. In constituting the physical world, on this view, appearances concerning the physical world may play no special role. It is the structure and relations among experiences rather than their specific content that matters.

One might object that all mental states (or at least all perceptual states) are appearances of some sort, so that any view on which mental or perceptual states constitute reality is a view on which appearance constitutes reality and is therefore anti-realist. But anti-realist idealism makes a stronger claim connecting the *nature* of any nonmental reality to the specific *content* of appearances: roughly, for any nonmental fact p about concrete reality, what it is for p to obtain is for appearances that p (or closely related appearances) to obtain.[5] On the realist versions of idealism discussed earlier, this stronger claim is false: what it is for physical facts p to obtain is for certain structural roles to obtain. When we conjoin the further (possibly contingent) claim that in fact appearances play that role, the appearance-reality and the mental-physical connections follow as consequences.

Idealist views like these are naturally understood as versions of realism about the physical world, rather than versions of anti-realism. The physical world really exists out there, independently of our observations; it just has a surprising nature. Indeed, views of this sort are highly congenial to epistemological structural realism, which says roughly that science reveals the structure of the physical world but not its intrinsic nature. We can think of them as versions of *realist idealism*.

Realist idealism may sound like an oxymoron, but this is only because we tend to associate idealism with the narrow anti-realist variety and ignore the broad variety. Correspondingly, the widespread view that idealism has been refuted or defeated is best understood as a view about anti-realist idealism.[6] Certainly the most familiar objections to idealism are largely objections to anti-realist idealism. Realist idealism has not been subject to the same sort of searching assessment as anti-realist idealism.

Anti-realist and realist idealism tend to go with two quite different paths to idealism. Anti-realist idealism takes an epistemological path to idealism. It is most commonly driven by epistemological questions about skepticism and is typically associated with the sort of empiricism that resists postulating hypotheses that go beyond appearances. Realist idealism takes a metaphysical path to idealism. It is often driven by metaphysical questions about the mind and about physical reality and tends to go with the sort of rationalism that allows metaphysical hypotheses that go well beyond appearances if they help us to make sense of the universe as a whole.

From certain angles realist idealism can even be seen as a sort of naturalistic view (naturalistic idealism, perhaps?), on which idealism is put forward as a sort of scientific hypothesis to explain our experiences. In any case, it is idealism in this rationalist or naturalist spirit that I want to examine in this chapter. I will touch on anti-realist idealism along the way, but I will focus especially on realist idealism in order to examine its prospects.

A more traditional taxonomy of idealist views distinguishes subjective idealism, objective idealism, transcendental idealism, and absolute idealism. These varieties of idealism do not have clear standard definitions, and they are often characterized as much by appeal to paradigmatic proponents (Berkeley, Schelling, Kant, and Hegel respectively) as to specific doctrines. For present purposes I will set aside the last two. Kant's transcendental idealism is not really a version of idealism in the metaphysical sense I am concerned with here. It is sometimes called a version of epistemological idealism:[7] at most it is idealist about the knowable phenomenal realm but not the unknowable noumenal realm, so it is not idealist about reality in general. Absolute idealism is typically associated with a number of Hegelian doctrines concerning teleology and rationality, and I do not have a clear sense of how these doctrines bear on the mind–body issues I am concerned with here. The label is occasionally used more straightforwardly for an idealism grounded in the mental states of a single cosmic entity, but to avoid the resonant Hegelian overtones I will give that view a different label below.

As for subjective and objective idealism, these labels correlate with at least three different distinctions. First is a version of the anti-realist/realist distinction above: reality is wholly constituted by the way things appear to be (subjective), or it has some mental nature external to how things appear to be (objective). A second distinction concerns whether the fundamental mental states are had by a subject (subjective) or by some other sort of entity or no entity at all (objective). A third distinction concerns what sorts of minds constitute reality: for example, human minds like ours (subjective) or a cosmic mind (objective). These distinctions are to some extent independent of each other, and the labels also bring enormous historical baggage, so for clarity I will use different language to mark the relevant distinctions here. To mark the first distinction, I will speak of anti-realist vs. realist idealism. To mark the second distinction, I will speak of subject-involving and non–subject-involving idealism. To mark the third distinction, I will speak of micro-idealism, macro-idealism, and cosmic idealism.

The third distinction is especially important for our purposes. Micro-idealism is the thesis that concrete reality is wholly grounded in micro-level mentality: that is, in mentality associated with fundamental microscopic entities (such as quarks and photons). Macro-idealism is the thesis that concrete reality is wholly grounded in macro-level mentality: that is, in mentality associated with macroscopic (middle-sized) entities such as humans and perhaps nonhuman animals. Cosmic idealism is the thesis that concrete reality is wholly grounded in cosmic mentality: that is, in mentality associated with the cosmos as a whole or with a single cosmic entity (such as the universe or a deity).[8]

For historical examples of each: Leibniz's view has at least a flavor of micro-idealism, with all reality grounded in the mental states of monads, although his monads may include macro and cosmic entities as well as micro-entities. Berkeley looks like a macro-idealist, at least before God enters his picture, and other British empiricists such as Hume and Mill have elements of this view. Many of the 19th-century German and British idealists (e.g. Fichte, Schelling, Hegel, and Bradley) as well as Hindu and Buddhist idealists (e.g. from the Advaita Vedanta and Yogācāra schools) at least tend in the direction of cosmic idealism.[9]

These three versions of idealism correlate fairly strongly with three existing philosophical views: micropsychism (the thesis that microphysical entities have mental states), phenomenalism (external reality is grounded in appearances), and cosmopsychism (the universe has mental states). Micro-idealism entails micropsychism, but not vice versa: there can be non-idealist micropsychists who hold that microphysical entities have mental and non-mental properties fundamentally (perhaps mass and charge are mental, and space and time are nonmental?). Cosmic idealism entails cosmopsychism but not vice versa, for the same sort of reason. Macro-idealism does not entail phenomenalism (a nonphenomenalist macro-idealist might hold that reality is constituted by non-appearance-involving mental relations among macrosubjects), and phenomenalism does not entail macro-idealism (a cosmic phenomenalist might hold that reality is partly or wholly grounded in appearances to a cosmic mind, and a micro phenomenalist could in principle say something analogous about micro minds), but the two views at least naturally go together. One could in principle speak of micropsychist, phenomenalist, and cosmopsychist idealism, but I will use the shorter labels for brevity and clarity.

There are also combined views on which more than one of the three sorts of minds is fundamental. For example, Berkeley can be understood as a cosmic/macro idealist, on which both a cosmic mind (God's) and macro minds (ours) are fundamental. Some emergent panpsychists may be micro/macro idealists, holding that both micro and macro minds are fundamental. There is also room in principle for micro/cosmic and micro/macro/cosmic idealism.[10]

In what follows I will examine the prospects for micro-idealism, macro-idealism, and cosmic idealism, looking also at combined versions along the way. I will not attempt to give compelling arguments for these views over alternative views, but I will examine their merits and their challenges. I will focus especially on the merits of these views as a solution to the philosophical mind – body problem. Here the constraints are to give a satisfactory theory of (i) the physical world, (ii) consciousness, and (iii) the relation between them. I will argue that all of these views face significant challenges, but that micro-idealism and especially cosmic idealism have some promise as an approach to these issues.

2. Macro-Idealism

I will discuss macro-idealism only briefly, as it is perhaps the version of idealism that is least motivated by the mind–body problem and least promising as a distinctive solution to it. It is also (in its phenomenalist guise) the version that is the most familiar in the existing literature, with familiar strengths and weaknesses. I do not have a great deal that is new to say about it (and readers should feel free to skip this section), but a few observations may be useful in drawing out the logical geography.

Macro-idealism holds that the mental states of humans and perhaps other macroscopic systems are fundamental, and that all of reality is grounded in these states. The first question for macro-idealism, as for any sort of idealism, is: how do these mental states ground facts about the physical world? Macro-idealists commonly answer: in virtue of appearance. Roughly speaking, the fact that it appears that the physical world is a certain way grounds its being that way. The second question is: how can there be illusions and hallucinations, where appearance is not a guide to reality? Macro-idealists commonly answer: physical facts are grounded in something like normal appearances, or coherence among multiple appearances, so that illusions and hallucinations are abnormal appearances or appearances that do not cohere properly with other appearances. The third question: how can there be unperceived parts of physical reality, such as the unperceived tree in the quad, or a rock on Mars? Macro-idealists commonly answer: these entities are grounded either in appearances in a cosmic or divine mind (God experiences the tree in the quad), thereby leading to cosmic or macro/cosmic idealism, or in (naturally or nomologically) *possible* experiences by macroscopic subjects (if we experienced going to a certain location on Mars, we would experience a rock).

Classical phenomenalism answers all three questions: facts about physical reality are grounded in coherence among facts about possible appearances (Mill's "permanent possibilities of sensations"). Phenomenalism is often understood as a semantic thesis (*semantic phenomenalism*): statements about the physical world are analyzable as statements about possible experiences. This semantic thesis naturally leads to a metaphysical thesis (though there is certainly room to accept one without the other, for those who strongly separate semantics from metaphysics): facts about the physical world are grounded in facts about possible experiences. We can call this metaphysical thesis *weak metaphysical phenomenalism*. This thesis does not entail idealism, since it is consistent with there being further nonmentally-grounded facts lying behind the mentally grounded physical facts: for example, noumenal facts lying behind appearances. However, a version of idealism is entailed by *strong metaphysical phenomenalism*, which says that all facts are grounded in facts about possible experiences.

Strictly speaking, strong metaphysical phenomenalism entails only a qualified version of idealism: reality is not wholly grounded in actual experiences, but it is grounded in naturally possible experiences, or powers or potentialities or conditionals involving experiences. By allowing fundamental powers or potentialities or conditionals, this view arguably says that there is an irreducibly nomic or modal aspect of reality as well as an irreducibly mental aspect, thereby qualifying the idealism. But as long as the modal truths in question wholly concern the mental, the view seems still idealist enough for it to deserve the name.

There are many traditional objections to phenomenalism, but in my view the most important objection to strong metaphysical phenomenalism is the *explanatory objection*: the truths about possible experiences demand explanation, and this view gives them none. For example, it is true that the table looks a certain way to me, and that from a different angle it will look a certain related but different way to me, and if I come back tomorrow it will once again look a related way to me, and so on. There is an order and coherence among these possible experiences that calls out for explanation. Standard nonphenomenalist views of the external world explain this by invoking a single physical table that causes the relevant experiences. A classical phenomenalist cannot do this, since the physical table is grounded in the possible experiences Rather, each truth about possible experience is taken as fundamental. So we have an enormous array of related fundamental truths, with no explanation for the relations. In effect, strong metaphysical phenomenalism gives an extraordinarily complex theory of fundamental reality and should be rejected for the same reasons that we usually favor simple theories of fundamental reality.[11]

In response to this objection, weak metaphysical phenomenalism and semantic phenomenalism can allow further facts that causally explain the facts about possible experiences, as long as they deny that these facts are physical facts. For example, Berkeley invokes facts about a divine mind in this role. Other phenomenalists may invoke structural facts about an underlying structural reality, or unknowable noumenal facts. These views are not entirely stable, since once one has underlying facts in the picture that causally explain physical appearances, there is some pressure to say that these facts themselves constitute the physical facts. But they are at least consistent. The further-fact response does little to save strong metaphysical phenomenalism (of the macro variety) and macro-idealism, however, as it allows facts that are not grounded in the mental states of macrosubjects. As a result, many semantic or weak metaphysical phenomenalists end up augmenting their macro-idealism with a non–macro-idealist account of external reality: perhaps cosmic idealism, micro-idealism, ontological structuralism, or noumenalism.

Perhaps the most promising macro-idealist response to the explanatory objection is to suggest that the regularities in our experience are explained by intra-experiential laws of nature. On one version of the view, the world is wholly experiential, but there are intra-experiential laws saying that experiences evolve just as they would if there were certain laws of physics, boundary conditions, and psychophysical laws. An initial objection is that a law like this amounts to the existence of an external world, so that the view is not truly idealist. But given that the existence of intra-experiential laws is consistent with idealism, it is at least not obvious why this complex law should be inconsistent with idealism. Perhaps a more decisive objection is that the law should be rejected on abductive grounds. The baroque hypothesis on which experiences are set up to mirror a simple physical world provides a worse explanation of our experiences than the simpler hypothesis on which the physical world exists and produces our experiences directly.[12]

Because of the explanatory objection, I think that the epistemological route through phenomenalism to idealism is not especially compelling. That said, I think there is a structuralist cousin of this route that has some promise for epistemological purposes. On this route, instead of holding that physical truths p are grounded in normal appearances that p, one holds roughly that they are grounded in the normal cause of appearances that p (and in related mutual causal roles). This leads to a structuralist view on which reality as we conceive of it is grounded in experience along with a structured network of causes that bring about those experiences. This view avoids the explanatory worry above, while still giving us some purchase against skepticism. Like phenomenalism, it reclassifies many apparently skeptical hypotheses (such as evil genius, brain-in-vat, and Matrix hypotheses) as hypotheses in which the apparent physical facts really obtain (see Chalmers 2005, 2012: excursus 15, 2018). As a result, certain forms of global skepticism may be ruled out as incoherent. Because this epistemological structuralism about the external world invokes external causes of experiences, it goes beyond macro-idealism. Instead it tends to lead to ontological structuralism, noumenalism, or perhaps micro or cosmic idealism about physical reality.

Is there room for a structuralist and non-phenomenalist version of macro-idealism? In the case of micro-idealism and cosmic idealism, there is a broadly structuralist nonphenomenalist view on which physical states are constituted by (broadly causal) relations among the mental states of micro-subjects or a cosmic subject. In principle there could be a broadly structuralist macro-idealism in which physical states are constituted by causal relations among the mental states of macrosubjects. In practice, this view is somewhat undermotivated and it is hard to make it work, not least because much of what goes on in the physical world seems not to be reflected in the states of macrosubjects. For example, it is hard to see how the location of a particle in a part of the universe far from conscious life could be constituted by the conscious states of a standard macrosubject (where it is at least somewhat easier to see how states of microsubjects or a cosmic subject could do this). Perhaps the view could posit a ubiquity of macrosubjects, or macrosubjects with unusually complex mental states, or perhaps it could deny reality where there are no macrosubjects, but by this point the view seems to have little to recommend it over micro-idealism or cosmic idealism.

In principle there can be phenomenalist idealism without macro-idealism. A cosmic phenomenalist or a microphenomenalist could hold that reality is grounded in appearances to a cosmic mind or to micro minds, via a general metaphysical principle connecting appearance and reality. Berkeley's invocation of God suggests a view of this sort (or perhaps a version of macro/cosmic phenomenalism, with appearances in both human and divine minds grounding physical reality). One can also find at least some elements of cosmic phenomenalism in Buddhist and Hindu versions of idealism, in which cosmic experience and appearance-reality principles play a central role. As for microphenomenalism, one can perhaps find a flavor of the view in interpretations of Leibniz on which matter is constituted by monads' perceptions of matter. Cosmic phenomenalism and microphenomenalism have less need than macro-phenomenalism to appeal to merely possible experiences, since there may be cosmic or micro-experiences corresponding to every part of physical reality, but one can still reasonably raise the question of what explains the order among the cosmic appearances or the micro-appearances.

Interestingly, there are a few recently discussed views with roots in contemporary science that have some flavor of macro-idealism.

Some views of this sort arise from quantum mechanics, which is sometimes associated with idealist-sounding slogans such as "observation creates reality". Perhaps the best-known view here is the interpretation on which consciousness collapses the quantum wave function (Wigner 1961; Stapp 1993; Chalmers and McQueen forthcoming). This view works best when consciousness is present only in macrosubjects, since wave function collapse in microsubjects is hard to reconcile with known quantum interference effects at the microscopic level. However, this view is standardly understood as a version of dualism rather than a version of idealism, with a causal rather than a constitutive connection between consciousness and a nonmental wave function. Anti-realist views are occasionally put forward where the wave function state itself is constituted by observers' experiences (some versions of so-called quantum Bayesianism have something of this flavor), but these views are very much subject to the explanatory objection to phenomenalism.

It is also possible to combine quantum mechanics with a structuralist rather than a phenomenalist route to idealism. One view of this sort grounds the wave function of the universe in the structure and dynamics of cosmic experience. This view leads most naturally to cosmic idealism or perhaps to cosmic/macro-idealism (if observer consciousness collapses the wave function) rather than to macro-idealism. For a macro-idealist version, one needs quantum states to attach fundamentally to macro systems but not to cosmic systems, perhaps because quantum entanglement extends to the macro level but not the cosmic level. The mind–body relation will be particularly tidy if person-level systems such as brains have their own fundamental quantum states, constituted by isomorphic structure and dynamics in person-level experience. This "quantum holist" view (as I called it in Chalmers 2017) will in principle be macro-idealist (or perhaps micro-/macro-idealist), but it faces serious challenges, not least because it postulates person-level experience whose structure is quite unlike the apparent structure of our own experience. It is also not easy to see how quantum entanglement can stably remain somewhere around the person level rather than spreading to the cosmic level (or collapsing to the micro-level), thereby yielding something closer to cosmic idealism or micro-idealism.

A second relevant view is the integrated information theory of consciousness put forward by Giulio Tononi (2004). Tononi makes the idealist-sounding claim that only consciousness has intrinsic existence, and he also says that consciousness is present only in causal systems with a positive amount of integrated information, which entails that conscious systems must be macrosubjects at least in the sense of having two or more components. If we understand this view as a version of macro-idealism, the obvious question concerns the status of single-component systems and perhaps other unconscious system: they are needed to explain the dynamics of the universe, but they do not truly exist? Here the macro-idealist reading of Tononi's view seems to suffer from problems analogous to those of phenomenalism. With only macro-conscious states, too much about the world is unexplained; once we grant reality to the non-conscious states that help explain things, the view looks much less like idealism.

A final potential form of macro-idealism with roots in cognitive science is Donald Hoffman's "conscious realism" (2008). Hoffman first argues (drawing partly on psychophysics) for an "interface theory of perception" on which the objects we perceive exist only as experiences (roughly as on traditional sense datum views) and experiences may be misleading as a guide to objective reality. He then argues for conscious realism, on which the objective world consists entirely of conscious agents. It is not entirely clear whether Hoffman's conscious agents are all macrosubjects. If they are, his view can be understood as a sort of intersubjective phenomenalism, and it faces a severe version of the explanatory objection to phenomenalism. If they are not, the views can avoid the explanatory objection by postulating microsubjects associated with every physical particle or perhaps a cosmic subject, but then the view becomes a form of micro/macro or cosmic/macro idealism.

3. Micro-Idealism

Micro-idealism is the thesis that all concrete facts are grounded in facts about the mental states of (or mentality associated with) fundamental microscopic entities, such as quarks or photons.[13]

Micro-idealism entails panpsychism, understood as the thesis that some fundamental physical entities have associated mentality, but the reverse is not the case, for a number of different reasons. The first reason turns on a delicate terminological issue: whether cosmopsychism, the thesis that the whole universe has mental states, counts as a version of panpsychism. If we define panpsychism as I just have here and adopt a version of cosmopsychism on which the universe is a fundamental physical entity, then this sort of cosmopsychism entails panpsychism. If we define panpsychism as the thesis that some fundamental microphysical entities have mental states, then cosmopsychism does not entail panpsychism. Both definitions are common, but on balance I think it makes sense to define panpsychism in terms of fundamental physics (as I have in previous work) rather than microphysics, so that cosmopsychism counts. On this approach we can use Strawson's term *micropsychism* for the thesis that some fundamental microphysical entities are associated with mental states. This then yields a first reason why panpsychism does not entail micro-idealism: micro-idealism entails micropsychism, so non-micropsychist versions of panpsychism such as cosmopsychism are inconsistent with micro-idealism.

Even narrowing our focus to micropsychism, there are a number of reasons why micropsychism does not entail micro-idealism. First, *nonconstitutive* micropsychists deny that the mental states of macrosubjects are grounded in those of microsubjects. These theorists include emergent micropsychists, who holds that macrosubjects are strongly emergent from microsubjects, and autonomous micropsychists, who holds that macrosubjects do not wholly depend on microsubjects. There are idealist versions of these views, but they reject micro-idealism for micro/macro-idealism. Second, some *nonreductionist* micropsychists may allow that there are fundamental nonmental properties in the world (for example, biological or normative properties) that are not constituted by properties of micro-entities. Third, *impure* micropsychists will allow that some fundamental microscopic entities have fundamental nonmental properties (e.g. spatiotemporal properties), perhaps in addition to fundamental mental properties. By embracing fundamental nonmental properties, nonreductionist and impure micropsychists reject idealism entirely.

We could exclude all of these views by focusing on constitutive, pure, reductionist, versions of micropsychism, thereby yielding the micro-idealist thesis that all facts are grounded in facts about the mental states of micro-entities. One might call this thesis *grounding micropsychism*, but I will typically speak just of micro-idealism for clarity.

The basic motivations for micro-idealism are closely related to the standard motivations for panpsychism. A common route to both is the route canvassed at the start, conjoining the successes of science, the problem of consciousness, and the inscrutability of matter, along with a desire to see consciousness closely integrated with the physical world and playing a causal role. These motivations typically lead to versions of micropsychism and micro-idealism where micro-entities have experiences (rather than other mental states). We might call these experiences microexperiences, contrasted with our own macroexperiences. It is these experience-involving views that I will focus on here.

In "Panpsychism and Panprotopsychism" I mounted a Hegelian argument for panpsychism, arguing that panpsychism can be seen as a sort of synthesis of the best aspects of materialism and dualism and the worst aspects of neither. Specifically, it respects the data of both the conceivability argument for dualism and the causal argument for physicalism. In effect, panpsychism is ideally suited to hold on to the three constraints: the irreducibility of consciousness, the causal role of consciousness, and the causal closure of the physical world.

The sort of micropsychism that satisfies these constraints is *constitutive Russellian micropsychism*. Russellian micropsychism (in its experience-involving version) holds that microexperiential properties *realize* microphysical properties, in that they play the causal roles associated with microphysical properties. For example, physics characterizes mass in terms of its role. Russellian micropsychism says that a microexperiential property realizes mass by playing that role, thereby serving as the "intrinsic nature" of mass. Constitutive micropsychism holds that these microexperiential properties collectively constitute (or ground) macroexperiential properties in subjects such as ourselves. In effect, Russellian micropsychism gives microexperiences a causal role, while constitutive micropsychism allows macroexperiences to inherit a causal role from those at the microexperiences, thereby avoiding the interaction problems for dualism.

Micro-idealism is naturally seen as a sort of constitutive Russellian micropsychism. If all facts are grounded in truths about mental states of microsubjects, then facts about mental states of macrosubjects are so grounded (yielding constitutive panpsychism), and facts about physics are so grounded (strongly suggesting Russellian panpsychism). So micro-idealism seems well-suited to satisfy the data of irreducibility of consciousness, a causal role for consciousness, and causal closure of physics.

At the same time, we have already seen that micro-idealism goes beyond mere micropsychism, in at least three respects: it is a constitutive, pure, and reductionist version of micropsychism. In principle it also goes beyond constitutive Russellian micropsychism in these respects, but perhaps the most natural and most common versions of constitutive Russellian panpsychism are reductionist and micropsychist. The key respect in which micro-idealism goes beyond constitutive Russellian micropsychism is its purity: it holds that *all* (and not merely *some*) fundamental properties of micro-entities are mental.

This purity is the source of a number of the distinctive strengths and weaknesses of micro-idealism. First, the strengths. In holding that all fundamental properties are of the same kind, micro-idealism offers a simple and unified monistic view of nature. By contrast, impure versions of panpsychism have both mental and nonmental properties at the fundamental level, yielding a sort of property dualism. Simplicity considerations seem to militate in favor of purity here. Second, micro-idealism yields a relatively comprehensible picture of fundamental reality, in that in principle we may be able to grasp the fundamental properties, while impure views tend to leave it quite obscure what the non-mental properties might be. One might endorse a sort of ontological structuralism about the non-mental properties, but this would yield an odd mix of ontological structuralism about some microphysical properties and nonstructuralism about others; or one might suppose they have their own intrinsic natures, but then it is quite unclear what those might be. Finally, pure panpsychism avoids the inter-action problem of making sense of mental-nonmental interaction, in favor of the arguably easier problem of mental-mental interaction. Together the issues of unity, comprehensibility, and interaction provide a powerful case for taking micro-idealism seriously.

Second, the weaknesses. Some real challenges to micro-idealism arise from it having to handle all fundamental microphysical properties. Even in a classical physics framework, there are challenges, the first among which is the challenge of space and time. Perhaps it is not so hard in principle to see how microexperiential properties might ground monadic properties and quantities such as mass and charge, as long as they have an appropriate scalar structure. But it is much harder to see how they will ground fundamental relational properties, as spatiotemporal properties seem to be.

Here the worry is that spatial properties seem to involve certain fundamental relations – distance relations, on a standard view – between fundamental physical entities. Pure Russellian panpsychism requires that these relations are realized by fundamental experiential relations between microsubjects. But it is very hard to understand what a fundamental experiential relation between distinct subjects of experience might be. The most basic experiential properties that we know about seem to be monadic properties of individual subjects. What sort of basic experiential relations between subjects might there be, that can play the role of spatial and temporal relations?

Micro-idealists might respond in a few different ways. First, they might try to find some experiential relation that can do the job. One familiar relation is the relationship of co-consciousness – but this holds between the experiences of a subject and it is not at all easy to see how it extends to a between-subjects relation. Others include the relationship of empathy, or of mental perception between subjects' perceiving each others' mental states, or of joint attention. All of these are more naturally analyzed in terms of individual mental states than as fundamental relations, though. Perhaps some other familiar or unfamiliar experiential relation could do the job. But there is at least a major challenge for this approach in making sense of these relations and of the picture of conscious subjects that emerges.

Second, a micro-idealist might offer a nonrelational grounding of spatiotemporal properties. One approach is to accept a substantivalist view of space or space-time on which these are single substances, and on which objects have spatiotemporal properties by being related to that substance. A micro-idealist version of this picture presumably requires that the substance here be mental, yielding an element of cosmic idealism in the picture, or perhaps a sort of microcosmic idealism, if there are fundamental microsubjects bearing relations to the fundamental cosmic subject that constitutes space-time. That view is no longer a form of micro-idealism, though, and it also once again faces the question of what the experiential relations between microsubjects and cosmic subject might be. Another approach is to analyze spatiotemporal locations as intrinsic monadic properties of fundamental entities – something like a set of intrinsic co-ordinates, say – which might then be realized by corresponding microexperiential properties. But this would require at least an unorthodox view of physics that would be particularly difficult to square with modern approaches.

Third, a micro-idealist might deny that spatiotemporal properties are fundamental in physics. This move to "emergent spacetime" (that is, weakly emergent space-time) has become increasingly popular in recent physical theories, where numerous theories that attempt to unify quantum mechanics and relativity (including string theory, loop quantum gravity, and causal set theory) have prominent versions in which space-time is derived from more basic structure. However, on most such views the more basic structure involves more basic high-dimensional spaces. If these spaces involve fundamental relational properties, this just moves the bump in the rug. One tempting move here is to invoke a sort of spatiotemporal functionalism that grounds spatiotemporal structure to causal structure, thereby reducing the problem of space-time to the (somewhat easier?) problem of causation, discussed next. However, for this move to help, we still need a fundamental physics without any fundamental spaces that are constituted by quasi-spatial relations. Most current emergent space-time theories do not have this character (even causal set theory involves a sort of geometry at the fundamental level), so this move requires a large bet on the character of future physical theory.

Finally, a micro-idealist might allow nonexperiential spatiotemporal properties in their picture of the world, while arguing that this does not compromise their idealism so badly as to rule out the label. Certainly there is some intuition that if the world consisted wholly of minds in time, where time is not given a mental analysis, this is reasonably close to a version of idealism (although it should be noted that Kant's "refutation of idealism" involved arguing that time cannot be wholly mental). If the world consists wholly of minds in space-time, where space-time is not given a mental analysis, then the idealism is weakened further, but perhaps the view has at least an idealist flavor. I think we should acknowledge that these views are not idealist in the strict sense defined at the start of the chapter, but perhaps they are close enough to be interesting. For example, if all truths are grounded in the mental properties of microsubjects along with their spatiotemporal relations, that would still seem closer to idealism than to other traditional views. So qualified relatives of idealism remain a possibility here.[14]

A related challenge concerns causal and dispositional properties of fundamental physical entities. Russellian panpsychism holds that these properties have mental properties as their categorical bases, but on a common view dispositions are distinct from their categorical bases and are not metaphysically grounded in those bases. But how can dispositional facts then be grounded in mental facts, as micro-idealism requires?

Responses to the challenge of causation largely parallel responses to the challenge of space-time. First, the micro-idealist might seek a mental grounding of dispositions, perhaps grounding them in active experiences such as that of the will. Second, the micro-idealist might reject fundamental dispositional properties, as Humeans do. Third, a non-Humean micro-idealist might allow fundamental causal/dispositional truths that are not wholly analyzable in mental terms, while holding that this does not compromise their idealism beyond recognition. As with the phenomenalist view that appeals to potentialities and powers regarding appearances, a world including fundamental dispositions to have experiences still seems idealist at least in spirit.

Perhaps the most interesting option here is the first. Mørch (forthcoming; see also this volume) has argued for a *phenomenal powers* views on which phenomenal states are or metaphysically ground certain causal powers or dispositions. For example, the experience of pain might ground a disposition to avoid certain situations, while the experience of love might ground a disposition to associate with certain people. On one version of this view, the phenomenal state without the power is inconceivable and metaphysically impossible (even if the power without the phenomenal state is conceivable and possible). If this view is correct, it offers the intriguing prospect of a micro-idealist view in which all microphysical dispositions and laws are grounded in the distribution of phenomenal states and the phenomenal powers that they ground. This would be an especially pure version of idealism.

These twin challenges of space-time and causation offer distinctive challenges to micro-idealism that impure versions of micropsychism do not face. Other major challenges to micro-idealism include two challenges faced by micropsychism in general.

One such challenge is the challenge of holism. It is arguable that contemporary physics does not deal in fundamental micro-entities. Instead, fundamental properties (including fields, functions, and the like) attach holistically to systems and perhaps ultimately to the universe as a whole. For example, quantum mechanics invokes wave function properties that in general are not possessed by single particles, but rather by systems of particles and perhaps ultimately by the universe as a whole. In addition, it is sometimes suggested (e.g. Schaffer 2003) that there may be no lowest or smallest level of entities in physics, but an infinite chain of ever-smaller entities. If any of these views are correct, there are no fundamental micro-entities to be realized by microsubjects, and there are no fundamental properties possessed by these entities to be realized by microexperiences. If we take a Russellian panpsychist approach to views of this sort, we will be led toward cosmopsychism and perhaps cosmic idealism rather than micropsychism and micro-idealism.

The other challenge is the famous combination problem (James 1895; Seager 1995). How do the microexperiences of microsubjects collectively constitute the macroexperiences of macrosubjects? Here there are at least three versions of the combination problem, concerning subjects (how do microsubjects yield macrosubjects?), qualities (how do microqualities yield macroqualities?), and structure (how does microphysical structure yield macroexperiential structure?).

Some panpsychists respond by endorsing emergent micropsychism, where macrosubjects and/or macroexperiences are fundamental, causally emerging from microsubjects rather than being metaphysically grounded in them. The analogous move for a micro-idealist is to embrace a sort of micro/macro-idealism. These views tend to raise all the macro-micro interaction problems that faced versions of dualism: how can fundamental macrosubjects and macroexperiences play a causal role in a causally closed microphysical/microexperiential world? The move to micro/macro-idealism in effect removes one of the major potential attractions of panpsychism and micro-idealism.

Other panpsychists endorse constitutive micropsychism, but then they have to solve the combination problem, or at least make a case that a solution exists. I have discussed and raised problems for a number of approaches to the combination problem in "The Combination Problem for Panpsychism" (Chalmers 2017), and I will not recapitulate them. Here I will just note that micro-idealism is a form of constitutive micropsychism, so the combination problem looms at least as large for it, and if anything micro-idealism tends to sharpen the problem. Where impure panpsychists can appeal to nonmental properties as well as mental properties to explain how the combination works, micro-idealists are restricted to mental materials from the start, which rules out some possible options and reduces the range of options generally. So the combination problem is a serious challenge for micro-idealism.

Overall: micro-idealism can be initially motivated by the same considerations as panpsychism, including the argument from irreducibility of consciousness, the causal role of consciousness, and the causal closure of the physical. It receives some extra motivation (relative to non-idealist panpsychism) by considerations of simplicity, comprehensibility, and interaction. But it also faces significant extra challenges from space-time and causation, as well as the more general challenges from holism and the combination problem. Some of these problems are very serious. Arguably the combination problem is the most serious, followed by the problems of space-time and of holism. So while there are significant attractions to micro-idealism, its prospects are somewhat questionable.

4. Cosmic Idealism

Cosmic idealism is the thesis that all concrete facts are grounded in facts about the mental states of (or the mentality associated with) a single cosmic entity, such as the universe as a whole or perhaps a god.

Cosmic idealism entails cosmopsychism, the thesis that a cosmic entity has associated mentality.[15] Cosmopsychism does not entail cosmic idealism, for roughly the same reasons that micropsychism does not entail micro-idealism. First, nonconstitutive cosmopsychists (e.g. emergent or autonomous cosmopsychists) deny that the mental states of macrosubjects are grounded in those of the cosmic subject. These panpsychists will at best be cosmic/macro idealists. Second, impure cosmopsychists will allow that the cosmic subject has fundamental nonmental properties (e.g. spatiotemporal properties) as well as fundamental mental properties. Third, some nonreductionist cosmopsychists may allow that there are fundamental nonmental properties in the world (for example, physical, biological or normative properties) that are not constituted by properties of the cosmic subject. As with micropsychism and micro-idealism, we could exclude these three views by focusing on constitutive, pure, reductionist versions of cosmopsychism, thereby yielding the cosmic idealist thesis that all facts are grounded in facts about the mental states of the cosmic subject.

The basic motivations for cosmopsychism and cosmic idealism are closely related to the motivations for panpsychism and micro-idealism. As with these views, cosmopsychism and cosmic idealism can be jointly motivated through the success of science, the problem of consciousness, and the inscrutability of matter. In particular, experience-involving versions of cosmopsychism and cosmic idealism hold out the promise of accommodating the irreducibility of consciousness, the causal role of consciousness, and the causal closure of the physical.

The sort of cosmopsychism that satisfies these constraints is *constitutive Russellian cosmopsychism*. To understand this view, start with a basic "priority monist" view (Schaffer 2010) on which the universe as a whole is fundamental, and on which it has fundamental cosmophysical properties: perhaps distributional properties concerning the distribution of matter in space-time, perhaps wave function properties, or perhaps something else. Russellian cosmopsychism (in its experience-involving version) says that cosmoexperiential properties realize cosmophysical properties by having their structure and playing their causal roles. In effect, cosmoexperiential properties are the causal basis of cosmophysical dispositions. Constitutive cosmopsychism holds that these cosmoexperiential properties collectively constitute (or ground) the macroexperiences of macrosubjects such as ourselves.

In effect, constitutive Russellian cosmopsychism is a view on which the world as a whole consists in the interplay of complex physics-structured experiential states in the mind of a cosmic subject. Russellian cosmopsychism gives cosmic experiences the structure and the causal role of physical states, while constitutive cosmopsychism allows macroexperiences to inherit a causal role from cosmic experiences. Cosmic idealism is certainly a form of constitutive cosmopsychism: if all facts are grounded in truths about mental states of the cosmic subject, then facts about macroexperiences are so grounded. Cosmic idealism does not entail Russellian cosmopsychism, but the most natural realist version of cosmic idealism is Russellian: the Russellian strategy seems the best way for cosmic mental states to ground states of the physical world.

What are the cosmic experiences like? We need not take a stand here. To start with analogs of familiar human experiences, the basic cosmic experiences might be perceptual: perhaps the cosmos undergoes a series of quasi-visual experiences roughly mirroring the evolution of the universe. They might be cognitive: perhaps the cosmos has a stream of conscious thought that mirrors the universe's physical dynamics. They might be imaginative: perhaps the cosmos is in effect imagining states with the structure of the universe. Or perhaps most likely, these states may be quite unlike any human experience, with a distinctive phenomenology of their own that realizes the universe-level structure and dynamics of physics.

The key respect in which cosmic idealism goes beyond constitutive Russellian cosmopsychism is its purity: it holds that all (and not merely some) fundamental properties of the cosmic subject are mental. As in the case of micro-idealism, this purity is the source of both strengths and weaknesses for cosmic idealism. As with micro-idealism, it has strengths stemming from unity and comprehensibility of the fundamental properties, as well as a particularly straightforward story about causal interaction, which comes down to mental-mental interaction in the mind of a single subject. As with micro-idealism, it also faces distinctive challenges concerning space-time and causation, as well as some more general challenges.

It is with respect to these challenges that cosmic idealism gains much of its distinctive motivation, at least relative to micro-idealism. The problem of space-time is less of a challenge for cosmic idealism than it is for micro-idealism. In both cases we are challenged to find experiential relations that can realize spatiotemporal relations – but it is easier to find experiential relations in the mind of a single subject than between subjects. For example, there are relations of co-consciousness, phenomenal feature binding, relative distribution in a sensory field, and so on. One could even imagine that space-time as a whole is realized by complex spatiotemporal experiences of a single cosmic subject. There are still many questions to answer (for example, concerning how relativistic phenomena could be realized experientially), but the initial obstacle seems significantly smaller.

As for the problem of causation, the same range of options is available for cosmic idealism as for micro-idealism, but in some respects these options are more attractive in the cosmic context. If we have to admit irreducible causal relations or dispositions, admitting such relations within the mind of a single subject (rather than between subjects) seems particularly idealist in spirit. The Mørch-style move of saying that cosmic experiential states ground the relevant dispositions is particularly attractive in this context, as it seems particularly natural for experiential states to ground dispositions to have further experiences within the mind of a single subject.

What about the more general challenges for micro-idealism: holism and the combination problem? Holism is of course no problem for cosmic idealism, and it serves as one of the major motivators for moving from micro-idealism to cosmic idealism in the first place.[16] Independently of idealism: if there are no fundamental physical micro-entities, this motivates a move to holistic physical entities such as the universe as a whole with holistic physical properties. In an idealist context, we need only combine this independently motivated move with the claim that these holistic physical properties are realized by mental properties.

An analog of the combination problem, by contrast, is a significant issue for cosmic idealism and for related versions of cosmopsychism. This is the problem of how cosmic experiences can constitute the ordinary macroexperiences of subjects like us. In earlier work I called this the "decomposition problem". Albahari (this volume) objects that this label makes it sound like the universe is decomposing and recommends "decombination problem" instead. However, this awkward neologism is also somewhat misleading in suggesting that the universal mind must be a combination of the macro minds. Instead, I will use the simple label of the "constitution problem" for the issue of how the cosmic mind constitutes macro minds. As a bonus, this label can be used to cover the analogous combination problem for micro-idealism and constitutive micropsychism (how do micro minds constitute a macro mind?), bringing out that there is a unified problem for both views. Strictly speaking the constitution problem arises only for constitutive versions of both views (emergent panpsychists deny that fundamental minds constitute macro minds), but these are certainly the views that are subject to the most serious combination/decomposition problems.

As with the original combination problem, the constitution problem for cosmopsychism and cosmic idealism has at least three subproblems. The subject constitution problem is that of how a cosmic subject can constitute macrosubjects. The quality constitution problem is that of how cosmic experiential qualities can constitute macroqualities. The structure constitution problem is that of how cosmic experiential structure can constitute macroexperiential structure.

All of these problems are serious. The quality and structure constitution problems are very closely related to the corresponding combination problems for panpsychism, and the range of options is similar (the main options discussed by Chalmers 2017 all apply here, with the same strengths and weaknesses), so I will set them aside here. The subject constitution problem is perhaps more distinctive in the cosmic case, and I will focus on it.

The subject constitution problem for cosmic idealism is that of how a cosmic subject can constitute macrosubjects such as ordinary human conscious subjects. It is at least not easy to see how this can happen, and there are arguments that it is impossible. For example, a straightforward conceivability argument (analogous to conceivability arguments against constitutive panpsychism mounted by Goff 2009) holds that one can conceive of the cosmic subject with all of its cosmic mental states without any further distinct subjects, and in particular without any macrosubjects. This claim may be derived from a more general claim that for any group of subjects one can conceive of any one of them without the others, or it may be offered as independently plausible in this specific case. Either way, given a link between conceivability and metaphysical possibility, it follows that it is metaphysically possible that the cosmic subject exists without macrosubjects; and given a link between metaphysical possibility and constitution or grounding, it follows that the cosmic subject cannot ground macrosubjects.

Many responses are possible. The first is to move to nonconstitutive cosmopsychism, giving up on the requirement that there be a constitutive connection between the cosmic mind and macro minds. One could endorse emergent cosmopsychism, holding that macro minds are strongly emergent in some way from the cosmic mind, or autonomous cosmopsychism, holding that macro minds do not wholly depend on the cosmic mind. Idealist versions of these views give up on straightforward cosmic idealism and instead move to a version of cosmic/macro-idealism on which both cosmic and macro minds are fundamental.[17]

A common way to arrive at this sort of view is to adopt cosmopsychism as an account of the physical world, while allowing that our own minds are not constituted by the physical world or its realizers. This is an important view, but it has very much the flavor of dualist views of the mind–body relation, and it suffers from analogous problems of interaction. For example, do the macro minds affect the physics-constituting aspects of the cosmic mind (thereby threatening causal closure of physics, as with interactionist dualism), or do they have no effect on it (thereby threatening the intuition that consciousness affects the physical world, as with epiphenomenalism)? The view may have some advantages over dualism in that the interaction will at least be mental-mental rather than mental-nonmental, and unity and comprehensibility provide considerations in its favor. But the view seems to give up on the initial promise of keeping the best aspects of materialism and dualism and the worst aspects of neither.

To keep this promise, one needs a constitutive solution to the constitution problem. This requires constitutive cosmopsychism, on which macrosubjects are genuinely constituted by (metaphysically grounded in) the cosmic subject and its mental states. Here there are a few strategies in the literature.

The first is *identity cosmopsychism*, on which macrosubjects are identical to the cosmic subject. This view avoids the conceivability argument by denying any subjects distinct from the cosmic subject, but it encounters twin immediate objections. First objection: macrosubjects are distinct from each other, so they cannot all be identical to the cosmic subject. Second objection: the cosmic subject has experiences that each macrosubject (like me) is not having, so they cannot be identical. If identity cosmopsychism is to retain anything like the standard logic of identity, it must presumably respond by saying that in fact all of us are identical to each other, and all of us in fact are having all the experiences that the macrosubject has. The cost is that both of these claims seem to be obviously false. The task for the identity cosmopsychist is to explain away their apparent falsity as some sort of illusion.

A natural strategy here suggests that the cosmic subject undergoes some sort of *cognitive fragmentation* into different components, modes, or guises, each of which lacks access to the other components. Kastrup (2017) suggests an analogy with dissociative identity disorder (DID): in effect, each macrosubject is an alter (of many multiple personalities) of the cosmic subject. Of course, the metaphysics of DID is controversial, with some arguing that multiple subjects are present, but it is common to hold that there is a single fragmented subject here. On a natural characterization, the subject has multiple modes or guises that lack access to the other modes. The subject has the experiences of all the alters, but under the mode of one alter they will lack cognitive access to the experiences (perhaps including simultaneous experiences) associated with other alters. In effect, the subject's access is relativized to modes. If we use the fragmentation model to understand cosmic idealism, we can then suggest that the experiences that seem to belong to a single macrosubject in fact belong to the cosmic subject under a certain mode, and under this mode we do not have cognitive access to the experiences we are simultaneously having under other modes.

Of course, this view raises many questions. There are many disanalogies between the universe and a DID subject, and it is not at all clear how to find analogous within-subject fragmentation at the level of cognitive processes in the universe. The view is also massively revisionary about our minds and our relations to one another. It makes our ordinary mode of existence pathological, since in this mode we are unaware of the vast majority of experiences we are having.[18] This entails a massive failure of introspection, as our ordinary beliefs reflect a near-complete lack of knowledge about our own consciousness. This failure is at least uncomfortable for people who are realists about consciousness, though analogous phenomena on a more limited scale are familiar. One analog is found in Ned Block's cases where phenomenal consciousness overflows cognitive access (Block 2007): we might think of cosmic fragmentation as involving phenomenal overflow on a very large scale. Still, identity cosmopsychism along with cognitive fragmentation seems a coherent view that is worth taking seriously.

The alternative is *non-identity* constitutive cosmopsychism, on which there are multiple subjects who are not identical to the cosmic subject but whose existence and experiences are grounded in the existence and experiences of the cosmic subject. One view is that the multiple subjects are experiential parts of the cosmic subject or that they are subsumed by the cosmic subject (Goff 2017). A related if somewhat more obscure view (Mathews 2011; Shani 2015) is that macrosubjects are "vortices" in the consciousness of a cosmic subject. An obvious objection to the first view is that parts of a subject are not usually subjects – there does not seem to be a separate subject who has just by visual experiences – and even if there is, the existence of such a subject does not seem to be necessitated merely by the existence and experiences of a cosmic subject. The same goes for subsumption and for vortices in consciousness. Goff (2017) gets around this by supposing that the cosmic subject has nonmental as well as mental properties ("consciousness-plus") and that these unknown and unconceived nonmental properties can in principle explain the subsumption of cosmic subjects.[19] In postulating these fundamental nonmental properties, however, Goff gives up on cosmic idealism for a sort of cosmic property dualism.

A final strategy is to deflate subjects of experience or to eliminate them entirely. Views like this are familiar in the Buddhist tradition, which denies the existence of the self and is often understood to deny the existence of subjects as well (at least in ultimate reality). On views of this sort, there are experiences but no subjects that have them; or at least, any bearers of the experiences are very much unlike the primitive persisting entities that we have in mind when we think of subjects. This non–subject-involving view is often combined with a sort of idealism on which conventional reality is grounded in conventional appearances, and in which all this is grounded in cosmic experience at the ultimate level. This picture at least tends to suggest a view on which macroexperience is grounded in non–subject-involving cosmic experience in ultimate reality.[20]

On a non–subject-involving cosmic idealist view, there is cosmic experience but no cosmic subject. It might then be argued that with no subjects there is no subject constitution problem to solve. Of course, this does not eliminate the problem entirely. Presumably experiences still come bundled into relatively unified groups (corresponding to what we thought of as subjects), and we still need to know how a cosmic bundle of experiences could constitute a macro bundle of the sort I seem to have. This problem is by no means straightforward (on the face of it one could run a conceivability argument against it analogous to the one for subjects), but perhaps the problems for it are at least more tractable than the corresponding problems for non–subject-involving views. One cost is then to make sense of experiences without subjects of experience. I am not sure I can do this, but many theorists have at least tried, and again the view is certainly worth taking seriously.

To sum up the discussion of the constitution problem for cosmic idealism: I think that as with the combination problem for micropsychism, the constitution problem is a very serious one, but there are at least some avenues for solving it (especially the identity cosmopsychist avenue) that are more promising than analogs in the micropsychist case and that are worth exploring further.

Of course, there are also any number of possible further objections to cosmic idealism. One potential objection holds that mental properties require nonmental properties lying behind them to causally sustain their structure and dynamics. Cosmic idealism is perhaps better placed than macro-idealism to answer this objection, by developing a picture on which cosmic experiences are both fundamental and causally closed, so that they need no further causal sustaining. But it is certainly a challenge to develop a detailed account of cosmic experience with the appropriate form.

Another issue is the *relationality problem*.[21] As Moore stressed in his "refutation of idealism" (1903), experience seems to be relational. In an experience (e.g. a sensation of blue), a subject is aware of some object (e.g. the subject is aware of blueness). Moore held that this object is itself non-experiential (in contemporary language, it is neither identical to an experience or grounded in experience), which entails that idealism is false. Contemporary representationalist views can avoid this consequence by holding that experience relates us to some abstract property (such as blueness) or proposition (e.g. that some object is blue). As noted at the start of the chapter, an idealist need not hold that abstract objects are grounded in experience. Still, if the fundamental experiences (e.g. in a cosmic subject) represent a mind-independent world in which entities have mind-independent properties such as blueness, and if there is no world independent of the cosmic subject, then it is hard to avoid the conclusion that the cosmic subject is hallucinating, which is at least odd.

Cosmic idealists might respond in a number of ways. If they retain a relational view of experience, they could accept that cosmic experience is hallucinatory, or they may hold that cosmic experience is nonperceptual: perhaps the cosmic mind merely imagines the relevant states of affairs, in which case no hallucination need be involved. Alternatively, they could argue that the relational experiences of a cosmic subject are veridical. For example, cosmic subjects might represent structural properties which are instantiated in their world, or they might be unlike ordinary human subjects in that they represent only experiences and not a mind-independent world. Still, combining cosmic idealism with a relational view of experience seems to make the relational structure of experience at best somewhat marginal to the role of experience in constituting the world. At least on a realist version of idealism, it looks as if experience could have constituted reality just as well if it were not relational.

A more radical but perhaps more principled response denies that cosmic experience is relational at all. As Allinson (1978) observes, this response to Moore is available to so-called "non-dual" views of experience in the Eastern traditions, such as the Advaita Vedanta and the Yogacara schools. On these views, experience at a fundamental level does not involve a duality between subject and object and does not involve a relational structure whereby subjects are aware of objects. For example, it may involve states of pure awareness without objects, or perhaps pure qualities without awareness, or something harder for us to comprehend. It is by no means straightforward to make sense of nonrelational experience, but if it is possible, it has some attractions in avoiding the problems of relationality at a fundamental level.

A related issue specific to cosmic idealism is the *austerity problem*. The issue here is that the cosmic mind in the present picture (whether relational or nonrelational) looks extremely austere, and very much unlike a mind as we normally think of it. Its basic experiential structure and dynamics is tied to the structure and dynamics of physics. There seems to be little or no rationality in this structure. There seems to be very little thinking, valuing, or reasoning. It is not really clear why, if there is to be a cosmic mind, it should be as austere as this.

The cosmic idealist faces a choice point here. On the first option, the cosmic mind has experiences that are wholly isomorphic to the structure of physics. This is the option taken by *austere Russellian cosmopsychism*, where the cosmic subject has mental states with structure and dynamics that realize physical dynamics, and has no more mental states and no more structure and dynamics than this. This option faces the austerity problem.

The second option is to postulate that the cosmic mind has experiences that go beyond the structure and dynamics of physics. One could adopt a non-Russellian cosmopsychism where the structure and dynamics of physics is absent from cosmic experience, but this view has trouble in recovering physical truths. A somewhat more attractive version of this option is *enriched Russellian cosmopsychism*, where the cosmic subject has experiential states with the physical structure and dynamics, but also has other mental states with further structure and dynamics. These further mental states might make the cosmic mind much less austere and more mind-like. The cost for this option is a sort of excess baggage problem: the world has more structure than physics suggests, and we have to postulate supra-natural structure and dynamics beyond what natural science suggests. The extra mental states seem to play no direct role in constituting physical states of the universe, and one might worry that they will be entirely epiphenomenal with respect to the universe we observe.

That said, there are arguably enriched Russellian cosmopsychist models where the extra mental structure plays a role in sustaining physical dynamics. For example, on one model the cosmic subject is a rational being somewhat like you and me, except vastly more intelligent and with enormously greater cognitive resources. Such a being may have an interest in imagining and simulating universes, perhaps to learn what will happen in universes given various conditions. If the cosmic subject fully simulates a universe like ours in its imagination, its imaginative states will then have very much the structure and dynamics of physics in our universe. These imaginative states themselves may be somewhat austere, but they will be driven by further mental states of the cosmic subject in which values and rationality inhere. A model like this allows for a much less austere cosmic subject, perhaps at cost of making the mental states that constitute our universe something of a sideshow in its mind.

One might even adapt Bostrom's simulation argument (2003) to argue that it is quite likely that a cousin of this sort of cosmic idealism is true. A simplified version of the simulation argument says that many simulated universes will be created in the lifetime of a universe containing intelligent life, and there will be more beings in simulations than outside simulations, so it is very likely that we are in a simulation. One could additionally argue that most simulations will be done within the minds of simulating beings. The great majority of simulating beings will be superintelligent beings, and these beings will have little need to run simulations on separate computers. Instead they will have the resources to run simulations directly in their own computational minds. If so, most beings in the cosmos will exist in universes realized by the minds of simulating beings.

The idealism suggested by this simulation argument is admittedly subject to some qualifications. One is that it is far from obvious that the simulations in question will need to be conscious. The idealism may well involve constitution by non-conscious mental states, which may themselves have underlying non-mental grounds. Another qualification is that on this view the cosmic subject will not constitute the entire cosmos, but it will at least constitute everything in our universe. Whether idealism or some other view is true of the cosmos as a whole remains a further question.

I conclude that there is significant motivation for cosmic idealism. It shares the general motivations for panpsychism, which are strong, and has some extra motivation in addition. Compared to micro-idealism, it deals much better with the problems of space-time and of holism, and it at least has some extra promise in dealing with the problem of causation and the all-important constitution problem. Compared to non-idealist forms of panpsychism and panprotopsychism, it has some advantages in simplicity and comprehensibility, while it has both benefits and costs with respect to the constitution problem. I do not know that the constitution problem can be solved, but there are at least avenues worth exploring.

Overall, I think cosmic idealism is the most promising version of idealism, and is about as promising as any version of panpsychism. It should be on the list of the handful of promising approaches to the mind–body problem.

5. Conclusion

I do not claim that idealism is plausible. No position on the mind–body problem is plausible. Materialism is implausible. Dualism is implausible. Idealism is implausible. Neutral monism is implausible. None-of-the-above is implausible. But the probabilities of all of these views get a boost from the fact that one of them must be true. Idealism is not greatly less plausible than its main competitors. So even though idealism is implausible, there is a non-negligible probability that it is true.

Notes

1. Thanks to participants in the NYU Shanghai workshop on idealism and in the ANU philosophy of mind work-in-progress group. For written comments, thanks to Miri Albahari, Eddy Keming Chen, Bronwyn Finnigan, Hedda Mørch, Bill Seager, Itay Shani, and Trevor Teitel.
2. I recall either hearing this epigram in conversation or reading it somewhere, with the sense that it came from the school of recent British idealists such as John Foster, Howard Robinson, and T. L. S. Sprigge. To my surprise no one I have consulted (including Robinson) remembers the saying, so perhaps I hallucinated it or it was the invention of one of my conversational partners. Any leads are welcome!
3. The rise of materialism: e.g. Armstrong (1968), Feigl (1958), Lewis (1966), Place (1956), Putnam (1960), Smart (1959). The dualist response: e.g. Chalmers (1996), Foster (1991), Jackson (1982), Kripke (1980), Nida-Rümelin (1997), Robinson (1982) (with support from Nagel 1974 and Levine 1983). The festival of panpsychism: e.g. Brüntrup and Jaskolla (2017), Chalmers (2013), Goff (2017), Mathews (2003), Rosenberg (2004), Seager and Allen-Hermanson (2015), Skrbina (2009), Strawson (2006) (with support from Chalmers 1996, Griffin 1998, and Nagel 1979). The stirrings of idealism: Adams (2007), Albahari (this volume), Bolender (2001), Foster (2008), Goldschmidt and Pearce (2017), Kastrup (2017), Meixner (2017), Pelczar (2015), Yetter-Chappell (2017) (with support from Foster 1982, Sprigge 1983 and Strawson 1994, as well as cosmopsychists cited later). Of course there is an enormous amount of idealism in pre-20th century philosophy (Indian, Tibetan, British, German, and so on) but due to lack of expertise I am engaging with historical material only superficially.
4. That is, mental facts are facts involving only mental properties. Mental facts might involve logical and/or singular constituents in addition to properties: so e.g. $\exists x Mx$ and Ma both count.
5. Some subtleties: The definition of anti-realist idealism can either include or exclude microphenomenalist and cosmic phenomenalist views (discussed in the next section), depending on whether or not the relevant appearances are limited to those in observers like us. For it to include nonphenomenalist views where there are experiences but no physical objects, we should allow the definition to be true vacuously. For it to exclude versions of Russellian panpsychism on which structural roles fix the reference of physical terms to mental properties that play those roles (so that perhaps electron-appearances play the electron role and are therefore electrons), the "what it is" claim should probably be understood as conceptual or epistemic equivalence rather than metaphysical equivalence.
6. The assumption that idealism must be antirealist is reflected in a question in the PhilPapers Survey (Bourget and Chalmers 2014): "External world: idealism, skepticism, or non-skeptical realism". The question tacitly acknowledges the possibility of skeptical realism but not of idealist realism. 4.3% accepted idealism. The figure would probably not have been much higher if realist idealism were explicitly acknowledged (and only 0.4% indicated that they accepted more than one answer), but the phrasing brings out the way that views of this sort tend to be ignored. (Mea culpa.)
7. Another common taxonomy distinguishes metaphysical idealism (reality is fundamentally mental) from epistemological idealism (all knowable facts are mental), conceptual idealism (our concepts constrain facts about reality; Rescher 1973; Hofweber 2017), and explanatory idealism (the mental plays some role in explaining all facts about reality; Rescher 2007; Ross 2017). My focus in this chapter is firmly on varieties of metaphysical idealism.
8. I say "mentality associated with" in order to make these three varieties of cosmic idealism consistent with non–subject-involving views that reject the idea that mentality requires something to bear on mental states. If we assume a subject-involving view (or a non–subject-involving view that allows bearers that are not subjects), one could change this expression to "mental states of" here and throughout this article.
9. Among contemporaries, it is easy to read Strawson (2006) as a micro-idealist (though his view is consistent with cosmic idealism). Pelczar (2015) is a macro-idealist, and Kastrup (2017) is a cosmic idealist. Others discussed ahead hold combined views, or hold versions of panpsychism and cosmopsychism without full-on idealism.

10. Among contemporaries, Foster and Robinson can be read as cosmic/macro idealists in the Berkeleyan mould, while Albahari and Yetter-Chappell can be read as cosmic/macro idealists of a somewhat different sort. Adams offers both cosmic/macro and micro/macro alternatives. Emergent panpsychists such as Mørch, Seager, and Rosenberg might be read as micro/macro or perhaps micro/macro/cosmic idealists.

11. Pelczar (2015) holds that sensation conditionals are all primitive but argues that they can be nonreductively explained in terms of a relatively small subset of sensation conditionals: they are naturally necessitated by those sensation conditionals that constitute the basic laws of nature and the associated boundary conditions. This subset is nevertheless still enormously large and complex: every way we look, the laws of physics seem to be true. As a result the view is very much subject to a version of the explanatory objection: the order among these sensation conditionals constitutes a remarkably complex coincidence, and is much better explained if the appearances are caused by a separate domain in which the laws are true. Pelczar concedes that the complexity is a disadvantage of his view, but holds that separate-domain views have even worse problems.

12. A sophisticated macro-idealist view in this class has recently been put forward by Markus Müller (2019). On Müller's view, there is a sequence of experiences governed by a single fundamental intra-experiential law: a given experience in the sequence is determined by its algorithmic probability conditional on earlier experiences (where the algorithmic probability of a sequence is higher when the sequence is generated by a short algorithm). The effect is that experiences start out random but that effective intra-experiential laws (shortish algorithms that generate experiences) may stabilize over time. However, it remains unclear why these intra-experiential laws should take a form that suggests an external world, with a domain of lawful interaction among non-experiential entities. The simplest intra-experiential laws will involve simple interactions among experiences, with no need for even an apparent external world.

13. I don't know of any philosopher who is committed to micro-idealism. Perhaps the nearest is Roelofs (2014), who favors micro-idealism but does not rule out cosmic idealism. Strawson (2006) looks like a micro-idealist but has more sympathy with cosmic idealism. Many other panpsychists turn out to be emergent panpsychists (e.g. Mørch and Rosenberg), cosmopsychists (e.g. Goff and Shani), impure panpsychists (Goff again), or neutral monists (e.g. Coleman 2012).

14. Adams (2007) and Strawson (2006) both seem to allow that space-time may not be mentally analyzable. Adams calls the view "mere panpsychism", holding that non-ideal space-time gives up on idealism. Strawson seems to hold that idealism is consistent with minds existing in non-ideal space-time.

15. Recent proponents of cosmopsychism include Mathews (2011) (under the name "cosmological panpsychism"), Jaskolla and Buck (2012) ("panexperiential holism"), Nagasawa and Wager (2017) ("priority cosmopsychism", which is roughly what I am calling constitutive cosmopsychism), Goff (this volume and 2017), and Shani (2015). See also Albahari (this volume) and Miller (2017) for discussion. Cosmopsychism is sometimes understood as the more specific thesis that the universe (or the cosmos) has mental states. This definition excludes many divine forms of cosmic idealism, so it is not entailed by cosmic idealism as defined earlier. Of course one could also define cosmic idealism more narrowly to exclude divine versions, but then we would need a fourth category of divine idealism. At least for present purposes it is more straightforward to treat the divine and non-divine versions of cosmic idealism and cosmopsychism together. My own focus is very much on non-divine versions, but much of what I say also applies to divine versions.

16. On the other hand, as Einar Bohn pointed out to me, the "what if there is no lowest level?" objection to micro-idealism is paralled by a "what if there is no highest level?" objection to cosmic idealism. If there is no cosmos (instead just infinitely embedded universes), the cosmos cannot serve as a cosmic subject.

17. Broadly autonomous versions of cosmic/macro-idealism (macro minds are autonomous from the cosmic mind) seem to fit the work of Foster (2008), Robinson (1982), and perhaps Adams (2007), while broadly emergent views (macro minds emerge from the cosmic mind) are adopted by Albahari (this volume) and Yetter-Chappell (2017).

18. According to some versions of this view, we can occasionally get hints of other fragments of our experience or become more lucidly aware of our underlying cosmic experiences. For example, some Buddhist traditions suggest that certain meditative practices (e.g. Dzogchen practice in Tibetan Buddhism) can help us experience the fundamental mode of consciousness.

19. For similar reasons, panprotopsychist views that appeal to unknown protomental properties have certain advantages over pure panpsychist (idealist) views when it comes to the constitution problem. Arguably we understand experience well enough to see that subjects of experience cannot constitute distinct subjects; but because we do not understand the relevant protomental properties, we do not have correspondingly strong reasons to deny that they can constitute subjects of experience. On the other hand, panprotopsychist theories have to deal with a nonexperience–experience gap (many theorists hold that only experience can constitute experience), and pure panpsychist views have the advantage of relative comprehensibility.

20. It should be noted that not all Buddhists are idealists. Idealism is most common in the Yogacara school, but even there, there is a vigorous contemporary debate about whether Yogacara involves metaphysical or epistemological idealism. See Arnold (2008), Finnigan (2017) and Trivedi (2005) for discussion.
21. Thanks to Daniel Stoljar for pressing this problem for idealism.

References

Adams, R. (2007). 'Idealism Vindicated'. In P. van Inwagen and D. Zimmerman (eds.), *Persons: Human and Divine*. Oxford: Oxford University Press, pp. 35–54.

Albahari, M. (this volume). 'Beyond Cosmopsychism and the Great I Am: How the World Might Be Grounded in Universal "Advaitic" Consciousness'. In W. Seager (ed.), *The Routledge Handbook of Panpsychism*. London: Routledge.

Allinson, R. E. (1978). 'A Non-Dualistic Reply to Moore's Refutation of Idealism'. *Indian Philosophical Quarterly*, 5: 661–8.

Armstrong, D. M. (1968). *A Materialist Theory of the Mind*. London: Routledge and Kegan Paul.

Arnold, D. (2008). 'Buddhist Idealism, Epistemic and Otherwise: Thoughts on the Alternating Perspectives of Dharmakirti'. *Sophia*, 47: 3–28.

Block, N. (2007). 'Consciousness, Accessibility, and the Mesh Between Psychology and Neuroscience'. *Behavioral and Brain Sciences*, 30: 481–548.

Bolender, J. (2001). 'An Argument for Idealism'. *Journal of Consciousness Studies*, 8 (4): 37–61.

Bostrom, N. (2003). 'Are We Living in a Computer Simulation?' *Philosophical Quarterly*, 53 (211): 243–55.

Bourget, D., and Chalmers, D. J. (2014). 'What Do Philosophers Believe?' *Philosophical Studies* 170: 465–500.

Brüntrup, G., and Jaskolla, L. (2017). *Panpsychism: Contemporary Perspectives*. Oxford: Oxford University Press.

Chalmers, D. J. (1996). *The Conscious Mind: In Search of a Fundamental Theory*. Oxford: Oxford University Press.

Chalmers, D. J. (2005). 'The Matrix as Metaphysics'. In C. Grau (ed.), *Philosophers Explore the Matrix*. Oxford: Oxford University Press, pp. 132–76.

Chalmers, D. J. (2012). *Constructing the World*. Oxford: Oxford University Press.

Chalmers, D. J. (2013). 'Panpsychism and Panprotopsychism'. *Amherst Lecture in Philosophy*. www.amherstlecture. org/chalmers2013. (Reprinted in Brüntrup and Jaskolla (2017), pp. 19–47.)

Chalmers, D. J. (2017). 'The Combination Problem for Panpsychism'. In Brüntrup and Jaskolla (2017), pp. 179–214.

Chalmers, D. J. (2018). 'Structuralism as a Response to Skepticism'. *Journal of Philosophy* 115: 625–60.

Chalmers, D. J., and McQueen, K. (forthcoming). 'Consciousness and the Collapse of the Wave Function'. In S. Gao (ed.) *Consciousness and Quantum Mechanics*. Oxford University Press.

Coleman, S. (2012). 'Mental Chemistry: Combination for Panpsychists'. *Dialectica*, 66: 137–66.

Feigl, H. (1958). 'The "Mental" and the "Physical"'. *Minnesota Studies in the Philosophy of Science*, 2: 370–497.

Finnigan, B. (2017). 'Buddhist Idealism'. In Goldschmidt and Pearce (2017).

Foster, J. (1982). *The Case for Idealism*. London: Routledge.

Foster, John (1991). *The Immaterial Self: A Defence of the Cartesian Dualist Conception of Mind*. New York: Routledge.

Foster, J. (2008). *A World for Us: The Case for Phenomenalistic Idealism*. Oxford: Oxford University Press.

Goff, P. (2009). 'Why Panpsychism Doesn't Help to Explain Consciousness'. *Dialectica*, 63 (3): 289–311.

Goff, P. (2017). *Consciousness and Fundamental Reality*. Oxford: Oxford University Press.

Goff, P. (this volume). 'Micropsychism, Cosmopsychism, and the Grounding Relation'. In W. Seager (ed.), *The Routledge Handbook of Panpsychism*. London: Routledge.

Goldschmidt, T., and Pearce, K. (2017). *Idealism: New Essays in Metaphysics*. Oxford: Oxford University Press.

Griffin, D. R. (1998). *Unsnarling the World-Knot*. Oakland: University of California Press.

Hoffman, D. (2008). 'Conscious Realism and the Mind – Body Problem'. *Mind and Matter*, 6: 87–121.

Hofweber, T. (2017). 'Conceptual idealism without ontological idealism'. In Goldschmidt and Pearce (2017).

Jackson, F. (1982). 'Epiphenomenal Qualia'. *Philosophical Quarterly*, 32: 127–36.

James, W. (1895). *The Principles of Psychology*. New York: Henry Holt.

Jaskolla, L. J., and Buck, A. J. (2012). 'Does Panexperiential Holism Solve the Combination Problem?' *Journal of Consciousness Studies*, 19: 190–9.

Kastrup, B. (2017). 'An Ontological Solution to the Mind – Body Problem'. *Philosophies*, 2: 2. DOI:10.3390/philosophies2020010.

Kripke, S. (1980). *Naming and Necessity*. Cambridge, MA: Harvard University Press.

Levine, J. (1983). 'Materialism and Qualia: The Explanatory Gap'. *Pacific Philosophical Quarterly*, 64: 354–61.

Lewis, D. (1966). 'An Argument for the Identity Theory'. *Journal of Philosophy*, 63: 17–25.

Mathews, F. (2003). *For Love of Matter: A Contemporary Panpsychism*. Albany: State University of New York Press.

Mathews, F. (2011). 'Panpsychism as Paradigm'. In M. Blamauer (ed.), *The Mental as Fundamental*. Frankfurt: Ontos Verlag, pp. 141–55.

Meixner, U. (2017). 'Idealism and Panpsychism'. In Brüntrup and Jaskolla (2017), pp. 387–406.

Miller, G. (2017). 'Can Subjects Be Proper Parts of Subjects? The Decombination Problem'. *Ratio*, 30 (2). DOI:10.1111/rati.12166.

Mørch, H. H. (forthcoming). 'Phenomenal Powers Panpsychism'.

Mørch, H. H. (this volume). 'The Argument for Panpsychism from Experience of Causation'. In W. Seager (ed.), *The Routledge Handbook of Panpsychism*. London: Routledge.

Müller, M. 2019. Law without law: from observer states to physics via algorithmic information theory. arxiv:1712.01826 [quant-ph].

Nagasawa, Y., and Wager, K. (2017). 'Panpsychism and Priority Cosmopsychism'. In Brüntrup and Jaskolla (2017), pp. 113–29.

Nagel, T. (1974). 'What Is It Like to Be a Bat?' *Philosophical Review*, 4: 435–50.

Nagel, T. (1979). 'Panpsychism'. In *Mortal Questions*. Cambridge: Cambridge University Press, pp. 181–95.

Nida-Rümelin, M. (1997). 'Is the Naturalization of Qualitative Experience Possible or Sensible?' In M. Carrier and P. K. Machamer (eds.), *Mindscapes: Philosophy, Science, and the Mind*. Pittsburgh: Pittsburgh University Press, pp. 117–44.

Pelczar, M. (2015). *Sensorama: A Phenomenalist Analysis of Spacetime and Its Contents*. Oxford: Oxford University Press.

Place, U. T. (1956). 'Is Consciousness a Brain Process?' *British Journal of Psychology*, 47: 44–50.

Putnam, H. (1960). 'Minds and Machines'. In S. Hook (ed.), *Dimensions of Mind*. New York: New York University Press, pp. 138–64.

Rescher, N. (1973). *Conceptual Idealism*. Oxford: Blackwell.

Rescher, N. (2007). 'What Sort of Idealism Is Viable Today?' In P. Basile and L. McHenry (eds.), *Consciousness, Reality and Value: Essays in Honour of T.L.S. Sprigge*. Heusenstamm: Ontos Verlag, pp. 67–78.

Robinson, H. (1982). *Matter and Sense*. Cambridge: Cambridge University Press.

Roelofs, L. (2014). *Combining Minds*. Ph.D. thesis, University of Toronto. https://tspace.library.utoronto.ca/handle/1807/69449.

Rosenberg, G. H. (2004). *A Place for Consciousness*. Oxford: Oxford University Press.

Ross, J. (2017). 'Idealism and Fine-Tuning'. In Goldschmidt and Pearce (2017).

Schaffer, J. (2003). Is there a fundamental level? *Nous* 37: 498-517.

Schaffer, J. (2010). 'Monism: The Priority of the Whole'. *Philosophical Review*, 119: 31–76.

Seager, W. E. (1995). 'Consciousness, Information, and Panpsychism'. *Journal of Consciousness Studies*, 2: 272–88.

Seager, W. E., and Allen-Hermanson, S. (2015). 'Panpsychism'. In E. Zalta (ed.), *The Stanford Encyclopedia of Philosophy*, Fall edition.

Shani, I. (2015). 'Cosmopsychism: A Holistic Approach to the Metaphysics of Experience'. *Philosophical Papers*, 44: 389–437.

Skrbina, D. (ed.) (2009). *Mind That Abides: Panpsychism in the New Millennium*. Amsterdam: John Benjamins.

Smart, J. J. C. (1959). 'Sensations and Brain Processes'. *Philosophical Review*, 68: 141–56.

Sprigge, T. L. S. (1983). *The Vindication of Absolute Idealism*. Edinburgh: Edinburgh University Press.

Stapp, H. P. (1993). *Mind, Matter, and Quantum Mechanics*. Berlin: Springer.

Strawson, G. (1994). *Mental Reality*. Cambridge, MA: MIT Press.

Strawson, G. (2006). 'Realistic Monism: Why Physicalism Entails Panpsychism'. *Journal of Consciousness Studies*, 13 (10–11): 3–31.

Tononi, G. (2004). 'An Information Integration Theory of Consciousness'. *BMC Neuroscience*, 5: 42.

Trivedi, S. (2005). 'Idealism and Yogacara Buddhism'. *Asian Philosophy*, 15: 231–46.

Wigner, E. P. (1961). 'Remarks on the Mind – Body Question'. In I. J. Good (ed.), *The Scientist Speculates*. London: Heineman, pp. 284–302.

Yetter-Chappell, H. (2017). 'Idealism Without God'. In Goldschmidt and Pearce (2017).

INDEX

Note: Page numbers in *italics* indicate figures; page numbers in **bold** indicate tables.

Printed in Great Britain
by Amazon